# Recent Titles in Social Hi

## Herskovits Award Winners

*Colonial Conscripts*
Les Tirailleurs Sénégalais
in French West Africa
1857–1960
MYRON ECHENBERG

*The Moon is Dead! Give Us Our Money!*
The Cultural Origins of an African Work Ethic in Natal
c.1843–1900
KELETSO E. ATKINS

*Cutting Down Trees*
Gender, Nutrition & Agricultural Change
in Northern Province, Zambia
1890–1990
HENRIETTA MOORE & MEGAN VAUGHAN

*Feasts & Riot*
Revelry, Rebellion, & Popular Consciousness
on the Swahili Coast
1856–88
JONATHAN GLASSMAN

Social History of Africa

# Violence & Memory

## One Hundred Years in the 'Dark Forests' of Matabeleland

# Violence & Memory

## One Hundred Years in the 'Dark Forests' of Matabeleland

JOCELYN ALEXANDER
JOANN MCGREGOR & TERENCE RANGER

James Currey
OXFORD

Heinemann
PORTSMOUTH, NH

David Philip
CAPE TOWN

Weaver Press
HARARE

James Currey Ltd
73 Botley Road
Oxford OX2 0BS

Heinemann
A Division of Reed Elsevier
361 Hanover Street, Portsmouth, NH 03801-3912
Offices and agents throughout the world

David Philip (Pty) Ltd
208 Wertmuller Centre
Claremont 7708
South Africa

Weaver Press
PO Box 1922
Avondale, Harare

© Jocelyn Alexander, JoAnn McGregor and Terence Ranger, 2000
First published 2000

1 2 3 4 5 04 03 02 01 00

ISBN  0-85255-692-6  (James Currey cloth)
ISBN  0-85255-642-X  (James Currey paper)
ISBN 0-325-07033-4 (Heinemann cloth)
ISBN 0-325-07032-6 (Heinemann paper)

**British Library Cataloguing in Publication Data**
Alexander, Jocelyn
   Violence & memory : one hundred years in the dark forests
   of Matabeleland. - (Social history of Africa)
   l. Violence - Zimbabwe - History - 20th century 2. Insurgency
   - Zimbabwe - History - 20th century 3. Zimbabwe - History -
   1890-1965 4. Zimbabwe - History - 1965-1980
   I. Title  II. McGregor, JoAnn   III. Ranger, T. O. (Terence
   Osborn), 1929-
   968.9'1

**Library of Congress Cataloging-in-Publication Data**
**available on request**

Typeset in 9/10 pt Palatino by Long House, Cumbria, UK
Printed and bound in Great Britain by
Woolnough, Irthlingborough

# Contents

## *Introduction*

## Part I
## Conquest, Eviction & Nationalism

### 1
### *Life in the 'Dark Forests'*
*Violence & Images of the Land, 1893–1930*

### 2
### *The Violence of the State*
*Forced Migration & its Consequences*

### 3
### *The Violence of the State*
*The Second Colonial Occupation*

### 4
### *The Rise of Nationalist Violence*

### 5
### *The Transition to Guerrilla War*
*1962–1976*

# Part II
## Wars & their Legacies

# List of
# Maps & Photographs

# List of
# Acronyms & Abbreviations

| | |
|---|---|
| ANC | African National Congress |
| AP | Assembly Point |
| CID | Criminal Investigation Department |
| CIO | Central Intelligence Organization |
| CNC | Chief Native Commissioner |
| Conex | Department of Conservation and Extension |
| DA | District Administrator |
| DC | District Commissioner |
| DSA | District Security Assistant |
| LDO | Land Development Officer |
| LGPO | Local Government Promotion Officer |
| LMS | London Missionary Society |
| NC | Native Commissioner |
| NDP | National Democratic Party |
| NPA | Native Purchase Area |
| PA | Provincial Administrator |
| PNC | Provincial Native Commissioner |
| TLA | Tribal Land Authority |
| UANC | United African National Council |
| WHO | World Health Organization |
| Zanu | Zimbabwe African National Union |
| Zanu(PF) | Zimbabwe African National Union (Patriotic Front) |
| Zanla | Zimbabwe African National Liberation Army |
| Zapu | Zimbabwe African People's Union |
| Zipa | Zimbabwe People's Army |
| Zipra | Zimbabwe People's Revolutionary Army |
| ZNA | Zimbabwe National Army |

# *Acknowledgements*

This book was a collective enterprise, and we are heavily indebted to the very many people who made it possible. Most importantly, we would like to thank those we worked with most closely in the Shangani, either as researchers and writers in their own right, or as interpreters – Richard Dube, Nicholas Nkomo, Japhet Masuku, Benoni Mkandla, Calistus Mkwananzi, Nathaniel Mpofu, Mark Ndlovu, Kilikiya Nyathi and Martin Sibanda. They showed extraordinary skill and tact in what were often sensitive contexts; their friendship, encouragement and criticisms were invaluable. The particular roles they played are spelt out in detail in our introduction. We are also indebted to the great number of people we interviewed who spent valuable time telling us about their often traumatic experiences. We depended on the support of the many district councillors, the council chairmen J. Gabheni Sibanda and Leonard Nkomo, District Administrators Jack Nhliziyo and Robert Mlala, and Provincial Governor Welshman Mabhena. The staff of the Panke Guest House and the Kusile Guest House extended the warmest of welcomes to us. In Lupane, Danisile Hlavangana generously opened her home and became a lasting friend. In Nkayi, Auxilia Mabhena and MaNgwenya were always the kindest of hosts. The companionship of these friends made our stay in the Shangani memorable and exceptionally enjoyable.

In Bulawayo, Shari and John Eppel and Judith Todd welcomed us into their homes. We are grateful for their warm friendship and for their insights into Zimbabwean history and politics. Special thanks are due to historian and author Pathisa Nyathi, who read our manuscript with meticulous care, providing detailed comments on our text, remedying our (otherwise inadequate) Ndebele spelling, and sharing his knowledge of Zapu's history and early operations in Matabeleland. We are also indebted to oral historian and archivist Mark Ncube.

We were affiliated to the Department of History in the University of Zimbabwe during our research. We are grateful for the support of Professor Ngwabi Bhebe and his enthusiasm for the history of Matabeleland. He and the other members of the History Department provided us with a valuable and well-informed forum for debate at the International Conference on the Historical Dimensions of Democracy and Human Rights in Zimbabwe, held at the University of Zimbabwe in September 1996. Other institutions in Zimbabwe also facilitated our research in various ways. We would like to thank the staff of the Bulawayo Records Office and the National Archives of Zimbabwe for their help, and the Research Council of Zimbabwe for granting us permission to undertake this project.

In Oxford, we were based at St Antony's College, where the African Studies group provided a friendly environment for writing and debate. Professor William Beinart continued to offer us kind support long after this book should have been completed. Many colleagues and friends in Oxford have also contributed in various ways to this book. Marieke Clarke enthusiastically shared her work on the London Missionary Society archive in SOAS, her findings on Queen Lozikeyi and her love for the history of Matabeleland. The late Ioan Bowen Rees generously shared his records and understanding of the Inyathi missionary Aurfryn Rees. Other Zimbabweanists, particularly Richard Werbner, Norma Kriger and Eric Worby provided valuable feedback on particular sections of the book. Mark Leopold gave much appreciated comment and advice. Other scholars in Oxford, Keele, Yale, Cape Town and elsewhere, as well as the members of the Britain Zimbabwe Society, provided a forum as well as helpful comments on numerous seminar presentations.

Our research would not have been possible without finance from the Leverhulme Trust and the Economic and Social Research Council. The former funded Jocelyn Alexander and Terence Ranger. JoAnn McGregor was funded primarily through the ESRC, on grant no. R00023 527601, with an additional grant from the Leverhulme Trust.

Finally, we would like to thank our respective families, partners and close friends for their tolerance and support, particularly Dori Kimel, Mark Leopold and Shelagh Ranger. Encouragement from the late Gordon McGregor made his loss in the course of this research easier to bear.

# Note on Orthography

This book comprises a history of two modern districts – Nkayi and Lupane – that have taken the place of the old Shangani Reserve. In the text, we use the term 'Shangani' as a shorthand for the two districts, although the term is no longer current.

For the sake of clarity, we have standardized our spellings of names and places. We have used the post-independence spellings throughout our text, even where we refer to the colonial period, except inside quotations or when referring to archival sources. In such instances, current spellings are included in brackets where the correspondence between old and new terms is not obvious. We have spelt interviewees' names as they were given to us.

# Maps

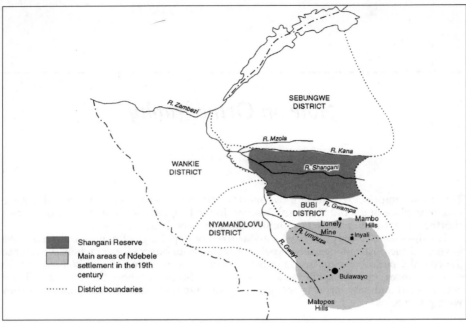

Map 1 The Shangani Reserve in late nineteenth-century Southern Rhodesia

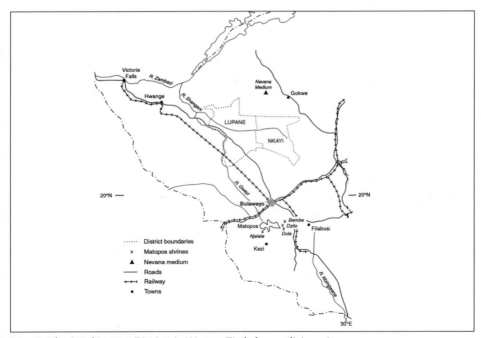

Map 2 Nkayi and Lupane Districts in Western Zimbabwe: religious sites

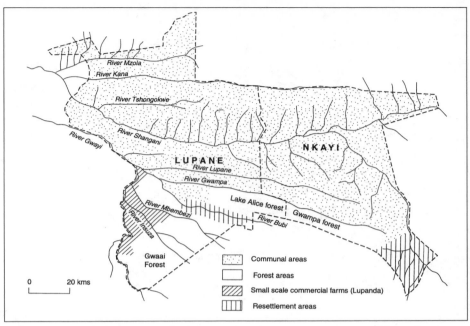

Map 3  Lupane and Nkayi Districts: land use

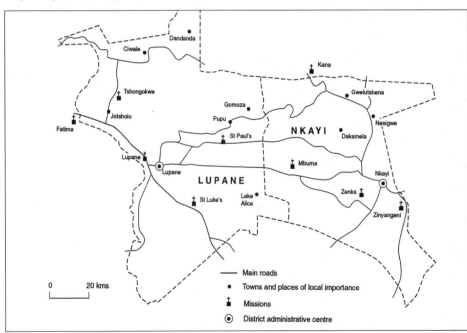

Map 4  Nkayi and Lupane Districts: missions and places of importance

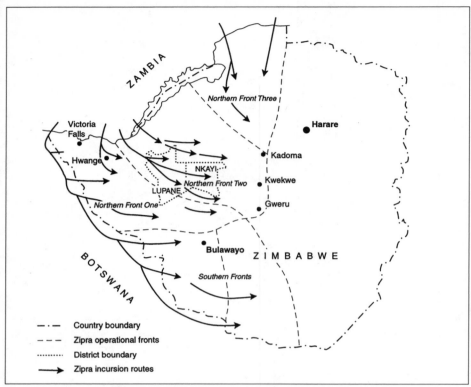

Map 5  Zipra incursions and operational areas

1 'The Last Stand' of the Allan Wilson Patrol, killed in the Shangani, 4 December 1893 (National Archives of Zimbabwe)

2 Lobengula's envoys, ca.1890 (Photo courtesy of Ben Shephard)

3 Soldiers burning African homes, Matabeleland, 1896 (Photo courtesy of Ben Shephard)

4  Joshua Nkomo

5  Zipra guerrillas addressing Zapu men in Lupane (J. Brickhill)

6  Zipra guerrillas addressing Zapu women in Lupane (J. Brickhill)

7  Zipra guerrillas drilling

8  Zipra guerrillas in action in the bush

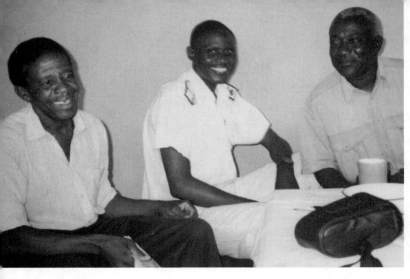

9  The research team: Japhet Masuku and Nicholas Nkomo with ex-Zipra nurse Hlanganani Ndebele in Dagamella Clinic

10 The research team: Jocelyn Alexander, Councillor Paulos Mhlotshwa and Nicholas Nkomo at Tshakalisa

11 The research team: Benoni Mkandla and the Shangani river in flood.

12 The research team: Calistus
Mkwananzi and family

13 The research team: Terence Ranger
with Nevana and Njelele  messenger
Mlingo Ncube, Dakamella

14 The research team: JoAnn McGregor with Nicholas Bhebe and family, resettlement village 24B

15 Panke
baobab tree

16 MaNcube,
shrine keeper at
Njelele

17 Former Zipra
guerrillas
returning from a
cleansing
ceremony at
Njelele

18  Njelele messenger and Bubi evictee Lina Moyo at her homestead rain shelter

19  Njelele messenger and Filabusi evictee
Chithekile Mhlanga

20  The Gusu forests of Matabeleland North

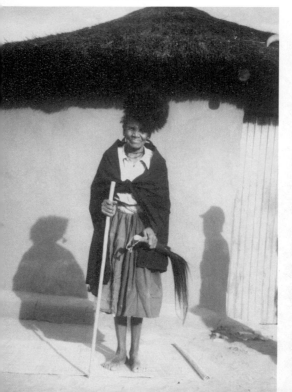

# Introduction

Our book is called *Violence and Memory* because violence has so powerfully shaped history and the memory of the past in Matabeleland. The story we tell concerns the remote, forested wilderness of the Shangani Reserve in northern Matabeleland, an area set aside as the Ndebele 'homeland' in the aftermath of the settler conquest of King Lobengula's Ndebele state. It is the story of the settlement of a sparsely populated, disease-ridden frontier and its transformation into the rural heartland of a nationalist movement, the Zimbabwe African People's Union (Zapu). The Shangani proved crucial to Zapu's war effort against the Rhodesian regime; after independence it gained notoriety as a refuge for former guerrillas who returned to the bush as 'dissidents'. Violence is a constant theme in Shangani history from the time of the wars of conquest of 1893 and 1896, through the particularly severe history of forced evictions and agrarian intervention in the colonial era, the nationalist resistance and intense state repression of the 1960s, the liberation war of the 1970s and, finally, the devastating post-colonial violence of the 1980s.

We wanted to write about Matabeleland in part because silence has surrounded the history of this region of Zimbabwe. As we talked to people in the districts of Nkayi and Lupane (into which the old Shangani Reserve was divided in the 1950s), we found that this silence had produced a profound sense of exclusion from national memory, and that the idea of writing a history of the Shangani inspired great enthusiasm. This sense of exclusion was, above all, the product of post-independence political and military conflict. As in other countries born of liberation wars, Zimbabwe's new leaders explicitly built their legitimacy on their nationalist and liberation war credentials. But their version of nationalist history was decidedly partial. Zimbabwean school books and official histories celebrated the successes of the ruling Zimbabwe African Nationalist Union (Patriotic Front) (Zanu(PF)) and its guerrilla army, Zanla. The contribution of Zapu – which was the loser in the national elections of 1980 and whose supporters were concentrated in Matabeleland – was downplayed or denigrated. Zanu(PF) politicians and the state-controlled media cast Zapu and its guerrilla army, Zipra, not as heroic liberators and nation-builders, but as a threat to the country's hard-won independence. The brutal campaign of violence directed against Matabeleland in the 1980s powerfully confirmed its exclusion from the nation. All of this has given remembrance of the past, and the telling of history, a particular significance in the 1990s.

The enthusiasm we found within the Shangani for the writing and telling of history has influenced this book in profound ways. We have benefited from unusually rich collaboration and sources. The three of us worked closely with a team of Zimbabwean

1

researchers. They used their special experience to collect material not readily available to us. Our research would not have been possible without them. Nicholas Nkomo, guerrilla commander of the Shangani during the liberation war, worked alongside us for much of our field work; Nkomo and a team of other former Zipra commanders – Richard Dube, Kilikiya Nyathi and Mark Ndlovu – also worked independently, interviewing guerrillas and encouraging them to record their own life stories. Nkomo's unpublished autobiography, 'Between the Hammer and the Anvil: The Autobiography of Nicholas Nkomo', is a remarkable document. We have drawn on it at length in our book, and we hope that the richness of the excerpts we have used may encourage its publication and recognition in its own right. Nkomo's mediation was also important to the relationship we were able to establish with former Zipra dissidents. Nathaniel Mpofu moved tirelessly round Nkayi recording the history of the Shangani's wide variety of churches. He, too, wrote a valuable autobiography which has greatly enriched our narrative. Japhet Masuku, Callistus Mkwananzi, Benoni Mkandla and Martin Sibanda accompanied one or other of us in the course of our research as interpreters and research assistants. They gave us the benefit of their knowledge of the people of their home areas in Nkayi and Lupane and so much more besides. Our understanding of Shangani history was immeasurably deepened as we worked, talked and travelled with them daily.

In addition to drawing on such a wide range of researchers, we have enjoyed an unusual, perhaps unique, access to written sources. The staff of the National Archives in Harare made available to us their very large deposit of material on the Shangani up to the 1960s. But we were also able to obtain rich archival material for the decades after that. The Governor of Matabeleland North, Welshman Mabhena, gave us his total support; the Provincial and District Administrators opened their archives to us; District Councillors in both Nkayi and Lupane gave us not only valuable interviews, and pointed us to many other informants, but also made council papers available to us. As a result we have a continuous administrative record from 1897 to 1985 and are the first researchers to be able to make such full use of the official correspondence of independent Zimbabwe. This has meant that every chapter in this book is based both on oral and on archival sources.

Although this book has been a collaborative enterprise, and has drawn on much local support, our historical reconstruction is different from any local narrative. We have drawn on the archival as well as the oral material in telling our story. And we have seen the way in which oral testimony has been shaped by the moment of recall in the 1990s. This has produced an inevitable tension in the book, stemming from our use of 1990s' recollections both as 'memory' and as evidence in historical reconstruction. In the course of our narrative, we have tried to be sensitive to – indeed, explicitly to discuss – the influence of the present on the oral histories we collected. But we have also tried to construct the most plausible version of events from the sources that were available to us. Where we have found perspectives and interpretations to vary, we have endeavoured to highlight these differences.

Inevitably, however, to give shape to our overall narrative of such a turbulent history as that of Matabeleland we have had to privilege some interpretations over others. Our richest oral sources, and the individuals whom we found to be the most eloquent tellers of their history, were often former nationalist leaders. It is their perspective, more than any other, that our book represents, though even then critically. Former Zapu leaders in the Shangani acted historically – and often act in our book – as spokespeople for broader communities of Shangani residents, and their perspective is in many ways widely shared. After all, they were often individuals who wore many hats at once – nationalist activist, church leader, shrine adept, teacher, etc. We have been careful to note dissenting voices and points of controversy where these have emerged through our interviews. But the Shangani is unusual – perhaps exceptional – in the way that nationalist party institutions and ideology came to be locally rooted. In moving through the districts of Lupane and Nkayi, it was difficult to find adults who, at some time in their past, had not been politically active. Zapu membership reached into every family, if not every home. In the 1980s, the residents of the Shangani were subjected to extreme violence collectively as supporters of Zapu, and this is reflected in many individual life stories. For this reason, the biographies and testimonies of local nationalist leaders are particularly revealing of the history of the Shangani.

Our primary aim in writing this book is to tell the history of the Shangani from the perspectives of those who live there, drawing on their own recollections. We hope that many of the people we interviewed will recognise themselves in this book. We also hope every interested Zimbabwean will be able to read our text. We have tried to avoid specialist language, which to the general reader may seem like mere jargon. But in the remainder of this introduction, we would like to spell out the broader significance of this history to African studies generally and Zimbabwean historiography in particular, before turning to a more detailed consideration of our methods and sources.

*Violence and Memory* investigates the relationships between anti-colonial resistance, nationalism, ethnicity and religion, and the more recent history of the guerrilla and post-independence wars. It is rooted in understandings of a particular landscape and environment, in the language of everyday political discourse, and in local interpretations of history. It is a narrative which is central to an understanding of Zimbabwean nationalism and to the formation and character of the post-colonial state. The perspective of this now silenced periphery is particularly revealing: it is on such margins that the workings of central power are often most clearly expressed and most sharply felt.[1] A recovery of the Shangani's history is important in its own right as well as for Zimbabwean history more generally. As the first historical study of this region, the book provides a corrective to the abundant recent scholarship on Zimbabwe which has focused so much on eastern and central Zimbabwe and so-called 'Shona' histories and legacies.[2] The book provides new insights into the impact of the great evictions of Ndebele speakers in the 1940s and 1950s; it is the first analysis of Zapu's 'rural nationalism'; the first extended account of Rhodesian Front administrative policy and theories of 'group democracy'; the first independent account of Zipra's civilian relations in the liberation war; the first general academic analysis of the post independence conflict; and the first detailed account of the role in this history of the important religious institutions and peoples of northwestern Zimbabwe.[3]

[1] Using the perspective of the margin to explore the centre is a common starting point for a range of recent anthropological and historical writing. See E. Worby, 'Tyranny, Parody and Ethnic Polarity: Ritual Engagements with the State in Northwestern Zimbabwe', *Journal of Southern African Studies*, 24, 3 (1998), p. 563.

[2] There are, of course, numerous studies of other regions in Matabeleland. The main texts are R. Werbner's *Tears of the Dead. The Social Biography of an African Family* (Edinburgh, IAI, 1999), which gives a vivid insight into the experience of one Kalanga family; T. Ranger, *Voices from the Rocks. Nature, Culture and History in the Matopos Hills of Zimbabwe* (Oxford, James Currey, 1999); N. Bhebe, *Benjamin Burombo: African Politics in Zimbabwe* (Harare, College Press, 1989). Also see N. Bhebe's long delayed *Zapu and Zanu. Guerrilla Warfare and the Evangelical Church in Zimbabwe* (Gweru, Mambo Press, 1999).

[3] On the religious institutions and peoples of the northwest see E. Worby, 'Maps, Names and Ethnic Games: the Epistemology and Iconography of Colonial Power in Northwestern Zimbabwe', *Journal of Southern African Studies*, 20, 3 (1994), pp. 371–92 and 'Remaking Labour, Reshaping Identity: Cotton, Commodification, and the Culture of Modernity in Northwestern Zimbabwe' (PhD, McGill University, 1992); R. Holst, 'Continuity and Change. The Dynamics of Social and Productive Relations in Hwange, Zimbabwe, 1870–1960' (M.Phil, University of Zimbabwe, 1993); G.T. Ncube, 'A History of North-West Zimbabwe, 1850–1950s: Comparative Change in Three Worlds' (M.Phil, University of Zimbabwe, 1997).

Our book focuses on the hidden political history of the Shangani, which has been submerged beneath the master-narrative of official Zimbabwean nationalism. But there are further hidden histories which we go some way to uncovering. We explore the Shangani's pre-colonial and pre-Ndebele histories, which were overlain first by a modernizing Ndebele public identity and then by pan-ethnic nationalism. We were able to recover these older hidden histories not least because they refused to remain buried at moments of anguish and crisis. They provided an important resource in the renewed moral debate of the 1990s, in efforts to heal and commemorate the dead, in attempts to come to terms with the past, and in local debates over power, community and relations with the land. We return to some of these issues below, as we discuss the book's contribution to academic debate under the themes of the post-colonial state, nationalism, war and violence, ethnicity, religion and landscape.

Much recent literature in African studies has been preoccupied with understanding the current 'African crisis'.[4] Academic writers from a range of disciplines have sought to counter the popular yet inadequate explanations offered by 'state collapse' and 'ethnic conflict'. These are widely used as a shorthand means of deciphering violence and anti-democratic practice across Africa, and have tended to naturalize conflict rather than further its understanding.[5] In this context of disillusion with corrupt, authoritarian and violent regimes, writers have looked for new insights into the origins of intolerance. They have revisited nationalism and the repressive late-colonial context in which nationalists mobilized support, and they have sought to excavate a deeper history in order to shed light on what Patrick Chabal has referred to as the 'retraditionalisation' of contemporary African political discourse.[6] These need not be contradictory approaches: as Francois Grignon has argued with reference to Kenya, one reading of Bayart's *Politics of the Belly* is that a traditionalist idiom has served to reinvent essentially colonial 'governmentalities'.[7]

These analyses are notable for having moved away from the stark opposition of collaboration and resistance, towards a concern with relationships of 'promiscuity' or 'convivial tension' between government and governed. As Eric Worby has argued, 'the new literature ... has begun to give us something else: an indigenization of the concepts used to capture the qualities and sensibilites of post-colonial power, and an attention to how popular imaginings of those qualities become themselves constitutive of the facts of subjugation'.[8] While we are concerned to explore the language and culture of local

---

[4] See, *inter alia*, M. Mamdani, *Citizen and Subject. Contemporary Africa and the Legacy of Late Colonialism* (Oxford, James Currey, 1996); P. Chabal, *Power in Africa* (London, Macmillan, 1994); P. Chabal and J.P. Daloz, *Africa Works: Disorder as Political Instrument* (Oxford, James Currey, 1999); J.F. Bayart, *The State in Africa: The Politics of the Belly* (London, Longman, 1993); J.F. Bayart, S. Ellis and B. Hibou, *The Criminalization of the State in Africa* (Oxford, James Currey, 1999); A. Mbembe, 'Provisional Notes on the Postcolony', *Africa*, 62, 1 (1992), pp. 3–37.

[5] See P. Richard's discussion of the naturalization of conflict in R. Kaplan's influential article 'The Coming Anarchy: How Scarcity, Crime, Overpopulation, Tribalism and Disease are Rapidly Destroying the Social Fabric of our Planet', *Atlantic Monthly* (February 1994). P. Richards, *Fighting for the Rainforest. War, Youth and Resources in Sierra Leone* (Oxford, James Currey, 1996). Also see D. Turton (ed.) *War and Ethnicity: Global Connections and Local Violence* (New York, University of Rochester Press, 1997) and, for the Matabeleland conflict, J. Alexander, J. McGregor and T. Ranger, 'Ethnicity and the Politics of Conflict: The Case of Matabeleland, Zimbabwe', in E. W. Nafziger, F. Stewart and R. Väyrynen (eds), *The Origins of Humanitarian Emergencies: War and Displacement in Developing Countries* (Oxford, Oxford University Press, forthcoming).

[6] See Chabal and Daloz, *Africa Works*, pp. 45–92.

[7] F. Grignon, 'Understanding African States' Governmentalities: The Case of Kenya', paper presented at the Institute of Commonwealth Studies, London, December 1996.

[8] E. Worby, 'Tyranny, Parody and Ethnic Polarity: Ritual Engagements with the State in North-

politics, our narrative remains open: it deliberately avoids a single overarching inter-pretation of the historical relationships between rulers and ruled in Zimbabwe.

Nonetheless, this book does allow a response to recent literature. Mahmood Mamdani's *Citizen and Subject* has been particularly influential in its revisionist account of nationalism and its focus on the late-colonial origins of the authoritarian post-colonial state. Mamdani sees nationalist mobilization as a reflection of the 'bifurcated' colonial state. This state accentuated difference by separating urban from rural, and one ethnicity from another under systems of indirect rule. In the rural areas, nationalism was tainted with and came to reproduce the authoritarian practices and understandings of chiefly rule and subjecthood. In urban centres, nationalism was preoccupied with racial discrimination and citizenship – the main concerns of an educated, urban elite. Mamdani's provocative opening question with regard to resistance and ethnicity is whether anti-colonial struggle took the form of 'a series of ethnic revolts against so many ethnically organized and centrally reinforced local powers – in other words, a string of ethnic civil wars? In brief, was not ethnicity a dimension of both power and resistance?'[9]

Our Zimbabwean narrative does not fit comfortably with these depictions of African politics. Late colonialism did of course influence nationalism. Intense colonial repression and war ruled out open, democratic practice and tolerance of alternative views. It fostered what could be termed a 'culture of authoritarianism' that was certainly compatible with the state socialist ideology of nationalist leaders at the time, as well as a 'traditionalist' discourse which stressed strong leadership and unquestioning loyalty.[10] The late-colonial period has dominated recent debates over the role of 'traditional' authorities. The colonial meanings attached to the tribal categories of 'Shona' and 'Ndebele' certainly facilitated the government's stigmatization of Zapu as an ethnic, as well as a political, threat after 1980. But our history of a rural nationalist stronghold does not allow a dichotomous treatment of rural and urban nationalism in the way Mamdani suggests: key figures moved between positions of authority across the town-and-country divide; notions of citizenship were well developed in both areas and not only amongst an urban elite; in the light of post-independence state violence in Matabeleland, ethnicity has come to seem more important in popular revisitations of nationalist divisions than it ever seemed at the time to those at the bottom of the movement. We speak of 'rural national-ism', but we do so in a way that does not root it solely in local grievances or ethnicity to the exclusion of the wider meanings and linkages which were intrinsic to its success.

Our narrative also allows a response to arguments about the 'retraditionalization' of post-colonial politics. The language and ideas of nationalism, rights and citizenship were central to the politics we describe. Ethnicity was not the only, or most important, arena of moral debate, as John Lonsdale appears to suggest for Kenya when he argues that moral ethnicity 'is a much more trenchant critic of the abuse of power than any Western political thought'.[11] While tradition and Western political ideas are at times counterposed in the political discourse of the Shangani, it would be misleading to think of a traditionalist discourse as separable from Western ideas: the two have been inextri-cably intertwined for too long.

---

[8] (cont.) western Zimbabwe', *Journal of Southern African Studies*, 24, 3 (1998), p. 562, citing A. Mbembe, 'The Banality of Power and the Aesthetics of Vulgarity in the Post-Colony', *Public Culture*, 4, 2 (1992), pp. 1–30; Bayart, *Politics of the Belly*, and others.

[9] Mamdani, *Citizen and Subject*, p. 8

[10] Our own material on the traditionalist idiom of loyalty and respect is, of course, an Ndebele one. However, for a comparable argument rooted in a Shona idiom which defends the culture of 'black people' as 'a weapon strong enough to bring about stability, humanity, unity, loyalty and respect', see Innocent Madzana, 'Decolonising Minds', *Moto*, 195 (April 1999), p. 2.

[11] See B. Berman and J. Lonsdale, *Unhappy Valley 2. Violence and Ethnicity* (Oxford, James Currey, 1992), p. 467.

We situate our analysis of post-colonial conflict firmly in political rivalry – in the Zanu(PF) government's desire to efface Zapu as a significant political counterweight, and in the insecurities of the first years of independence in which a legitimate and 'majoritarian' Zanu(PF) government sought to consolidate its power. Violence in post-colonial Zimbabwe was the product not of a disintegrating state nor of ethnic antagonism – it was in no way the result of a 'retraditionalization' of politics. Rather, it was the consequence of the excesses of a strong state, itself in many ways a direct Rhodesian inheritance, and a particular interpretation of nationalism. As in more well-known African wars, notions of generations-old tribal antagonism came to be used by the military during the conflict, and civilians subjected to state violence came to see the war as both political *and* ethnic in intent.[12] Though popular understandings of tribal opposition and memories of persecution were not causes of the conflict, they were elaborated and hardened during it, and have been sustained in public and private memory since the conflict's conclusion.

It would be misleading to consider the broader relevance of our text only in relation to debates over contemporary African politics, and certainly the narrative we tell is not intended solely to serve this purpose. *Violence and Memory* also contributes to wider debates over nationalism *per se*. Our analysis is new partly because of our sources and approach. Rather than drawing on the testimony of senior nationalist leaders, we explore the views of influential local figures – their motives, language and ideas, their debates with national party leaders, guerrillas and wider society. And we investigate how these Shangani leaders created a rural nationalism which gave wider meaning to local grievances and protest. In Zimbabwean historiography, and indeed in African studies more generally, this perspective is rarely explored, though the work of Peter Delius, Greet Kershaw and Steven Feierman has begun to show the potential of such an approach in the rather different contexts of South Africa, Kenya and Tanzania.[13] Much writing on rural nationalism in Zimbabwe has either assumed that peasants were intrinsically nationalist, and so conflated a long history of various forms of resistance and protest into a proto-nationalist trajectory, or that peasant consciousness could be treated as autonomous from nationalism.[14]

In contrast, we explore the character of rural nationalism in terms of its changing social base and ideological content. Nationalism embodied the ideals of freedom, democracy, equality and restoration of the land to the people of Zimbabwe; it was also a movement able to accommodate a range of local issues reinterpreted as an essential part of these broader ideals. The goals of ousting the colonial regime and transforming the nature of the state linked the two. We show how the social base of nationalism in the Shangani shifted from a modernizing, Christian elite to a wider constituency tolerant both of traditional religious ideas and social groups stigmatized as 'backward'. This history fills a more specifically Zimbabweanist gap by telling the story of the making of

---

[12] For other cases where ethnicity was mobilized in the course of a conflict (rather than acting as its cause) and subsequently dominated popular understandings of conflict, see G. Prunier, *The Rwanda Crisis: 1959-1994. History of a Genocide* (London, Hurst, 1995); R. Lemarchand, *Burundi: Ethnic Conflict and Genocide* (Cambridge, Cambridge University Press, 1995); and essays in K. Fukui and J. Markakis (eds), *Ethnicity and Conflict in the Horn of Africa* (Oxford, James Currey, 1994), notably D. Turton, 'Mursi Political Identity and Warfare: The Survival of an Idea', and W. James 'War and "Ethnic Visibility": the Uduk on the Sudan-Ethiopia Border'.

[13] P. Delius, *A Lion Amongst the Cattle: Reconstruction and Resistance in the Northern Transvaal* (Oxford James Currey, 1996), G. Kershaw, *Mau Mau From Below* (Oxford, James Currey, 1997); S. Feierman, *Peasant Intellectuals: Anthropology and History in Tanzania* (Madison, University of Wisconsin Press, 1990).

[14] We are explicitly arguing a different case from T. Ranger in *Peasant Consciousness and Guerrilla Warfare* (London, James Currey, 1985).

Zapu's rural nationalism, whose grassroots organization and relationships with guerrillas have only begun to be explored in the academic literature.[15]

This history of nationalism remains powerful in local political discourse today. The history of the Shangani, as it was told to us in the mid-1990s, was in many ways dominated by the nationalist past. It has become commonplace to speak of the present as a 'post-national' era[16] – a time of global information flows, international economies, and weakened states, marked by the passing away of the first generation post-colonial heads of state. And in Zimbabwe at the time of writing, criticism of the Zanu(PF) government and its nationalist project has become increasingly acute. Yet our book is the story of people who want to be incorporated into nationalist history, who want their contribution recognized, and who feel that the nationalist goals they fought and suffered for were not only valuable in themselves, but remain one of the principal means through which they can hold the state to account. In the Shangani, moral debates over the political practice of both local and national leaders constantly refer back to nationalist promises and ideals. The values of nationalism are regularly held up in a favourable light against what are seen as the corrupting and exclusive practices of 'tribalism'. In this context, 'ethnicity' and 'nationalism' cannot be subsumed into each other, or used interchangeably. Each has a separate history and invokes different meanings. By making this argument, we are not suggesting that nationalism is intrinsically a positive force, simply that it *can* be used as a moral counterweight to much criticized post-colonial governmental practice.[17] Nor are we making any claims about its future use: the passing away of the older generation of political activists will undoubtedly have an important impact on political discourse, and the use of historical memories of nationalism by a younger generation is likely to be very different.

By providing new insights into the liberation and post-independence wars, our study contributes to debates over warfare and violence in Africa, particularly with regard to the ideologies and motivations that have sustained insurgencies across the continent. Even in anti-colonial wars, or wars fuelled by destabilization, by cold-war antagonisms or discontent over decolonizing settlements, people's motivations for supporting armed insurgencies have proved resistant to generalization.[18] Although the story of nationalism and guerrilla war in the Shangani is the source of much pride, the recollections of the 1990s through which we tell this history are not the straightforwardly triumphalist, glorifying narratives familiar from the early 1980s in Zimbabwe, or from

---

[15] See J. Brickhill, 'Daring to Storm the Heavens: The Military Strategy of Zapu, 1976–1979', and D. Dabengwa, 'Zipra in the Zimbabwe War of National Liberation', both in N. Bhebe and T. Ranger (eds), *Soldiers in Zimbabwe's Liberation War* (London, James Currey, 1995).

[16] See P. Chabal, 'The African Crisis: Context and Interpretation', in R. Werbner and T.O. Ranger (eds), *Postcolonial Identities in Africa* (London, Zed Books, 1996), pp. 29–55.

[17] In this respect we wish to distance our analysis both from an approach which sees nationalism as inherently good and from those which cast it as an intrinsically negative force. The former is exemplified by much of the 'heroic' nationalist literature produced by the Dar es Salaam School, the latter by B. Davidson, *The Black Man's Burden: Africa and the Curse of the Nation State* (London, James Currey, 1992) or, in a different context, E. Hobsbawm's analysis of nationalism in Eastern Europe in *The Age of Extremes. The Short Twentieth Century, 1914–1991* (London, Abacus, 1995).

[18] In addition to Zimbabwean debates over rural ideologies and motivations, reviewed in T. Ranger and N. Bhebe (eds), *Society in Zimbabwe's Liberation War* (London, James Currey, 1995), also see the accounts of post-colonial Mozambique which followed the publication of C. Geffray's *A Causa Das Armas. Antropologia da Guerra Contemporanea em Mocambique* (Porto, Ediçoes Afrontamento, 1991), such as K. Wilson, 'Cults of Violence and Counter-Violence in Mozambique', *Journal of Southern African Studies*, 18, 3 (1992), pp. 527–82; W. Minter *Apartheid's Contras. An Inquiry into the Roots of War in Angola and Mozambique* (London, Zed Books, 1994). For a discussion of recent East and West African wars, see C. Clapham (ed.), *African Guerrillas* (Oxford, James Currey, 1998).

comparable heroic and fervent accounts of transition, liberation and revolution else-where.[19] The oral testimonies we collected were not blind to pain or to the divisions that were part of the course of nationalist mobilization, repression and guerrilla war. From local recollections, we have been able to tell the story not only of battles won and the enemy outwitted, but also of the conflicts between party leaders and guerrillas, the struggles over Christianity during the war, the violence against witches and sellouts and the devastating effects of the Rhodesian use of poisons. The moral debates over these painful episodes live on powerfully in memory today. Our study contributes to the historiography of the liberation war by putting local nationalist leaders and nationalist ideology at the centre of our account, allowing us to explore the interaction between guerrilla and rural nationalist ideologies, and the wartime conflicts and debates which shaped rural politics.

The history and memory of the liberation war is important not only in itself, but also as a point of contrast with the conflict of the 1980s. Our analysis of the conflict from the point of view of those at the receiving end of state violence – civilians, local Zapu leaders and armed 'dissidents' – throws new light on this conflict. By charting the activities and fate of the Shangani's Zapu leaders after independence, we reveal the profound differences between guerrilla relations with nationalists during the liberation war, on the one hand, and 'dissident' relations with civilians after independence on the other. We also reveal the differences in the ideologies which sustained – or rather, failed to sustain – civilian support for armed dissent. If, as we argue, nationalism was the defining ideology of the liberation war and provided guerrillas and civilians with a common cause, the war of the 1980s found no such uniting force. The former Zipra guerrillas who became dissidents saw themselves as persecuted victims in a war in which tribalism had replaced nationalist ideology, but also saw themselves as perpetuating Zipra's struggle. Yet they never succeeded in finding common cause with the Shangani's nationalists, who, though initially sympathetic to their plight, came to suffer at their hands and even to blame them for the excesses of the state violence that followed. We show the devastating effects of state violence in the 1980s, and explore the ways in which it shaped people's perceptions of the Zimbabwean nation, their ideas about the central and local state, and their understanding of history.

*Violence and Memory* also dwells on attempts to commemorate and heal this violent past, and thus contributes to a growing literature on the politics of memory.[20] We build on Richard Werbner's study of state remembrance and popular memorialization of the Zimbabwean liberation war, showing how the proclamation and enactment of official memory of the liberation war has sought to silence, often with very direct repression, all alternative memories.[21] In Matabeleland, it remains difficult and dangerous for people to seek to erect monuments to those slain in the 1970s, let alone those who died at the hands of the state in the 1980s. Even the creation of official provincial Heroes' Acres to honour the fallen of the liberation war in Matabeleland lagged far behind other provinces, and has provoked a highly sceptical response.[22] Memorialization has thus been forced into

---

[19] The historiography of Zimbabwe's guerrilla war is discussed in Ranger and Bhebe, *Soldiers in Zimbabwe's Liberation War*. The key text marking the transition from heroic accounts to less sanguine interpretations is Norma Kriger's *Zimbabwe's Guerilla War. Peasant Voices* (Cambridge, Cambridge University Press, 1992). Comparable transitions have marked the literature on Mozambique, Eritrea and elsewhere.

[20] See, for example, the collection of essays in R. Werbner (ed.), *Memory and the Post Colony. African Anthropology and the Critique of Power* (London, Zed Books, 1998).

[21] R. Werbner, 'Smoke from the Barrel of a Gun: Postwar of the Dead. Memory and Reinscription in Zimbabwe', in Werbner (ed.), *Memory and the Post Colony*, pp. 71–99.

[22] Personal communication from Japhet Masuku, who attended the official opening of Matabeleland North's Heroes' Acre in August 1998.

Introduction                                    9

the realms of silence, of private arenas of discourse, and of possession and ritual. Our narrative details how local efforts to commemorate and heal the past have drawn not only on the history of nationalism and the wars of the 1970s and 1980s, but have delved into deeper pasts. People have looked for points of comparison and contrast, for 'traditions' of commemoration, cleansing and healing; they have searched for the best interpreters of economic crisis, disease and ecological calamity, and for the most powerful and 'authentic' mediators between living and dead. To find these they have looked to the nineteenth century, to other phases of Shangani history, and to histories previously hidden.

Because of the variety and persistence of these efforts to deal with the past, we find that Zimbabwe's experience is different from interpretations of other African post-colonies, such as the Zairian 'postcolonial beyond' described by de Boek, where 'we find ... no past and no future, no memory and no oblivion, no dead and no living'.[23] Despite all the dangers and difficulties, there *are* means in Matabeleland, as elsewhere in Zimbabwe, for using the past and for making from it understandings of the present, and hence imagining a future. Unlike other parts of the continent where warfare persists, the extreme violence of the Matabeleland conflict *did* come to an end, in however a coerced and one-sided way and at whatever price in the suppression of public memory, in the Unity Agreement of December 1987. The articulation in Zimbabwe of what Richard Werbner calls 'a right of recountability ... the right, especially in the face of state violence and oppression, to make a citizen's memory known, and acknowledged in the public sphere', can seem unthinkable to commentators from other parts of Africa.[24]

In addition to contributing to the study of nationalism, war and the post-colonial state, *Violence and Memory* contributes to debates over ethnicity. Our analysis of ethnicity follows recent understandings in the East African literature which have combined a sensitivity to social constructions of ethnicity with an emphasis on the experience of ethnic divisions as 'real', 'natural' and 'ancient'.[25] The silence over Matabeleland's history has had effects beyond those already detailed, in that it contributes to the popular conception of the region in nineteenth-century terms, as the home of 'the Ndebele' – and 'the Ndebele' continue to be envisaged as fierce immigrant warriors and raiders. This image has been a source of historical pride to many modern Ndebele speakers and of historical resentment to many modern Shona speakers. But it is an image which casts a dangerous shadow over both the past and the present. It was used by government forces to devastating effect during the violence of the 1980s, and has allowed both Zimbabwean and foreign observers, as well as many Zimbabwean citizens, to see the conflict in terms of 'tribalism', as the inevitable result of deep-rooted animosities between 'Ndebele' and 'Shona'.[26] Such tribal images flourish in Zimbabwe today.

Although the Shangani has gained notoriety as a dissenting and solidly Ndebele heartland, we are able to show how ethnically, linguistically and culturally complicated the notion of Ndebele identity is. Almost everyone in the Shangani came to speak Ndebele and to identify themselves as such, but the process through which this occurred was a complex one, and in many ways an unexpected development for an area

23 Filip de Boek, 'Beyond the Grave: History, Memory and Death in Postcolonial Congo/Zaire', in Werbner (ed.) *Memory and the Postcolony*, pp. 21–57.
24 R. Werbner, 'Beyond Oblivion: Confronting Memory Crisis', in Werbner (ed.), *Memory and the Postcolony*, p. 1. Following a presentation on Matabeleland at a seminar on the South African Truth and Justice Commission, held in the University of Cape Town in 1998, participants from Rwanda, Mozambique and Zaire made comments to this effect.
25 See Turton (ed.), *War and Ethnicity*; Fukui and Markakis (eds), *Conflict and Ethnicity in the Horn*.
26 For an analysis of media reporting in Zimbabwe, see J. Alexander and J. McGregor, 'Representing Violence in Matabeleland, Zimbabwe: Press and Internet Debates', in T. Allen and J. Seaton (eds), *The Media of Conflict. War Reporting and Representations of Ethnic Violence* (London, Zed Books, 1999).

on the margins of the nineteenth-century Ndebele state, inhabited largely by people who were not descendants of the immigrant Nguni warriors of popular stereotype. In the first decades after the defeat of the Ndebele regiments, the fragmentation of the former state allowed a reassertion of pre-Ndebele cultural traditions by previously incorporated peoples who settled in the Shangani. The importance of Ndebele language and history grew within the Shangani over the colonial period, as evictions brought waves of Ndebele-speaking evictees into the Reserve from the 'white' land to the south, and as Ndebele became the language of administration and authority. But the consolidation of Ndebele as the dominant public identity did not rule out the existence of alternative identities, and did not translate into ethnic politics. Nor were the meanings attached to being Ndebele static: Ndebele identity was not only about a warrior past, but was also reinscribed with meanings of modernity and (a much contested) moral authority. In the period of nationalist activism, the Shangani was resolutely loyal to Joshua Nkomo's leadership and to the Zapu tradition, but Zapu never mobilized as an 'Ndebele' party either locally or nationally.

Few texts on nationalism and ethnicity in Africa would be complete without a consideration of the role of religion. The religious history we tell in this book is in many ways a reversal of the usual story in Southern Africa. Although nationalism offered the 'grand narrative' which structured rural leaders' telling of the Shangani's history, their accounts were also powerfully influenced by Christian ideas and beliefs. The first nationalist activists in the Shangani were Christian progressives whose Christianity was a key source of self-identification, and was intimately tied up with ideas about modernity and nationalism. That Christianity, nationalism and a modernising ethos should be linked is hardly new in southern African history, and is equally commonplace in Zimbabwe's past.[27] But unlike the familiar outline of Christian history elsewhere in Zimbabwe, the Christian history of the Shangani began late, after the Second World War, with the arrival of thousands of evictees from alienated land in other parts of Matabeleland. Independent churches were brought into the Shangani on the backs of immigrants, rather than arising out of protest against local missions. The missionaries followed the evictees, and construction of churches and schools began on a significant scale only after the evictees' arrival. The balance of agency between missionaries and locals was thus very different from that described in classic histories of southern-African Christianity.[28] Our study resonates in many ways with the process of late Christian arrival which Maxwell describes among the Hwesa people of Eastern Zimbabwe, where it similarly accompanied large-scale evictions of the modernizing Manyika. He notes that 'Bengt Sundkler has long been at pains to point out the role of African agents in the continent's Christian history. To his "refugee" and "returnee" movements for Christianization there must now be added "eviction" movements.'[29]

But the relationship between religion and nationalism was more complex than this suggests – 'traditional' religion also played a central role. An understanding of this relationship is crucial for an interpretation of contemporary 'traditionalist' critiques of central government. We argue that in the early twentieth century, when the Shangani

---

[27] Recent studies which throw light on the relationship between Christianity and nationalism include T. Ranger, *Are we not also Men? The Samkange Family and African Politics in Zimbabwe 1920-1964* (London, James Currey, 1995); D. Maxwell, *Christians and Chiefs in Zimbabwe. A Social History of the Hwesa People, c. 1870s–1990s* (Edinburgh, IAI, 1999); R. Elphick and R. Davenport (eds.), *Christianity in South Africa. A Political, Social and Cultural History* (Oxford, James Currey, 1997).

[28] See, for example, Jean and John Comaroff, 'Through the looking-glass: colonial encounters of the first kind', *Journal of Historical Sociology*, 1, 1 (March 1998).

[29] Maxwell, *Christians and Chiefs*, p. 117.

was populated by fragmented groups of settlers of diverse origins and languages, the important Nevana spirit medium provided at least some cultural cohesion. When waves of Ndebele-speaking immigrants arrived from the south over the course of the twentieth century, the Shangani became a zone of competition between Nevana and the network of shrines at the Matopos, notably Njelele, in Matabeleland South. Nationalism was led by modernizing Christians, but it also sought to incorporate older cultural and religious traditions. The Nevana medium, the Njelele shrine, and their many adepts and envoys in the Shangani, have all played an important role in the different phases of Shangani history. Local traditional religious leaders and the major religious centres were used by nationalists, guerrillas and dissidents to further their cause. And from the 1960s onwards, these religious traditions became an intrinsic part of nationalist symbolism and legitimization. After independence, the relationship between nationalists and the shrines provided people with an idiom of accountability, and a model of the relation- ship between leaders and led, as mediated by ancestral spirits and the High God, Mwali.[30] This idiom of accountability was legitimated by virtue of its 'traditional' status, yet made its moral claims on leading government figures by virtue of the use and appeals made to its religious leaders by nationalists.

This consideration of the politics of traditional religion leads us to the final area of concern of our book and a further realm of traditional religious signification and meaning – the landscape. The 'dark forests' of the Shangani were more than a backdrop for the history we tell.[31] Ideas about the forested landscape of the Shangani as 'dark' and 'threatening', as a place of refuge, rebels, outcasts, wild animals and hostile spirits had a profound influence on the course of this history. The image of the 'dark forests' has resonance for many periods of Shangani history and is central to its recounting. It provides the backcloth to stories of the rebels who lived and fought in the forests in the uprisings of 1893 and 1896; it is a defining image in African immigrants' accounts of their initial encounters with a hostile land, of struggles with wild animals, of the depredations of malaria and the poisonous plants of the veld; it is invoked in the telling of tales of rebellious protesters who took to the bush in riots against colonial 'develop- ment', of the succession of guerrillas who made hideouts in the forests and used the bushy land to strategic advantage, and of 'dissidents' who returned to the protection of the forests after independence. People's understanding of their history as a process of taming a wild and hostile land remains powerful today, not least in shaping attitudes towards development initiatives.

Ideas about the environment have been important in other ways as well. Cycles of epidemic disease and drought feature as regular markers in narratives of Shangani history. Interpreting these events has provoked intense moral and political debate which has itself influenced subsequent events. Epidemics provided occasions for elaboration of the relationship between violence and disease, and for reflection on relations with neighbours and leaders, both secular and religious. Drought inspired criticism of leaders and demands for accountability, post-war cleansing and an apology for the violence of the past. Attitudes to land and environment are interwoven into this political history – they have shaped both its course and its telling.

---

[30] See Ranger, *Voices from the Rocks*, for a full account of the Mwali shrine and nationalism.
[31] Much recent writing has emphasized the power of landscape imagery on the course of history in Zimbabwe and other parts of Africa. See for example, Ranger, *Voices from the Rocks*; D. Moore, 'Clear Waters and Muddied Histories: Competing Claims to the Kaerezi River', *Journal of Southern African Studies*, 24, 2 (1998); K. Middleton, '"Who Killed Malagasy Cactus?" Science, Environment and Colonialism in Southern Madagascar (1924–1930), *Journal of Southern African Studies*, 25, 2 (1999); H. Moore and M. Vaughan, *Cutting Down Trees: Gender, Nutrition and Agri- cultural Change in the Northern Province of Zambia, 1890–1990* (London, James Currey, 1994).

## Authorship, Methods and Organization

This book has been a collective endeavour. It is the equal result of the research, analysis and writing of three scholars. Over the last three years we have shared the research from beginning to end. There is not a chapter of this book which does not draw on the work of all three of us, and which we have not rewritten in response to the comments of others. For this reason we have not indicated the authorship of chapters, and have not indicated in the footnotes which of us transcribed a file or carried out an interview. Every interpretation and conclusion of this book is endorsed by all of us. But the conventions of authorship greatly undervalue the contribution of our Zimbabwean collaborators mentioned above, without whom our research would not have been possible. There are many other people who have also contributed to this research in different ways and whom we mention below.

We divided the tasks of research as follows: one of us worked in the archives in Harare and Bulawayo and shared in some of the fieldwork; one of us carried out fieldwork in Lupane and noted documents held there; one of us did the same in Nkayi. We photocopied and exchanged our archival notes and interview transcripts so that each of us has had access to the full range of evidence. Findings in the archives raised new questions to be pursued in fieldwork; findings in fieldwork demanded the discovery of new archival sources and reinterpretation of old. After drafting chapters, we have exchanged, discussed and rewritten them to the satisfaction of all of us.

Our archival material has been collected and assessed by the established canons of historical research. The list of sources at the end of this book will show what an extensive official archival record exists even for the 'remote' and 'peripheral' Shangani. Mission sources are, however, much less rich than elsewhere, partly because large-scale missionary work began so late and partly because the particular churches involved had little interest in historical and ethnographic record. (As Father Odilo, founder of the Catholic Marianhill mission in Lupane, says: 'If I had been a Jesuit, I would have been able to create a rich record. But I was only interested in conversions!') We have filled in the religious history of the Shangani by means of interviews and the written texts of Nathaniel Mpofu. But we have had access to records for periods, and on topics, hitherto not explored. In particular, we have been able to analyse Rhodesian Front policies in the late 1960s and 1970s.

We carried out our fieldwork between 1994 and 1996, making our entry into the two districts of Nkayi and Lupane through district administrators and councils. The councillors in turn provided us with an introduction to local communities. We found that, throughout the Shangani, the political leaders of the 1990s were the nationalist leaders of the 1960s; the councillors themselves had often been born into the homes of political activists, indicating a remarkable continuity in both activism and representation. We asked local councillors in each of the districts' more than twenty wards for introductions to religious and traditional leaders, to people who could speak for different generations of migrants, and to nationalist leaders of the old Zapu hierarchy. We also asked to speak to former guerrillas, and former refugees. We moved systematically around each ward in the two districts in this way.

When we entered communities through trusted local political leaders, many people proved keen to tell their stories, sometimes for hours at a time, and occasionally extending over several days. Others, of course, given such a turbulent history, were fearful and suspicious, and a small number declined our request for an interview. Some – particularly the former guerrillas and dissidents – decided they would prefer to write their own stories for us rather than be interviewed. For many, the pain of the past – particularly, but not only, that of the 1980s – was not just history. It was a living present and difficult to retell – people 'are still dying from their wounds', they would speak of being 'already dead'. While local political leaders, as community spokespeople, often had a well-developed 'public' narrative of Shangani history and of their own role in it, many others did not have seamless accounts which they could retell without reliving the personal suffering and loss they had experienced. Even the more 'distanced' of public narratives were full of pain. We will not forget the experience of interviewing people who have survived so much.

Over the period of our fieldwork, we conducted more than 300 interviews. Our main method of interviewing was to collect life histories, making the interviews as informal and conversational as possible, but covering a range of topics of interest to us. Typically, we would begin by asking how the interviewee's family came to the Shangani, and would cover the whole sequence of Shangani history through to the 1990s. Often these interviews turned into group discussions, as friends and relatives of the interviewee turned up and joined in. Sometimes the interviews were more focused on the particular experiences, interests and specialisms of the interviewee. Although we conducted a large number of interviews, we have not used these sources quantitatively in our narrative. However, the sheer volume of material we collected, and the systematic coverage of all wards and most, if not all, of the important local leaders, gives us confidence in weighting the statements we make in our text. We interviewed every chief and headman in the two districts and every significant religious leader. Where important nationalist leaders had moved to town or had passed away, we were able to find others who could tell us their history.

By telling our history of the Shangani through the recollections of those who live in the districts today, our account inevitably misses out on the perspective of certain key actors in this history. Under-represented in our interviews are former liberation war 'collaborators'. Although we interviewed all the chiefs in the district (most of whom could be classified as wartime collaborators) and a number of people who worked for the war, we have interviewed few locals who fought for the Rhodesians and have interviewed no former Rhodesian soldiers deployed in the Shangani. Similarly, in writing our history of the violence of the 1980s we have not been able to draw on interviews with former members of the security forces, though we were able to speak to some of those who joined the ruling party in the midst of the 1980s conflict, as well as local representatives of the state such as police officers and district administrators. We were also able to draw on a very rich and unique range of archival sources for the 1980s, revealing of the actions and views of government officials.

Our book falls into two main sections. Part I (Chapters 1 to 5) covers the Shangani's history from the wars of 1893 and 1896 to the transition to guerrilla war in the late 1970s. Part II (Chapters 6 to 11) concerns the wars of the 1970s and 1980s, and the subsequent period of reconstruction, development, and attempts to come to terms with the violent past.

We begin with the imagery of the 'dark forests' which has become so central to the telling of Shangani history, using this as a way to discuss the expansion of settlement in the sparsely-populated forests in the decades after the 1896 rebellion, as the Ndebele regiments dispersed, and the nineteenth-century state broke up. This period saw the immigration into the Shangani of disparate groups of people formerly incorporated into the Ndebele state, and of aristocratic Ndebele chiefs and royals; it saw complex processes of accommodation and adaptation to the environment and new neighbours.

In Chapter 2 we turn to the massive evictions that followed the Second World War, and which brought politicized, Christian, Ndebele-speaking evictees from Matabeleland South into the Shangani's dark forests. The dramatic encounter between these evictees and the people they found in the forests produced the Shangani's most enduring social and political cleavage, a cleavage which nationalism sought to overcome, but whose significance in local politics remains. A divisive process of naming accompanied the initial interactions between these groups, in which the progressive evictees cast locals as the epitome of all things primitive, labelling them with a range of usually ethnic names now reinscribed with new meanings of backwardness. Ideas about the Shangani environment as 'dark' and 'hostile' were reinforced as newcomers were struck down with malaria, as cattle died of veld poisoning and disease, and as people struggled to recreate 'civilized' open spaces through the back-breaking work of clearing trees.

The arrival of the evictees was followed by a period of intensified colonial 'development' which we describe in Chapter 3. This post-World War Two 'second colonial occupation' provoked resistance so intense that its results were scarcely noticeable on the *physical* landscape of the Shangani. Its critical effects were on the *political* environment, producing angry, riotous mobs and severe state repression. In Chapter 4 we turn to the rise of nationalism, and explore its relationship to ongoing protest against agrarian interventions. We show how nationalism came to be rooted in the two districts through the evictee communities, but how the imperatives of mobilization demanded an incorporative attitude towards the much stigmatized locals, as well as a tolerance of 'traditional' religion, which posed new challenges to the leadership of the Christian nationalists.

The transition from nationalism to guerrilla war is the subject of Chapter 5. We discuss the Rhodesian Front's elaboration of traditionalist policies and the consequences for the Shangani's chiefs, whose political views increasingly diverged from those of the growing nationalist movement. As state repression escalated, the impetus to local protest given by the incursion of Zapu guerrillas in the mid-1960s was of particular significance. The state's successful campaign against these guerrilla incursions resulted in torture and detention for local nationalists, and demoralization for the party membership. Over the early 1970s, the Shangani's party leaders struggled to keep clandestine structures active. Open protest became more intermittent and fragmented, but preparations for the reception of guerrillas nonetheless continued.

Part II begins with the start of full-scale guerrilla war in the Shangani. Our reconstruction of the liberation war in Chapters 6 and 7 is based on both civilian and guerrilla testimony. We use these recollections to explore the activities and perceptions of the range of government forces deployed within the Shangani. We focus on the central mediating role of local nationalist leaders and the intense moral and political debates over nationalism, military strategy, the use of violence and the role of religion which characterized the war years and powerfully shaped the character of local nationalism.

Chapter 8 turns to the period after the ceasefire, to the process of guerrilla assembly and the brief window of peace when Zapu played a crucial role in reconstruction. We explore the subsequent breakdown of this emerging new order, and its terrible implications for the former Zipra combatants who fled the newly-integrated army and returned to the forests of the Shangani, taking up arms once again as 'dissidents'. Drawing on the testimony of dissidents themselves, we give a substantially new interpretation of the 1980s conflict. The government response to the presence of armed dissidents in the Shangani is the topic of Chapter 9. Here we draw on civilian recollections of their relationship with dissidents, before turning to their accounts of the devastating effects of the government's heavy-handed effort to purge dissidents from the communities in which they lived. Government intervention took the form of a campaign of grotesque repression in which violence was used indiscriminately against civilians as well as more selectively against party activists. The notion of Shona revenge for nineteenth-century Ndebele raiding was used explicitly in this campaign. People in the Shangani came to see themselves as persecuted for their ethnic identity as well as their political affiliation.

The legacies of this period for people's attitudes towards the state and for development after the return of peace comprise the topic of Chapter 10. Through three case studies we explore how memories of state violence live on in the interpretation of, and response to, development initiatives as diverse as land-use planning, community-based wildlife management, and state efforts to control malaria. Other aspects of the past also bear on understandings of development in the 1990s – particularly the authoritarian development initiatives of the 'second colonial occupation', and the long struggle to 'civilize' the Shangani.

The final chapter of the book is in many ways a commentary on the whole narrative of Shangani history. By exploring efforts to confront the legacies of war, to commemorate the fighters and those who died, we see how people continue to make use of the whole sweep of Shangani history, from the nineteenth century to the 1980s. Resolutions of previous eras of violence are part and parcel of the healing of more recent phases. The positive values of local nationalist ideology – incorporating ideas about democracy and human rights as well as about the relationship between nationalists, ancestral spirits and Mwali – have shaped debates over drought, over cleansing, over the accountability of leaders. Such ideas testify to the hope for a better future, for a constructive national politics which is both inclusive of all citizens of Zimbabwe and responsive to all parts of the country.

# Part I

## Conquest, Eviction & Nationalism

# 1

# Life
# in the 'Dark Forests'

## Violence & Images of the Land
## 1893–1930

### Introduction

This book is about the vast block of land designated as the Shangani Reserve by colonial occupiers in 1894. Located on the northwest frontier of the nineteenth-century Ndebele state, the Shangani lay far from the central areas of Ndebele settlement. It was a place renowned for its dense hardwood forests, its expansive, waterless ridges of Kalahari sands, its wild animals, tsetse fly and mosquitoes. Today, the Ndebele idiom used to describe the forests is '*amagusu amnyama*', literally the 'dark forests'. The people of the Shangani explain that the *gusu* forests[1] are 'thickets to be afraid of', they are 'dark and fearful, full of lions, spirits and other scary things', 'places of tall, crowded trees and no people'; in the past, they were places of outcasts 'where witches were thrown to live'.[2] The image of the *gusu* forests as dark and threatening is a powerful and evocative one, central to the way people narrate their lives in the Shangani. It is in many ways a fitting image for a region whose history has been one of violence, displacement and disease.

Most of the people who live in the Shangani today are the descendants of waves of immigrants forced to move from the open country of the Ndebele state's heartland into this little-known frontier over the course of the twentieth century. These largely Ndebele-speaking immigrants draw on the image of the *gusu* as dark and fearful in telling of their encounter with a strange and hostile land. A similar idiom has at times been invoked by European missionaries, travellers and administrators in describing what was a notoriously impenetrable terrain. But the images of the forest are more diverse than this suggests. At different junctures in the course of the twentieth century, the forested landscape and the history of the Shangani have been reimagined by both Africans and whites.

Before exploring these images, let us begin with an account of a definitive episode in the history of Matabeleland generally and of the Shangani in particular. The series of events which occurred on and after 4 December 1893 are central to the depiction of the *gusu* forests as a place of refuge and rebellion, darkness and disease. Memories of these events would be drawn upon many times in the decades that followed. They would be reworked, commemorated and given new meanings.

---

[1] *Igusu* (pl. *amagusu*) is the correct Ndebele form of '*gusu*' and refers specifically to the Kalahari sands forests. We use the term *gusu* because the prefix is usually dropped in English.

[2] Interviews with Fotsholo Tshuma, Jotsholo, 25 August 1996, Wilson Fuyana, Lupanda, 19 September 1996, Callistus Mkwananzi, Jotsholo, 5 December 1994, Nkosembi Khumalo, Lupane, 5 April 1996.

December 4, 1893 was the day on which King Lobengula's Ndebele warriors killed to a man the members of the Alan Wilson Patrol at a place called Pupu, deep in the forests of the Shangani. That same day King Lobengula disappeared, never to be seen again. Lobengula had fled north from the Ndebele state's capital, Bulawayo, following its occupation by troops of the British South Africa Company and imperial forces. He had sought out the protection of the *gusu* forests, long a place of refuge and retreat. The jubilant L.S. Jameson and Cecil Rhodes dispatched a column in pursuit of the King under the command of Major Forbes and Alan Wilson. Overly confident after previous successes and poorly armed and equipped, the column moved slowly, spending much time looting Ndebele cattle.[3] At Pupu, a small advance patrol led by Major Alan Wilson encountered the King's forces. The entire 30 strong patrol was killed before midday. Chief Mina Sivalo Mahlangu's vivid account of the battle was recorded by the missionary Bowen Rees:

> Wilson's party in their distress dismounted and laid down, making a fort to themselves with their horses, the whitemen in the centre. By this time, the Matabele had so surrounded them, that there was no opening to escape, so the white regiment fought inside their fort. ... We fought from sunrise until mid-day. All the white party were killed with their horses, and a great number of the Matabele perished in the same battle. ... Some of the latter escaped death by hiding under the bodies of those who were killed. In the afternoon the Matabele picked out their dead to bury them, and on the morrow they did likewise. Others were covered with the branches of the trees and bushes, both Black and White. Not a garment was taken away from the dead; they were all left as they fell to be devoured by the vultures and the wolves [wild dogs, presumably].[4]

The main body of the column under the command of Major Forbes also came under attack and scarcely managed to escape after twelve hours of fighting. Abandoning all plans of rescuing the Wilson patrol, Forbes began a 'panic-stricken retreat', in which the column was attacked twice more.[5] Sivalo recounted how, 'The Whitemen ran away up the valley of the Shangani. On their journey they were saved on account of the Maxim guns and the Matabeles were saved on account of the trees.'[6]

The battle in the Pupu forests was the last time King Lobengula was seen. Rumour has it that he fled north, either crossing the Zambezi river into Zambia or remaining in hiding in the forests of the northwest to be buried in an unknown place. Ndebele elders have yet to agree upon, or fully reveal, the long-kept secret of Lobengula's fate. The battle has provoked other disagreements as well. Contemporary actors and later historians have disputed whether the battle signified the total defeat of the Ndebele kingdom and a collapse of its military capacity, or whether the Ndebele remained 'essentially unpacified'.[7] Whatever the significance of the battle, the remaining Ndebele

[3] For an account of the Alan Wilson patrol, see J. Cobbing 'The Ndebele under the Khumalos', PhD, University of London, 1976, pp. 368-70, citing: the Diary of W. Napier, November–December 1893, entries for 26 November, 3, 4, 12 and 16 December 1893, Hist. MSS CR2/1/1; H.L. Stevens, *The Autobiography of a Border Policeman: A Narrative of War and Adventure in Bechuanaland and Matabeleland* (London, 1927), pp. 277–81; Correspondence of H.H. Williams to his mother, 20 December 1893, Hist. MSS WI 13/1/1.

[4] Testimony witnessed and translated by Bowen Rees, and published in the *Bulawayo Chronicle*, March 1918 [undated excerpt]. Also see the *Bulawayo Chronicle*, 12 March 1918.

[5] Cobbing, 'The Ndebele under the Khumalos', pp. 369–70.

[6] Mina Sivalo Mahlangu in the *Bulawayo Chronicle*, March 1918 [incorrectly cited as Mahlana].

[7] See T. Ranger, *Revolt in Southern Rhodesia 1896-7. A Study in African Resistance* (London, Heinemann, 1967); Cobbing, 'The Ndebele Under the Khumalos', p. 370.

chiefs and royals were to be major actors in the events that followed, and would once again mobilize and command regiments of warriors in the second uprising of 1896.

They certainly had good cause to rise again. After 1893, the Ndebele were treated as a conquered people. The entire Ndebele heartland on the highveld around Bulawayo was alienated to white settlers; Ndebele cattle were looted on a grand scale.[8] The Land Commission of 1894 defined the Ndebele 'home' as the inhospitable Shangani and Gwaai Reserves, areas which whites disdained and which the Ndebele had used less for settlement than for hunting, grazing and refuge.[9] Although land alienation had little immediate impact on the Ndebele – only a tiny fraction of 'European' farms were actually worked in 1895 – the looting of Ndebele cattle most certainly did. Julian Cobbing estimates that 100,000 head were taken by mid-1894, and when rinderpest struck in February 1896, remaining herds were further decimated. The quarantine and shooting-control measures were interpreted as a continuation of Company cattle seizures, and preparations for a new uprising accelerated.[10] The hardships associated with this interim period were particularly acute in the remote Shangani, which had become a temporary refuge for Ndebele warriors and civilians, and where terrible famine and disease struck.[11]

The Shangani witnessed similar crises after the 1896 uprising when its forests once again became a place of refuge and the redoubt of rebels. Before their retreat into the Shangani, the intransigent northern group of rebels were based just to the south of the Shangani Reserve on the lower Bembesi river and in the Mambo hills. Its leaders included influential Ndebele royals and chiefs, such as Nyamanda (Lobengula's eldest son and candidate for succession to the kingship), Queen Lozikeyi (Lobengula's senior wife), and another son, Tshakalisa. Nyamanda, according to Cobbing, 'acted as "co-ordinator"' with other chiefs, amongst whom were Madliwa and Sikhobokhobo. Queen Lozikeyi distributed bullets at the outset of the war.[12] Although the uprising was initially quite successful, the arrival of imperial forces and subsequent shortages of ammunition and food brought about a desperate situation. The Europeans deliberately targeted standing crops and destroyed stored grain. By July, shortages resulted in 'feuds over grain, and struggles by the chiefs and "die-hards" to prevent the people from surrendering through lack of food.'[13] These internal fissures were exploited by the Europeans – Dakamela, for example, surrendered in August, having been attacked by Madliwa for his reluctance to fight, and was subsequently used to rout other rebels. But many members of the recalcitrant northern group surrendered only in December 1896, several months after the first of Rhodes' negotiations with the southern Ndebele chiefs.

The latter part of 1896 was a time of famine all over Matabeleland, but starvation was 'particularly acute' in the north.[14] Here not only had the 1895–6 harvest failed and stored food been deliberately burnt in the war, but refusal to surrender delayed early planting the next year, and locusts damaged what little grew. Native Commissioner (NC) Val Gielgud, based in Inyathi, reported a 'very terrible' situation in January 1897, with whole families dying of starvation. The following month he travelled north, crossing the Shangani River into yet more stricken areas, where news had come in that

---

[8]  Ranger, *Revolt*, pp. 102–4.

[9]  R. Palmer, *Land and Racial Domination in Rhodesia* (London, Heineman, 1977), pp. 28–33.

[10]  Cobbing, 'The Ndebele Under the Khumalos', p. 374.

[11]  J. Iliffe, *Famine in Zimbabwe 1890-1960* (Gweru, Mambo Press, 1990), p. 21.

[12]  Her distribution of ammunition is recorded in Gielgud to CNC, 19 July 1898, LO5/6/1, cited in Cobbing, 'The Ndebele Under the Khumalos', p. 409.

[13]  Cobbing, 'The Ndebele under the Khumalos', p. 422.

[14]  The famine was the direct result of the war rather than lack of rain or crop pests, as Iliffe has convincingly argued, though the BSAC tended to blame nature. Iliffe, *Famine in Zimbabwe*, pp. 21–4.

people 'grind up the skins of rinderpest oxen and cook the powder for food'; 'On the banks of the Shangani there are a good many people living on the pith of the palm trees.'[15] Gielgud described how the desperate food situation had sparked further violence from the retreating regiments:

> The Matabili have completely scattered all the 'rolis' in the country north of Manyeu's kraal … they have plundered them of food, arms, seed and goods … and are now living in their kraals. We came upon a few of these wretched people wandering about and looking for roots, etc.[16]

Others relied upon game, digging large pits and driving the game into them with cordons. Elders in Ilihlo recounted how: 'People would dig holes … the animals would be driven into the area, channelled by the fences into the holes. Inside the holes were sharpened poles so that the animal would be pierced as it fell into the pit. This was done during the war with the whites because food wasn't around, granaries were burnt, cattle were scattered. … Starvation made them do that. People had eaten their *amabhetshu* [skin aprons] and sandals out of starvation.'[17] The hunting pits of the 1890s famine still scar the landscape of the Shangani, stretching in lines along the major rivers.

Disease increased the toll. In April Gielgud reported:

> The cause of death in most cases is fever. The prevalence of fever this year even among people inhabiting old kraals is very great. … I estimate that nearly one fourth of the population of this District have died since the beginning of the rebellion, from wounds, hunger and disease. … The people who have suffered most are those who were awkward in surrendering, for the people who surrendered first planted early and their crops were already big when the locusts appeared in large numbers.[18]

Iliffe concludes that, elsewhere in Zimbabwe, 'there was no "famine that killed" to match that in northern and western Matabeleland'.[19]

This history of violence, and the Shangani's role as a forested hideout for rebels as well as a place of disease and suffering, came to have a powerful resonance with later historical episodes. The events of the late nineteenth century and the landscape of the dark *gusu* forests would be reimagined by Africans and whites in various ways over the next century, as we recount in this and subsequent chapters. Below, we explore some of the late nineteenth-century and early twentieth-century representations of Shangani history and landscape.

## Images and History in the Gusu Forests

The image of the Shangani which emerged in the context of the 1890s uprisings was partly shaped by earlier decades. White travellers before the wars portrayed the *gusu* forests as wild and unoccupied, as a place of violence and an inhospitable buffer zone between Ndebele raiders to the south and Kololo/Lozi raiders to the north. This image was reinforced by parallels with the events of the uprising itself. But it was only one of

[15] Carnegie to Thompson, 20 September 1896, SOAS CWM (M) 2/6/A; NC Gielgud to CNC, 5 February 1897, LO/5/6/8 f.217, cited in Iliffe, *Famine*, p. 26.
[16] Val Gielgud to CNC, 20 March 1897, LO/5/6/8, f.350, cited in Iliffe, *Famine*, p. 26.
[17] Interview with Tafi Dube, Mangwa Mate and David Ndlovu, Ilihlo, 29 March 1996.
[18] Val Gielgud to CNC, 3 April 1897, LO/5/6/9, f.47, cited in Iliffe, *Famine*, p. 28, note 48.
[19] Iliffe, *Famine*, p. 30.

many images of the Shangani forests in the nineteenth and early twentieth centuries. The 1894 Land Commission sought to recast the Shangani as an area long integrated into the Ndebele polity and economy and hence as a fitting 'home' for Ndebele settlers. As Ndebele chiefs began to move into the area with their large herds of cattle, administrators elaborated a tradition of Ndebele use of the forests and cast it as the chosen home of Ndebele royals.

African images of the land were as varied as white. The conventional Ndebele idiom of today casts the *gusu* forests as 'dark' and 'threatening', and emphasizes the emptiness of the land, said to be fit only for wild animals. But there were Africans living there in the nineteenth century and probably much earlier, and they had different views of the forest. As Ndebele speakers moved into the Shangani during the first decades of the twentieth century, they, too, created new ways of life in the *gusu* forests. They became acquainted with its earlier settlers and adopted some of their ways of using and propitiating the land. They came to read the landscape for niches of opportunity, to see that the 'dark' and sandy *gusu* ridges were broken up by fertile valleys, wetlands and rich black soils. The areas they settled ceased to be the domain of fearsome alien spirits as the land was imaginatively possessed through religious shrines and tales of ancestors and earlier inhabitants.

Meanwhile, however, Ndebele politicians and progressives deplored Ndebele settlement in the forests. They continued to insist that the forests were dark and uninhabitable – at least for Christian cultivators using modern farming methods. In their various demands for a Matabele National Home, they certainly did not envisage the forests of the Shangani Reserve as its core, but asked for open land closer to Bulawayo. Missionaries shared these perspectives, deploring that the Ndebele converts who had moved to the Shangani had lapsed from a Christian life into the paganism of the dark *gusu* forests.

We propose to take in turn each of these images – and the realities that underlay them – and through their interplay to try to arrive at the outlines of the history of the Shangani Reserve up to the 1930s.

## Violence and the Empty Land

The first European accounts of the Shangani and its history came from travellers and missionaries who had moved through the region in the decades before the uprisings of the 1890s. They represented the *gusu* forests as wild, uninhabited, impenetrable; they saw the Shangani's history as a story of violence and refuge from marauding Ndebele regiments based further south.

The classic nineteenth-century text was written by Thomas Morgan Thomas, a missionary at the new London Missionary Society (LMS) mission at Inyathi. Although Inyathi lay within striking distance of the Gwampa river (which would mark the Shangani Reserve's southern border), missionaries rarely crossed it to travel northwards. But in 1867, Thomas was given permission by the Ndebele King to travel to the Zambezi, 'a journey of two or three months through the pathless wilds.'[20] Between the Bembezi and the Zambezi rivers, wrote Thomas, a distance of 200 miles, 'we could not expect to see another human being' and would be solely in 'houseless and wild beast-abounding forests.' Three days out, Thomas and his party saw a fire. They romantically speculated that 'some one of the Zambezi tribes was on its way to retaliate upon its cruel [Ndebele] aggressors', but it turned out to be an Ndebele hunting party. Between the Gwampa and the Shangani they saw no people and game in abundance – elephant, rhino, buffalo, wild pigs, antelope.[21] But when they reached the Tshongokwe and Kana

[20] T.M. Thomas, *Eleven Years in Central Africa* (London, Snow, 1872), p. 361.
[21] *Ibid.*, pp. 364, 365.

valleys, Thomas found 'signs of former habitations and cultivation'. His guides told him that:

> forty years ago ... the whole country was thickly inhabitated by the Amatonga and the Abayaye tribes; but the Makololo [to the North] and the Amandebele [to the South] hemmed them in on either side, and compelled them to submit or flee. Thus one of the most beautiful and fertile countries in Central South Africa was entirely depopulated and left to be the habitat of wild beasts and reptiles, which are found there now in great abundance and variety.[22]

Other travellers arrived at the Inyathi LMS station only to abandon their plans to reach the Zambezi by way of the Shangani territory because of reports of lack of water or the refusal of carriers to enter the forests.[23] The intrepid F.C. Selous, of course, *did* manage to penetrate the Shangani bush, travelling south from the Shangwe area to Inyathi in 1878. 'I tried to get a guide,' wrote Selous, 'as the intervening country is uninhabited,' but he could not afford the wage demanded. So 'there was nothing for it but to strike straight through the country in a southerly direction'. Selous arrived at Inyathi exhausted and without having seen any occupants of the forests.[24]

After the defeat of the Ndebele state in the uprisings of the 1890s, administrators began to explore the huge new districts for which they were responsible, and began to elaborate on this picture of the land and its history.[25] In August 1898, C.L. Carbutt was sent through the Shangani Reserve to the territory of the Shangwe chiefs which lay to the north and northeast. 'Next to nothing was known of the country,' Carbutt remembered. So he set out with twelve armed Africans and ten pack ponies. Moving north from the Gwampa river on the southern border of the Reserve, they passed through 'dense teak forest with a thick, thorny undergrowth'; at Nkayi they had to pick up 'an expert tracker' to get them to the kraal of the Shangwe paramount, Sileya. All the way there and back they saw 'much game' but very few people and these fled at their approach.[26] In 1903, De Lassoe, NC of Sebungwe to the north of the Shangani, opined that the Tonga movement and settlement south of the Zambezi, 'was stopped by the struggles in Matabeleland ... whence the powerful Zulu invaders drove hordes of fugitives northwards'.[27]

Southern African historians have good reason to suspect such claims of exterminating raids and depopulated valleys. Julian Cobbing, for example, rejects the idea of a 'scorched-earth belt' in the Shangani area in favour of explaining the sparse population in terms of the 'unfavourable climate or soil-conditions, wild animals and tsetse fly, or to the disinclination of those peoples who did exist there to show themselves to Europeans armed with rifles.'[28] But although it appears that the *gusu* had long been

---

[22] *Ibid.*, p. 368.

[23] Eduard Mohr, *To the Western Falls of the Zambesi* (London, Sampson Law, 1876); C.G. Oates (ed.), *Frank Oates, Matabeleland and the Victoria Falls* (London, Kegan Paul, Trench and Co., 1889).

[24] F.C. Selous, *A Hunter's Wanderings in Africa* (London, Richard Bentley, 1895), p. 323.

[25] As NC Val Gielgud trekked north from Inyathi after the 1896 uprising, he vividly described the trackless wastes of the Shangani and the 'mountains, jungles and swamps' to the north of it. Val Gielgud's patrol to the Zambezi, 8 January 1898, NB 6/5/2/2. The Chief Native Commissioner, Matabeleland, remarked in March 1898 that the Zambezi River belt was 'separated from the main portion of Matabeleland by a large uninhabited tract of country', Annual Report, CNC, 31 March 1898, NB 6/1/1.

[26] C.L. Carbutt, 'Reminiscences of a Native Commissioner', *Native Affairs Department Annual* (NADA), 1924.

[27] Annual Report Sebungwe/Mafungabusi, 31 March 1903, N 6/1/3.

[28] Cobbing, 'The Ndebele Under the Khumalos', p. 150.

inhabited, there is also evidence for depopulating violence, both in the subsequent pages of this chapter and in other historical studies.[29]

As we shall see, the white image of the Shangani in the nineteenth century as empty of anyone save fugitives was inaccurate and overdrawn. Nevertheless, it may well be correct in its emphasis on violence and disruption. Shangani memories go back to the violence of the nineteenth century – to the overthrow of the pre-Ndebele Lozwi state by the Swazi regiments who cleared the way for the arrival of the Ndebele. They tell of Ndebele disruption of Tonga settlements south of the Zambezi valley, of capture and raiding, of flight and hiding from the regiments, as well as of incorporation and of political and economic relations between 'subject' peoples and the rulers of the Ndebele state. A series of detailed government investigations into the origins of the Shangani population, based on interviews conducted in the 1960s and 1970s, also complicate and contradict the image of the forest as uninhabited. These oral and administrative sources give a striking picture of dislocation and movement to and fro through the forests. They portray a disrupted and depopulated marginal frontier but, as we show below, not a completely uninhabited one.

### The 'Ideal' Ndebele Home

Given all these European and administrative images of the Shangani forests as wild, deserted and subjected to the depradations of itinerant Ndebele warriors, we may well ask how the Land Commission of 1894 managed to declare the area ideal for Ndebele settlement and to set it aside as the Shangani Reserve, the primary 'homeland' for the Ndebele.

Essentially, this was an act of crude expediency, inadequately backed by travel within or survey of the territory concerned. The Commissioners did not go north of the Shangani, and questioned only four witnesses.[30] It was hardly worth their while to go to much trouble, after all. The core land of the Ndebele state had already been granted out to companies and individuals, so there was no land to allocate as a Reserve except areas outside the nineteenth-century limits of Ndebele settlement. Hence the peripheral location of the two huge Reserves of Shangani and Gwaai. But the Commissioners offered some sort of intellectual justification as well. In place of the old image of the

---

[29] The following studies touch on the Shangani and surrounding regions. Godfrey Ncube's 'A History of North West Zimbabwe, 1850–1950s: Comparative Change in Three Worlds', M.Phil., University of Zimbabwe, 1994, pp. x, xii, xiii, describes how in 1862 an 'Ndebele invasion destroyed the Nambya state'; how 'people retreated from the more open settlements of previous periods to patches of defensive granite hills, separated by uninhabited forests'; how Portuguese slaving disrupted Zambezi Valley societies; how 'agricultural self-sufficiency' in the region was undermined both by Ndebele raids, European traders and adventurers from the south. For suggestions of the *gusu* as uninhabited in the late eighteenth century, see Reinier Holst, 'Continuity and Change. The Productive Dynamics of Social and Productive Relations in Hwange, Zimbabwe, 1870–1960', M.Phil., University of Liverpool, 1993, Appendix One. 'The Banyama Tribe'. Compiled by the Nambya Cultural Assocation, Hwange, 1988. Chet Lancaster's study, *The Goba of the Zambezi: Sex Roles, Economics and Change* (Norman, University of Oklahoma Press 1981), pp. 15-17, describes the Goba population of the central Zambezi as made up of waves of rebels and refugees from the south – 'people known as Tonga, or rebels against Shona kings', and later people fleeing 'Ngoni and Matabele migrations and raids in the nineteenth century.'

[30] Robin Palmer notes that even the BSAC's own historian described the Commission's enquiry as 'somewhat perfunctory', *Land and Racial Domination in Rhodesia* (London, Heinemann, 1977), p. 32, citing H.M. Hole, *The Making of Rhodesia* (London, 1926).

Shangani territory as empty forested land, devastated in the past by Ndebele raids, the Commission argued that the Ndebele had made use of both the Shangani and the Gwaai Reserves, and that they had established political relations with the peoples of the north.

Two Ndebele headmen testified that Lobengula grazed large herds of his own cattle on the Gwampa on the southern border of the Shangani. 'This river was the King's grazing ground. He would never allow us to graze our cattle there. The King had large troops of oxen which he kept for slaughtering purposes.'[31] Moreover, there had been populations briefly resident both south and north of the Shangani River. The Gwampa valley on the southern boundary of the reserve 'was at one time occupied by the Matabele – in Umzilikazi's time. They lived about the junction. After a time Umzilikazi withdrew his people because they were too much scattered.'[32] As for the abandoned kraals which Thomas had seen on the Kana River (at the Reserve's northern limit), these were not the result of Ndebele raiding but had been part of the Ndebele state. 'Our Amaholies [subordinates] used to live on the Karna river, but they left because the fever was so bad.'[33] Although Palmer notes that much of their evidence was vague and unreliable,[34] the headmen's references to Ndebele herds are supported by oral histories from the Shangani today, as well as recent historical studies. Ndlovu Mpimbili told how his father, a member of the Ndebele Igabha regiment, had left herds of cattle in the Gwampa and Lupane valleys; historian Godfrey Ncube argues that royal cattle were grazed on the Gwaai river, right up to its junction with the Shangani; Julian Cobbing remarks on royal herds tended by the Insuka regiment on the Gwamayaya tributary to the Shangani.[35]

The Commission undoubtedly went too far in asserting that Lobengula had intended to settle on the Shangani – 'to remain there permanently to cultivate, make gardens and to locate the tribe there.'[36] But from colonial documents and oral sources, there is evidence of much Ndebele movement through the forests, of some interaction with scattered 'subject' peoples living inside or on the margins of them, and of considerable interaction with the peoples who lived to the north of the Shangani. Thus, the Tonga leader Somanyanga, originally from the Zambezi valley, was not captured by the Ndebele, but requested and was given asylum by Lobengula just to the south of the borders of what became the Reserve. 'Somanyanga was never in a regiment', his descendents recall. 'When he visited Lobengula's settlement, he asked to be given a place with his own people. He asked for sanctuary and protection. He wasn't conscripted. So he was allocated a special place for Tonga people … He had to look after the King's cattle.'[37] And as we shall see below, there were other Ndebele subjects also living in the forests – including people who claimed Lozwi, Nyai, Shangwe, Tonga and Kalanga descent. Some of these preferred not to 'interact' with the Ndebele, and chose

---

[31] Evidence of Umjane [Mtshane], 16 October 1894, *Matabeleland. Report of the Land Commission of 1894 and Correspondence Relating Thereto*, June 1896, C-8130, pp. 8–9.

[32] Evidence of Inqubgubo [Ngubongubo], 23 October 1894, *Ibid*. p. 11.

[33] Evidence of Umjane [Mtshane], *Ibid*., p.9. A map attached to the Commission's Report showed the area north of the Kana as 'depopulated but formerly inhabited by Abeyaye and Batonga'.

[34] Palmer, *Land and Racial Domination*, p. 32.

[35] Interview with Ndlovu Mpimbili, Isilwane, 14 September 1996. Interview sources also make reference to royal herds in the Gwaai, e.g. interview with Tafi Dube, Mangwa Mate and David Ndlovu, Ilihlo, 29 March 1996. Ncube 'A History of North West Zimbabwe', p. 221; Cobbing 'The Ndebele under the Khumalos', p. 170.

[36] *Matabeleland. Report of the Land Commission of 1894*, June 1896, pp. 8–9.

[37] Interview with Dulini Sicha Ncube, Edward Mdwaleni et al., Headman Ndabambi's kraal, Lupane, 20 September 1995. See also M.E. Hayes, November 1975, file CHK 6/LU, Ndabambi, Provincial Administrator's Office, Bulawayo.

to hide instead: the Kalanga forefathers of Sibigwapi Mhlanga, for example, had settled in the fertile wetlands of Shabulana in the Shangani, but during 'Lobengula's war' they fled 'out of the way of the fighting' and hid in the *gusu* forests at Ngamo.[38]

There were also some Sili, or 'bushmen' in western Shangani. Although most were said to have 'hidden in the bush' like Mhlanga during Lobengula's reign, some had economic relations with the Ndebele. They were used as expert hunters, and were also famous for their *muti*, or medicine. Descendents of former warriors and early settlers in the Shangani remember how 'the Sili were known as great hunters, they would round up meat' for influential Ndebele leaders. The Ndebele leader Tshayamatole, who was said to be Lobengula's doctor and companion during his final flight to Pupu, would 'have Sili hunting for them, bringing him meat'.[39] We shall return to the diverse late nineteenth-century forest dwellers below.

Although some few Ndebele subjects did live within the Shangani or on its margins during Lobengula's reign, there were much larger and more important populations to the north of what became the Reserve. The Ndebele had economic and political interactions with these people, resulting in much movement through the forests in the late nineteenth century. The Shangwe leaders and tobacco traders to the north east were particularly important,[40] and in 1893 the King was said to have sent to the Shangwe chiefs for appropriate seed.[41] There were also important interactions with the Tonga in the Zambezi valley.

Colonial administrators portrayed these interactions with populations to the north of the Shangani as evidence of Ndebele overlordship. When they went on their arduous explorations to the north, they were accompanied by senior Ndebele who already knew the region well. In 1897, Assistant Native Commissioner Green went on patrol to the Zambezi. He was accompanied by Ndonsa, 'late chief of the Zambezi District by Lobengula's appointment', who was essential to the expedition because of 'his past position, knowledge of the Natives, the country and the language.' Ndonsa guided the patrol across the Shangani and Kana Rivers. He was greeted with great respect – and with much fear by the people of Sijabile, who feared his revenge for the death 'of his principal Induna, Sinagoma'.[42] In March 1898, NC Gielgud furthered the idea of an extensive Ndebele overlordship by describing the Shangwe chiefs as 'only vassal indunas to Utshukulu, [Ndebele] Induna of Enqojini'.[43]

In this line of reasoning, tobacco trading with the Shangwe was 'tribute'. When Carbutt patrolled Shangwe country in August 1898, he was accompanied by 'Tshoko [Madliwa], a Kumalo and near relation to Lobengula' who had enjoyed jurisdiction over the Shangwe in Lobengula's time. The Shangwe paramount, Sileya, 'paid an annual tribute of tobacco to the Mandebele king, every year collected at Nyoka's kraal, and thence the annual convoy set out carrying the tobacco to Bulawayo.'[44] One of the Shangwe chiefs, Nemangwe, 'acted as their representative in carrying messages and tribute to Lobengula'. But the relationship was not just one way: Nemangwe was also wife-provider to the great rain maker of the north, Nevana, 'the famous rain doctor of

[38] Interview with Sibigwapi Mhlanga and others, Ndlovu school, 18 September 1995.

[39] Interview with Antony Magagula, Tafila Tshuma *et al.*, Masungamala, 7 February 1996.

[40] See B. Kosmin, 'The Inyoka Tobacco Industry of the Shangwe People: The Displacement of a Pre-Colonial Economy in Southern Rhodesia, 1898–1938', in R. Palmer and N. Parsons, *The Roots of Rural Poverty in Central and Southern Africa* (London, Heinemann, 1977).

[41] *Matabeleland. Report of the Land Commission of 1894*, June 1896, pp. 8–9.

[42] Report by Green to Robert Lanning, Native Commissioner, Shiloh, 14 December 1897, NB 6/5/2/5. Sinagoma is remembered in the Shangani, as 'chief in the Zambezi', with 'duties ... to ferry Lobengula's soldiers across the river'. Interview with Gibson Ndlovu, Ndimimbili, 11 March 1996.

[43] Annual Report, Inyathi, March 1898, NB 6/1/1.

[44] Carbutt, 'Reminiscences of a Native Commissioner'.

Matabeleland', to whom Lobengula himself sent tribute.[45] There was obviously much Ndebele transit through the Shangani forests in the course of these activities.

Although it is highly unlikely that Lobengula intended to settle in the Shangani, the fact that his last battle took place at Pupu and the speculation that his grave lay close to the northern boundaries of the Shangani Reserve, gave the territory resonance for Ndebele traditionalists. Administrators thought that Queen Lozikeyi, who had accompanied Lobengula on his flight north, knew where he was buried and that she organized annual sacrifices at his grave. 'Persistent' rumours told how Lobengula had summoned his warriors and told them he would 'disappear like a needle in the grass'. And that he had laid spiritual claim to the land: 'I shall either throw myself down a precipice or disappear in a pool of water. Everything will, however, remember me: the people, land, hills, rocks, trees, grass, cattle, dogs.'[46]

Impressed by all these resonances – and by the practical need to clear African cattle from 'white' land – administrators abandoned their image of the Shangani as desolate. Instead they began to preach its virtues as Ndebele homeland. They were delighted that one of Lobengula's sons, Tshakalisa, was the first important Ndebele to make his home in the Shangani Reserve. They tried to persuade Queen Lozikeyi herself to settle there.[47] In this they did not succeed, but before long, aristocratic Ndebele chiefs were moving in with their cattle. Tshoko/Madliwa was already in the area by 1900; Sivalo went to an area north of the Shangani river in 1906;[48] Sikhobokhobo moved into the Shangani in 1910; Tshugulu in 1912; Dakamela in 1913; Nkomo/Nkalakatha in 1920.[49]

These new colonial chiefs were a diverse group. Their appointment and movement into the Reserve in some ways reproduced nineteenth-century structures of status and authority, and in some ways introduced changes. All the colonial chiefs were Nguni, that is part of the Ndebele aristocracy who were descendants of the Ndebele immigrants from today's South Africa. Some – such as Sikhobokhobo and Madliwa – had been important regimental chiefs during the 1896 war,[50] but others had not headed regiments and were contemptuously brushed aside by Lobengula's sons. In July 1919, for example, the King's eldest son, Nyamanda, objected strongly to chief Sivalo's appointment as curator of the late Queen Lozikeyi's estate. 'Sivalo was a most unsuitable person to appoint, as he was a man of no standing and had been employed

---

[45] Monthly Report, Sebungwe, January 1906, N 6/4/7; Superintendent of Natives, Bulawayo, to CNC, 15 November 1926, S 138 92.

[46] Mbizo, 'Mtikana ka Mafu', *NADA*, 1926, pp. 56–7.

[47] After 1896 Lozikeyi lived at the Queens' Kraal, Bembesi, south of the Shangani. In August 1914 CNC Taylor minuted that it was 'probable that Losegeyi will in the near future ask for permission to move into the Shangani Reserve'. But she continued to live at Queens' Kraal until her death in February 1919. Memorandum by CNC, 17 August 1914, N 3/19/3.

[48] Correspondence about Sivalo's move is contained in file L 2/2/117/43. The CNC explained that 'owing to the increase of stock and inadequacy of water and grazing area ... he is compelled to seek new ground'. The administration at first tried to persuade him to go to the Gwaai Reserve but he refused. Eventually, the CNC was able to report that Sivalo's objections to the Shangani Reserve 'have been overcome'. CNC to Chief Secretary, 26 April 1906; 18 June 1906.

[49] These dates are given in the Nkayi Chiefs' files held in the Provincial Administrator's office in Bulawayo, CHK 6/Nkayi.

[50] Sikhobokhobo is widely remembered by Shangani residents to have been a regimental chief, and is described as such by Cobbing, 'The Ndebele under the Khumalos'. The administrative files misleadingly downplay his authority by noting Sikhobokhobo's father had been 'entrusted with the care of the royal milking cattle' under Lobengula and been appointed as a chief only after 1896. DC Nkayi to PC, 4 March 1966, CHK 6 Nkayi, Sikhobokhobo. Chief Menyezwa who moved into Lupane after the Second World War, was another case of a chief who could claim descent from a regimental leader.

by the late King merely as a dresser of hides to make skirts for the Queens.'[51] The current chief Sivalo gives a more prestigious pedigree for his predecessor, claiming that he first guarded and then fired Lobengula's headquarters at Bulawayo in 1893 and that he was entrusted with the royal children when Lobengula wanted them surrendered to the whites.[52] Nevertheless, even this was far from having been a regimental *induna*.

Other chiefs were appointed because they had sided with the whites during the uprising. Tshugulu was made chief because he had brought in one of the die-hard rebels hiding in the Shangani forests at the end of the war: he had 'showed his valour in 1896 by apprehending Potshwana [Mpotshwana (Ndiweni) who] had caused terror to the white settlers'.[53] Dakamela, as we saw earlier, was influential in 1896, but was attacked by other Ndebele leaders of the northern group of rebels when he turned to collaboration. Administrative files describe Dakamela as son 'of one of Mzilikazi's most famous Inyanga [traditional healer]' who was 'appointed a chief by the Government after the Rebellion.'[54]

Most of the headmen who moved into the Shangani in this period were not members of the Ndebele aristocracy, but were descendants of incorporated peoples of varied status and history. Some had a history of interaction with the new colonial chiefs under which they served, some had been their *abalisa* (headmen) in the nineteenth century, and many had a history of tending royal cattle, serving in regiments, or had personal connections with Nguni leaders of one sort or another. These headmen, in addition to being Ndebele, commonly also claimed a pre-Ndebele Lozwi, Nyai, Kalanga or Tonga history.[55]

The chiefs who moved into the Shangani Reserve in the early twentieth century left most of their people behind. Although the influential Sikhobokhobo had the authority to call members of his regiment to follow him,[56] other chiefs arrived with more cattle than people. All of the chiefs owned large herds, which included beasts with the royal ear-mark. 'White land-owners wanted these cattle off the land, but they did not wish to lose the rents and labour of the chiefs' followers.' In 1919 the Bubi district Annual Report confessed that, despite all the propaganda about the virtues of land between the Gwampa and the Kana, 'the bulk of the population is not in the Reserves. ... The chiefs, being the large stock owners ... have been the first to have to leave the farms and go into the Reserves.'[57] Next year, the Report noted that the chiefs had 'left their former tribal areas and removed with only a small following' into the Shangani.[58] Many of the chiefs' former subjects remained on 'white' land close to the core of the old Ndebele state, while their new subjects in the Shangani often had little connection to them.

[51] NC Carbutt to Supt. of Natives, Bulawayo, 29 July 1919, N 3/19/3. Nyamanda may have had his own reasons for objecting to Sivalo, who had been an ally of Lozikeyi with whom Nyamanda was on bad terms, personal communication, Marieke Clarke.

[52] This account was given to Marieke Clarke and District Administrator Jack Nhliziyo in August 1993.

[53] Draft speech for installation of Chief Tshugulu, August 1988, CHK Nkayi General.

[54] M.E. Hayes' report on Dakamela, October 1975, CHK Nkayi Dakamela. According to the missionary, Bowen Rees, Dakamela was 'an *isanusi* – a smelling out doctor' during the reign of Lobengula. Bowen Rees to Mr Hawkins, 23 July 1914, CWM, South Africa Incoming, Box 76, Folder 4, SOAS.

[55] For example, headman Ngubo and headman Lupahla claimed a Lozwi history as well as an Ndebele history; headman Ndabambi claimed a Tonga history in addition to an Ndebele history; headman Majaha claimed a Kalanga and Ndebele background.

[56] Interviews with Elias Sibanda, Malandu Ncube and Luka Sibanda, Kana, 5 December 1995; Mhlotshwa Majaha Moyo, Majaha, 5 October 1995.

[57] Annual Report, Bubi, 1919, N 9/1/22.

[58] Annual Report, Bubi, 1920, N 9/1/22.

## A Long-settled Land

There is another history of the land between the Gwampa and the Kana rivers – a secret history which in some ways contradicts both white and Ndebele representations. The 'empty', 'dark' and 'threatening' forests of Ndebele and European imagination had in fact been inhabited for generations. In the early twentieth century, Ndebele claims to suzerainty were challenged by the claims of older polities, both Lozwi and Tonga. However, these Lozwi and Tonga histories also tell a tale of violence, disruption and movement.

The memory of the Lozwi ruler Mambo survived the subsequent reigns of the Ndebele Kings Mzilikazi and Lobengula. In 1926, when Albert and Rhodes Lobengula were collecting cattle in the Reserve to create a fund to buy a Matabele National Home, J.W. Posselt noted that descendants of the Lozwi Empire opposed the idea on the grounds that they were the true owners of the country, of which they had been robbed by the Swazi and Ndebele.[59] In the Shangani today, there are people of Lozwi and Nyai descent who recall the rule of Mambo. Jeremiah Moyo recounted how his forefather had served Mambo as an *inyanga* when they fought the Swazis.[60] Similarly, Ndlovu Mpimbili recalled, 'when our forefathers came, it was before the Ndebele. They found Mambo and Tumbale'. In times of war, they defended Mambo with their 'good charms'.[61]

After Mambo's defeat by the Swazi regiment and his followers' subsequent subjugation to the Ndebele, both Moyo and Mpimbili's forefathers were incorporated into the Ndebele state. Moyo described a history not of capture, but of living as the 'King's people' within the Shangani; Mpimbili told of how his grandfather became a Ndebele warrior, and was given the name 'Isilwane' or lion, because he was 'brave as a lion'. Neither claimed uninterrupted settlement in the Shangani during the reigns of Mzilikazi and Lobengula. Moyo's forefathers had lived to the south of the Shangani. They 'vacated' their land when the Ndebele arrived on the advice of the Inyathi missionaries, moving to 'empty' land in the Shangani which they then occupied through the late nineteenth century.[62] Mpimbili said his grandfather Isilwane was told by Lobengula in 1893 to return to the area in the Lupane valley where he had left cattle with other people of Tonga, Sili and Lozwi descent. From that time on, his grandfather occupied the valley.

As the Ndebele state fragmented after the uprisings, such incorporated people sustained or revived pre-Ndebele traditions. The descendants of these older polities had sometimes, like Moyo's family, lived in the Shangani for a considerable time before the appointment of Ndebele chiefs in the first decade of the twentieth century. Other families had a more interrupted history of using, or living in, the Shangani. But many such, like Mpimbili's, were among the first to remake their homes there as the Ndebele regiments dispersed in the aftermath of 1896. So by the time the Ndebele chiefs moved into the Reserve, each found their areas already populated, if far from densely. Chief Tshoko/Madliwa, for example, found south-eastern Nkayi sparsely populated, 'but for a few Balozwi who had been living in the area for some time. The majority of his people [were] of the Lozwi and Nyai.'[63]

[59] J.W. Posselt to CNC, November 1926, S 138 92, 1923–1933.
[60] Interview with Kungwa Jeremiah Moyo, Gomoza, 13 March 1996. Administrative reports for south-western Nkayi note that: 'the original inhabitants of this area are the Balozwi Tribe who were followers of chief Mambo. They were considered by chief Mambo as fine witch-doctors.' Report on Area C, LDO J. Richardson, January 1958, S 2208/1/25.
[61] Interview with Mpimbili Ndlovu, Isilwane, 14 September 1996.
[62] The centre of the Lozwi state was on the plateau to the east of the Shangani. It is unclear how extensive settlement was in the *gusu* areas.
[63] Delineation Report, Nkayi, Chief Madliwa, June 1965, S 2929. For similar comments on chief Nkalakatha's area, see Report on Zone B, January 1958, S 2808/1/25.

By the time the colonial chiefs arrived, then, southern and eastern parts of the Shangani were occupied by people who had been variously incorporated into the Ndebele state, but who could also claim Lozwi or Nyai descent and, as such, ownership of the land. There were other non-Ndebele claims to the land as well. Headman Mfungo, for example, who came to be based in Gokwe District to the north-east of the Shangani, was descended from rain-making chiefs overthrown by the Shangwe paramount. In addition to his longstanding ritual role as an intermediary to the Nevana medium, he also claimed once 'to have controlled the area from the Zambezi to the Shangani.'[64] Chief Mkoka (initially a Lozwi fugitive, who is said to have 'become Tonga' through marrying Tonga wives) was based north of the Shangani reserve in the mid-twentieth century but claimed his predecessors had settled and ruled 'a large tract of country' which included the Shangani as well as territory to the north.[65] While this is undoubtedly an exaggeration, there are many Tonga people now living in northern Lupane who describe their fathers and grandfathers as having been among Mkoka's subjects.[66]

A Tonga history was particularly important in the north and west of the Shangani. Most of the Ndebele chiefs who moved into the Shangani in the early part of the century settled in the eastern half of the Reserve. In the west, there was little Ndebele immigration until the 1950s, and the Ndebele chiefs who would rule there – Mabhikwa and Menyezwa – lived in the Forest Areas to the south of the Reserve in the early part of the century. Many of the Tonga-speaking people the chiefs found on their arrival were keen to defend their Tonga identity, and to distance themselves from the Ndebele and Ndebele history – a history in which they tended to be cast as slaves or captives. They continued to speak Tonga and pursue their own cultural activities in the early part of the century – indeed Tonga is still spoken by some 'original' settlers in the north and west of the Shangani today.

Ndebele-speaking settlers who moved into the western Shangani in the early twentieth century speak of moving into 'Tonga country', or of the Tonga as being 'owners of the *gusu*' when they arrived.[67] Native Commissioner Posselt's map of the 'Approximate Distribution of Tribes and Languages' – which showed 'Batonka' populations to the west of the Shangwe and to the south of the Shangani river as far as the junction of the Gwampa and the Gwaai – may well have been based on reliable information.[68] Posselt's tribes are depicted as overlapping and, certainly in the Shangani, any implication of rigid and fixed boundaries between 'Lozwi', 'Nyai', 'Tonga', 'Shangwe' and so on would be highly misleading. As we have seen, family histories testify to much mixing and a fluidity of identification which was conceived of in political rather than essentialized 'tribal' terms. The case of Mkoka demonstrated the fluidity of Lozwi and Tonga language and identifications; being part of the Ndebele state certainly did not rule out other identities.[69] The contrasts between Lozwi/Nyai settlement in the south,

---

[64] Delineation Report, Gokwe, Mfungo, S 2929/7/3.

[65] Delineation Report, Gokwe, Chief Mkoka, S 2929/7/3.

[66] Interviews, Tonga elders, Dandanda, 10 December 1994; group interview, Ndimimbili, 11 March 1996; group interview, Lusulu, 26 February 1996.

[67] Interviews with W. Fuyana, Lupanda, 18 September 1996; Luta Inyati, Jotsholo, 3 March 1996.

[68] The Posselt map is reproduced in the 1927 issue of *NADA*. For a discussion of Posselt's map, see Eric Worby, 'Maps, Names, and Ethnic Games: The Epistemology and Iconography of Colonial Power in Northwestern Zimbabwe', *Journal of Southern African Studies*, 20, 3, September 1994, p. 386.

[69] Tonga is a particularly slippery label. As David Beach points out 'the word *tonga*, suggesting either "subject" or "chiefless" people, was used by various Bantu-speaking people at various times to mean different groups from Lake Malawi to Delagoa Bay, including the Lakeside Tonga of modern Malawi, the Valley Tonga of the middle Zambezi, the Sena speaking Lower Zambezi Tonga, the Tonga of the bay of Inhambane and the Tonga-speakers who eventually covered

Shangwe settlement in the northeast, and Tonga settlement in the west was far less clear cut, and far more mixed by the early twentieth century than either we or Posselt have made it appear. Nor were these populations stable over the nineteenth century. As with the Lozwi/Nyai, Tonga settlement was profoundly disrupted. Many Tonga men were incorporated into the regiments or lived as Ndebele subjects, while others fled and hid, only recreating Tonga communities in the Shangani after 1896.[70] They could, however, make connections with an earlier Tonga expansion into the region, and they could claim 'ownership' of the land prior to that of the Ndebele immigrants who would settle the Shangani in large numbers after the Second World War.

Let us look briefly at the evidence for Tonga settlement in the region before and during the time of the Ndebele. Hitherto Zimbabwean historiography has hardly considered the existence of an 'upland' Tonga population on the Zimbabwean side of the Zambezi. It is standard to write of both the Valley and the Plateau Tonga so far as Zambia is concerned.[71] But in Zimbabwe the Tonga are often thought of as being a riverine people, up until the displacements caused by the building of the Kariba Dam. The latest historian of the Zimbabwean Tonga, Godfrey Tabona Ncube, however, describes dense Tonga settlement along the Kana, Mzola and Tshongokwe rivers of the Shangani until the Ndebele raiding of the mid-nineteenth century forced a retreat to the Zambezi valley.[72] Our interviews suggest on-going, sparse Tonga settlement in the northern river valleys through the late nineteenth century, with individual Tonga families living as far south as the Gwampa river.[73] During the reign of the Ndebele, the biggest and southernmost group of Tonga-speakers seems to have been that of Soma-nyanga. As mentioned above, they lived south of the Gwampa as Ndebele subjects.

The evidence for a significant pre-Ndebele Tonga expansion is much greater for the Tonga polities of the north-central plateau than for the Shangani. Stanlake Samkange collected oral traditions in the Chivero district of Tonga armies conquering extensive areas of the plateau.[74] David Beach writes of the Ngezi dynasty of Rimuka, who were recorded by the Portuguese as being a 'Tonga' people in the midst of Shona/Karanga chieftancies. Beach believes that the Rimuka polity was in place by the seventeenth century and represented the south-eastern limits of Zambezi Tonga penetration.[75] He includes the Ngezi chieftaincy – and possibly other now vanished Tonga dynasties – among the group of peoples whom the Portuguese called 'Roro', but who have now been lumped together with the 'Zezuru' sub-ethnicity. The great rainmaker of the northwest, Nevana, claims to come from this 'Roro' area and the mediumship may therefore have originated from a plateau settlement which was once part of a 'Tonga' belt stretching from the Zambezi.[76]

[69] (cont.) almost the whole area between the Sabi, the Plateau and the Delagoa Bay. Certain Shona dynasties used it to mean their Shona-speaking subjects.' Beach, *The Shona and Zimbabwe, 900–1850* (Gweru, Mambo Press, 1980), p. 158.

[70] Some Tonga families said they had sought out their current homes as places of refuge 'fleeing raiding'. See, for example, interview with Widness Tshuma, Sibombo, 15 December, 1996.

[71] In the writing of Elizabeth Colson, for example. See *The Plateau Tonga of Northern Rhodesia. Social and Religious Studies* (Manchester University Press, 1962) and *Social Organization of the Gwembe Tonga* (Manchester University Press, 1960).

[72] Ncube argues that, 'The Tshongokwe valley represented the southernmost area ever occupied by the Tonga in Zimbabwe.' Ncube, 'A History of North West Zimbabwe', p. 284.

[73] For example, interview with Mpimbili Ndlovu, Isilwane, 14 September 1995.

[74] Samkange Archives, The Castle, Harare.

[75] D. Beach, *A Zimbabwean Past: Shona Dynastic Histories and Oral Traditions* (Gweru, Mambo Press, 1995), p. 53.

[76] J. Alexander and T. Ranger, 'Competition and Integration in the Religious History of North-Western Zimbabwe', *Journal of Religion in Africa*, 28, 1, 1998, pp. 3–31.

It seems very unlikely, however, that there were ever Tonga armies or dynastic polities in the forested country between the Kana and the Gwampa rivers. Chiefs Mfungo and Mkoka probably had some influence in the region but it is not clear if they and their subjects can meaningfully be called 'Tonga', and it seems more likely that it was recognition of the rain-making powers and spiritual prestige of the Nevana medium and other rainmakers which gave some coherence to the scattered settlements of the Shangani territory. (The present Nevana medium claims spiritual control of the whole region from the Zambezi River to the Botswana border at Plumtree!)

Today there remain traces of Tonga settlers in the names of trees and rivers all over the Shangani territory. Colonial administrators recorded myths about the origins of names, and we also collected such stories – they are often contradictory in their detail, but nonetheless concur in the remembrance of a non- or pre-Ndebele history. At Zenka, south of the Shangani river, 'the main shrine is at a tree which is said to be unique in the district. Legend has it that the tree was brought by one Nzenka from the Zambezi very many years ago and planted there', close to the Zenka salt-pan. The tree was obviously very old and of a type which grows only in the Zambezi Valley; Nzenka himself was said to be buried beneath it; it attracted people from a considerable distance to rain-making rites. 'If somebody stumbles upon it by accident he will see a very big snake looking after it.'[77] At Jotsholo, on the Shangani River's southern banks, 'the original inhabitants of the area were scattered Tonga peoples. They gave the area the name Jotsholo, meaning a large or immense thing. This related to a huge baobab tree'.[78] The river Kafulafula in Manguni area 'comes from a Tonga word meaning "springing from the ground"'.[79]

Other names testify to the huge diversity of languages and varied descent of the 'original' settlers. Thus the name of the Bopoma river comes from a Nanzwa word meaning 'water is boiling from the ground'; the river Gababe owes its name to a Shangwe word meaning 'a plain where people died in great numbers in one go'; the name of the Mangwizi river is derived from a Lozwi word meaning 'drink water before you cross the river or else you die.'[80] One version of the origin of the name Shangani itself is that it is a corruption of the Kalanga word 'Hankano', or junction, and was first applied to the junction of the Shangani and the Gwaai rivers.[81] The tree-shrine at Panke – 'one of the biggest baobab trees I have ever seen', wrote M.E. Hayes in 1975 – is said to derive its name from a Lozwi pioneer.[82] Nyai and Tonga settlers regarded Panke as the most important of rain-making shrines; their rainmakers would 'go inside the hole' in the tree 'and dance'.[83]

We have argued that there was significant, if mobile, Lozwi and Tonga settlement in the Shangani prior to the establishment of the Ndebele state. We have also argued that the idea of depopulating violence from the mid-nineteenth century had some validity, though it has often been exaggerated. In the early twentieth century the Shangani continued to draw settlers of diverse origins. Many Tonga and others came from the north. Although people moved for varied reasons, hunger in the Zambezi valley and in the land north of the Shangani certainly played an important part. In the first decade of the century the Tonga, Mawela, came south with his younger brother and son-in-law,

[77] M.E. Hayes report on Headman Mpande, October 1974, CHK 6 Nkayi, Headman Mpande.
[78] D.K. Parkinson, 'Lupane Notes', *NADA*, 1980.
[79] District Commissioner, Nkayi to Secretary, Geographical Names Society, 22 January 1963, Nkayi LAN 1/Gen., 1962-1970.
[80] *Ibid*.
[81] SGP, 'Native Nomenclature', *NADA*, 1934.
[82] M.E. Hayes, Report on Headman Malunda, October 1975, CHK 6 Nkayi. Hayes said that the people of several other headmen also went to Panke.
[83] Interviews with Albert Hadebe, Lutsha and Headman Mlume, Gwampa, 2 October 1995.

escaping hunger in Pashu's country. They aimed 'to come near' to the Ndebele in Bubi so that 'they could trade with them if there was hunger'. 'They wanted the swamps around Gwaai, but they were afraid of lions, so they moved to the Shangani.' Mawela set up his own *mtolo* (rainshrine) and was recognized as the 'owner' of the area in the early decades of the twentieth century.[84] Others arrived to escape 'crowding', 'looking for wet places' or game, and to escape tsetse fly. Tsetse-control measures, implemented north of the Shangani in 1910, displaced Chief Mkoka and many of his people, forcing them to move into the Shangani.[85]

Other people who had originated in the Zambezi valley, and had been captured and incorporated into the Ndebele regiments, moved northwards as the Ndebele state fragmented after 1896. Some intended to return to their former homes in the Zambezi region, but instead settled in the Shangani. Others who had become labourers in the mines or in Bulawayo town decided to establish homes which were less far away from work than the distant Zambezi valley. Sometimes they had married Tonga wives in the Shangani.[86]

This increasing settlement of the formerly incorporated or subjugated people originally from the northwest generally pre-dated the movement into the Shangani of former members of the Ndebele state who had no prior connection with the region. In this period, the area was remembered as dense bush, and even these 'original' settlers would often draw on the Ndebele idiom of the 'dark forests' in telling of their settlement. The Lozwi, Council Sibanda, for example, recalls how 'the place was *emaguswini amnyama* [in the dark forests] – it was difficult to return home. If my home was north, I'd head south.' His parents would beat a drum 'to draw you home. It was difficult even to find where the drumming was coming from. That was the problem of the forests.'[87]

## The Development of Forest Cultures

Not only did the settlers in the Shangani territory come from many different places; the land itself was very varied, despite its image of being unremittingly dark and threatening. The whole art of being a pioneer settler in this country lay in finding niches – a fertile valley; wet vlei areas; parts of the *gusu* bush which would give good yields and which could be identified by particular trees or shrubs; places free of fly or poisonous plants where cattle could graze; places regularly visited by game and good for hunting. It was the river valleys which attracted almost all settlement. But people familiar with this territory came to see the *gusu* not as universally dark, but as highly differentiated: 'The *gusus* are all very different', one such explained. 'When you choose fields in the *gusu* there are about five types of trees which are of very great assistance in choosing your spot: *mqhobampunzi*, *isihlangu*, *igonde*, *umvagazi* and *mkusu* ... grasses can also help.'[88]

Despite the diversity of settlers in the early twentieth century, it is possible to discern some broad patterns in the way the forests were used. Fields and settlements tended to be small. 'The natives huddle together', ran a report of 1919, 'in very small collections of two or three huts, without any fence around them, and usually unperceivable by reason

---

[84] Interview with Boda Nkomo, Sobendle, Lupane, 27 November 1994.

[85] Interviews with Widness Tshuma, Sibombo, 15 December 1994; Madube Ncube, Sibombo, 16 December 1994; Tonga elders, Dandanda, 10 December 1994.

[86] See interviews with Sabelo Mhlanga, Mpofu Ncube, Patison Mpofu and David Ncube, Lupaka, 9 February 1996.

[87] Interview with Council Sibanda, Mateme, 12 December 1995.

[88] Interview with Magwaza Ndlovu, Pupu, 20 February 1996. Magwaza's family came originally from Plumtree but settled among the Tonga and Shangwe. Magwaza grew up in the Shangani.

of the surrounding thick bush which is never cleared away.'[89] And this is certainly the picture drawn by later arrivals,who claimed that those they found in the Shangani 'only scratched the soil'. Early settlers recall that 'there were very few villages, they were miles apart. Our means of communication then was beating drums.'[90] One major distinction was between the northwest Shangani, where the early settlers had no cattle, and the southeast, where Ndebele aristocrats were settling with sizeable herds and where some of the 'originals' also had cattle of the indigenous type known as *amanjanja*. These cattle-owners proved attractive to the earlier settlers. Luka Sibanda, a Nyai, recalls how 'the introduction of cattle was so popular', allowing people to plough larger lands, reap bigger harvests and, if they were close enough to the stores which began to open in the southeast, to trade for goods.[91]

Access to cattle had implications not only for how much land was used, but for which parts of the landscape were chosen for cultivation. While all settlers needed to be close to water and so built their homes along the main river valleys and tributaries, they did not always cultivate the same soils. Many 'originals' who lacked draught power avoided the fertile, heavy black soils of the valley bottoms, known as *isidaka*, but those with cattle actively sought them out. The Tonga in particular often used the lighter soils on the edge of the *gusu* forests rather than cultivating right down in the valleys. These sandy *gusu* soils were well-suited to the Tonga staple of bulrush millet, *inyawuthi*. Those who planted the *gusu* margins did not clear the trees completely, but burnt the land and pruned the tall trees, cultivating for a few years until the soil became exhausted, and then moved on. But those who chose the *isidaka* planted sorghum and maize, and could replant year after year.

Although many men were at some point in their lives migrant labourers and travelled to the mines and towns to the south, hunting was perhaps the chief source of male prestige, and certainly is central to oral recollections of the early decades of the twentieth century. One Ndebele-speaking arrival from the south described the society of Lozwi/Nyai and Tonga which he found as follows:

> The people were great hunters. They would compete in hunting, even the old men. The more animals you kill, the more pride you have. At the end of the month, a father or adult who had not killed enough kudu or eland or water buck would not be allowed to drink beer with the elders – he'd be with the boys or women. These people, as hunters, they had only little patches of kaffir corn, just for beer brewing. Their pride was in meat.[92]

And the prestige of hunting was certainly not just a matter of Tonga and Lozwi culture. Antony Magagula, a Nguni descended from the Swazi regiment, recalled how, in his childhood in the Shangani, men used to kill lions: 'We were still men! Remnants of the warriors. If you saw a lion, you went for it ...'; '... we'd kill lions single-handed'.[93]

The prevalence of wild animals made it difficult and dangerous to move through the bush, particularly in more sparsely populated areas. A Tonga elder described the days when:

> if you wanted to make a trip, you'd walk at midday in the scorching sun to avoid the animals. Around 3 p.m. we'd start building a shelter for the night, high up in a tree. We'd see lions and elephants from our tree shelters. It was dangerous. On

---

[89] Nielsen to Chief Staff Officer, 21 March 1919, NGB2/4/1.
[90] Interview with Luka Sibanda, Kana, 5 December 1995.
[91] Interview with Luka Sibanda, Kana, 5 December 1995.
[92] Interview with Albert Hadebe, Lutsha, Gwampa, 4 October 1995.
[93] Interview with Antony Magagula, Masungamala, 7 February 1996.

those trips we'd need water, so we'd take calabashes. ... The area was wide and there was no water when you crossed the *gusu.* ... [If we ate meat] the lions would smell the meat and would come. They'd be eating the bones and scraps down below the tree. We never thought the land would be clear as it is now.[94]

In this kind of country, a 'big man' had to be involved in hunting. A well-remembered twentieth-century big man was the Sili, Ngabetsha. His wealth was based on his role as guardian of powerful herbal medicines used against lions and his knowledge about hunting. He had many wives and many Tonga junior sons-in-law who worked for him to win his daughters. 'Ngabetsha was friendly to the *amagotsha* [tsetse-control hunters] because they sought advice from him. He told them where to find the animals. They brought him meat for that.'[95] Ngabetsha could provide medicine, 'and you could take that *muti* [medicine] and go next to a tree and touch it and become invisible. You can approach game without being seen, heard or smelt ... Lions couldn't damage us.'[96]

The people of the forest built communities and wider connections through religion. Almost everywhere religious rituals focused on tree-shrines. Some were concerned with hunting; others with rain and fertility. In the western Shangani there were *mpane we nyama* 'trees for game' set in groves of *umpane* and *ichithamuzi* trees.[97] One such was in western Lupane: 'Hunters used to go to that tree and ask permission before hunting.' The tree, called Lupanda, was itself said to crave meat – 'if Lupanda doesn't get meat it kills the hunter.'[98] Elsewhere, ritual was much more focused on rain and, as agriculture grew in importance, the hunting shrines themselves came to have significance as rainshrines.[99] *Mtolo* shrines for ancestral veneration and rain-making ceremonies were by far the most common and most important local religious sites. They were established at particularly striking trees, and were often founded by the first generations of settlers.[100] Such ritual centres were common to the Lozwi, Nyai, Tonga and Shangwe settlers, and our oral testimonies provide rich accounts of activities based around them. As an early Nyai settler recalled:

> We used to play drums, *amachukwana*, and an old lady would collect up all the young children and paint their bodies with wood ash in stripes from the waist up, and they would be sent to sweep the area. Then they would congregate at the [*mtolo*] tree, and the *wosana* [rain spirit mediums] would dance and dance. Then there was feasting on meat and beer before all went to the river to wash.[101]

The shrines constituted a loose hierarchy. At the lowest level, there were the many *mtolos*, which were usually trees. Some of these were more important than others, and could attract people from quite a wide area. These *mtolos* were linked to higher-level religious centres. In northern Shangani, for example, communities would send envoys

---

[94] Interview with Chief Kavula, Lubimbi, 25 March 1996.

[95] Interview with Jeli Mlotshwa, Matshiya, 8 March 1996.

[96] Interview with Fotsholo Tshuma, Jotsholo, 8 March 1996.

[97] Respectively, *Colophospermum mopane* and *Lonchocarpus capassa.*

[98] Interview with Gabheni Sibanda and Pahlane Moyo, Lupanda, 3 April 1996. Lupanda, which became the name of Lupane's Native Purchase Area, originally referred to the hunting tree. It was said to draw on Kalanga traditions.

[99] Interview with Fotsholo Tshuma, Jotsholo, 8 March 1996.

[100] Wetlands and pools were also commonly sacred sites, or *amalinda.*

[101] Interview with Mavelalitshone Mpofu, Matshiya, 19 January 1996. For a missionary account, see Charles Celt Thomas, 'Thomas Morgan Thomas. Pioneer Missionary, 1828-1884', ms, National Archives, Zimbabwe, p. 63.

to an old woman, Bamwali, at Ciwale, bringing water from her pool before dancing at their local *mtolos*. Bamwali was a mysterious figure, fluent in all the major languages of the area and herself of disputed descent. She lived surrounded by lions – 'you had to go near and clap hands, then they'd give you space to pass, but you must not swerve from the path.' 'She was like God,' recalls one Tonga elder, 'so you could never know the whole story.'[102] In northeast Shangani, Sigwegwe was another important medium. After he died, his grave became a pilgrimage site: it 'was protected in the traditional way – they made a shelter with grass, a triangular shape. Every year in October, we would get water and pour it over the grave to cool it.'[103] At the top of the hierarchy were the two most important religious foci of western Zimbabwe – the network of shrines at the Matopos in Matabeleland South, notably Njelele, and the Nevana medium in today's Gokwe district. In the early part of the twentieth century, the Nevana medium seems to have been by far the most important pilgrimage centre.[104] Communities from all over the Shangani would send deputations to Nevana for rain and for seed to be blessed. Most of the intermediate level religious sites were also linked to the Nevana medium. For the communities of the Shangani forest, the rain ceremonies and the movement to and fro between Nevana and the *mtolo* in many respects defined both a local and a wider community in the years after the disruptions of the 1890s.

The individuals responsible for rain were usually called *wosana*, and were possessed by rain spirits of the same name. Much has been written about the *wosana* associated with the High God cult of the Matopos.[105] But in the Shangani, most of the early settlers' *wosana* went to the Nevana medium. Some communities had a further division of responsibility for rainmaking: the *wosana* would lead the ceremony at the local *mtolo*, but messengers called *abahambi bendlela* would make the trip to Nevana or Njelele. The politics of rainmaking was often highly contested – individual rainmakers and shrines regularly fell in and out of favour.[106]

In Tonga communities, the term *mpande* described an individual possessed by rain spirits, and the *mpande* often played a comparable role to the *wosana* (today, some people use the terms interchangeably). Cosmas Ncube argues that the *mpande* was the key ritual figure, and the 'basis of societal unity' in nineteenth-century Tonga society. To the north of the Shangani Reserve, there were several Tonga shrines where particularly famous *mpande* performed, and which were visited by people from northern Lupane. Bila pool in Lubimbi was one such place, named after a prominent *mpande*. According to Tonga elders, Bila used to 'go right in' to the pool at the hot springs 'and come out later without a scratch, carrying green mealies, sweet reeds and melons.'[107] In addition to *mtolo*, each Tonga clan would have a shrine called a *numba* which hosted ancestral spirits. They were located in the homeyard and tended by the *mpande*.[108]

[102] Interviews with Fuba Ncube and Chief Kavula, Lubimbi, 9 February and 25 March 1996.

[103] Interview with Luka Mpofu, Mtshabi, 16 October 1995.

[104] Nevana is discussed in Alexander and Ranger, 'Competition and Integration in the Religious History of North-Western Zimbabwe'.

[105] See R. Werbner, *Ritual Passage, Sacred Journey* (Manchester University Press, 1989).

[106] The description given here is echoed in the reports of M.E. Hayes and Rhodesian administrators. These provide much valuable information on rainmaking activity, but they tend towards an overly static picture due to the practice of interviewing only one rainmaker for each chief or headman. They thus give no sense of the diversity in each area, or of the different views of competing rainmakers. See, e.g., report of C.J.K. Latham, March 1967, S 2929/5/1/1; M.E. Hayes, report on headmen Fanisoni and Mtenjwa, October and November 1975, CHK 6.

[107] Interview with chief Kavula, Lubimbi, 25 March 1996 and Class Mudenda Dube, Lubimbi, 26 March 1996. Described also in Cosmas Ncube, 'Tonga Ritual: A Way of Constructing Reality', BA Honours Thesis, Religious Studies, University of Zimbabwe, 1987.

[108] Cosmas Ncube refers to these as *intumba*, but in the Shangani, the term is often pronounced *numba*.

Religious figures such as these played a critical role in the early parts of the twentieth century, not only in ensuring rain and fertility, but in protecting against illness and crop pests – a role that was central to the disease- and epidemic-prone Shangani. The 1918 influenza pandemic (known as *'ifureza'*) and the locust plagues of 1920 and the mid-1930s are widely cited as historical markers and periods of crisis. 'Frazer came in like a strong wind from the south,' recalled one elder who had been a migrant labourer and returned home to procure 'preventive medicine' and 'protect' his village in the Lupane valley. 'It was a sickness, that when you contract it, you just drop dead. Lonely Mine [in Inyathi] came to a standstill.' As the workers fled home, the forests were filled with the bodies of those 'struck down in the bushes'.[109] Not long thereafter, the first of two plagues of locusts hit. In each instance, the Nevana medium, the *wosana* and *mpande* were consulted. Maintaining good relations with ancestral spirits was critical to life in the *gusu* forests in uncertain times such as these. As settlers arrived in the Shangani from all directions in the first decades of the twentieth century, religious sites proliferated, religious leaders competed, and connections were remade with ancestors and times gone by.

## Ndebele Immigrants and the Forest Cultures

It was into this society of small riverine settlements, scattered between the arid *gusu* ridges and marked by a hierarchy of shrines, that the aristocratic Ndebele chiefs and their people began to move in the early twentieth century. It was a society which in many ways was re-asserting its autonomous identity after the collapse of the Ndebele state. Tonga informants in western Shangani describe how their ancestors had been incorporated into Ndebele regiments. But

> after the war my grandfather worked in a kitchen in Bulawayo, and built his home near Ngabetsha [the Sili hunting expert and big man]. He collected female relatives who had also been captured by the Ndebele and arranged Tonga husbands for their daughters from amongst the Tonga migrant labourers in Bulawayo. We continued speaking Tonga and we had a … *numba*, which was handed down from the grandfathers. … When we were fighting we couldn't continue doing that, but as soon as the fighting stopped, we started it again … the beads used in it were the original ones, taken from the Zambezi.[110]

Such forest dwellers lived in an environment which Ndebele settlers often portrayed as profoundly threatening. It was one thing to hunt, graze cattle or pass through the Shangani forests, as Ndebele speakers had done in the nineteenth century, but quite another to build villages and cultivate. The current chief Sivalo relates how his family moved from Bulawayo into 'land for wild animals. We never liked this part of the country. We were forcibly moved. … Now we are here but we still don't like it'.[111] But the Ndebele newcomers had to make the most of their new environment and of the people amongst whom they found themselves.

As we have seen, there were no Tonga or Shangwe or Lozwi chiefs in the Shangani, though there were plenty of 'big men', and plenty of powerful ritual specialists.[112] The incoming Ndebele chiefs soon established themselves as political, and even judicial,

[109] Interview with Mr Mate, Matonsi Sibanda and others, Endamuleni, 7 March 1996.

[110] Interview with Fuba Ncube, S. Mhlanga, Mpofu Ncube, et al., Lupaka, 9 September 1996.

[111] Statement at meeting of Nkayi chiefs, August 1993, communicated by Marieke Clarke.

[112] There were, however, non-Ndebele chiefs on the northern borders of the Shangani, such as the Tonga chief Kavula and chief Mkoka.

authorities. The influence of the Ndebele language spread as it became the language of authority in the Shangani. But as we have also seen, many of the chiefs' subjects were concerned to assert their older identity, even if they had at one time been Ndebele warriors or subjects and might also assert an Ndebele identity under certain circumstances. As the earlier settlers claimed ritual authority over the land and were numerically significant, there was often a good deal of accommodation and adaptation on the part of the Ndebele aristocracy and those who moved into the forests with them.

At one extreme, this involved recognizing local authority over the land, intermarrying and even adopting an 'original' language. Thus some of the 'Tonga' around Pupu, north of the Shangani, are 'not pure Tonga. They came from Bubi and took Tonga wives, changed their language and became Tonga.'[113] More commonly, however, and certainly for men of Nguni heritage, a Tonga or Lozwi wife would have no choice but to accommodate to the Ndebele husband. Many Ndebele, and particularly the aristocrats, looked down on Tonga and Lozwi as inferior. The earlier settlers also had little choice but to accept Ndebele as the language of administration and communication with the outside world, even if the Ndebele immigrants in turn learnt to communicate in Tonga, accepted some of the locals' means of propitiating the land, and interacted with them on a day-to-day basis.

Paulos Mhlotshwa describes how his grandfather came into central Shangani in 1911 with Prince Tshakalisa, *sintingantinga seNkosi* (beloved son of the King), in search of grazing for their large herds. He described Nguni interactions with the Tonga of the Shangani in the following way:

> The Nguni/Tonga relationship was very friendly. Tshakalisa was respected because he was the son of the King, and he took the Tonga as his children and didn't harass them. If the Tonga had problems of starvation, they came to Tshakalisa because he had access to the Native Commissioner and white people, so he could get assistance. The Tonga here spoke Tonga when we came here, they even taught Tshakalisa Tonga. At the same time they were interested in Ndebele. ... In our Nguni culture, we didn't have rain ceremonies, we depended on the Tonga, on Sibalaboyi [the *mpande*]. Tshakalisa said, it looks like we need rain. Can you do something and we will all follow. So we would collect young ones, brew beer, gather under a tree, and clap and dance. Sibalaboyi had a vision of when rain would come and he would tell Tshakalisa. ... The ceremony was under the *mtolo* tree. We use the same one now and there is still a Tonga *wosana*.[114]

Nor did the Ndebele incomers only adopt 'original' religious rituals. They also adapted to some aspects of the local economy. Many found that the local, smaller, *amanjanja* cattle did better in the bush than cattle from the plateau grasslands. Some also began to plant *inyawuthi* – bulrush millet – even though it was often stigmatized by Ngunis as 'an offence to the ancestors'. As Jeli Mlotshwa, whose Ndebele-speaking family moved from Umguza in the south to Lupane in 1917, recalled:

> We learnt to plant *inyawuthi* here. There [in Umguza] it was only sorghum and maize. We got our *inyawuthi* from the Tonga. ... We didn't remove the trees, we'd

[113] Interview with K.K. Nyati, Pupu, 2 April 1996.
[114] Interview with Paulos Mhlotshwa, Tshakalisa Business Centre, 25 November 1995. Sibalaboyi himself had originated in the Zambezi Valley; had left there as a guide to a white traveller; ended up in Francistown; left the white man's employ and migrated back towards the Zambezi. He settled instead in the Gwampa valley. He established a *mtolo* in the Zambezi, at Gwampa and then in Tshakalisa's area, when the Prince asked for his help with rain. His son, England Ngwenya, cannot speak Tonga. Interview with England Ngwenya, Tshakalisa, 6 December 1995.

just plant around them. … We used to plant like the Tonga, burning the trees, then the crops would be good in those sites. We didn't have gardens as such, but a little patch next to the homes to give the unmarried sons as a test to see if he could organise it. We didn't plant in the wetlands, only small patches of *mbanje* [marijuana], no vegetables. … We'd plant in the *gusu*.[115]

These first immigrants also hunted. Both the memories of these early settler families and written records reveal the continued abundance of wild animals and the importance of hunting skills. Bowen Rees, travelling through the Reserve in 1914, reported lions everywhere. At chief Madliwa's he was offered fine beef from a beast killed by a lion who 'had paid a midnight visit among his herd of cattle'. At Prince Tshakalisa's 'we had quite a lively time with lions'. Eight lions came close to the kraal and 'on account of these lions on the path, we had to wait a day longer at Jakalisa's kraal until we were assured that the road was clear.'[116] Chief Sikhobokhobo was remembered to have shown himself a true leader in his youth by dealing with the wild beasts of the Shangani: 'the young chief was strong and brave and became renowned for the killing of lions. On one occasion he was attacked by a lion but he fought it and killed it.'[117]

Early colonial criminal cases arising from events in the Shangani – where there were no police or lock-ups – dealt almost exclusively with hunting and hunters. White adventurers travelled through the Reserve on hunting parties to shoot eland, sable and roan. They recruited men at Tshakalisa's or Madliwa's, gave them guns and employed them 'to go with us and hunt'.[118] A rape case in 1917 presents a picture of the environment – of Lozwi kraals strung along the Shangani river and flanked by game-filled bush. The Lozwi girl, Yega, going to the river for water with her aunt, was accosted by a stranger who 'offered to give them meat'. He took them first to 'a temporary hut in the bush', which had been erected 'by some Dutchmen who were shooting game at Shangani'; suspecting the worst, the aunt escaped, leaving Yega to be raped several times. Next day he took her to a platform in the bush, where game-meat was drying, 'a long way from any kraals'. Yega managed to escape; her rapist was caught by people from the Lozwi kraals, out searching for the missing girl.[119]

For locals in the Shangani, hunting with guns had been rare prior to this period. During the nineteenth century, European hunters, and Ndebele gun-hunters seeking elephant had penetrated the area, some men absorbed into the regiments had used guns, and a minority of migrant labourers had bought muzzle loaders with their wages. But after 1910, guns proliferated and a substantial class of local gun-hunters arose. These men, called *amagotsha*, were employed by the Rhodesian state as part of its new game-elimination campaign against testse.[120] The state shooting campaign was initially focused on the Shangani/Gwaai confluence and along the Kana river on the Shangani's northern border. In May 1922, the Native Commissioner, Bubi, strongly urged an extension of the programme southwards to protect the Shangani Reserve against an expansion of the fly by the employment of 'about fifty good native shots, at 20/- per mensem, and, of course, the meat and skins of the animals shot by them'. In addition,

[115] Interview with Jeli Mlotshwa, Lupane, 8 March 1996.
[116] Bowen Rees, 'Lions on the Path', 23 July 1914, CWM, South Africa Incoming, Box 76, Folder 4, SOAS.
[117] District Commissioner, Nkayi to Provincial Commissioner, 4 March 1966, CHK 6 Nkayi Sikhobokhobo.
[118] Rex v J.H. Hoare, 26 May 1913; Rex v W.T. Dymott, 21 August 1914; Rex v N.G. Von Petty, 9 February 1915; Rex v J.W. Morrison, 22 April 1915, D 3/23/2 and 3. The criminal offence was giving firearms to Africans.
[119] Rex v Magodi, 19 October 1917, D 3/23/4. Magodi was a 'labourer' from north western Rhodesia.
[120] See John Ford, *The Role of Trypanosomiases in African Ecology* (Oxford, 1971), p. 320.

Special Permits to Shoot Game would be issued to Reserve residents in the north-west Shangani.[121] By 1930, there were 37 Government rifles and 7 rifles owned by Africans in use in this zone; in January 1932, when unpaid African hunters were 'busy with their lands', though 'still using their rifles in the intervals', the Native Department proposed to pay 20 full time gun-hunters in the western Shangani.[122] The number of guns was certainly much higher as hunters from the northern borders (only later incorporated into the Nkayi/Lupane districts) went uncounted in these figures.

Many of these gun-using *amagotsha* were Tonga who now replaced their snares and the occasional highly dangerous muzzle-loader with modern rifles. Chief Kavula recalls their impact:

> All our forefathers were *amagotsha*. They were the ones who chased all the animals. We were both angry and happy about that. Happy because the lions were cleared away but angry because our favourite game meat was also chased away. The *amagotsha* would kill and we would eat all the meat. ... People bought cattle from the Ndebele with money from that *gotsha* work ... it seemed so much money, you could buy quantities and quantities of goods. ... Some of the *amagotsha* accumulated many wives.[123]

Though hunters resented the fact that only whites were allowed to shoot elephants and that hunting outside the confines of the campaign remained prohibited, they were delighted that dangerous predators, such as lions and hyenas, were being destroyed.[124] And *amagotsha* derived other benefits from the campaign. They became patrons, able to distribute abundant meat to their clients. Some converted their wealth in game meat into wives, and as the tsetse belt was driven north, into cattle. These established themselves as local big men. When the wave of Ndebele evictees arrived in Lupane in the early 1950s, they found the *amagotsha* still in operation – and plenty of game still present:

> Elephants, kudu, eland, wild dogs, hyena, these were the most fearful animals. Lions, yes, but only passing, itinerant. I remember in 1952 the Pupu river had lots of elephants, there were swamps along the river and they'd get stuck there and would be trying to pull each other out from the marsh. They'd call Native Commissioner Hall to dispatch *amagotsha* hunters. Then we'd feast on the meat.[125]

The tsetse-eradication programme marked a change from earlier ways of hunting. And there were many other changes to the Shangani economy in the first three decades of the twentieth century. We have already mentioned the Ndebele chiefs' introduction of large herds, and the growing importance of traders in the southeast. As tsetse retreated north, and people began to accumulate savings from work on the mines and farms of Matabeleland, as well as from South Africa, they, too, were able to buy *mabula* – Afrikander cattle – from sources such as the white rancher, Majaha.[126] When the first

---

[121] Native Commissioner, Bubi to Superintendent of Natives, Bulawayo, 18 May 1922, G 1/3/2/16.

[122] Native Commissioner, Inyathi to S/N/Bulawayo, 9 January 1932, S 3024/1/1.

[123] Interview with Chief Kavula, Lubimbi, 25 March 1996.

[124] See J. Alexander and J. McGregor, 'Wildlife and Politics: Campfire in Zimbabwe', *Development and Change*, 31, 3, 2000.

[125] Interview with Titus Sibanda Moyo, Pupu, 20 February 1996.

[126] Daniel Ncube, son of immigrants who had moved north from Bulawayo to Binga but who then returned southwards to avoid tsetse, recalls that early settlers on the Kana river 'had plenty of cattle ... *mabula*, Afrikander. We bought the cattle from a European to the east of here, called

white traders set up in the Shangani in 1914, Bowen Rees was 'ashamed to mention the fact that white traders are in occupation of the Shangani Reserve' while the London Missionary Society was still debating whether to send a missionary there.[127] By the 1920s, there were white shopkeepers at Dakamela's and at Nyaje, known respectively as Mafuta, fat, and Mamenemene, crooked. People traded small quantities of grain in these shops in exchange for clothes and beads. 'When we were young', recalls Paul Sibanda, 'there was nowhere to sell our produce, no stores. The closest was Mafuta at Dakamela … It was at this Mafuta store that we learned you could sell crops – 20 litres of corn for 1 shilling and 6 pence. That's where we started buying shirts.'[128] Mafuta also ran ox-drawn wagons which plied between Dakamela and Lonely Mine and which, up to the late 1930s, were the only form of transport in the Shangani. Some settlers in the south of the Reserve, particularly those with cattle, were able to market surplus grain, and farmed on a more extensive scale.[129] But these changes did little to modify life in the remote forests of northern and western Shangani.

## Ndebele Repudiation of the Shangani Reserve

While all these adaptations and interactions between Ndebele immigrants and 'originals' were going on, there was simultaneously an articulate critique of the whole idea that the Shangani Reserve could possibly become an Ndebele National Home. This had both a 'traditionalist' and a 'progressive' dimension.

Prince Tshakalisa might have settled in Shangani, but his brother, Nyamanda, leader of the Matabele National Home Movement, would have nothing of it. At a meeting with the Administrator in April 1920, Nyamanda declared:

> The Shangani Reserve is a wild forest. … The native reserves are in the wilds; they are full of mosquitoes and wild beasts. I have visited my brother Tshakalisa's land in the Shangani Reserve. It is too far away. [Must I go] into a far country to be finished off by disease and wild animals? Must I go and live alone in a forest? The Reserves are too far away from Bulawayo, the centre of this country.[130]

Later in the 1920s, Albert and Rhodes Lobengula might tour the Shangani Reserve demanding 'royal' cattle from the chiefs – Rhodes even seeking a permit to go shooting around Dakamela's – but the money gained from sale of the cattle was intended for purchase of land on the plateau close to Bulawayo.[131]

Meanwhile, Christian missionaries and their converts on the plateau were deploring the way of life which many Ndebele already in the Shangani had come to adopt. The London Missionary Society began to prepare to follow up its migrating converts as early as the late 1890s. Its missionaries began with optimism. Bowen Rees thought well

---

[126] (cont.) Majaha. Our fathers were working for Majaha, that's how they bought the cattle, and bought them very cheaply.' Interview, Kana, 28 November 1995.

[127] Bowen Rees to 'my dear Mr Hawkins', 23 July 1914, CWM, South Africa Incoming, Box 78, Folder 4, SOAS.

[128] Interview with Paul Sibanda, Gampinya, 19 October 1995.

[129] In 1921 'over 5,000 bags of grain were traded to store-keepers and supplied to Lonely Mine'. Annual Report, Bubi, 1921, N 9/1/24. Of course, much of this would not have come from the remote Shangani, as the huge Bubi district extended as far south as Bulawayo.

[130] Interview with Nyamanda, 19 April 1920, N 3/19/4.

[131] S 138 92, 1923-1933. Chief Sikhobokhobo robustly replied that if they wanted any of *his* cattle they would have to take him to court.

of the 'vast forests of mpane and mahogony trees', believing that 'soil that could produce such trees could grow food stuffs,' and that Ndebele settlers would 'find ample building materials close to hand.'[132] But soon the missionaries had good reason to deplore the survival of 'pagan' religion in the thickets: in 1901 Shangani was described as 'our furthest, darkest and hardest outstation ... about 40 miles away from the nearest centre of civilisation'. Even the prize convert, Matambo, could make little impression there. In 1903 Matambo, 'after years of toil and prayer' was only able 'to reap a few grains on the Shangani River.' Then Tshakalisa, Sikhobokhobo, Sivalo and Dakamela, all of whom were supporters of the LMS, moved into the Shangani Reserve. Bowen Rees implored the LMS headquarters to send missionaries after them; he and Matambo were prepared to repay part of their own salaries; but in 1909 headquarters imposed stringent economies. A missionary drive was out of the question.

In 1914, Rees toured the Reserve. At Sikhobokhobo's he found a night school where herd boys and young girls gathered around a blazing fire which kept the beasts away: 'we did sing until our songs came back to us in the echo from the primeval forests. And so the seed was sown'. Rees still longed for a permanent mission in the Shangani. 'We need a missionary in the Shangani Valley and another in the Gwampa Valley', he wrote. 'We shall then reap the *cream* of the Ndebele people'.[133]

By 1915, four more of Rees' Inyathi out-stations had moved into the Shangani from Bubi as the result of a wave of evictions. In 1916, a European missionary, Brown, was at last sent to reside in the Reserve and to try to water the seed. At Dakamela's 'people could hardly believe that I would live there' but greeted him warmly; at Tshakalisa's, he found that the Prince had built a brick house. It seemed as if the flag of Christian progressive civilization was flying in the wilderness. Yet Brown also reported that 'the majority of the people are in gross heathenism and some of the people who were under the influence of the Gospel, having lived away there in the forests, have lapsed into heathenism.' Next year, Brown found Tshakalisa, 'a friend and a gentleman', anxious to support the LMS. Yet though 'the mature folk and the elders heartily welcome us, [they] still cling to their heathen customs.' In 1919 Brown ceased to live in the Shangani – he had suffered badly from malaria and his superiors believed that no married missionary could live there with his family. Thereafter, Brown merely 'itinerated' in the Reserve, leaving the Ndebele 'adherents' of the LMS who had moved north into the Shangani with little structured support.

As for the 'original' inhabitants, Brown had few good words for them:

> The Matabele tribe forms only a portion of the people in Shangani Reserve. Many of the other people belong to what is called the Zambezi tribe and they are practically inaccessible at present. They refuse to come to our services and when the evangelist or preacher approaches their kraal they steal out and away into the forest and hide. Living away here in the forest the natives are able to indulge in all their heathen customs. Witchcraft and superstition are rampant.[134]

Moreover, people who had refused to accept the Christian way of life on the Inyathi mission farm itself also moved north into the thickets. So 'in 1927 people came from Bubi, from the LMS mission at Inyathi, because of the policy of the missionaries which said that all polygamists must go to the forests. Those people were abaLeya and Lozwis and Nyai. These abaLeya came from the Zambezi River; they were brought down here

---

[132] Bowen Rees, 'Social Conditions of Native Populations' circa 1910. We owe this text to Rees' grandson Ioan Bowen Rees.

[133] Inyathi Report, 1914, CWM Incoming, SOAS.

[134] These citations are taken from notes on the London Missionary archive at the School of Oriental and African Studies made by Marieke Clarke.

by Mzilikazi. When Mzilikazi got lost, these Leyas guided him back. Then the mission-aries ordered them out and they stayed here [in Shangani] because it was too far to go to the Zambezi.'[135] By 1936, W.W. Anderson was writing from the Shangani that the LMS had 'nothing to rejoice about ... One longs to see a re-awakening and a turning towards Christ among the Ndebele.'[136]

It became axiomatic among the Protestant Ndebele farmers and missionaries of the plateau that the Shangani Reserve was a place of pagan culture, fit only for wild beasts and wild men; incapable of supporting large-scale plough cultivation; bereft of clinics and schools. Their political spokesmen totally repudiated the land. In December 1920, a petition to the British Government from African Methodists described the Gwaai and Shangani Reserves as 'barren and useless'; in the late 1920s, Industrial and Commercial Workers Union speakers in Bulawayo attacked the government for planning to send the Ndebele away into the 'land of windmills' and boreholes, 'where only animals can live.'[137] When, after the Second World War, it was the turn of these plateau Protestants to be moved to the dark *gusu* forests of the Shangani, they approached it in a temper far different from the followers of Tshakalisa and Sikhobokhobo.

---

[135] Interview with Headman Manomano, *et al.*, Manomano, 17 October 1995.

[136] W.W. Anderson to T. Coker Brown, 3 March 1936, LMS South Africa, 1936, SOAS.

[137] The Methodist petition is in A 3/18/39/21; ICU speeches are reported in S 84/A/301.

# 2

# The Violence of the State

## Forced Migration & its Consequences

### Introduction

When the Shangani Reserve was proclaimed in 1894, and for many years thereafter, it was thought of by whites as a zone of violence and criminality – the site of battles; a refuge for bandits and murderers; a hide-out for those who wanted to avoid tax or missionary teaching. By the 1930s and 1940s, its official image had completely changed. It was now seen as a deeply rural site of peace. After all, by that time the turbulence was all in the towns, with ethnic faction fights, cultural nationalism and working-class militancy. 'Any advance in political thought or revolutionary ideas,' noted one Native Commissioner, 'may be expected to stem from the industrial areas ... Those who remain behind in the Reserves have been well content.'[1]

Although, as we shall see, a good deal was going on under the surface, the Shangani Reserve seemed to officials to be locked in a world of day-to-day complacency. 'The Reserve appears to be free from unsettling political influences,' its Native Commissioner reported in 1933.[2] In 1939 he reported hardly any crime – most prosecutions were for 'non-registration of marriages'. 'The natives have been loyal and law-abiding and no attempts at "resistance" have been made.'[3] In 1943, a company of the Rhodesian African Rifles toured the Reserve seeking recruits. Only four came forward. 'Soldiering is foreign to this generation of natives,' concluded the Native Commissioner.[4] In 1945 – the year of the railway strike, which caused 'lively comment' among 'the more articulate labourers' in neighbouring Nyamandhlovu district – there was still no response in the Shangani as far as the NC could see. 'Very little interest is shown for any matter concerning the welfare of anyone beyond the immediate vicinity of a man's home,' he concluded. 'Larger interests do not hold him.'[5] In 1946, there was still no police post or lock-up in the Shangani. 'The punishment of an offender depends on his willingness to wait patiently at the office until a police patrol can be summoned from Inyati.'[6]

By 1946, however, administrative officials were bemoaning rather than celebrating this apparent state of lethargic acquiescence. 'This district owing to its unfortunate

---

[1] Annual Report, Hartley, 1952, S 2403/2681.
[2] Annual Report, Shangani Reserve, 1933, S 235/511.
[3] Annual Report, Shangani Reserve, 1939, S 235/517.
[4] Annual Report, Shangani Reserve, 1943, S 1051.
[5] Annual Reports, Nyamandhlovu and Shangani Reserve, 1945, S 1051.
[6] Annual Report, Shangani Reserve, 1946, S 235/518.

geographical position has for years suffered from the defect of "out of sight, out of mind".' People were uninterested in wider issues because there were hardly any schools. There were hardly any clinics either, and 'nature decides the issue by the survival of the fittest'. The Shangani Reserve had barely been administered and had 'been left far too long in the peace and solitude of the Gusu.'[7] These were the words of an administrator infected by the post-war ideology of development and facing 'a constant battle against the odds' in 'a backward district'. But the Native Commissioner had a more immediate motive for demanding change. He estimated that some 5,000 Africans from 'European land in adjoining districts' would be moving into the Shangani in the coming year. 'This large influx of detribalised natives' was bound to threaten law and order and to introduce subversive ideas.[8]

## Eviction and Forced Migration

The Rhodesian state, in fact, had embarked on a programme of institutional violence in the form of forced evictions. At long last the implementation of the 1930 Land Apportionment Act, so long deferred in Matabeleland, was to be carried through. Africans on 'white' land were to be removed to the Reserves, by force if necessary. This policy involved suffering everywhere but evictions into the northwest were exceptionally harsh, even by Southern Rhodesian standards. As we shall see, the deaths and hardships which resulted from being forcibly dumped in the disease-ridden wilderness were built into the evictees' collective historical memories. The Shangani became a zone of violence once again; the imagery of the *gusu* forests as dark and fearful became more vivid than ever in the minds of evictees.

For decades, it had been clear to officials that force was going to have to be used to get 'the Ndebele' to move into the Shangani Reserve. From the mid-1930s, Native Commissioners had been lamenting that Africans evicted from one farm in the Bubi district would find refuge on another, or on Crown Land, and that they refused to move into the Shangani. In 1935, the Reserve was 'not popular as malaria is present' and water was scarce; there were no markets for produce and an abundance of wild animals. In 1936, the NC again commented that, despite all warnings that the Land Apportionment Act would eventually be enforced, Africans showed 'the greatest reluctance' to go into the Reserve. 'Belief that many parts of the Reserve are unhealthy for Native occupation are not altogether unfounded,' he admitted. In 1938, those evicted from 'white' farms were still moving onto Crown Lands and ignoring the Commissioner's warning that there would soon 'be no alternative but to move to the Shangani Reserve.' He noted that malaria had again been 'troublesome' in the Shangani. By 1945, however, African reluctance was being forcibly over-ridden.[9]

By this time, the Native Commissioners were using a new and dehumanizing vocabulary. 'Depopulation was continued throughout the year,' recorded the Bubi Commissioner. Africans from Crown Lands and from occupied and unoccupied 'white' farms had been 'removed to Shangani Reserve'. In 1946, the year that the Commissioner for the Shangani was asserting that 'the peace and solitude of the Gusu' must be broken, his counterpart in Bubi was congratulating himself that the 'depopulation' of his district had almost been completed. 'Considerable opposition in the nature of "passive resistance" was shown but the scheduled areas have now been vacated almost in toto.' The bulk of the 'displaced persons' had gone into the eastern Shangani or into the newly-created Lupane Native Area in the west of the old Shangani reserve.[10]

---

[7] *Ibid.*

[8] Annual Report, Shangani Reserve, 1946, S 235/518.

[9] Annual Reports, Bubi, 1935, 1936, 1938, 1939,1943.

[10] Annual Reports, Bubi, 1945 and 1946.

Nor was it merely a matter of 'depopulating' Bubi district. The Shangani and Lupane were to be used for the forced resettlement of Africans from all over central and southern Matabeleland. Rupert Meredith Davies, who came to Southern Rhodesia from East Africa in 1948 to take up the post of Assistant Director of Agriculture, later recalled that one of his first tasks was:

> a big resettlement exercise mainly in Matabeleland. Squatters on vacant farms, European land; squatters in African Purchase Areas that hadn't been taken up but were going to be taken up … I must say, I felt very sorry for a lot of these people, because they were sent to most difficult country, what I'd call baboon country. Wild animals, elephants, lions, the lot. There was no suitable land available. And it wasn't good land … I tried to induce the Administration to put some of these squatters on to irrigation schemes [in the Sabi] … but they wouldn't have it.[11]

Despite Davies' pity, it was in fact the Ministry of Agriculture, in alliance with white farmers, which was demanding the total eviction of Africans from 'European' land. The Native Department itself was appalled at the difficulties of the enterprise and was constantly seeking to obtain land on which to resettle Africans within their original districts. It was to the Minister of Agriculture and Lands that a Bubi settler, D.E. Williams, wrote in 1942 to complain that the Native Department was buying up land and threatening to squeeze whites out. 'We (the Bubi [farmers]) have 40 odd sons and daughters born here [now] with the forces – what sort of guardians are we of their heritage?'[12] The Minister backed the Bubi farmers in 1942 and his successor took the same line in 1947. In that year, Patrick Fletcher, now Minister of Agriculture, attacked the policy of finding relief land for Africans on an *ad hoc* basis:

> Today the economy has changed and the native has no more right to a farming area than the European. … It would be stupid for us to fly in the face of nature in the case of the native. … It is impossible to relax until the Native Department acknowledges the relentless progress of evolution.[13]

Fletcher was insistent that Africans had to be removed from all contested areas in Matabeleland: from Matobo, Fort Rixon and Filabusi.

In his 1947 Annual Report, the Native Commissioner, Shangani, lamented that 'the Reserve, owing to its size, is apt to be regarded as the dumping ground for surrounding Districts. Preparations are already being made for the movement of large numbers of Natives and cattle from the Fort Rixon area to the Lupani sub-district.'[14] In 1948, there was large-scale movement from Fort Rixon – it would be 'most unwise to accept any further large movements'.[15] The peace and solitude of the *gusu* had been well and truly broken.

In 1950, C. Bisset, the Native Commissioner, Lupane, received a bitter lesson in the political realities of eviction. He hoped to integrate a reasonable number of incomers into a development plan for his district, but he discovered that it was instead a mere 'dumping ground'. On 2 October 1950, he wrote privately to the Chief Native Commissioner:

---

[11] Interview with Rupert Meredith Davies, 17 November 1983, ORAL/241, National Archives, Harare.
[12] D.E. Williams to Minister of Agriculture, 22 July 1942, S 2588/1978.
[13] Minister of Agriculture, memo, 1 September 1947, S 1516/47.
[14] Annual Report, Shangani, 1947, S 1051.
[15] Annual Report, Shangani, 1948.

I am given to understand that this is the only district that can take people but there is a limit and a definite one – the 'gusu' forest areas which are without water, and the character of the soil. ... I came to Matabeleland with a fresh and open mind and after 18 months I can see that this Reserve [Shangani] and Lupani area are very different propositions to some of the Mashona Reserves with a decent rainfall and less cattle.

Calculating on the agreed basis of 30 acres per beast, the area was already overstocked. 'I am short of over 100,000 acres for the present human and stock population'; and 'the land available is not sufficient for the families I am asked to settle'.[16]

On 2 November, however, the Chief Native Commissioner attended a planning meeting at which it was decided that some 800 further families must be moved into the Shangani in 1951. Priority areas for eviction were Matobo and Filabusi/Fort Rixon in Matabeleland South. On 7 November, the CNC replied to Bisset:

I am afraid that the whole question is very difficult ... As you know, the Minister promised in the House that all Natives on Crown Land be moved within 5 years, and he has told me to draw up a five year plan showing exactly how many Natives from each Province I will move each year and to where they will go. This as you may imagine is a very difficult, in fact well nigh impossible task ... My difficulty is that as Shangani-Lupani is at the moment the only area in Matabeleland available for the transfer of displaced Natives, and I have to move 815 families next year ... you will have to be content with an assessment of 20 acres per beast.[17]

Still more families were moved into the Shangani and Lupane in 1952, when the long resistance of the Filabusi people was finally broken.

These later compelled migrations were attended by greater force than the movements from Bubi. Those had been compulsory but the people had been ill-prepared to resist. People in Matobo, Fort Rixon and Filabusi, however, had fought hard against eviction. In the Matopos National Park, they set up their own resistance organisation, *Sofasonke*; elsewhere they called in the assistance of Benjamin Burombo and the African Voice Association. They took government to law and compelled an amendment to the Land Apportionment Act before they could be evicted. So the final evictions were accompanied by displays of state coercive power.[18]

The *Rhodesia Herald*'s report of the Filabusi 'depopulation' in September 1952 depicted a dawn operation, drawing upon 'a strong force of police, European and Native'. 'What was described by a police official as a show of passive resistance soon crumpled.'[19] The strong force of police then went on to Matobo district for further dawn raids. 'We used to go out with the police and we'd encircle a kraal at about 4 a.m. in the morning and put them on lorries', a Native Department official cheerfully remembered.[20] 'Ring-leaders' of opposition were handcuffed and thrown on to the trucks.

[16] C. Bisset to 'Dear Mr Powys Jones', 2 October 1950; NC Lupane to PNC, 2 October 1950, S 2086/1995.
[17] CNC to NC Lupane, 7 November 1950, LS 100/3B/50.
[18] The story of the Matopos resistance is told in T. Ranger, *Voices From the Rocks. The Modern History of the Matopos* (Oxford, James Currey, 1999). The story of the Filabusi resistance is told in J. Alexander, 'The State, Agrarian Policy and Rural Politics in Zimbabwe: Case Studies of Insiza and Chimanimani Districts, 1940-1990', D.Phil. thesis, Oxford, 1993.
[19] *Rhodesia Herald*, 9 September 1952.
[20] Interview with Richard John Powell, 3 July, 21 August and 5 September 1978, Oral/22, National Archives, Harare.

The state violence of the 'depopulations' and especially of the dawn evictions is vividly remembered in Nkayi and Lupane today. Julia Kimeta Sibanda, who was removed from Bubi in 1950, recalls, 'We were moved by the Government by force. We were not used to this area. We knew nothing about this area. We were not happy. We came here in lorries and were just dumped. ... People just had to comply though they tried to refuse.'[21] The Filabusi evictees of 1952 evoke stronger imagery:

> We waged a war of words with the whites for five years [recalls Paul Mapetshwana Moyo] when they were trying to evict us. When the whites realized the situation was getting worse and worse, those whites sat and discussed and one day we woke in the morning – it was so bad, trucks all over and we were arrested and handcuffed. It was a ground and air operation. ... It was an abnormal situation, it was war. They kept bringing people and dumping them at boreholes. ... The place was *gusu* and there were a lot of animals. You just couldn't move easily, the bush was so thick. Leopards and hyenas were catching our animals here on this spot.[22]

After this Filabusi eviction, the Native Commissioner, Bubi, belatedly wondered whether the forced migrations had been worth their cost. 'It is no use pretending that the recent movement of Natives has not caused a great deal of hardship. No man likes to be uprooted and see his home destroyed before his eyes.' The evictions gave 'plenty of ammunition to demagogues'. 'All this has been lawful,' he concluded, 'but in all the circumstances has it been expedient?'[23]

## The Experience of the Forced Migrants

These dramatic events have become part of a heroic epic which is central to twentieth-century Ndebele history. It was given characteristic expression after Zimbabwe's independence in February 1982, when the *Chronicle* carried a story entitled 'Bulldozed and Beaten They Carved a New Life':

> Thirty years ago whole settlements of people in many parts of Matabeleland were uprooted and moved to open up new frontiers in remote parts of the province. They came from Filabusi, from Belingwe, from Fort Rixon, the Matopos, from Kezi and numerous other places. They resisted, using all the tricks in the book, including legal action, but it did not help ... It was a heart-rending defeat. When the bull-dozers moved in with chains to pull down the houses of those who would not move, the people reluctantly threw in the towel and loaded their possessions on to the African Development Fund trucks that took them off into the unknown. Some found themselves at Gomoza, in the Lupane district ... in the sandy wastes of the Wankie Communal Land, in the Tjolotjo West jungles. ... They found great problems. But amid this harassment and hardship, the people have carved out for themselves out of virgin jungles a life that is the envy of those who remained at their old settlements [and have become] the most prosperous cattle farmers of any corner of Zimbabwe.[24]

This myth expresses an important self-perception. People whose parents were forced migrants have become self-motivated pioneers, pressing ever further north in search of

---

[21] Interview with Julia Kimeta Sibanda, Mkalati, 23 August 1995.
[22] Interview with Paul Mapetshwana Moyo, Gampinya, 19 October 1995.
[23] Annual Report, Bubi, 1952, S 2403/2681.
[24] *Chronicle*, 1 February 1982. The report did admit, however, that in a good year 'the water problem is a thorn in their flesh and in a bad year it becomes a matter of life and death'.

new opportunity. But, of course, it leaves out very many things. It leaves out the subsequent violence – the violence of state intervention in rural production and land-holding; the nationalist sabotage campaign in Nkayi and Lupane and its repression; the guerrilla war; the repression of the 1980s. This sequence of violence is the topic of the chapters which follow.

But it also leaves out the people who were already settled in these so-called 'virgin jungles'. The evictees were not entering an empty land. Their interactions with the 'originals' of the *gusu* forests is the subject of the rest of this chapter; so too is the ideology which eventually enabled them to dominate the earlier settlers politically, and to come to terms with their environment.

## The Self-perceptions of the Evictees

The men and women who were forcibly re-settled in the Shangani had a clear self-image. They defined themselves as Ndebele but not as traditionalists. They were people of the school and of the store and of the market. They were 'dressed' people. They were plough-using farmers. They were literate Christian adherents of the missions. In all these ways they saw themselves as differing totally from the 'original' inhabitants of the Shangani.

These self-consciously 'progressive' identities were often of recent origin. Mpulazi Msipa, who moved from Fort Rixon into Lupane, gives a revealing description of his own 'conversion' to modernity:

> In Fort Rixon … some people lived in the mountains and others in the plains. … Now, those in the plains were proud … they were church people, following the missionaries. They were now cultured, civilised, in trousers. Those who put on trousers wanted refined mealie meal. Skin aprons [*amabhetshu*] went with millets – those were the primitive ones. Those with mealie meal were on the right track. They held the Bible as their literature and were trying to follow a new type of living. Those in the hills were still primitive, washing was not an accepted part of life. … Those in the plains tried to persuade those in the hills to follow their way of life, tried to pull them down. … We were up in the hills in our *amabhetshu* when I was a child. … But the church penetrated, attracting the small ones, rounding them up for education … I married … when I had come down from the hills into the plains, out into the open. We felt the hills were darkness, full of wild animals and we joined the church.[25]

The recency of such 'conversions' meant that the new identities were yet more passionately defended. Being dumped in the forests of the Shangani seemed like being made to go back to the hills. The earlier inhabitants of the dark *gusu* forests seemed like the primitives of the hills.

Of course, there were many evictees who had only imperfectly undergone the con-version experience. Some of them were not Christians; some were illiterate; some were unsuccessful farmers. For many, being 'Ndebele' was hardly something that could distinguish them from the Shangani population, many of whom also spoke Ndebele. Although some evictees were descendents of the Nguni aristocracy, who had migrated from the south in the nineteenth century, most were the descendents of incorporated peoples and claimed other identities as well as Ndebele. And as we saw in Chapter 1, by the time the evictees arrived the Shangani had already become home to a mixture of Nguni immigrants and many earlier settlers who had long been incorporated into the Ndebele state.

---

[25] Interview with Mpulazi Msipa, Lupanda, 28 March 1996.

Nevertheless, whatever the exceptions and complications, the progressive Ndebele stereotype was strongly articulated by the evictees. It served many functions. It exposed the violent injustice of removing such a people from schools and stores and markets and dumping them in the bush. It enabled the dispossessed to set about making a new life with self-confidence and high morale. It justified their claims to leadership, even in an environment so strange to them. Moreover, it enabled them to make an alliance with other progressives, both white and black.

Strong expressions of the Christian modernizing image also came from missionaries. Thus in December 1945, a Bubi Presbyterian missionary, J. Tallach, objected strongly to the eviction of his flock into the Shangani:

> They have built neat houses, laid out nice gardens and generally improved their living conditions far beyond those of their fathers. Some have gone to consider-able expense; they have bought timber, doors, windows and in some cases even cement. ... We shall greatly err if we regard this improvement as something spasmodic and artificial – something removed from the deepest feelings of the people. ... The improvement of most of them has been steady and continuous; it has been accepted at a cost, it has entered into the very foundations of their social life, and it has now become a necessary part of their way of life. Things like neat cottages, flowers, clean yards, trim hedges, tables, chairs, clean clothes, clean children, a main Mission with all its encouraging influences, the habit of sending children to school ... are things which have become necessary to them. ... They cannot be robbed of them without experiencing a deep resentment.

Tallach contrasted all this with 'the planting of them in a backward reserve'. Men who now went to work in Bulawayo could not be expected to cycle the 125–170 miles to and from the Shangani Reserve. Families would be divided. 'To ask decent Christian-living people to take their families and to begin at the bottom [in Shangani Reserve] is to ask more than any human being might be expected to give.'[26]

The missionary's plea for a moment touched the heart of the Chief Native Commissioner, who wrote in January 1946 that it would be contrary to natural justice to remove such people to 'a remote rural area'.[27] The Native Commissioner, Bubi, was inflexible, however:

> The Shangani Reserve itself is vividly portrayed as a dismal jungle of savagery and superstition. The impression is given that as soon as they arrive there the people will revert to cannibalism and voodoo practices. In actual fact this country is superior ... and there is an unlimited supply of timber and grass ... I cannot agree that these men will be so discouraged that they will sink back to a sub-human way of living. They will not be allowed to do so.[28]

The evictees had no intention of allowing themselves to do so either. And when they got to the eastern Shangani or to Lupane, they found allies in the missionaries who were arriving there. In Lupane, Catholic missionaries had begun to operate only in 1944, when Father Odilo Weeger became 'Rector of the Shangani District'; his first mission station, St Fatima's, was established only in 1948; St Luke's hospital, in Lupane proper, was opened in April 1950.[29] Father Odilo remembers Lupane in the mid-1940s as 'quite

---

[26] J. Tallach, Ingwenya, to Chief Native Commissioner, 8 December 1945, S 2588/1978.
[27] Chief Native Commissioner to Acting Provincial Native Commissioner, 21 January 1946, *ibid.*
[28] NC Bubi to PNC, 6 February 1946, *ibid.*
[29] 'Mission Work of the Mariannhill Missionaries in Zimbabwe, 1896–1980', ms., Bulawayo, 1982, pp. 50–52.

a wild district, with dense forests, wild animals and perennial streams. To begin with, there were very few people because the area was unassigned. So we were poised to serve when the big movements in began'.[30]

Dr J.F. Davis-Ziegler, who opened St Luke's, soon found herself surrounded by Fort Rixon evictees. 'They were moved before I was aware. It was whole groups.' But from the beginning she worked closely with the newcomers:

> I can note the difference between indigenous people here in the Gwampa Valley. They are very backwards. They are full of witchcraft, down south, in the Gwampa Valley and towards the Bubi, and at the Shangani, the indigenous people were full of witchcraft. Whereas the people from Fort Rixon they brought schools, they were more educated, they were different people, well-dressed, much more advanced than those indigenous people at the Shangani and in our area. You could notice that these people would accept us much quicker when we had to introduce something. Whilst the local people here, I could strangle them at times. We had the hospital and they would come late and they are full of witchcraft.[31]

The evictees valued this kind of alliance with the missions. They drew on old Ndebele ideas about the *gusu* as dark and threatening, which dovetailed with, and were reinforced by, missionaries' identification of the Shangani forests with darkness and evil:

> People didn't like to come here [remembers a Bubi evictee] because the forest was dark and full of animals. People wanted to stay in the farms, the open places, not the dark forests – *amagusu amnyama* – the thick, dark forests. When you are in Bulawayo, people will ask you where you are from. If you say Nkayi, they will say, 'Oh! *Amagusu amnyama*'.[32]

They wanted to create 'open places'. In 1957 the Native Commissioner, Lupane, reported on six families from Filabusi who had been 'settled in undeveloped Gusu country. Although they only moved in during September, they soon set to work building huts and clearing the thick forest. One old Matabele matron, used to the open grassland of her former home, when asked how she liked the place, replied: "Fine, but oh! for the trees".'[33]

By 1957, many trees had been felled and many open places created. The evictees set about their task with a proper Christian zeal. But they largely had to rely upon themselves as Christian pioneers rather than on the patronage of a mission station. The experience of those Fort Rixon evictees who found themselves close to newly-built Catholic missions and hospitals was an uncharacteristic one. In most places, the evictees had to bring their Christianity in with them.

As we have seen, missions had been slow to penetrate the Shangani. The early efforts of the London Missionary Society (LMS) had been undercut by shortage of money and withdrawal of missionaries. Other denominations had not hastened to take advantage of the LMS retreat. By 1932, there were LMS, Seventh Day Adventist and Presbyterian teachers in the Reserve but still only twenty schools altogether, overwhelmingly concentrated in the southern part of Shangani. The post-war evictions were both a challenge and an opportunity. The LMS missionaries at Inyathi watched 'family after family heading for the Shangani Reserve, a scotch cart piled high with their possessions,

---

[30] Interview with Father Odilo, Bulawayo, 7 January 1995.
[31] Interview with Dr J.F. Davis-Ziegler, St Luke's, Lupane, 24 January 1995.
[32] Interview with Lazarus Sibanda, Malindi, 7 September 1995.
[33] Annual Report, Lupane, 1957, S 2827/2/2/5.

and men, women and children following behind driving the cattle and the goats', finding it 'a moving and rather pathetic sight'. They took comfort in the fact that there was an LMS station in the Shangani, ready 'to receive them'. LMS schools in the Reserve grew from twelve to twenty-eight between 1946 and 1950, and in 1947 a new station was opened in Lupane.[34]

But this expansion – and similar efforts by other mission churches – was nothing like enough to meet the need. 'Educationally our people have struck their tents, and are on the march,' wrote Reverend Amos Mzileti, minister in charge of Inyathi district, in 1950. 'They are bursting into civilisation overnight. But whither?'[35] The evictees had to rely on self-help. 'As soon as they built their rough shelters,' wrote an Inyathi missionary, 'where they would live until they had time to build the more permanent pole and dagga huts, they had also put up a shelter for a church, and planned to erect a more permanent structure which would serve as church building and school classroom.'[36] 'Although there was no preacher,' remembers one Free Presbyterian evictee, 'they held prayers in their huts to keep the Lord's Day as members of the church.'[37] The balance between missions and African Christians changed. The evictions muddled up people from all over central Matabeleland. There was no possibility in Lupane and Nkayi for zones of denominational monopoly as there had been on the plateau. The continuity and growth of churches depended more upon individual Christian settlers than upon evangelists.[38]

Christianity was important to these people as a modernizing ideology – a sign of civilization. But Christian commitment arose out of much more than arrogance and discrimination. People suddenly removed from ancestral lands, markets and amenities and dumped in the wilderness, needed some way of asserting their membership of a wider community and some way of asserting the significance of their lives. Nathaniel Mpofu, who interviewed members of so many churches on our behalf, is himself a convinced member of the Free Presbyterian Church. He lives in a modest house and has put most of his money into building a Presbyterian conventicle. His religion gives him a connection with a global debate about faith and culture – himself running a traditional dance group as well as preaching on Calvinism, he is a strong supporter of Lord Mackay in his confrontation with Free Presbyterian intolerance in Britain. His belief in pre-destination makes sense for him of the history of the northwest over the past thirty years.[39]

The evictees brought not only mission Christianity. Before their arrival there were no independent African churches in the Shangani. Independency normally emerges as a reaction to an intensive period of mission evangelism. But in the Shangani independent churches came in on the backs or in the minds of evictees. Today there are very many independent churches in Nkayi and Lupane. Nathaniel Mpofu interviewed members of the Apostolic Holy Church in Zion; the Zion Christian Church; the Ruponiso Faith Apostolic; the Twelve Apostles; the Galilee Faith Apostolic Church; the Apostolic Holy Church in Zion and the Evangelist Jerusalem Church of God. Only a few of those interviewed spoke of breaking away from Shangani mission churches for doctrinal reasons, though Thabani Moyo described how his mother, an evictee from Bubi into 'the

[34] P. S. King, 'Post-War Expansion', in Iris Clinton, *These Vessels. The Story of Inyati, 1859–1959* (Bulawayo, Stuart Manning, 1959), p. 84.
[35] *Ibid.*, p. 78.
[36] *Ibid.*, p. 84.
[37] Interview between Nathaniel Mpofu and Elijah Mpofu, 17 November 1995.
[38] There was in effect a Catholic monopoly in Lupane, at least so far as infrastructure and services were concerned, but even here denominational adherence was very diverse.
[39] Interview with Nathaniel Mpofu, Somakantana school, 29 August 1995. These ideas are further developed in J. Alexander and T. Ranger, 'Competition and Integration in the Religious History of North Western Zimbabwe', *Journal of Religion in Africa*, 28, 1, 1998, pp. 3–31.

thick forests of the Shangani Reserve', left the Free Presbyterians and joined the Twelve Apostles because their worship was 'more relaxed' than Calvinism.[40] In other cases, evictees brought these churches with them, like the people who had been staunch members of the Jerusalem Church of God in Bubi and who set it up in Nkayi after they had been resettled there, or the evictees from Dromoland who brought 'their prophets and those who pray for the sick' with them in 1956, establishing the Apostolic Holy Church of Zion in Nkayi.[41] These Apostolic and Zionist churches were also a product of 'modernization' but unlike the disciplines of mission Protestantism, they spoke more to its stresses than to its aspirations. For this reason they were destined to spread rapidly in Nkayi and Lupane during the violent decades which were to come.

## The Evictees meet the 'Originals'

These reluctant immigrants, deeply suspicious of the forests and fearful of the wild beasts which inhabited them, were now to meet the 'originals' who had made their home in the black forests. The first encounters are vividly remembered by both sides, no doubt in legendary form.

Sometimes the two groups literally stumbled across each other. An old local, Luka Sibanda, who lived at Nzamani on the Kana, thus recalls his discovery of the evictees from Filabusi:

> To start with when these Filabusi people came they were dropped at night. In the morning there was something very peculiar – we heard cocks crowing in the bush, and similarly the Filabusi people heard cocks crowing along the stream. So we both had to investigate. The Filabusi people found old homes and we found people just dropped in the bush. ... No-one introduced us.[42]

Sometimes an elaborate and alarming introduction took place, with the Native Department officials warning each group about the other. In October 1995, in Gampinya, Nkayi, we interviewed a spokesman for the evictees, Paul Mapetshwana Moyo, together with a spokesman of the earlier settlers, Paul Sibanda. Sibanda remembered that: 'We were called to Dagamela dip before the Filabusi people came. We were told, "You people at Kana must move inland, there are people coming from Filabusi and they are witches and thieves and have venereal diseases".' For his part, Moyo recalled that, 'We were told, "Go there to the forest, and if you misbehave, watch out because those people have got *ulunyoka.*" *Ulunyoka* is something that stops love affairs – it affects the bodies of the lovers – they will find their genitals missing, or they will get stuck while having sex, so that they die.'[43] Today Moyo and Sibanda dismiss these alarming caricatures as mere colonial 'divide and rule'. Influenced by the later development of nationalism, they emphasize their achievement of unity. Sibanda insists that the originals refused to move away: 'We asked, "Are they white or black?" They said they were black so we said "Let them come!".' Moyo insists that the Filabusi people said, 'They are not animals, they don't have horns. We can live with them.'

But as we shall see in a later chapter, nationalist unity was not so easy to achieve. White divide-and-rule tactics everywhere took a long time to overcome and in many places it did not require white strategies for immigrants and earlier settlers to develop

---

[40] Interview between Nathaniel Mpofu and Thabani Moyo, 6 December 1995.
[41] Interviews between Nathaniel Mpofu and Mdala Ncube, 10 November 1995; Solomon Juba, 19 October 1995.
[42] Interview with Luka Sibanda, Nzamani, 5 December 1995.
[43] Interview with Paul Sibanda and Paul Mapetshwana Moyo, Gampinya, 10 October 1995.

damaging stereotypes of each other. Even today, derogatory stereotypes of the 'originals' persist and social cleavages between earlier settlers and evictees often continue to play an important part in local politics. The evictees' basic perception of the divide between the two was the contrast between their modernity and the locals' backwardness.[44] 'They lived like animals in the forest,' many evictees told us; evictees described differences related to all aspects of life from dress, deportment and gender relations to how homes were built and kept, how fields were tended, whether and which type of cattle were kept, and attitudes towards religion and education. Such distinctions were often rendered in ethnic terms.

The Ndebele identity of the incomers was in many ways a recent construct, derived partly from the cultural nationalism of the towns, partly from a history of contact with missions, as well as from older relations with the nineteenth-century Ndebele state. But above all, it was an assertion of modernity. There lay, ready-to-hand, all the ethnic labels which colonial administrators and missionaries had used in the past to highlight the backwardness of the 'Tonga' or the 'Shangwe'.[45] In the mouths of the evictees, these names carried with them historical implications of inferiority derived from the nineteenth-century Ndebele categories of *amahole* (subordinates or slaves) or *abathunjiweyo* (captives). So the 'Shangwe' were subordinates who had paid tribute to the Ndebele state in tobacco; the 'Lozwi' and 'Nyai' were the conquered people of the Rozwi empire; the 'Tonga' or 'Zambezi' were those raided and enslaved from the valley; the 'Sili' were the inferior hunters of the bush.

The complex intermixing which had characterized earlier settlement in the Shangani sat uneasily with these block, ethnic identifications. The populations amongst whom the evictees found themselves contained people from many different origins, and included many Ndebele-speaking settlers and some Nguni families. The evictees were themselves a diverse bunch. Locals slowly discovered similarities, as Luka Sibanda recounts: 'People at first thought the Filabusi people were Ngunis but at ceremonies [where songs were sung] we realised there were a lot of tribes, and some of those were the same as us here – that "eyah, eyah" cannot be found in Nguni, only Kalanga, and we heard it.'[46] But the evictees ignored such commonalities and distinctions. 'The original people of this place are mainly Tonga,' says an evictee in Pupu. 'Of course when we talk of Tonga, some are Shangwes and the Khumalos were Ndebele [but] from the point of view of those of us who were arriving here, we couldn't really distinguish between them all, even from the way they were living, it seemed just the same to us.'[47] The blanket labels imposed by the evictees said more about their perceptions of backwardness – and of their own modernity – than about ethnicity.

The locals resented and resisted this process of labelling. An elderly Lozwi from the Kana valley recalled, 'They called us Sankwes even though we weren't ... Sankwe was

---

[44] This topic is discussed in detail in J. Alexander and J. McGregor, 'Modernity and Ethnicity in a Frontier Society: Understanding Difference in Northwestern Zimbabwe', *Journal of Southern African Studies*, 23, 2, 1997, pp. 187–201; T. Ranger, 'African Identities: Ethnicity, Nationality and History. The Case of Matabeleland, 1893–1993', in Joachim Heidrich (ed.), *Changing Identities* (Berlin, 1994), and 'The Moral Economy of Identity in Northern Matabeleland', in Louise de la Gorgendiere, *et al* (eds), *Ethnicity in Africa* (Edinburgh, 1996). Also see E. Worby, 'Maps, Names and Ethnic Games: The Epistemology and Iconography of Colonial Power in Northwestern Zimbabwe', *Journal of Southern African Studies*, 20, 3, 1994, pp. 371–92.

[45] Ironically, the Native Department was now transforming its own evaluation of ethnic difference, seeing the evictees as 'loud-mouthed gentlemen', as a 'vociferous and truculent element'. The Tonga were now seen as dignified, loyal traditionalists. See Ranger, 'The Moral Economy of Identity'.

[46] Interview with Luka Sibanda, Kana, 5 December 1995.

[47] Interview with Mvumindaba Ncube, Pupu, 16 February 1996.

used derogatorily by the Filabusi people to mean people who have nothing but snuff.'[48] Sometimes people simply moved away from the evictee settlements. The evictees particularly stigmatized the Tonga and Sili – to them all locals were primitive, but the Tonga and Sili were by far the most backward. Faced with contempt and insult, the Sili, who had once lived throughout Lupane, moved westwards into Tsholotsho. Many Tonga in Lupane moved north in a veritable exodus to Lubimbi and Binga. In Nkayi, too, 'when the Ndebele came the Tonga ran away to Binga and Gokwe'.[49]

Sometimes the local response took the form of counter-stereotyping. The earlier settlers had their own terms for the incomers. One of these was historical – *amadzviti* – a term used by Tonga speakers in northern and western Lupane, meaning 'invaders' and invoking the violence of the nineteenth-century Ndebele regiments. Others were merely descriptive – *amadeluka* – meaning 'the dumped ones', or terms denoting the geographical origin of the evictees such as *amaFilabusi*. But these terms were less derogatory than those applied by the evictees, and sometimes evictees' aggressive displays of modernity led the earlier settlers to apply to the evictees as a whole high-status labels such as *amaNguni* – Ndebele aristocrats – or *amabhunu*, Boers or whites. The latter name was applied to evictees because they 'stayed close to white people, they wore trousers, ate with spoons and had churches'. The Tonga 'wore fewer clothes ... didn't wash much and had holes through their noses. The women wore mini-skirts and had knocked out their four front teeth. They thought that was beautiful.'[50] The Lozwi Council Sibanda recalls, 'We were very low – I still remember I wore *amabhetshu*, just a piece in front ... The Essexvale people were very smart, we admired them, they looked like town fellows.'[51] Just as evictee labels for their new neighbours primarily connoted backwardness, the earlier settlers' names for the evictees – whether geographical, historical, ethnic or racial in origin – took on meanings of modernity and power.

These stereotypes were in themselves a sort of intellectual and cultural violence. But there were also images based on perceptions of violence in itself. Evictees depicted the Tonga as free of all discipline – 'for them, killing a person was not a big thing'.[52] Tonga ceremonies were seen as orgies of mindless violence:

> We went to each other's funerals [recalls an evictee]. The Tonga used to dance on the grave of the dead person until it was flat, completely flat so that you couldn't know there was a person buried there. ... In the past, the Tongas used to bring dangerous spears to funerals, barbed ones. ... Once when there was an *umbuyiso* [the ceremony to bring back the spirits of the dead] for a Tonga we experienced a very hard situation. The two teams [of Tonga drummers] faced each other and wanted to stab each other. ... We fled and watched from afar. No one died. The Tonga old folk warned the youthful teams, 'Look here. If you continue doing this, the Ndebele aren't used to it, so they will go away and you'll remain alone drinking beer'.[53]

For their part, Tonga-speakers feared attending Ndebele funerals 'because the Ndebele

---

48   Interview with Luka Sibanda, Kana, 5 December 1995.

49   Interview with Peter Mantanka Ndhlovu, Mhutshaphansi Dip, 13 December 1994.

50   Interviews with Luta Inyathi, Jotsholo, 3 March 1996; elders, headman Mbanjwa's kraal, 18 November 1994.

51   Interview with Council Sibanda, Mateme, 12 December 1995.

52   Interview with P.C. Mahlamvana, Sobendle, 31 January 1996.

53   This Ndebele stereotype was not baseless. The early criminal cases for Sebungwe District, which included the Tonga areas of what is now Binga, include several accounts of affrays at Tonga funerals. D3/8/1.

carried knobkerries'.[54] It is clear that fear of evictee violence was deep-seated. It partly derived from historical memory – the Ndebele 'had that military history, so the Tonga did not want to stay with them. They could remember the abductions, the raiding, the violence'.[55] And the newcomers were sometimes not averse to reminders of this violent past: 'At beer drinks,' recalls one evictee, 'the Ngunis would take up their knobkerries and hit the Lozwis – we were harsh.'[56]

At first, the evictees had little economic or political power. They had lost their investments in farming and, though they brought most of their cattle with them, many died from eating the poisonous plant *mkhawuzane* in the *gusu*. They faced the back-breaking toil of cutting down trees and destumping. They had lost their well-built brick houses. Some had lost their stores, and it was many years before African storekeepers were to emerge in the Shangani. Women had to share in clearing away the trees, and had lost their well-tended gardens and homeyards. Children were now far from schools, and were especially vulnerable to the many new diseases of the forests. For some time, most evictee families were fully occupied with establishing themselves and surviving in their new environment.

The evictees' position was also undermined because they were regarded as highly suspect by the colonial administration, which policed them closely. Those who had been leaders of the opposition in Matobo or Fort Rixon or Filabusi were separated from each other and scattered over the Reserve. 'Because we were coming from Filabusi,' says Sabhuku Gayela, 'the whites said we were so stubborn so they broke us up into groups of 15, 15, 15, with long distances in between. They said we'd cause trouble if we were together, so they divided us up.'[57]

The evictees' traditional spokesmen were given no official recognition. In the eastern part of the Shangani Reserve, which had been proclaimed as Nkayi district, the existing chiefs were now given power over the incomers as well as the earlier settlers. Chiefs' areas were defined and demarcated and the Native Department officials supported their authority against any challenge. The great majority of the evictees in Nkayi ended up in the large areas allocated to chief Madliwa and chief Sikhobokhobo; a few came under Nkalakatha, Tshugulu or Dakamela. The Filabusi evictees came into Madliwa's area with three of their own headmen: 'There was a struggle to reinstate them as head-men here [recalls a Filabusi man]. It took two months for us to change our *situpas* [registration books] from Filabusi to Nkayi. People were resisting. [But] our headmen were never approved.'[58]

The western side of the Shangani Reserve was now added to unassigned land and forest land to make the new Lupane district. Here there were no chiefs. In 1945 chief Mabhikwa Khumalo came in from Bubi and was given authority over by far the greater part of Lupane. He was seen by the whites as the best sort of Ndebele chief – an authoritarian disciplinarian. But the Filabusi evictees placed in his area condemned him as a typical white distortion of tradition: though he had been an influential person in the nineteenth century, he had not been a regimental chief. The evictees recalled how they:

> refused to go under chief Mabhikwa. [Voice activist] David Mabhena was the outspoken one. He said: 'No, we've never been ruled by a Khumalo as a chief, we can only live under a Khumalo as a king, a Khumalo who is a descendent of [King] Lobengula.' … He was saying this at a meeting with the DC and the chief. … We stayed for five years without a chief.

[54] Interview with Mvumindaba Ncube, Pupu, 16 February 1996.
[55] Interview with Boda Nkomo, Sobendle, 27 November 1974.
[56] Interview with Moffat Mbombo, Mateme, 23 November 1995.
[57] Interview with Sabhuku Gayela, Gwelutshena, 6 December 1994.
[58] Interview with Paul Mapetshwana Moyo, Gampinya, 19 October 1995.

Having been refused a chief of their own, they elected a headman – Goduka, who was 'son of Dlodlo, one of the great [regimental] chiefs of the south' – and finally accepted the authority of Chief Menyezwa, rather than Mabhikwa, because Menyezwa, who had entered Lupane in 1947 from Figtree, was 'also an original chieftaincy, not like Mabhikwa's father, Mlonyeni, who was a cook to the queen [Lozikeyi], elected by a woman. We couldn't accept that'.[59] Fort Rixon evictees came into Lupane in 1948 with two chiefs, Makhosi and Dlamlomo, but neither was recognized.

The evictions were traumatic and frightening, both for the incomers and for the locals. For both, they involved a transformation of familiar landscapes. Dr Davis-Ziegler recalls that in Lupane before the arrival of the evictees:

> there were long distances in between. ... If I wanted to visit people from one kraal I had to walk half an hour until I got to the next kraal. And that's what people liked. I remember quite well that when more and more people moved in a woman moved out and I said 'But you are not living here any more. Why?' 'Oh, I couldn't live here any more. I had such a long way to walk to the bush, going to the lavatory, because we were too dense together.'[60]

For their part, the evictees found the *gusu* forests a great obstacle to open social inter-course: 'There was no open place,' recalls a woman from Bubi.'You had to cut the trees, men and women both.'[61]

But if both evictees and 'originals' were profoundly shaken, it was the former who gradually began to take the initiative, despite their lack of economic and political power. Their cultural self-confidence eventually gave them dominance in the societies of Nkayi and Lupane. They refused to be influenced by the practices of the locals; increasingly the locals copied them. In the decades which followed, it was the evictees who took most of the social, economic and political initiatives.[62]

Variation upon the Theme: The Creation of Lupanda Native Purchase Area

The Land Apportionment Act provided not only for possessory segregation and the division of the country into zones of exclusive white and black occupation, it also provided for the creation of special Native Purchase Areas (NPAs) where African Master Farmers could purchase significantly larger plots than those available in the Reserves. It proved hard to attract applicants to the Native Purchase Areas set up in Matabeleland, but nevertheless some voluntary migration to the NPAs took place at the same time as the forced evictions.

The Carter Commission, which made the proposals on which Land Apportionment was based, recommended that the extreme western part of the Shangani Reserve be excised from it and established as a Native Purchase Area. This NPA came to be called

---

[59] Interview with Enos Dube, Timothy Moyo and Magwaba Nkomo, Matshokotsha, 12 March 1996. Mabhikwa was a Khumalo, but not from one of the royal houses.

[60] Interview with Dr Davis-Ziegler, St Luke's, 24 January 1995.

[61] Interview with Julia Kimeta Sibanda, Mkalati, 23 August 1995.

[62] The argument here is not dissimilar from that advanced by Jean and John Comaroff about missionaries among the southern Tswana in the nineteenth century. Heavily outnumbered as they were, the missionaries had the cultural initiative. They brought about a 'state of colonialism' which laid the foundations for the later colonial state. Jean and John Comaroff, 'Through the looking-glass: colonial encounters of the first kind', *Journal of Historical Sociology*, 1,1,March 1988. The evictees into Nkayi and Lupane, who brought with them so many Protestant missionary assumptions, also had the cultural initiative. If we may anticipate a later chapter, it might be said that they brought about a 'state of nationalism' which laid the foundations for the later national state.

Lupanda, after the hunting tree which we described in Chapter 1. Settlers began to arrive there from 1945 onwards. These were yet more uniformly and self-consciously Christian and progressive than the evictees. Most of them came from the environs of major mission stations in Matabeleland South. Many were Seventh Day Adventists from around Solusi, adherents of the London Missionary Society, or Methodists. They tell a now-familiar story of arriving when the area was still a forest full of lions and inhabited by primitive people – Tonga, Sotho, Kalanga and Sili. N. T. Mlilo, son of an evangelist from Mtshabezi Mission, tells a typical tale:

> When we arrived it was a real thicket, we'd never seen anything like it. We'd hear hyenas howling at night. My wife said 'Have you brought me here to kill me?' She threatened to leave. … We had problems with all sorts of animals. … The originals were just broadcasting *inyawuthi* [bulrush millet] under the trees. They'd never seen a cultivator. … If they see [sic] you going to school, they thought it was useless.[63]

Some of these Christian progressives refused to compromise with local religious beliefs and practice. The *Lupanda* tree-hunting shrine now fell into one of the NPA farms. An ardent Seventh Day Adventist took over the plot. 'I can't stay here with a tree said to have gods,' he said. The sequel is told by one of the 'originals' still resident in Lupanda: 'It was the first target. So he brought heaps and heaps of firewood to burn the tree and it was totally burnt. We felt so disturbed by his action.'[64]

Those already resident in Lupanda, therefore, often felt as despised by the incomers as their counterparts in the rest of the Shangani. Yet everywhere, the locals had two strengths which we must end this chapter by considering. They were accustomed to the disease patterns of the Shangani, and particularly to the malaria which took such a dreadful toll on the incoming evictees and Purchase farmers. And they knew about the environment, and how best to propitiate it.

## Explaining the Malaria Epidemics[65]

As we have seen, people from the plateau had been reluctant for decades to go to the Shangani Reserve because of their fear of disease, and particularly malaria. When the forced evictions began in the 1940s, these fears proved fully justified. The first people resettled in the Shangani from the plateau suffered badly from malaria. From 1948 onwards, the disease reached epidemic proportions among the evictees. By 1951, when Filabusi people were being ordered to move to Lupane, they refused on grounds of the danger to their lives.

In July 1951, a test case was heard in the Filabusi court. One Sibuzana was charged with refusing to obey the order to move to the Shangani Reserve. Benjamin Burombo's African Voice Association hired lawyers and Sibuzana was represented by two Bulawayo advocates, Davies and Newham. These put Holl, the Filabusi Native Commissioner, through a taxing cross-examination. The latter was obliged to admit that he had no personal knowledge of the area to which Sibuzana was to be removed, together with 420 other families:

> The area is sparsely populated. It is probably hotter than here. It has the reputa-tion of having malaria there. Veld poisoning of cattle is said to be prevalent … It is a fair statement for them to say they would be pioneers.

[63] Interview with N.T. Mlilo, Lupanda, 1 April 1996.
[64] Interview with J. Gabheni Sibanda, Lupanda, 3 April 1996.
[65] Malaria is discussed more extensively in J. McGregor and T. Ranger, 'Displacement and Disease. Epidemics and Ideas about Malaria in Matabeleland, 1945-96', *Past and Present*, 2000, No. 167.

A delegation had gone to visit the area and one of them, Vungusa, testified.

> There is no water and no thatching grass there. There are also mosquitoes which are a danger to our children and our children will suffer from illness. … We think we would die if we went there. … We spoke to natives there. They said the place had a lot of illness caused by mosquitoes.[66]

Holl asserted that he had received assurances from the Native Department that 'they are making adequate provision to contain the malaria position'. In fact, the evictions were a brutal gamble with people's lives. In 1950 the Southern Rhodesian Director of Preventive Services, D.M. Blair, met with the World Health Organization (WHO) Regional Malarial Consultant for Africa to discuss priorities in a campaign against the disease. The effective use of insecticides and prophylactics during the Second World War encouraged the WHO to believe that vast areas of Africa could be freed from malaria. But Blair made it clear that his government's first priority was to open up areas hitherto closed to white enterprise because of the malaria risk. The second priority was to protect African agricultural and industrial employees so as to improve their productivity. No eradication campaigns were planned in the Reserves. In passing Blair remarked that: 'Movement of native population from higher areas to more malarious areas is normally accompanied by high infant mortality and almost paralysing morbidity in adults and children.' But he made no proposals to respond to this situation, even though the evictions from the plateau were already well underway.[67]

The results were regularly reported by the Native Commissioners for Nkayi and Lupane and as regularly deplored by African mission intellectuals. In 1948, 'malaria was responsible for the largest number of deaths' among Fort Rixon evictees in Nkayi; in Lupane the 'malarial season was worse than usual' and 'the people recently moved to this sub-district from Fort Rixon have been particularly affected'. In March 1949, malaria was reported to be still 'rife amongst the people who were moved … last year'.[68] Writing from the London Missionary Society station in the Shangani Reserve, E. Gwebu described how he had watched the thousands of evicted people being dumped in the forests of the Shangani. He thought that it was clearly part of a plan to create 'a white Rhodesia' by expelling all Africans 'to the Zambesi depression, that low-lying, malarial and tsetse-fly region … Steeping the African people in the unhealthy lower-lying region is murderous. Can the British still say that they are better than Hitler?'[69]

Gradually preventive measures were taken; pools in the Shangani river were sprayed with malariol; quinine and mepracrine were distributed. But these measures were ineffective. In March 1952, the Native Commissioner, Lupane, was obliged to admit that, despite the spraying of huts, 'the people, especially those from Matobo district, suffered from malaria … It was impossible to get those suffering badly from malaria to the clinic. Of the people that moved from Matopos, numbers of the women left the district, taking their children with them.'[70] Matobo evictees vividly remember the

---

[66] Rex v Sibuzana, 27 July 1951, S 2263. Sibuzana was acquitted because of defects in the eviction order. After amendments to the Land Apportionment Act, Holl told the people that they would have to go whether they liked it or not.

[67] Draft answers to WHO questionnaire, May 1950; D.M. Blair, 'Malarial Control. Southern Rhodesia', August 1950, S 2413/400/78/8.

[68] Annual Report, Shangani, 1948; quarterly reports, Lupane and Shangani, June 1948, December 1948, March 1949.

[69] E. Gwebu to Thompson Samkange, 20 June 1947, Samkange Papers, Harare, cited in Terence Ranger, *Are We not Also Men? The Samkange Family and African Politics in Zimbabwe 1920–1964* (London, James Currey, 1995), p.107.

[70] Quarterly Reports, Lupane, December 1951 and March 1952. Matobo chiefs and elders were so moved by the sufferings of evictee wives that they resolved to make divorce easier and cheaper.

malaria crisis. Pilot Ncube, who was re-settled at Pupu in Lupane in 1951, recalls:

> People were really struck down. I remember some even going back to Kezi because of the malaria deaths and only later coming back for the second time. My uncle had two wives, and the wives said: 'No, we can't remain here where our children are dying.'[71]

A charitable Christian evictee wrote to the *Bantu Mirror* to say that 'the good Native Commissioner, Lupani, is trying to destroy malaria. ... Nevertheless, malaria does not spare long people who are not used to this part of the country.'[72]

These sufferings intensified the resentment felt by evictees against the coercive Rhodesian state. Father Odilo recalls for Lupane that:

> When people were moved in they were filled with animosity. The area was completely different from their homes. ... Malaria was devastating. Many, many people died of malaria. When you talked to people they were bitter. They would say 'Rhodes promised us that we could stay in the Matopos. Now we have been moved among the mosquitoes, the tsetse, the midges and into the thickets.'[73]

The malaria epidemic also intensified the tension between evictees and locals. Both thought that malaria which killed was something new, different from either the endemic disease in the Shangani or their experience of illness on the plateau. Non-fatal diseases of the rainy season, including fevers, were known as *inyongo*; traditionally they were believed to be caused not by mosquitoes but by unwise over-consumption of fresh, sugary and green foods. There were many well-known treatments for *inyongo*, particularly purgatives and emetics. But these remedies were powerless against the malaria epidemic of the late 1940s. Nor did it do the evictees any good to follow the long-established advice of healers, who recommended that travellers take soil and water from their home area, mix it with the soil and water of the new place, and drink the infusion.

This 'new' disease had to be explained. Some originals thought that the evictees had brought it with them, along with many other deplorable manifestations of the modern world:

> We had aches and pains before but not malaria. We lived along the Shangani [river] being bitten by mosquitoes, and if they had carried disease we would all be dead. We think those from Matabeleland South brought it with them when they came, because that is when we saw it strike.[74]

Others thought that the evictees suffered because of their arrogance, their ignorance of the forest environment and their contempt for its local custodians. 'The new arrivals suffered when they came. *Inyongo* greeted them because they did not belong in this place.'[75]

---

[71] Interview with Pilot Ncube, Lupahlwa, 2 April 1996. Daveti Sibanda, interviewed on the same occasion, recalled that 79 men and 15 women from Kezi died in the first year. 'It was terrible. Before we left Kezi, we had been told we would die: "There is death in that place", we had been told. There was nothing we could do. No doctors, nothing.'

[72] *Bantu Mirror*, 15 March 1952.

[73] Interview with Father Odilo, Bulawayo, 7 January 1995. For the promises of Rhodes see Terence Ranger, *Voices From the Rocks. A Modern History of the Matopos* (Oxford, James Currey, 1999).

[74] Interview with Mudenda Dube, Lubimbi, 23 March 1996.

[75] Group interview, Ndimimbili, 11 March 1996.

The incomers also thought that malaria was a product of their new and feared environment. The locals could handle it – 'they did have some way of preventing the *inyongo* we found here' – but they kept their remedies and their knowledge to themselves. So far as the evictees were concerned, the Shangani was by definition an uncontrollable place, full of wild animals, tsetse and ticks:

*Inyongo* has always been in this place ... because it is infested with animals. It was the 'air' from the animals which caused the problem. Animals breathe out a different air from people, so it came from them. Animals cannot live well with people. Because we were breathing the air from animals we got sick. It infects the air, the soil and the water and it comes out with the grass. The only cures we knew for *inyongo* were not effective in this environment.[76]

## The Struggle over Rain and Fertility

Yet the evictees believed that they *did* have some means of exerting control over the new environment. They brought with them not only mission and independent Christianity but also long-established connections with Mwali, High God of the Matopos, and especially with the Njelele shrine in the south-west of the hills.[77] Cult messengers had long been moving between Njelele and the areas in Bubi, Matobo and Insiza from which most of the evictees came. Very many Christians there had combined church and school attendance with observation of the ecological rituals of the shrines. Especially in times of drought, they sent seed to be blessed and messengers took gifts of black or red cattle to the priests. Although the Matopos shrines pre-dated the Ndebele Kingdom, and their priests were all drawn from subject peoples rather than from the Nguni aristocracy, they had, by the 1940s, come to seem part of a composite Ndebele heritage.[78]

The oral tradition of the new Ndebele cultural nationalism insisted that Mzilikazi and Lobengula had venerated the shrines as well as befriending the missionaries. Thus one of Joshua Nkomo's close associates, Nzula Ndebele, an evictee to Hwange in the 1950s, insists both on his Nguni ancestry and his faith in Njelele. He holds that the Rozwi Mambo advised Mzilikazi how to govern the country. People from all over came to Njelele to ask for rain and to carry out 'various things involved in that mountain, including traditions of the various nations of Zimbabwe'. Mzilikazi continued to respect and make use of Njelele; so did Lobengula; so too did Nyamanda. Nzula Ndebele himself first went to Njelele in 1945, 'accompanying the chiefs of Northern Matabeleland'.[79] Missions, the Matopos and memories of militarism all played their part in the modern Ndebele identity.

In any case, many of the Ndebele-speakers who were forcibly resettled in Nkayi and Lupane were descended from the Kalanga, Venda and Nyubi peoples who had long been associated with the shrines. In fact a powerful 'rain-goddess', *uMtaka Mlimu* or *Shoko*, an emissary from Njelele, lived at Inyathi in the 1940s. She danced for rain and gave out doctored seeds. Then she left for Nkayi, where she spread the influence of Njelele.[80]

[76] Interview with Dokotela Ncube, Jabiwa, 10 March 1996.

[77] For a fuller discussion see Alexander and Ranger, 'Competition and Integration'.

[78] For an account of these processes see Ranger, *Voices From the Rocks*.

[79] Interview with Nzula Ndebele, Lobengula township, 28 January 1995. Nzula claimed that representatives from Hwange and Binga also went to Njelele, by way of Mzilikazi's grave at Entumbane. 'The right way to go to Njelele is to go first to Entumbane.' The synthesis between Ndebele history and identity and the Mwali cult could hardly be more complete.

[80] Interview with Jeremiah Khabo, Inyathi, 15 August 1993. It was this woman who visited the

Some convinced Christians among the evictees – particularly members of the Zionist and Apostolic churches – repudiated any connection with the Matopos. But many more saw no contradiction between a modernizing and progressive image and veneration of Mwali. The resentful incomers carried their Christianity to the Shangani. They also aspired to retain their connections with Njelele.

These connections offered important advantages in their new environment. Ndebele chiefs could claim no ancestral control over this alien land; for several years Ndebele evictees did not understand how best to farm it or where they could safely graze cattle. As we have seen, the long-settled Tonga, Nyai and Shangwe local population certainly did understand the environment and had pioneered its use. It was all very well for Christian progressives to boast that they knew how to plough or that they held Master Farmer certificates, but in their new *gusu* environment they could also benefit from local knowledge about soils and vegetation – even if they were reluctant to do so. They also had to know how to obtain rain and to ensure fertility. But here, too, they were adamant that they could rely on their own resources. Like previous Ndebele immigrants, the evictees encountered a network of indigenous *mtolo* rainshrines but, unlike many earlier settlers, they did not wish to acknowledge the superior power of indigenous rituals. What they sought to do was to take over the *mtolos* or set up their own and incorporate the area into the Njelele rainshrine system. Messengers went from the new evictee communities to the Matopos, not to Nevana.

These processes were, however, resisted. In those areas which sent to Nevana, the locals maintained that only they and their rainshrines could ensure fertility; only they knew the land and knew how to speak to its 'owners'. A complex struggle ensued. In this context, at least, the evictees did not have a monopoly of cultural initiative.

Two interviews from Nkayi illustrate the dynamics of the contest – and its varying results. From one part of Nkayi comes the testimony of a Filabusi evictee, Yona Sibanda: 'The locals didn't wear clothes, women wore nothing on top. They were living a primitive life. They were a mixture of Shangwe and Tonga … People here respected [the] Thursday [rest day], they were going to Nevana. We stayed at Njelele and made the locals go there too.'[81] From another part of Nkayi comes the testimony of a local, Mbitshana Sibanda:

> In 1952 the Filabusi people came here. … Before 1947 there was plenty of water. There were rivers here. We had big trees called *ichithamuzi* and rain fell from those trees in October. The trees had big snakes in them. … When the new people came they cut all our customs, we were afraid to say the name of our own tribe. So we became Ndebele and followed their customs. The Ndebele were rich, they had been living with white people, they came with sugar. … The *ichithamuzi* trees were a Mgoba custom. The custom was broken so there is no rain from those trees. The people who came here found the snake in the trees and killed it, and so ended the customs. … It was at that time that the rivers became dry. … We were going to Nevana. When the rain failed we talked to those people and they adopted our customs. … The Filabusi people tried to get rain [from Njelele]. The rain came only from our own *mtolo*. Now everyone goes to the old tree.

Mbitshana emphasizes how overwhelming the incomers were, but it was the locals who

---

[80] (cont.) supposed grave of Lobengula in 1943. *Bantu Mirror*, 6 November 1943. She was one of a sequence of such women messengers. In 1928, for example, the Gwelo Annual report described 'a native woman known as Gogo operating in the Bubi district, who is the reputed deputy of Salugazana, some sort of High Priestess or Rainmaker. Gogo is credited with the power of producing the seed at will by scratching it up from the ground'. S 235/506.

[81] Interview with Yona Sibanda, Mkalati, 19 December 1994.

had the connection with Nevana and 'the ones who should go to Nevana should be the old ones'.[82]

Oral testimonies, supported by the careful records of the ritual situation in every chief's and headman's area made in the mid-1970s by M.E. Hayes, present a very complicated picture of a highly contested issue. But a contrast can be drawn between the attitude of the early generation of Ndebele newcomers, including many of Nkayi's chiefs, and the later generation of evictees. In Nkayi, evictees were mostly resettled under Chiefs Madliwa and Sikhobokhobo, who had long established an interaction with local religion. Madliwa sent messengers every year to Nevana with gifts of cloth and beads; he sent a Lozwi messenger as 'the most suitable man to be used as a messenger to Nevana'. Sikhobokhobo also sent yearly to Nevana, his messenger being chosen 'because he is a Shangwe and will therefore have no language problems when he consults Nevana'.[83] Militant Filabusi advocates of Njelele were thus going against chiefly ritual practice as well as the practice of the local *mtolos*.

Although evictees took over some *mtolos* and went so far as to desecrate others, there was often a compromise. In Chief Dakamela's community, for instance, the main messenger to Njelele was Mlingo Ncube, who had come as a child from Bubi in the 1930s. He first went to Njelele in 1952, but thereafter went as often to Nevana as to the Matopos. When we interviewed him, he identified four other *wosana* in the Dakamela area: Timlefu, a Nyai, goes to Njelele only; Banyana Ndhlovu, a Leya, goes to both Njelele and Nevana; Lisi Ndhlovu, a Venda, and Sonini Ncube, a Tonga, go to Nevana only. Chief Dakamela contributes to cattle gifts for Njelele, but the Nevana medium regularly visits his kraal to perform rain dances.[84]

When Chief Mabhikwa arrived in Lupane in 1947, however, he was not initially as prepared to acknowledge local ritual sites. His home was situated close to a major Tonga ritual centre at Jotsholo, which comprised three large baobabs used for rain-making and named after Tonga ancestors, but Mabhikwa would have nothing to do with it at first. He insisted on keeping his links with Njelele. 'In case of drought they send to Matopos,' recorded Hayes in 1975. When he arrived, Mabhikwa brought with him 'a very strong Hosana who used to be successful at inducing the spirits to provide rain.'[85] But even the autocratic Chief Mabhikwa could not entirely over-ride Tonga religious feeling – Hayes' report does not reflect the accommodation he was forced to try to reach with local Tonga ritual leaders. Mabhikwa ploughed so close to the ancestral baobabs at Jotsholo that one of them fell down. The chief had to apologize to outraged Tonga elders in order to avert drought. He came to recognize the importance of local rain ceremonies, to consult local Tonga ritual experts, and to send emissaries to Nevana as well as to Njelele.[86]

Although Chief Mabhikwa himself was forced to compromise relatively soon after his arrival, the Filabusi evictees were often more stubborn. Those dumped in Mzola in the far north of Lupane had rejected Chief Mabhikwa. Their headman, Goduka, 'didn't consult the Tongas', he and his people 'had our own *wosanas* who had come from Fort Rixon with us and they went to Njelele'.[87] In his 1975 report, Hayes described how

[82] Interview with Mbitshana Sibanda, Gampinya, 8 December 1994.
[83] Hayes' reports on Madliwa and Sikhobokhobo, October 1975, CHK 6 Nkayi, Provincial Administrator's Office, Bulawayo.
[84] Interview with Mlingo Ncube, Dakamela, 25 August 1995.
[85] Hayes report on Mabhikwa, November 1975, CHK 6/LU, Provincial Commissioner's Office, Bulawayo. Hayes interviewed a man who entered Lupane with Mabhikwa, Giyane Mpofu. Giyane was a Nyai, whose grandfather had been a *wosana*; Giyane himself was initiated at Njelele in the 1920s and thereafter went annually to the shrine, driving black cattle as a gift.
[86] Interview with Sabhuku Ngwenya, Jotsholo, 24 November 1994.
[87] Interview with headman Goduka, 2 December 1994.

Goduka had switched to Nevana, and was using the important Tonga envoy, Sigoriko, also used by Mabhikwa.[88] But this move was far from complete. In 1994, headman Goduka described how 'we're still trying to negotiate with the people. Those who come from Fort Rixon still go to Njelele, but the Tongas along the Kana, the indigenous people, are consulting Sigoriko … Both groups hold their own ceremonies'. The twenty-year-old process of 'handing everything over to Nevana' was still underway.

Although the locals' knowledge of the land gave them some purchase in their relations with the evictees, their influence was limited. A Tonga elder, who still carries out rain ceremonies at the Jotsholo baobabs, described how the Tonga,

> pretended to join and live with the Ndebele. Others were shy and had to leave. The Ndebele were very proud, so it was difficult for us to live with proud people who belittled us. The Ndebele abused us, calling us poor, insulting us, they thought we were just nothing, worthless. The Tonga sacred places were respected but the Tonga people were treated just like animals.[89]

Still, there is some evidence of Ndebele evictees coming to treat the Tonga and other 'originals' with more respect. The Siziba family live at Memuka dip in northern Nkayi, where they were dumped in 1952. They had been political activists in Filabusi. Old Sibangwa Siziba, now in his mid-eighties, remembers their arrival:

> We were dumped at the borehole. When we first came there were very many diseases, and many died of malaria. Our cattle died. There were many people living here, all scattered about. There were Tongas around Kana and Shangwe here. They were afraid of us new people and were very hard to mix with. But they had plenty of ideas. We saw the respect they gave to each other and saw they had many traditions. … They had their *mtolos* for rain and they were calling us and we were going there for respect. … Every area had a representative to go to Nevana. We were not allowed to go. We were foreigners. But we gave them money to take.

His son Jaconia, who *has* been to Nevana many times since his first visit in 1977, added: 'We respected these people and accepted Nevana.'[90]

Underlying the complex and varied pattern of these interactions since the early 1950s, two broad processes can be detected. One is that the idea of Nevana became more systematized and his network more centralized as a response to the arrival of advocates of Njelele. The other was that the many Ndebele who came to accept Nevana began to work him into their versions of Ndebele history and identity, just as Njelele had been so successfully absorbed. By the 1970s, traditions of the Gokwe rainmakers' relationships with Lobengula had been developed and the Nevana medium had come to speak Ndebele as well as Lozwi, Shangwe and Tonga.

## Conclusion

The coerced eviction of so many people from the plateau set Shangani society in turmoil in all the ways we have described. The image among administrators of the *gusu* as a

---

[88] Hayes' report on Goduka, Mzola, November 1975, CH.6/LU. The report describes how 'they have been looking for a new envoy and have decided to enlist the services of Sigoliko ... because he is the senior member of the family of that name who were living in the area when Goduka moved in.'

[89] Interview with the Ngwenya family, Jotsholo, 24 November 1994.

[90] Interview with the Siziba family, Memuka, 26 August 1995.

place of peace and solitude had been thoroughly shattered; the Ndebele understanding of the *gusu* as a fearful and dark place became more powerful than ever as evictees suffered hardship, disease and death after being dumped in the Shangani forests. But the Rhodesian state could not rest content with its first violent movement of families. It felt compelled to follow them up – establishing police posts and lock-ups for the first time; imposing punishment when there were clashes at funerals and beer drinks; giving support to the challenged authority of the chiefs. It also had to take notice of the impact on the Shangani environment of the rapid multiplication of its human and cattle population. As we have seen, the calculations of experts about acceptable carrying capacities had been over-ridden for political expediency in the course of the evictions. The consequences were bound to involve ever-increasing state intervention – to resettle people away from the crowded valleys, to de-stock cattle, and to discipline the discontented evictees. The violence of eviction was to be followed by a Rhodesian version of what historians of East and Central Africa have called 'the second colonial occupation'.

# 3

# The Violence of the State
## The Second Colonial Occupation

### Introduction

After the Second World War there was a great intensification of colonial regulation throughout British colonial Africa. The loss of India made Africa seem like the last chance for imperial economic development. State control of the British economy during the war made official direction of production respectable. It was development orthodoxy that, under direction, African peasant production could be made vastly more efficient and profitable. So almost everywhere colonial officials enforced conservation rules, imposed plans for rural settlement patterns, divided up land for cultivation and grazing, and experimented with title rights. It was a process which involved a great multiplication of the number and type of officials deployed in the rural areas, met widespread resistance, and it was a process which involved the use of police, and sometimes troops, to break this resistance. It is not surprising, therefore, that these post-war interventions have been described as 'the second colonial occupation'.[1]

Southern Rhodesia was not, of course, a typical British colony. Its 'native policies' were generated locally. Its post-war aspirations for economic development were based on the anticipated triumphs of white production rather than on peasant improvement. Nevertheless, in Southern Rhodesia, too, the post-war period saw the deployment in the African rural areas of greatly increased numbers of administrative and technical staff. There was official interference in African peasant patterns of residence, production and inheritance – in many areas for the first time. All this was connected to the great evictions and removals described in the last chapter. Doubled or tripled populations could only be accomodated in the Reserves, it was held, if urgent measures were taken to enforce conservation and to improve farming efficiency. In the more remote Reserves, certainly, the notion of a 'second colonial occupation' is a useful way of imagining the impact of the new policies.

Nowhere were the changes more striking than in the area of the old Shangani Reserve. For decades, the Reserve had been part of a much larger administrative district, fitfully visited by the Native Commissioner, Inyathi. But by the mid-1950s, it had been divided up into two administrative districts, Lupane and Nkayi, each with its Native Commissioner, Assistant Native Commissioner, two or three Land Development

---

[1] The first, and still the best, description of the 'second colonial occupation' is D.A. Low and J.M. Lonsdale, 'Introduction: Towards the New Order 1945–1963', in D.A. Low and A. Smith (eds), *History of East Africa: Volume Three* (Oxford, Oxford University Press, 1976).

Officers and their Field Assistants, and ten or so African Agricultural Demonstrators. Where once the Reserve had possessed no police post or lock-up, police were now regularly deployed to enforce agricultural rules and to prosecute offenders. In Nkayi in 1961, there were over a thousand prosecutions for refusal to dip cattle; there was an 'upsurge of prosecutions during the last two months of the year to figures unheard of in this district'; these related especially to refusal to pay taxes. The police had become essential to routine administration:

> During the tax drive Police made their radios available to us and worked tire-lessly serving processes. CID and Police investigating teams sometimes with riot squads were commonplace in the district, a spotter aircraft was used, and the local gaol burst at the seams several times. ... The local police force were busily maintained at several times its normal strength.[2]

There was a similar transformation of official knowledge about the area. When the Shangani Reserve was first allocated in 1894, its features were virtually unknown; for decades after that most of the bush remained untraversed. By 1960, however, almost every square inch of Nkayi district had been surveyed. The 1958 annual report described how roads and land allocations were being planned 'from air photographs'; on the basis of this aerial survey, detailed maps of each zone of the district were being drawn up; soil pits had been sunk and vegetation classified. As the Native Commis-sioner proudly boasted, 'Nkayi is the first district in which such planning has taken place'. The district would be completely mapped by the end of January 1959 and land use planning would be completed by the end of June.[3] In December 1958, the Native Commissioner told his provincial superior that he had been 'really getting to know the area from aerial photographs'.[4] The 1959 report indeed claimed that 'land classification had been completed on the aerial mosaics'. The district had learnt from errors elsewhere and had resolved to develop 'a cut-and-dried plan before any field work actually took place.' As a result, Nkayi had become a model for the whole country. A Native Agricul-tural Conference met there in December 1959 and 'unreservedly endorsed everything that was being done'.[5]

All this came as a great surprise and an unwelcome shock to the people evicted from the plateau. They had wanted to be close to Europeans and to markets and had enthusiastically pursued improvements in their methods of farming in order to extract the maximum advantage from their position. But having been forcibly removed from areas of white settlement and dumped far away from markets, they thought that the least they might expect was to be left alone. As the Native Commissioner, Lupane, found in 1955, his first foray into land planning was met with 'unanimous and vociferous opposition' from the Filabusi evictees. They claimed that:

> when they were removed from Filabusi they were told that once settled in their new abodes they would be left alone entirely, to do as they liked and live happily ever after: and now here was the Government breaking their backs again.[6]

This attitude remains entrenched in oral memory today. In October 1995, P.M. Moyo, a Filabusi evictee to Gampinya in Nkayi, insisted that 'when we were forcibly moved, we were told no white man would follow us here ... Then the Conex [Conservation and

---

[2] Annual Report, Nkayi, 1961, S 2827/2/2/8.
[3] Annual Report, Nkayi, 1958, S 2827/2/26. The aerial photographs had been taken in 1955.
[4] Native Commissioner, Nkayi to Provincial Native Commissioner, 4 December 1958, S 2808/1/25.
[5] Annual Report, Nkayi, 1959, S 2827/2/2/7.
[6] Annual Report, Lupane, 1955, S 2827/2/2/3.

Extension officers] came. We came with the kraalhead Senza Khumalo. The Conex said, "You, kraalhead, this is your area." They marked fields in the dense bush … We were told we were going to the forest where we could do our will, and here came these Conex people.'[7]

The new policies were no more popular with the earlier settlers who in the past *had* been more or less left alone to do their will. They had come to think that the niches which they had identified in the Shangani environment were incontestably theirs to exploit. Thus one of the early migrants who had arrived with Chief Sikhobokhobo recalls how they had settled down to 'farm right in the middle of the Gwampa Valley.' After 1952, and as part of planning mainly aimed at the incoming evictees, these locals were moved into the bush. 'We found it very difficult to clear the thick bush for fields. The land wasn't fertile either. If you ploughed in the valley you didn't need fertilizer, but up here without manure and fertilizer you can't reap anything.' The people were outraged: 'It was our legitimate right to plough in the valley'.[8]

To both evictees and early settlers, the new order did look pretty much like a new colonial occupation.

## The Development of Official Agrarian Planning

Such intrusions into African peasant production took place everywhere in Southern Rhodesia after the Second World War and they have been analysed by a number of scholars.[9] State intervention in the Shangani, however, is particularly interesting to examine. Agricultural experts faced a uniquely demanding challenge to come up with effective methods to improve production in the arid and unobliging *gusu*. There was an unusually explicit political motivation in the implementation of official agrarian policies in the Shangani. And there was a particular intensity in the response both of evictees and locals. The experience of the 'second colonial occupation' in the Shangani became a powerful part of memories of the illegitimacy of the colonial state – memories to which we will return in later chapters.

Before the Second World War, official endeavours to improve African agriculture and stock-management in the Shangani Reserve were restricted to rhetorical gestures. In 1925, for example, Native Commissioner Farrer of Bubi called together at Inyathi Industrial school all the chiefs of his huge district, including those of the Shangani. His oration was rich in ironies. He wished to speak, he told them, on matters of 'agricultural interest, improvement of your stock, improving your dwellings, and the industrial training of your people.' He made it clear that: 'you are not called here for the purpose of being ordered to do these things. I am only going to point out to you the benefits which you will derive'. Farrer then proceeded to present a secular version of Christian improvement ideology.

---

[7] Interview with P.M. Moyo, Gampinya, 19 October 1995. Similar opinions were expressed in many other interviews.

[8] Interview with M.M. Moyo, Majaha, 5 October 1995.

[9] See, e.g., J. Alexander, 'The State, Agrarian Policy and Rural Politics in Zimbabwe: Case Studies of Insiza and Chimanimani Districts', PhD, Oxford, 1993; M. Drinkwater, *The State and Agrarian Change in Zimbabwe's Rural Areas* (London, Macmillan, 1991); B.N. Floyd, 'Changing Patterns of Land Use in Southern Rhodesia', PhD, Syracuse, 1959; S. J. Mhlabi, 'The effects of and African responses to the Land Husbandry Act of 1951 with special reference to Ntabazinduna Communal Land', BA History Honours thesis, University of Zimbabwe, 1984; Terence Ranger, *Peasant Consciousness and Guerrilla War in Zimbabwe* (London, James Currey 1985); Ranger, *Voices From the Rocks* (Oxford, James Currey, 1999); Guy Thompson, 'Cultivating Conflict: the Native Land Husbandry Act in Colonial Zimbabwe', PhD, University of Minnesota, 1998.

He pointed out that all the work on white farms was actually done by African labour. Africans ploughed and manured and planted and cultivated. 'You know how to do it.' But at home they did not try to do it. Instead they left cultivation to the hoe agriculture of their wives: 'You are men ... Men are never beaten when they want to do a thing. Why do you let these things beat you? Why don't you show that you are men and can do the things which you see the white men doing?' Farrer then embarked on a bit of colonial historiography. 'The white men took away the country because you were doing nothing with it. The Ndebele only lived on the people they raided.' But today, things had changed. The whites had left Africans with land and cattle.

> We don't want to make soldiers of you or slaves like you did with some of the people you captured. We want to make men of you ... breeding good cattle, growing plenty of good corn ... to sell to enable you to buy good clothes and good food and to build good houses to live in and to pay for your children to go to school.

He waxed particularly eloquent about their 'round huts with small doors' – just like those of the nineteenth century: 'We white people live in big houses with big doors and windows and wash our clothes, we get plenty of wind through our houses and wind drives disease away.'[10]

The chiefs largely replied in the fixed rhetorical terms of such occasions – they were as children compared to the whites; they depended on the administration as a father. But they made some shrewd practical points too. They lacked capital and they lacked labour. 'We shall not be able to grow crops like you because we cannot pay labour to do the work.' Nor did they enjoy cleared and open land. 'We have got lots of trees in the forest.' Above all they did not have markets. As Sikhobokhobo complained two years later, 'they were told that stores would be established in the Reserve. But the stores only sold rubbish and afforded no profitable market for cattle and produce.'[11] In short, Farrer's address was no more than empty, and in the circumstances impudent, rhetoric. Even he, in his 1925 Annual Report, admitted that perpetual evictions had made Africans into 'wanderers', with no confidence that the whites would leave the Reserves themselves alone if they proved fertile. There was no incentive for them to 'improve'.[12]

In any case, even when bits of Farrer's advice were taken, they turned out to be very mixed blessings. Thus, in 1932, it was noted that ploughs were now in use everywhere except along the Kana river, where Tonga cultivators still used hoes. But the ploughs had proved to be 'instruments of destruction rather than of benefit', bringing about 'destruction of grazing and timber' and the rapid turn-over of impoverished land. A single Agricultural Demonstrator, stationed at Dakamela's, made 'no impression on the consciousness of the mass'.[13]

By 1943, the Native Commissioner, forseeing the postwar implementation of Land Apportionment, reported that:

> Owing to the nature of the country the bulk of the population has settled all along the river banks and in the valleys. Large tracts of country, especially between the Shangani and Kana Rivers are vacant, chiefly owing to the lack of water. ... The

[10] Meeting between NC Bubi and Inyathi Chiefs, 1925, S 607. Tshugulu, Sikhobokhobo and Mlege were present as well as several Bubi chiefs, 7 headmen and 44 kraalheads.
[11] Meeting between the Governor and Chiefs, Shangani Reserve, 6 August 1927, *ibid*. The 1935 Bubi annual report admitted that in the Shangani Reserve 'lack of markets give the native no encouragement to better his method or increase his crop'.
[12] Annual Report, Bubi, 1925, S 235 503.
[13] Annual Report, Shangani Reserve, 1932, S 235 510.

implementation of the Land Apportionment Act will require the Reserve to carry a larger population than hitherto, especially from the Inyati area. It is anticipated that the present population will be more than doubled from this source alone. Unless utter confusion and congestion through overcrowding and overstocking is to be avoided, development, not only of water supplies, but also culling of stock and centralisation must be immediately installed.

The NC envisaged the introduction of compulsion. 'A few judiciously placed contour ridges and supervision of the methods of ploughing' were required. As for:

the question of improvement of stock [it] must be taken out of [the Africans'] hands altogether. The matter is a national one ... It has been proved that the native is incapable of looking after or improving his one source of security. The obvious solution is a strict culling of his herd and the compulsory acquisition by him of an approved bull.[14]

Boring of water holes began at once, many of them in the river valleys where water was readily reached.[15] But there was no de-stocking and little centralization or compulsion, though officials increasingly called for it. Thus in 1946 the NC, Shangani, declared that 'compulsory development is the only remedy for the present state of affairs. Reserves must be controlled and lands restricted.'[16] By 1947, there had already been 'heavy movements of natives from the Bubi District' but still no land-use planning:

The implementation of the Land Apportionment Act at too great a rate only solves the problems of one district by the creation of more acute difficulties in others. Large movements of natives into areas which have not been centralised only accelerates the rate of damage to the natural resources.[17]

The evictees from Bubi were, in fact, not settled by Land Development Officers or Native Commissioners but were able to move about and to select their own land. They made straight for the black soils of the river valleys – the *isidaka* – which they could cultivate with their ploughs and oxen. As David Msebele, originally from Bubi and founder of the Catholic Mission at Fatima, recalls, 'We didn't plant anything in the *gusu*... We used to just plough in the *isidaka*.'[18] Douglas Siso, who came into Lupane from Bubi in 1952, chose:

Tshongokwe because of *isidaka* soils. There was good grazing land and the *isidaka* was good for ploughing. The government hadn't pegged stands for us by this time. You could just choose where you wanted to put your home. The government didn't really come in to control land use. We were allocated 10 acres, but you could plough more if you wanted to.[19]

Ruben Dube and other Bubi evictees, now settled around St Paul's in south-eastern Lupane, recall that 'there were no stands at that time. We chose to live together. We settled ourselves in fact, organizing ourselves as we had done in our old neighbour-

---

[14] Annual Report, Shangani Reserve, 1943, S 1051.
[15] On the history of water development in Nkayi, see F. Cleaver, 'Water as a Weapon: The History of Water Supply Development in Nkayi District, Zimbabwe', *Environment and History*, 1, 3, 1995, pp. 313–35.
[16] Annual Report, Shangani Reserve, 1946, S 235 518.
[17] Annual Report, Shangani Reserve, 1947, S 1051.
[18] Interview with David Msebele, Jabatchava, 23 January 1996.
[19] Interview with Douglas Siso, Bulawayo, 8 March 1996.

hood.' Some of these Bubi evictees had gone first to Dakamela's and then across the river to Sikhobokhobo's before moving back south of the Shangani 'because members of the family were working in town and there was no bridge'.[20]

This freedom of settlement did little to avoid overcrowding in the more fertile wetlands. But it allowed for the development of agrarian interaction between the newcomers and the earlier settlers. There was exchange of seeds and techniques. Successful settlers from Bubi had good harvests and were able to sell or barter surplus maize to locals. Thus Douglas Siso recalls that local Tonga did 'various jobs for us' in return for surplus maize. Other locals now acquired cattle and began themselves to move down into the river valleys and to cultivate the *isidaka* soils. 'We moved down into the wetlands when we got cattle,' says Jeli Mlotshwa.[21]

It was only with the arrival of the militants from Filabusi that land-use planning and resettlement began to be connected, though even then arrangements were made very hurriedly. In June 1954, the Native Commissioner, Nkayi, reported that the Reserve was centralized 'for Filabusi settlers only'. At that point, indeed, he did not think that assessment and allocation of land anywhere else in the district should take place for at least five more years because of problems of 'administration and stock control'.[22]

## Agrarian Intervention and Social Discipline

Things were in fact about to change radically and the second colonial occupation was about to gain speed in Nkayi and Lupane. The prime reason for this change of policy was as much political as agricultural. Jocelyn Alexander has shown that, in general, as agricultural intervention became the hallmark of the second colonial occupation, the colonial technical branches gained dominance over the administrative. Rhodesian Native Commissioners were extremely (and in the overall African context, perhaps uniquely) powerful figures. But however much Native Commissioners might have hankered after compulsion, legislation such as the Native Land Husbandry Act of 1951 was not their work but the work of agricultural 'experts'. Application of the Act demanded survey, demarcation and allocation on a huge bureaucratic scale.

Alexander remarks that it was only when African resistance to the imposition of the Land Husbandry Act threatened law and order that the Native Commissioners regained the initiative.[23] In the Shangani, however, considerations of political discipline went hand in hand with those of agrarian 'improvement' from the very beginning. Thus in April 1955, Native Commissioner Trollip wrote from Nkayi to his Provincial Native Commissioner. He explained that Filabusi evictees had been centralized in 1952 at boreholes north of the Gwelo river and along the Kana valley, each family getting ten acres:

> They were given verbal instructions not to move from their stands or to exceed their arable allocations, but no written orders were issued as the whole movement operation was too rushed. These instructions have been ignored. ... It is well known that these people caused a lot of trouble in Filabusi over the movement, and I feel that it is a matter of urgency that something be done about their activities in this district before they get out of hand.

He noted that it had not been intended to apply the Land Husbandry Act to Nkayi for

[20] Interview with Ruben Dube *et al.*, Malunku, 6 March 1996.
[21] Interview with Jeli Mlotshwa, Matshiya, 8 April 1996.
[22] NC Nkayi to PNC, 29 June 1954, S 2808/1/25.
[23] Alexander, 'The State, Agrarian Policy and Rural Politics'.

some years, but there seemed little point in making formal allocations to the Filabusi people now, and then having to go through the whole process again later. Trollip therefore asked that an assessment committee be set up under the Act for the zone in which the Filabusi evictees lived, and that thereafter there should be rapid implementation of the Act's provisions.[24]

These disciplinary considerations weighed with the Provincial Native Commissioner who endorsed the recommendations in April. In August 1955, the Secretary for Native Agriculture put the case to his Minister:

> In 1952 Natives living on Crown Lands in the Insiza District were moved to the Shangani Reserve and were allotted ten acres each in the area it is now wished to proclaim. These Natives have disregarded their demarcation and extended their lands. They are politically minded and the PNC has requested that the area should receive early priority.

The Minister approved.[25]

Oral informants recall these new interventions clearly. One of the 1952 Filabusi evictees, P.M. Moyo, recalls the arrival of technical staff, the marking of 'fields in the dense bush', and the enforcement of boundaries. 'That marking didn't affect the originals. They could plough as much as they liked. We didn't honour that ten-acre limit – we cleared as much land as we liked. But people were arrested for this.'[26]

The first Land Husbandry Zone in Nkayi – Zone A1 – was proclaimed in the Filabusi evictee area, north of the Shangani. The Annual Report for 1955 reported that the district field staff were fully occupied in Land Husbandry appreciation there. The Filabusi people had protested and refused to point out their holdings; a kraalhead had been prosecuted; people were now collaborating 'under protest and without enthusiasm'. Things had been so managed that the compulsory introduction of what the state's experts regarded as 'modern' agriculture into Nkayi was being resisted by the district's most self-consciously 'modern' men and women.[27] Two definitions of 'modern' had in fact come into conflict. African 'modernizers' were primarily concerned with adopting new seeds, ploughs, etc. so as to produce more effectively for the market. The state's emphasis on reducing field sizes, moving fields from the *isidaka* into less fertile *gusu* areas, destocking, and requiring labour on contour works undermined such accumulation. From the African point of view, to resist field allocations and destocking was in no sense anti-modern.

In Lupane, too, the same pattern prevailed. The district's first Land Husbandry Zones, A1 and B1, lay south of the Shangani, in an area where many Filabusi evictees were concentrated. There, too, the announcement of the Act's operation was greeted with 'unanimous and vociferous opposition' from the Filabusi people.[28]

The Land Husbandry Act, of course, involved much more extensive interventions than had been contemplated in the past. It meant assessment of arable and grazing land. It meant development of water resources so that residential stands could be sited away from the river valleys, and development of roads so that they could be reached. It meant allocation of arable rights to individual landholders, and stock-grazing permits. It meant calculation of 'carrying capacity' for stock and a commitment to destocking. It meant compulsory conservation work so as to make permanent rather than shifting cultivation possible. It also meant that some people would not get arable or grazing

[24] NC Nkayi to PNC, 4 April 1955, S 2808/1/25.
[25] Memo to Minister of Native Affairs, 8 August 1955, S 2808/1/25.
[26] Interview with P.M. Moyo, Gampinya, 19 October 1995.
[27] Annual Report, Nkayi, 1955, S 2827/2/2.
[28] Annual Reports, Lupane, 1956 and 1957, S 2827/2/2/4 and 5.

rights. In Nkayi and Lupane, as elsewhere, implementation of the Act would mean the creation of a class of landless youth. But above all, what the act really implied in the old Shangani Reserve was a remaking of the agrarian landscape.[29]

## The Emergence of an Agricultural Policy for the Shangani

Land Husbandry was first applied in Nkayi and Lupane for political as well as agricultural reasons. Native Department staff in Nkayi and Lupane were often obsessed by the intransigent problems of their districts and the difficulties of disciplining articulate and disaffected evictees. They sometimes regarded technical officers as juniors very much at their command.[30] Nevertheless, they came to realize that agricultural reform could not be determined solely by administrative convenience. As early as 1952, indeed, the Native Commissioner for the Shangani Reserve admitted that 'for the past few years all activity has been directed to the settlement of natives moved from other districts. In consequence agriculture has to a great extent been neglected'. It had now become 'necessary to deal with the backlog of development work in areas inhabited by the original population', and a start had been made by ordering that cattle were not to be depastured in valleys and vleis during the summer months.[31]

As we have seen, in 1955 the emphasis shifted back again to the ex-Filabusi evictees. But gradually Land Husbandry assessments and land planning extended to cover the whole of Nkayi and Lupane, and the technical experts came to determine policy. By 1957, a Land Husbandry zone had been established north of the Shangani river, in Lupane, as well as in three zones south of it. Technical staff were working on defining farming and grazing rights: 'All the staff were somewhat inexperienced in land allocation and conservation planning and it took some little time to settle down to the rhythm of the work.' In Nkayi in 1957, the original Zone A1 north of the Shangani, containing 'almost a quarter' of the Reserve, had been assessed for demarcation and allocation; two other Zones, B and C, 'comprising nearly two thirds of the Reserve, have reached the final stages of kraal appreciation and should be ready for assessment early in the new year.'[32]

Then, in 1958, there was a pause, imposed on the Native Commissioners from outside the districts. The Native Agriculture Department was worried that the initial surveys and assessments had been too rapidly and superficially carried out. It recommended a shift from Zone appreciation to Unit assessment. The Native Commissioner, Lupane, reacted bad-temperedly:

> The people are holding back and doing as little as possible to improve their lands until the Act is applied. Unless we apply the Act and issue rights in the near future agricultural progress is likely to retrogress. At the moment the people do not know where they stand and the sooner we clear up the position the better ... I see no point in holding back the application of the Act for the sake of complicated surveys.

He found himself in the worst of both worlds. A common-sense man like himself

[29] H.J.R. Henderson, 'Legislation and Land-use Planning in Rhodesia: An Example of Recent Landscape Evolution in the Nkai Tribal Trust Land', *Swansea Geographer*, 15, 1977, pp. 56–9.
[30] Interview with Rupert Meredith Davies, 17 November 1983, ORAL/241, National Archives, Harare. 'A lot of the District Commissioners', remembers Davies, 'treated the Land Development Officers as if they were boss-boys.'
[31] Annual Report, Shangani Reserve, 1952, S 2403/2681.
[32] Annual Reports, Lupane and Nkayi, 1957, S 2827/2/2/5.

would have favoured allowing 'shifting cultivation [to] go on for many years and only good could come from it', because much of the forest would have been cleared. Instead, he had been required to implement Land Husbandry – and now that was in suspension![33]

His colleague in Nkayi was more positive. Noting that 'due to the lack of Field Staff and change of policy in implementing the Native Land Husbandry Act at Nkai, the programme has had to be postponed', he added that even in Zone A1 'allocation has been discontinued as it is feared that re-assessment may be necessary'. Nevertheless, he favoured thoroughness – 'the Land Husbandry Planning which is at present in progress will be invaluable in the redistribution of the population in the near future'.[34] Thereafter, this process of thorough planning continued. The year 1959 was spent in Nkayi planning the Reserve 'into units once the land-use classification had been completed on the aerial mosaics'. At last everything was in readiness for implementation of the Act. 'All the staff are facing the next season with confidence'.[35]

This confidence was misplaced. The process of consideration, survey and assessment had taken too long. By 1960 and 1961 the rise of African protest politics, which is the subject of the next chapter, made implementation of Land Husbandry impossible in Nkayi and Lupane. In Lupane in 1961:

> Political agitators, who encouraged opposition to the Land Husbandry Act, inter- fered with the work that had been planned for the year. In the case of three units work was brought to a standstill. There have been a number of prosecutions.

In Nkayi 'Land Husbandry work did not proceed well and smoothly' even though 'the working year opened with a fully staffed team operating from headquarters in Zone A2'. Faced with resolute African opposition, two of the three Land Development Officers left the district in the second half of the year. 'Freedom-ploughing' across the boundaries of demarcated holdings was widespread; there was an urgent necessity for Land Inspectors to police and prosecute offences, 'without which the work of the past few years is liable to be set at naught'. The Native Commissioner was gloomy about the future: 'I fear for the personal safety of all field staff when the Land Husbandry operations start again next winter'.[36]

In fact, Land Husbandry was about to be abandoned as government policy. In some ways its history in Nkayi and Lupane had been an elaborate exercise in futility, succeeding in provoking but not in controlling the African populations of those districts. Still, although Land Husbandry as such was never enforced in the Shangani, an overall agricultural strategy had emerged during the 1950s, parts of which *had* been implemented and which continued to shape official interventions into African agriculture well into the 1970s.

The basic premise of this strategy was that the population of the districts had to be more evenly distributed. In Lupane in 1955, it was noted that 'the district is a very difficult one in which to work. There has been no centralization; almost all the people live and cultivate in the river valleys, and the "gusu" country, 80% of the district, is virtually untouched.' In Nkayi in 1956 'an endeavour is being made to distribute both humans and animals as evenly as possibly throughout the district'; nevertheless, as late as 1958, it was still being reported from Nkayi that the river valleys 'were grossly over- populated and over-stocked' and that 'at least half the population will have to be

---

[33] Annual Report, Lupane, 1958, S 2827/2/2/6.

[34] Annual Report, Nkayi, 1958, S 2827/2/2/7.

[35] Annual Report, Nkayi, 1959, S 2827/2/2/7.

[36] Annual Reports, Lupane and Nkayi, 1961, S 2827/2/2/8. Annual Reports are unavailable after 1961.

moved and be more evenly distributed.' In both districts there was a desperate search for water supplies in the *gusu*.[37]

What this policy involved in practice can be seen from detailed Zone assessments. As we have seen, Zone A1 in northern Nkayi, largely east of the Nyaje river, was the first to be proclaimed. It included the 'original Lozwi' of Chief Madliwa and many evictees from Bubi and Filabusi. The people 'had concentrated along the valleys' and there was 'only one road along the main valley'. A hundred miles of new road had to be cut through heavy timber; boreholes had to be dug in the *gusu* and land allocations centralized around them.[38]

W.L. Moncrieff's report on Zone A1 in May 1956 revealed the movements that had already taken place there and what remained to be done:

> There are two subsidised headmen, Manguni and Sibangelana, resident in the area, both of whom are under chief Madhliwa. Kraalheads total 154 and their followers are scattered. When they are centralised this will be remedied. ... When natives from the Filabusi district were moved into Zone A1 during 1952, their kraals and homes were centralised. Since then, however, considerable movement has taken place. Lands have been extended and in most instances the timber strips between lands have been cultivated and it is often impossible to locate the original lands. The lands allocated were all of 10 acre blocks, no extra land being allowed for additional wives. Some of the soil is very poor. At about the same period, the old inhabitants residing along the Kana Valley and who in previous years had had their lands in the Valley were prohibited from further ploughing in the Valley and were allocated lands in the gusu. Some of the older residents have moved their kraals into lines but generally speaking the whole area will have to be centralised and lands allocated. ... Villages are scattered but where centralisation has taken place they are in lines on the high ground, usually in the vicinity of a borehole.[39]

In the plan, all these new centralized villages were to be made accessible to motor traffic. All sponges and vleis were to be fenced off. A systematic system of rotational grazing would be introduced. A Pasture Research Officer, making a grazing assessment of the zone in the same month, found that distribution of stock was bad. He recommended 'application where possible of a system of veld management. A 2 Paddock 1 Herd or a 4 Paddock 3 Herd system with fire would be suitable.'[40] In the past there had been 'very little European supervision'. This must be replaced by constant direction and control by LDOs.[41]

This and other zone reports reveal the scale of the intervention required to carry out official agricultural policy. In the end, the administration did not command the resources to implement such plans or to cow African opposition. Moncrieff reported in May 1956 that 'when appreciation of lands commenced [in Zone A1], a great deal of opposition was met with. After the meeting with the Acting Native Commissioner at Ngenungenu towards the end of November 1955, the inhabitants agreed to permit of the measurement of their lands on the understanding that the authorities realized that they were opposed to the Act. It was stated at the time that they would oppose the Act

[37] Annual Reports, 1955, 1956 and 1958, S 2827/2/2/2-7.
[38] Annual Report, Nkayi, 1956, S 2827/2/2/4.
[39] Report on Zone A1, W.L. Moncrieff, Field Assistant, NHLA, 24 May 1956, S 2808/1/25.
[40] Pasture Research Officer, Memo, 22 May 1956, *ibid*.
[41] The same Land Husbandry file also contains assessments of Zones A2, B and C. These all reveal the same desire for centralization, for spreading out the human and animal populations, and for tight control over production and stock management.

again when it came to allocating the lands after the Assessment Committee had met'. And oppose it they did.

## The Problem with Official Agricultural Policy

Land Husbandry failed in Nkayi and Lupane not only because of shortages of resources or intensity of African opposition. It also failed because its underlying agricultural philosophy was badly flawed.

As we saw in Chapter 1, the Shangani area was made up of innumerable micro-environments. The original settlers had sought out productive niches within and on the margins of the *gusu* and in the fertile wetlands of the valleys. But Land Husbandry planning units were too large to allow for such variety. 'The striking feature of Nkai', noted the Assessment Committee for Zones A2, B and C in July 1959, 'is the tremendous variation in soil and vegetation types which make it a very difficult area to plan.'[42]

And if it was difficult for the planning process to recognize areas of rich potential within the *gusu*, it was also hard to know what use could be made of the rest of the *gusu* area. In the midst of all the confident statements about the need to spread out the population, there were repeated notes of pessimism about the *gusu*. The Lupane Annual Report for 1955, noting that 'the "gusu" country, 80% of the district, is virtually untouched', added: 'Whether, in fact, this so-called wasteland can be profitably used for agriculture remains to be seen.'[43]

The search for water in the *gusu* often failed. In Nkayi in 1958, 'on the whole drilling was not successful, especially on the gusu ridges in Zone C.'[44] In the early 1950s, the boreholes necessary for further settlement were located in river valleys, thus actually increasing the density of population there. As a report on Zone B, Nkayi, pointed out in 1958, 'due to the past siting of boreholes in valleys, heavy population concentrations are found along them as well as the length of the Shangani and Gwelo rivers wherever suitable arable soil is available.'[45]

Equally unsuccessful were attempts at demonstration plots in the *gusu*. In 1955 a 'gusu fertility experiment' was set up in Lupane by the Native Agriculture Department. A six-acre plot had been cleared, ploughed and fenced, preparatory to planting. But by 1958, it was lamented that the experimental plot had 'proved very little. The plot is isolated and the depredations of wild buck and springhares introduce a factor which to a great extent negates the scientific value of the experiment.' The plot had been abandoned.[46]

The *gusu* plot was not so isolated, however, as to escape local notice. Its failure is today joyously remembered:

The soils we were using were the *isidaka* down by the river [recall a group of Bubi evictees]. The government did try to move people from the rivers in the 1950s and 1960s at the time when politics was starting. The government didn't want people living down there, they wanted them to be up on the *gusu*. It was about the time when the Filabusi people arrived here. People were objecting to that because the *gusu* was not a good place for making a field because there are thickets. No one had lived up there before.

Mahamba yedwa [the Land Development Officer] had a field right in the *gusu*

---

[42] Assessment Committee report, 17 July 1959, S 2808/1/25.
[43] Annual Report, Lupane, 1955, S 2827/2/2/2.
[44] Annual Report, Nkayi, 1958, S 2827/2/2/7.
[45] Report on Zone B, January 1958, S 2808/1/25.
[46] Annual Reports, Lupane, 1955 and 1958. S 2827 2/2/3 and 2/2/6.

to show people how to use that soil and develop their agriculture. But because it failed, so people were not convinced. He planted maize, groundnuts and sorghum in his demonstration plot, but the maize tassled when it was only knee height. It was a useless crop despite being a good year. We youth were working in Bulawayo at that time and when we came back home you could see the plot from the buses. We used to laugh at it – the whole bus would be leaning to the windows to see it. We had to ask questions about the demonstration plot in Lupane. We saw it was always green, but it never improved, the crops never ripened properly. So we had to ask the Native Commissioner: 'Why is the land always green and never ripening?' You couldn't expect much from that soil, because it was as poor as river sand. Mahamba yedwa had applied manure, but it had still failed – he might as well have put manure into the river bed. It was a complete failure. In the meantime, the crops in our own gardens were very successful.[47]

This failure confirmed the evictees' view that 'the *gusu* was only good for wild animals'. Everything tried on the plot – maize, groundnuts, round nuts, sorghum, 'new drought resistant crops' – was equally disastrous. (Significantly, no attempt was made to plant bulrush millet, the crop long planted by the earlier settlers on more fertile patches of the *gusu*.) 'The main aim of the plan was to get people settled in the *gusu*. If he had been successful we would all have been forced up into the *gusu* to follow his methods.'[48]

In any case, by this time the Native Agriculture Department was also beginning to think that the *gusu* could never be planned and allocated. In May 1959, the Director wrote to the Under Secretary, that the 'main problem in the Nkai District is whether 207,000 acres of undeveloped, waterless area should be developed at a cost of £153,000 so that families may be settled there. It might be that this money would be better spent on some other development scheme.' He thought that 'an investigation into the whole gusu problem should be one of the priority tasks of the Planning Officer'. The Under Secretary agreed and instructed the Provincial Native Commissioner that pending such an inquiry, 'we should concentrate on the full utilisation of the fertile soils in Nkai and Lupane for the implementation of the Land Husbandry Act, and leave for the time being any development of the "gusu" ridges.' Money would be better spent on irrigation; work in the *gusu* 'might prove to be a complete waste of time and effort'; Land Husbandry rights should only be granted 'in respect of the better soils of the area'.[49]

The implementation of Land Husbandry planning in Nkayi and Lupane had been suspended the previous year pending further survey. The Native Commissioner, Lupane, complained bitterly that there was little point in 'complicated surveys which even if they prove that the greater part of the area is not suitable for occupation will certainly not provide an alternative'. If all the population was to be settled in Lupane then the *gusu* just had to be used.[50]

These weaknesses meant that well-founded and rational opposition could be and was voiced to Land Husbandry planning on agricultural rather than political grounds. In May 1961, for instance, Native Commissioner McLean of Nkayi reported to the Provincial Native Commissioner on the points raised at eleven meetings held in Zone B2:

---

[47]  Interview with Josiah Ndlovu, Enoch Ncube and Ruben Dube, Malunku, 6 March 1996.
[48]  Interview with ex-Bubi evictees, Malunku, Lupane, 6 March 1996.
[49]  Director of Native Agriculture to Under Secretary, 1 May 1959; Under Secretary to PNC, Matabeleland, 2 May 1959. S 2808/1/25.
[50]  Annual Report, Lupane, 1958 S 2827/2/2/6.

Ideas and opinions put forward and worthy of note are as follows:
People along the rivers such as the Gwampa, Lupane, Lukampa, Singwangombi etc this year have excellent crops in their lands in the river vleis. They realise that they will be moved out into the gusu – and are opposed to such a move, on the grounds that the gusu will not give them crops to compare with their present ones. This has some truth in it, but I told them that ploughing these areas will ruin them, and that unploughed as they are they constitute the only dependable winter grazing.

Typical gusu land will not give a reasonable return after 3 or 4 years crop raising on it – no matter what rejuvenation measures are taken. There may be truth in this and I have made it the subject of a separate inquiry.

People argued that there were 'unoccupied adjacent European areas available for native settlement' and that the Shangani Reserve was only overcrowded because of the government's programme of eviction; they also argued that jobs in towns should have been created before the Act was implemented. 'There is something in this', McLean admitted. The Provincial Native Commissioner's comment was merely that these same complaints 'have been made on all occasions over the last ten years.'[51]

## Legacies of Land Husbandry and Centralization

The abandonment of Land Husbandry planning did not mean the end of 'the second colonial occupation' in Nkayi and Lupane. As we shall see, there continued to be direct official intervention in production and conservation, focusing particularly on the compulsory construction of contours; there continued to be arrests and prosecutions; if anything, administration became more rather than less authoritarian. The Land Husbandry period came to stand in the memory of the people of the Shangani as a monument to the arrogance of experts who did not really understand the environment; subsequent enforcement of contours was bitterly resented and is often spoken of as having 'started the war'. Nevertheless, there was one important difference between the first and successive phases of the 'second colonial occupation': interventions became more focused and were more rigorously and continuously enforced, because the fate of Land Husbandry stood as a warning against over-elaboration and over-ambition.

Land Husbandry planning itself was abandoned in 1962. After all the furore over Nkayi's unequalled mapping and planning, it comes as a surprise to read a letter from Noel Hunt, District Commissioner, Nkayi, in November 1964. Writing to his predecessor, D.E.F. Gumprich, now District Commissioner, Gwelo, Hunt evoked a vanished era:

I am told that land allocation actually took place north of the river while you were here. Can you recall how far the exercise actually got, please? Were grazing rights issued? Were land rights issued? If so, do you recall where they are? I can find no Land Husbandry Registers here. The Inspectorate may be moving into the area to deal with those who have extended their lands, etc, and the record will obviously be needed.

Gumprich replied that some records must surely be around somewhere.[52]

---

[51] E.D.K. McLean, 'Native Land Husbandry Act – Start of Implementation in Residual Area of District Under Chief Madhlisibanda', 19 May 1961, S 2808/1/25.

[52] Hunt to Gumprich, 5 November 1964; Gumprich to Hunt, 14 November 1964, LAN 1/GEN, 1062–70, Nkayi. Gumprich remembered that while he was at Nkayi in 1959 'the area was subdivided into units, and it was found that some of the units were overcrowded and people would

When in 1969 a Five Year Development Plan was drawn up for Nkayi, it was as if the Land Husbandry programme had never been:

> The main settlement has taken place along the main rivers. ... These heavy concentrations are undesirable. However, past attempts to secure water on the Kalahari sand areas of the district have not proved very successful and there can be no settlement in these areas until such time as water is made available.[53]

On the other hand, the Land Husbandry years did leave some mark in at least some parts of the Shangani. In 1977 the geographer, H.J.R. Henderson, wrote an article on 'legislation and land-use planning in Rhodesia', taking an area in Nkayi as an example of 'recent landscape evolution'. Henderson compared air photography from 1955 with later photographs from 1964 and 1971. He took units 142 and 143, north of the Mangwizi Valley, as his case study. He found that 'the 1964 photography, taken after the abandonment of Native Land Husbandry planning, shows how the plan had been put into operation. The arable plots stand out clearly, with a homestead adjacent to most of them.' The 1971 photographs, however, revealed that 'while the basic settlement pattern remained, it is evident from the landscape that the planning system had broken down. The number of arable plots had been greatly extended though the number of home-steads had not changed significantly.' He concluded that while the Act was 'a failure in many senses', it 'did leave its imprint on the landscapes of the Tribal Trust Land'. Areas which were planned under the Act had not reverted 'in geographical terms to anything resembling the unplanned state. Settlement has remained where it was placed by the planners.'[54]

The Mangwizi valley was not representative, however. Elsewhere it was not Land Husbandry but the earlier concentration and centralization of evictees which left its mark on the Shangani landscape, and which had begun to change the way the evictees themselves regarded the landscape.

## Land Husbandry and Nationalism in Nkayi and Lupane

The oral memory of the Shangani retains a great variety of opinions about the relation-ship of Land Husbandry to the rise of nationalism. General histories of Zimbabwean nationalism often see resistance to Land Husbandry as crucial to the making of an alliance between nationalist leaders and peasant producers. In Nkayi and Lupane, things are remembered as somewhat more complicated. No-one denies that there was successful nationalist opposition to the Act, but many people dispute that opposition to Land Husbandry *amounted* to nationalism. In the Shangani, nationalism is thought of as something much more fundamental and extensive than mere resistance to official agrarian policy.

Some informants insist that people resisted official interference in their patterns of residence and production even before they became consciously nationalist. M.M. Moyo, descendant of those who came in with Sikhobokhobo and settled in the Gwampa valley

---

[52] (cont.) have to move into other units, but before this could be done boreholes had to be sunk.' Both he and McLean made allocations but 'for part of the area, especially under Chief Madhliwa, allocation was stopped as the people threatened the tractor driver and other people employed on demarcation.'

[53] DC Nkayi to PNC, 26 February 1969, LAN GEN/1, 1967-1970, Nkayi.

[54] Henderson 'Legislation and Land-Use Planning in Rhodesia'. Henderson cites J.R.V. Prescott, 'Overpopulation and overstocking in the Native Areas of Matabeleland', *Geographical Journal*, 52, 1961.

in Nkayi, recalls that his father was arrested for resisting removal from the 'middle of the valley' after 1952. But in his view 'the resistance to moving from the valley wasn't politically motivated. It was simply our legitimate right to plough there. It wasn't politics.' Moyo knows what 'politics' is, since his father, his brothers and he himself became radical nationalists.[55] Douglas Siso, a Bubi evictee into Lupane and later a nationalist official and restrictee, makes the same distinction. 'The thing people were really against was the vaccination of the cattle. They were strongly opposed to that ... The police were brought in to do forced injecting. It was the community as a whole and not the party who were organising the resistance to the injections. It was just a popular resistance.'[56]

Others maintain that opposition to Land Husbandry was merely one manifestation of an already existing nationalist consciousness. The current Chairman of Nkayi Council, Leonard Nkomo, says that 'nationalism was not the result of the Land Husbandry Act which did not materialise here. Because they were *already* political the people resisted this thing.'[57] Senzani Ngwenya, herself an evictee from Bubi and later a Zapu provincial official, remembers that 'in the 1960s we were clandestinely active, we joined political parties and were given cards which were hidden somewhere not to be seen. Being forced to dig contours was a contributing factor in the rural area, but it was not the main aim of politics. It was part of the bigger question.'[58] Anthony Magagula, also from Bubi and a National Democratic Party/Zapu activist, says that 'land was a key issue' in politics, but that neither evictions nor Land Husbandry implementation were 'the main focus'. 'Our platform was that the country was ruled by the whites, the economy was not in the hands of blacks, all the resources of our rich country were in the hands of the whites. The land blacks were living on was useless, some of us were dumped in the *gusu*, we were campaigning for the government to give us fertile land.'[59] 'We fought here for these Filabusi people to be able to go back to their home', says the early settler Paul Sibanda. 'We didn't fight to stay in this sandy area, we fought for rich land.'[60]

Being able to grasp the 'bigger question' was a matter of education rather than merely of experiencing interference in production and residence. 'It was because of education, that is how our eyes were opened, that is how we came to know we were oppressed.' For this reason, many people maintain that the evictees were able to understand nationalism in its full sense, while the 'originals', living away in the *gusu*, could at first only react to immediate provocations.[61] 'The NDP was talking about issues like we Africans being oppressed', says P.M. Moyo, 'that we had no freedom.'[62] In any case, the evictees thought from the beginning in nationalist terms rather than in terms of local 'peasant consciousness'. Local solutions were no use to them. They had not wanted to be in this locality at all; they wanted their old land to be returned. Only a national solution could achieve this.

As we explore further in the next chapter, this discussion raises important general issues. Nationalism had to be *made* in the rural areas rather than just imported or imposed; we need to understand not just the nationalist exploitation of local grievances, but the emergence of rural nationalism as such. To achieve this, attention needs to be focused on the local leaders who fostered a rural nationalist consciousness and

[55] Interview with M.M. Moyo, Majaha, 5 October 1995.
[56] Interview with Douglas Siso, Bulawayo, 8 April 1996.
[57] Interview with Leonard Nkomo, Nkayi, 9 February 1995.
[58] Interview with Senzani Ngwenya, Singwangombe, 21 February 1996.
[59] Interview with Anthony Magagula, Lupanda, 22 December 1994.
[60] Interview with Paul Sibanda, Gampinya, 19 October 1995.
[61] Interview with Pilot Ncube and Daveti Sibanda, Lupahlwa, 2 April 1996.
[62] Interview with P.M. Moyo, Gampinya, 19 October 1995.

mobilized rural protest against local oppression as part of this endeavour. But before turning to these issues, perhaps we may conclude here that nationalism in Nkayi and Lupane was very much a response to 'the second colonial occupation' in the totality of its manifestations – to forced eviction and intervention by the colonial state – rather than to Land Husbandry as one temporary form of it. In any event, it is clear that nationalism assumed a significance in the Shangani in the early 1960s which it has never since lost. The development of this nationalism by the evictees and its extension to the earlier settlers of the Shangani is the subject of our next chapter.

# 4

# *The Rise of Nationalist Violence*

## Introduction

We interviewed many nationalist leaders in the Shangani and our book reflects their articulation of public memory. This does not make it, we hope, mere 'nationalist history', but we have certainly been seeking to write part of the history of nationalism. In Zimbabwe today, it almost goes without saying that a critical history of nationalism is essential: many of the fundamental issues which affect Zimbabwean society arise out of the promises, the disputed character and the failures of nationalism. Elsewhere in Africa it may be true that not only 'nationalist history' but the history of nationalism have to be discarded – because the nation was never imagined; because nationalist rhetoric has proved to be empty; because the nation state has withered away; because class formation and class struggle is manifestly more important than nationalist politics; because ethnicity has become the key local unit of cultural mobilization against globalism; because cities exercise influence over hinterlands which cut across several national boundaries.[1]

In Zimbabwe, too, much nationalist rhetoric has proved to be empty. 'Nationalist history' is today denounced both by political commentators[2] and by historians of trade unions or of 'civil society'.[3] Worse still, the nation was imagined after 1980 so as to

---

[1] For a review of the catastrophes of nationalism see B. Davidson, *The Black Man's Burden: Africa and the Curse of the Nation State* (London, James Currey, 1992). Examples of post-nationalist history include: J. F. Bayart, S. Ellis and B. Hibou, *The Criminalization of the State in Africa* (Oxford, James Currey, 1999); P. Chabal and J-P. Daloz, *Africa Works. Disorder as a Political Instrument* (Oxford, James Currey, 1999); S. Ellis (ed.), *Africa Now. People, Politics and Institutions* (London, James Currey, 1996).

[2] For a denunciation of nationalist history in Zimbabwe see Lupe Mushayakara, 'Africa's Greatest Curse is Partisan Scholarship', *Zimbabwe Independent*, 5 February 1999.

[3] The most recent criticism of 'nationalist history' in Zimbabwe is B. Raftopolous and I. Phimister (eds), *Keep on Knocking. A History of the Labour Movement in Zimbabwe, 1900-97* (Harare, Baobab, 1997). In his preface the Secretary General of the Zimbabwe Congress of Trade Unions, Morgan Tsvangirai, writes that 'the history of the labour movement has usually been subordinated to the struggles of the nationalist elite [and] the complex relationship of the movement to the growth of nationalist parties and nationalist ideology has frequently been simplified to suit the triumphalist views of nationalist history.' In their introduction Raftopolous and Phimister describe how in the historiography of the 1980s 'radical voices were increasingly drowned out

exclude the history and experience of the western third of the country. In this way, men and women in Matabeleland who were committed nationalists found themselves in conflict with the nation state. Zimbabwean nationalism turned out to be authoritarian rather than emancipatory, and we are under no illusions that had Zapu rather than Zanu won the 1980 elections things would have been very different. At the level of its leadership, Zimbabwean nationalism in 1980 was commandist; both parties were equally committed to the one party state and the executive presidency.

Yet despite all this, the nation and nationalism remain critical concepts in contemporary Zimbabwe. The Zimbabwean state has certainly not withered away. Some of the most effective opposition ideologies are rooted in the ideals of an original, democratic and uncorrupted nationalism. In western Zimbabwe in particular, local politicians hold tenaciously to such a vision, using it as the foundation of a moral critique of the state of the nation.

To make this case, however, we need to offer a definition of what we mean by nationalism, a notoriously protean term, and to clarify our use of the phrase local or rural nationalism. A minimal definition of nationalism, of course, is support for the sequence of mass nationalist parties – the African National Congress (ANC), the National Democratic Party (NDP), and the Zimbabwean African Peoples Union (Zapu) – over the thirty years from the ANC's relaunch in 1957 to Zapu's merger with Zanu in 1987. By this definition, Nkayi and Lupane were certainly 'nationalist' at least from 1961, when they were a stronghold of the NDP, through to 1987. Even after the merger of Zapu into Zanu(PF), the old local leaders of Zapu, now within the united Zanu(PF), continued to be elected as councillors.

But this certainly is a minimalist – and in some ways a circular – definition. One has to ask what made these parties nationalist, as well as what made their members in the Shangani nationalists. Nationalism was, of course, anti-colonial but this is not sufficient to distinguish it from previous local protest associations in the areas from which the evictees came, like Sofasonke which grouped the inhabitants of the Matopos against eviction, or from 'tribal' protest associations, like the organization of the old Nqama regiment, Sofasihamba, in Wenlock, or from regional protest associations, like the Matabele Home Society.[4] All these bodies were also in their own way anti-colonial but none had a national focus nor possessed an ideology of a national right to land, justice and respect. Their claims to land were much more local and historically specific.

Many people in Nkayi and Lupane had been members of one or other of these bodies before their forced resettlement in the Shangani. But in the Shangani they could not sensibly belong to associations which derived legitimacy from claims to an area which they no longer occupied, or a tribal grouping which excluded most people. Even the wider claims of the Matabele Home Society – to represent 'the Ndebele' – carried less weight when the much-vaunted promises made by Cecil Rhodes to 'the Ndebele' had been dishonoured. Moreover, in the Shangani the evictees were acutely aware of ethnic complexity and diversity. They became suspicious of the divisive potential of 'tribalism', associating it with heavy-handed colonial strategies of divide and rule. So instead of tribally or regionally based protest, they developed what we refer to as local nationalism.

This nationalism was ethnically inclusive. It drew on an understanding that the fate of Africans was determined at the territorial political centre – the evictees knew that the Rhodesian Government had to pass an amendment to the Land Apportionment Act before it could forcibly remove them from Filabusi and Matobo, and they attributed the

[3] (cont.) by the supporters of the newly triumphant nationalism ... Various studies praised unity and nation-building over class struggle, as they celebrated the post-1980 dispensation as the best of all possible worlds.' pp. xiii–xiv.

[4] See T. Ranger, *Voices From the Rocks. Nature, Culture and History in the Matopo Hills of Zimbabwe* (Oxford, James Currey, 1999).

daily interference in their modes of production and living to the workings of the Rhodesian state. Focusing on the state as the source of oppression and discrimination, Shangani nationalists went beyond opposition to particular legislation, such as the Land Husbandry Act, or particular official interferences, like contouring. They developed an ideology of their rights, as citizens of an African nation, to land and resources, to dignity and freedom.

The Shangani's nationalists included many migrant labourers and individuals who spent periods in both urban and rural environments, and whose political activism spanned the two. Rural party committees were intimately connected with their urban counterparts in Bulawayo. Rural and urban leaders alike drew on the vocabulary and experience of the wider African anti-colonial struggle.[5] Joshua Nkomo became the leader of nationalists in Nkayi and Lupane not because he was 'Ndebele' (being in fact Kalanga by birth) but because he had come to represent the African workers and residents of Bulawayo.

In all these ways the activists of the Shangani were clearly nationalist. Yet the nationalism of Nkayi and Lupane was not merely externally derived: it had its own character, its own social base. Rural nationalism in the Shangani was a significant local variant of the Zimbabwean movement as a whole.

Historians need to study the way rural nationalisms such as these were established and made, instead of either taking nationalist ideology for granted or viewing it as a straightforward expansion from the towns. This is a proposition more readily plausible in Zimbabwe, where the guerrilla war of the 1970s was fought in the rural areas, than it is in intensely urbanized South Africa. In Zimbabwe, analysis of resistance has concentrated on the peasantry; in South Africa on the proletariat and urban youth.[6] But even in Zimbabwe, little attention has so far been paid to the distinctiveness of local nationalisms.[7] Although the ideas of urban-based movements were critically important, to build a rural movement, local leaders had to establish a rural social base and redefine issues of local concern within the frame of a nationalist project.

It is in many ways possible to argue that rural nationalism in Nkayi and Lupane was more 'nationalist' than many other parts of the country. Elsewhere in Zimbabwe, nationalist leaders sought to build on rural ideologies of ancestral title to the land or exploit deep cleavages between chiefly houses.[8] But the evictees could claim no such

---

[5] During the open mass nationalist period in the Shangani, there was frequent recourse to terms derived from the anti-colonial movement in Congo/Zaire - sellouts were called 'tshombe' after the secessionist leader of Katanga, and nationalist youth were called 'zhanda', or gendarmes.

[6] There have been as many books and articles about resistance in Soweto as about the guerrilla war in Zimbabwe's rural areas. See Clive Glaser, '"We must infiltrate the Tsotsis": School Politics and Youth Gangs in Soweto', *Journal of Southern African Studies*, 24, 2, June 1998, and the references there given. A path-breaking study of rural nationalism in South Africa is P. Delius, *A Lion Amongst the Cattle. Reconstruction and Resistance in the Northern Transvaal, 1930–94* (Oxford, James Currey, 1997).

[7] General accounts of African nationalism in Zimbabwe which do not pay attention to rural differences include: M. Meredith, *The Past is Another Country* (London, Pan, 1980); W. Nyagoni, *African Nationalism in Zimbabwe* (Washington, University Press of America, 1978); N. Shamuyarira, *Crisis in Rhodesia* (London, Deutsch, 1965); M. Sithole, *Zimbabwe: Struggles Within the Struggle* (Salisbury, Rujeko, 1979). Sithole emphasises ethnicity as a cause of nationalist faction but his analysis mainly deals with ethnicity in exile rather than with local rural nationalism.

[8] The district in which rural nationalism was first entrenched was Sipolilo, which provided by far the most detainees when the African National Congress was banned in 1959. Preliminary research suggests that long-standing disputes over ancestral land and deep divisions within the Sipolilo chieftaincy powered local nationalism there. The Sipolilo Annual Reports for 1959 and 1961 provide a detailed analysis of nationalist support; many files attest to long standing

ancestral rights to land in the Shangani – many wanted to leave the district altogether and to return to areas close to the towns and markets, a prospect which would certainly require a revolutionary political upheaval. Nor were chiefly politics as important in the Shangani as elsewhere – there were no powerful rival claimants and chiefly units were widely seen as arbitrary and artificial. As we shall see, chiefs in the Shangani did develop forms of opposition politics which were effective constraints on the state. But the opposition politics of the chiefs was different from the nationalism of most of their people. This allowed the Rhodesian administration to play one off against the other. But while nationalists might attack chiefs as stooges, their aim was not to replace a bad chief with a good chief. Their aim was to replace what was from their point of view a bad state – one which removed people from a viable environment and dumped them in wild forests, one which commanded and demanded – by what they dreamt of as a good state, which would cease discrimination, provide services, restore markets and be accountable to them as citizens. (Of course, the post-colonial nation state turned out not to be like this at all.)

Although the character of nationalism differed from one part of Zimbabwe to another – and perhaps in some rural areas nothing that can be called nationalist developed at all – there were not such wide variations as in many other African contexts. In Northern Rhodesia/Zambia, for example, the history of negotiations with African kings and chiefs, and the practice of Indirect Rule, meant that anti-colonial, 'nationalist' politics was very different in Barotseland from that among the Bemba or among the Tonga.[9] The belated development of Rhodesia Front ethnography did little to create such deep 'tribal' differences. Even a consciousness of 'Shona' identity was a development of the 1950s, part of the same movements of ideas which produced nationalism itself. 'Shona' nationalism was not at this stage very different from 'Ndebele' nationalism; distinctions within them were much greater than distinctions between them; Zapu itself remained a national party, with key 'Shona' leaders, right through the 1980s.[10]

In other parts of Africa, nationalist parties were put together by forming coalitions of strikingly contrasting regional class interests. Even in impoverished Tanganyika, the class character of TANU's allies varied widely from region to region, from the leaders of wealthy and powerful producer cooperatives in the north to immiserated coastal peasants.[11] We have seen that in the Shangani there was a clear-cut difference between the self-image of the Christian progressive and of the 'original' traditionalist. But this cleavage did not emerge primarily as a class division, and Rhodesian state interventions aimed to undercut entrepreneurs and to equalize cattle and land holdings. There were great differences between Reserves close to Harare with many schools, stores, clinics and those in the northwest with hardly any. But neither differences within areas nor differences between areas ran as deep as in Tanzania. Uneven as it was, Rhodesian colonial capitalism had not produced the gross contrasts which existed, say, in Mozambique and which made an effective nationalist movement so difficult to develop there.[12]

[8] (cont.) grievances over 'ancestral land'; file S2929/2/5 contains the October delineation report for Sipolilo.

[9] S.N. Chipungu (ed), *Guardians in their Time. Experiences of Zambians Under Colonial Rule, 1890–1964* (London, Macmillan, 1992).

[10] The current attempts to revive Zapu under the name Zapu 2000 as a party in and for Matabeleland ignore the party's history as a national movement. See, e.g., Mercedes Sayagues, 'New Party has Bulawayo on the boil', *Mail and Guardian*, 30 April 1999.

[11] J. Iliffe, *A Modern History of Tanganyika* (Cambridge, Cambridge University Press, 1979).

[12] The very wide regional variations in Mozambique's modern history of nationalism and war emerge clearly from the Special Issue on Mozambique, *Journal of Southern African Studies*, 24, 1, March 1998. See also J. Penvenne, 'Mozambique: A Tapestry of Conflict', in D. Birmingham and P. Martin (eds), *History of Central Africa. The Contemporary Years Since 1960* (London, Longman, 1998).

Rural nationalisms in Zimbabwe each had their own history and social base, their own dynamics of incorporation and exclusion. In the Shangani, the pioneers of nationalism were Christian modernizers. But as confrontation with the state intensified, many teachers, preachers and storekeepers became identified as at best 'moderates' and at worst 'sellouts'. Furthermore, the need to develop a nationalism which embraced the 'originals' as well as the evictees meant an appeal to multiple histories and to multiple religious legitimations. Local nationalism became less Christian and more 'traditionalist' over time. Both the Nevana medium and the Mwali cult were appropriated to Shangani nationalist ideology. In so far as it was Christian, radical youth and guerrillas chose to work with Zionist and Apostolic churches rather than with the local representatives of mission Christianity.

But despite its changing character, Shangani nationalism never ceased to be genuinely national in its aspirations. Members of Zapu in the 1960s were keenly aware that they worked together in the party with people all over Zimbabwe. With clearly national aspirations, they committed themselves to violence against the state more rapidly and enthusiastically than most rural areas in Rhodesia, or than most local nationalisms elsewhere in south-central Africa. In 1959, when the African National Congress was banned and the Emergency declared, Nkayi and Lupane were peacefully unaffected. A mere two or three years later – by 1961 and 1962 – the two districts were proverbial in administrative circles as centres of violent radical nationalism. There were widespread campaigns of sabotage. In 1962, there were 'mobs' rampaging through the forests around Pupu in Lupane, ambushing police trucks, releasing prisoners, and marching on the homes of African collaborators. In the mid 1960s, there were guerrilla incursions into the area, the most effective of which aimed to establish itself in rebellious Pupu, where it could call not only on the symbolism of the 1893 war and of Lobengula's last battle, but also on the traditions of more recent nationalist violence.

In August 1995, we interviewed Julia Kimeta Sibanda, wife of the vice-chairman of Nkayi Council, Yona Sibanda. With a gleam in her eye, she remembered the violence of the early 1960s, 'What we did we destroyed schools, dip tanks, bridges everything that belonged to the Government. We were taking the decisions. We were sending the youth to do it, both boys and girls. We were now making petrol bombs. We are now acting as men.'[13] Today there is a general, if ambivalent, glorification of memories of nationalist destruction in Nkayi and Lupane, amounting almost to a stereotypical memory.

Julia Kimeta Sibanda insisted, like other Shangani nationalists, that nationalism was not merely a negative opposition to the evictions, to Land Husbandry and to the interference of the Rhodesian state. For them, nationalism was about 'freedom' and 'equality' and 'dignity'. They would not have been won over by belated Rhodesian concessions of an Ndebele 'national home' or even by the revival of the Ndebele Kingship, which radical conservatives like Noel Hunt contemplated. In this respect we concur with Susan Geiger's insistence that nationalism was not something introduced from outside or above. We do not single out women in our narrative, as she does, but we certainly second her assertion that local activists 'constructed, embodied and performed … nationalism'; that they continued to believe in it; and that instead of focusing exclusively on the failures of the nation state after independence, the historian should examine a continued 'positive sense of nationalism' at the grass-roots, based on 'dignity, self-respect, equality, pan-ethnic solidarity'.[14]

These themes will be fleshed out in the chapters which follow. This chapter traces the making of nationalism in the Shangani. Later chapters describe its development; its persistence; its agonies; its confrontation with the nation state.

[13] Interview with Mrs Julia Kimeta Sibanda, Mkalati, 23 August 1995.
[14] S. Geiger, *Tanu Women. Gender and Culture in the Making of a Tanganyikan Nationalism, 1955–1965* (Oxford, James Currey, 1997), pp. 7, 14, 15, 204.

## The Politics of the Chiefs

In the 1940s, the chiefs of the Shangani Reserve expressed resentment at their isolation and at growing official interference. They did this in two ways. First, they made use of official representative institutions. Second, they sought to ally themselves with urban politicians. In both modes, they and their headmen spoke as Ndebele, raising issues of Ndebele tradition and demanding justice for Matabeleland.

During the Second World War, the Rhodesian government sought to bring the chiefs of the Shangani Reserve together in a Native Council. There was little enthusiasm and, although the first initiatives were taken in 1939, it was not until August 1943 that Chiefs Nkalakatha, Madliwa, Madhlisibanda Sikhobokhobo, Myinga Dakamela, Mabhikwa and their headmen voted unanimously to set up a Council. It first met in June 1944.[15]

From the beginning, the chiefs used the Council to complain about lack of development. At the first meeting, Mabhikwa was particularly articulate. He 'said that the Reserve was a long way from all towns and peopled entirely by Africans and that a large school was essential for the development of his people'; he noted 'that the Reserve was far away from medical facilities, was low lying, hot and unhealthy besides being a very large area. It had only one clinic at the extreme eastern end ... He asked for more clinics', a maternity ward and a resident doctor.[16] Others complained about the poor roads and the bad treatment of men conscripted in the Reserve for work on white farms.

The same issues came up at the August 1945 meeting but all the Native Commissioner could do was to promise that things would improve once the war was over. 'As regards a doctor, the Government would no doubt station one here when the war against Japan was over and doctors were released from the forces.' When further representations were made, however, the Medical Director thought it would be at least 'two or three years before further Clinics could be built in the Shangani Reserve'. The Inspector of Education merely noted that schools could be left to the missions. The chiefs linked the continued backwardness of the Reserve to their ambiguous position as tribal authorities, resulting from the fact that many of 'their people' had chosen to remain close to schools and clinics in Bubi rather than to follow them into the Shangani wilderness. Nkalakatha complained 'that many of his people resident in the Bubi district refused to join him in the Reserve as they did not wish to move further from the town of Bulawayo. He stated that he could not control people in two districts.'[17]

The Council of October 1946 repeated demands for clinics, roads and school and still nothing was done. By the time the chiefs and their people met again in October 1948, they were thoroughly disillusioned with the futility of making polite representations to government. They complained that there were still no additional clinics and that the Reserve remained as remote and backward as ever. Meanwhile, as the second colonial occupation got under way, they were being exposed at Council meetings to exhortations about agricultural improvement and threats of official intervention. The Council was attended by the Provincial Agriculturalist, by an Animal Husbandry Officer and a Land Development Officer. 'The meeting was reminded that ploughing in the valleys must cease otherwise our water supplies would disappear. The lands would soon be centralised and allocated. Ploughing up and down slopes would not be allowed.'

In response, a new note of conservative radicalism was struck. Speakers pointed out 'that segregation was the white man's policy' and stressed 'that Native areas should be reserved for Native effort.' It was unanimously agreed that 'no Europeans be allowed to

[15] Minutes of the Shangani Reserve Native Board, 10 August 1943, S 2584/4251. Mabhikwa was not yet resident in the Reserve but he was included because 'he has a very large following under Headman Nduna and is keenly interested in the establishment of a Council'.

[16] Minutes of the Shangani Reserve Council, 5 June 1944, *ibid*.

[17] Minutes of the Shangani Reserve Council, 6 August 1945 and appended correspondence, *ibid*.

open stores in the Reserve; that they should be shown the way back to their towns as Natives are prevented from opening stores in European areas.' They demanded that 'Government be asked to provide more land for the growing native population, pointing out that large areas of land were occupied by but few Europeans.' Chief Sivalo spoke against destocking and chief Dakamela demanded additional winter grazing areas. The meeting refused to elect councillors:

> There was a feeling of distrust and fear that the Native Commissioner did not represent the views of the people, but that the Native Commissioners made the decisions, using the Councils to pretend that the decisions were the wish of the people. The inadequate medical treatment available to such a large district was the subject of strong comment.[18]

On the second day, Chief Sivalo 'spoke on the recently formed branch of the Matabeleland Home Society and asked if certain matters could be discussed'. The chiefs, in short, were seeking to replace official forms of representation. Representatives of the Home Society had visited the Reserve shortly before the Council meeting and had promised that the Society would take up all the issues bothering the chiefs – the lowness of their own salaries; the constraints on their authority; the need for clinics, hospitals and schools; the need for more land to accomodate evictees and to avoid de-stocking; the need, in short, for a just deal for Matabeleland.[19]

In fact, the Shangani Reserve chiefs had long been supporters of the Matabeleland Home Society. Some of them had been involved with the pre-war movement to restore the Ndebele Kingship; in 1945 all Shangani 'chiefs, headmen and elders of the Amandebele' backed the Society's demand that Ndebele royals be buried near Mzilikazi's grave at Entumbane; Chief Myinga Dakamela became a Vice-President of the Society in 1945; the great MHS conference of December 1945, which organized a pilgrimage to Mzilikazi's grave, and which called for a Chiefs' Assembly in Matabeleland, was attended by Dakamela and Mabhikwa. By 1948, the MHS had moved under the influence of its executive secretary, Sipambaniso Manyoba Khumalo, to a more radical political position. It had added questions of eviction and destocking to its long concern with Ndebele traditional issues. This made the society the ideal ally for the conservative radicals of the Shangani Reserve.[20]

When the chiefly members of the Shangani Reserve Council and their followers met in June 1949:

> they declined to elect new members. The principal speakers were the chiefs and previously elected members of the Council while the rest of the people present merely nodded approval. They stated one after the other that they could see no need of a Council, that they thought that they might be committed to matters which they would be unable to decide, that they already paid enough taxes, that Native Commissioners wished to hide behind Councils and pretend that they were carrying out the wishes of the people, that they had been told that the dip tanks belonged to the people yet they had to pay 1/- per beast and were arrested if some of the cattle got lost and did not dip. The highlight of the meeting was 'We have never seen the constitution of the Native Council but the Matabeleland

---

[18] Minutes of the Shangani Reserve Council, 22 and 23 June 1948; NC to PNC, 6 July 1948, *ibid*.

[19] PNC to CNC, 17 July 1948, *ibid*.

[20] 'Matabele Home Society', S 2584/4251. Sipambaniso, the son of one of the earliest women property holders in Bulawayo and a member of the royal family, was involved in the 1948 general strike. Through him the Shangani Chiefs were linked with all the important elements in Bulawayo Ndebele politics.

Home Society had a constitution which is being taken to the High Court in Bulawayo and the Government will be forced to recognise the MHS as the "Voice of the People".'[21]

The Native Commissioner discovered that one of the previously elected members of the Council, Mguni, was now secretary of the local MHS branch; that Sipambaniso had held several meetings in the Reserve 'and my chiefs and headmen have been invited to attend meetings and join the society. To my knowledge, Chiefs Sihlangu, Solomon, Nkalakatha and Madliwa have attended these meetings and are probably members of the society ... There is no doubt that these people are in touch with the subversive elements in Bulawayo ... That these meetings held by the MHS are political is clear from the topics discussed, i.e. more land for Africans, destocking, labour for repairs to roads, Land Apportionment and the exclusion of European traders.' His Dip Supervisor and Land Development Officer had received letters asking them to attend meetings of the MHS 'to discuss dip tank affairs as there is great dissatisfaction'.[22]

For the next two years, the influence of the Matabeleland Home Society dominated Shangani politics. In March 1949, an MHS meeting in the Reserve decided to send Reverend E. Gwebu and Makuni Mabhena as its representatives to a meeting with the Secretary of Native Affairs. They were to raise 'treatment of Chiefs and Headmen', education, clinics, destocking. 'The subject of destocking is always discussed at meetings'.[23] When the meeting took place, it was attended by Chief Dakamela, who urged that 'there was urgent need for elevating the standard of education to Standard VI' and that government should set up a school in the Reserve. Instead of destocking, 'where possible cattle be allowed to move to cattle posts or grazing areas which at present are not being utilised.'[24] In November 1950 'a meeting of all Chiefs, Headmen and followers' insisted that they did not want a Council. 'The majority are members of the MHS and they have asked that the Society be recognised as the medium of expression.'[25]

The Native Commissioner was scornful of the idea. 'The MHS no more represent the bulk of the people than does the Queens Club or the Sons of England represent the majority of the people of Southern Rhodesia.'[26] On the other hand, if only the chiefs themselves could be separated from the MHS and encouraged to take on their 'traditional' role as spokesmen, that would be fine. When, in January 1951, a further meeting declared that it neither wished for a Council nor representation by the MHS, but asked 'that the chiefs be recognised as their mouthpieces', the Native Commissioner and Provincial Native Commissioner hastened to agree. So did the Assistant Secretary, Administration, who wrote in February 1951 that 'if we could foster this attitude and build up the chiefs it would go a long way to overcome the many demagogic Native associations, societies, etc who allege they represent Native interests.' Local officials declared that recognition of the chiefs was particularly important since 'considerable numbers of Natives are to be moved into the Shangani District' and these might bring undesirable politics. But 'if the authority of the chiefs is fostered then we in this district will be in a strong position'.[27]

Thereafter, the MHS faded away. Sipambaniso died in 1952. More populist bodies,

---

[21]  Quarterly Report, Nkayi, June 1949, S 1618.
[22]  Quarterly Report, Nkayi, June 1949, S 1618.
[23]  'MHS. Deputation to the Secretary of Native Affairs', April 1949, S 2584/4251.
[24]  Note on meeting, June 1949, *ibid*.
[25]  ANC Nkayi, to NC Lupane, 28 November 1950. S 2797/2453.
[26]  NC Lupane to PNC, 5 December 1950, *ibid*.
[27]  NC Lupane to PNC, 10 January 1951; Assistant Secretary, Administration, to PNC, 12 February 1951; PNC to NC, Lupane, 21 March 1951, *ibid*.

like Benjamin Burombo's African Voice Association took up rural grievances. The Rhodesian administration succeeded in separating the Shangani chiefs from formal politics. They made increasing use of the chiefs against the protest movements initiated in Nkayi and Lupane by evictees. But there was a price to be paid for this alliance. The chiefs might want to impose discipline upon their new subjects, but they were no more enthusiastic than before about many aspects of official policy, especially destocking. Using the chiefs in Nkayi and Lupane really meant that destocking could not be carried out there.

## Official Uses of the Chiefs

As early as 1945, the Native Commissioner, Shangani, was urging that chiefs should be chosen carefully and given 'real and extended authority over their people. We have the organization but still lack the leaders among the people themselves.' In 1946, NC Cockcroft began the complicated business of demarcating the Reserve 'into chiefs' areas to establish tribal control which is sadly lacking owing to the present confusion'. By 1947, the demarcation was complete and everyone in the Reserve had been registered as belonging to the chief in whose area they resided. In 1948 efforts were being made to sub-divide the chiefs' areas into bounded headmanships. This invented 'traditional' structure was in place to receive the evictees from Matobo, Filabusi and Essexvale.[28]

In 1952 the Native Commissioner was able to rejoice in the establishment of a Provincial Chiefs' Assembly. 'For the natives it means that they have a channel through which they can communicate their views. With this facility the necessity for Associations and Societies has fallen away and they should very soon become moribund.' In 1953 the NC, Nkayi, rejoiced in the success of this strategy. The Assembly offered 'a traditional avenue'; even the Filabusi evictees had merely asked for 'a chief of their own' so that they could fit into the system.[29] Soon the district officials were praising their chiefs. In Lupane, Chief Mabhikwa was 'virile, autocratic, inclined to be selfish, but useful'; in Nkayi, Chiefs Nkalakatha and Dakamela were Master Farmers and strong advocates of progressive agriculture. In 1957 both were rewarded with medals at the Royal Indaba in the Matopos.[30]

These chiefs stood by the government during the crisis of Land Husbandry. They banned nationalist meetings in the Reserves. In Lupane in 1961:

> Chiefs and headmen have remained loyal to the Government during a very difficult period and have carried out their duties well ... A few months ago chief Mabigwa gave this Department strong support when there was fairly widespread opposition to the Land Husbandry Act. He is a stern disciplinarian and is very intolerant of any defiance on the part of his people.[31]

Richard John Powell, who was posted to Lupane in October 1961, later recalled that 'the district was slightly subversive. They have an outstanding chief called Mabikwa. He is a great disciplinarian. His people had been defying him over the Land Husbandry Act. There'd been a period without an N.C. and I think he felt slightly let down. He was keen to prosecute.' Powell brought in an officer from the Ministry of Justice to set up emergency hearings and this 'very quickly restored law and order in Mabikwa's area. Mabikwa was most appreciative ... He had no time for lack of discipline and I am afraid

---

[28] Annual Reports, Shangani Reserve, 1945, 1946, 1947, 1948.
[29] Annual Report, Shangani, 1952; Nkayi, 1953.
[30] Annual Reports, Lupane, 1955, S 2827/2/2/2; Nkayi, 1957, S 2827 2/2/5.
[31] Annual Report, Lupane, 1961.

Lupane was undisciplined at that time ... It's a peculiar district. It's made up largely of resettled Africans and they don't seem to have the roots of people who sort of have grown up traditionally in an area.'[32]

In Nkayi in 1961, the chiefs 'acquitted themselves like men'. The Native Commissioner thought that they might 'not be able to keep on doing so if they were not given effective protection against nationalism. 'We will be in a sorry state if we lose the loyalty of these men.'[33]

But the chiefs also pursued their own agenda. This was clearest in the case of Mabhikwa. When he came into Lupane, Mabhikwa brought with him a herd of 550 cattle. He had negotiated for the grant of a thousand acres of land on which to settle his immediate followers and to graze his herd. The Assistant Native Commissioner, Lupane, did not at first welcome Mabhikwa's arrival. 'He cannot possibly pasture all these cattle on his 1000 acres,' he wrote in July 1946, 'nor should he be allowed to try to do so. I recommend that he be limited to 100 head of cattle. Other Natives in the area are being limited to 20 head. Mabhikwa has been warned that he will not be allowed to place his cattle with members of his following and so evade his limit.' Mabhikwa 'has ploughed down an entire valley which wanders through the land selected by him, and he would have liked us to follow the line of his lands, adding what he considered suitable grazing land, regardless of symmetry and other people's rights. This I was not prepared to allow.' But the Assistant Native Commissioner's severity soon had to be relaxed. Other officials stressed the advantage of Mabhikwa being able to gather his people around him and to maintain discipline. In the event, he kept most of his cattle or lent them out to followers.[34]

Thereafter, Mabhikwa took his own line on government agrarian policy and, in particular, stoutly resisted destocking. In 1955, 'he publicly opposed the increase in poll tax and was decidedly luke-warm about – if not anti – the Land Husbandry Act'.[35] If, as we have seen, he came to view Land Husbandry as a matter of discipline, Mabhikwa became famous for his opposition to culling. In 1958, it was noted that he 'is feared and has a firm hold', and also that he had 'achieved some notoriety' by 'expressing views about destocking' in the African *Home News*.[36] Indeed, that paper had carried on 15 June 1957 a report of the Matabeleland Chiefs Conference. Mabhikwa said that destocking in his area 'was being done by two distinct forces simultaneously, namely the Government and the tsetse fly'; he was so persuasive that the Minister of Native Affairs, 'obviously moved', promised to come to Lupane himself and undertook that meanwhile no destocking would take place. On June 22, the *News* hailed Mabhikwa as 'a well-respected chief', one of the few loved by his followers. On 8 November 1958, the *Home News* reported that Mabhikwa had walked out of the Chiefs Conference in disgust over destocking. 'Chief Mabikwa loves cattle, and for the sake of keeping his cattle he might even be prepared to relinquish his position of chief. It is understood that he was deeply hurt when the subject of the reduction of cattle was brought up at the Chiefs Conference.'[37]

Mabhikwa was not called upon to choose between his chieftainship and his cattle. He had become much too important an ally of the administration for that to happen. He was regarded as 'a fine old African ... a true Matabele'.[38] Ironically, as we saw in

[32] Interview with Richard John Powell, 3 July, 21 August and 5 September 1978, Oral/22, National Archives, Harare.
[33] Annual Report, Nkayi, 1961, S 2827/2/2/8.
[34] ANC Lupane to PNC, 24 July and 7 August 1946, S 2806/1995.
[35] Annual Report, Lupane, 1956, S 2827/2/2/4.
[36] Annual Report, Lupane, 1958, S 2827/2/2/6.
[37] *Home News*, 15 June and 22 June 1957; 8 November 1958.
[38] Interview with J.F. Davis-Ziegler, St Luke's, Lupane, 24 January 1995. There is a striking photograph of the old Mabhikwa and an admiring biography in D.K. Parkinson, 'Lupane Notes', *NADA*, 1980, pp.142–3.

previous chapters, the Filabusi evictees refused to accept him as chief because he was not descended from one of the nineteeenth-century regimental chiefs. But to the whites he was the very archetype of the traditional Ndebele chief. 'Mabikwa's a real character', declared Native Commissioner Powell. 'He speaks very little English, but if you can speak Sindebele you realise what a character he was.' A later Commissioner, Noel Hunt, included Mabhikwa among 'the hereditary aristocracy' which he so much admired:

> They'd been ruling these people ever since they emerged from the Congolese forests ... They know how to rule blacks. When the white man came to Rhodesia, you didn't have to consult any Mashona or Karanga or anybody else at all because they'd all been conquered and defeated by the Amandabele. The de facto rulers of every square inch of land and the de facto rulers of every single head of cattle in Rhodesia were the Amandebele.[39]

Love of his own cattle seemed only natural in a strong Ndebele chief like Mabhikwa. He was able to influence Land Husbandry assessments. A meeting on Zone A1 in Lupane noted that there had been no previous destocking there but that the African members 'consider the present stocking rate satisfactory.' The white officials sided with Mabhikwa, accepting his estimate that the zone could carry 5,000 head of stock and over-ruling the representative of the Natural Resources Board who wanted a much lower figure.[40] Oral informants today recall Mabhikwa's achievement:

> This place was never pegged [remembers Mr Magagula]. That was because of resistance from Mabhikwa. We were extremely lucky regarding destocking. It was government policy but in this area it was defused because Chief Mabhikwa owned lots of cattle and he was outspoken and refused.[41]

Mabhikwa was the most outstanding example, but other chiefs also managed to protect their people against destocking, and this part of the Land Husbandry pro- gramme was never carried through in the Shangani. The evictees lost up to half of their herds from the poisonous plant *mkhawuzane*, disease and wild animals when they moved into the area; thereafter, many beasts died from drought and some from tsetse. But at least the authoritarianism of the chiefs was balanced by their successful resistance to destocking.[42]

## The Development of Rural Nationalism

By 1961, as we have seen, the chiefs confronted violent mass nationalism. The adminis- tration's predictions, a bare ten years before, that political associations would wither and die now seemed ridiculous. Yet right up to 1959, district Annual Reports for Nkayi and Lupane repeated that there was little formal political activity in the Shangani. Where had mass nationalism come from?

To this there are two extreme and completely opposed answers. The official answer was that nationalism was a poison from outside. Administrators were, of course, aware of the past political activism of the evictees. But by the late 1950s, they had persuaded

---

[39] Interview with Richard John Powell, 3 July, 21 August and 5 September 1978, Oral/22; interview with Noel Hunt, 27 November 1983, Oral/240, National Archives, Harare.

[40] Assessment Committee report, Zone A1, Lupane, 11 June 1956, S 2827/1/1.

[41] Interview with Antony Magagula, Lupanda, 20 December 1994.

[42] The only area in which destocking was carried out was in the relatively small area of Chief Menyezwa in Lupane.

themselves that the evictees had settled down to farm and that they were still too divided from the 'originals' to be able to come together in a nationalist movement. 'I find the inhabitants of this Reserve pleasant people', wrote Native Commissioner Bisset, adding that political associations 'are not inspired by the Reserve people but are importations from the urban areas.'[43] In 1957, when the African National Congress was refounded, the Lupane Annual Report declared that 'none of the African political or semi-political parties have as yet any following among the permanently settled rural people'. In 1958 the Native Commissioner believed that 'the majority of the people are politically dormant [and] there is no indication that Congress is active in the district'. In Nkayi, too, there were no Congress activities reported. As we have seen, in 1959, when a state of emergency was declared, Congress banned, and its national and local leaders detained, no-one was detained in Nkayi or Lupane. 'The emergency was shrugged off as being one of those things.'[44] The Shangani seemed an island of rural peace in a sea of political troubles.

Soon, however, nationalist serpents were introduced into the Eden. In 1959, the 'hard-core' of the Congress restrictees were sent to Gokwe; later that year the Gokwe group was split up 'and some of the worst ones were sent to Lupane'. Native Commissioner Powell, who had been dealing with the Gokwe restrictees, 'sort of followed' the hard core to western Lupane. Powell found the restrictees 'far worse than anything we had anticipated and it made a complete difference to life'. His Head Messenger told him: 'These are wild animals, they are not human. Why does the Government bother with these people? Shouldn't we just go out at night with a shotgun?'[45] Noel Hunt found that one of the restrictees, James Robert Chikerema, 'exuded such an atmosphere of evil that I couldn't stay in the same room with him. I used to sweat and the hair on the back of my neck used to stand up. ... He made me wish I was wearing a crucifix so that I could hold it.'[46]

These were, of course, wildly paranoiac responses to the ANC restrictees.[47] But to the Native Department they provided some explanation for the sudden change from the passivity of 1959 to the resistance of 1961. 'In Lupane,' recorded the 1961 Annual Report, 'the restricted persons seem to have influenced many neighbouring farmers. There was an active branch of the National Democratic Party in the Native Purchase Area and frequent political meetings were held. Elsewhere in the district political agitators encouraged opposition to the implementation of the Land Husbandry Act. People ploughed outside their allocations and ploughed contours and grass strips. Excessive intimidation was resorted to.' Nkayi was too far away for the influence of the restrictees to account for the new 'arrogant and reckless' contempt for authority. Nevertheless, here too it was 'the lies and irresponsible promises of the nationalists' which the Native Commissioner blamed. In short, the trouble was imported from the towns. 'Considerable importance seems to have been attached by the NDP [National Democratic Party] to their operations in this district. Several visits to the district were made by Joshua Nkomo.'[48]

A very different account is given by some long-time nationalists in the Shangani. They see nationalism there as very deep-rooted and with a local history of more than a decade before the explosions of 1961. In this view, the NDP and its successor, the Zimbabwe African Peoples Union (Zapu), were merely the latest in a series of 'parties'

[43] Quarterly Report, Nkayi, June 1949, S 1618.
[44] Annual Reports, Lupane and Nkayi, 1957, 1958, 1959, S 2827 2/2/5-7.
[45] Interview with Richard John Powell, 1978, Oral/22.
[46] Interview with Noel Hunt, 1983, Oral/20.
[47] Terence Ranger visited the Lupane restrictees in 1961, together with the African Sisters of the Church of St Francis, and recalls sitting around the camp fire singing Methodist hymns!
[48] Annual Reports, Lupane and Nkayi, 1961.

to which nationalists in Nkayi and Lupane had owed allegiance. Thus Julia Kimeta Sibanda describes how she was a member of 'the party' – the African National Voice – in Bubi before her eviction to Nkayi in 1950.[49] 'When I got here I found some people who were not of the party so I had to recruit them. No woman was not allowed to join the party. They wanted all women to join in to make a voice. I said to women, let's all join for independence.' She was first arrested in 1957 as 'dangerous to the public'; thereafter she held office in Congress, the NDP and Zapu. Throughout, her struggle was against state authoritarianism, if not always successfully. In this view, Shangani nationalism bided its time. It gave notice that if Land Husbandry were implemented, there would be resistance. Meanwhile, it was necessary to bring in the 'originals' alongside the evictees. By 1961, it was ready for confrontation with the state.

Opposite though they were, these two views could sometimes be combined. Thus the Native Commissioner, Nkayi, asked himself 'just why the district was so receptive to the lies and irresponsible promises of the nationalists', and replied:

> I think the main causes are land shortage and the fact that during the 1950s a large proportion of disgruntled people were moved here from land problem spots such as Filabusi, Fort Rixon and the like. These people have been particularly robust supporters of subversion and have seriously infected the original inhabitants of the district with it.[50]

Nevertheless, neither view can be sustained. Plainly, nationalist opposition in the Shangani was not suddenly fomented from outside in 1961. But equally, there was no easy nor smoothly continuous development of an internal nationalism.

## The African National Voice

Before they were evicted from Filabusi, Fort Rixon, the Matopos and Essexvale, many of the people who ended up in Nkayi and Lupane had been supporters of the African National Voice Association. The leader of the Voice, Benjamin Burombo, had been concerned with evictions into the Shangani since 1950. In that year he tried to help Africans living on Westcote Farm, Nyamandhlovu, to avoid being evicted to Lupane. He failed in the end and had to advise them in December 1950 to 'obey the instructions of the Government', promising them that he would assist them when they got to their new homes.[51] But Burombo had more success in the Matopos, Filabusi and Essexvale, where the Voice called in lawyers from Bulawayo who were able to frustrate evictions until government could push through amendments to the Land Apportionment Act.[52]

As we have seen, the evictees made much play with their Ndebele identity. Unlike the Matabeleland Home Society, however, the Voice was a proto-nationalist organization, stronger outside Matabeleland than within it. At its Annual General Meeting in March 1952, the twenty-six chiefs who attended came from Gwelo, Fort Victoria and

---

[49] The 'party' was Benjamin Burombo's Voice Association, though Julia Kimeta herself insists that it was the Industrial and Commercial Workers Union (ICU) led by Masotsha Ndlovu. Ndlovu, leader of the ICU in the 1930s, had come out of political retirement to join Burombo in the late 1940s.

[50] Annual Report, Nkayi, 1961, S 2827 2/2/7.

[51] Native Affairs Memorandum 52, Special Branch, 2 January 1951. A collection of these Memoranda is now lodged with the University of Natal in Durban. We are grateful to Professor Philip Warhurst for making his notes and photocopies available.

[52] The best treatment of Burombo's career and of the Voice is Ngwabi Bhebe, *Benjamin Burombo. African Politics in Zimbabwe 1947–1958* (Harare, College Press, 1989).

Salisbury; officials elected at the meeting came from Bikita, Rusape, Salisbury, Buhera, Zaka, Mutare and Chipinga. Matabeleland was represented only by a provincial secretary, Isaac Sibanda.[53] But the Voice admirably represented the radical Christian progressive identity of the evictees. Burombo frequently quoted the Bible, asserting that 'if Government arrested him it would be arresting the Bible'; God had laid down that each nation should have its own country and Africa was intended for Africans. Instead of evicting Africans, the government should send Europeans back to their homelands. He instituted what was to become the regular nationalist practice of opening his meetings with the African hymn '*Ishe Komborera Africa*', rather than with 'God Save the King'. A Voice member in Filabusi told the Native Commissioner in February 1951 that 'it was against the law of Jesus to move them'. Another added that 'the removal was contrary to British justice', and Burombo's ability to make use of Bulawayo lawyers and his promises to take the issue to the British government spoke to the modern sensibility of the evictees.[54]

By May, 1951 the Rhodesian government was seriously alarmed that the Voice would be able to combine strike action in Bulawayo with resistance to eviction in the rural areas. Burombo was hailed as a 'saviour' by the Rhodesdale Africans who were threatened with eviction to Gokwe; the Voice was very strong in Filabusi, where there was a 'grim and serious' determination to resist removal to the Shangani. In July 1952, Burombo called members of the association from Filabusi, Rhodesdale and the Matopos to Bulawayo; he 'condemned Lupani and Kana', and promised them that there would be no evictions for five years.[55] In August 1952, Voice members from Filabusi and the Matopos attended a protest meeting against eviction in Essexvale, excluding police from the gathering. In this way, a Central Matabeleland protest movement was being coordinated.[56]

But the moment of truth was at hand. On 31 August 1952, a strong police force 'descended without any warning on a number of kraals' in Filabusi, the inhabitants 'being somewhat overwhelmed by the force brought to evict them'. The police moved on to the Matopos and to Rhodesdale. Essexvale Africans, cowed by this example, began to move voluntarily.[57] After this, the Rhodesian Government stopped worrying about Burombo. They mocked his protestations at a Voice meeting in November 1952 'assuring Africans removed from Filabusi, Hadane [Essexvale], Matobo and Rhodesdale that they hadn't been forgotten'. By mid-1953, the Special Branch was confident that Burombo's failure to prevent eviction and destocking had caused widespread disillusion. 'He has completely lost face with his followers and presents a rather dismal picture compared to his heyday in 1951.'[58]

Oral evidence shows that many evictees did not blame Burombo, whom they believed to have done his best to help them. Still, their eviction had certainly been a serious defeat for the Voice. And it was difficult for them to resume political activity in their new homes. Most evictees had quite enough to do to fell trees and clear bush for farming. Voice radicals were scattered:

> I was active in the Voice in Bulawayo [recalls Mkandla Maragwa] ... We continued with the Voice after the evictions. The issues were pure politics ... They took those who were vocal members first – to show people that their leaders

[53] Native Affairs Memorandum 64, March 1952.
[54] Native Affairs Memoranda, 53, 54, 56.
[55] Native Affairs Memoranda, 56, 65, 66, 67, 68.
[56] Native Affairs Memorandum 69.
[57] Native Affairs Memorandum 70.
[58] Native Affairs Memoranda 73, 79 and 84. Burombo promised the evictees that a commission would be set up consisting of three Voice members and two government representatives to tour Lupane, Nkayi and Gokwe. No such commission was formed.

couldn't win. They split the leaders up, sending some to Nkayi and some to Tsholotsho. We leaders tried to keep in contact with one another, sending all communication via Bulawayo, using the structure of the Voice. Burombo didn't come out to Lupane because the movement was restricted but we ... held and attended underground meetings. But it was very difficult ... We were defeated within a couple of years. When we first settled, they put strangers as our neighbours so there could be no strong communication. They did it deliberately. We soon came to have no power and we were just abiding.[59]

Over and above all these difficulties was the fact that the Voice programme was designed for evictees and not for 'locals'. 'We were fighting to go back where we came from,' says Maragwa, himself from Filabusi. 'We were not happy being here.' There could only be Voice organization in the Shangani in areas where the evictees were particularly concentrated.

Despite all this, there *was* some Voice activity, especially in Nkayi north of the Shangani, where many Filabusi evictees had been located, and where a Filabusi Zionist church leader was also a Voice activist. 'A few loquacious leaders of the African Voice appear to have a certain amount of influence over a fairly large number of people in the area north of the Gwelo River,' wrote the Native Commissioner, Nkayi in 1955.[60] One of these 'loquacious leaders' was Lakatshona Samuel Ndebele who is remembered by people in Nkayi as a pioneer of nationalism, and who is perhaps the outstanding example of political continuity in the Shangani. Lakatshona was from chief Maduna's area in Filabusi and had been a key organizer in the Industrial and Commercial Workers Union there. He worked closely with Masotsha Ndhlovu and later with Benjamin Burombo. In 1952 he was moved to northern Nkayi. He was a leading figure in opposition to contours in the mid-1950s; he went on to become NDP and then Zapu chairman for northern Nkayi and to spend several stints in detention.[61]

Lakatshona and others managed to organize a series of Voice meetings in northern Nkayi. In March 1954, Burombo himself met Filabusi evictees in the Kana valley.[62] In May of the same year, the *Bantu Mirror* reported a 'huge crowd' at a Voice meeting in north Nkayi. Burombo demanded that clinics be built 'to fight against fever', and urged that, instead of land being restricted, Africans should be given more and better land.[63] In 1955, as we have seen, the area of the Filabusi evictees was proclaimed as Zone A1 under the Land Husbandry Act. The Native Commissioner reported that 'opposition was met with by the natives refusing to point out their lands. This opposition was inspired by the African Voice Association'. In October 1955, local Voice activists called a meeting to coordinate resistance. In Ngwabi Bhebe's summary of a police report:

Many of those who attended the meeting were the same people who had been uprooted from Filabusi and dumped in the Shangani Reserve. The assembled people said that they had come from Filabusi and had been given land to plough. In order to show their defiance against the Land Husbandry Act and the Native Department which applied the Act, 'they were going to extend their existing lands without authority and that they would make their lands as big as they liked.' They declared that they were not going to have anything to do with the LDOs, the Demonstrators and other agricultural officers. 'One person said that

[59] Interview with Mkandla Maragwa, Mzola, 2 December 1994.
[60] Annual Report, Nkayi, 1955, S 2827 2/2/2.
[61] Interview with Lakatshona Samuel Ndebele and Andrea Mhlanga, Gwelutshena, 5 December 1994.
[62] Native Affairs Memorandum 91.
[63] *Bantu Mirror*, 15 May 1954.

the Native Commissioner should be called upon to take his Demonstrators away. If he refused, they should be told to go back to the district they were born in and teach their fathers how to plough and leave the people in Shangani Reserve alone.'

Those attending the meeting left their registration cards at home and used Voice membership cards as their only proof of identity.[64]

By this time, Voice activists in Nkayi were far outrunning the parent association. In 1955, Burombo himself was ill; only three people turned up at a Voice meeting in Bulawayo in April; young radicals in the towns were turning to the Youth League. Only in Nkayi did the name of the Voice still mean anything much. Voice activists there were still opposing pegging of lands, movement away from river valleys, etc., in 1956 and 1957.[65] By this time, the Native Department had come to regard the Filabusi adherence to the Voice as almost traditional rather than political. Native Commissioners constantly reported from both Lupane and Nkayi that there were 'no political activities'. And in 1958, even the Voice loyalists gave up. In March of that year, Voice delegates from Nkayi came into Bulawayo to inquire into the association's finances. They went on to meet a Bulawayo radical, Gibson Frazer Sibanda, to discuss with him the possibility of opening a branch of the African National Congress.[66] In April 1958, Burombo died.

It is clear, then, that however important leaders like Lakatshona Samuel Ndebele turned out to be in the rise of Shangani nationalism, the Voice did not initiate the general nationalist movement in Nkayi and Lupane. Its history was not merely a matter of succession from the Voice to Congress to the National Democratic Party and at last to Zapu. By the time of Burombo's death hardly any of the 'originals' had been brought into the Voice. We have seen from Maragwa's testimony that there certainly were Voice militants in Lupane, but by 1956, the Native Commissioner could remark that: 'the district has its quota of agitators and potential trouble-makers [but] there do not seem to be any organized followings of any of the known African associations'.[67] Even in Nkayi, Voice opposition was limited to one of the Land Husbandry zones. Yet Voice activists *did* introduce some key nationalist ideas into the Shangani and some of them went on to be important leaders of the later nationalist movements.

## The Movement into Congress and the National Democratic Party

The Voice had been carried into niches in Nkayi and Lupane by groups of evictees. The entry of the subsequent nationalist parties worked rather differently. They began pre-eminently as urban organizations and news of them had to seep into the countryside. The first of the series of modern nationalist movements was the revived African National Congress, formed in September 1957. It was led by Joshua Nkomo and had an active Bulawayo branch. But in the Matabeleland countryside it was strong only in Nkomo's own home area in Matobo. Its entry into the Shangani was uneven.

Nevertheless, some oral informants date their consciousness of politics to the formation of the ANC. Many of these were Shangani labour migrants in Bulawayo. Thus Timothy Mthethwa of Mateme in Nkayi says that 'it was in Bulawayo that I joined politics. I joined the ANC and became branch secretary.' Mthethwa did not return home during the ANC period, staying in Bulawayo and becoming chairman of the Radio

[64] Assistant Constable Tongesayi, 'Report of a Meeting held at Ngomambi Dip, Bava, 3 October 1955', cited in Bhebe, *Benjamin Burombo*, pp. 107–108.

[65] Annual Reports, Nkayi, 1956 and 1957, S 2827 2/2/6 and 7.

[66] *Bantu Mirror*, 24 March 1958. For the career of Sibanda see Ranger, *Voices From the Rocks*.

[67] Annual Report, Lupane, 1956, S 2827 2/2/4.

Workers Union.[68] But other labour migrants carried the news of the ANC and its message back to the villages. 'Politics started in Tshongokwe in 1957,' says Douglas Siso, an evictee into Lupane from Bubi. 'I still remember being visited by Sikwili Moyo ... We were told that after independence we'd be free and could do whatever we wanted. Our first activities were to conscientise people on the aims and objectives of the party.'[69] Micah Mpofu of Manomano remembers that 'the political influence came in 1957 as far as I'm concerned. The political influence came because we were enslaved and wanted to be free. The African National Congress came here first, from the urban areas. People could come on the buses and alert the locals, talking to people and educating them about politics. In the ANC time the political talk was in the villages'. There were not yet formal party meetings nor branch structures.[70] The ANC period in Nkayi and Lupane was one of gradual establishment of a political consciousness invisible to the Native Commissioners.

Urban labour migrants came from the 'original' inhabitants of the Shangani as well as from the evictees. So urban political experience gradually began to change the balance of political radicalism in Nkayi and Lupane. In the Kana valley in Nkayi, for instance, the local Nyai and Lozwi were first introduced to nationalist politics by the Filabusi evictees:

> When the Filabusi people came here [recall the Nyai Elias Sibanda and the Lozwi Daniel Ncube] politics wasn't active amongst us. The Filabusi people capitalized on that so that most of them became political leaders, chairmen, despising us. Monies were misused, some got rich through us.

But Malandu Ncube, a Kana Lozwi, describes how he himself got 'this political influence from political meetings in Bulawayo' and that when he returned home 'the idea of the Filabusi people leading us had to vanish.'[71]

The ANC was banned in February 1959 with no visible repercussions in the Shangani, but by the time its successor, the National Democratic Party, was formed in January 1960, many of the people of Nkayi and Lupane were ready for organized nationalism. This was partly a matter of the pressures of Land Husbandry Act implementation; it was partly a matter of the seeping through of nationalist ideas; and, at times, it led to a growing commonality of interest between the 'originals' and evictees.

In October 1995, we interviewed a spokesman of the 'originals' and a spokesman of the evictees in Gampinya in northern Nkayi, who explained these changes. The evictee spokesman, P.M. Moyo, had come from Filabusi and been a Voice activist: 'We were very involved with Burombo. He stayed at my father's home and we participated fully in political activities. The old people could even brew beer for Burombo. When we came here these people were not politically active.' The Filabusi people were told by the Native Department how primitive the 'originals' were; the 'originals' were told how wicked the evictees were. 'These people here were regarded as very good,' says Moyo, 'while we were regarded as very bad people. But on arrival we united and lit the fire.' The 'original' spokesman, Paul Sibanda, agreed: 'We were being destocked, they were being evicted. It was the same, so we decided to join and resist again.' Moyo summed up: 'We defeated this divide and rule ... When political activities started, all of us participated and these people here also went to prison and some died.' It was, however, a slow process. The Filabusi men arrived in 1952, but the 'originals' were not drawn into

---

[68] Interview with Timothy Mthethwa, Mateme, 1 December 1995.
[69] Interview with Douglas Siso, Bulawayo, 8 April 1996.
[70] Interview with Micah Mpofu, Manomano, 17 October 1995.
[71] Interview with Elias Sibanda, Daniel Ncube and Malandu Ncube, Kana, 28 November and 5 December 1995.

the Voice nor even into the ANC. 'The first party here was the National Democratic Party in 1961.' It had taken nearly ten years for the various peoples of Gampinya to combine and even then Moyo had to be the organizer 'because there was no political activity previously. With the NDP there was no district. I was the only one. Later, people joined and district structures were formed.'[72]

Moyo's NDP message was 'about we Africans being oppressed. We had no freedom.' This was a message which had begun to resonate with the 'originals'. They continued to insist that only they *knew* the land and that incomers had to subscribe to their rituals for fertility and rain. But the evictees and subsequent nationalist teaching had given them a new idea – that Africans *owned* the land. One 'original' told us that, intoxicated with this new idea, and realising that the whites would not like it, he had gone into the forest and whispered to the trees, 'We own this land.' Soon all the kraalheads in Gampinya were members of the NDP. The same thing began to happen elsewhere so that the NDP was much more widespread than the Voice or Congress had been. Its organizers realized that they must bring the 'originals' in. In Mlume Ward in Nkayi, for instance, the descendants of the original Sikhobokhobo migration had been 'only concerned with work and *isitshwala* [the maize staple] – we weren't aware that things were changing. All we thought about was our cattle.' But 'the political spirit crept in in the 1960s'. Headman Majaha, a Kalanga of the Sikhobokhobo migration, 'was very popular, people loved him. So when this political spirit was at its highest, people came to to him and said, "We know without you it will not succeed." They asked him to represent them and gave him party cards. The old man accepted and became NDP.'[73]

The NDP network was thinly spread over the Shangani. 'The NDP officials were very few,' says Josiah Ndhlovu of Malunku, 'so we covered a very large area.' They sold membership tickets and organized secret meetings in 'bushy places', once again taking advantage of the Shangani's dark forests.[74] Party members observed a similar discretion. 'In the 1960s', says Senzani Ngwenya, 'we were clandestinely active, we joined political parties and were given cards, which were hidden away somewhere, not to be seen.'[75] Yet there were several important nuclear zones of NDP activism, and later of Zapu, from which nationalism spread into the rest of the Shangani. All over the two districts, it was the areas where evictees were concentrated that became the most important foci of nationalism – the Filabusi and Fort Rixon concentrations in Mzola, the Bubi evictees in Tshongokwe, the Esigodini evictees in Mateme, the Filabusi concentrations north of the Shangani and along the Kana in Nkayi, and many other areas besides, all became centres of activism. However, a full understanding of how nationalism was localized in the Shangani requires a more detailed understanding of the history of such core areas. Below we focus on three such.

## Nuclear Areas of the NDP and Zapu: Lupanda

One of the key NDP zones in Lupane was the Lupanda Native Purchase Area. As we have seen, the western part of the original Shangani Reserve had been set apart for purchase by Master Farmers under the Land Apportionment Act of 1930. Before the Second World War, it remained very thinly populated by Lozwi, Tonga, Kalanga, Nambya and some Sili. After the war, farms began to be taken up by African entrepreneurs but many of the 'originals' remained on the land, some as lease-holders. And there was still

---

[72] Interview with P.M. Moyo and Paul Sibanda, Gampinya, 19 October 1995.
[73] Interviews with Headman Mlume and family, Nkoni, 2 October 1995; 'Headman' Mhlotshwa Majaha Moyo, 5 October 1995. Majaha was imprisoned and deposed for his pains.
[74] Interview with Josiah Ndlovu, Malunku, 6 March 1996.
[75] Interview with Senzani Ngwenya, Singwangombe, 21 February 1996.

plenty of wild bush in which to put unwanted men. In late 1959, seven of the ANC 'hard core' were sent there; in August 1960, these were joined by three more restrictees.

As we have seen, the Native Department demonised the ANC restrictees who were sent to western Lupane and held them responsible for corrupting the whole district. This was a grotesque overstatement but the restrictees did nevertheless play an important stimulating role. We are fortunate to have the personal account of one of them, Maurice Nyagumbo. He was sent to Lupane in August 1960 together with two colleagues. They found themselves in thick *gusu* and were afraid during their first night even to look for water for fear of wild animals. But soon they discovered that they were only about fifteen yards away from a borehole used by several NPA plot-holders. They were restricted to a fifteen-mile radius, which included shops and churches.

But they found a total 'lack of communication between us and the local farmers' who had been warned by the Native Commissioner that they would lose their plot titles if they helped the restrictees. Nyagumbo remembered that, 'The local farmers had been told that the restrictees were rapists and murderers who were being rusticated and should not be talked to.' He recalls that the restrictees had a hard time making connections with the locals. When Nyagumbo and his friends tried to join a beer drink all the men disappeared into the bush and the women and children into the house; when they went to the local Methodist church on a Sunday morning, everyone else broke off in the middle of a hymn and walked out.

But the ice began to break, according to Nyagumbo, when the restrictees had a fight with the Native Commissioner and his police. Local farmers offered to help pay for their defence, telling them how grateful they were to the restrictees 'for having beaten up what they called *umthakathi*, the devil'.[76] When the NC was transferred to Beit Bridge, the restrictees became local heroes. It was their opportunity:

> We now wanted to organise the whole area and to establish an NDP branch there. The first thing we wanted was to organise a big rally where NDP officials would be invited to speak ... the first political rally in this part of the country.

Thousands attended and listened to several NDP leaders from Bulawayo. A branch was established. Early in 1961, Joshua Nkomo himself visited Lupane. The restrictees asked the local branch to organize a resounding welcome for him, and 'every farmer turned out to greet Nkomo whom they had not seen before'. By May, when the restrictees were sent to Gokwe, the NDP was well established in Lupanda.[77]

Many aspects of Nyagumbo's account are endorsed by oral memory. Yona Dube came from Matobo to take up one of the Lupanda farms in 1952. He recalls:

> The ANC had its detainees near headman Lupahla's place. Malaba and myself were influenced by those detainees. Because of [the Native Department's] fear they'd influence me, their boundary was about 1 kilometre east of here, just across the river. This is when we joined politics. They allowed us to cross the river but they refused to allow the detainees to visit us. When we crossed over the river to this place it was at night to discuss matters. ... We visited them out of interest,

---

[76] *Umthakathi* is more commonly translated as 'witch'.

[77] Maurice Nyagumbo, *With the People. An Autobiography from the Zimbabwe Struggle* (London, Allison and Busby, 1980), chapter 14, 'Lupane Restriction Camp'. Nyagumbo blames his and other restrictees' initially cold reception in part on the fact that they were Shona speakers, and argues that locals believed that 'politics was a Shona way of life'. Questions of ethnicity do not arise in the accounts of Lupanda locals, and Nyagumbo certainly underestimates the previous political connections of the region. Some of the Lupanda activists had in fact already joined politics in town.

because we had complaints about our then government. That is when I joined and became a member. From there we went into the NDP.

Dube himself became organizing secretary and Malaba chair of the branch. Dube recruited members at church services, at boreholes – 'in fact any place with water could do'. He and Malaba 'formed branches as far as the Shangani', at St Luke's, along the Bubi river and in chief Mabhikwa's headquarters at Jotsholo. 'But all that was the work of the detention, all the branches were set up after the detainees were brought here.'[78] Thereafter Dube remained a political activist in Zapu, although 'the government was very rough, especially the Special Branch'. But 'you become a bit mad when you get involved in politics'. Even the Lozwi headman Lupahla became involved. As he remembers, 'NDP/Zapu was very strong in the Purchase Area. I myself was part of the struggle.'[79]

Japhet Gabheni Sibanda, chair of the Lupane Council after independence, gives an account of Lupanda nationalism which combines the influence of the restrictees with his own earlier political involvement and later activism. It well illustrates how the NDP spread out from the core areas of its formation into the Shangani:

I had already joined the NDP in 1961 and when I left [confinement] in Hwange I came home here [to Lupanda] and met with political detainees like Patrick Matimba, Maurice Nyagumbo, Henry Hamadziripi and others. During that time there were no party branches and districts, but I started organising for the party since I was given a bicycle to do the work. I travelled as far as Tshongokwe, where prominent people like Robert Mlala and Joseph Maseko joined. I even went as far as Tsholotsho, to chief Mathupula's area, where I mobilised the people there.[80]

In Tshongokwe, some 50 miles from the Lupanda detention centre, urban migrants had long been members of the ANC and NDP, but told of the detainees' 'critical influence on local politics'. Luta Inyati, an NDP member in Bulawayo recalls, 'Those influences converged – those detainees encouraged us to be very active.'[81]

### Core Areas: The Zinyangeni Nationalists

When Maurice Nyagumbo got to Gokwe he found that the branches there had been brought under the direction of Welshman Mabhena, the super-efficient NDP secretary of Nkayi district.[82] Welshman was a product of another NDP nucleus, the area around the London Missionary Society church and school at Zinyangeni. Today Zinyangeni is derelict, with the church in disrepair and the mission houses in ruins. Only the concrete base of Welshman Mabhena's house remains – the building itself was destroyed by Zanu Youth in the 1980s. It does not look like the powerhouse of Nkayi nationalism. And yet it was.

Welshman himself was born there. His Christian name reflected the influence of the early Welsh missionaries of the London Missionary Society, just as his career reflected their radical anti-imperialism. His father was an early LMS convert, itinerant preacher, cook and caretaker of the mission station in Nkayi, who eventually became minister at

---

78 Interview with Yona Dube, Lupanda, 22 February 1996.
79 Interview with Headman Joko Lupahla, Lupanda, 13 December 1996.
80 The citation is an extract from an interview between K.K. Inyathi and Japhet Gabheni Sibanda prepared for the council elections in the mid-1990s.
81 Interviews with Siponono Mlotshwa and Mr Dlakama, Ngombane, 27 February 1996 and Luta Inyati, Jotsholo, 3 March 1996.
82 Nyagumbo, *With the People*, p. 152.

Zinyangeni. He had been a supporter of the Industrial and Commercial Workers Union in the late 1920s and of the Matabele Home Society in the 1940s. Today Welshman asserts that 'my politics has just been a continuation of my father's work for the people'. Welshman himself went to South Africa to train as a teacher. He came back to the main LMS school at Inyathi in 1948, just as the parents of many pupils were being evicted from Bubi into the Shangani Reserve. Their essays on their return from their holidays were all about malaria and the death of cattle; the white headmaster thought that it was Welshman, rather than the experience of eviction, that underlay these subversive writings. Welshman left Inyathi and went back to Zinyangeni as a 'farmer'. Well-educated and a product of the LMS tradition of political critique, he joined the African National Congress. When the ANC was banned, Welshman invited the aged radical, Masotsha Ndhlovu – who had been an activist with the ICU, the Voice and the ANC – to come to speak at Zinyangeni as an inspiration to younger men. Welshman joined the NDP as soon as it was founded and by May 1961, when Nyagumbo arrived in Gokwe, had become the coordinator of a vigorous cluster of branches.[83]

Welshman's main ally and closest friend was Ronald Sibanda who had come to Zinyangeni as a teacher. Sibanda was a man of restless energy and fierce political commitment. He was secretary of the ANC branch which Welshman chaired, and became the most articulate spokesman of the NDP in Nkayi. Both men saw themselves as pre-eminently Ndebele. Sibanda later got into trouble within Zapu in Zambia for denouncing the 'Kalanga' faction. Both also saw themselves as modernizers and entrepreneurs. Before long Sibanda left teaching at Zinyangeni and opened a string of stores in Nkayi.[84]

The old LMS connection was useful to Mabhena and Sibanda. There had long been an LMS church at Chief Dakamela's; one of the teachers in the LMS school there was John Dakamela, who had studied at Hope Fountain under three pioneer nationalists, Robert Mugabe, Tennyson Hlabangana and Patrick Rubatika. Welshman was John's cousin. He often visited Dakamela, together with Ronald Sibanda and a third Zinyangeni activist, Sampson Ndebele. Usually they were trailed by police. The NDP was soon established at Dakamela's.[85]

These men emerged as spokesmen for Nkayi. In July 1960, Sampson Ndebele told the *Bantu Mirror* that 'the tribesmen in the Shangani Reserve were disturbed and that there was almost no cooperation with the local Native Affairs Department.' Ndebele complained that the implementation of Land Husbandry meant great disruption. 'People are being forced to destroy their expensive homes and move to another spot. No compensation is offered … Many young men have been rendered landless. Nothing is done with the consent of the people of the Reserve.' Ndebele pointed out that: 'most of the people in his area had been moved by Government Order from Filabusi to Shangani as recently as 1952 and had been urged by the Government to build sound and permanent homes, which they did.' Now they had to 'move to a new spot to start again from the beginning'.[86]

The attempted enforcement of Land Husbandry, as the most visible aspect of the second colonial occupation, gave the NDP a target for non-cooperation and sabotage. By the second half of 1961, Welshman's machine was ready to go into action. The result was described by the Native Commissioner, Nkayi:

> The efficient administration of the district was attacked from almost every angle, amongst which forms of attack the following might be noted – handing in of dip

[83] Interview with Welshman Mabhena, Bulawayo, 21 October 1994.
[84] Interview with Welshman Mabhena, Bulawayo, 19 January 1995.
[85] Interview with John Dakamela, Dakamela, 24 August 1995.
[86] *Bantu Mirror*, 9 July 1960.

cards, blockage of dips, refusal to dip, widespread illegal meetings, boycott of cattle sales, mass refusal to pay personal and arrear native tax, mass refusal to be vaccinated and tuberculosis tested, ploughing at will in allocated areas, and general intimidation throughout the district making the work of the police in detection and bringing to book extremely difficult.

The Zinyangeni activists had stimulated a populist movement which had some apparently paradoxical results. 'The LMS received a setback,' reported the Native Commissioner, 'in the apparently wilful burning down of its school at Gampinya.' In Lupane, storekeepers came secretly to tell the Native Commissioner how pleased they were that the NDP had been banned, since when the party was active 'storekeepers were placed in a most difficult position and expediency virtually compelled them to join the party.' The former teachers, progressive farmers and storekeepers, Welshman Mabhena and Ronald Sibanda, now led a movement which appeared to be growing distrustful of both teachers and store owners.[87]

This movement of sabotage divided Shangani nationalists. Some entered into it with enthusiasm – we have seen Mrs Julia Kimeta Sibanda's vivid recollection of her role in the destruction of schools, dip tanks and bridges, in 1961 under the NDP and in 1962 under Zapu. Others accepted it as the only way to communicate their desires. 'We wanted to rule ourselves,' says one, 'So this was our way of talking.'[88] Yet others remained nationalists but disapproved of the burning of schools and clinics which in the past they had so much desired. 'They belonged to us,' says the NDP headman Lupahla in Lupanda Purchase Area. 'If you destroyed them you'd be committing suicide.' The sabotage was 'pure hooliganism' in his view, the work of 'very dangerous youth'.[89]

There were some who despised and rejected nationalism because of the violence. 'The nationalists were active here,' says Levy Ndhlovu, an evictee from Essexvale and a Presbyterian headmaster in Lutsha in Nkayi, 'but they were doing things to show they were ignorant. We were being led by people who never went to school.' He participated in sabotage because he was forced to do so – 'those unlearned people knew how to beat'.[90] The nationalist violence of 1961 and still more of 1962 began to break up the composite evictee identity, which had combined Christian progressive dedication to education and modernity with a nationalist claim to own the land. The evictees had originally despised 'originals' for wearing skins, while they themselves paraded smart trousers, shirts and jackets. But when seven Nkayi men appeared in court in Que Que in September 1961 'as a sequel to disturbances in the Reserve recently' they chose to assume traditional dress even though they were almost certainly evictees:

The seven men attracted great attention here, as they all came dressed in their traditional dress and went through the town and the locations to the great amusement of many people. Some authorities of the Court tried to persuade these men to go and dress in modern dress but they would not.

The *Daily News* illustrated its story with a photograph of the men in headrings and carrying knobkerries and shields as a clear statement of militant intention.[91] And certain items of 'traditional' attire – particularly fur hats and knobkerries – became increasingly familiar symbols of the nationalist cause.

[87]  Annual Reports, Nkayi and Lupane, 1961, S 2827 2/2/8.
[88]  Interview with Headman Mlume's son, Nkoni, 2 October 1995. Mlume himself held much more conservative views.
[89]  Interview with Headman Joko Luphala, Lupanda, 13 December 1994.
[90]  Interview with L. M. Ndhlovu, Lutsha, 3 October 1995.
[91]  *Daily News*, 14 September 1961.

On the other side, of course, there was increasing regime violence. As early as September 1961, the NDP wrote to Prime Minister Edgar Whitehead protesting against 'the reign of terror perpetrated by the Police' in Nkayi. But two more plane loads of police were flown into Nkayi on 31 November to join those already on the ground. 'The troubles are said to have spread to every part of the District,' reported the *Daily News*, adding that Chiefs Nkalakatha and Dakamela had been given police protection.[92] The NDP was banned on December 9, 1961. Soldiers and police poured into Nkayi; taxes were collected at gunpoint. At the end of December Joshua Nkomo publicly protested that the army had been flogging people in Nkayi.[93] Very many NDP officials and supporters were arrested in Nkayi, as well as in Lupane. 'We were constantly in and out of arrest,' says one ANC/NDP activist in Lupane. 'It was a game of repeated arrest. All of the Tshongokwe group of politicians were picked up. My home was constantly visited by soldiers, police and CIDs.'[94]

Nevertheless, when the Zimbabwe African People's Union emerged less than a week after the NDP ban, most nationalists in Nkayi and Lupane moved into the new party. In 1962, sabotage intensified. 'When Zapu came in,' says Micah Mpofu of Manomano, a member of the ANC and NDP before he joined Zapu, 'people organised. Only those active and with a clear mind could participate. Our leaders remained from the NDP time, they were very active. As Zapu came in, Zapu tried to knock at the door and the door couldn't be opened, so Zapu came up with new tactics – the blocking of roads, destroying dips and government institutions.'[95]

The Zinyangeni nationalists, closely watched and harassed as they were, remained the best able to speak out in 1962. In April, Ronald Sibanda led a Zapu delegation, which also included Sampson Ndebele, to meet with the Minister of Native Affairs, Jack Quinton. They presented a petition alleging that the chiefs were holding meetings for the United Federal Party; that a 'witch-hunt for leaders of Zapu was now in progress in the Reserve'; that the army had intimidated people and that 'the unusual ransacking of the army into our villages was unwarranted.'[96]

An official 'verbatim report' of the meeting has been preserved, which illustrates very clearly that the door was firmly closed to Zapu's knocking. Quinton and Chief Native Commissioner Stanley Morris spent most of it abusing the delegation in what became a monologue rather than a discussion. Quinton began by stressing that,

> there is a system of Chiefs, Headmen and Kraal Heads and that is where your complaints should be laid. You know perfectly well that the Chief's authority is to represent the African people's views in the rural areas and the Government is not going to have the Chief brought into disrepute.

During the disturbances, a chief's court had been burnt down and a chief's grain hut. 'The people of Nkai should be ashamed.' Quinton said that he had no intention of visiting Nkayi to see for himself, but that he would,

> take this matter up strenuously with your Chiefs because there has been a tradition, a highly respected tradition that the people make their grouses or grievances to the Chiefs ... delegations of this type are something quite new. ... When the Government has the whole country to deal with it cannot look in

---

[92] *Daily News*, 2 December 1961. The paper reports at least 300 arrests since the arrival of the police reinforcements.

[93] *Daily News*, 21 December 1961.

[94] Interview with Douglas Siso, Bulawayo, 8 April 1996.

[95] Interview with Micah Mpofu, Gonye, 17 October 1995.

[96] *Daily News*, 4 April 1962.

isolation at the small grievances of individuals. It must look at the well being of the African people as a whole.

In any case, 'any delegation coming from a place like Nkai should come to apologise to Government for the appalling trouble they have created for their people over the past few months.' People were being prosecuted for breaking dipping laws. LDOs and demonstrators had been chased out of Nkayi. It was because of all 'these acts by the people in Nkai that the Police and Military went into Nkai and you have nobody but yourselves to thank.'

Morris then objected to Sibanda's presence. He was not a resident of Nkayi, where 'he has no land rights, no cattle rights' and 'is merely a trader'. A restriction order had been issued 'prohibiting him from entering any part of the Nkai Reserve except where his store site is', and the chiefs had now asked for his total removal. Quinton refused to allow Sibanda to speak, and then himself went through the points in the petition. 'I am not prepared to allow any public meetings if the Native Commissioners do not want them.' As for the inequalities of black and white land ownership, 'the Europeans in this country have bought their land and the African people have not, and if you buy a motor car you do not expect anybody else to interfere with it.'[97]

Sibanda got little chance to argue a case during this interview, but he was as intransigent as Quinton in his public statements. In July, he led another delegation to Bulawayo to complain that Africans in government employment in Nkayi were being ordered to register as voters or lose their jobs. Sibanda dismissed Quinton's reply to the earlier complaints as 'evasive' and insisted that political intimidation was a daily reality in Nkayi. 'Several of us here and many others like us are virtually under house arrest.'[98] Sibanda himself had been given two months notice to quit Nkayi. He had told the Chief Native Commissioner 'that his political beliefs will still find expression wherever he is restricted.'[99]

In August, a further wave of arson in Nkayi emphasized the fragmentation of the Zinyangeni tradition. Two classrooms were burnt down at Zinyangeni itself. The *Daily News* reported that local people believed that the teachers there were working for the United Federal Party's Build a Nation Campaign.[100] Later in the month, it was reported that Chief Nkalakatha was greatly perturbed by the arson. Sibanda had been prohibited from entering any African area.[101] On August 7, the Chief Native Commissioner sent a secret memorandum to his Minister:

> The security position in Nkai district is fast deteriorating and, I fear, will be back to what it was towards the end of last year. Chief Sikhobokhobo's court-house was burnt to the ground. ... At private meetings Ronald Isaac Sibanda has advocated violence in the following forms:
> Arson, destruction of dip tanks, attacks on Chiefs and Headmen, attacks on farms, petrol stations, the Native Commissioner's office at Nkai and Police Families who are alone.

[97] Verbatim Report of a Meeting of the Minister of Native Affairs and a Delegation from the Nkai District, 4 April 1962, S 2827/1/11.
[98] *Chronicle*, 6 July 1962.
[99] *Daily News*, 9 July 1962.
[100] *Daily News*, 7 August 1962. It should be noted, however, that F. Mzamba, who was educated at Zinyangeni and later employed by the mission, disputes the party's responsibility for the arson there. Mzamba was an ally of Welshman's and joined the NDP in 1960 later becoming a member of Zapu. He says that Zinyangeni school 'was burned by a man who we wouldn't let in the party. We thought he was a sellout ... You could say he was against missionaries and education.' Interview, Nkayi, 3 November 1994.
[101] *Daily News*, 15 August 1962.

Sibanda can well be described as a dangerous political fanatic who will go to any lengths to gain recognition for himself in the eyes of Zapu.

The CNC enclosed an anonymous letter received by the Native Commissioner, Nkayi. Signed 'Furious' it denounced the scheme of land allocation 'which will only cause extreme provocation which will result in many regrettable loss of lives – you as well. The answer to this is not the use of GUNS but to co-operate with the people. This letter of warning has been written with the approval of the entire Nkai … If you are not prepared to co-operate with the people, go back to wherever you came from – not Africa. This is an African country. The use of the gun has failed everywhere.' The CNC nevertheless advocated another resort to the gun. People ploughing in grazing areas had to be prosecuted; and to do this 'it will be necessary to take very strong security precautions and arrange for equally strong mobile columns of Police to be available as we had to do in the same area last year.'[102]

The police in Nkayi were given their head. In September, prosecutions began; on 4 September three youths complained 'of alleged assaults and intimidation by the Nkai police', they having been deprived of food, assaulted and forced to confess to arson.[103] At the end of the month, six restriction orders were served on Zapu officials, including Welshman Mabhena who was restricted to an area in Essexvale where he had 'neither home nor relatives'.[104] According to Welshman, the police went further, planting explosives in his house and that of Ronald Sibanda. The explosives were found in a raid while he was at home and in early November 1962 he was arrested and charged with 'illegal possession of four sticks of explosive and some detonators'. He was sent to prison for five years, and thereafter held in restriction areas and prisons until 1978. Sibanda escaped prosecution since he was in Bulawayo when the police raid on his home took place. But he soon slipped out of the country to Zambia where he joined other Zapu activists who had opened an office in Lusaka, and was later joined by Zapu's leaders when they left Tanzania.[105]

## Core Areas: The Pupu Uprising

A week after the Chief Native Commissioner's memorandum of 7 August 1962, however, Zinyangeni and Nkayi had been displaced as the focus of official disquiet by a hitherto apparently passive bush area of Lupane. Pupu, the third and last core zone discussed in this chapter – though by no means the only other core area in the two districts – was certainly different from Zinyangeni. Pupu shared with other core areas a history of evictee settlement, but in other respects Pupu was unique.

Far from being at the heart of radical Protestantism, Pupu represented an extraordinary mixture of religious traditions. It contained the site of Lobengula's last battle, where the Allan Wilson patrol had been killed to a man. For many years, the Native Department carried out an annual ritual there. The Native Commissioner in Inyathi would send word to Pupu that he was coming to visit 'the graves'; old people would clean up the area of the battlefield and slash grass all along the Pupu river, where stood a *mtswiri* tree, 'where the King was seated, his last command post, the last instructions he gave'. The Native Commissioner 'was coming *emalindeni*, to the sacred places'; he visited the battlefield and the tree and then went on across the Kana river to the place in Chief Pashu's country where Lobengula's grave was supposed to be

---

[102] Secret Memorandum, Morris to Quinton, 7 August 1962, S 2827/1/11.
[103] *Daily News*, 4 September 1962.
[104] *Daily News*, 26 September and 5 October 1962.
[105] Interview with Welshman Mabhena, 27 October 1994.

situated.[106] Although this ritual commemorated a battle important to Ndebele history, the ritual was an invention of the Department of Native Affairs. (It was not until the first Zapu guerrillas arrived in the later 1960s and came to the battle field and *mtswiri* tree that the past was remembered in a different way and new forms of commemoration were stimulated.)

But all around the battlefield lived Tonga, Shangwe, and Lozwi 'originals'. The Lozwi Mpunyuka, who became a headman under Mabhikwa, had acted as 'chief' before Mabhikwa came, and there were memories of the *Mambos*, expressed through spirit possession and historical narrative. The 'originals' had a sacred place near Pupu, 'a dangerous place with many wild animals'. They also had their own *mtolo* rainshrines, one of which was the *mtswiri* tree. A woman, UmtakaWillie, was messenger for the area to the great rainmaker, Nevana, in Gokwe. The locals tried to persuade the evictees from Fort Rixon, Matobo and Bubi, arriving in the dense bush of Pupu, also to send offerings to Nevana.

The evictees brought both mission and Zionist churches with them to Pupu. Titus Sibanda Moyo, a former guitarist in a Bulawayo band, became a member of the New Holy Full Gospel Church in Zion in Bulawayo and its leader in Pupu. He gained the nickname 'Papa' (Pope) and itinerated in neighbouring areas, building up converts to Zionism.[107] And to add to all this religious complexity, one Mnindwa Nyathi arrived at Pupu in 1950 and came to live close to the battlefield. Nyathi had been living as 'a church goer' in the Bulawayo townships, but the death of his third child led him to consult a *sangoma* – a medium of Nguni spirits – who told him to go to Pupu and to sort out his problems with the spirits of the dead there:

Initially Mnindwa was a church goer but then he couldn't accept natural deaths. The *izinyanga* [traditional healers] said the spirits were angry. ... The spirits started to have the need to be reinstated on him by the *ukuthwasa* ceremony (a kind of initiation ceremony, to know more about medicines and spirits)..., entirely contrary to his religious beliefs.

Nyathi was told 'by the Njelele Voice' that he must go to a Shona healer in Gatooma for six months training. The family contributed cattle for his expenses. When Nyathi emerged as a qualified healer, he at once took action which symbolically united Nevana and Njelele. 'He went straight away to Nevana', who gave him snuff. Then he went to Njelele, to offer snuff to the Voice. There he was given 'power from the shrine, from the Voice'. He never used herbs or charms in his healing but worked directly with Mwali's divine power. Indeed, he was told at Njelele: 'Now you will be my spokesman over here, north of the Shangani. Go and perform the duties of the shrine north of the Shangani ... Mnindwa worked like the *ilitshe* [rock] not like an *inyanga*. He was here as the representative of *ilitshe* himself.'

He established a large healing village in the *gusu* at Pupu, often housing hundreds of patients at a time. These patients, brought to his village by bus, worked on his huge fields, carrying fertile anthill soil to them and building fences round acre after acre. As well as healing he also made rain, after appeals to the *mtolo* and Nevana had failed. And as his son, Kilikiya Nyathi – Zapu activist and Zipra guerrilla – insists: 'My father was also a politician. Politicians themselves used to come and visit him here from throughout the country for advice.'[108]

Perhaps all this historical and religious complexity made Pupu an area where

---

[106] Interview with Magwaza Ndlovu, Pupu, 20 February 1996.
[107] Interview with Titus Sibanda Moyo, 20 February 1996.
[108] Interview with Kilikaya Nyathi, Mvumindaba Ncube and Tandiwe Nyathi, Pupu, 16 February 1996.

differences of ethnicity and ideology could be synthesized. At any rate, the leading nationalist in Pupu, Simon Ntonisa Siwela, made a special effort to bring the 'originals' 'into the Zapu fold, so that we should move as one. Muntumubi Ncube really came up strongly in our support. So then we were ready by the time the action had begun.' And 'Papa' Moyo moved about the area, ostensibly on Zionist business, but in reality preparing people for this action.

The action was to be part of Zapu's sabotage campaign. By August 1962 Pupu was strongly Zapu. Two activists, Pilot Ncube and Daveti Sibanda, recall:

> We started buying cards at the time of the NDP clandestinely. As time went on, there was the *zhii* [uprising] in Bulawayo. Then there was the uprising here. It all started with a meeting here in the bush when it was decided that we would destroy all government property. We said it was high time now to take up arms against the government. The meeting went on for two to three days. ... Only locals [not Bulawayo leaders] were at that meeting. We slept in the bush and our wives brought us food.[109]

Soon this Pupu 'crowd' was to burst into the press headlines. On August 10, the *Chronicle* reported that 'security measures were being tightened' in Lupane, but that nevertheless a wave of arson had broken out. Then came a sensational headline on August 15: 'KNOBKERRIE MOB AMBUSHES POLICE PATROL. Frees 3 held for questioning in connection with burnings.' A patrol of one white and three black police had been ambushed in 'dense bush' by 'a crowd of sixty Africans armed with knobkerries ... The ambush took place a few miles from the Allan Wilson Memorial.'

Subsequent trial evidence revealed that the white constable, who had been driving the police truck, had been carrying both a .22 rifle and a shotgun 'but did not go for his firearms because he thought such action in face of such a large mob might lead to unnecessary bloodshed'. For their part, the 'mob', having secured the release of the prisoners 'appeared to lose interest in the police', and vanished into the 'thick bush'.[110]

Next day there was further news. 'Two Native Department officials had been threatened at a kraal near Pupu by a crowd of nearly 100 Africans.'[111] These were two agricultural demonstrators, Solomon Japhet and G. Ncube. Some hundred people had marched to Japhet's kraal as soon as the prisoners had been released from police custody. The crowd abused him for reporting the men to the police and told him that he must leave at once, otherwise they would 'burn him and his house'. Some youths said: 'You are lucky we are being accompanied by old men. Had it been only us, young men, we would have killed you.'[112] The crowd went on to where Ncube was working in the fields and took him to his home where he was called 'a sell-out', a 'tshombe'. But he was not assaulted.[113]

Although there had been no physical violence, the affront to the authorities was the most spectacular yet reported from any rural area in the country. As soon as the ambush and release of prisoners was known on August 14, Inspector Gilmour went to the Shangani river with 12 white and 19 black police, all heavily armed:

> They visited various kraals to find the people responsible for the trouble. But they saw only women and young children. The next day a police reserve aircraft joined

---

[109] Interview with Pilot Ncube and Daveti Sibanda, Lupahlwa, 2 April 1996. The influence of the riots in Bulawayo on the timing and pattern of rural sabotage should not be underestimated.
[110] *Chronicle*, 15 August and 17 October 1962.
[111] *Chronicle*, 15 and 16 August 1962.
[112] *Chronicle*, 6 October 1962.
[113] *Chronicle*, 27 October 1962.

them to help scour the Pupu River area. At dawn on August 16, as they were going down the river valley, they saw smoke in the hills across the river. They crossed a vlei … and went up the heavily wooded hillside. Guided by the aircraft, they approached the top of the hill where they saw three camp fires. The Africans, busy watching the aircraft, were taken completely by surprise. After a melee, when the startled Africans started rushing about, they were gathered together, 97 being arrested.

Dogs were used in the operation. Later that day the *Chronicle*'s reporter saw the arrested men, guarded by armed African constables, 'in the centre of the make-shift police headquarters which were erected only two years ago'.[114]

Nationalist elders in Pupu vividly remember this day. 'When the government forces came,' says Daveti Sibanda, 'they came prepared for a full confrontation, for war. There were many arrests and people were seriously beaten.' Others recall 'those huge dogs'. The whole episode is today evoked as 'the war of the dogs'.[115] The next month Zapu was banned throughout the country and the army again deployed in Nkayi and Lupane. The severity of this repression made it far from inevitable that there would be subsequent violent encounters between nationalists and the regime in the Shangani. But the arrival of armed guerrillas from Zambia would provide a new opportunity for confrontation.

## Religion and Nationalism in the Shangani

There was a complex interaction between religion and nationalism in the Shangani. At the time of the Voice, when nationalism was exclusively the ideology of evictees, it was also above all the ideology of Christian evictees. Their belief that Africans owned the land had biblical foundations. The 'traditional' religion of the 'originals', with their *mtolo* trees and their recourse to Nevana seemed to belong to another, quite different universe of thought. We have seen that the tradition of the London Missionary Society was important for the beginning of Zinyangeni nationalism. The Calvinist theology of the Free Presbyterians also led many of their members to political consciousness. The staunch Presbyterian, Nathaniel Mpofu, in 1960 became a full member of the church at Mbuma mission and also 'a member of the Party (NDP) and a staunch supporter of the leadership of Joshua Nkomo'.[116] And there was a radical strain in Lupane Catholicism. Father Xavier, who had been based at Tshongokwe mission North of the Shangani – a place where evictees had been dumped and which became a prominent focus of protest and sabotage at the same time as Pupu – was outspoken regarding police brutality and torture during the severe repression. He was deported. Several of the Irish and Spanish fathers from Matabeleland made a political decision to leave Southern Rhodesia and work for the nationalist cause in the camps in Botswana. One of them was Father Francis, who returned to Lupane in the 1980s. These examples from their missionaries reflected and further validated the nationalism of many African Catholics.

Yet from the beginning, the Christian nationalism of the Shangani was different from that of other areas. It is often said, for example, that Zionist and Apostolic churches were apolitical and stood aloof from nationalism. This was certainly not true in Nkayi and Lupane, where one of the Voice leaders north of the Shangani was a Zionist from Filabusi and one of the coordinators of the Pupu action was the Zionist, 'Papa' Moyo.

As we shall see, Zionists – with their perceived prophetic and healing power –

---

[114] *Chronicle*, 17 August and 5 October 1962.
[115] Interviews with Titus Sibanda Moyo, Pupu, 20 February 1996, Daveti Sibanda, Pupu, 2 April 1996.
[116] Autobiography of Nathaniel Mpofu, December 1995.

continued to work with young nationalists and then with guerrillas right through the 1970s. But already by 1962, things had begun to change for mission church stalwarts. Churches and mission schools were targets of the arson campaign; teachers were suspected of working for the government. And as nationalists began to turn to revived traditional religion, many Protestants found themselves in difficulty. At the same time as local rainshrines and other aspects of 'tradition' received new respect in the Shangani, nationalist leaders made a more general appeal to central shrines. Joshua Nkomo had made a famous pilgrimage to the Mwali shrine of Dula in the eastern Matopos as long ago as 1953, and by the early 1960s, it was widely believed that the Mwali cult endorsed the nationalist movement. 'Politicians' went to Mnindwa Nyathi at Pupu who was thought of as Njelele's representative north of the Shangani. And as the 'originals' came into the nationalist movement, so the Nevana medium too was recruited. The current medium, Samson Tewasira, recalls that 'Nkomo sent high-ranking representatives, at the time of *zhii* ... to ask the spirits for power for the young men to fight victoriously.'[117]

All this presented serious difficulties for many Christian nationalists. Nathaniel Mpofu was distributing Free Presbyterian literature in Nkayi in December 1961. When he came to the church station at Nzalikwa he found that the local preacher was holding 'a feast to appease the spirit of his ancestors'. The literature Mpofu was distributing condemned even Christmas Day as 'a heathen celebration', let alone *isangoma* ceremonies of Nguni spirit possession. This material had fallen into the hands of local politicians 'who were suspicious of [government] agents who were going about identifying the members of the National Democratic Party. I was then suspected to be one of them. The members of the NDP were now planning to punish me for handing out such literature.' One NDP member warned him secretly not to enter into any debate because his every word was being scrutinized:

> When I went back to the house the festival table was set and the feeding was starting. I and my friend joined the table. One of the men told the house that I stayed away from my home during the December holidays because I was working as a missionary in collaboration with the suppressive government to suppress people's traditional way of life, saying that festivals such as this one were a heathen practice that should be stopped and that people connected with the church should be told to stop henceforth preaching to people.

Mpofu left quietly and went home where he found an NDP pamphlet demanding that dipping and taxes be stopped and that 'churches should stop preaching because they are working together with the suppressive government.' He left his school to stay with his in-laws 'because there were people going about beating sell-outs. I was named as one of them because I was preaching the gospel of the white man.' In the event he was lucky. A group of NDP youth were sent to burn his house and school. The leader of the youth 'knew that I was a member of the Party' and saved him. Mpofu took refuge with his political mentor, Japhet Ncube, a teacher at Zenka mission, cousin of the youth activist Dumiso Dabengwa, who further 'indoctrinated me into the Party's ideology'. Ncube, who acted as interpreter to white missionaries at communion services, resolved his own dilemma by accepting an NDP scholarship to study outside Rhodesia. In April 1962, Ncube left for Northern Rhodesia. Mpofu remained behind to serve both church and party as well as he could manage.[118] This turned out to be an early hint of much

[117] Interview with Samson Tewasira, Gokwe, 19 September 1995.
[118] The autobiography of Nathaniel Mpofu, December 1995. In January 1963, Mpofu was sent to open a school at Somakantana. He found himself threatened with witchcraft by local people who wanted a Zapu activist as teacher.

more serious tensions between the two loyalties which, during the war itself, would amount to threats on his life. In this period, however, local Christian leaders were only beginning to come under suspicion.

By 1962, membership of Zapu and commitment to its policy of sabotage and confrontation had become central to the life of very many people in the Shangani. While the modernizing, Christian evictees retained their dominance of the local nationalist movement, there were indications of tensions to come, and some attempts to reconcile with and mobilize the 'originals' and members of other religious traditions of the Shangani.

# 5

# The Transition to Guerrilla War

## 1962–1976

### Introduction

Our last chapter dealt with the development of nationalism in Lupane and Nkayi between 1952 and 1962. It was able to draw on an abundance of sources. But the period from the banning of Zapu in 1962 to the opening of an effective guerrilla war in 1976, which is the subject of this chapter, is much more difficult to reconstruct.

Zimbabwe operates a thirty-year rule for access to its state archives and problems of accessioning mean that this is in practice more like a thirty-five year rule. Few files in the National Archives run beyond 1962; the last available district annual reports relate to 1961. Thanks to the generous support of the Governor, Provincial Administrator and District Administrators, we were given access to Matabeleland North provincial and district files for the period between 1962 and 1985. But these have only survived very incompletely. There is a list of Lupane district files for the late 1960s and early 1970s dealing with destocking, with conservation, with eviction from forest areas, and even with such exciting topics as 'Riots, Subversion and Detainees' and 'Military Matters'. But all of these were withdrawn and destroyed in the late 1970s.

Press coverage is also much less useful for this period. The *Daily News*, that invaluable source for African politics, was banned in August 1964 on the same day as the final proscription of the nationalist parties.[1] The Bulawayo-based *Home News* ceased to report on the politics of Matabeleland when its editor was restricted in Gonakudzingwa in the southeast. The *Chronicle* was less interested in, or informed about, the underground struggles of the late 1960s than it had been in the Pupu 'riots' of 1962. Even oral reminiscence in Nkayi and Lupane is often confused about the dating and sequence of the confrontation between the Internal Affairs department and local nationalists; many of the key local nationalist figures spent much of this period in detention and moving between the rural areas and town.

This chapter has been pieced together from a variety of sources. Files on chiefs and headmen exist both at the Provincial Administrator's offices in Bulawayo and at the District Administrator's offices in Nkayi and Lupane. Where the Lupane files for the late 1960s and early 1970s were all destroyed, the Nkayi files have mostly survived,

---

[1] Elaine Windrich, *The Mass Media in the Struggle for Zimbabwe. Censorship and Propaganda under Rhodesian Front Rule* (Gwelo, Mambo Press, 1981), p. 61; Eugene Wason, *Banned: The Story of the African Daily News, Rhodesia 1964* (London, Hamish Hamilton, 1976).

though alas without anything on 'riots, subversion and detainees' or on 'military matters'. We have been able to draw on the oral memoirs of Nkayi's most ferocious District Commissioner, Noel Hunt, as well as on the invaluable testimonies of local activists. Moments of particular significance, like the Rhodesian Front's Unilateral Declaration of Independence (UDI) in November 1965, the guerrilla incursion of 1966 or the efforts of the Pearce Commissioners to test African public opinion in 1972, have generated rich clusters of evidence.

We have thus been able to draw a picture of the Shangani during these critical years of transition to full guerrilla war. There is more in our account than there should be about chiefs and headmen because the Rhodesian administration was so obsessed with them and most of the reports and records dealing with them have survived.[2] There is a bias towards Nkayi because of the destruction of the Lupane files. But it seems unlikely that the archival record necessary for a more balanced picture will ever now be recovered.

Various themes nevertheless emerge strongly. One is that the history of nationalism at district level has a quite different chronology from its history at national level. Even in 1961 and 1962, when the NDP and Zapu were legal parties, all party meetings in the Reserves of Nkayi and Lupane were illegal and party officers were constantly being arrested. The ban on Zapu in late 1962 and the final ban on all nationalist parties in August 1964 had much less effect in the Shangani than in the towns. The confrontation between the administration and Zapu went on in Lupane and Nkayi despite the bans.

It also went on despite the split in the nationalist movement in 1963. Late in that year there emerged a new party, the Zimbabwe African National Union (Zanu), led by Ndabiningi Sithole and supported by Herbert Chitepo, Enos Nkala, Robert Mugabe and others. It denounced Joshua Nkomo for his alleged inactivity and promised a policy of confrontation. In the towns, much of 1963 and 1964 was taken up with fierce in-fighting between Zapu and its rival Zanu. After the ban on both parties and the detention of their leadership in 1964, the initiative passed to their representatives in exile. The two parties, both initially based in Zambia, competed with each other to organize armed incursions into the country. Zanu made no impact in Nkayi and Lupane and there was no diversion of energies in the two districts, where Zapu continued its underground struggle with the Rhodesian state. Local rural leaders of nationalism could not now interact with their party's leaders in the towns. But the experience of Shangani detainees in prisons and restriction areas, where they met Zapu activists from all over the country, now offered them a 'schooling' which they put to use when they returned to Nkayi and Lupane. And they eagerly awaited their first contact with the guerrillas sent in by Zapu's leaders in exile.

It is important to stress, however, that although Zanu had no influence on the Shangani in the 1960s and 1970s, the division between Zapu and Zanu *does* have a major influence on the way the violence of those years is remembered in Nkayi and Lupane. After Zanu(PF)'s victory in the 1980 elections, the role of Zapu and its armed wing, Zipra, was consistently downplayed in the national media. The first encounter between Zanu guerrillas and Rhodesian forces at Chinhoyi became celebrated as the beginning of the liberation war. Nothing was said about Zapu's guerrilla operations, such as those which reached Lupane and Nkayi in 1966. Our informants were thus especially keen to highlight the guerrilla arrival at Pupu and to search out for us the people who were principally involved.

During the fourteen years between 1962 and 1976, there were periods of 'peace' from

---

[2] The material about Rhodesia Front traditionalism presented in this chapter is made available here for the first time. Of course, traditionalist policies were not implemented only in Nkayi and Lupane. A discussion of these policies in the wider national context is T. Ranger, 'Zimbabwe and the long search for independence', in D. Birmingham and P. M. Martin (eds), *History of Central Africa. The Contemporary Years Since 1960* (London, Longman, 1998).

the administration's point of view: after l966, when guerrilla incursions more or less ceased; or when arrests of local officials crippled nationalist structures for a time; or when there was a lull in state agricultural intervention and in protest against it. But the second theme of the chapter is the increased commitment to violence both by the state and by local nationalists. District Commissioners discussed – and implemented – schemes of collective punishment; the police and army used torture to gain information about guerrillas; administrative officials rejoiced when chiefs took the law into their own hands and flogged nationalists. There were also periods in which the nationalists resorted to 'peaceful' tactics – working through legally recognized African National Council branches in 1972 or during Joshua Nkomo's attempts to negotiate a settlement with Smith. Nevertheless, on the nationalist side, too, there was an increasing readiness to go beyond sabotage to more intensive violence – to recruit young men for guerrilla training; to aid guerrillas when they managed to get into the Shangani; to beat up 'sell-outs'. The extraordinary intensity of the confrontation of the late 1970s – when District Commissioners were themselves killed and when the Rhodesian regime resorted to extremes of violent repression – was not inevitable. But there was little in the history of the decade before it to make it unlikely.

A major theme of this chapter, then, is the persistence and chronology of the nationalist confrontation with the state. Another theme is that of the state's persistence through all this with interventions in African agricultural production. The transition from the 'modernizing' and 'revolutionary' policy of the Land Husbandry Act to the 'conservatism' of Community Development certainly did not bring the second colonial occupation to an end. It merely meant that the activities of offical experts were directed through so-called 'traditional' channels. While the Land Husbandry Act had removed the power of land allocation from chiefs, under Community Development, the new Tribal Land Authorities, chaired by chiefs and headmen, became theoretically responsible not only for allocation but also for conservation of land. In practice, the pressure for conservation measures came from the regime's technical officers. These went on pretending that they could 'modernize' African agriculture in the Shangani despite the fierce resistance aroused by enforced contouring. We were astonished to discover that as late as 1975 a widespread and intensive campaign to impose contours was being waged in Nkayi and Lupane – and being resisted just as strongly as earlier agricultural interventions had been. The priorities of the second colonial occupation continued right up until the intensification of the guerrilla war which brought about the end of the Rhodesian state.

A fourth theme is the continuing ambiguity of this alliance between the state and the chiefs within the system of Community Development. The administration strove desperately to find the 'right' chiefs – which meant men who were traditionally legitimate but at the same time 'progressive' as far as farming and education were concerned; commanding the support of their people but simultaneously totally loyal to the state. The Rhodesia Front came to need chiefs so badly that it could hardly bring itself to depose even the 'worst' of them. Meanwhile, there were a series of running battles between chiefs and administrators over cattle management and over 'tradition'.

A fifth theme is that of the interaction of religion and politics. During the emergence of the African National Council under Bishop Abel Muzorewa in order to oppose the Anglo-Rhodesian constitutional settlement in 1972, African ministers and teachers of mission churches came once more to play a role in local African politics. They later fell once again under deep nationalist suspicion. At the same time the administration was competing with the nationalists to gain the support of regional rainshrines and some chiefs were seeking to make use of witchfinders and witchcleaners as part of their 'traditional' authority.

In what follows, we seek to bring out these themes in the course of a largely narrative account of the years 1963 to 1976.

## Building up the Chiefs and the Declaration of UDI

In the early months of 1963, as the army withdrew once again from Nkayi and Lupane, and as hundreds of nationalist activists went to prison or into restriction, the Internal Affairs Department set about building alternative structures in the Shangani.[3] It was believed that the Land Husbandry Act had undercut the authority of the chiefs and the basis of traditional community. 'Chiefs and Headmen are not popular in this district today,' admitted the Native Commissioner, Nkayi, in March 1961, 'Land Husbandry implementation being the main cause of this.'[4] Now that implementation of the Act had been abandoned, every effort was to be made to build up the chiefs as leaders of organic communities.

In February 1963, the Secretary for Internal Affairs wrote to all District Commissioners telling them new legislation would 'make possible the setting up of Tribal Trust Lands Authorities'. It was essential to 'know the boundaries of Chiefs' tribal areas' so that these could be gazetted. In March, District Commissioner Ferguson of Nkayi sent in his map of chiefs' areas.[5]

Later in 1963, Noel Hunt became District Commissioner of Nkayi. Hunt was an extreme enthusiast for 'traditional' autocracy:

I am a great believer in the tribal system [he told a National Archives interviewer in 1983]. I think it is a superb system, absolutely grand. Just use the damn thing, get rid of all your ridiculous European ideas and use it – it is magnificent, it works every time. It can cope with any problem whatsoever … It would cope with over-population. There would be an awful lot of corpses about the place. Once you've got away from the sort of sickly belief that human life is sacred, life becomes a hell of a lot easier.

Hunt wished to give chiefs the power to banish people from their tribal areas and thus to make them 'non-persons'; he encouraged chiefs to take the law into their own hands and to punish nationalist opponents; he contemplated the restoration of the Ndebele monarchy:

Well, why not? These chaps were rulers and realists. You don't think that grubby little gangsters like [the nationalist leadership] would get anywhere against chaps like that do you? You've got the right blokes together in the right place and you know the right powers they've got. So you can say, 'Now what I want you blokes to do is so and so, how're you going to do it?' If they say 'We're going to cut everybody's right hand off', you've got to say 'Yes, OK, have you got a sharp knife?'[6]

Hunt never succeeded in his ambition to hand over tribal areas to chiefs and let them do whatever they liked within them. Even the Rhodesia Front, he thought, was full of

[3] The Internal Affairs Department had replaced the Native Affairs Department in 1962. Native Commissioners became District Commissioners (DCs), and Provincial Native Commissioners became Provincial Commissioners (PCs) at the same time.

[4] NC Nkayi to PNC, 13 March 1961. The Native Commissioner argued in favour of allowing assemblies solely composed of chiefs and headmen to make decisions on who should succeed to office. There should be no general meetings of the people of a headmanship. 'I am not in favour of giving the populace a chance to snipe at their native authorities.' Nkayi H/M Manguni, Provincial Administrator's Office, Bulawayo.

[5] Secretary, Internal Affairs, to all stations, 25 February 1963; DC, Nkayi to PC, 22 March 1963, LAN 1/GEN, 1962–1973, Nkayi, Bulawayo Records Office.

[6] Interview with Noel Hunt, 27 November 1983, ORAL/240, National Archives, Harare.

'breast-beaters, bleeding-hearts, and men of goodwill'. Such men 'were so frightened that some poor black man should be oppressed (and oppression is the nature of Africa) we had all sorts of mechanisms to make it impossible for anyone to do an efficient job of oppressing him.' Nevertheless, as we shall see, Hunt did his best as an 'oppressor' and he promised his chiefs that he would back them up when they used their authority. Chiefs who were already adequately authoritarian were publicly rewarded. In 1964, for instance, Mabhikwa went on the chiefs' tour to Pakistan, Egypt, Jordan, Italy, England, Scotland, South Africa and the Transkei.[7] In the same year the Lupane and Nkayi chiefs attended the Domboshawa Indaba with the Labour Secretary of State for the Commonwealth.[8]

What Hunt really could not overcome was the idea that Community Development was about 'development' as well as about 'community'. Left to himself, he would have withdrawn all official support for schools and clinics and left Africans to get on with agriculture in their own way. His chiefly areas would have been autarkies as well as autocracies. The official doctrine of Community Development was different – first you defined the 'community' and then you stimulated 'development' within it. Early in 1965, while Hunt was still District Commissioner in Nkayi, an elaborate delineation exercise was carried out there, part of a massive nationwide survey.

Delineators in Shona-speaking areas tended to assume that the authority of chiefs came from the endorsement of ancestral mediums, and to define 'community' in terms of shared ritual. In Matabeleland, and certainly in Nkayi and Lupane, chiefs were not ritual figures and delineators did not bother to explore local religion. The delineator in Nkayi was A.D. Elliott. In June 1965, he reported on his findings. The core of an Ndebele 'community', said Elliott, lay in the concept *ukuthonisa*, which meant 'not only to try a case, but to govern or administer'. A community was best defined 'as those villages which comprise a common judicial authority', from which people took their cases to a *mlisa*, 'a person under the chief who controls a number of kraal heads on behalf of the chief.' Many cases could be determined by the *mlisa*; those that could not were sent on to the chief. The chief controlled his whole territory, or *ilizwe*; the various *abalisa*, or headmen, controlled their *izigaba*. So far as land was concerned, 'the chief is the overall land authority for his *ilizwe*' and the *abalisa* were 'delegated land authorities for their *izigaba*'. The main aim of the delineation report was, in fact, to establish boundaries for the headmen's *izigaba* within the chiefly territories already laid down.

Development projects, wrote Elliott, ideally came up from below. A village, or group of villages, would bring proposals to the *mlisa* and his court; he in his turn would approach the chief. If the project was approved 'a *komiti* will be formed to act as the executive body responsible'. The functional community 'in tribal areas has been found to be the *isigaba* … The community board will in fact be nothing more nor less than the *mlisa*'s council, *inkundhla* … It cannot be overstressed that all our activities and efforts in the tribal areas should be channelled through these'.

Elliott then reported in detail on each chief and his chieftancy area or *ilizwe*, following this up with a report or a recommendation upon the number and role of the headmen, *abalisa*. He gave an account of the history of the chieftainship – noting in some cases that the initial appointments had broken Ndebele rules. Elliott was well aware that the Ndebele chiefs of Nkayi controlled very mixed populations. He made a survey of the

---

[7]  D.K. Parkinson, 'Lupane Notes', *NADA*, 1980, p.143.

[8]  Noel Hunt gloried in his chiefs' response to Domboshawa. Chief Myinga Dakamela returned totally disillusioned with Arthur Bottomley – 'He's not an Nkosi at all, is he? He talks just like those Europeans who work on the railways.' The extremely aged Sikhobokhobo Madhlisibanda was delayed on his return from the Indaba because his truck had broken down. 'He yelled and screamed, he had to go home … I have been away for seven days. I want to have a woman.' 'I thought it was to his credit,' commented Hunt. ORAL/240, National Archives.

complex ethnic make up of each *ilizwe* – the unit of Community Development in Matabeleland was to be a matter of governance rather than of common 'blood' or culture. Elliott thought that 'the Ndebele chief or headman is not nearly so involved in spiritual matters as is his Shona counterpart'. Finally, he reported on 'the felt needs' of each community.

Elliott found the chiefs responsive to the whole exercise. Chief Tshugulu and his son, for instance, 'pressed me to discuss with them for a second time some of the principles of community development and local government'. He also found popular suspicion that Community Development was just Land Husbandry under another name. Headman Mpande 'stated that his people are suspicious of the Community agent operating in the area as they feel he is connected with Land Husbandry and is aiming at the destocking of their herds'. (These perceptions were acute. Different sorts of 'knowledge' were being recorded in the Rhodesia Front surveys than had been collected during the era of land-use plans, but boundaries, contours and control remained as important as ever.)

Finally, Elliott found sharp memories of recent nationalist protest. 'Up until recently, Headman Sibangelana was reasonably popular with his people, but certain elements moved into the area damning him as the man who had introduced the Land Husbandry Act.' Sibangelana was a Lozwi headman under Chief Madliwa; he was under attack from evictees from Filabusi. Elliott thought he should be supported.[9]

The following year Elliott 'delineated' Lupane. But it took time to map and proclaim the recommended *izigaba* as Tribal Land Authorities and executive development units. Meanwhile the District Commissioners of Nkayi and Lupane concentrated on demarcating valleys and vleis under the Natural Resources Act. Conex (the Conservation and Extension services) moved in large numbers of Extension Assistants; Chiefs and headmen were sent on a Conservation Course. In June 1965, 'demarcation of the Lupani Valley streambanks continued … 119 cease cultivation warnings have been issued in the section of the valley to date … Conservation of the Kataza Valley [in Nkayi] by Conex made good progress initially'. Nationalist resistance was not dead, however. 'During the month the Extension Staff met with opposition due to intimidation by a certain group. The Inspectorate were requested to investigate. It was decided to move into the area and serve orders where necessary, but the people showed hostility and refused to give information. The Police were contacted and seven arrests were made. Prosecutions are pending.'[10]

Oral testimony is agreed that the arrests of 1962 had badly wounded Zapu in Nkayi and Lupane. 'The arrests of the 1960s really weakened the structures,' recalls Senzani Ngwenya. 'They weakened the party as a whole'. 'I was jailed for two years,' remembers Micah Mpofu. 'Many of the leaders were detained – Samuel, Joel, Elias Tshuma, Ngavele Mhlanga, Sigomba Tshuma, Mango, Douglas Tshuma … While I was away, the party was not active because most people were arrested and detained.'[11] Possession of a knobkerry, wearing a fur hat or sporting a beard – the 'uniform' of Zapu – were sufficient grounds for arrest. Some key party leaders lost their lives. 'Matshipisa Tshuma was tied behind a land rover and dragged after the destruction of the Tohwe dip. He later died [from his injuries].'[12]

Nevertheless, a good deal of the nationalist structure remained. Youth action groups – *Zhanda*, or gendarmes, a term imported from Zaire – had been operating secretly during

---

[9]  Delineation of Communities: Interim Report, A.D. Eliott, June 1965, S 2929.

[10]  Group Inspector, Lands to Provincial Commissioner and Resident Commissions, Lupane and Nkayi, 2 July 1965; Assistant Provincial Conservation and Extension Officer to Provincial Commissioner, 4 March 1966, LAN 1/GEN, Nkayi.

[11]  Interviews with Senzani Ngwenya, Singwangombe, 21 February 1996; Micah Mpofu, Gonye, 17 October 1995.

[12]  Interview with Johnson Mpofu, Malindi, 12 September 1995.

the sabotage campaign of 1961 and 1962 and they continued in being after 1963. 'There was an underground movement,' recalls one former youth activist in Tshongokwe. 'We'd assess who was brave and who was not ... There is a party saying that the youth is the backbone of the nation ... They saw to it that they were the spearhead of fighting the enemy.'[13] In some cases, women took over the functions of their detained husbands. And it was still possible for whole communities to be mobilized. In 1965, the people of the Mlume/Majaha headmanship destroyed the dip at Zwelabo. A police helicopter came, soldiers were deployed, and there were many arrests. 'That day we had a beer brew,' remembers the present headman Mlume's wife, 'and the army drank all my beer'.[14] Headman Majaha was denounced to the authorities, arrested, detained and deposed.[15] And as we have seen, nationalists could mobilize resistance to valley demarcation.

Between 1963 and 1965, Hunt waged ruthless war on Zapu leaders and supporters. He was an ardent advocate of collective punishment and, although this was not yet adopted as government policy, Hunt managed to carry it out in Nkayi: 'What happened was that ... they were refusing to dip their cattle, or some bloody thing, so I disconnected all the boreholes; there was no water for them, which was highly effective.' Jack Nhliziyo, who was District Administrator, Nkayi, during our fieldwork, remembered Hunt well. 'He was a man with an evil heart. He used to drive about the district by himself. When he came across women pumping water, he would say to them: "Good, pump as much as you can, that is the last water you will have from this hole". People would explain to him why they objected to dipping, etc. and he could have understood if he had listened. But he just wanted to force everything.'[16]

So far as Hunt was concerned, the remaining influence of Britain stood between him and total control of his district. When he disabled the boreholes, a local Catholic missionary phoned the Justice and Peace Commission in Salisbury; the Commission in turn phoned London; the British Government phoned Ian Smith; and within twenty-four hours Hunt was called to account by the Provincial Commissioner. Smith's declaration of independence from Britain seemed a moment of triumphant significance and Hunt's memory of it is vivid. On November 11, 1965, he was in a 'dirty' little store 'at the bottom end of Nkai', 'full of blacks and everybody talking and nobody listening, as usual, and on the counter there was a radio blaring away'. Hunt recognized Smith's voice and heard him declare UDI:

All of a sudden the blacks started listening too. And when I went out and got into my truck and drove off, word had spread all over the tribal area that something terrible had happened, that the white man had taken over the country and was going to rule it and he'd kicked the British out. And wherever you went the Africans were taking their hats off and sitting down by the side of the road and clapping their hands.

Everyone expected a rule of terror, 'and believe me, the Chiefs were one hundred percent behind us on that ... They thought we were going to get busy and kill every damn Afro-Nat in Rhodesia.' The day after the broadcast, Hunt went to a cattle dip in Nesikwe. One of the royal Khumalo family lived there. When Hunt arrived, the Khumalo 'was standing there with a sjambok in his hand and he'd hauled out every

---

[13] Interview with Mr Dlagama, Ngombane, 27 February 1996.

[14] Interview with Headman and Mrs Mlume, Nkoni, 2 October 1995.

[15] Noel Hunt, D.C., Nkayi to Provincial Commissioner, 26 November 1965; Hunt to Majaha, 17 February 1966. Hunt warned that while Majaha 'has long been known as a strong nationalist sympathiser', his son Mnindwa was 'even more virulently nationalist'. H/M Mlume (Majaha), Nkayi.

[16] Interview with Jack Nhliziyo, Bulawayo, 8 February 1995.

Afro-Nat (they all knew who these people were), he'd lined them up and he was flogging them. "Ha, my friend, Ian Smith has taken the country over." … The bloke just stood there and took it.' Hunt, of course, was delighted.[17]

## The Guerrilla Incursion of 1966

A nationalist response to Hunt's triumphalism was not long in coming. Early in April 1966, a group of eight Zapu guerrillas set out from Zambia. They were not the first armed men to be sent into Matabeleland but they were the first to proceed in what became the classic pattern, entering the country by foot and interacting with the civilian population.[18] Partly because they were the first guerrillas anyone in Lupane and Nkayi had seen and hence are vividly remembered, and partly because of their remarkable achievement in living within the area for three months and undertaking the training of locals, it is worth recounting their story in some detail.

They crossed the Zambezi and spent nine days without food in Hwange; then they shot a rhino, took its liver, and ate it on their walk to Lupane. The guerrillas were making their way first to Pupu and then to northern Nkayi – the two best known areas of nationalist militancy in 1961 and 1962. They came armed not only with rifles and machine guns but also with the names of the leading Zapu activists in these areas.

There were several reasons for choosing Pupu. 'This is a good place for guerrillas,' says K.K. Nyathi, who later became a guerrilla himself, 'because there is plenty of bush.'[19] Pupu was not only deep within the 'dark' forests, but was also the site of the 1893 battlefield and of Lobengula's tree and hence a place implicit with traditions of Ndebele heroism. Yet Pupu was also a place where 'true' Ndebele lived among many Lozwi, Nyai and Tonga 'originals', many of whom had been drawn into the nationalist movement and had taken part in the demonstrations of 1962. There were two Shona-speaking guerrillas among the eight and the group saw itself as part of a campaign for national (rather than ethnic) liberation.

Despite all these advantages, both guerrillas and civilians were cautious to begin with. The story of their interactions has a marvellous flavour of Lupane rusticity and of life in the *gusu* forests. The guerrilla commander, Fineas Dapona, had been given the name of Pilot Ncube as an important local contact. But neither Dapona nor any of the other guerrillas were from Lupane or known to the locals. Early in the morning, one day in April 1966, two of the band emerged from the bush at Pilot's vegetable garden in the

---

[17] Interview, Noel Hunt, ORAL 240, National Archives of Harare.

[18] Zapu started to infiltrate guerrillas in 1964 but, before this, individuals had smuggled weapons into the country from as early as December 1962, for use in sabotage operations in the vicinity of Bulawayo. One of the first such caches was kept in Lupanda purchase area in Lupane by a farmer whose son, Abraham Nkiwane, had brought the weapons from Zambia via Victoria Falls, where security control was still 'extremely lax'. He left them at his father's home, proceeded to consult Joshua Nkomo, then still in detention in Matabeleland South. The weapons were retrieved by Findo Mpofu and security forces only discovered the cache when Tobias Bobylock Manyonga was arrested by the police at a roadblock near Zvishavane (interview by Pathisa Nyathi with Abraham Nkiwane, 1998). Ellert describes how 'the astonished Police Constable who examined Manyonga's vehicle found a number of Vintage Thompson and Lancaster sub-machine guns, .45 calibre ammunition and hand grenades. A second load was found at Hwange at the same time'. H. Ellert, *The Rhodesian Front War* (Gweru, Mambo Press, 1993), p. 9. In September 1964 an armed group of Zapu members entered the country by bus from Living-stone, Zambia, and then travelled by hired car to the extreme south of Matobo, where they attacked Dube ranch. Interview with Elliott Ngwabe, Esiphezini, 4 September 1998.

[19] Interview with Kilikiya Nyathi, Pupu, 16 February 1996.

*mateteni* (swamps) on the Pupu river, 'the place where cows get stuck'. They greeted Maluso Ndhlovu, the old man employed to tend the garden, and offered him a splendidly Shangani false identity. 'We're policemen. We've been sent to look for those illegally shooting animals along the river.' Pilot was off selling pigs in Lupane town; he was sent for; and around noon he arrived at his garden, where he agreed to provide them with mealie meal for which they would pay, they promised, when their police salaries came at the end of the month.[20] Meanwhile, the guerrillas dug a pit in the forest where they stored arms and ammunition and another pit for their sleeping quarters.

After some time, the guerrillas thought they could trust Pilot, though he was still unsure whether he could trust them. They asked him to bring the most influential elders; he 'called Jive Nyathi and Paul Nkomo, the senior old people of the area'. The guerrillas showed them 'pins bearing Josh's [Nkomo's] photo' and proclaimed their Zapu identity. Pilot still feared that they might really be police, so he denied any knowledge of Nkomo or of Zapu. But 'they continued, knowing that everyone had bought such pins: "You all contributed five shillings each at the meetings. We are what you got for your money." The three elders were told that they must greet each other every morning with the query 'How are the children?' as a signal that all was well. Then they were told to convene a general meeting of men from eight nearby villages. Four of the guerrillas attended, 'fully kitted out' and carrying their guns. They set up a food supply rota and promised that 'we'll start training you'. The *zilo* (rest day) – Thursday, because Pupu lay in Nevana's zone – was to be used for training. First they were taught how to use 'military types of knives' – Pilot says it took seven weeks. Then they were taught how to disassemble and assemble guns, all eight guerrillas now being involved. Finally they were taught 'how to build shelters in the bush, properly prepared and camouflaged.'

Meanwhile, the Rhodesian Police knew of the guerrilla incursion, had tracked their spoor through Hwange, and came round the villages showing people photos of some of the guerrillas and promising rewards. But, by this time, mutual trust had been established between the fighters and the locals. The guerrillas came at night to Pilot's home and in turn showed him where they lived in the bush.

Soon some locals were even more deeply involved. One of the guerrillas, Lazarus Masuku, was injured in a shooting accident, and Finneas Dapona decided to take him to hospital. They left their uniforms and weapons behind and the new commander, Robert Mpofu, decided to recruit and train two local youngsters. One of these was Daveti Sibanda, a leading Zapu youth militant. He recalls that he was 'very clear politically, as this was the home of Zapu. The guerrillas only required introduction.'[21]

Rhodesian searches of the area intensified. Dapona and Masuku had been captured on their way to hospital and under torture had revealed the general area of their hide-out. One day Rhodesian police were seen making their way directly towards it, but by 'a miracle' a duiker distracted their attention. The guerrillas decided that they must split up into two groups of four. A new camp was begun in another part of Pupu. But as one of the Shona-speaking guerrillas, Elijah Chifunya, was digging the pit, Steven Pausa Moyo came looking for his cattle in the bush. He was curious to know what Chifunya was doing. 'I'm digging a spring hare.' 'But why such a big hole?' Moyo noticed that Chifunya's Ndebele was poor. He went back and reported to his *sabhuku*, Jotamu Mkandla.

'Mkandla was a good boy to the government' and had been promised a reward of £60 if he discovered the guerrillas, so he went straight to Headman Ngubo, who in turn reported to the police. When the police did not immediately come, Mkandla became

---

[20] For this and for much of the narrative which follows we draw on the interview with Pilot Ncube and Daveti Sibanda, Lupahlwa, 2 April 1996.

[21] Interview with Daveti Sibanda, Lupahlwa, 2 April 1996.

over-eager and went himself to the second hideout. The four guerrillas were waiting; they fired on the approaching men and Mkandla was killed. Daveti recalls that 'our aim was to drop one person, any person, a lesson to the people not to interfere.' In particular, they wanted to kill a representative of the 'collaborating' class, a *sabhuku*, a headman or a chief. 'The Chief, Mabhikwa, couldn't be killed because he wasn't a sell-out.' But the meddling Mkandla, who 'envied money and not his life', was a suitable victim.[22]

The guerrillas decided that they had made Pupu too hot to hold them. They sent Chifunya and Chabungu ahead into Nkayi, and soon the other six followed them. Pilot Ncube and the other elders were left to face the Rhodesian music. Police went through all the schools, offering sweaters and other gifts to children. 'In one school, a child said: "My father gives food to people in the bush."' So the father was arrested together with many others. They were 'tortured, put in coffins and dropped from the air'.[23] Pilot himself recalls how he and 21 others were arrested and tortured. Meanwhile, Chifunya and Chabangu had been taken by the Rhodesians in Nkayi:

> Chabangu was tortured, they tied him around a tree, putting leg irons on his feet and handcuffs around his hands. They'd then attached the chain of the handcuffs to the jeep and driven the jeep forward away from the tree ... That is when he revealed the ammunitions dump up the Pupu river. So they found it and that was the end of our section.[24]

Two trials were held in Bulawayo, one for the guerrillas and one for their civilian helpers. Two of the guerrillas, Robert Mpofu and Sikhosana, who had shot Mkandla, were sentenced to death; the others got 21 years each. Each of the civilians got five years in Khami.

The Pupu incursion increased the level of violence in Lupane. For all the sabotage and arson and intimidation in Zapu's confrontation with the state, Mkandla was the first person to be killed by the nationalists. On the Rhodesian side, beatings and torture – sometimes fatal – became habitual ways of extracting information. The same was true for Nkayi, where the guerrillas went after leaving Pupu.

The contact man for the guerrillas there was Paul Mapetshwana Moyo, 'a prominent party member', who lived at Gampinya in northern Nkayi. 'This place was thick bush', he remembers, and the guerrillas 'decided to dig homes in the ravines', deep holes with rags to sleep on. Moyo went off to sell hides in Gweru and while he was away the guerrillas were arrested at his home. He came back to find soldiers sleeping around his house and helicopters parked on the ground. 'I'd never seen such a terrible army around.' He and his neighbours were taken to Gomoza for questioning. 'The entire people had been rounded up – as many people as there are leaves here.' They were severely tortured: 'One day we were taken by landrovers and tied hand and legs and hung upside down from a tree and beaten by logs. They could drag you behind a landrover ... Six people died in the Gomoza camp.' Some of the civilians got long jail sentences. Moyo was sent to Khami for only three months but was then restricted to Gonakudzingwa for five years.[25]

Noel Hunt has given his own account of combatting the guerrillas:

> There was a lot of unrest over land ownership in Nkai district at the time, and this fell in with the classic guerrilla thing ... exploit a local grievance, and there they

[22] Interview with Daveti Sibanda, Lupahlwa, 2 April 1996.
[23] Interview with Kilikiya Nyathi, Pupu, 16 February 1996.
[24] Interview with Daveti Sibanda, Lupahlwa, 2 April 1996.
[25] Interview with P.M. Moyo, Gampinya, 19 October 1995.

were exploiting it. And I kept on stamping on them, every time they did it – never had so much fun in my life.[26]

But while Hunt was having fun, the Rhodesian administration was disconcerted by the Pupu incursion. It lasted much longer and the guerrillas made much more effective contact with civilians than in any other guerrilla operation of this period. It seemed to show that, as Daveti Sibanda claimed, 'the guerrillas only required introduction' to achieve widespread support.

## Making Contours and the Coming of the Pearce Commission

However significant for the future the Pupu incursion was, its immediate effects were to set back the nationalist cause. Zapu had shown itself unable to meet the force of the Rhodesian government head on and incapable of protecting its sympathizers. The guerrillas seemed to have achieved nothing. Around Pupu itself, 'politically, people were not clear, they thought we were bringing them problems. Others were relatives of Jotamu Mkandla who had been shot.'[27] 'Up to the 1970s,' recalls 'Papa' Moyo, the Zionist activist at Pupu, 'the political climate was looking down. Because the momentum was reduced … as the result of the arrests.'[28]

Moreover, the Rhodesian regime had learnt how to prevent guerrilla groups from getting as far as Pupu. In 1971, leaks from the Rhodesian intelligence services were picked up by newspapers in France, South Africa and Zambia. These claimed that Rhodesian intelligence had infiltrated both Zapu and Zanu in Zambia; that they always had full details of operational plans with the result that guerrillas were rapidly captured and suffered 'death, imprisonments and tortures'; moreover, 'the actions of the security forces have apparently planted fear in the minds of even those who were ardent local supporters of the freedom fighters.' In particular, the leaks described in detail joint operations by Zapu and the South African ANC in August 1967. Two guerrilla groups, code-named Luthuli and Lobengula, 'slipped across the Zambezi in dugout canoes'. They were well-trained and well-armed. 'Their mission was to penetrate Rhodesia, establish base camps and guerrilla training facilities in the Nkai and Tjolotjo areas.' But neither group got further than 130 kilometres into Rhodesia. The Lobengula group was 'chased across Wankie game reserve and finally smashed in an engagement at Verney's Pan'.[29]

However self-interested these leaks were, they nevertheless more or less accurately described the situation of Nkayi and Lupane nationalists. After 1966, they were on their own, with the party's national leaders in restriction or exile, and with little prospect of immediate guerrilla arrivals. Oral informants say that from 1967 onwards the strategy of local confrontation was supplemented by recruitment and sending out of youth for guerrilla training.

[26] Interview with Noel Hunt, 27 November 1983, ORAL/240. Hunt dates these incursions to 1967 and 1968, though we have found no oral recollection of them. He is presumably describing one of these later incursions when he writes of 'one bunch' which hid themselves in 'an underground place' and could not be found for some time. 'I walked right over them there, I think a couple of times, because we found letters and tapes from them when we finally knocked them off, describing how this bloke in a white bush shirt had walked over them twice. They were lying there with a light machine-gun on me.'

[27] Interview with Pilot Ncube, Lupahlwa, 2 April 1996.

[28] Interview with Titus Sibanda Moyo, Pupu, 20 February 1996. The key local leader, Simon Ntoniswa, was sent to Gonakudzingwa for five years.

[29] *Times of Zambia*, 21 September 1971, drawing on reports in *La Spectacle du Monde* and the *South African Financial Gazette*.

An example of such combined activities is given by J. Gabheni Sibanda, Zapu activist in Lupanda, who was very active in organizing the escape of political detainees into Zambia as well as organizing resistance in Lupane. Like many of the important Lupane nationalists, Gabheni divided his time between Bulawayo and his rural home. He remembers:

> One day there was a man who was sought by the army and police. This was announced over the radio. We went to see him and met him at night. His name was E. Ndlovu. We quickly organized transport for him that same night and drove ... quickly to the Zambezi River where this man crossed the river to Zambia. ... After that I lost my job [in Bulawayo] and came back home to Lupanda. Again I was tasked with the underground movement ... The Vic Falls road was being tarred. All bulldozers had stopped operating because of sanctions. People were called up to come and were forced to work to provide manual labour which made many people into slaves on the roads. I campaigned against that vigorously. We used to write placards and put them on trees telling people not to go and work as slaves.[30]

Meanwhile, the apparatus of Community Development was gradually being put in place. Each chief had his own Council; in 1969 Tribal Land Authorities were gazetted. They at once issued Grazing and Cultivation Bye-Laws. Those for Tshugulu, Nkalakatha, Sikhobokhobo and Sivalo Tribal Land Authorities (TLAs) have been preserved on file. They state that their purpose is to ensure 'that the land available within the tribal area for grazing and cultivation is preserved, managed, used and developed to the best advantage of the inhabitants'; they empower the TLA to prohibit areas for grazing or cultivation; declare areas to be under the control of a kraalhead or group of kraalheads who wish 'to introduce a scheme for improving the quality' of grazing or arable, so that no outsider can use the land and any member of the kraals who uses it badly can be excluded. The TLA could compel conservation measures, have them carried out at the land-user's expense, or 'forthwith withdraw the consent given to the offending tribes-man to use that land'. The time had come, it seemed, for another effort at compelled conservation.[31]

An Nkayi informant recalls:

> The District Commissioner would summon the chiefs to his office and say the contours are a must. The chiefs and headmen would tell the people to do it ... This made the chiefs and headmen very unpopular ... Next would come the Conex people with the District Assistants and guns.[32]

The files now held at the Nkayi District Administrator's office are full of reports on how well, or badly, this particular chief or headman was doing in enforcing 'conservation' – indeed, in the annual rating given to traditional authorities, marks were given for 'contours' as well as for 'loyalty'.[33]

---

[30] Interview with J. Gabheni Sibanda, Lupanda, November 1994. Gabheni had used school-children to write the placards; when the children were picked up by the police 'I said release the children, admitted the case and we were brought to court and were sentenced to two years in jail.'
[31] These bye-laws are in LAN 1/GEN, Nkayi.
[32] Interview with D.C. Moyo, Manomano, 17 October 1995.
[33] The assessment of Headman Mziwaphansi, for example, rated him as good for loyalty to the state, for influence over his people, for his conduct of spiritual matters, and his support of the Dakamela Council, but poor for 'support on conservation and grazing schemes'. It was noted that he was 'dominated by Chief Dakamela and follows his unprogressive attitude towards

H.R. Henderson, whose article on Land Husbandry we cited in Chapter 3, went on to discuss with approval the effects of the newer system. In 1971, a third comprehensive aerial photograpic record was compiled for Nkayi, and Henderson was able to compare this to the aerial photographs of 1955 and 1964. He found that, while the exact allocations of Land Husbandry were no longer maintained, the district had not 'in general reverted in geographical terms to anything resembling the unplanned state', and that 'planning under the Land Tenure Act appears to have made a reasonably successful start in the Nkai district, mainly because it has operated within the context of the tribal society to which it has been applied.' Henderson took Headman Huba Moyo's *isigaba* as an example, pointing out that the area did not coincide with the previous Land Husbandry planning unit. But during the early 1970s 'a plan had been agreed and construction of conservation crests and water ways was in progress.'[34]

However, despite the setbacks to nationalism, these new planning processes were still meeting with opposition. In October 1970, the Lands Inspector, Lupane, wrote a long report to the District Commissioner, Nkayi, about his recent 'safari' through that district. The Inspector found that district officials had 'a most comprehensive set of maps and statistics' and that they were 'going about the conservation drive in a well organised manner'. In 1969, 3,000 acres had been pegged in various parts of Nkayi, 'with a certain amount of resistance'; this year a further 10,000 acres had been pegged. 'The District Commissioner anticipated a certain amount of trouble once the rains started properly, in cases where cultivation was to cease in the pegged areas'; he was standing ready to prosecute uncooperative kraalheads. At Singwangombe, he found that none of the ten men previously prosecuted as uncooperative 'have done a thing since being prosecuted and therefore early action will have to be taken by me'.[35]

People disliked contours – the *amakandiwa* – intensely. There was outrage at not only having to dig them but also having to pay for them. Enormous labour was required, yet people commonly thought that contours on the sandy soils of the *gusu* were futile as water inflitrates rapidly, rather than running off the surface to make gulleys. Many informants told us that contours 'started the war'. 'With the introduction of contours, that's when people resisted,' says Moffat Mbombo, from the north-east Nkayi/Gokwe border. 'Many people joined the political struggle through the pain of the contours.'[36] In the same area Timothy Mthethwa was detained both in 1968 and 1969 'because they thought I'd organised people here to refuse the contours'. Since 1965, Timothy had been a member of 'underground Zapu. We called it "the church of the orphans".' The imposition of contours gave him a chance to come above ground.[37] In Gampinya, Paul Mapetshwana Moyo, returning in 1971 after his five years' detention for helping the guerrillas in 1965, found that:

> in 1971 we had contours. They were introduced by force. We had to dig them and pay for them. If you didn't dig them, you couldn't plough. The Conex would dig a square hole at the end of the contour and that was called a policeman. If you ploughed there you would be fined.

[33] (cont.) conservation'. Headman Nhlanganiso was rated poor on everything; Headman Mpande was sober and loyal but bad on projects and conservation. 'High percentage Nats. Frightened man, can't assert his authority.' These particular assessments were made in 1976 and can be found in a Nkayi file which also contains kraal assessments from that year.

[34] H.J.R. Henderson, 'Legislation and Land-Use Planning in Rhodesia: An Example of Recent Landscape Evolution in the Nkai Tribal Trust Land', *Swansea Geographer*, 15, 1977. There is an extraordinary avoidance of the political in Henderson's article. By 1977, when it was published, all land-use planning in Nkayi had been engulfed by war.

[35] Lands Inspector, Lupane to District Commissioner, Nkayi, 26 October 1970, LAN 1/GEN, Nkayi.

[36] Interview with Moffat Mbombo, Mateme, 7 December 1995.

[37] Interview with Timothy Mthethwa, Mateme, 1 December 1995.

Then there came storm drains, which Moyo thought 'were not actually doing anything. It was only a punishment.' He settled down to organizing resistance.[38]

Into this situation came the visit of the Pearce Commission to test African opinion on the Smith/Home constitutional proposals agreed by the Rhodesian and British governments in 1971. The Pearce Commission arrived in Rhodesia in January 1972. The chiefs, gathered together for the purpose, told the commissioners that they accepted the proposals. Then the commissioners broke up to tour the country and to test African public opinion. A condition of their visit was that 'normal political activity' was to be allowed. The African National Council was formed, under the leadership of Bishop Abel Muzorewa, to express opposition to the proposals. Branches of the Council were legally formed all over the country. Moreover, in order to create a constructive climate, an instruction was issued that no prosecutions should proceed under the Land Tenure Act without the explicit approval of the Attorney General.[39]

The results of all this in the Shangani were striking. Those who had refused to make contours had an amnesty from prosecution. Old Zapu branches revived and mobilized their members. 'Around the time of the Pearce Commission there was mobilization here,' says 'Papa' Moyo from Pupu. Pilot Ncube had returned to Pupu in 1971 from his five years detention for helping the guerrillas; 'on my return, I rejoined the party, taking the post of organizing secretary'. Pilot took the lead in instrumenting the rejection of the proposals.[40] Wide-ranging political activities were planned at St Paul's in eastern Lupane.[41] In western Lupane, the Lupanda activist, Gabheni Sibanda, returned from Bulawayo to organize the 'no' campaign. Moffat Mbombo from Mateme in north-eastern Nkayi thinks that 'the formation of branches, districts etc., was at the time of the [African National Council].'[42]

The return of restrictees and the persistence of Zapu's underground organizers presented the two Pearce Commissioners who toured the Shangani with a well-organized and effective public rejection. The chiefs affirmed their support; every public meeting affirmed its opposition:

> All too often the public meetings followed the same pattern. Large crowds, well organized and drilled, were dominated by a few politically active cheerleaders, the presence of two or three of whom was sufficient to stifle any public debate. ... We saw the same faces of cheerleaders and ex-detainees at every meeting.

The Commissioners decided that the verdict of public meetings was based on ignorance and intimidation. They therefore paid attention only to their private meetings with individuals. On this basis they found that Nkayi favoured the proposals and that Lupane did not.[43] The overall Commission report agreed that 'there was a greater degree of

---

[38] Interview with P.M. Moyo, Gampinya, 19 October 1995.

[39] DC Nkayi to PC, 15 July 1972, LAN 23. Rural Development Planning, Dev 82/84, Nkayi, Bulawayo Records Office. There was a debate between the Commission and the Rhodesian government about what constituted normal political activity. The Secretary for Internal Affairs, Hostes Nicolle, told them that 'normal political activity operates only through the tribal system as modified by legislation, which means that it is restricted to working within the tribal machinery and this machine does not permit individuals to appoint themselves as independent leaders, because to do this would clearly undermine the established authority, cause it to collapse and culminate in chaos.'

[40] Interviews with Titus Sibanda Moyo, Pupu, 20 February 1996; Pilot Ncube, Lupahlwa, 2 April 1996.

[41] Interview with Enoch Ncube, Malunku, St Paul's, 6 March 1996.

[42] Interview with Moffat Mbombo, Mateme, 7 December 1996.

[43] *Report of the Commission on Rhodesian Opinion under the Chairmanship of the Right Honourable the Lord Pearce*, Cmnd.4964, London, May 1972, pp. 178–9, 200.

support for the proposals in Matabeleland North than in the remainder of the country' because of the following factors: the sparse population of Matabeleland North; its 'tribal existence remote from the influence of the cities'; the fact that 'the political organizations have probably not penetrated some of the outlying areas'; the 'low degree of comprehension' in the province. [44]

A certain amount of fruitless ink has been spilt in attempts to explain why Nkayi 'favoured' the proposals, and it has been seriously suggested that this 'home of Zapu' was politically backward. It is clear, as Judy Todd suggested in 1972, that it was the two Commissioners rather than Nkayi district who were out of step. Their report 'was worthy of the pen of the Rhodesian Ministry of Internal Affairs'. 'What does an ex-detainee look like?', she asked rhetorically. 'I would like to know, as one day I hope to be an ex-detainee myself.'[45] Both the commissioners had served for many years in Northern Rhodesia. They reacted against the degree of Zapu/ANC success in Nkayi and Lupane rather than against political immaturity.

Some of the details are interesting. The Purchase Farmers of Lupanda – brought into nationalist politics by the original African National Congress restrictees – were solidly against the proposals. Because of Muzorewa's leadership of the African National Council and the prominent role of other clergy, like Canaan Banana and Henry Kachidza, many teachers and black clergy came back into the nationalist fold in 1972. Still, the identity of those in Nkayi who opposed Muzorewa and the ANC is also interesting.

One of them, for instance, was the Reverend Aaron Ndebele of the Free Presbyterian Church in Nkayi, who told the Commission that rejection of the proposals would result in 'economic and political suicide' and 'bring hero-worship for Bishop Muzorewa and his ANC – an organization sponsored by the World Council of Churches and open supporters of terrorism.'[46] Nathaniel Mpofu, whose autobiography we quoted earlier and who in 1972 was still trying to establish himself as a Presbyterian minister, records his many struggles with Ndebele. Ndebele was buying cows and 'renting them in a ranch' and often going off to inspect them instead of preaching and teaching, 'spending his time more like a farmer than a minister'. By contrast, Mpofu, who was posted in 1971 to work under Ndebele at Ingwenya Mission, was despised as 'a man come from the bush'. Despite his fervent Calvinism, Mpofu 'was beginning to look at the church work in contrast with the political situation. The church government was now suppression and not free. I stopped working at the mission because at the end of the day I would be labelled as an informer to the white people.'[47]

## Refurbishing the Tribal System

The Shangani's rejection of the constitutional proposals despite the stand taken by the chiefs outraged the Department of Internal Affairs. The major theme of the period between 1972 and the large-scale guerrilla incursions was the government's attempts to bolster the chiefs and to fine-tune the 'traditional' system. In the later part of 1972, prosecutions for conservation offences began again and chiefs were supported by strong official and police action. At the same time, there was rethinking of the bases of Community Development.

In February 1973, the Secretary, Internal Affairs, circulated all administrators in Southern Rhodesia. 'In the past,' he admitted, 'we have had some unfortunate

---

[44] *Ibid.*, p. 61.
[45] Judith Todd, *The Right to Say No. Rhodesia 1972* (London, Sidgwick and Jackson, 1972), pp. 175–6. Judith Todd was in detention at the time she wrote her book.
[46] *Rhodesia Herald*, 12 February 1972.
[47] Autobiography of Nathaniel Mpofu.

experiences in using the tribal system, notably in our conservation drive, but these disappointments resulted not from the tribal structure or organization as such but perhaps from using incorrect levels of the organization.' It was important to support the chief and the headman. 'But the important level is the *musha/imizi* level', the level of the village.

So it was urgently necessary to recognize and identify 'the small sub-communities making up these tribes. These sub-communities consist of groups of people bound by a common spiritual and family allegiance, who within a definable area live, cultivate and graze their stock.' *Imizi* were to be identified not just by counting kraals since they might consist of several linked kraal populations. 'The information required can only be obtained in the field by questioning the people themselves. This work can be done by community advisers, district assistants or agricultural demonstrators.' Once the *imizi* had been identified, all future development operations should be based on them. 'This requires the establishment of a clearly defined boundary on the ground between the village and its neighbours. This boundary in most cases did not exist previously ... The boundary so established must be marked on an aerial photograph and then transferred to a map.'[48]

Little more than three years before the guerrilla war consumed Nkayi and Lupane, its administrators embarked on yet another project of survey, delineation and mapping. The District Commissioners for Matabeleland North met in April 1973 and agreed on the new policy. At the end of the month, the Provincial Commissioner instructed them to proceed with delineation, since only 'when this has been done with the boundaries defined and mapped, and the basic statistic extracted for each area, can we start on any effective planning'.[49]

The new policy took time. In October and November 1975, an experienced administrator, M.E. Hayes, travelled through Nkayi and Lupane interviewing every chief and headman about religion and ritual – topics left out of the original delineation exercise of ten years earlier. Hayes' findings on rainshrines and spirit possession revealed the complex division of responsibility between the evictees and locals.[50] As late as 1976, assessments of every kraal in Nkayi were being carried out, revealing all their ethnic, religious and social complexity. We have worked through the kraal assessments for Chief Tshugulu's area. Some kraalheads assessed came originally from Hwange, Bubi, Fort Rixon, Filabusi, etc. Some boasted that their 'ancestors came from Zululand with Mzilikazi' accompanied by 'the Matabele Nation'; others claimed to be indigenous to the area. Some said that their tutelary spirits were *Isangoma*, others that they were *Ujukwa*, others insisted that they were Apostolics and recognized only the Holy Spirit. Some named traditional herbalists as their recognized healer; many answered with 'Dr Decker at St Paul's'. Kraalhead Mbangwa Ncube, under Headman Mpande, Chief Tshugulu, told assessors that he was a member of the African National Council and attended ANC meetings at other kraals; very many of the kraalheads under Headman Fanisoni, also under Chief Tshugulu, felt confident enough to define themselves as members of 'ANC Nkomo'.[51]

[48] Secretary, Internal Affairs, Circular, February 1973 and Annexure A, LAN 23, Rural Planning, Dev 82/84, Nkayi.

[49] Provincial Commissioner to District Commissioners, 30 April 1973, *ibid*.

[50] Hayes' reports are in chiefs' and headmen's files in the Provincial and District Administrator's offices. By interviewing each chief and headman and their main rainmakers (and excluding those not recognised or used by these authorities), however, the report gives a misleading picture of stability and consensus on what was a highly contentious question.

[51] These kraal assessments also included details of cattle holdings and methods of land allocation. In one kraal a man owned 42 cattle, 26 acres and had two wives and 21 children; six fellow residents owned no cattle at all though all had not less than six acres of land. A full analysis of

## The Ambiguities of Tradition

By 1976, the whole Community Development structure was being swallowed up in war. The mapping of *imizi* threatened to disrupt the simple idea of 'traditional' Ndebele chiefship. But in any case, well before that, the policy had revealed many ambiguities and weaknesses.

It was essential to the policy, for instance, to delineate and map chiefs' areas. These had been laid down by Native Commissioner Cockroft in the late 1940s. Faced with a 'chaotic situation', he made 'some arbitrary decisions'.[52] As a result, disputes between chiefs raged right through the Rhodesian period. In 1963, the District Commissioner, Nkayi, reported the grievances of two 'outstanding chiefs', Dakamela and Nkalakatha, who both had small areas and whom he wished to reward with much more territory. These disputes were still unresolved in 1968 when there was also 'a sharp dispute' between Chiefs Sikhobokhobo and Sivalo. Another attempt was made at a final delineation of chiefs' areas in 1969, though 'it is a possibility that difficulty will be experienced, in which case it may be necessary to make some arbitrary settlement.' It was not until September 1970 that tribal areas were finally published in terms of the Land Tenure Act.[53] But disputes still went on into the 1970s.

The effect of such disputes can best be illustrated by the case of Chief Dakamela. Dakamela was in many ways the model chief of Nkayi district. In 1956, he had been awarded the Bledisloe Medal and been described by his Native Commissioner as a 'very able chief' and 'without a doubt the best Master Farmer in the district', who 'by his good example has influenced a large percentage of his following into better methods of agriculture, so that his area is the most productive in the district.' The Native Commissioner thought that when Land Husbandry allocation was complete, Dakamela's 'area will be the most progressive in the district'.[54] Dakamela rotated crops on 16 acres of land; used manure; possessed brickbuilt farm buildings and a good deal of farm machinery.

In December 1961, Dakamela specifically asked the Native Commissioner to convey 'a message of thanks to the Prime Minister of Southern Rhodesia for the firm action that has been taken against the National Democratic Party'.[55] In 1962, he was invited to attend the opening of parliament; in 1963, he was awarded the Queen's Silver Medal; in 1965, he attended a funeral service for Winston Churchill and also a Conservation Course for chiefs. In 1968, when financial allowances were increased for Nkayi chiefs to £420 a year, only Dakamela got an additional £60. In 1970, he received the Independence Commemoration Decoration. In 1971, when he was a leading member of the Council of Chiefs, he was described as commanding 'terrific respect in the district, albeit as a dictator'.[56]

But, by the 1970s, the former model farmer was becoming known as opposed to most conservation measures. The reason was that his gazetted area was so small. In 1967, he had complained that he was 'settled in a farm of other chiefs'.[57] He owned large herds of cattle, many of which were lent out to his people. There was not enough grazing land in

---

[51] (cont.) these assessments, which are in a large Nkayi file, would obviously be very valuable for an economic and social profile of the district in the late 1970s.

[52] DC Nkayi to PC, 9 September 1970, LAN 1/GEN, 1962–1970, Nkayi.

[53] DC Nkayi to PC, 22 March 1963; DC to Secretary, Internal Affairs, 18 March 1968; Secretary, Internal Affairs to PC, 5 July 1968; Secretary, Internal Affairs to PC, 4 October 1969; DC to PC, 9 September 1970, *ibid.*

[54] NC Nkayi to PNC, 14 July 1956, file, Chief Myinga Dakamela, Nkayi.

[55] Assistant NC to PNC, 13 December 1961, *ibid.*

[56] DC to PC, 7 April 1971, *ibid.*

[57] Myinga Dakamela to PC, 7 August 1967, *ibid.*

his own area so 'for many years', it was reported in 1971, 'the Dakamela people have been grazing their cattle in adjacent areas. The increasing pressure on the land in these areas is causing friction ... Consequently, when cattle were moved into the area of Sikhobokhobo, violated reserved grazing areas and trespassed on cultivated land, it was inevitable that trouble would ensue.' For their part, Dakamela and his people announced that 'they would punish any person preventing the free movement of stock.' In April 1971, there was an affray in which some of his people 'suffered a minor skull-bashing' in Sikhobokhobo's land and others were fined in courts there for damage to crops. Dakamela had 'a sense of complete frustration, for his area is stocked at the rate of one beast to three acres and he himself owns about 1,000 head of cattle alone'. His area amounted to only 35,000 acres, much of which was waste. He feared great stock losses. He was ready neither to destock – Internal Affairs asserted that his area was 65% overstocked – nor to use up land by making contours.[58] When presented with a cultivation and grazing plan for his area by government agriculturalists, Dakamela flatly refused it. He also refused to command his people to work on contours, saying 'that nothing would be done unless government did it all'.[59]

This problem was not confined to Dakamela's people. 'The delineation of firm boundaries was bound to cause trouble where past grazing had been on an "at will" basis.' Now the chief's *izigaba* had to be the unit of land management and all grazing and cultivation carried out within it. Dakamela called for a Commission of Inquiry into these arrangements; in 1973, he was still 'pushing more of his starving stock from his hopelessly overstocked area' into neighbouring areas.[60] So far from being the most fertile and progressive area in the district, Dakamela's 35,000 acres were now regarded as barren and worked out.

But despite all this, Dakamela continued to be essential to the Rhodesia Front system. In 1974 he was elected to the Senate. In 1975, while he was still complaining bitterly about his frontiers and failing to implement conservation, he was granted Emergency Powers as a District Authority 'to counter terrorist activities'. He could arrest without a warrant, and deal with anyone on the spot who caused 'feelings of hostility toward yourself', including administering 'moderate correction' in the shape of whipping or the seizure of property.[61] The same year he was rated 'very good' for loyalty, power, control over spiritual matters; 'good' for interest in schools; but 'poor' for support of conservation and grazing schemes. 'If only his area was as impressive as his decorations,' wrote the assessor. In 1976, a similar assessment found that 'he continues to rule his area with an iron hand. However conservation-wise his area is literally "bombed out".'[62]

The Nkayi Headman's files reveal in a rather different way the problems for traditional authorities over conservation. Unlike Dakamela, many headmen were expendable. Headman Mpande, for example, first had to deny that he was spreading rumours blaming his chief for 'introducing contours', and was then prosecuted in May 1972 under the Natural Resources Act for failing to ensure that contours in his area were properly maintained; Headman Mlume, whose predecessor had been removed for participating in demonstrations against contours, complained in 1970 that he was being abused as a 'Tshombe' – a sellout – because he supported them.

In May 1975, Noel Hunt, now high up in the Internal Affairs Department, sent a memorandum suggesting how to combat 'the decline in power and prestige of the tribal hierarchy begun during the Pearce Commission and compounded by the present

---

[58] DC to PC, 7 May 1971, *ibid.*
[59] Memo, 'Chief Dakamela', n.d. *ibid.*
[60] DC to PC, 28 November 1973, *ibid.*
[61] DC to Chief Dakamela, 15 August 1975, *ibid.*
[62] Chiefs' Assessments, 1975 and 1976, *ibid.*

detente exercise'. Hunt suggested that Chiefs' Councils should levy rates on cattle and land holdings. The District Commissioner, Nkayi, M.J. Hood, clearly had Dakamela in mind when he ruefully commented that he could not see 'such a revolutionary change' appealing to any of his Chiefs' Councils. 'One of my chiefs is reputed to own over 1000 head of cattle which even at 10c per head per annum will be liable to pay $100, not to mention the tax which should be imposed on his lands.'[63]

Dakamela's case reveals the predicament of the authorities when dealing with an able and strong chief. So, too, does the case of Chief Mabhikwa. His support was so critical to the regime that it was prepared to extend all sorts of favours to him, the building of an airstrip so that he could fly to visit 'his people' at Inkosikazi; assistance with 'the new house that he is building'; compensation for land taken over by the expansion of the Tribal Trust Lands Corporation agricultural estate (though his people were moved off fertile black soils in the Shangani valley with no question of compensation).[64]

The case of Chief Madliwa Tshoko, on the other hand, shows what happened when administrators were presented with an eccentric and incompetent chief. Kuya Madliwa emerges from the files as drunken, adulterous, peculating and unpredictable. He feared attempts on his life by Zapu supporters and would do little to provoke them. 'At a recent meeting in the Sabawisa area,' wrote the District Commissioner in September 1969, 'he was at pains to point out that [contours] were a Government action and that since they ruled they would have to be done ... I have had the greatest difficulty in obtaining any co-operation at all and in many instances he has obviously been obstructive in a very subtle manner, e.g. when told peggers required good sight he promptly sent in two candidates with only one eye and the other less than 50% effective.'[65] His behaviour undermined 'the whole structure as it exists at present'; his salary was regularly reduced; in 1972, he was prosecuted for cattle theft and judicial corruption, but the conviction was set aside, much to the District Commissioner's fury. A chief was needed under the Natural Resources Act, he wrote, but to allow Madliwa 'to continue in office is to ridicule the tribal system, embarrass the chiefs and undermine the administration'.[66] Madliwa was still in office in 1976, when he reportedly called African District Assistants 'the Dogs of the District Commissioner'; however, it was 'not an opportune time to depose him'.[67]

The most interesting issue raised by Madliwa's case, however, concerns what was meant by 'tradition'. The evictees rejected his authority (as they also did Mabhikwa's) as 'untraditional'. But Madliwa was a strong supporter of 'traditional religion' and in particular of divining, witch-finding and witch-cleansing. In June 1964, Noel Hunt reported that Madliwa had called in a 'witchdoctor from another district', paying him £16 'to ascertain what had caused the death of two children'. 'He asked my permission to do this – itself hardly the act of a sensible man – and later sent a deputation to seek permission again.' Hunt explained the terms of the Witchcraft Suppression Act. But Madliwa later 'sent in the witchdoctor to introduce himself before he began work'.[68]

It seems clear that Madliwa thought that Hunt, who was so strong a traditionalist and who is remembered by informants as urging them to pray to the rainshrines and to their ancestors, would endorse chiefly action against witchcraft. And there had been a

[63] N. Hunt to PC, 9 May 1975; DC, Nkayi to PC, 27 May 1975, SMO Miscellaneous 1974 and 1975, Nkayi.
[64] Tribal Trust Lands, General, LAN 9; Tilcor Irrigation Projects, General, AGR 16.
[65] DC, Nkayi to PC, 15 September 1969, Chief Madliwa, Nkayi.
[66] DC Nkayi to PC, 27 February 1973, *ibid.*
[67] DC, Nkayi to PC, 10 November 1976, *ibid.*
[68] DC, Nkayi to PC, 16 June 1964, *ibid.*

long history in the Shangani of dispute between administrators and chiefs over the issue.[69]

Under Direct Rule the Native Commissioner, Bubi, had launched a personal crusade against witch-finding. In 1909, he had taken up the death of Chief Ngege, blamed on the witchcraft of his brother, Mleya, as an opportunity to deal what he hoped would be a final blow to what he called 'bone-throwing'. With the support of the Chief Native Commissioner, he laid on a show trial.[70] Of course, a show trial could not end divination. The practice went underground. Demands that it be legitimated surfaced again in 1951, when the evictions were producing so many tensions and there were so many deaths from malaria. 'There was not a chief present,' it was asserted at one Provincial Assembly, 'in whose country there were not 10 or 20 witches killing people and the witchdoctors should be allowed to deal with them'.[71]

Under the modified Indirect Rule of Community Development, many chiefs quietly began to assume responsibility for controlling witches. In 1975, Hayes found that the contemporary *isangoma* was 'in fact, a witch finder'; he also found that Chief Mabhikwa's court in Lupane had heard witchcraft cases the month before his visit.[72] Oral informants tell us that witchcleansers moved through the Shangani in the early 1970s. But the eccentric Madliwa was the only chief who kept on presenting the Internal Affairs Department with the dilemma of whether witch-finding should be regarded as 'traditional'. In September 1969, he declared that he saw 'no necessity for people informing the kraalheads before they visit certain witch-doctors'. The District Commissioner complained that Madliwa had supported an *isangoma* who had 'made strong anti-government comments'.[73] Internal Affairs dealt with this by holding that *they* supported traditional 'religion' and that the nationalists made use of 'witchcraft'. By supporting witch-finders, Madliwa was showing that 'he is in sympathy with the nationalists'. In 1973, the District Commissioner found a good 'traditional' explanation for Madliwa's behaviour – he had been driven crazy as a result of 'his ancestors' displeasure for the Tshoko family accepting a chieftainship which tradition forbade'.[74] In effect, the District Commissioner was now siding with the troublesome evictees!

## The Ambiguities of Development

In the unreal period between the departure of the Pearce Commission and the arrival of Zipra guerrillas in large numbers, while the Internal Affairs Department was trying to discover the 'real' traditional system and Joshua Nkomo was trying to negotiate with Ian Smith, a sort of quiet fell on the Shangani. District administrators, as well as trying to 'develop' through the chiefs, also attempted some development plans of their own. One of District Commissioner Johnstone's pet schemes was the development of an export business in *ilala* palms. But the 'development' project which was to have the greatest repercussions in the future was the attempt to establish a wildlife and bird-watching zone in the Gwampa Valley. It was a form of 'development' which seemed to

[69] Terence Ranger, 'Patterns of Witchcraft Belief and Control in Northern Matabeleland', November 1996.

[70] Annual Report, Bubi, October 1909, N6/4/10; Rex versus Mzungu and Simelwane, 19 October 1909, D3/23/1.

[71] Minutes of the Midlands Provincial Assembly, 28 October 1951 and 27 August 1952, S 2796/2/1.

[72] M.E. Hayes, November 1975, CHK 6/LU/Mtenjwa and Mabhikwa, Provincial Administrator's Office, Bulawayo.

[73] DC to PC, 15 September 1969, *ibid.*

[74] DC to PC, 27 February 1973, *ibid.*

Africans to favour animals and birds over human beings and to reverse decades of clearing the land of wild beasts, of making it 'civilized'.

This project was first conceived by the Rhodesian Forestry Commission, 'half-owners of the Gwampa Valley', who introduced a multiple-use policy in the forests south of the Gwampa, under which 'wildlife that is compatible with forestry is being fostered.' The Commission gave concessions for 'hunting safaris' along the Gwampa.[75] In July 1975 the Forester, Lupane, approached the District Commissioners of Nkayi and Lupane, proposing that Internal Affairs join in the scheme, since 'both our departments are becoming more wildlife/conservation conscious'. His emphasis was on birds – 'the number and variety of the species on the [Gwampa] system is nothing short of fantastic.' Lake Alice and every other dam and pan in the valley should be proclaimed as sanctuaries. The District Commissioners enthusiastically agreed.[76]

This benevolent sounding project – the direct ancestor of the contemporary Campfire scheme for the Gwampa discussed in Chapter 10 – in fact involved a good deal of human policing and displacement. In 1970, the Forestry Commission announced that 1,250 people were to be removed from Lake Alice and Gwampa Forests. There were 'mass moves' out of the forests into the northern Gwampa area in Nkayi and into Chief Mabhikwa's area of Lupane. These moves gave rise to 'all manner of rumour'.[77] Meanwhile, the Forestry Commission instituted and policed severe regulations against those who still remained on their land. Permit-holders were expelled for 'possessing snares', hunting without permission, and for cultivating streambanks. In October 1974, Forest Guard I.M. Ngwenya issued the following notice:

All habits written below are not allowed … to extract honey from the forest … burning of the veldt is an offence. Carrying an axe is an offence. Going about in the company of dogs is an offence. Going about with a spear or a wire is an offence. Never you walk along with either a dog or an axe.[78]

All this was creating a very different sort of forest culture from that of the nineteenth or early twentieth centuries. The displacement and regulation was very deeply resented. In 1965, when the first attempts to regulate use of the Gwampa Valley were being made, the Group Inspector of Lands was optimistic that 'any scheme to use the valley legally and with a certain amount of tenure … will meet with co-operation.'[79] But the idea of the valley as a game and bird safari area met with a very different reception. People living on the Tribal Trust Land side of the Gwampa objected strongly to the influx of families evicted from the Forest. They resisted the imposition of constraints on their own cultivation, herding and hunting. Contemporary memory adds these Forest evictions and this attempt to establish animal sanctuaries to the forced building of contours as the oppressive acts of illegitimate colonial government.

District Commissioners were also engaged in development projects designed to improve communications or agricultural production. The possibilities of irrigation were

[75] Memorandum on Gwampa Valley Conservation, Fritz Meyer, Conservation Organizer for the Rhodesian Ornithological Society, August 1975, LAN 23 Nkayi.

[76] Forester, Lupane to District Commissioners, Lupane and Nkayi, 29 July 1975; District Commissioner, Nkayi to Forester, Lupane, 26 August 1975, LAN 23 Nkayi.

[77] Meeting between Forestry Commission and Internal Affairs, 5 June 1970; Acting DC Nkayi to PC, 12 June 1970, LAN GEN/1 Nkayi. PC to DCs, 23 October 1970; PC to Secretary, Internal Affairs, 26 May 1971, LAN 23 Nkayi.

[78] The original of this notice of 3 October 1974 was in Ndebele. We quote from the translation made for the DC, LAN 23 Nkayi.

[79] Group Inspector, Lands to Provincial Commissioner and Native Commissioners, 2 July 1965, LAN 1/GEN Nkayi.

explored. Five Year District Development Plans were drawn up. But not much came of all this. The people of the Shangani were low on the development priority list. 'The people of Nkai District have in the past been uncooperative,' noted the Provincial Commissioner, urging postponement of a large irrigation scheme on the Shangani river. They had now to prove that they were ready to assist in their own development.[80] In 1972, District Commissioner Johnstone of Nkayi set out his estimates for Development Fund expenditure over the next four years. The Government should be prepared to pay for roads, he thought, but 'local government must play a large part in any expenditure on soil conservation and water supplies and until they are making this contribution no consideration should be given to further Primary Development.'[81] Given the fixed view of the evictees that government should meet all costs of developing the wilderness in which they had been dumped, and the opposition shown to every conservation scheme, it was very unlikely that 'local government' was going to contribute to 'Primary Development' expenditure.

In any case, the Development Fund was increasingly drawn on for security rather than for development purposes. In May 1975, District Commissioner Hood asked that money be used 'in the interests of security and Tribal Land Authority flying' for an airstrip in 'the extreme north-west most inaccessible part of my district'. Later that year, the Development Fund was in any case cut by 15%. By March 1977, it was being used to pay for Adams grenades for protection of chiefs and administrative personnel; by July 1977, there was not enough available to maintain dipping services throughout the year.[82]

## Conclusion

When the guerrilla war began in earnest, the Shangani was still ideal insurgent territory. 'Apart from the Huggins Bridge and a small causeway at Fanisoni upstream,' wrote the District Commissioner, Nkayi, 'the District is divided by the Shangani River. It is possible to cross with wheeled vehicles only during the dry season.' Despite all the efforts of the past years, the population was still heavily concentrated 'along the main rivers', leaving large areas of *gusu* very thinly populated and open for guerrilla encampments. In fact, 'the water level has dropped and several boreholes no longer yield', so that some people were abandoning *gusu* sites. There was still little marketing of agricultural or any other produce; womens' clubs were growing but were being given little or nothing practical to do; there was still 'no regular goods service to Nkayi'.[83]

It was not much to show. And if development had been unsuccessful, so too had the attempt to win support by reinventing tradition. The people of Nkayi and Lupane remained unconvinced that any local solutions – still less those of Community Development – could be found for their problems. They remained committed to a national solution and to nationalism. They awaited the return of the men they had sent out to be trained as guerrillas.

By 1976, the Internal Affairs officials well understood the difficulties of winning hearts and minds. District Commissioner Hood of Nkayi responded in September of that year to a proposal for a structured youth movement 'to instil a feeling of patriotism'. It was a good idea, he said, but Internal Affairs must stay right out of it:

[80] PC to Secretary, Internal Affairs, 28 February 1967, LAN/GEN 1, 1967–70, Nkayi.
[81] Memorandum, DC, Nkayi to PC, 22 September 1972, LAN 22 1972–8, Nkayi.
[82] *Ibid.*
[83] DC, Nkayi to PC, 'Five Year Development Plan: Nkai District', 26 February 1969, LAN/GEN 1, 1967–1970, Nkayi.

Regrettably at this time Internal Affairs could not engender these feelings as in the eyes of many of the people, no doubt due in the main to the propaganda put out by Nationalists, who have labelled us as oppressors here merely to ensure that they dig their contours, dip their cattle, have their lands pegged, make them accept councils and pay taxes.[84]

[84] DC to PC, 8 September 1976, LAN 23 Rural Planning. Dev 82/84, Nkayi.

# Part II

## Wars &
## their Legacies

# 6

# The Liberation War
# in the Shangani

By the mid-1970s, the violence of conquest, of forced migration, of state agrarian policies and of political repression had long shaped the Shangani, giving its inhabitants an unusually refined understanding of state power, as well as of strategies of resistance, accommodation and adaptation. The colonial machinery had not, however, faced any real threat since the wars of the 1890s. Eighty years later, and more than ten years after the first incursions of Zapu guerrillas, the Rhodesian state faced its first real challenge. The genesis of this challenge in the evolution of Zapu's military strategy, the consequences for Rhodesian administration and counter-insurgency, and memories of state violence are the topic of this chapter.

In exploring this period of the Shangani's history, we draw primarily on the testimonies of guerrillas and civilians. Guerrilla accounts of the war are rich in their analysis of the military threat posed by the Rhodesian forces, and vivid in their depiction of the formative experiences of military training and political education, of the tactics and skills deployed in the field. We use guerrilla accounts to explore the development of Zipra strategy and the rapid process through which control of the Shangani was wrested from the Rhodesian state. The unarmed inhabitants of the Shangani faced the same Rhodesian units as the guerrillas, but remembered them in different ways. Civilians were concerned to make moral distinctions between the various state forces. Their accounts highlight an often neglected aspect of the war's history: the role played by paramilitary forces.[1] A focus on these forces reveals the central role of moral judgements about war in shaping memories of violence.

## Guerrilla Insurgency, 1976–79

Zanu's breakaway from Zapu in 1963 set the stage for the development of distinctive

---

[1] N. Bhebe and T. Ranger discuss the lack of attention paid to paramilitaries in their 'Volume Introduction: Soldiers in Zimbabwe's Liberation War', in N. Bhebe and T. Ranger (eds), *Soldiers in Zimbabwe's Liberation War* (London, James Currey, 1995), pp. 22–3. Studies of the 'protected villages' in eastern Zimbabwe have begun to explore the role played by paramilitaries in social change. See particularly the recent studies of H. Schmidt, 'Love and Healing in Forced Communities: Borderlands in Zimbabwe's War of Liberation', in P. Nugent and A.I. Asiwaju (eds), *African Boundaries: Barriers, Conduits and Opportunities* (London, Pinter, 1996), pp. 183–204, and M. Kesby, 'Arenas for Control, Terrains of Gender Contestation: Guerrilla Struggle and Counter-Insurgency Warfare in Zimbabwe 1972–1980', *Journal of Southern African Studies*, 22, 4, 1996, pp. 561–85.

military strategies and for ongoing and extreme antagonism between the two parties. It would also politicize the writing of the liberation struggle's history. Zapu's armed wing, Zipra, has not received anything like the attention of its counterpart Zanla. There are few academic studies of Zipra; its role in liberating the country has been belittled in official accounts. There is a need both to redress the balance empirically so as to comprehend military strategy and interactions with civilians in Zipra areas, and to respond to the deep sense of grievance which Zapu and Zipra veterans feel over the marginalization of their history.

The two most important published accounts of Zipra strategy are the recent works of Dumiso Dabengwa, Zipra's former head of intelligence, and Jeremy Brickhill, both of whom write as insiders to Zipra's struggle, and both of whom are explicitly concerned to rectify a distorted history.[2] Their accounts are invaluable for the insight they provide into the vexed relationship with Zanu, the struggle to recruit cadres, the role of external backers, and the debates and constraints which shaped Zipra's military strategy. We also draw on the autobiography of, and interviews with, Nicholas Nkomo, and, largely indirectly, the accounts of over 80 former Zipra guerrillas. Nkomo became commander of the Shangani and surrounding regions in the later stages of the war, and he has worked closely with us in our field research.[3] His account is central to a reconstruction of the dynamics of war in the Shangani.

In significant ways, the history of Zimbabwe's liberation movements is one of failed attempts at unity and of military innovation in the face of an intransigent and powerful enemy. Dabengwa and Brickhill stress Zapu's position of strength vis a vis Zanu in the 1960s, a position which allowed Zapu to scorn early attempts to unify the two movements.[4] This position was disastrously undermined in the early 1970s as Zapu was racked by internal divisions. The turmoil cost Zapu its contacts with the Mozambican liberation movement, Frelimo, thus consigning Zapu to rear bases in Zambia. Several of Zapu's senior leaders, as well as a large number of guerrilla recruits, defected to Zanu, dramatically altering the balance of power between the two armies.[5]

Subsequently, Zapu reorganized and formally launched Zipra, the Zimbabwe People's Revolutionary Army. The early seventies were spent recruiting anew, and launching sabotage, ambush and landmine campaigns in Zimbabwe.[6] But plans for a larger offensive were delayed by renewed attempts to unite the two military forces, and by political negotiations. A joint military command was finally initiated in November 1975, under the auspices of Zipa (the Zimbabwe People's Liberation Army). Zipa's reign was troubled and brief. Zipra leaders had from the outset been extremely critical

---

[2] See Jeremy Brickhill, 'Daring to Storm the Heavens: The Military Strategy of Zapu, 1976–1979', and Dumiso Dabengwa, 'Zipra in the Zimbabwe War of National Liberation', both in N. Bhebe and T. Ranger (eds), *Soldiers in Zimbabwe's Liberation War* (London, James Currey, 1995).

[3] See N. Nkomo, 'Between the Hammer and the Anvil: The Autobiography of Nicholas Nkomo', ms., 1996. In addition to our own interviews, Nkomo and three other former Zipra guerrillas – Richard Dube, Mark Ndhlovu and K.K. Inyati – carried out structured interviews with former Zipra guerrillas. A number of guerrillas also wrote autobiographies. While this material informs our discussion here, we do not explore it in great detail. See J. Alexander and J. McGregor, 'Zipra Guerrilla Narratives', Oxford, 1998, for a fuller consideration.

[4] Dabengwa, 'Zipra', pp. 29–30. Zanu had at this time a tiny number of recruits. See Bhebe and Ranger, 'Volume Introduction: Soldiers in Zimbabwe's Liberation War', p. 12.

[5] On Zapu's divisions and their consequences, see Dabengwa, 'Zipra', p. 31; Owen Tshabangu, *The March 11 Movement in Zapu – Revolution Within the Revolution for Zimbabwe* (Heslington, Tiger Papers, 1979); D. Moore, 'The Zimbabwe People's Army: Strategic Innovation or More of the Same?', in N. Bhebe and T. Ranger (eds), *Soldiers in Zimbabwe's Liberation War* (London, James Currey, 1995), p. 76.

[6] See Brickhill, 'Daring to Storm the Heavens', pp. 54–55; Dabengwa, 'Zipra', pp. 30–32.

of Zanla's military capacity, and severe conflicts in the Tanzanian Zipa camps in June 1976 brought their participation to an end after only six months.[7]

Following its withdrawal from Zipa, Zipra intensified recruitment and set about elaborating a new military strategy notable for its development of a conventional capacity. Over half of all recruits arrived in Zambia in 1977. Operational areas grew dramatically and semi-liberated zones were established. In 1978, Zipra began deploying conventionally trained forces, particularly artillery and anti-aircraft units. In November of that year, Zipra's High Command formulated the Turning Point strategy.[8] This important innovation was intended to allow Zipra to consolidate control over semi-liberated areas by introducing additional regular forces. These areas would then be used as bases from which to launch attacks on the hitherto untouchable Rhodesian garrisons and towns. The strategy involved the transfer of half the Zambia-based High Command into Zimbabwe and the strengthening of communications, the reorganization of many guerrillas into larger groupings (detachments and brigades), and the movement of war material, particularly heavy weaponry, into the country. While Zipra did not fully deploy its conventional forces before the negotiated ceasefire, the Turning Point strategy marked Zipra as a unique liberation army in terms of its training, sophisticated weaponry, and military innovation.

The evolution of Zipra strategy had important implications for the Shangani. The Shangani stood at the heart of Zipra's Northern Front, falling under the second of three Northern Front divisions (Northern Front Two or NF2).[9] The Northern Front as a whole provided the main avenue of entry into the country and by far the majority of Zipra guerrillas were deployed within it. It contained the first semi-liberated areas, and it was from the protection of the 'dark' Shangani forests that offensives were to be launched on the towns and communications of the highveld.[10] Under the Turning Point strategy, Nicholas Nkomo was appointed deputy commander of NF2, thereby becoming the most senior commander based inside the front.

Within the Shangani, Nkomo came to designate areas under his command as 'green', 'yellow' or 'red'. Green implied a semi-liberated area through which Rhodesian forces could pass but could not maintain a presence, yellow indicated contested control, and red meant full Rhodesian control. As Zipra drove back Rhodesian positions along the Zambezi river in 1977 and guerrillas entered the country in unprecedented numbers, Nkomo was able to expand his control over what would become NF2 with remarkable speed. Broadly, he contends that, in 1976, the Rhodesians enjoyed full control of Nkayi and Lupane; 1977 was a year of transition from red to yellow, after which the districts began to change to green. Zipra first established control of large parts of northern Lupane, and then simultaneously moved eastwards along the river valleys into Nkayi, as well as southwards within Lupane. This was not always an easy process: Nkomo contends that, in contrast to the facility with which guerrillas entered most of Lupane and western Nkayi, the expansion into eastern Nkayi was difficult. This area was penetrated relatively late, and it seems Rhodesian counter-mobilization had been effective in creating a network of informers and in preventing the full use of the Zapu networks which played such a critical role in easing guerrilla advances elsewhere. Nkomo stresses the importance of military victories in changing the balance of allegiance and establishing Zipra as a credible force in these areas.[11]

[7] See Moore, 'The Zimbabwe People's Army', pp. 74–5, 80–81; Dabengwa, 'Zipra', pp. 33–5.
[8] On the Turning Point strategy and the subsequent Zero Hour Operation, see Brickhill, 'Daring to Storm the Heavens', pp. 49-66; Dabengwa, 'Zipra', p. 35.
[9] In addition to Nkayi and Lupane, NF2 encompassed Binga, Gokwe, Inyati, Kwekwe and Gweru Districts. Northern Front 1 stood to the east, and Northern Front 3 to the west of NF2. There were also two Southern Fronts.
[10] See Brickhill, 'Daring to Storm the Heavens', p. 61.
[11] Interview with Nicholas Nkomo, Nkayi, 8 September 1995.

By 1978, Nkomo regarded areas north of the Shangani in both districts, together with the Lupane purchase areas and Gwaai forest, as green. Local party leaders referred to these areas as 'Zambia'. Most of the region south of the Shangani fell into yellow and red zones, the red zones being limited to the immediate vicinity of the administrative centres of Nkayi and Lupane and the militarily protected sub-offices, all of which hosted large numbers of armed personnel on a permanent basis. The yellow zones were constantly contested and were some of the most violent for civilians. In red zones, Zipra did not seek to launch attacks, but guerrillas – including senior commanders such as Nkomo himself – moved within them to collect intelligence while Zapu agents used their stores to secure supplies. In early 1978, Nkomo was ordered to expand control south of the Shangani and more units – including regular forces – were moved in.[12]

Nkomo's control over the Shangani was greatly strengthened by the implementation of the Turning Point strategy in late 1978. Thereafter, many of the guerrilla units in the region were organized into five detachments of (initially) around 100 men each, allowing for attacks on larger units of Rhodesian forces and better-protected targets.[13] A sixth group, which came to call itself Pamodzi, operated within NF2 outside Nkomo's command from late 1976, for reasons which stemmed from conflicts between this group's commanders and the High Command based in Zambia.[14] Nkomo allowed Pamodzi to operate without interference, a strategy which seems to have been success-ful in containing the potential confusion and violence among guerrillas which such a split might have caused.[15] Nkomo's five main detachments, each responsible for a geographical area, were supplemented by smaller, mobile guerrilla units, as well as other units. These included an intelligence unit of Zipra's National Security Organiza-tion answerable to his deputy, Tshaka Moyo, and special units of engineers and instructors, the latter being tasked with training recruits within the country.[16]

Nkomo's logistics also greatly improved after the Turning Point. He established radio

---

[12] Nkomo, 'Between the Hammer and the Anvil', Appendix, p. 10.

[13] Spear Detachment, commanded by Velemu, operated in Lupane; Striker Detachment was deployed in Nkayi and commanded by Stalin; Parirenyatwa Detachment was deployed in Gokwe and commanded by Brighton Majaha; Vulindlela Detachment was commanded by Christopher Fuyane and operated in Silobela and Zhombe; and Madiliza Detachment operated in Nkosikazi and Inyati.

[14] Nkomo comments that this unit 'had its own problems with the High Command', and suggests that they may have rebelled initially due to the killing of their commander in the High Command. Pamodzi, led by Sandhlana Mafuta and Castro, did not fall under Nkomo's command until the ceasefire. (Nkomo, 'Between the Hammer and the Anvil', Appendix, p. 9; Interview with Nkomo, Nkayi, 19 December 1994.) Brickhill, 'Daring to Storm the Heavens', footnote 15, notes that the split was one of the 'few active revolts inside the country by Zipra forces'. He contends that this unit refused to comply with High Command orders after a Rhodesian attack in which they suffered high casualties. Other accounts stress their anger over inadequate supplies and the Zipra leadership's comfortable life outside the country. (Interview between Norma Kriger and a former Zipra guerrilla, August 1992.) The Selous Scouts may well have had an impact on the split: Ron Reid Daly and Peter Stiff, *Selous Scouts. Top Secret War* (Alberton, Galago, 1982), pp. 406–8, say the Selous Scouts were 'stirring things up all the time'. They are not correct, however, in placing 'Lipson' amongst the rebel leaders with Mafuta. Lipson seems to have sympathized with Mafuta, but was a commander of the loyal Parirenyatwa Detachment.

[15] Pamodzi's breached relationship with the High Command weakened it in the end: the unit suffered from a lack of supplies and low morale, and experienced regular desertions to the detachments under Nkomo's command. Interview with Nicholas Nkomo, Nkayi, 19 December 1994.

[16] See Nkomo, 'Between the Hammer and the Anvil', Appendix, pp. 9–11.

communication with the Zambian-based High Command and writes that the new lines of command – stretching from Zambia to his mobile headquarters in the Gwampa valley and on to detachment commanders – facilitated 'effective troop control and prompt decision-making'.[17] A new military logistics structure was established for transporting arms, ammunition and medicine from points near the Zambezi to the Gwampa headquarters, as well as for guiding reinforcements from the rear. As the semi-liberated zones expanded, a steady flow of reinforcements and material arrived, including regular infantry reconnaissance units and additional heavy weaponry.

Nkomo's hold on the region had become very strong indeed. In the latter half of 1979, Zipra's deputy political commissar in the High Command, Richard Dube, arrived in Lupane with two new guerrilla detachments of 120 men each, known as Chinamano and JD, as well as two Strella anti-aircraft missile launchers (guerrillas had previously used machine guns against air attack). Dube's only losses in coming to Lupane were suffered while crossing the Zambezi – some of the new arrivals told Nkomo that they thought the area, 'had never had enemy forces because they said that since they crossed the Zambezi up to Gwampa they never saw nor heard about Rhodesians'.[18] Nkomo was on the point of launching attacks on concentrated Rhodesian forces at the adminis-trative centres and protected sub-offices when the negotiated ceasefire was called in December 1979.

The dense *gusu* forests, so long a defining feature of the Shangani, proved crucial to Nkomo's advances. They offered essential cover and were often untraversed by roads. Guerrillas' knowledge of the bush allowed them to evade Rhodesian troops and to launch ambushes upon them when they were vulnerable; their relationship with local Zapu leaders brought them detailed intelligence on Rhodesian troop movements and provided geographic and topological information to facilitate the planning of such ambushes. The rare areas of the Shangani which lacked forested cover were given evocative names such as 'Ogaden', and were vividly remembered as places of danger and death.[19]

Nkomo details the means by which guerrillas planned their advances. Red areas, where Rhodesian troops were concentrated in large numbers in bases, were not attacked directly as guerrillas lacked the firepower necessary to do so without heavy losses. Within green areas, guerrillas tried to minimize contacts so as to avoid reprisals and allow the consolidation of control. The majority of ambushes were concentrated in yellow zones, particularly along roads, so as to deny Rhodesians access to existing green zones and to expand the areas under guerrilla control. As the war progressed, regular Rhodesian forces such as the Rhodesian Light Infantry and the mounted Grey's Scouts suffered heavy losses when they sought to move outside their bases. Their links to barracks, supplies and reinforcements were weakened by ambushes on the main tarred roads and repeated sabotage of the Bulawayo–Victoria Falls railway line. Guerrillas and Zapu youth regularly blocked secondary roads with trees, a tactic in use since the disturbances of the 1960s. The Rhodesians responded by investing in road construction, and deploying community development staff and forced labour to road building.[20] The roads built during the war – particularly the 'fighting road' which linked Kwekwe to the Victoria Falls Road, spanning the breadth of Nkayi and Lupane – were

---

[17]  *Ibid.*, Appendix, p. 11.

[18]  *Ibid.*, Appendix, p. 12.

[19]  'Ogaden' was the name given to the much dreaded open lands between Sagonda and Skopo in Nkayi by Nicholas Nkomo's deputy, Tshaka Moyo. Interview with Nicholas Nkomo, 22 Novem-ber 1995.

[20]  A former community development officer recalled: '... you were simply told, go and build a road there... It was difficult to mobilize anyone. The roads were for the benefit of the govern-ment personnel travelling safely.' Interview, Jotsholo, 19 November 1994.

important for government troop mobility, but they were far from safe: the dense roadside bush facilitated the laying of mines and ambushes. Nkayi's DC was killed in one such ambush in 1979, an event which occasioned much celebrating. 'We jumped up and down we were so excited,' one party chairman recalled.[21]

The ambush and mine tactics used by the expanding guerrilla forces in the Shangani proved effective against the Rhodesian regular forces. The Rhodesian arsenal was not, however, limited to conventional means. Zipra's successes led the Rhodesians to turn to unconventional tactics, tactics which they had already used to considerable effect in Zanla operational areas. The elite Selous Scouts were the key unit involved in these operations. The Scouts were created specifically to operate in areas where regular troops could no longer move. They rallied behind the credo 'the ends justify the means'; their 'all-important task' was to 'improve the kill rate and they were not too fussy about how this was achieved'.[22] They specialized in 'turning' captured guerrillas, and sending them back to infiltrate and attack guerrilla units, as well as to sow confusion amongst, and to alienate, the guerrillas' civilian supporters. One way in which the latter was accomplished was through staging horrific killings of civilians. It is difficult to identify the perpetrators in many such cases but some, such as the notorious murder of Dr Decker at St Paul's hospital, seem likely to have been the work of Selous Scouts. Guerrillas vehemently deny involvement in Decker's death, arguing that she and her hospital staff were known for assisting them with medicines. Nonetheless, many civilians angrily blamed guerrillas for her murder.[23]

The Selous Scouts achieved their most devastating successes through a campaign of poisoning.[24] Knowing that guerrillas depended upon civilians for the supply of clothing, food and other goods, the Selous Scouts set out to infiltrate supply networks and to poison the goods which passed through them. Various poisons were used, including a type of organophosphate known as parathian which was 'impregnated into the fabric of clothing so that poisons would be absorbed through soft body tissue ... where prolonged contact could be achieved ... After exposure to the poison ... the victim would experience symptoms which included bleeding from the nose and mouth and a rise in temperature.'[25] Thallium and a rat poison called warfarin were used in food and drink.

The strategic importance of NF2 may help to explain why it was the Zipra military division most severely affected by poisoning. Zipra commanders claimed that 'Rhodesian poisoning was the most effective' strategy used against them: Nicholas Nkomo claimed that more guerrillas died in NF2 through poisoning than in battle.[26]

---

[21] Interview with Johnson Mpofu, Malindi, 12 September 1995.

[22] H. Ellert, *Rhodesian Front War: Counter-insurgency and Guerrilla Warfare 1962-1980* (Gweru, Mambo Press, second ed., 1993), pp. 124, 142.

[23] E.g., Interview with Musa Dube, Lake Alice, 19 February 1996.

[24] The most detailed accounts of poisoning and other Selous Scout operations are Ellert, *Rhodesian Front War*, pp. 124–61; J. Brickhill, 'Zimbabwe's Poisoned Legacy: Secret War in Southern Africa', *Covert Action*, 43, 1992/93, pp. 4–59; K. Flower, *Serving Secretly. An Intelligence Chief on Record, Rhodesia into Zimbabwe 1964–1981* (London, John Murray, 1987). Also see P. Stiff, *See You in November. Rhodesia's No-holds Barred Intelligence War* (Alberton, Galago, 1985). Guerrillas in NF2 found proof of the poisoning after the ceasefire when suspect items of clothing were sent for forensic testing. Interview with Nicholas Nkomo and Richard Dube, Bulawayo, 4 September 1996. For a discussion of poisoning in Zanla operational areas, see J. Nhongo-Simbanegavi, 'Zimbabwean Women in the Liberation Stuggle: Zanla and its Legacy, 1972–1985', D. Phil, University of Oxford, 1997.

[25] Ellert, *Rhodesian Front War*, pp. 142, 144.

[26] Interview with Nicholas Nkomo and Richard Dube, Bulawayo, 4 September 1996. Nkomo estimated that between 50 and 70 guerrillas died as a direct result of poisoning within a few

Peter Stiff notes that within the Rhodesian CIO, 'It was said that there were some months when Sam Roberts [responsible for concocting the poisons] had killed more terrorists than the Rhodesian Light Infantry.'[27] As we explore further in Chapter 7, these losses severely tested the Zipra commanders as guerrillas, unsure of the cause of the deaths, turned on civilians. Commanders faced widespread insubordination and guerrilla morale plummeted. Attacks were all but halted for a brief period and reprisals against civilians dramatically undermined support networks.

In addition to the use of poisons, the Rhodesians may have used other forms of chemical and biological warfare in the Shangani. Nicholas Nkomo cites a case where guerrillas found Napalm canisters after an air attack, and Napalm was certainly used elsewhere.[28] There was also an anthrax epizootic in the Shangani which caused severe loss of livestock, some loss of (largely civilian) life and a good deal of confusion.[29] Zipra commanders believed the epizootic to be the result of Rhodesian action. Unlike the poisoning, however, former CIO officers have not admitted to spreading anthrax. Suspicion lingers nonetheless. As Meryl Nass has noted, the number of cases was wholly unprecedented and the epizootic persisted for an unusually long period of time. The pattern of distribution was also abnormal: the disease was confined to national borders and, within them, affected only Africans. Nass concludes that anthrax could have been spread by air – biological warfare techniques were within the Rhodesians' capacity. Moreover, the epizootic could be seen as advantageous to the Rhodesian war effort because it hit at civilians', and hence guerrillas', means of sustenance.[30]

To people in the Shangani, this logic made sense and they tended to blame the Rhodesians for the spread of anthrax. As a result, it was the legitimacy of the Rhodesians rather than that of the guerrillas which suffered. As one Zapu leader explained, 'We felt [the spread of anthrax] was deliberately done by the regime because they suspected we could kill the animals and give the meat to the freedom fighters, and this way they could die.'[31] People remember seeing planes drop a white powder on fields and pastures, and believe this caused anthrax and other illnesses; some recall soldiers sprinkling 'small pills' into dams which 'killed the fish, and poisoned cattle which then became bearers of anthrax'.[32] Others – including guerrillas and their commanders – thought anthrax was introduced by cattle stolen from the commercial farms which had been purposely infected with the disease.[33] But understandings of anthrax and other diseases were not always so clear cut. Some linked anthrax to the explosion of tick populations which resulted from the breakdown of veterinary

---

[26] (cont.) months. Nkomo's second in command, Tshaka Moyo, was himself a victim and very nearly died. Interview with Nicholas Nkomo, Nkayi, 19 December 1994.

[27] Stiff, *See You in November*, pp. 308–10.

[28] Nkomo, 'Between the Hammer and the Anvil', Appendix, p. 11. Also see David Martin and Phyllis Johnson, *The Struggle for Zimbabwe* (London, Faber and Faber, 1981).

[29] After the cease-fire, Assistant Provincial Veterinary Officer Dr Tony Taylor estimated that 10,000 cattle had died of anthrax in Nkayi and Lupane and that 1,200 people were being treated for the disease. See *The Chronicle*, 10 January 1980, 12 February 1980.

[30] M. Nass, 'Zimbabwe's Anthrax Epizootic', *Covert Action*, 43, Winter 1992/93, p. 13. Nass cites Zimbabwean physician J.C.A. Davies who wrote extensively about the epizootic. See, e.g., J.C.A. Davies, 'A Major Epidemic of Anthrax in Zimbabwe', part 1, *Central African Journal of Medicine*, 29, 1983, pp. 8–12.

[31] Interview with Alson Tshabalala, Malindi, 12 September 1995; Yona Dube, Lupanda, 22 February 1996.

[32] Interview with V.J. Ndhlovu, Mateme, 23 November 1995. Also, e.g., Interviews with Rainfall Msimanga, Mathendele, 13 September 1995; Alson Tshabalala, Malindi, 12 September 1995; Lutha Mhlanga, Malandu, 22 November 1995.

[33] Interview with former Zipra guerrilla Benjamin Ncube, Mabayi, 21 September 1995.

restrictions and services.[34] Many simply associated the disease with the polluting nature of gunfire and smoke.[35]

Rhodesian counter-insurgency strategies as a whole profoundly shaped Zipra tactics and advances in the late 1970s. The training in, and deployment of, these military tactics also shaped guerrilla memories of war, serving as an important register of Zipra identity as well as a point of comparison with Zanla's methods of confronting the same Rhodesian enemy. As in Nicholas Nkomo's account of the Shangani, many Zipra guerrillas emphasized the ways in which their training, and the development of new strategies, prepared them for confrontation with the Rhodesians in the field. Guerrilla accounts are often told as a series of ordeals or rites of passage which served to turn boys into men, and men into professional soldiers able to combat such an awesome enemy. They laid great stress on military training and political education in these processes.

The training camps played a central role in guerrilla accounts. It was here that the recruits were given war names, symbolizing their transition from civilian to soldier. And it was here that they were trained in warfare. The rigorousness of this process was often a source of surprise. On his arrival in Zambia, Nicholas Nkomo believed 'all that was needed was for us to be shown how to use guns, to be issued with guns, and then straight away we would go home and fight the Rhodesians'.[36] Instead there followed a rigorous and lengthy programme of physical training and drills, instruction in guerrilla tactics, weapons handling, bushcraft and politics. Those guerrillas who were inducted into Zipra's conventional forces relate their advanced training and knowledge of sophisticated weaponry in detail. The emphasis on rigorous training expressed itself in heartfelt declarations: 'I loved to be a well-trained soldier with discipline because that was [the] Zipra gospel of power,' wrote Mjoni Mkandla.[37]

Training also regularly involved international travel and political revelation. Guerrillas came to see that the struggle was against 'the system' rather than against the whites. They learned the principles of socialism from political instructors, from visits to the Soviet Union, Cuba and elsewhere, or from reading revolutionary texts. For one guerrilla, Che Guevara was the key: 'That is the man … who spiritually turned me into a soldier', into a man of 'steel nerves'.[38] For Nicholas Nkomo, it was his training in the Soviet Union which shaped his socialist beliefs. In many of the guerrilla accounts, the description of political instruction takes on the quality of an epiphany, a moment of realization. Guerrillas often held, 'before, we were ignorant'. These new political ideas were added to those which guerrilla recruits brought from their homes – a great many had cut their teeth in the Zapu youth or had come from families with a long history of nationalist activism.

If guerrillas' lengthy training gave them a powerful belief in their military capacity and political understanding, it was also a period in which many suffered the most traumatic experiences of the war. These experiences were in part owed simply to the hardship of camp life – the food shortages and harsh discipline, and the intensive Rhodesian bombing campaigns of the last years of the war. But they were also owed to the divisions which marred Zapu and Zipra and, much more powerfully, the relations between Zapu and Zanu. The latter were critical in shaping the views which Zipra

---

[34] Some suspected that the ticks (which included unfamiliar species) were introduced deliberately: 'because it was war … they could have been dropped from the air'. Interview with J. Ndlovu, E. Ncube and R. Dube, Malunku, 6 March 1996.

[35] Interview with Hole Tshuma, Jibajiba, 21 January 1996; also, e.g., Roy Mpofu and Luka Mgayo, Sebhumane, 14 December 1995.

[36] Nkomo, 'Between the Hammer and the Anvil', p. 8.

[37] Autobiography of Mjoni Mkandla, 18 January 1995.

[38] Interview with Patson Sikhumbuzo Mabuzo, n.d.

guerrillas held of Zanu and its armed wing Zanla, and are deserving of some exploration here. The worst cases of inter-party conflict accompanied the formation of Zipa in
1976. Zipra accounts of the breakdown of Zipa do not focus on ideological, ethnic or
strategic differences, but on the malice and megalomania of Zanla and the treachery of
its external backers – the Mozambicans or Chinese or Tanzanians.

Accounts of the fighting between Zipra and Zanla in the Tanzanian camps of Mgagao
and Morogoro in June 1976 are some of the most lengthy and bitter passages in guerrilla
accounts. Zipra guerrillas recalled the Chinese instructors and Tanzanian Defence Force
siding against them. They recalled being disarmed, discriminated against and
persecuted – many only narrowly escaped with their lives.[39] In Morogoro, food shortages
provoked violence betwen Zipra and a much larger number of Zanla guerrillas. Zipra
were disarmed by the Tanzanians, but nonetheless managed to disarm Zanla in turn
and, having gained control of a machine gun, killed several of their oppponents and
subsequently managed to escape to Zambia.[40] The veteran Nkayi nationalist, Leonard
Koro Nkomo, vividly described the treatment of the approximately 800 Zipra recruits
living in Mgagao in 1976: 'We were becoming thin, there was no food. Zanla was telling
us to thin up so we can kill you properly with no resistance.' A fight broke out on 6 June
over access to the kitchens:

> The Zanlas searched us, took all the valuables, money, all blankets, all jerseys
> were taken. … Before long one of our instructors was going from our group to the
> barracks and the Zanlas attacked him with an axe. They cut his head and killed
> him. … The Zanlas ran to get armed – we had not even a knife. They started to fire
> at us with the help of the Chinese instructors. They were firing with machine
> guns in an 'L' formation.

The Zipra guerrillas scattered, and those who were caught were killed: 'They found one
Zipra and they told him to say "down with Nkomo" and he said "forward with
Nkomo" and they shot him. The Zanlas were picking up corpses and burning them so
that you only found fingers.' Koro estimated over 50 Zipra recruits were killed in this
battle alone – among them Nicholas Nkomo's brother.[41]

Nkomo's own involvement in Zipa very nearly ended in his demise. He was sent to a
Zipa camp in Mozambique after his return from training in the Soviet Union and
Tanzania, and subsequent to the first outbreaks of internecine violence. Zipra's reception
did not augur well: 'We were regarded as people who had come to join Zanla and not
Zipa as we had been told. We were forced to denounce our party, Zapu, and its leader-
ship.' Nkomo recounts how his Zipra comrades were beaten, imprisoned and tortured.
He managed to escape – by fleeing on foot from Mozambique to Botswana – after a
Zanla recruit (whose parents had been Zapu) informed him of a plot on his life.[42] Such
stories filtered back through the ranks of Zipra guerrillas as survivors made their way
to Zambia, and powerfully hardened the existing antagonism between Zanla and Zipra.

These antagonisms were transferred into the Zimbabwean battlefield. Where Zipra
met Zanla, they faced each other as enemies. Zipra guerrillas' accounts of their
professional training and conduct served as a regular point of contrast with what they
uniformly depicted as the shoddy training and pointless politicizing of Zanla. Zanla's
all night mobilizational meetings, known as pungwes, were much scorned, and
contrasted negatively to Zipra's liaison with party committees:

[39] E.g., Interview with Andrew Ndlovu, 28 October 1995.
[40] Interview by Pathisa Nyathi with Eddie Sigoge, 1998.
[41] Interview with Sesabo Leonard Koro Nkomo, Nkayi, 20 December 1994. Also see Autobiography
of James Chauke, n.d. and interview with Ambrose Zikale, Dongamuzi, 21 December 1995.
[42] Nkomo, 'Between the Hammer and the Anvil', pp. 17–18. Also see Autobiography of Joseph
Moyo, February 1995.

As far as political structures were concerned [recalled Patson Sikhumbuzo], the locals did it themselves with no interference from the fighting men. We had no time to organize bush rallies and sing in the mountains. ... The men with whom I served were highly trained in both modern warfare and guerrilla warfare, they were soldiers not armed politicians! Therefore, sloganeering and singing were not their appetite.[43]

Other guerrillas went even further, denouncing Zanla guerrillas as cowardly and exploitative of civilians.[44]

Zipra guerrillas' emphasis on their professional training gave a military focus to their accounts. Their main concern with regard to the Rhodesian forces was with those units which posed a military threat – the Selous Scouts, the regular units. There were distinctions here: battles with regular units were recounted with military pride, but the unconventional tactics, especially the poisoning campaign, were a source of fear, trauma and confusion. They posed a threat which was not readily visible, that could not be easily confronted with the weapons at guerrillas' disposal. Those units which did not pose a significant military threat were near absent from guerrilla accounts. Guerrillas rarely came into contact with the armed contingents of Rhodesian farmers who entered the peripheries of the Reserves in pursuit of stolen cattle, or the police reserve forces who moved outside their camps in search of civilian informers. They regarded the paramilitary forces deployed against them as laughably incompetent and cowardly – some guerrillas even said they 'pitied them' because they suffered such high casualty rates as a result of their poor training and inadequate weaponry.[45]

Civilians assessed military forces on a very different basis. In contrast to guerrillas' focus on training and tactics, on experiences outside the country, civilians' accounts were shaped by moral judgements of the various Rhodesian forces which deployed violence against them.

## Civilian Memories of Soldiers, Paramilitaries and Administration

To understand the central role which soldiers and particularly paramilitaries came to play in civilians' lives, we must first consider the nature of wartime administration in the Shangani. Administrators in Nkayi and Lupane had relied increasingly on force since the nationalist uprisings of the 1960s. They had long depended on the police and army, on intimidation, detention and torture. However, the arrival of significant numbers of guerrillas after 1976 ushered in a new era which both drastically limited the aspirations and effectiveness of administration and required new levels of force. Government development work was paralysed as officials came under attack, and the minimal array of administrative tasks which could still be carried out relied on armed escorts. The police and intelligence services increasingly depended on the armed police reserve, stepped up their recruitment of civilian informers, and detained and tortured unprecedented numbers of suspects.

One of the first moves the administration took to counter the guerrillas was a 'hearts and minds' campaign, launched in 1976. District Commissioners and the army held meetings around the district, warning civilians against the brutality of 'terrorists', and exhibiting photographs of atrocities said to be committed by them. They sought to demonstrate the government's strength by showing pictures of the devastating conse-quences of the bombings in Zambia, and by publicly laying out the corpses of guerrillas

---

[43] Interview with Patson Sikhumbuzo, 28 February 1995.
[44] E.g., Interview with Saymore Nkomo, 26 September 1995.
[45] Interview with Hlanganani Ndebele, Dakamela, 15 September 1995.

killed in battle.[46] Leaflets with similar information were dropped from airplanes around the district.[47]

These tactics often failed to convince: in places already familiar with guerrillas or where party committees remained influential despite increasing repression, people had a healthy suspicion of government motives, and worked to counter official propaganda. They were joined in this by the effective broadcasts of Zapu's Radio Zambia. Elsewhere, however, such tactics met with success, albeit often only in the short term. In Lupaka, for example (an area north of the Shangani which became a guerrilla stronghold after 1978), one group of civilians who lacked a long Zapu history recalled:

> They dropped leaflets from airplanes. Before we saw the boys, we thought it was all true. It was instilled into us: these people are really animals. They'll forcibly take away your wife, they're not decent. They showed us pictures, scenes of bombing in Zambia to terrify us more. When the boys arrived, we found it was a heap of lies.[48]

In other areas, such as parts of eastern Nkayi where guerrillas arrived late and government forces were concentrated, the Rhodesians seem to have been successful in instilling fear and recruiting informers, who were issued with two-way radios, and sometimes guns.[49]

After 1976, district administrative centres became increasingly isolated and reliant on armed units. Administration in remote parts of the district was undertaken from garrisoned 'protected sub-offices' at strategic roadside locations. These were established to provide an 'administrative base in an area badly affected by terrorism', a base for the police and army, and protection for chiefs and headmen.[50] The offices differed from the 'protected villages' predominant along the eastern borders of the country. They lacked the comprehensive restrictions on movement and the large, forcibly displaced populations; they were few in number and their influence was limited to nearby areas. Government centres in Nkayi and Lupane were largely populated by armed forces, civil servants, chiefs and headmen, and detainee populations numbering in the hundreds. They also attracted people who were (rightly or wrongly) labelled sellouts by guerrillas or Zapu party committees – many such, however, quickly moved on to the city of Bulawayo.

After 1977, the administration could no longer rely on chiefs and councils to provide even a minimum of administration in outlying areas. Chiefs' councils were placed under the DCs' 'management', a euphemism signalling their collapse. Some council employees even absconded with government funds and joined the guerrillas.[51] Chiefs and headmen often had to be brought to meetings by plane as roads could no longer be safely traversed. Though chiefs' relations with the state and Zipra were diverse, it

[46] E.g., Interview with Headman Mlume, Nkoni, 2 October 1995.
[47] On psychological operations, see J. Frederikse, *None but Ourselves: Masses versus the Media in the Making of Zimbabwe* (London, Heinemann, 1982), pp. 115–45.
[48] Interview with Fuba Ncube, Sabelo Mhlanga, Mpafu Ncube, Patison Mpofu and David Ncube, Lupaka, 9 February 1996.
[49] Interview with Rainfall Msimanga, Mathendele, 30 August 1995.
[50] 'Notes on the Role of the Ministry of Internal Affairs during the War: Lupane', File His 3, District and Tribal History and Custom, Lupane. In Lupane, protected sub-offices were created at Ciwale in the north of the district, and at Jotsholo, near the Tilcor (state farm) estate which functioned throughout the war. In Nkayi, Zwelabo, Dakamela and possibly a third site were designated as protected sub-offices. DC, Nkai to SIA, 8 December 1978, 38/7/3F Box 28924, File X 461/44, Nkayi.
[51] Autobiography of Sifiso Velani, Nkayi, 16 January 1995.

became impossible for any to continue to perform government tasks. Staying at homes
which were located far from the administrative centres risked their own lives, as well as
those of their families. Headman Jojo recalled his move into Nkayi centre in 1977:

> The situation was very tense here. I'd left the family behind. It was hot on the
> guerrilla and the government side. It was difficult for me to talk to my son – as
> soon as I talked to him, they would say I was a sellout and I'd given him a
> message so he should be killed as a sellout. And the government thought I was
> harbouring guerrillas because I had such a big home – so both sides were
> dangerous.[52]

Following the killing of four of Nkayi's headmen in 1978, the administration evacuated
all those chiefs and headmen who did not already live near administrative centres and
protected sub-offices to the district centres.[53] Others moved of their own accord,
including many headmen and Chiefs Madliwa and Sivalo, the latter having been
prompted to do so after two attacks from guerrillas in late 1977 in which he and his
relatives suffered beatings and rapes, and his house and car were destroyed.[54] Others,
such as Chief Sikhobokhobo, were warned to move out by guerrillas.[55] Only Chief
Menyezwa stayed with Zipra during the war, after escaping from the protected sub-
office to which he had been forcibly moved by the government. Only two chiefs
remained at their homes under government protection. In Lupane, Chief Mabhikwa
lived adjacent to the protected Tilcor estate and was given his own paramilitary force,
while Chief Dakamela in Nkayi remained at the Dakamela protected sub-office, behind
barbed wire, protected by paramilitaries and accessible to government forces by air.
Kraalheads, the lowest rung of Rhodesian administration, on the whole stayed at home
and threw in their lot with the nationalists: many were, in fact, Zapu chairmen.

DCs relied ever more heavily on their paramilitary forces, the District Security
Assistants (DSAs) from 1976, and the auxiliary forces in the last desperate year of 1979.[56]
Under Martial Law, introduced in December 1978, 'administration' came to mean the
'enforcement of the regulations by punishing tribesmen in the area of an ambush,
landmine or damaged dip tank by the collection and sale of cattle from these areas as
compensation for the damage done [to government property]'. A dusk-to-dawn curfew
was put in place. DSAs and auxiliaries undertook 'small administrative tasks' while
also being 'used extensively in an aggressive role' alongside the regular security forces.[57]
From the local point of view, the DC had become 'a soldier'.[58]

These military and paramilitary units had overlapping roles, and often moved
together in joint operations. The hierarchies to which they were answerable, as well as
their responsibilites and composition, were variable between regions, were often
confused, and changed over time.[59] Though their tasks were separately defined in theory,

---

[52] Interview with Headman Jojo, Nyamazana, 11 December 1995.

[53] Headmen Manguni, Faroni, Siphunyuka and Sibangelana were killed. Headman Nhlanganiso
was beaten so severely by guerrillas that he was paralysed. See Per 5 files, DA's Office, Nkayi.

[54] Interview with Chief Solomon Sivalo, Sivalo, 12 December 1994.

[55] Interview with Chief Sikhobokhobo, Sikhobokhobo, 16 December 1994.

[56] Although District Security Assistants are popularly known as 'DAs' in the Shangani, we refer to
them as 'DSAs' throughout this book to avoid confusion with the post-independence District
Administrators who are also known as DAs.

[57] 'Notes on the Role of the Ministry of Internal Affairs during the War: Lupane', File His 3, District
and Tribal History and Custom, Lupane.

[58] Interview with Johnson Mpofu, Malindi, 12 September 1995.

[59] See P. Moorcraft and P. McLaughlin, *Chimurenga! The War in Rhodesia 1965–80* (Marshalltown,
Sygma/Collins, 1982), pp. 59–62.

in practice, groups of soldiers often moved with the paramilitaries. Nonetheless civilians drew strong distinctions between the different government forces which they faced in the late 1970s.

Civilian evaluations of government forces depended partly on the degree to which they used violence, but their actions were also assessed in moral terms, and set against implicitly defined ideas about the acceptable conduct of war. Civilians tended to portray violence in the course of military engagements between guerrillas and soldiers as 'normal', and sometimes portrayed the punishment of those who supported the opposition as an expected – though painful – military act. Civilians' harshest condemnations were reserved for the opportunistic use of force for personal gain, status and revenge.

In the estimation of civilians, the regular units of the Rhodesian army were judged the least bad of all government forces. Though they were often ruthlessly violent towards civilians, they were also seen as lacking prejudice, as a 'professional' fighting force. They lacked prejudice because they were outsiders, unknown to local people and unfamiliar with their personal histories and disputes. They were professional because they were primarily concerned with fighting guerrillas, not with personal gain or status. The majority of occasions on which they directed violence against civilians occurred in the course of contacts with guerrillas, or in following up such contacts (though follow-ups were at times conducted jointly with, or delegated to, the CID and paramilitaries). Civilian accounts of Rhodesian forces' violence focused on their retaliations in areas where guerrillas had launched attacks or had eaten or slept. Such actions were often based on accurate intelligence from informers, trackers or police investigations (the latter relying on beating and threatening villagers). Retaliation generally took the form of shooting cattle, burning homes, beating and sometimes shooting suspects, or taking them for interrogation. Beatings were at times fatal, while those who were taken away did not always return.[60] Philip Bhebe remembered how, 'when [the soldiers] discovered guerrillas had been in a village, people were beaten. This was a common thing ... They also burned villages. I remember one Mangena who was the District Chairman. He'd harboured the guerrillas and when the security forces came they shot all 21 of his cows and burned his houses.'[61]

In contrast to the soldiers, the poorly-trained and equipped DSAs and auxiliaries were considered neither unprejudiced nor professional.[62] They were invariably compared unfavourably to soldiers by civilians. They were described as 'rougher', prone to looting, and as 'untrained people excited by carrying guns'.[63] Paramilitaries' attacks on civilians and their property were often explained not in terms of military goals, but in terms of the weak moral character and desire for status of the individuals involved. As Paul Ndebele explained: 'Some [DSAs] were delighted to handle a gun ... They enjoyed eating free food, to be seen eating canned beef and baked beans. They took delight in insulting us. They were proud of their good food and gun.'[64]

---

[60] E.g., Interviews with Mhlotshwa Majaha Moyo, Majaha, 5 October 1995; D.C. Moyo, Gonye, 17 October 1995.

[61] Interview with Philip Bhebe, Mateme, 14 September 1995. Soldiers regularly shot or confiscated cattle found outside of their kraals under the curfew. E.g., Interview with H. Masuku, Sebhumane, 30 November 1995. There is some evidence that soldiers became more 'ruthless with people' – more often shooting them and their cattle, and burning huts – towards the end of the war. Group Interview, Mateme, 23 November 1995.

[62] See Moorcraft and McLaughlin, *Chimurenga!*, pp. 59–62.

[63] Interviews with Bishop Moyo, Mathendele, 13 September 1995; Tshata Mguni, Sessemba, 6 October 1995.

[64] Interview with Paul Ndebele, Mjena, 8 December 1995.

Recruitment into the DSAs was largely voluntary,[65] and the majority were deployed within their home districts where they operated amongst people they knew well. Many early recruits were government employees, and these men often acted as leaders. Chiefs' messengers were given key roles 'because they knew the area';[66] DC's messengers were 'used to pinpoint Zapu leaders'.[67] Former community development officers, dip tank attendants and forest rangers were also prominent amongst the DSAs. Some highly disreputable whites were also involved in the DSA command: one such was found guilty of rape, stock theft and public violence after the ceasefire.[68] But for many Africans, joining the DSAs was their first entry into government service. Their primary motivation was said to be financial gain. As one Zapu leader recalled, 'Local people joined the DSAs for money. They got salaries and they used to "pay" themselves – they raided homes and took money and there was nowhere to report.'[69] But former DSAs themselves gave more varied explanations of their motivations. One such joined up out of fear after guerrillas told him they would 'visit' him at his home, a promise he took as a threat.[70]

The areas most severely affected by the DSAs (as well as by regular Rhodesian forces) were those easily accessible by road, particularly areas Zipra regarded as yellow. Moving away from the road or into the green areas proved too dangerous because of the risk of guerrilla attack, while the red areas were populated by the DSAs' own relatives, friends and others loyal to the government. In the most hard-hit yellow areas, civilians existed in the worst kind of limbo, neither under government control, nor within the relatively safe green zones of the guerrillas. They were often trusted by neither government forces nor guerrillas, and both carried out retaliatory attacks. As Jeli Mlotshwa, whose home is less than 5 kilometres from the base of the Lupane DSAs, recalled, 'The DSAs moved around looking for the boys, then the boys wanted the DSAs. Both sides would beat if you didn't speak something palatable. Among us, we'll sell each other out – locals could report to the DSAs, the child of so and so is among the boys. So then it was an offence.'[71]

Punitive raids by DSAs were common in these zones, and were vividly remembered for the extreme forms they took. A Zapu leader recalled the behaviour of DSAs in one such area:

> If the DC was given information that a certain village had given food to the guerrillas, he would send the DSAs there to beat people or shoot and kill, or burn the whole village, or confiscate property, get the cattle. Or if they found you ploughing before 9 AM [under the curfew], they would take your team of oxen straight to their camp and only give you your yoke and chains back later. The oxen would be eaten.[72]

The DSAs' behaviour was remembered as overly cruel, even maniacal: they didn't just burn homes but, 'If you tried to get your property out, they'd take those things from

---

[65] However, in the vicinity of Lupane district offices, civilians also refer to recruits being forcibly taken for both the DSAs and the police reserve. E.g., Interview with Councillor Sibanda, Gwampa Ward, 1 March 1996.

[66] Interview with Johnson Mpofu, Malindi, 12 September 1995.

[67] Interview with H. Masuku, Sebhumane, 30 November 1995.

[68] See *The Chronicle*, 21 February 1980.

[69] Interview with Alson Tshabalala, Malindi, 12 September 1995.

[70] He explained: 'I went to the DC's office and I told him, "I'm going to join you because this is where the nearest gun is." … If people promise to come to your home carrying a gun, well, you think that they are likely to kill you.' Interview with Mjubek Tshuma, Lupane, 27 August 1996.

[71] Interview with Jeli Mlotshwa, Matshiya, 8 March 1996.

[72] Interview with Johnson Mpofu, Malindi, 12 September 1995.

you and put them in the fire';[73] they didn't just kill suspects, 'They killed everything, all the donkeys, the goats, even the chickens.'[74] Beating – to extract information on the whereabouts of guerrillas, or simply on suspicion that a home had hosted guerrillas – was common and, again, extreme. 'The DSAs were the worst. They beat people to death in public places. Wherever they found a suspect – at stores, schools, boreholes – they'd call people to come and watch,' remembered a former Zapu youth chairman.[75]

The DSAs' cattle confiscation duties were a source of particular resentment, partly because DSAs (unlike soldiers, who at any rate more often shot than confiscated cattle) kept the cattle for their own use: 'At times beasts would be taken as a fine for nothing ... [One DSA commander] would impound quite a number of cattle. He wouldn't take them to the DC, but just put them in his kraal, just loot from villages straight to his home.'[76] DSAs were also judged as cowardly for their use of civilians as shields during cattle confiscations.[77] DSAs were in fact vulnerable to attack while moving large herds of cattle to the district offices. They were highly visible and were often unaccompanied by regular soldiers while undertaking such work. Civilians who hoped to get their cattle back had an added incentive for reporting such raids to guerrillas. Guerrillas enjoyed some notable, and popular, successes in stopping what a kraalhead described as 'all that nonsense'.[78] A Zapu youth leader remembered an instance in which, 'A herd of cattle was being driven from Komayanga to Nkayi, so the youth alerted the guerrillas. ... Around Sibuyu, they were ambushed and shot at – all the DSAs were killed there.'[79]

It was not only the DSAs' punitive role and cattle confiscations that left such a bitter memory, but also their partiality. They were accused of protecting their own families and villages from cattle raids, of settling personal disputes. In Lupane, many DSAs were recruited from families of government workers living in Shabulana, adjacent to the district offices. As Marcus Zulu explained, 'that is why the people of Shabulana were not affected by this cattle confiscation. They had their own people amongst the DSAs who could divert that to other areas.'[80] DSAs used their positions to settle old scores and to target the wealthy. As one Zapu leader recalled: 'If Sibanda's son got a job as a DSA and Sibanda hated Tshabalala, then the DSAs would be sent there to wipe out the whole village. That's how quite a lot of people lost their property. DSAs called rich people sellouts and looted from them.'[81] In confiscating cattle, 'The DSAs knew who had many cattle, they would go straight to those homes.'[82]

DSAs were also well aware of the likelihood of retaliation by guerrillas against families they visited. They were said to eat or sleep overnight in wealthy homes out of jealousy, or in homes believed to support the guerrillas, in an effort to leave them vulnerable to reprisals. In Pupu, the large and wealthy homestead of the famous evictee healer Mnindwa, who was said to receive his powers from Njelele, provided just such a target: even during the war, his home was always full of dozens of visitors in search of treatment. His family recalled:

DSAs collected a number of cattle from the villages around. Then after collecting them, they kraaled them here in this home. They had the idea of making

[73] Interview with Luka Msipa and Anna Nyathi, Mzola 55, 21 March 1996.
[74] Interview with Mr Dlakama, Ngombane, 27 February 1996.
[75] Interview with D.C. Moyo, Gonye, 17 October 1995.
[76] Interview with Rainfall Msimanga, Mathendele, 13 September 1995.
[77] Interview with Titus Sibanda Moyo, Magwaza Ndlovu, Pupu, 20 February 1996.
[78] Interview with Nduna Ndaza, Dlobodlobo, Lupaka, 5 February 1996.
[79] Interview with D.C. Moyo, Gonye, 17 October 1995.
[80] Interview with Marcus Zulu, Shabulana, 24 March 1996.
[81] Interview with Johnson Mpofu, Malindi, 12 September 1995.
[82] Interview with Chain Moyo and John Ndlovu, Bububu, 23 March 1996.

Mnindwa seem like a sellout to the local community and the guerrillas. The Smith regime knew Mnindwa was helping the guerrillas through advice and healing. They wanted the guerrillas to turn against him.

But the family was protected from retribution in this instance. The DSAs were intercepted by guerrillas, and some were killed, as they left the area. The family claimed Mnindwa had been responsible for protecting them: 'It was the power of the old man Mnindwa. He didn't like war. Even ... during the liberation war there were fewer incidents in this home. There was hitting rather than death.'[83] Others were not so fortunate, however, and retaliation against those who had been forced to shelter or feed DSAs was all too common.[84]

The paramilitaries used their familiarity with local communities in other ways as well. Government intelligence drew on their knowledge of Zapu committees – they were the 'guides' for the government forces, the ones who 'pointed out the Zapu homes'[85]: they 'knew who were the chairmen, and they could bring them in [to Nkayi] and beat them'.[86] Zapu faced severe obstacles mobilizing in closely contested zones as a result. Provincial party member Mrs Senzani Ngwenya recalled the difficulties of organizing in the vicinity of the district offices and protected sub-offices:

> Mzola [close to the Ciwale protected sub-office] was difficult because there were so many DSAs. Also Endamuleni and Ndembwende because they were near to the offices. The problem is that these DSAs were on the government side. ... It's not that the majority of the population resisted the ... party officials. People were willing, but because there were DSAs living with them, they were intimidated and threatened. That's why we had to go into the difficult areas to prove they had the right to join. Also around Nkayi was a problem. Some places around the centres would be OK and others difficult, it all depended.[87]

Guerrillas operating in Nkayi and Lupane concurred that areas with large, permanent DSA forces were especially problematic for party members. Chief Dakamela's continued presence at his heavily guarded home was one such thorn in the guerrillas' side: 'The locals were sympathetic, but we had a problem with Dakamela because there was a camp there and so people couldn't come in the open because of the DSAs and soldiers ... People who the Rhodesians thought were supporting us were killed and beaten.'[88] People from the area remember neither DSAs nor guerrillas with any warmth.

The DSAs' use of their local knowledge, and exploitation of power to settle scores and accumulate wealth set them apart from regular soldiers, placing them in the most vilified of categories from the civilians' point of view. They are remembered not only as extremely violent, but as a status-seeking, self-interested and cowardly force. Civilian memories of the second paramilitary unit – the auxiliaries – are in some respects similar to those of the DSAs. They too were undisciplined, renowned for looting and violence and were said to be prepared to use their new power for their own interests. However, accounts of the auxiliary forces also differed in important respects: the auxiliaries were overwhelmingly forcibly recruited, were even less well controlled, and suffered major

[83] Interview with Kilikiya Nyathi, Mvumindaba Ncube and Tandiwe Nyathi, Pupu, 16 February 1996.
[84] E.g., Interview with Mpulazi Msipa, Lupanda, 28 March 1996.
[85] Interview with Siponono Mlotshwa and M. Dlakama, Sobendle, 27 February 1996. Also, e.g., Interview with B.J. Ndhlovu, Sebhumane, 30 November 1995.
[86] Interview with Lazarus Sibanda, Malindi, 7 September 1995.
[87] Interview with Senzani Ngwenya and Hole Tshuma, 21 February 1996.
[88] Interview with Hlanganani Ndebele, Dakamela, 15 September 1995.

defections to Zipra. The auxiliaries in the Shangani were certainly the most dys-
functional force in the Rhodesians' counterinsurgency strategy.

In contrast to the DSAs, the forcibly recruited auxiliaries were often known as 'call
ups'.[89] Some of the auxiliary units which operated on the margins of Nkayi and Lupane
were created as an armed wing of Bishop Abel Muzorewa's UANC at the time of the
April 1979 internal settlement elections. As a former Zapu activist in Tshongokwe
recalled: 'They forced [that] … to give an appearance of UANC support. The idea was to
make them like Banda's young pioneers, a party army.'[90] Though the UANC had some
support elsewhere in the country, it had little or no support in Nkayi and Lupane, and
the UANC did not bother to campaign in the districts after the war's end. Most of the
auxiliary units in the Shangani were not, however, aligned with any political party, but
were simply 'young tribesmen of unknown political views, recruited locally to form a
"home guard"' in the last stages of the war.[91]

Forced conscription into the auxiliary forces occurred in various ways. In Lupane,
people were rounded up in the immediate vicinity of district offices and sub-offices or
from sweeps into nearby areas; in Nkayi attempts were made to recruit from detainees.
We deal first with the Lupane case. Forced recruitment was necessary because of the
speed required and the lack of volunteers – the war was at its height and many young
men had left to join Zipra, while those who remained behind were often part of the
Zapu youth. Recruitment relied heavily on coercion and trickery: 'They'd go from
village to village,' elders in Lupanda recalled, '… they'd say, "we're taking boys to
work, not to kill them." All the able-bodied were called for work, but only to discover
that it wasn't a job but war.'[92] The scarcity of young men often led to the conscription of
the old. People recall fleeing to Bulawayo or hiding in the bush during the recruitment
sweeps for the Jotsholo and Ciwale forces: 'If they found a man they would just take
him, so we used to hide in the *gusu* during the day. … Later I ran because I saw an
elderly man being recruited,' one recalled.[93] Kraalhead Mapendere described his
recruitment as follows:

> A meeting was called by the DC for people to go to Mzola 5. No one knew why
> they were meeting. … With no explanation, they were all abducted, bundled into
> trucks and taken away to Gwaai siding where they were trained and given
> uniforms. … Then they were brought back and their first task was to go out into
> the villages and get all the men from the homes – it was at this point that I was
> taken from my home. I was trained at [Ciwale protected sub-office], given a gun
> and a uniform. After training we were supposed to patrol. But the old people like
> myself couldn't undertake such strenuous activity so we guarded the camp.[94]

In Lupane, auxiliaries were nominally placed under the control of often reluctant chiefs
or headmen who lived at the district offices or protected sub-offices. However, there is

---

[89] Others called them 'amakhaki' or 'amacoffee' due to the colour of their uniforms (which they
    had in common with the DSAs), or 'dzagudzagu' from the notoriety of the units from neigh-
    bouring Gokwe district, as explained below.
[90] Interview with Mr Dlakama, Jotsholo, 27 February 1996.
[91] See report in *The Chronicle*, 25 February 1980.
[92] Interview with Tafila Tshuma, Matobolo Ndebele, Antony Magagula, Mthoniselwa Mlotshwa,
    Pioni Ndlovu, Masungamala, 7 February 1996.
[93] Interview with E. Dube, Mzola, 26 November 1994. Some men who were rounded up were later
    rejected for being too old. Interview with Tafila Tshuma, Matobolo Ndebele, Antony Magagula,
    Mthonsiwela Mlotshwa, Pioni Ndlovu, Masungamala, 7 February 1996.
[94] Interview with Kraalhead Mapendere, Mzola, 3 December 1994.

little evidence that the chiefs had any day-to-day role in, or control over, these forces. Prominent chiefs like Mabhikwa in Lupane managed to retain their legitimacy despite the deployment of the auxiliaries in this way.[95] Only Headman Goduka, placed at the head of the Ciwale auxiliaries, is said to have played a more active, even 'commanding', role, and was condemned by many for doing so.[96]

The forcible recruitment of these units often proved counterproductive. Lupane's DC complained of the problem of providing the units with a stable leadership, and their failure to reduce Zipra influence even in the immmediate vicinity of the protected sub-offices where they were based. To say the auxiliaries lacked 'stable leadership' was a vast understatement: mass desertions and defections of reluctant leaders were common, and are a particular feature of memories of the Ciwale force. According to Kraalhead Mapendere:

> Many ... recruits left for Zipra, it was chaotic. The armed patrols used to go out with guns and radios and then never come back. Those who had deserted with radios used to call their mates at the base [Ciwale protected sub-office]. It was a crisis. Because so many were deserting, they began to suspect ring leaders in the camp, an organized defection. Some auxiliaries were taken to Khami prison for that reason. ... Zipra never attacked the camp, it was too useful to them, providing troops, intelligence, guns and radios.[97]

In Nkayi, auxiliary recruitment proved even more disastrous. In early 1979, the Rhodesian Psychological Operations Unit attempted to recruit from among the hundreds of detainees held at the Nkayi police station. The conversion tactics were decidedly crude. According to Henrick Ellert:

> Groups of detainees were instructed to chant pro-government songs and were subjected to lectures on the merits of the Rhodesian governmental system compared to the evils of Communism and Socialism. Detainees who seemed submissive were taken to be early converts and allowed freedom to move in and out of the camp. Those who refused to sing the required verses were forced into tiny cells behind the Nkai police camp and kept in darkness. At frequent intervals, high-volume loudspeakers would pour pro-government slogans and chants into the concrete rooms, deafening the prisoners. Those who resisted were beaten or starved.

Two hundred of these men were subsequently given a month's military training, and posted to Silobela Police Camp in neighbouring Kwekwe district, where they were charged with patrolling for Zipra guerrillas. Ellert records the result:

> One week later it was discovered that the non-political force had deserted *en masse* to Zipra. The POU scheme was hastily abandoned but the tragedy of this story was revealed by the desperation of the Rhodesians who were now prepared to try virtually any plan no matter how remote the chances of success.[98]

---

[95] Luta Inyathi maintained that Chief Mabhikwa had argued – unsuccessfully – against the deployment of auxiliaries for his protection, and had refused them entry into his home. Interview, Jotsholo, 3 March 1996.

[96] Interview with E. Dube, T. Moyo and M. Nkomo, Mashokotsha, 12 March 1996.

[97] Interview with Kraalhead Mapendere, Mzola, 3 December 1994. Accounts of these defections are a recurrent theme in interviews in Mzola. See also interview with E. Dube, 26 November 1994.

[98] Ellert, *Rhodesian Front War*, pp. 191–2.

It appears that Zapu was able to organize such defections in other areas as well: Jeremy Brickhill describes an incident in September 1979, apparently in Lupane, in which 144 auxiliaries were recruited to Zipra.[99] These defections notwithstanding, the remaining auxiliary forces were able to wreak considerable havoc, not unlike that meted out by the DSAs.

The UANC-aligned auxiliary units based in neighbouring Gokwe district, which harrassed the northern borders of Nkayi and Lupane, had a different composition and reputation from local units. They were seen as not only violent, greedy and un-disciplined, but also as political and tribal. According to Henrik Ellert, these units were specifically intended to exploit ethnic differences. They were comprised over-whelmingly of Shona speakers, and were used to mobilize support amongst the mainly Shona speaking population of Gokwe as against the largely Ndebele speaking Zipra guerrillas.[100] In Nkayi and Lupane, the Gokwe auxiliaries were dubbed *Dzagudzagu*, a Shona word meaning 'directionless', or 'swaying about hopelessely'. Though some of the Gokwe *Dzagudzagu* units were locally recruited, others were brought in from distant Shona-speaking areas. One such unit persecuted and killed prominent Tonga- and Ndebele-speaking Zapu leaders in Gokwe with such ferocity that a large group moved across the border into Lupane. They recalled: '*Dzagudzagu* were under Muzorewa. They were all Shonas. They were not locals of here, they were brought in from deep inside Mashonaland. ... We stayed [in Gokwe] with the [Shona speaking] Rhodesdales evictees, and it was not them. ... It was youth from Masvingo, Zaka.'[101]

All over northern Nkayi and Lupane, the *Dzagudazgu* are remembered for their brutality and looting. As one Zapu leader in northern Nkayi recalled,

> *Dzagudzagu* came here a lot, from 1979. Those were the most troublesome people. They stole a lot from our homes during the curfew. ... If the *Dzagudzagu* came to a village they would drive people away and then just loot. If they had a meeting at Manoti, they would just come here and take a beast to slaughter. ... The *Dzagudzagu* would order people to climb a tree and just fall out. Many got injured. Along the Kana, they would just shoot in this direction indiscriminately – cattle, goats – just for fun. Once they shot a woman in the thigh, and once they shot a small child.[102]

Another *Dzagudzagu* group which operated in northern Lupane were remembered for their curious practice of carrying bows and arrows, as well as for raiding into Lupane and for terrorizing Lupane residents who took grain to a Gokwe grinding mill.[103] Such cross-border attacks heightened the *Dzagudzagu's* reputation as violent, foreign youth, and served to harden the ethnic divide along the Gokwe border.

Though the Shangani's DSAs and auxiliaries are vividly and angrily remembered, they do not seem to have brought about the major social disruptions described in the literature on the paramilitaries and protected villages in the east of the country. The paramilitaries' interactions with civilians in the Shangani were less intense: they did not live among their wards, nor were people systematically displaced into new, con-centrated and heavily regulated settlements. The abuses of Nkayi and Lupane's

[99] Brickhill, 'Daring to Storm the Heavens', p. 69. Other forces, such as the reserve police force and army, also suffered occasional defections. Interviews with Marcus Zulu, Shabulana, 24 March 1996; Nicholas Nkomo, Nkayi, 9 September 1995.

[100] Ellert, *Rhodesian Front War*, p. 189.

[101] Interview with Mlole Sibanda, Canaan Ndlovu, Nyembezi Ndlovu, Mrs Dube and others, Lusulu, 26 February 1996.

[102] Interview with Elias Sibanda, Kana, 28 November 1995.

[103] Interview with S. Moyo, Dandanda, 30 March 1996.

para-military forces were limited in geographical extent, and to intermittent visits. These young men could not mount a challenge to senior male figures, nor substantially alter gender and generational relations as Schmidt and Kesby argue was the case in protected villages.[104] Abuse of women by the paramilitaries is not a prominent feature of civilian memories of the war, though it certainly occurred.[105] The paramilitaries' violence, looting and partiality left other marks on the memory of war: they were the most vilified of armed men, judged and condemned in accordance with an implicitly defined understanding of the morality and rules of war.

## Conclusion

The latter half of the 1970s brought dramatic change to the Rhodesian state's authority in the Shangani as Zipra mounted the first real military challenge since conquest. The violence of this confrontation was remembered very differently by civilians and guerrillas. Guerrilla narratives focused on training and political education, tactics and strategy, and on their main military foes, the Rhodesian regular forces and the Selous Scouts. These were often proud stories about becoming fearsome professional fighters. For guerrillas, the violence which was remembered as most traumatic was that which occurred in the training camps. The conflicts with Zanla would go on to powerfully shape guerrilla attitudes to the ceasefire and to the new political dispensation of the 1980s. Civilians, in contrast, remembered the violence of regular soldiers primarily as part of their military confrontation with the guerrillas, casting it as an inevitable, if painful, consequence of war. Their most intense condemnation was reserved for the local men who joined the paramilitaries. They were censured for their use of their guns and local knowledge to settle scores, to accumulate, to seek status. Their actions were not remembered as part of the engagement of two armed forces, but as an illegitimate source of terror for their neighbours.

Vivid as memories of the Rhodesian forces were, their influence was greatly restricted in the last years of the war. In the very large areas which comprised Zipra's green zones, it was the presence of guerrillas which was the more significant in shaping daily life. It is to the complex interactions between guerrillas and civilians that we now turn.

---

[104] See Schmidt, 'Love and Healing', on abuse of women and social change. Kesby, 'Arenas for Control', emphasizes the problem of such abuse for masculinity and the authority of older men.
[105] Schmidt, 'Love and Healing' p. 188, cites newspaper coverage of such cases. See also, discussion in H. Schmidt, 'The Social and Economic Impact of Political Violence in Zimbabwe, 1890-1990: A Case Study of the Honde Valley', PhD, Oxford, 1996; J. Nhongo-Simbanegavi, 'Zimbabwean Women in the Liberation Struggle'. Local people also remember rapes, e.g., Interviews with Anthony Magagula, Lupanda, 22 December 1994; Lazarus Sibanda, Malindi, 7 September 1995.

# 7

# Guerrillas & Civilians

Studies of the interactions of guerrillas and civilians in Zimbabwe's liberation war are among the most sophisticated and detailed of their kind. However, these analyses have focused almost exclusively on the history of regions that the nationalist party Zanu and its guerrilla army, Zanla, came to dominate. Zapu's rural nationalism, and the party's interaction with Zipra guerrillas, differed significantly. Here we explore three main aspects of the war: mobilization and legitimacy, patterns of political, social and religious change, and the ways in which civilians and guerrillas alike sought to cope with violence.

Studies of the relationships between Zanla guerrillas and civilians expound diverse and sometimes contradictory arguments, but they agree on one general point – that guerrillas' entry into rural communities demanded an adaptation to local agendas and ideas. David Lan has emphasized the 'assimilation of Zanla guerrillas into established peasant categories'. He argues that 'it was necessary first for guerrillas to win the approval of the ancestors, to be seen as their tools, almost, one might say, as the passive mediums of their will.'[1] Terence Ranger explains how guerrillas 'came to admire the determination of the peasantry and to support them in their quintessentially peasant political programme – for the recovery of the lost lands and the cessation of state interference in production'.[2] David Maxwell describes guerrilla ideology as 'essentially weak', mass mobilization as 'pragmatic rather than ideologically determined': 'Although the war had globalizing effects,' he concludes, 'local agendas proved more salient.'[3] Norma Kriger describes guerrillas' unsuccessful appeal to 'cultural nationalism' and their consequent resort to force. She argues that gender, generation and other inequalities in villages 'may be more important motivating factors than peasant grievances arising from their externally oriented relationships'.[4]

[1] D. Lan, *Guns and Rain. Guerrillas and Spirit Mediums in Zimbabwe* (London, James Currey, 1985), pp. 225–6.

[2] T. Ranger, *Peasant Consciousness and Guerrilla War in Zimbabwe. A Comparative Study* (James Currey, London, 1985), pp. 177–8, 182.

[3] D. Maxwell, *Christians and Chiefs in Zimbabwe. A Social History of the Hwesa People c.1870s–1990* (Edinburgh, IAI, 1999), p. 120.

[4] N. Kriger, *Zimbabwe's Guerrilla War. Peasant Voices* (Cambridge, Cambridge University Press, 1992), p. 19. More recent discussions of Zanla/civilian relations include: J. Nhongo-Simbanegavi, 'Zimbabwean Women in the Liberation Struggle. Zanla and its Legacy, 1972–1985', Phd, Oxford, 1997, and; H. Schmidt, 'The Social and Economic Impact of Political Violence in Zimbabwe, 1890–1990: A Case Study of the Honde Valley', PhD, Oxford, 1996.

If the literature on Zanla areas stresses the predominance of local agendas in motivating civilian support for guerrillas, and in shaping guerrilla mobilization strategies, the single academic study of Zipra mobilization has painted a rather different picture. Jeremy Brickhill argues that Zipra guerrillas did not need to draw on local sources of legitimacy such as spirit mediums and church leaders but could simply announce themselves as 'Nkomo's boys', i.e., as followers of Joshua Nkomo, the long time leader of Zapu. They were able to build on Matabeleland's two-decades-old nationalist tradition, and to work exclusively through the rural Zapu party hierarchy.[5] We follow Brickhill in emphasizing the importance and depth of explicitly nationalist commitment, and the crucial role of the rural party in mediating between guerrillas and civilians: nationalism was the legitimizing ideology of the war in the Shangani, and nationalist identifications and institutions were strengthened and broadened over its course. Zipra guerrillas did not need local mediums, church leaders and diviners to legitimize their arrival and purpose in a local idiom. However, contra Brickhill, guerrillas did appeal to these actors in order to deal with injury and illness, fear and danger, and Zapu's rural nationalists were themselves not so secular.

This is not, however, the whole story of the war, for within the discourses and institutions of nationalism there were important divisions and differences among rural social groups, between them and guerrillas, and within guerrilla ranks. Below, we explore the moral and practical debates, and the transformations in popular nationalism, brought about by the escalation of guerrilla war. We focus largely on the semi-liberated or 'green' areas, and to a lesser extent on the 'yellow' areas where control was contested between the Rhodesian state and Zipra.

As in earlier chapters, our oral sources are undoubtedly influenced by the current desire for Zapu and Zipra contributions to the war to be included in the nation's history as well as by the judgement that the liberation war was a legitimate struggle (in contrast to the post-independence violence). The accounts are not, however, blind to the pain of living through war, nor are they silent on the moral questions and political controversies posed by violence. As such, they are revealing of debates that took place during the war years themselves. Some wartime stories have nonetheless become almost mythical: they are recounted and elaborated all over the Shangani in different forms; they remain a topic of debate and are still probed for their meaning.

## Civilian Mobilization and Guerrilla Logistics

The arrival of large numbers of guerrillas in Nkayi and Lupane after 1976 restricted the state's administrative and military activity – it also placed substantial new demands on Zapu committees. The party had survived the repression of the 1960s and 1970s to varying degrees. In the mid-1970s, local Zapu leaders' efforts to expand branch and district committees, and to improve communication with the central party through provincial levels, were greatly stimulated by the arrival of small groups of guerrillas. Guerrillas' and party leaders' assessment of the strength of the party at this juncture differ: guerrillas tend to emphasize their own role in reviving and forming new committees while party leaders stress Zapu's uninterrupted heritage. These views are not necessarily incompatible. Where detention and repression had been severe, Zapu 'committees' at times consisted of no more than one or two individuals. In such instances, it is remarkable that Zapu survived at all, but it is also true that guerrillas needed to stimulate the establishment of full committees and oversee an expansion of

---

[5] J. Brickhill, 'Daring to Storm the Heavens: The Military Strategy of Zapu, 1976–79', in N. Bhebe and T. Ranger (eds), *Soldiers in Zimbabwe's Liberation War* (Harare, University of Zimbabwe Press, and London, James Currey, 1995), pp. 48–73.

party activity. Proximity to administrative centres also played a role: as discussed in Chapter 6, both guerrillas and party leaders agreed that the areas where it was most difficult to organize Zapu committees were those near to large concentrations of government forces, be they paramilitary or regular units.

In addition to reviving defunct committees and forming new ones where none existed, the arrival of guerrillas provoked other changes. While guerrilla demands acted as the spur to change, party leaders maintained an important level of autonomy and initiative in meeting new challenges. As guerrilla numbers increased, Zapu leaders coped with their demands, and the stresses of war more widely, by elaborating a moral economy of supply, trying to uphold norms of law and order, and widening the social basis of the party's membership and leadership.

Meeting guerrillas' logistical needs was the principal force behind Zapu's wartime expansion. Guerrillas' demands were far reaching: they relied on civilians for food, cigarettes, clothes, boots, medicine and intelligence. Party committees organized these supplies. The main executive committees were largely responsible for bringing goods from outside the districts, while women were responsible for providing and cooking food, washing and mending clothes. Youth were charged with scouting and carrying messages, delivering food and supplies to guerrillas, and a host of other activities. The logistical demands of guerrillas required a new set of roles to be undertaken by different social groups as well as a greater level of involvement across a broader section of rural society.

The first meetings between guerrillas and civilians in the Shangani were very different from those described for Zanla operational areas. In eastern Zimbabwe, the stereotypical account of the first encounters with Zanla guerrillas has civilians demanding proof that they were not wild beasts with tails. Guerrillas had first to be 'humanized'. Such was rarely the case in the Shangani where the existence of guerrillas and their purpose had long been known, and where guerrillas came equipped with the names of key party leaders. In Pupu, they made straight for the home of Pilot Ncube, the Zapu leader who had hosted their colleagues in the 1960s. Ncube recalled, 'When the first group of 1970s guerrillas arrived they came straight to me. "Are you Pilot Ncube?" they said. "We got your name from Zambia because you helped our comrades well in the 1960s, so now we're also here to ask for your assistance".'[6] Even in less well-known areas, Zapu members remembered that Zipra 'asked for the homes of the chairmen, the secretary. They knew who were the supporters. They knew the leaders in each corner.'[7] Party leaders' main concern was not guerrillas' humanity but their authenticity. As Zapu leader Micah Mpofu recalled:

> We asked [the guerrillas], 'How can we identify you? It could be a trap.' They had to identify themselves with certain documents [about the party hierarchy and constitution] that they carried, by the type of equipment they had, and they had to politicise us – the party – in the ways to resist. That's how we recognised a true freedom fighter.[8]

This difference is significant: guerrillas who operated in the Shangani did not generally face long periods of suspicion during which they might rely heavily on violence to gain material and political support.[9] In the Zanla area of Mutoko, Norma Kriger has argued that coercion and material calculation played a key role in civilian support for

---

[6] Interview with Pilot Ncube, Pupu, 2 April 1996.
[7] Interview with Lazarus Sibanda, Malindi, 7 September 1995.
[8] Interview with Micah Mpofu, Gonye, 17 October 1995.
[9] This was particularly true for the 'green' zones. In 'yellow' zones, guerrillas' entry was less straightforward, and more liable to rely on coercion.

guerrillas. Adults complained of the costs of providing support, while guerrillas and youth used their coercive power to attain higher levels of consumption.[10] In contrast, providing logistical support for guerrillas in the Shangani was, in general, one of the least contentious issues of the war. Civilians' accounts often focus on bravery, political commitment and cooperation, rather than coercion and complaint. The ingenuity which went into obtaining supplies was a source of great pride, and the methods used have sometimes remained a closely guarded secret up to today.[11]

Mobilization to meet logistical needs was legitimized through, and understood as part of, the long nationalist history of the Shangani. It built on the previous experiences of party activists. Prior to the onset of war, party subscriptions had been the principal means of raising funds. These were collected through the party hierarchy and passed on to provincial committees. In wartime, the demands of the guerrillas necessitated new methods of raising funds, such as holding beer drinks, and widening party member-ship.[12] Wartime demands also required negotiating alliances with people in town, migrant labourers, local businessmen, missions and bus operators in order to acquire and transport goods. Nkayi and Lupane had long had close links with the urban areas, and these were now exploited in new ways. Those with jobs in town or locally were particularly important in acquiring commodities, 'because they could buy those things as if they were their own'.[13]

The rural–urban transport system played a key role. Just as they helped to smuggle guerrilla recruits out of the country, bus drivers and conductors helped to disguise the movement of supplies within Zimbabwe. People remember in great detail which bus companies, and which drivers and conductors were sympathetic to the guerrillas, and which had to be avoided.[14] Zapu leaders developed ingenious techniques for smuggling items through Rhodesian soldiers' road blocks, such as stuffing goods into the spare wheels of buses or burying them in maize sacks.[15] One man remembered: 'You would buy new clothes, then go into a house and put the new clothes on, and take your clothes to the laundry – then they would be put in a parcel and if someone checked the parcel all they would see would be old clothes.'[16] The daring and trickery these 'secret supply teams' required to successfully carry out such tasks was, and still is, a source of great pride.

Supplies were also negotiated from local storeowners, workers in logging companies and Forestry Commission compounds, as well as from the government run Tilcor agricultural estate in Lupane.[17] Storeowners all over the two districts played an

---

[10] Kriger, *Zimbabwe's Guerrilla War*, pp. 140–9.
[11] Revealing the techniques involved could still cause unease a decade and a half after the war. A minority refused to talk about such matters. E.g., Interview with Tshata Mguni, Sesemba, 6 October 1995.
[12] Interview with Council Sibanda, Kwesengulube, 12 December 1995.
[13] Interviews with Johnson Mpofu, Malindi, 12 September 1995; Enos Kanye, Nkayi, 27 November 1995.
[14] E.g., interviews with Mhlotshwa Majaha Moyo, Majaha, 5 October 1995; N. Khumalo, Dandanda, 16 June 1995; Councillor Mlotshwa, Lupaka, 8 February 1996.
[15] E.g, interviews with Paulos Mhlotshwa, Tshakalisa, 25 November 1995; Councillor Mlotshwa, Lupaka, 8 February 1996; group interview, Gomoza, 13 March 1996.
[16] Interview with Mhlotshwa Majaha Moyo, Majaha, 5 October 1995; also, interviews with Yona Dube, Lupanda, 27 February 1996; group interview, Ndlovu school, 18 September 1995.
[17] Zipra guerrillas allowed the Tilcor estate to continue functioning during the war and set up a party branch amongst workers. Interview with former worker, 22 February 1996. A party branch was also established among Forestry Commission workers. Group interview, Masungamala, 7 February 1996. Zipra negotiated with labourers of sawmills and timber companies to obtain supplies. Interviews with Yona Dube, Lupanda, 27 February 1996; Chain Moyo and J. Ndlovu, Bububu, 23 February 1996.

important role in the supply of manufactured goods, particularly clothing and shoes.[18] One local party leader explained: 'We made friends with the local storeowners and politicised them, and we asked them to include our consignments in their orders.'[19] Some leading businessmen were in fact already 'politicized', having joined the Zapu youth movements in Bulawayo in the 1960s.[20] A Gokwe businessman even succeeded in supplying a semi-liberated area of northern Nkayi with a grinding mill.[21] While they remained open, the rural network of Roman Catholic missions also played an important role, particularly in the supply of medicine. A party youth leader described the assistance from Kana mission: 'The hospital helped the guerrillas. ... Youth were closely in touch with the mission. We would get tobacco from the mission, clothing, shoes and medicine for the guerrillas. We'd come with prescriptions to be filled – vaseline, disinfectant.'[22] St Paul's and St Luke's hospitals in Lupane played comparable roles.

Relations with storeowners, missions and bus operators were not, however, un-problematic. Missions, bus companies and stores were – correctly, of course – suspected by Rhodesian forces of supplying guerrillas. Some stores were closed, or had their supplies (with or without the owner's knowledge) infiltrated with poisoned clothing, food and drinks by the Rhodesians. Missions walked a particularly fine line between the pressures of guerrillas and security forces. Many suffered attack from both sides when their loyalties came under question, and only one – St Luke's in Lupane, located on the tarred Bulawayo/Victoria Falls Road – remained open for the duration of the war. Bus operators likewise fell under close scrutiny. Rhodesian forces regularly searched buses while guerrillas used the Zapu networks to ascertain which buses should be attacked, and which allowed to operate – party chairmen objected vehemently when guerrillas attacked buses indiscriminately.[23] One party leader recalled: 'There were two buses here, Godhlwayo and Wankie ... The Godhlwayo driver was sympathetic, but the Wankie driver was not ... He was heavily beaten by the guerrillas and nearly died.'[24] Under such circumstances, the support which guerrillas and Zapu leaders were able to mobilize from these sources, and the commitment of certain priests, bus drivers, and storeowners is all the more remarkable.

In addition to the key role of rural and urban workers, those with businesses and those working in institutions, almost every home played a role in providing food for guerrillas. Under wartime conditions of scarcity, it was important that guerrilla demands should be evenly spread, and the party worked hard to mitigate excessive pressure on any one home.[25] One woman party leader recalled how women

> would distribute [cigarettes] according to village, say three packets in each village so that in case the guerrillas came to you, you could spare some cigarettes. After one or two days, we met to see who was visited. Then if another group of guerrillas arrived they could be directed to a village that still had some.[26]

Though women's logistical role was mainly domestic, the domestic tasks they fulfilled

---

[18] On the cooperation of store owners, see, e.g., group interview, Ndimimbili, 11 March 1996; interview with John Ndlovu, Daluka, 25 January 1996; group interview, Lake Alice, 19 February 1996; group interview, Mathendele, 13 September 1995.

[19] Interview with Micah Mpofu, Manomano, 17 October 1995.

[20] E.g, interview with Jeremiah Moyo, Nkayi, 21 September 1995.

[21] Interview with Leonard Nkomo, Nkayi, 15 December 1994.

[22] Interview with Elias Sibanda, Kana, 5 December 1995.

[23] E.g., Interview with Tallus Ndlovu, Gwelutshena area, 6 December 1994.

[24] Interview with Mhlotshwa Majaha Moyo, Majaha, 5 October 1995.

[25] E.g., Interview with Tallus Ndlovu, Gwelutshena area, 6 December 1994.

[26] Interview with Sisigile Ncube, Mathendele, 13 September 1995.

were far from pre-war norms. With many men absent in detention or because they had joined the guerrilla forces, women's responsibilities increased, extending even to decisions about allowing guerrillas to cache arms within their yards.[27] Nor was food preparation an easy task, particularly in the 'yellow' areas where Rhodesian forces still patrolled. Keeping sufficient food at home to feed guerrillas, yet disguising this from Rhodesian search parties required particular ingenuity, as well as tight coordination among homes and with guerrillas such that demands were evenly spread. Supplying guerrillas became more difficult everywhere in the last year of the war when guerrilla numbers increased substantially. As Musa Dube, Zapu committee member in the 'green' area of Lake Alice, recalled: 'They could demand chicken. Some could provide but others were unable. ... To the people it was a very big problem, not in the sense that people didn't like that, they appreciated, friendship was there, simply it was not easy to meet their demands.'[28] Guerrillas were expected to eat the same food as civilians, and not to demand special treatment such as the slaughtering of animals. While there were many cases of coercion and excessive demands made by guerrillas, notably towards the war's end, these were not generally portrayed as the norm, nor were they regarded as normatively acceptable. A logistical moral economy developed between Zipra guerrillas and their supporters away from government influence in the Shangani, and abrogations were condemned within the discourse and institutions of nationalism.

If providing food to guerrillas was the most common role played by women in the war, it was not the only one. Many women entered, voluntarily or involuntarily, into relationships with guerrillas. These were a source of great concern to the elder male Zapu chairmen, who argued that such relationships were not an acceptable part of the struggle. Controlling such relationships relied, as in the control of other aspects of guerrilla behaviour, on the authority and sometimes audacity of party chairmen and their relationships with guerrilla commanders. Zapu chairman Arthur Ncube explained, 'It was difficult to control the young guerrillas. They tried to proposition girls, but we argued with them, saying, "That's not what you're here for". Those staying with us had a very good commander whom we could inform to prevent that.'[29] Commanders, of course, varied and there certainly were abuses. Rape was, however, described as exceptional (though there are many reasons why rape should go under-reported). Northern Front commander Nicholas Nkomo maintains there were harsh punishments for rape,[30] and chairmen and women both hold that many relationships were not forced, though they were beyond their control. Indeed, some guerrillas returned after the war's end to marry and pay lobola to the families of women with whom they had had wartime relationships.[31]

Though the role of Zapu committees, and of women within them, was profoundly changed during the war years, the presence of guerrillas brought about the most dramatic transformation to the role of local youth. Youth were often called upon to carry out the most dangerous tasks, such as scouting for enemy soldiers, carrying messages and alerting parents when guerrillas needed supplies. Members of the main

---

[27] Interview with Siponono Mlotshwa, Ngombane, 27 February 1996.

[28] Interview with Musa Dube, Aaron Dube and Ken Moyo, Lake Alice, 19 February 1996.

[29] Interview with Arthur Ncube, Tshongokwe, 6 December 1994. Also, e.g., interview with J. Gabheni Sibanda, Lupanda, 7 November 1994.

[30] Interview with Nicholas Nkomo, Nkayi, 9 September 1995. Former Zipra guerrilla Hlanganani Ndebele recalled a case where his unit disarmed and 'rehabilitated' a guerrilla found guilty of rape. He said others were sent to Lusaka for punishment. Interview, Dakamella, 15 September 1995.

[31] E.g., Interviews with Timothy Mthethwa, Kwesengulube, 1 December 1995; Sisigile Sibanda, Gwelutshena, 8 December 1994; Paul Ndebele, Mjena, 8 December 1995.

wings of the party regularly praised youth for their bravery and hard work – they were 'the real army of the people', as one Zapu chairman put it.[32]

While this role put youth at great risk, it also gave them unprecedented power as gatekeepers to the guerrillas. In our interviews, we asked systematically whether youth had posed a problem of control, as the excesses of youth in wartime had formed an important part of other accounts of the war.[33] Controlling youth was indeed a major challenge which the main branch of Zapu committees struggled to meet, though it does not seem to have been commensurate with that described by Norma Kriger for the Zanla area of Mutoko. This was due in part to the fact that it was unusual for youth to live with guerrillas or to rely on them for sustenance: they remained more closely tied to their own homes and to the party hierarchies. Party chairmen's descriptions of their efforts to keep control over youth focused on their duty to maintain 'law and order', to contain coercion within the confines of legitimate nationalist goals. Key in this was the authority of individual chairmen and their links to guerrilla commanders.

In many areas, chairmen said that they had kept youth in line, through a combination of their own longstanding authority, bravery, and good relations with guerrilla commanders.[34] Where youth committed crimes, they were often disciplined: in one instance the parents of a youth who had abducted and raped a young girl were forced by the Zapu committee to pay her parents a sewing machine in compensation.[35] In another case, it was guerrillas who were responsible for disciplining youth who had looted a store.[36] Nonetheless, there were many instances of young men abusing their power, and this aspect of the war was often described as one of the failures of nationalist and guerrilla authority. We return to this question with regard to the treatment of witches and sellouts below.

Meeting guerrillas' logistical needs thus required a new, and often difficult, level of cooperation among men, women and youth, among migrant workers and local producers, among store owners and employees of bus companies. The divisions of class, gender and generation were not the only divides which had to be wrestled with in this vast expansion of party activity: bridging the tensions between the evictees who dominated the Zapu committees and the earlier settlers of Nkayi and Lupane also became a matter of survival. David Maxwell has argued that Zanla guerrillas in the eastern district of Inyanga used the educated and politicized Manyika evictees of the area to mobilize their less-educated Hwesa neighbours.[37] In the Shangani, it was not the guerrillas who took the initiative to overcome a similar divide, but Zapu leaders themselves.

As discussed in previous chapters, in some areas a unity of purpose was achieved before the war. Elsewhere, the war brought a new rapprochement as sons from all groups were recruited into the armed struggle and joined the party youth, and as more 'originals' became prominent party activists. The logistical pressures at the height of the war consolidated such processes and brought about a significantly greater role for early settlers. In Kana, for example, one 'local' explained, 'To start with, locals were hesitant to become chairmen. This came later when people were conscientised. ... So this idea of Filabusi [evictee] people leading us had to vanish. ... The balance shifted in 1977.'[38] Likewise, in Sebhumane, Filabusi dominance was 'balanced out' by Tonga activists

[32] Interview with Micah Mpofu, Manomano, 17 October 1995. Also see Kriger, *Zimbabwe's Guerrilla War*, p. 184 and *passim*.

[33] See Kriger, *Zimbabwe's Guerrilla War*, pp. 180–6.

[34] E.g., interviews with Sibindi family, Panke, 24 November 1995; Paulos Mhlotshwa, Tshakalisa, 25 November 1995; D.C. Moyo, Manomano, 17 October 1995.

[35] Interview with Elias Sibanda, Kana, 5 December 1995.

[36] Interview with Josiah Ndlovu, Enoch Ncube and Ruben Dube, Malunku, 6 March 1996.

[37] Maxwell, *Christians and Chiefs in Zimbabwe*, Chapter 5.

[38] Interview with Elias Sibanda, Kana, 5 December 1995.

during the war.[39] Even in cases where early settlers were inadequately drawn into the party leadership, they were still drawn into the war effort – though they were some-times accused of not pulling their weight and of cowardice. One evictee Zapu chairman described the locals as 'fence sitters': 'Those from here don't want to be leaders. ... They didn't want to be in a den of lions so they let us lead.'[40] The inclusion of the previously derided earlier settlers on Zapu committees was one of the factors which significantly changed their character. It weakened the hold of a Christian and educated elite on political authority, and broadened the party's ethnic composition. This tendency was further strengthened by the antipathy that guerrillas expressed towards mission Christianity, as discussed below.

In sum, the enormous logistical demands of the later years of the war provoked a series of changes in the character of local nationalism in Nkayi and Lupane. The membership and roles of the party were greatly expanded, drawing youth, women, shop-owners, migrant labourers, bus operators and others into newly prominent positions. Perhaps most significantly, the imperative of a broad alliance required a firmer bridging of the divide between the evictee political leadership and the long-scorned earlier settlers. While nationalist structures vastly expanded in this period, and successfully coped with many of the demands of guerrillas, there were also tensions and difficulties. The nationalist leadership sought to cope with new challenges by developing a moral economy to regulate the provision of supplies, by trying to uphold norms of law and order in order to control the excesses of youth and guerrillas, and by initiating an ethnically and socially inclusive policy of recruitment so as to expand party representation. Though these party endeavours were not always successful, they demonstrated the institutional and ideological adaptability and resilience of the party, as well as the strength of local nationalist commitment.

## Debates over Guerrilla Goals and Beliefs

If the logistical demands of large numbers of guerrillas forced dramatic change in the nationalist institutions of Nkayi and Lupane, so did the Zipra guerrillas' own policies and beliefs. The guerrilla goal of driving government authorities from the rural areas, and the expression of guerrilla attitudes towards religious beliefs sparked political changes and moral controversy. Though the banishing of government authority was an explicit part of both Zapu and Zipra strategy, and was debated in terms of a shared nationalist commitment, guerrillas' beliefs, and means of achieving their goals, did not always sit easily with popular nationalism.

Ousting government representatives from the rural areas required dismantling the (usually unarmed) administrative hierarchy of chiefs, headmen and kraalheads, as well as preventing policemen, agricultural demonstrators, dip-tank attendants, teachers and others from working. Moral debate over the treatment of government employees between guerrillas and Zapu committees revolved around whether they should be killed, simply forced to stop working, or accommodated within the nationalist struggle. On the whole, guerrilla killings of active government servants were some of the least controversial of the war. Such individuals were, after all, working for 'the enemy', and some had a long history of open antagonism to nationalist activists. Let us first consider the administrative hierarchy of traditional authority.

From the early 1960s, Rhodesian governments had increasingly sought to use chiefs

---

[39] Interview with J. Mnethwa, H. Masuku, and B.J. Ncube, Sebhumane, 30 November 1995.

[40] Interview with Timothy Mthethwa, Kwesengulube, 1 December 1995. Zipra guerrillas, for their part, often sterotyped Tonga 'originals' as more trustworthy, because they were less interested in money and hence less liable to be 'bought' by the government, than the more wealthy evictees.

and headmen as a bulwark against rural nationalism, as well as putting them in the frontline of implementing unpopular agricultural regulations. In the Shangani, this strategy had widened what were never very close relations between chiefs and their constituencies. Chiefs were largely administrative creations whose legitimacy did not rest on an historical relationship to their followers. Chiefs' relations with the activist evictee communities had been particularly hostile, and their use in enforcing the building of contours in particular had alienated a much wider group. During the war, this history meant that local nationalists and guerrillas were often in agreement in designating chiefs and headmen as legitimate targets.[41] As discussed in Chapter 6, only two out of the large number of chiefs and headmen stayed with guerrillas during the war – the others fled or were evacuated to government centres, and not without a considerable death toll.

Further down the traditional hierarchy, the situation was more complex. Some guerrillas tended initially to regard kraalheads with suspicion: as Lupanda activist Gabheni Sibanda explained, 'all kraalheads were labelled "sellouts". You really had to prove yourself, showing your true colours.'[42] However, party leaders regularly drew a distinction between chiefs and headmen on the one hand and kraalheads on the other. Many kraalheads had had a long association with nationalism, and some were, in fact, party chairmen. Guerrillas were forced to modify their beliefs through discussion with Zapu committees.[43]

Civil servants were a more clear-cut guerrilla target: a number of agricultural demonstrators, veterinary officers and dip tank attendants were killed. However, it was also common, and preferred by party leaders, for employees first to receive warnings to leave their work. As one agricultural demonstrator remembered: 'If one was warned not to work and then agreed, the guerrillas would not harm you.'[44] Known nationalist activists who held, or who had held, government jobs were a source of intense debate. Sometimes guerrillas were condemned for their hasty execution, while the senior guerrilla command and local Zapu leaders tended to advocate incorporating them in the nationalist struggle, arguing that liberated Zimbabwe would need skilled people, and insisting on the valuable contribution they had made, and could still make, to the war effort. In Lake Alice, for example, NF2 commander Nicholas Nkomo intervened to stop guerrillas from killing a highly educated former senior policeman who was a member of the local Zapu committee.[45] Of course, guerrillas were not always in favour of execution: in Menyezwa, a 'yellow' zone not far from the Lupane offices, guerrillas insisted that the local Zapu members elect Gilbert Maphosa, a former agricultural demonstrator, as vice-chairman of the party, on the grounds that he would be less likely to fall under Rhodesian suspicion. Unfortunately for Maphosa, he was arrested, interrogated and beaten by government forces who wondered why he had not been killed or fled the rural areas.[46] Though party leaders and guerrillas agreed that individuals who refused to leave government employ were legitimate targets, party

---

[41] Nationalist leaders regularly condemned chiefs for their complicity in enforcing agricultural regulations and in repressing activists, and saw them as closely allied to white administrators. E.g., group interview, Gonye, 17 October 1995; group interview, Mateme, 23 November 1995.

[42] Interview with Gabheni Sibanda, Lupanda, 9 November 1994. Not all guerrillas were hostile to kraalheads: e.g., interview with former Zipra guerrilla Agrippa Mguni, Nesigwe, 19 November 1995.

[43] E.g., group interview, Gonye, 17 October 1995; group interview, Gampinya, 19 October 1995; Lakatshona Samuel Ndebele and Andrea Mhlanga, Gwelutshena, 5 December 1994; Kraalhead M.S. Ndhlovu, Dwala, 9 December 1995.

[44] Interview with Mr Maphosa, Menyezwa, 24 September 1995.

[45] Interview with Musa Dube, Aaron Dube and Ken Moyo, Lake Alice, 19 February 1996.

[46] Interview with Mr and Mrs Maphosa, Menyezwa, 24 September 1995.

leaders sometimes condemned cruel and humiliating executions. They recounted with horror stories of dip tank attendants who were forced to swim in, or drink, the dip water before being killed, or stories of veterinary officers being forced to eat raw meat before being shot.[47]

Whether, and which, civil servants should be considered legitimate wartime targets, and how they should be killed, were thus a source of debate amongst guerrillas and local nationalist leaders. Zapu leaders, often in alliance with guerrilla commanders, generally acted to contain killings: local nationalism tended to be incorporative and humane, to prefer personal rather than categorical evaluations of loyalty.

The treatment of civil servants was not the only component of the guerrilla assault on the government's rural presence that sparked debate: the closure of government services was another source of contention. Zipra's official policy was to close down, but not physically destroy, all services. However, guerrillas and youth often preferred destruction, sometimes out of sheer zealousness, and sometimes on the grounds that an independent Zimbabwe would have all new and higher quality services. In the case of schools, parents had often contributed labour and money to their construction. The evictee communities had struggled particularly hard to expand the scarce educational opportunities available in the Shangani. They regarded schools as an investment in their children's future; they saw attempts to destroy them as regressive, and were skeptical of guerrilla promises of future rebuilding. Zapu leaders debated with guerrillas over the value of education and its importance for the future. In Lake Alice, the Zapu branch chairman had remonstrated with youth and guerrillas who wanted to burn the school. He told them:

> If we win we will need educated people to rule. Even dip tanks, we need them. So if you destroy these things, then what? The commanders and local Zapu were against burning the school. … When the senior commanders came and agreed with us, we were very relieved.[48]

In Malindi, Zapu chairmen explained, 'In this area, we didn't want to slacken our responsibilities or allow vandalism. … We sat down with the guerrillas and told them if you say we must destroy these things, it is us who will suffer. We will need these … schools, so let's leave them. And they agreed.'[49] Party leaders cast their efforts to save schools as an heroic and dangerous struggle in which their forward-looking views on the value of education largely prevailed. Statistics compiled by the government on the closure and destruction of schools confirm their success: in both Nkayi and Lupane, while the vast majority were closed, less than a third were destroyed.[50]

The destruction of dips was less controversial than that of schools, as dipping had a history of coercion and was associated with taxation – many tanks had in fact been enthusiastically destroyed in pre-war protests, and the vast majority would be destroyed before the war's conclusion.[51] However, a side effect of the breakdown of veterinary services and dipping was the spread of cattle disease, particularly that carried by ticks. As the aim of closing dips was the restriction of government activity, guerrillas sometimes allowed individuals to run private dips. In Dongamuzi, for example, elders

---

[47] Interview with Mr Maphosa, Menyezwa, 24 September 1995.
[48] Interview, Lake Alice. Such accounts of debate were common, e.g., group interview, Manomano, 17 October 1995.
[49] Interview with Lazarus Sibanda, Johnson Mpofu and Alson Tshabalala, Matetshaneni, 12 September 1995.
[50] In 1977–8, 23 of Lupane's 64 schools were burnt and the remainder closed. In Nkayi, only 15 of 50 schools were destroyed or badly damaged. See *The Chronicle*, 12 May 1980.
[51] In Nkayi, 45 of 50 dip tanks were destroyed by the war's end. See *The Chronicle*, 17 January 1981.

recalled that, 'cattle started dying of tick-borne disease, so Zipra allowed individuals to purchase chemicals and use them in the dip.'[52] In short, Zipra's campaign to close down rural services was extremely successful, while party chairmen's efforts to preserve schools (if not always dips) from destruction occasioned debate among guerrillas and chairmen in which, more often than not, the views of chairmen won out.

The guerrillas' efforts to displace government authority were not restricted to the negative goals of killing, destruction and closure. They also had a positive agenda with regard to removing state restrictions on land use, an agenda which echoed the initiatives of the nationalist activism of the 1960s. Guerrillas' support for 'freedom farming' in the 1970s was extremely popular. It included the destruction of the hated contours, the movement of fields back into the fertile river valleys and of homes back into Forestry and 'European' land, the raiding of stock from white farmers – and celebratory feasting thereon – and the evasion of veterinary restrictions on the holding and movement of cattle in areas subject to tsetse controls. Some of these changes, such as the removal of restrictions on cultivation practices, were universal. Others affected only communities which bordered on 'European' and Forestry land. Their overall impact was to demonstrate the authority of Zipra and Zapu – rather than the government – over the land, and to realize some of the most longstanding of nationalist goals.

The driving out of government representatives and the removal of unwanted state restrictions on land use and settlement both had the effect of enhancing the authority of nationalists. Other aspects of guerrilla ideology, however, undermined this local political leadership. Crucial in this regard was guerrillas' antipathy to mission Christianity. Guerrillas consistently closed churches, prevented worship and cast stalwart mission Christian figures as sellouts. They argued that mission Christianity was a tool of the European, part of 'the white man's strategy to tame people and perpetuate colonialism'.[53] Guerrillas brought this attitude with them – it did not develop in response to local views regarding missions, as has been argued for both Zanla and Zipra areas elsewhere in Zimbabwe.[54] The origins of Zipra guerrillas' consistently hostile views towards mission Christianity probably lay in their training. Their views cannot be explained simply in terms of their own backgrounds: many guerrillas were in fact Christians (and some were deeply ambivalent about attacking churches).[55] Missions in Nkayi and Lupane had played an important role in the logistical support of guerrillas as well as in the history of nationalism. The early, evictee-dominated leaders of Zapu committees were often ardent members of mission Christian churches, and had struggled against and condemned the 'heathen' beliefs of the older settlers of the Shangani, causing great offence to their new neighbours in the process.

The guerrilla attitude to mission Christianity placed many of the evictee Zapu leaders in a difficult and dangerous position. Many were threatened or chastised for their beliefs. The Anglican Alexander Mabhena recalled, 'One could even die because of calling on God publicly.'[56] The Presbyterian Levy Mavolo remembers guerrillas refusing to pray, and warning him: 'Mdala [old man]! When your eyes are closed a bullet can enter there.'[57] LMS adherent and party chairman Timothy Mthethwa described how he

---

[52] Group interview, Chief Menyezwa's kraal, 15 December 1994.

[53] Interview by Nathaniel Mpofu with Timothy Gumede, UCCSA, Sivalo, 3 October 1995.

[54] See T. Ranger and M. Ncube, 'Religion in the Guerrilla War: The Case of Southern Matabeleland', in N. Bhebe and T. Ranger (eds), *Society in Zimbabwe's Liberation War* (London, James Currey, 1995), pp. 35–57.

[55] A former priest at Kana mission described how several Zipra guerrillas who were themselves former seminary students came to apologize to him for attacking the mission. Interview with Joseph Mkwebu, Nkayi, 14 December 1995.

[56] Interview by Nathaniel Mpofu with Alexander Mabhena, Somakantana, 5 October 1995.

[57] Interview with Levy Mavolo Ndhlovu, Lutsha, 3 October 1995.

was asked by a guerrilla, '"Do you pray in your meetings?" I said yes. He said, "Bring that God of yours and I'll shoot him!".' The Christians of Mthethwa's area stopped going to church, instead 'aligning' themselves with the religious practices of the earlier settlers: 'If we didn't do that we could have betrayed ourselves during the war – they could have pointed a finger at us, blamed us [for drought or misfortune],' he explained.[58]

Others refused to suspend their church activities, instead entering into debate with guerrillas in which they argued that Christianity was compatible with nationalism. The devout Presbyterian and staunch nationalist Nathaniel Mpofu, to whom we have referred in earlier chapters, is a case in point. Guerrillas came to his home and demanded to know 'why I was holding services and respecting the religion of the white man in an African country'. Mpofu launched into an explanation of the doctrine of pre-destination, arguing that, 'the war they were fighting was predestined by God', as was their victory. He explained the emergence of Zanu by likening Zapu leader Joshua Nkomo to Moses: 'The bible says that Moses was in the wilderness for forty days and that when he came back he found the people worshipping the golden calf. Joshua Nkomo was out of the country for forty days and when he came back he found people worshipping Zanu.' Mpofu and his church survived, but not without continued harrass-ment.[59] More commonly, churches were shut down for the duration of the war.[60]

Guerrillas' hostility to mainline Christian churches, did not, however, imply a secular, rationalist stance. Guerrillas regularly called on *izinyanga* and *izangoma* or *wosana* spirit mediums, as well as on Zionist and Apostolic prophets, to heal individual afflictions and injuries, and to ask for the support and protection of the ancestors, the Nevana medium and the Mwali High God.[61] Many healing churches flourished in the course of the war, encouraged rather than harrassed by guerrillas. 'They encouraged us to pray so that we would remember them in our prayers that they become victors of Zimbabwe,' recounted one Zionist leader.[62] The Vice-President of the Apostolic Holy Church in Zion recalled how 'during the war, many guerrillas came to us with their disease and some need[ed] prayers. So that when they are befallen misfortune in the war or some people seem to stand in opposition to or do not welcome them, so they come to me for prayers.'[63] A traditional healer told how he used to treat guerrillas who came to him 'suffering fainting, after walking long distances, also dizziness and fits. Some didn't want to hear loud sounds, like a crack or a clicking sound, that would send them into shock. What was needed was *muti* to eradicate it ... others came possessed by *amadlozi* [ancestral spirits].'[64]

---

[58] Interview with Timothy Mthethwa, Kwesengulube, 1 December 1995.

[59] See J. Alexander and T. Ranger, 'Competition and Integration in the Religious History of North Western Zimbabwe', *Journal of Religion in Africa*, 28, 1, 1998, pp. 3–31.

[60] E.g., interviews with Tshata Mguni, Sesemba, 6 October 1995; Ndola Ndhlovu, Siphunyuka, 29 November 1995; England Ngwenya, Tshakalisa, 6 December 1995.

[61] Instances of this kind are common both in accounts of Zipra behaviour, and in our interviews of Zipra combatants. E.g, interviews with Wosana England Ngwenya, Tshakalisa, 6 December 1995; Elias Sibanda and Daniel Ncube, Kana, 5 December 1995; former Zipra combatant Cleopas Sibanda, Mdlawuzeni, 16 September 1995; Phineas Ncube, Somakantana, 16 December 1994; former Zipra combatant Rainfall Msimanga, Mathendele, 30 August 1995; Tshata Mguni, Sesemba, 6 October 1995.

[62] Interview with Solala Edward Dube of the Zion Catholic Church by Nathaniel Mpofu, Novem-ber 1995. Such comments were common: see also Mpofu's interviews with Thabani Moyo of the Twelve Apostles Church, and Betty Mlophe of the Catholic Apostolic Church, both in November 1995.

[63] Interview by Nathaniel Mpofu with M. Nyathi, November 1995. Such accounts were typical.

[64] Interview with Sabelo Mhlanga, Mpofu Ncube, Patison Mpofu and David Ncube, Lupaka, 9 February 1996.

Many party leaders and ritual specialists recall that guerrillas were avid participants in *mtolo* ceremonies: 'They were very concerned about shrines – more concerned than we were!' remembered a group of elder men.[65] At the famous Panke tree, a gigantic baobob which had long been a sacred site, guerrillas asked the tree's keepers to carry out a special ceremony in 1978: 'We made it look like a normal ceremony, but it was for the guerrillas. The guerrillas came and put their weapons down and performed with us. … The elders were told to make it known to the ancestors that the young men had come to liberate them and to ask for protection.'[66] These appeals were less about legitimizing the war and the guerrillas' presence than about seeking ancestral spirit support, and finding ways of coping with illness and fear. Nor did appeals to the ancestors lead to any less rigour in adherence to military codes of conduct – while guerrillas may have danced at *mtolo* trees, they did not don the customary leg rattles which would have hindered a quick and silent escape.[67]

Guerrillas also made ritual links with the region's pre-colonial history. NF2 commander Nicholas Nkomo travelled to the grave of Lobengula's senior queen, Lozikeyi, in Inyathi where he buried two bullets, one from an FN rifle to symbolize the Rhodesian forces, and one from an AK-47 to symbolize the guerrillas. He placed the tips of the two bullets together in order to indicate that the country was at war once again.[68] The historic site of Pupu, where Ndebele warriors had routed the Alan Wilson Patrol in 1893, was particularly important. Guerrillas visited the grave and the *mtswiri* tree which had acted as Lobengula's 'command post'. Former guerrilla Agrippa Mguni remembered Pupu as 'a very respected area. We would select one of our members to talk on our behalf, to tell the ancestors we were here and ask for guidance.'[69] Kraalhead Magwaza Ndlovu, an early settler who was responsible for the Pupu shrine, recalled:

> When the multitude of guerrillas came, they encouraged us to go and *thethela* (propitiate the ancestors) there [at the grave]. Later we bought a black goat and celebrated there, slaughtered the goat. Then the guerrillas praised us for that. The guerrillas used to go to both the grave and the *mtswiri* tree.[70]

Guerrillas tried to prevent fighting near this site: the area was in fact remembered as a 'zone of peace' amidst the turmoil of war. Kraalhead Magwaza explained:

> There was no fighting around that area except for one day when … the Rhodesians shot and killed one guerrilla. … That is the only incident of fighting in the vicinity. That is what caused the guerrillas to try to destroy the Alan Wilson memorial with a bazooka in retaliation. That was the only noise around Pupu. It was a respected area.[71]

At times, Christian evictee party chairmen worked hand in hand with previously shunned traditional religious figures in order to meet guerrillas' needs. In Lupaka, for example, the Christian evictee Zapu leadership worked with *izinyanga* (traditional

[65] Group interview, Mabayi, 21 September 1995.
[66] Interview with Sibindi Family, Panke, 24 November 1995.
[67] Interview, Headman Mlume and family, Nkoni, 2 October 1995. The emphasis on both military vigilance and respect for the ancestors was commonly made by guerrillas. E.g., Interviews, former Zipra combatant Hlanganeni Ndebele, Dakamela, 15 September 1995; former Zipra combatant Benjamin Sibanda, Saziyabana, 11 October 1995.
[68] Interview with Nicholas Nkomo, Nkayi, 9 September 1995.
[69] Interview with Agrippa Mguni, Nesigwe, 19 November 1995.
[70] Interview with Kraalhead Magwaza Ndlovu, Pupu, 20 February 1996.
[71] Interview with Kraalhead Magwaza Ndlovu, Pupu, 20 February 1996.

healers) from the ranks of the earlier settlers in seeking to resolve the problem of spirit possession among guerrillas far from home – a matter which would normally have been resolved within the family. *Inyanga* Sabelo Mhlanga, an early settler in Lupaka, explained:

> If there was a problem of *amadlozi* [ancestral spirits], we had organized for that. The District Chair organized a party to go to the Matopos to ask about that. ... There was a certain cloth and beads brought by men from Njelele which could represent every ceremony from every place. So when a boy from Nkayi or Tsholotsho was brought here during the war, we would choose a special place, like a tree, and tie the cloth around the tree and use the beads. Even if the spirit is from a foreign place, it didn't matter. The beads and cloth were kept by Dhlodhlo [the Zapu provincial chairman]. Then in some cases that would be successful, and the spirit would leave the boy to do his duties.[72]

The guerrilla predeliction for drawing heavily on *izinyanga*, diviners and Zionists, while rejecting mission Christians (many of whose churches, clinics and schools were, at any rate, closed down), influenced broader social change within the rural areas, as well as the character of local nationalism. The dominance of modernizing Christians on the Zapu committees had already been diluted by the great expansion of party membership occasioned by the guerrillas' logistical demands; Zipra's specific hostility to mission Christianity tended to reinforce a marginalization of this aspect of local nationalism. The ideological content of nationalism thus shifted, while the long-standing struggles between evictees and the 'originals' of Nkayi and Lupane over religion was tipped in favour of the latter. In local activists' minds, the nationalism which emerged at the end of the war was linked far more explicitly to the pre-colonial history of struggle in the region and to the support of the ancestors, Njelele and the Nevana medium, than ever before.

### Witches and Sellouts: The Legitimacy of Violence

The violence and controversy associated with accusations of selling out and witchcraft within African communities far exceeded that which surrounded the treatment of civil servants, Christians and others.[73] These accusations provoked some of the most traumatic incidents of the war, and occasioned intense moral and political debate. Here again, shared nationalist goals framed divergent ideas about the legitimate uses of violence in wartime. Guerrillas were drawn into accusations of selling out and witchcraft based on local animosities; guerrillas and civilians both sought recourse to diviners in attempts to identify sellouts. At the same time, party leaders and guerrillas debated the legitimacy of such accusations in the broad terms of Zipra military strategy and Zapu's constitution.

Geography shaped the patterns of guerrilla violence against civilians: the contested yellow zones were particularly violent for civilians as they found themselves caught between guerrillas and government forces. Upsurges in guerrilla violence in the green zones were owed more to the successes of Rhodesian unconventional tactics, particularly the poisoning campaign. There was also a temporal pattern to wartime violence.

---

72 Interview with Sabelo Mhlanga, Lupaka, 9 February 1996.
73 For a fuller discussion of the issues in this section see J. McGregor, 'Containing Violence: Poisoning and Guerrilla/ Civilian Relations in Memories of Zimbabwe's Liberation War', in K. Lacy Rogers, S. Leydesdorff and G. Dawson (eds), *Trauma and Life Stories: International Perspectives* (London, Routledge, 1999).

Most people held that the war became more violent as it progressed, with the final months of the war being the worst of all.[74]

Although the literature on sellouts and witches – as well as many of our own inter-view accounts – tends to treat the two categories as one,[75] moral debates over legitimate violence in the Shangani often produced clear distinctions between the two categories. Zapu leaders and Zipra commanders played an important, and often successful, role in containing violence against civilians accused of witchcraft by rejecting the legitimacy of killing witches (but not proven sellouts) in terms of nationalist or military goals. The distinction between witch and sellout was important. David Lan has argued that guerrilla violence against witches/sellouts was popular among civilians, and helped to legitimize guerrillas by identifying them with struggles against evil.[76] But in the Shan-gani, the opposite was true – Zapu leaders and the Zipra command strove to control violence against witches precisely because it undermined support for guerrillas.

Other authors have analysed violence against sellouts and witches in a different way. Norma Kriger explains the patterns of sellout and witchcraft accusations in Mtoko by emphasizing the role of divisions within rural society which pitted youth against parents, women against men, and the less well-off and outsiders against the local African elite.[77] But in the Shangani, although jealousy of others' wealth was at times identified as the motivation for accusations and though women were often a target, charges of selling out and witchcraft were not interpreted as reflections of corporate class or gender interests – nor were they portrayed as a reflection of the rift between evictees and earlier settlers.

Civilian testimony in Nkayi and Lupane consistently blamed accusations of selling out and witchcraft on individual animosities motivated by greed and jealousy. Such animosities were very local and personal, sometimes intra-familial. The refrain 'it was all jealousy' was constantly repeated. 'If you hated your uncle, that was a reason for accusation, as a sellout or as a witch, just to get rid of you,' one Zapu leader argued.[78] Though most (but not all) executions were conducted by guerrillas and youth, those who held the gun were often portrayed as the innocent, or at least ignorant, instruments of such animosities. These wartime killings were understood as highly arbitrary, are remembered as deeply traumatic, and certainly had a lasting impact on intra-familial and intra-community tensions.

It is important to place accusations of selling out and witchcraft in their wartime context. There were, of course, genuine sellouts whose actions threatened the lives of both Zapu activists and guerrillas. The Rhodesians sought – with variable results – to cultivate informers through their psychological operations campaign, through threats and torture, as well as by offering cash rewards for information.[79] Some collaborators were issued with two-way radios, which they were able to use to devastating effect against guerrillas.[80] Killing 'real' sellouts was accepted as a necessary wartime act, but it

---

[74] This was the case in Zanla areas as well. See T. Ranger, 'Bandits and Guerrillas: the Case of Zim-babwe', in D. Crummey (ed.), *Banditry, Rebellion and Social Protest in Africa* (London, James Currey, 1986), pp. 386–90.

[75] See Lan, *Guns and Rain*, p. 170; R. Werbner, *Tears of the Dead: The Social Biography of an African Family* (Edinburgh, Edinburgh University Press, 1991), p. 150.

[76] Lan, *Guns and Rain*, p. 36.

[77] See Kriger, *Zimbabwe's Guerrilla War*, pp. 208–9.

[78] Interview with Elias Sibanda, Kana, 28 November 1995. We have many such examples. See McGregor, 'Containing Violence', for a more detailed discussion of the allocation of blame in such instances.

[79] See Chapter 6. Large cash rewards were offered for weapons and land mines as well as for information. Interview with Alson Tshabalala, Malindi, 12 September 1995.

[80] Interview with Paul Sibanda, Gampinya, 19 October 1995.

was very hard to prove guilt. Debates over the legitimacy of sellout killings hinged on whether or not there was convincing evidence, whether warnings were issued, whether there was an investigation. People's stories of sellout accusations emphasize the arbitrariness of killings based on a mere hunch or divination.[81] Individuals could fall under suspicion simply for travelling to places where government troops were stationed, such as the administrative centres of Nkayi and Lupane,[82] for an off-hand remark, or due to a visit by patrolling Rhodesian forces. As one Zapu chairman recalled:

> One of those who was killed [as a sellout] here, he was a gambler, he was playing cards – he said, 'You are trusting your youth, but I have my own youth too, which I will call.' Unfortunately for him, soldiers stopped at his place the next day. We don't know if he called them or not, but it fulfilled what he had said.[83]

Senior Zapu leaders themselves at times fell victim to accusation. Lupanda activist Gabheni Sibanda told of narrowly escaping execution by guerrillas on the basis of neighbours' grudges, only subsequently to be offered an apology.[84]

But if 'real' sellouts were obviously dangerous to the nationalist cause, and constituted a legitimate enemy during the war, this was not the case with witches. Though some arguments against killing witches were grounded in the desire not to take life, or in religious arguments that only God had the right to judge, the most powerful arguments against the killing of witches were cast in nationalist and military terms. Senior party leaders argued that killing witches was not part of Zapu's programme. One provincial Zapu leader, Senzani Ngwenya, confronted a group of guerrillas intent on killing an accused witch: she asked, 'Now, can you produce your constitution to show me you have been assigned to kill witches. Where is the document that gives you the power to kill witches? We are the leaders of Zapu and you are our soldiers. We don't know that constitution.'[85] Another party leader had sought to convince youth that witches 'were there when the earth was still young', that the party had 'nothing to do with that', that they were fighting for freedom for all – and even witches would one day be free to vote.[86] NF2 commander Nicholas Nkomo opposed the killing of witches on the grounds that they were not designated as targets in Zipra strategy: 'I was clear that we had no instructions to kill witches. So I gave these instructions to lower commands – no one can die because they are accused of being a witch.'[87] But these arguments were not always effective: as with sellout accusations, charges of witchcraft were widespread, and often targeted hated neighbours or the wealthy. They at times also took on a gendered edge, focusing on adulterous wives, or women thought to have caused fertility problems, or the death of a mother in childbirth. These 'witches' were identified through divination, or on the basis of suspicions held by party committee members.[88]

Zapu chairmen, in fact, played a pivotal role in the treatment of accusations of witchcraft. As Paulos Mhlotshwa explained: 'The problems depended on how strong or weak a chairman was. ... So the ground was loose – where the party chair was weak, people could go to kill witches, or the youth could even kill on the command of the

---

[81] On the arbitrariness of wartime accusations also see Werbner, *Tears of the Dead*, p. 150.

[82] E.g., interviews with A. Ncube, Tshongokwe, 6 December 1994; Mr and Mrs Dube, Mzola, 25 November 1994.

[83] Interview with Timothy Mthethwa, Kwesengulube, 1 December 1995.

[84] Interview with J. Gabheni Sibanda, Lupanda, 7 November 1994.

[85] Interview with Mrs Dlamini, Singwangombe, 21 February 1996.

[86] Interview with D.C. Moyo, Gonye, 17 October 1995.

[87] Interview with Nicholas Nkomo, Nkayi, 19 February 1996.

[88] E.g., interviews with Nathaniel Mpofu, Somakantana, 29 August 1995; Roy Mpofu and Luka Mgayo, Sebhumane, 14 December 1995.

party chair.'[89] Similarly, another party leader recalled: 'We had instances when the party chairman was strong enough to save the people, otherwise, if the party chair was weak, many would just die. At times, the chair wouldn't be consulted, you'd just hear someone had been killed.'[90] Where party officials themselves were involved in identifying and accusing witches, violence could easily escalate. But many senior party activists commonly acted to stop killings of both witches and sellouts. For example, Leonard Nkomo, one of Nkayi's most prominent Zapu leaders, returned home after being released from prison at the height of the war in 1978 to find a tense situation. He was known by many of the guerrillas in his home area:

> I had authority over those Zipras because of the Bulawayo Youth League. Many members of the youth league crossed the border when I was detained. So when they saw me in Jojo, they respected me, they knew me already. ... When I came from detention, some parents were being threatened, guerrillas would promise to kill them in two or three days. I told them that people have hatred and jealousies, these are the cause of the problems. People go to the guerrillas to say this one is an informer. ... I would say to the guerrillas, you can't make us fear you or we will desert you.[91]

This was not an isolated case. Party leaders frequently put their own lives on the line in order to protect those facing execution as witches or sellouts. In Panke, the party chairman sheltered an accused witch in his home, refusing to allow guerrillas and youth to take her for execution.[92] Other party leaders organized meetings to prevent deaths, physically obstructed arrests, and threatened guerrillas or reported them to their seniors.[93] It was a great source of pain to many party chairmen where they intervened too late.

If the party committees, in conjunction with the guerrilla command, were able to moderate much of the violence directed against sellouts and witches, there were nonetheless instances where killings spiralled out of control. This was particularly the case with regard to the numerous guerrilla deaths which resulted from the Rhodesian infiltration of poisoned food and clothing into guerrilla supply networks. As discussed in Chapter 6, this tactic was intended to strike at the heart of the relationship between guerrillas and civilians. It worked well in places where the source of the poisoned goods, and the cause of the guerrilla deaths, went undiscovered: in such cases, unexplained deaths were very often blamed on witchcraft.

One such case gained mythological status. It concerned the death of a woman accused of being a witch in Dandanda, northern Lupane. Her story is told by civilians all over the Shangani, and by guerrillas who operated in all parts of the Northern Front. It is a tale much elaborated upon and embellished in the telling – different versions are inconsistent and contradictory.[94] When guerrillas began to die mysteriously from poisoning in the area, the 'Dandanda witch' was accused of leading a Rhodesian-sponsored poisoning ring, and was tortured and killed by guerrillas.[95] She was said to

---

[89] Interview with Paulos Mhlotshwa, Tshakalisa, 25 November 1995.

[90] Interview with V.J. Ndlovu, Mateme, 23 November 1995.

[91] Interview with Leonard Nkomo, Nkayi, 15 December 1995.

[92] Interview with Sibindi family, Panke area, 24 November 1995.

[93] E.g., interviews with N. Khumalo, Mzola East, 16 June 1995; A. Magagula, Lupanda, 22 December 1994; J. Gabheni Sibanda, Lupanda, 7 November 1994; Paulos Mhlotshwa, Tshakalisa, 25 November 1995, and many others.

[94] The various versions of the tale are discussed at length in McGregor, 'Containing Violence'. We do not use names in citing interview sources for this story as it remains a painful and contentious episode for those involved.

[95] Interview with Nicholas Nkomo, 19 February 1996.

have supernatural powers which were evident partly in the death of women in childbirth within her family, but were revealed more clearly in the length of time it took her to die at guerrillas' hands and in a curse she made whilst burning to death. People told how she survived bayonetting and gunfire before being hurled into a fire; some said charms had to be broken (by jumping over an ammunition belt) before guns could be used against her. Even in the fire she could be heard talking and singing for some time. Some said that her body swelled and swelled in the fire, and when she finally died, a big black bird emerged from the smoke. As she died, she cursed the guerrillas, threatening death to those who had touched her body or participated in the bayonetting. When guerrillas continued to die from poisoning after her death, it served to confirm her powers, which were attributed to a type of 'doctoring' known as *uzimu* that protected her and caused her spirit to seek retribution.

As guerrillas continued to die in numbers, they and local Zapu chairmen expended much effort in trying to find the cause of the deaths and a solution. They consulted local *izinyanga* and Zionist and Apostolic leaders: 'We ran around … using both traditional and Christian ways of trying to find out about what were the causes of this disease which led to death,' recounted a Zapu leader, 'Our findings … were that they had killed certain witches. According to our traditional belief, some people are medicated traditionally, so then when he or she is being killed, that person will defend herself, even if she is dead, by means of revenge.'[96] They reached the conclusion that the killing of the 'Dandanda witch' was wrongful, and sought various means to pacify her spirit. One such was to offer compensation to her husband. A Zipra guerrilla who was also an *inyanga* recalled: 'When the dying got really bad, nine, five, three [guerrillas] would die each day. We knew there had been a mistake. So we went … to get cattle to pay for the damage we had done …, to compensate the husband of that woman … The local people came to me with some Zipras and I threw bones. I said they had wronged by killing that woman.'[97] According to another guerrilla, the husband confessed to having placed the charm himself and demanded six head of cattle and a virgin from the guerrillas as the means of breaking it.[98]

Few doubted that the accused woman was a witch, except members of her own family. Family members argued that she was not a witch, but was merely possessed by an *ihumba* spirit – an ancestral lion spirit harmful to the possessed individual but not to others – and that she had threatened the guerrillas as she died merely to protect herself. Her daughter-in-law recalled:

> As she was about to die, guerrillas had asked her to name another person who bewitches. She said, 'No, I don't know any, I don't want someone to lose their children because of me. I want to die alone. If you kill me, like this, you will carry your guns in twos or threes or fours'. It was a saying, and she meant that guerrillas would die, and those who survived would be carrying their dead comrades guns. She was just threatening them to try to preserve her life … she wasn't an *inyanga* or a witch … she had an ancestral spirit [*dlozi*], an *ihumba* spirit … you could hear her talking in the fire as she was burnt, singing in the flames … it took her a long time to die in the fire. They couldn't kill her quickly. She took time to die because of that *dlozi*.[99]

But the consequences for her relatives of the near-universal belief that she was a witch were severe. Younger female members of the family were also accused of witchcraft;

---

[96] Interview, 7 April 1996.
[97] Interview, 28 January 1996.
[98] Interview, 27 September 1996.
[99] Interview, 30 March 1996.

neighbours refused to enter the home; the husband and son were detained and interrogated by guerrillas. The son went mad on his release – he refused to sleep with his wife, talked incessantly and nonsensically about war and the guerrillas, and became obsessed with washing, going every few hours to the river to wash and try to clean himself.[100] The community as a whole was also suspected of harbouring additional witches. Guerrillas called mass meetings in the forest. Youth were sent to round people up and hundreds were forced to attend. Renowned *sangoma* spirit mediums and Zionist prophets 'smelt' out witches from amongst community members as they filed past those presiding. And people confessed to acts of witchcraft at these events. As a Zapu branch chairman recalled of a meeting presided over by both an *inyanga* and a prophet:

> It was so difficult at that gathering because people would be sniffed out by those two people. They'd tell a person, 'you have been doing x, using these things against this person at such and such a time'. And people would agree to that. Others, when accused said they did that unknowingly … Others were asked … 'Do you remember I caught you bewitching a person on that day?' Then people would agree. That was all out of terror. Me, as an individual, I can say that fear penetrated my body … the *inyanga* and the Zionist were seated and all the villagers would file past.[101]

In the largest of these meetings, fourteen people were killed, including Zapu leaders and important Tonga rainmakers.[102]

The breakdown in the relationship between the party and guerrillas over the issue of poisoning presented the Zipra command with tremendous problems in Dandanda as well as elsewhere. NF2 commander Nicholas Nkomo recalled: 'Sometimes we found ourselves doing no operations. [The poisoning] affected morale terribly. … Insubordination was a huge problem over this issue.'[103] Nkomo found the poisoning-inspired campaign against witches in full swing when he returned from a trip to Zambia. He describes the situation in his autobiography:

> I received reports from the commanders that all was not well in the areas of operation. Guerrillas were dying in big numbers from what they suspected to be poisoning from the local population. In turn, guerrillas were taking punitive measures against the locals in the form of burning them alive and other forms of revenge. This shocked me. I asked why these civilians were doing this and the reply was that they were being used by the Rhodesians to poison them through food. I had, on my arrival in Lupane, met a unit of guerrillas under the command of Magayisa which was wholly ill and the following day I got a report to the effect that four of them had died of suspected poisoning. I stood up to know if some kind of proof of the act could be available. Nothing was produced as proof. Having read about guerrilla wars in other countries like Algeria, etc., I suspected the hand of the enemy in this whole issue. I immediately called a meeting of the regional command in which we tried to find out what really was happening in ᴧe area. Guerrillas were so furious and were highly convinced that it was the locals who were responsible and on my insistence on proof, they were so angry with me to the point of telling me that it was a matter of time before finding myself in the same situation. We decided together with Tshaka Moyo [Nkomo's second in command] and the regional command to stop the rot once and for all and told the

---

[100] Interview, 30 March 1996.

[101] Interview, 7 April 1996.

[102] Interview with elders, Dandanda, 10 December 1994; interview, 7 April 1996.

[103] Interview with Nicholas Nkomo, Nkayi, 9 September 1995.

cadres not to take the law in their own hands. No shooting or killing of civilians by guerrillas was to be witnessed [before reporting to] the command ... [M]eetings and rallies were organised with the locals in these semi-liberated zones to find out from them what they thought was behind the dying of their sons ...[104]

Nkomo's interventions were effective. In Lake Alice, for example, where eight civilians were burnt as witches, Nkomo was credited with halting the killing. Party official Musa Dube recalled:

How to stop it? We couldn't do that. There was no way to stop it. But the commanders were the ones who really helped. They talked to the people strongly, threatened, [saying,] 'Look, we'll have war against each other. What evidence do you have?' It was those commanders who managed to calm it down.[105]

In Dandanda, Nkomo and other Zipra commanders organized meetings with guerrillas and junior commanders, telling them to stop the killings. They called large rallies in conjunction with senior Zapu leaders who also spoke out against the witch killings. These included influential figures such as Lupane's future MP and longtime activist Nkosembi Khumalo, and Leonard Nkomo, Nkayi's future council chairman. Religious leaders from other parts of Lupane were also drawn in. Many credit Papa Moyo, the Zapu leader and Zionist prophet from Pupu, with the final act of pacifying the witch's spirit. He performed a ceremony on her grave symbolic of pinning her spirit down.[106]

Zapu and Zipra efforts to alter supply routes, and hence prevent or stop guerrillas from dying were also critically important in halting the violence. Suspect local stores were boycotted by party supply teams, and new logistical networks were created. In some areas, a ban was instituted on all supplies which did not come directly through the party structures.[107]

The effects of the poisoning campaign, and the mythic stories which were elaborated around the Dandanda case, continue to reverberate in popular memory today. People are often unwilling to allocate blame for these violent events, describing them as simply a product of the wartime context. Some blame one 'wild' group of guerrillas who got out of control, while others see the violence as the fault of civilians willing to sell out their neighbours to guerrillas. In the words of Nkosembi Khumalo, 'All this witch-killing was led by peasants trying to bring their misunderstandings against themselves to the guerrillas which was wrong. ... People were selling their neighbours. ... The guerrillas were being misled by local people.'[108] The memory of this episode is ambivalent, torn between the desire to assign culpability on the one hand, and to make allowances for the cruelties so easily perpetrated in the fearful context of wartime on the other.

The violence against witches and sellouts forms an important and troubling part of civilians' and guerrillas' memories of the war, but it did not result in patterns of social or political change that can be generalized over the two districts. Where it was not contained, the violence struck primarily at the relationship between guerrillas and civilians. Though accusations drew on personal animosities and conflicts, the civilian deaths which resulted were not interpreted primarily in terms of class, gender, or the social divide between different generations of immigrants. Even in Dandanda, one of

---

[104] Nkomo, 'Between the Hammer and the Anvil', Appendix, p. 10.
[105] Interview with Musa Dube, Aaron Dube, Ken Moyo, Mtupane, 19 February 1996.
[106] Interview, 30 March 1996; interview with Titus Sibanda Moyo, Pupu, 20 February 1996.
[107] Nicholas Nkomo came to suspect the Rhodesians of poisoning, and hence focused on changing supply lines, as a result of his knowledge of comparable counter-insurgency tactics in Algeria.
[108] Interview with Nkosembi Khumalo, Mzola East, 16 September 1995.

Lupane's most recent frontiers of settlement, no one interpreted the witch-killings in terms of the divide between the long-time Tonga-speaking residents and the Ndebele-speaking newcomers, despite the fact that the accused witch's family had only arrived in 1976. The violence associated with witchcraft accusations was widely understood as illegitimate, as an aberration. Instances where it spun out of control were exceptional. Guerrillas in general, and the guerrilla command in particular, retained their legitimacy, even if particular groups of guerrillas did not. So, too, did the norms of popular nationalism.

## Conclusion

In Matabeleland North, the crucial wartime struggles over legitimacy focused on the goals and institutions of nationalism. These struggles centred around the party's adaptation to the logistical demands of guerrillas, the beliefs of the guerrillas themselves, and the particular challenges of wartime violence. Party leaders developed and sought to defend a moral economy of supply, an ethic of law and order, and a more inclusive party membership. These efforts brought dramatic change in the social base of the party, further broadening it from the Christian evictee political leadership to include many more youth, women, members of the previously derided earlier settlers of the region, and a host of others in new roles. Guerrillas' agendas also sparked change and controversy, perhaps most significantly with regard to religion and violence. The powerful nationalist traditions of Nkayi and Lupane, as well as the views of Zipra commanders, were crucial to containing violence. In all the realms of wartime debate and change, the overarching ideology of nationalism acted as a force for inclusion and humanity in the face of division and violence.

With all its violence and strains, the liberation war remains a source of pride for the nationalists of Nkayi. The memories of the 1980s, to which we now turn, could not have been more different.

# 8

# *Independence*
# *& the Dissidents*

The ceasefire of 21 December 1979 brought Zimbabwe's liberation war to a close. It was a time of optimism, as well as of on-going insecurity and violence. Many of the challenges of the transition to peace applied to the country as a whole. Everywhere, suspicious guerrillas had to turn themselves in to Assembly Points (APs), long-secretive political cadres had to come into the open, order had to be consolidated and elections held. There were also particular challenges facing regions loyal to Zapu. The loser in Zimbabwe's first national elections, Zapu soon found itself embroiled in political conflict, with devastating repercussions for its armed wing, Zipra.

This chapter focuses on the genesis of post-independence conflict. Our account draws on the perspective of those who are generally blamed for it – the former Zipra combatants who became what were called 'dissidents'.[1] Their experience has been little explored, in part because of the difficulty in doing so until recently but also because scholars and journalists have analysed post-1980 violence primarily in terms of the political interests of Zapu, Zanu(PF) and the South African state. These often partisan accounts have portrayed conflict as the product of an ill-judged bid by Zapu to claim the victory it had failed to gain through the ballot box,[2] as a cynical attempt by Zanu(PF) to use the incidents of violence in the early 1980s as a pretext to crush the only real obstacle to its total supremacy,[3] or as an attempt by South Africa to exploit tensions between Zanu(PF) and Zapu, whites and blacks, so as to leave its newly independent neighbour in disarray.[4] But none of these accounts have explored the motives, goals and

---

[1] See J. Alexander, 'Dissident Perspectives on Zimbabwe's Post- Independence War', *Africa*, 68, 2, 1998, for a fuller discussion of the views of dissidents.

[2] For fairly baldly pro-Zanu(PF) accounts see D. Martin and P. Johnson, 'Zimbabwe: Apartheid's Dilemma', in D. Martin and P. Johnson (eds), *Destructive Engagement: Southern Africa at War* (Harare, ZPH, 1986); E.P. Makambe, *Marginalising the Human Rights Campaign: The Dissident Factor and the Politics of Violence in Zimbabwe 1980-1987* (Lesotho, Institute of Southern African Studies, 1992); Ministry of Information, Posts and Telecommunications, *A Chronicle of Dissidency in Zimbabwe* (Harare, Government Printer, 1984).

[3] See J. Nkomo, *The Story of My Life* (London, Methuen, 1984); W. Spring, *The Long Fields: Zimbabwe Since Independence* (Basingstoke, Pickering and Inglis, 1986).

[4] See, e.g., Martin and Johnson, 'Zimbabwe: Apartheid's Dilemma'; J. Hanlon, *Apartheid's Second Front: South Africa's War against its Neighbours* (Harmondsworth, Penguin, 1986) and *Beggar Your Neighbours: Apartheid Power in Southern Africa* (London, James Currey and CIIR, 1986); Ulf Engel, *The Foreign Policy of Zimbabwe* (Hamburg, Institut für Afrika-Kunde, 1994).

organization of the dissidents themselves.[5] The reasons behind Zipra guerrillas' return to the bush have remained unclear.

The perspectives of the dissidents allow for a substantial reinterpretation of post-independence violence. On the basis of interviews with former dissidents, as well as with a larger group of former Zipra guerrillas,[6] we argue that post-independence insurgency was largely a result of distrust within, and then repression by, the newly formed Zimbabwe National Army (ZNA). Dissidents had neither political leaders nor political support, but the majority nonetheless maintained their loyalty to Zapu and tenaciously clung to their liberation war identity as Zipra guerrillas. The main body of dissidents sought to recreate Zipra structures, partly in response to the challenge of a dissident faction backed by South Africa. Though this would prove an unattainable goal, dissidents did not develop any particularly new agenda. They sought a return to an unrecoverable pre-conflict state, and saw the war as one for survival in which tribalism had replaced ideology. The views of dissidents throw light not only on the origins and development of Zimbabwe's post-independence war, but also on wider debates over the meaning and legacies of violence.

Before turning to dissidents' own stories, we first set out the context of escalating violence in the Shangani and more widely in the first years of independence.

## The Escalation of Violence: 1980–1983

The escalation of violence after the end of the liberation war built on the two guerrilla armies' regional patterns of recruitment and operation during the 1970s, and the history of animosity and distrust between the two armies and their political leaders. These patterns had left Zipra forces dominated by Ndebele speakers from Matabeleland while Zanla was predominantly Shona speaking. Operational areas maintained a significance in terms of political loyalties: voting largely, though not completely, followed ethnic and regional divisions, creating the possibility for conflict along these lines.[7] Zipra's capacity for conventional warfare was also a source of friction. Following Zanu(PF)'s victory in the February 1980 elections, the possibility that the clearly surprised and disappointed Zapu would use these forces, which were still based largely outside the country, to obtain victory by other means was a source of concern for Zanu(PF). These seeds of distrust and division fell on fertile ground in the early 1980s.

Immediately following the ceasefire, guerrillas were called upon to gather in designated Assembly Points (APs) from which they would be demobilized or integrated into the nascent ZNA. But many guerrillas refused to come in to APs, or made sorties outside them, and regularly cached arms and ammunition. Their motives were diverse. Most important was a pervasive fear that they would be bombed or attacked while concentrated in the APs – the Rhodesian Army was, after all, still very much intact. A

---

[5] Analyses of dissidents' goals and composition based largely on press reports include T. Ranger, 'Bandits and Guerrillas: the case of Zimbabwe', in D. Crummey (ed.), *Banditry, Rebellion and Social Protest in Africa* (London, James Currey, 1986); R. Hodder-Williams, 'Conflict in Zimbabwe: The Matabeleland Problem', *Conflict Studies*, 151, 1983, The Institute for the Study of Conflict, London.

[6] Over 20 former dissidents, or roughly a fifth of those who turned themselves in under the Presidential Amnesty of early 1988, were interviewed or wrote their own autobiographies. As discussed in Chapter 6, more than 80 former Zipra guerrillas were also interviewed or wrote autobiographies. Those former guerrillas who became dissidents are referred to by their war names or initials only.

[7] See L. Cliffe, J. Mpofu and B. Munslow, 'Nationalist Politics in Zimbabwe: The 1980 Elections and Beyond', *Review of African Political Economy*, 18, 1980, pp. 44–67.

significant group of guerrillas objected to the negotiated ceasefire as a 'sell out'. Others sought to campaign on behalf of their political leaders outside the APs, while some simply wanted to enjoy what they saw as the spoils of war. Problems also flowed from the continuation of conflicts whose origins lay in tensions within and between the guerrilla armies during the liberation war.

In 1980, Zanla troops seemed to have presented the greater problem. Under the ceasefire agreement, the two guerrilla armies were to move all troops into the APs in the seven days between December 29 and January 4 (later extended to January 7). Whereas Zipra largely kept to the agreed terms, Zanla held an estimated 40 per cent of its guerrillas outside the country in the pre-election period, and continued cross-border incursions after the stipulated date.[8] Zanla guerrillas inside the country were also a problem. They were repeatedly accused of leaving APs to 'campaign' for the elections. In the vicinity of the Matabeleland APs which they shared with Zipra, they were accused of abducting young girls, of murdering several civilians, and occasionally came into conflict with their Zipra counterparts.[9] According to the Commonwealth Monitoring Force, 'Zipra would obey orders and not over react ... but ... Zanla was unreliable, ill-disciplined and unpredictable.'[10] After the February elections, Zanla guerrillas were involved in a series of attacks on police stations in Mtoko, Mount Darwin and Gutu, some involving the use of rockets and resulting in the deaths of policemen.[11] Zanla guerrillas from Foxtrot AP in Gutu regularly left with their weapons and eventually had to be rounded up by police in mid-1980.[12] Newly integrated units of the ZNA were deployed against Zanla guerrillas from the X-Ray AP in Mtoko in late 1980 when they started ambushing vehicles along the Mtoko–Harare road, and attacked the police camp once again.[13]

On the Zipra side, Mike AP was the most serious trouble spot. Located at the abandoned St Paul's Mission in Lupane, it was the destination for Zipra guerrillas from Northern Front 2 (NF2), as well as a smaller number of guerrillas from Northern Front 1. By the end of December, the AP population exceeded 4,000. Tension at the AP had diverse causes, but most important initially was suspicion of the terms of the ceasefire (a suspicion shared by many Zanla commanders and guerrillas).[14] NF2 commander Nicholas Nkomo recalled both his own reaction to the ceasefire's terms, and the conviction among some of his men that they had been 'sold out to the forces of reaction':

> Having commanded my men in the field for such a long time, I had now the belief that I was the law itself. I had been enjoying utmost loyalty from my men, but I must admit here that when I assembled them to order them to the assembly point,

[8] Zanla chief of staff Emerson Mnangagwa himself cited the figure of 40 per cent. See N. Kriger, *Zimbabwe's Guerrilla Integration: Entitlement Politics* (book ms., 1996), p. 51, citing Rice, 1990.

[9] See press reports in *The Chronicle*, 11, 24 January 1980; 1, 13 February 1980; 2, 5 July 1980; Interview with former Zipra guerrilla Saymore Nkomo, 26 September 1995; P. Moorcraft and P. McLaughlin, *Chimurenga! The War in Rhodesia 1965–1980* (Marshalltown, Sygma/Collins, 1982), pp. 228–43; Kriger, *Zimbabwe's Guerrilla Integration*, Chapter Two.

[10] Kriger, *Zimbabwe's Guerrilla Integration*, p. 53, citing Report of British Ministry of Defence on the CMF, V84/B04 (obtained from the UK Ministry of Defence), p. 153.

[11] See *The Chronicle*, 25, 26, 28 August 1980; 6 September 1980. Zanla guerrillas were particularly hostile to the police due to the fact that Joshua Nkomo had been appointed Minister of Home Affairs, and thus held jurisdiction over the police force. See Kriger, *Zimbabwe's Guerrilla Integration*, pp. 77–8.

[12] *The Chronicle*, 8, 12, 16 July 1980. Incidents nonetheless continued to occur, e.g., see *The Chronicle*, 2 September 1980.

[13] *The Chronicle*, 1 November 1980.

[14] See Kriger, *Zimbabwe's Guerrilla Integration*, pp. 49, 83.

I almost triggered a rebellion against myself and above all the leadership of both Zapu and Zipra. ... Myself and my men in the field felt that, had the leaders had the real interests of their fighting men at heart, they would have consulted with the field commanders when the question of a ceasefire arose. Who had chosen St. Paul's as an assembly point for me and my men? Why had it to be St. Paul's, which in my own opinion provided no natural defence for us should the ceasefire breakdown. ... It was mentioned on the news that the agreement signed by the participants at Lancaster House, including the nationalist leaders, contained clauses entrenching the rights of the Rhodesian forces and the minority whites. What about us, the liberators? Nothing was said about safeguarding us. Nothing about our pensions for the many painful years we had spent in the bush, away from our beloved wives and children.[15]

Before moving into Mike AP to meet the January 4 deadline for guerrilla assembly, Nkomo sent reconnaissance units to report on conditions, then instructed groups of guerrillas to enter the AP while himself staying behind. Finally, 'sky shouts' by Zipra High Commanders convinced Nkomo it was safe to move. Once inside the AP, Nkomo deployed his forces against attack, and undertook further reconnaissance so that he and his men would not to be killed 'like sitting ducks'.[16]

The unequal treatment of the guerrilla armies in comparison to the Rhodesian forces deepened the sense of bitterness and suspicion: not only were the Rhodesians exempt from an equivalent assembly process, but they were put in a supervisory role, overseeing movement to the APs and guarding guerrillas after the withdrawal of the Commonwealth Monitoring Force. As Nicholas Nkomo recalled:

We were ordered never to take our weapons with us when going outside the camp, while forces of the colonialist regime did so with impunity. ... [Mike AP] looked like a restriction camp, or some kind of Gonakudzingwa, where our movement was restricted but that of the Rhodesian forces was free. They were even free to kill us around our Assembly Points because according to the Lancaster House agreement they were responsible for security around the enemy camps. The Rhodesian police based at Lupane Police Station were the same that we had fought against during the war of liberation.[17]

The ostentatious displays of power by the security forces, who toured the rural areas in military jeeps equipped with mounted machine-guns and flew regularly overhead in low flying planes, certainly did not help.[18]

Rhodesian forces were responsible for a large number of guerrilla (as well as civilian) deaths during the process of assembly at St Paul's. In the days immediately after the deadline for assembly, police opened fire on bus loads of guerrillas being transported to the AP as they passed through Lupane business centre; at Cross Jotsholo, a bus load of guerrillas was attacked by air.[19] Hearing of these incidents, many guerrillas decided not to move into the AP, or fled the AP to town, South Africa or the bush. Former Zipra guerrilla Andrew Ndlovu recalled the consequences of the Jotsholo incident:

---

15  N. Nkomo, 'Between the Hammer and the Anvil: The Autobiography of Nicholas Nkomo', ms, 1996, pp. 27–8.
16  Interview with Nicholas Nkomo and Richard Dube, Bulawayo, 4 February 1996.
17  Nkomo, 'Between the Hammer and the Anvil', pp. 27–8.
18  See Nkomo, 'Between the Hammer and the Anvil', p. 27; interview with former Zapu chairman, Gampinya, 19 October 1995.
19  Press accounts include *The Chronicle*, 8, 9, 12 January 1980.

Seven guerrillas were killed on the spot, and they were not decently buried. Up to now their bones are at Cross Jotsholo. Some guerrillas decided to stay in towns for safety. ... Some decided to go to Johannesburg to look for jobs and they never demobilized until now due to harrassment in Assembly Points.[20]

There were also practical reasons which delayed guerrillas' entry into the APs, and which made the deaths of latecomers particularly cruel: information about the process of assembly reached the NF2 command and guerrillas very late, and then many guerrillas had to walk a considerable distance to the pickup points for transport to the AP (Andrew Ndlovu's group, for example, was based some 70 kilometres from the pickup point).[21]

Tension continued even after the majority of guerrillas had entered the AP. Zipra guerrillas regularly left to visit girlfriends, wives, family, friends or healers, as well as to monitor the movements of the Rhodesians. Some such sorties ended in gun battles with Rhodesian police in which civilians, police and guerrillas alike were killed.[22] A number of refugees who arrived at the AP to register after the curfew were shot. In the face of such violence and insecurity, Zipra guerrillas continued to interact with local Zapu committees on a war footing. Zapu activists provided guerrillas with intelligence on the movements of Rhodesian forces, visited them inside the AP, nursed wounded guerrillas before they moved into the AP, and provided logistical support to those who were slow to enter.[23] Guerrillas often chose to sleep outside the AP.[24] Shops in Lupane business centre were closed once again, and people were afraid to move. Civilians no less than guerrillas believed that 'it was still war', that the deaths were part of a 'pre-arranged plan', that the Rhodesians were continuing to fight 'by stealth'.[25]

Tension rose within Mike AP for other reasons as well. Important in this respect was the issue of differential pay for rank and file guerrillas and their commanders.[26] Richard Dube – the former Mike AP commander and a member of the Zipra High Command – was flown in to ease tension over this issue after guerrillas had threatened the pay team and prevented them from leaving the AP. Later the same day, a grenade was thrown into Dube's room.[27] Others recalled tensions between guerrillas who had operated within Zimbabwe and those who had undergone conventional training – tensions which rose to the point of provoking desertions. As former guerrilla John Mjoni Mkandla recalled: 'At St Paul's there was no cooperation between guerrillas from the front and regulars. The problem was that regulars wanted to be in charge of the camp. So others disappeared up to now.'[28] Other potential tensions within the guerrilla ranks were overcome. Importantly, the errant Pamodzi detachment which had refused to obey the authority of the High Command during the war, was accepted as a self-contained detachment within the AP.[29]

Guerrillas' inactivity and confinement to a small space constituted a challenge in

[20] Interview by Mark Ndlovu with Andrew Ndlovu, 28 October 1995.
[21] Nkomo, 'Between the Hammer and the Anvil', p. 27.
[22] See, e.g., *The Chronicle*, 9, 12, 13, 22 February 1980, for incidents in the vicinity of Mike AP.
[23] Interviews with former Zapu youth, Malunku, 6 March 1996; former Zapu chairman, Pupu, 20 February 1996.
[24] Interview with Nicholas Nkomo, Nkayi, 8 and 9 September 1995; *The Chronicle*, 30 January 1980.
[25] Interviews with Councillor, Malunku, 6 March 1996; former Zapu chairman, Pupu, 20 February 1996.
[26] Pay was a problematic issue in Zanla APs as well. See Kriger, *Zimbabwe's Guerrilla Integration*, pp. 88–100.
[27] Interview with Nicholas Nkomo and Richard Dube, Bulawayo, 4 February 1996.
[28] Interview with John Mjoni Mkandla, 18 January 1995.
[29] Interview with Langford Ndiweni, 30 August 1995.

itself. Nkomo recalls introducing 'a programme of drills … to keep them busy'. But that created its own problems: commanders tried to introduce the British drilling system so as to prepare guerrillas for integration in the ZNA. But for guerrillas trained in the Soviet Union, adopting British drills was tantamount to selling out. As commanders Nicholas Nkomo and Richard Dube explained: 'In fact there was very great resistance to the British system of drilling. We were used to the Russian style. So this meant we were abandoning communism for capitalism. There was a lot of resistance to that.'[30]

The number of Zipra guerrillas in the Matabeleland North region who did not come in to APs, or left them subsequently, was significant. In February 1980, an election supervisor estimated that there were some 200 guerrillas roaming the northwest, campaigning for Zapu, engaging in robbery or behaving as if the war were still on by shutting down schools.[31] One such group was headed by a man called Tommy. Tommy had been what Zipra commanders termed a 'loose force' in the 1970s, meaning he had refused to obey the Zipra command structure. In 1980, he and his followers operated in northern Nkayi and southern Gokwe. Other groups who were afraid to enter the APs, or who did not believe the war should be brought to an end, operated particularly in Tsholotsho. According to Nicholas Nkomo, 'Quite a large unit of Zipras refused to come in [in Tsholotsho]. … Those guys thought all was lost with a negotiated ceasefire.'[32]

Such individuals were a problem for local Zapu leaders. Tommy and others like him called upon Zapu committees for support, used violence against those who refused, and opposed early reconstruction efforts such as the re-opening of schools. Zapu leaders were left with a 'big confusion': 'we were between the horns: Who was who? Who was in charge? The province [Zapu headquarters] or the people in the bush?'[33] Some travelled to Harare to seek clarification from Joshua Nkomo himself.[34] Zapu policy was clear: the war was over, guerrillas must enter the APs. Zipra and Zapu took extraordinary measures to ensure that the ceasefire was observed. Joshua Nkomo toured the rural areas demanding that guerrillas come in, rallying the support of Zapu committees behind him. Most dramatically, in May and June 1980, Zipra regular forces from the Gwaai AP, commanded by Charles Grey and Soneni Mdlalosi, rounded up some 400 errant Zipra guerrillas and delivered them to Khami prison.[35]

In early 1980, guerrillas who left APs were condemned by the political leaders of both parties. They were termed 'outlaws', 'unruly elements', 'bandits' or 'renegades'. But a semantic change occurred in the post-election period: armed men on the loose in Matabeleland came to be called 'dissidents', and the problem they represented was increasingly cast in political terms. After the opening of Parliament, Zanu(PF) politicians argued that dissidents were dominated by Zipra and motivated by disaffection over Zapu's electoral defeat.[36] While stopping short of suggesting Zipra commanders were responsible, Prime Minister Robert Mugabe accused 'organised bands of Zipra followers' of 'refusing to recognise the sovereignty of the government'.[37] Enos Nkala, the most prominent Ndebele in the ranks of Zanu(PF) Ministers, introduced a tribalist element and pointed the finger more directly at Zapu: he argued that dissidents were 'Ndebeles

---

[30] Interview with Nicholas Nkomo and Richard Dube, Bulawayo, 4 February 1996.

[31] See *The Chronicle*, 13, 22 February 1980.

[32] Interview with Nicholas Nkomo, 26 September 1995. Richard Dube interviewed a senior Zipra commander in 1994 who estimated that 1,000 Zipra guerrillas refused to come in to APs in early 1980.

[33] Interview with Councillor, Mateme, 7 December 1995. Also, interview with Councillor, Kana, 28 November 1995, 5 December 1995. See Chapter 9 for further discussion of party views.

[34] E.g., interview with former Zapu District Chairman, Tshongokwe, 6 December 1994.

[35] See *The Chronicle*, 10 May, 10 June 1980; *The Sunday News*, 2, 6 July 1980.

[36] E.g., see *The Chronicle*, 21, 23 May 1980.

[37] See *The Chronicle*, 27 June 1980. For earlier remarks see *The Chronicle*, 20 June 1980.

who were calling for a second war of liberation', and said they should be 'shot down'; he called for Zapu leader Joshua Nkomo – the 'self-appointed Ndebele King' – to be 'crushed'.[38] The attacks on Zipra dissidents went hand in hand with a much resented belittling of Zipra's role in the liberation war.[39] Zapu leaders responded by vehemently denying any connection to dissidents, pointing out that Zipra regular forces had rounded a large number up, and that Zanlas were responsible for far more chaos in the northeast.[40]

Former guerrillas were involved in a second, and ultimately more significant, type of conflict in late 1980. This violence would eventually produce a new type of 'dissident', as well as the conditions for sustained insurgency. Conflict stemmed from the decision to move thousands of guerrillas from rural APs to city suburbs – Chitungwiza in Harare and Entumbane in Bulawayo – in an effort to stop rural banditry and provide guerrillas with better accommodation: guerrillas had now been sitting in APs, often under uncomfortable conditions and with little to do, for many months.[41] However, and fatefully, the movement brought Zipra and Zanla into close proximity not only with each other but with their civilian supporters, providing an ideal situation for the exacerbation of tensions. Such tensions were, of course, not new. They had roots in the clashes between party cadres (many of whom later became guerrillas) at the time of Zanu's split from Zapu in 1963, the massacres – largely of Zipra guerrillas – in the Tanzanian camps in 1976, and the hostile relations between the two sides where they met on the battlefield.

Gun battles and other clashes between Zipra and Zanla guerrillas occurred at Chitungwiza in mid-October,[42] but the real problem arose at Entumbane. Zipra accounts of this conflict stressed the tensions created by a rally at White City Stadium at which Zanu(PF) Minister Enos Nkala told the assembled crowds that Zapu had 'declared itself the enemy of ZANU (PF)'; that the time had come to 'form vigilante committees', to 'challenge [Zapu] on its home ground. If it means a few blows we shall deliver them.'[43] Following the rally, party supporters clashed in the streets and guerrillas were drawn into the fray.[44] A two-day battle ensued which was brought to a close through the intervention of senior Zipra and Zanla commanders. Both sides blamed each other for initiating the violence, and Zipra commanders stressed that Rhodesian units had exacerbated the situation. The government subsequently conducted a search for weapons on Joshua Nkomo's farm in Mguza, moved an additional 500 Zanla guerrillas to Entumbane and arrested a number of Zapu officials in Bulawayo.[45]

This incident convinced many guerrillas of the possibility of further conflict. Distrust and tension spread to other APs and newly integrated units of the ZNA as stories and

---

[38] See *The Chronicle*, 30 June 1980; 7 July 1980. Also see Lawyers' Committee for Human Rights, *Zimbabwe: Wages of War* (LCHR, New York, 1986), p. 51, on Nkala's behaviour.

[39] Zapu women demonstrated in Bulawayo against what they saw as anti-Zipra bias. See *The Chronicle*, 23 June 1980, and Kriger, *Zimbabwe's Guerrilla Integration*, pp. 76–7, more widely.

[40] For Joshua Nkomo's reactions see, *The Chronicle*, 27 June 1980; 24, 28 July 1980; 22 August 1980.

[41] See Zanu(PF) Minister Eddison Zvobgo's comments on the move in *The Chronicle*, 11 September 1980. He was particularly concerned to bring the Zanla guerrillas in Mutoko under better control.

[42] See *The Chronicle*, 17 October 1980; 3 November 1980.

[43] Reported in *The Chronicle*, 10 November 1980.

[44] Interviews with former Zipra guerrillas Langford Ndiweni, 30 August 1995; Mbacanga Viko, 26 September 1995; and Innocent Gama, 27 September 1995. Also see T. Barnes, 'The Heroes' Struggle: Life after the Liberation War for Four Ex-Combatants in Zimbabwe', in N. Bhebe and T. Ranger (eds), *Soldiers in Zimbabwe's Liberation War* (London, James Currey, 1995), p. 122; D. Auret, *Reaching for Justice: The Catholic Commission for Justice and Peace 1972–92* (Gweru, Mambo Press, 1992), p. 164.

[45] See *The Chronicle*, 17, 19, 22 November 1980.

rumours about what had happened at Entumbane circulated amongst guerrillas and civilians. Zipra guerrillas stressed the daily tensions over fears that food was being poisoned; over who held the keys to the armouries; over the justness of punishments; over the rumoured disappearances of guerrillas supposedly sent for training courses and over bias against Zipra promotions.[46] At Entumbane, Zipra guerrillas believed that their Zanla colleagues had used heavy artillery which was, in theory, banned within the APs. Rank and file Zipra put great pressure on their commanders to allow them to import heavy weapons so as to even the odds in the event of further fighting. As one Zipra combatant explained:

> This fighting started and it was discovered Zanla had big weapons – mortars, bazookas, weapons which weren't allowed. This really caused friction among ourselves, between soldiers and commanders. Because commanders said no big weapons, but we knew Zanla had them.

Heavy weapons did, in fact, find their way into the Zipra camps at Entumbane, though by whose authority is not clear.[47]

Christmas and the advent of the new year nonetheless passed quietly, and were marked by conciliatory speeches from Nkomo, Mugabe, and even Enos Nkala.[48] But, in February 1981, a much larger conflagration took place, spreading from integrated ZNA units at Ntabazinduna, Connemara and Glenville to Entumbane once again. Zipra accounts and press reports of testimonies made to the Dumbutshena Commission of Enquiry which was established to look into the causes of conflict, indicated that fighting had often been set off by fairly minor incidents – an argument, a fist fight – but had then escalated rapidly, revealing a certain amount of preparedness on both sides, as well as the pervasiveness of fear and tension. In these clashes, the upper hand went to those who managed to gain control of the armouries, or of heavy weapons as in Entumbane. At Ntabazinduna, it was Zanla members of 1:2 Battalion who gained control of the armoury; but in one of the worst clashes, Zipra members of 4:1 Battalion at Connemara got there first and 'hunted down' their Zanla comrades.[49]

The outbreak of renewed violence at Entumbane led Zipra troops stationed in Gwaai and Essexvale to head for the city. Mugabe relied on still intact Rhodesian Army and Air Force units to stop their advance.[50] Again, fighting was only brought to an end through the concerted efforts of senior military figures of both sides. Subsequently, the Entumbane camps were broken up, and sent to shooting ranges outside Bulawayo. Guerrillas who had fled during the fighting were slowly rounded up and at least three battalions were eventually disbanded and distributed to other units.[51] Some guerrillas did not return to their units and arms were certainly cached by both sides in the aftermath of conflict,

---

[46] E.g., interviews with former Zipra guerrillas Mawobho Sibindi, December 1994; System Mkwananzi, December 1994; Attempt Siziba, 25 September 1995; and Madzokandevu, December 1994. Also see A. Seeger, 'Revolutionary Armies of Africa: Mozambique and Zimbabwe', in S. Baynham (ed.), *Military Power and Politics in Black Africa* (London and Sydney, Croom Helm, 1986), p. 152.

[47] Interview with former Zipra guerrilla, Attempt Siziba, 25 September 1995.

[48] See *The Chronicle*, 20, 29 December 1980; 1 January 1981.

[49] Interview with former Zipra guerrilla Innocent Gama, 27 September 1995. Also see, interview with former Zipra guerrilla Mbacanga Viko, 26 September 1995 and evidence presented to the Dumbutshena Commission reported in *The Chronicle*, 7, 14 May 1981 on Ntabazinduna; 6 May 1981 on Glenville.

[50] See Moorcraft and McLaughlin, *Chimurenga!*, pp. 238–9.

[51] See Martin and Johnson, 'Zimbabwe: Apartheid's Dilemma', p. 53; Seeger, 'Revolutionary Armies of Africa', p. 153.

adding to previous caches made during the war, the repatriation process, and in the tense months waiting in APs.

After this second period of fighting, political relations between Zanu(PF) and Zapu deteriorated. Mugabe noted, 'very sinister undertones, a definite organised pattern' to the conflict.[52] Zapu leaders denied a pattern and stressed the fears and tensions which had reigned amongst guerrillas since the first Entumbane conflict. Dumbutshena's report on the causes of the conflict was unfortunately never publicly released because, Mugabe complained, it did not clearly condemn either side, meaning it did not condemn Zipra.[53] Joshua Nkomo was nonetheless demoted from Minister of Home Affairs to Minister without Portfolio. This certainly worried Zapu and Zipra cadres. They were also concerned by the announcement in August 1981 of the arrival of 106 North Korean instructors and quantities of equipment and arms intended for training a special Fifth Brigade which, according to press reports, would be used to 'wipe out dissidents and criminals', including those found 'in the army'. The North Koreans were also to train a People's Militia. To no avail, Nkomo strongly objected to the secrecy surrounding the Fifth Brigade and expressed fears that it and the People's Militia would be used to achieve political goals.[54]

A rift between Zapu and Zanu(PF) which would not be healed until the Unity agreement of December 1987 finally occurred in February 1982. In that month, the Zimbabwean government announced it had discovered vast quantities of arms on properties owned by the Zapu company Nitram and around Zipra APs, and used this as grounds for confiscating the properties and sacking Nkomo and other Zapu ministers. Senior Zipra commanders – including former NF2 commander Nicholas Nkomo and Ambrose Zikale, a Zipra commander from Dongamuzi in Lupane – were subsequently arrested on charges of treason.[55] The evidence for a conspiracy was shaky: the existence of arms caches on both sides had been well known for some time, and both Zipra and Zanla had cached weapons after the Entumbane and other disturbances as insurance. The revelations regarding arms caches on Zapu properties were at any rate the result of tip-offs from white members of the Zimbabwean intelligence services whose evidence was decidedly suspect: they had already fled the country at the time of the 'discovery' to take up positions in the South African defence and intelligence establishment.[56] The evidence against Zipra commanders Lookout Masuku, Dumiso Dabengwa and others failed to convince a high court judge, but they remained in jail until 1986, nonetheless.[57]

After February 1982, the room for political conciliation disappeared. Mugabe treated the caches as definitive proof that Zapu had always been planning a coup, that it had held back forces and cached weapons 'to fight in a final struggle to overthrow a

---

[52] For Mugabe's comments, see *The Chronicle*, 13 February 1981. Zanla commanders and Enos Nkala were more explicit in their accusations. See *The Chronicle*, 16 May 1981; 5 June 1981.

[53] *The Chronicle*, 2 September 1982.

[54] See *The Chronicle*, 14, 21, 22, 25, 27 August 1981; 5, 10 September 1981.

[55] Zikale had been the commander of Zezane AP in Matabeleland South.

[56] See Engel's summary of the evidence available to date on the arms caches in *The Foreign Policy of Zimbabwe*, pp. 206–8. Norma Kriger, in a personal communication, notes that the timing of the 'discovery' was convenient in that it came after guerrillas in the APs had been either disarmed and demobilized, or integrated into the ZNA, thus making any collective military response from Zipra difficult.

[57] In 1985, Charles Grey, Kindness Ndhlovu, Tshili Nleya, Eddie Sigoge and other former Zipra commanders were also arrested on charges of planning a coup. See Engel, *The Foreign Policy of Zimbabwe*, p. 208; interview with Nicholas Nkomo, December 1995; Catholic Commission for Justice and Peace/Legal Resources Foundation, *Breaking the Silence, Building True Peace: A Report on the Disturbances in Matabeleland and the Midlands, 1980 to 1988* (Harare, CCJP/LRF, 1997), p. 70.

Zanu(PF) government if it came to power.'[58] Two subsequent incidents spurred the turn to a military response: in June 1982, Zipra guerrillas were implicated in an attack on the Prime Minister's residence, and shortly thereafter six foreign tourists were kidnapped and killed in Matabeleland North by dissidents.[59] Though Joshua Nkomo continued to condemn dissidents, Zapu was regularly charged with orchestrating their activities, and assertions of popular support for dissidents became increasingly common.

Throughout this period, South Africa fanned the flames, thus helping to justify Zanu(PF)'s military response. Tensions were first heightened by South African sabotage at Inkomo Barracks in August 1981, and a very nearly successful attempt to assassinate the Zanu(PF) leadership in December of the same year. The Zimbabwean Air Force was subsequently decimated in an attack on the Thornhill base in July 1982. In August of the same year, three white soldiers of the South African Defence Force were killed in a clash inside Zimbabwe. At the end of 1982, South Africa launched 'Operation Drama', an effort which involved recruiting and arming a Zimbabwean insurgent group, dubbed Super Zapu. Various South African agents, many of them recruited from the Rhodesian intelligence service, also played a key role in fomenting distrust.[60] But if South Africa skillfully heightened tensions between Zanu(PF) and Zapu, its interventions cannot wholly explain the developments within, and actions by, the ZNA, and their consequences for the burgeoning conflict.

### Creating an Insurgency: the ZNA and Fifth Brigade

Though the arms caches incident certainly had important political repercussions, the crucial factor in creating an insurgency lay in the consequences for Zipra guerrillas inside and outside the ZNA. Little attention has been paid to this aspect of the conflict, but interviews with Zipra guerrillas consistently indicated that their persecution at this time, rather than the political rift, was key in causing mass desertions. Many felt they had little choice but to flee or take up arms once again to save their lives. Though the Fifth Brigade (discussed below) is generally singled out as the only ZNA unit to have been overtly partisan, and it was certainly unique, many other ZNA brigades also strayed far from apolitical norms. So-called 'dissident sympathizers' and 'disloyal elements' were in fact purged, arrested or worse with such ferocity in 1982 that senior army officers subsequently had to make a tour of ZNA units to assure soldiers that 'they wouldn't be victimized for past affiliations.'[61]

Interviews with former Zipra combatants revealed that violence within the ZNA was widespread. Many alleged that Zipra guerrillas were killed, beaten or otherwise victimized. In several battalions, former Zipra guerrillas allege that they were segregated, disarmed, and some of their number were taken away never to be seen again.[62] At Silobela camp, where tensions already ran high between members of the two guerrilla armies, the arms caches incident provoked violence:

> Then it became very tense and all Zipra were regarded as dissidents and we were banned from leaving the camp. … Zipras were being killed in the camp. Some

---

[58] See *The Chronicle*, 22 March 1982.

[59] See CCJP/LRF, *Breaking the Silence*, pp. 29–30, 41–3.

[60] On South African involvement, see Engel, *Zimbabwe's Foreign Policy*, pp. 213–16; Hanlon, *Beggar Your Neighbour*, pp. 175–7, 183; Martin and Johnson, 'Zimbabwe: Apartheid's Dilemma', p. 352; CCJP/LRF, *Breaking the Silence*, pp. 29–30, 41.

[61] See reports in *The Chronicle*, 4, 29 October 1982.

[62] Interviews with former Zipra guerrillas Alfonse Sibanda, 14 October 1995; Maduna Nxobogo, 13 September 1995.

had left by foot to go to Bulawayo. Many Zipras fled. … Those colleagues who were targeted are still missing.[63]

In addition to those who fled, a great many more demobilized at this time.[64]

Leaving the army was no guarantee of safety: former Zipra combatants outside the army also faced increasingly severe persecution. Notably after the abduction of the six foreign tourists in July 1982, the security force presence in Matabeleland was greatly bolstered.[65] Battalions of the First and Second Brigades, police Support Units, and elite paratroop units worked in conjunction with the CIO in tracking down Zipra ex-combatants. Detention camps run by the CIO and army were established at various centres in Matabeleland between 1982 and 1984. Anyone believed to have aided or abetted dissidents, but particularly former Zipra combatants, members of the Rhodesian army, even serving members of the ZNA home on leave, were tortured and sometimes killed in these centres. In late 1982, demobilized Zipra guerrilla Mbacanga Viko recalled:

> ZNA patrols came to our home areas. If they found an ex-guerrilla, he was in trouble. At times they would be arrested, and sometimes they never came back. … I was taken and assaulted again and again. One day I was taken by the ZNA and brought to the airport at Plumtree where I was severely tortured with electric shocks and other means. They asked, 'Why did you leave the ZNA? Why are you sitting at home? Do you have guns?' They were accusing me of being a dissident at night. There were many people there, all Zipras.[66]

In the Shangani, detention camps for civilians and ex-combatants were established at St Paul's, Nkayi, Lupane and elsewhere. Ex-combatants were especially vulnerable to being picked up: they carried demobilization cards and travelled to towns monthly to collect demobilization pay.[67] Hundreds more were picked up in 'curfew and search' operations in Bulawayo.[68]

The actions taken against civilians and former guerrillas by integrated ZNA units in Matabeleland at this time caused others to desert. Twelve former Zipra guerrillas fled 3:3 Battalion in late 1982 in Plumtree after they were ordered to round up civilians for interrogation. One explained, 'I asked myself … is this what I fought for? If you go … being Zipra alone, parents ask us, "What kind of freedom is this?"' Timothy Moyo was with 1:1 Battalion in Nkayi in 1983 which 'carried out difficult operations against the people in search of dissidents'. He 'decided not to be part of this act' and fled.[69]

The desertion in 1982 of thousands of armed former Zipras from the ZNA and their

---

[63] Interview with Innocent Gama, 27 September 1995. The three battalions at Silobela (4:5, 4:6, and 4:7) were all severely affected. Interviews with M.N., December 1994; Sivumela Moyo, December 1995. Also see Alexander, 'Dissident Perspectives'.

[64] Kriger, *Zimbabwe's Guerrilla Integration*, p. 121, notes that a far higher percentage of Zipra guerrillas demobilized in 1982 and 1983 than Zanla.

[65] See Chapter 9 for further discussion of the repercussions of the tourist abduction.

[66] Interview with Mbacanga Viko, 26 September 1995. There were many such centres which existed for various stretches of time. See CCJP/LRF, *Breaking the Silence*. Dusk to dawn curfews were also instituted in the western regions. See Auret, *Reaching for Justice*, pp. 149–50.

[67] In October 1982 alone, 77 demobilized soldiers were arrested in Matabeleland when they came in for their pay. See *The Chronicle*, 3 November 1982. Also see Kriger, *Zimbabwe's Military Integration*, p. 122.

[68] Auret, *Reaching for Justice*, p. 149, records government reports that 452 'dissidents' were rounded up in Bulawayo in 'curfew and search' operations in July 1982.

[69] Interviews, December 1995.

persecution at home led to a vast increase in dissident violence in Matabeleland.[70] These dissidents were not the same as those of 1980. Their position was due to the deterioration of relations within the ZNA and targeting of former Zipras outside it, a situation which was to worsen dramatically with the deployment of the notorious Fifth Brigade to Matabeleland North in early 1983.

The Fifth Brigade was the product of an agreement signed with the North Koreans by Prime Minister Mugabe in October 1980, though plans for the brigade were only announced in August 1981.[71] The brigade was unlike any other unit of the ZNA. It answered directly to the Prime Minister, and not to the normal military chain of command. It was specifically intended for what were termed 'internal defence purposes'. Its North Korean training was both military and political; its communications systems were not compatible with other brigades; the brigade's soldiers wore a different uniform and used AK-47s rather than NATO issue assault rifles. The Fifth Brigade was intended to be unquestioningly loyal and thus recruitment and leadership positions were dominated by former Zanla guerrillas. The only former Zipra battalion commander was Eddie Sigoge, but his career, like that of other former Zipra officers, was brought to a premature end.[72] G.N. graphically described the experience of former Zipra guerrillas in the Fifth Brigade:

> We were said to be not loyal to the Government and were associated with dissidents. … [T]owards the end of our training, former Zanlas with no ranks at all were promoted to Lieutenants and now each platoon had two commanders, that is, former Zanlas understudying former Zipras. … At the end of the training, former Zipras were withdrawn from units and former Zanlas took over. At a passout parade the then Brigade Commander told the parade, 'From today onwards I want you to start dealing with dissidents. We have them here at this parade. … Wherever you meet them, deal with them and I do not want a report.'

Former Zipra guerrillas were subsequently attacked, demoted and posted to other battalions.[73] Those who remained in the brigade seemed to have been kept on solely for the instrumental purpose of including soldiers familiar with the Matabeleland terrain and Ndebele language. That notwithstanding, certain units had no Ndebele speakers among them, and relied on interpreters in the field.

At the brigade's passing out parade in December 1982, it put on a formidable fire show for the benefit of Mugabe and then President Canaan Banana. Mugabe handed over the brigade flag, emblazoned with the name Gukurahundi, to Colonel Perence Shiri, the brigade's first commander. The term Gukurahundi means 'early spring rains', and had been used by Zanu in 1979 in its slogan 'The Year of the People's Storm' or '*Gore reGukurahundi*'. Richard Werbner's Kalanga informants took the term Gukurahundi to mean 'the sweeping away of rubbish', and interpreted themselves as the

---

[70] The numbers of deserters is a matter of speculation. Drawing on the *Africa Contemporary Record*, Seegers, 'Revolutionary Armies of Africa', p. 153, fn 75, puts the number at 1,800; Hodder-Williams, 'Conflict in Zimbabwe', p. 15, estimates 4,000 deserted; the Lawyers' Committee for Human Rights, *Zimbabwe: Wages of War*, p. 32, puts the number at 1,000.

[71] '"Gukurahundi" – Ten Years Later', *Zimbabwe Defense Forces Magazine*, Vol. 7, No. 1, p. 33; Engel, *The Foreign Policy of Zimbabwe*, p. 205, fn 758.

[72] See '"Gukurahundi" – Ten Years Later', pp. 33–6. Sigoge was detained at Chikurubi Prison, and subsequently forced into early retirement.

[73] Interview with G.N., 1995. G.N. was demoted and posted to 4:8 Battalion from which he demobilized in November 1982. He was arrested in Bulawayo in June 1983, and interrogated and tortured on suspicion of being a dissident.

rubbish.[74] Mugabe told the brigade, 'The knowledge you have acquired will make you work with the people, plough and reconstruct.'[75] That it did, but not in the sense one might have hoped.

From its deployment in Matabeleland North in January 1983 until its withdrawal from Matabeleland South in late 1984, the brigade carried out a grotesquely violent campaign. As we explore further in Chapter 9, the Fifth Brigade justified its violence in explicitly tribal and political terms. It targeted party chairmen and civil servants, civilians at large, as well as former Zipra combatants, refugees, and anyone suspected of having crossed the border to Botswana in the course of the liberation war. Former Zipra combatants rarely survived an encounter with the brigade. Its violence played a key role in shaping the spread and character of dissidency.

## The Dissidents

The former dissidents we interviewed had all served as Zipra combatants and did not differ significantly in terms of age, education, employment or political background from the bulk of Zipra guerrillas. They were, of course, not the only ones to participate in violence in the 1980s: some civilians joined the dissidents and opportunists took advantage of the situation to rob or carry out vendettas. There was also a South African-backed group of dissidents, which we discuss further below. Nonetheless, it was former Zipra guerrillas who formed the backbone of the insurgent forces.

The view that these former guerrillas took up arms with a clear plan to 'overthrow'[76] the Mugabe government is not borne out by the testimonies of those we interviewed. Rather, they stressed the life-threatening pressures of what they called 'the situation' and their abandonment by their leaders, who were often in jail or who actively disassociated themselves from and condemned their activities.[77] Saymore Nkomo explained,

> Our party put us into this integration to form the National Army. Because of the problems we encountered there we left. We were made responsible though it was the party that put us there. We wouldn't have left if there were no problems. At the same time, these people blamed Josh [Nkomo], that he was responsible for our activities. [But] we were sent by the situation.[78]

M.D. added:

> When Mugabe won, Zapu said accept this. When Zapu said join the army we did, or the police. But then here comes this situation knocking on our door. We never had intentions to lead this life. We'd done our duty, we wanted to build our homes, what had we done wrong? … [I]n the 1980s war, no one was recruited, we were forced by the situation, all of us just met in the bush. Each person left on his own, running from death.[79]

---

[74] See Werbner, *Tears of the Dead*, pp. 161–2. Many of those interviewed in Nkayi, however, saw the term as simply a meaningless Shona name for the Fifth Brigade.

[75] '"Gukurahundi" – Ten Years Later', p. 35.

[76] As argued by Martin and Johnson, 'Zimbabwe: Apartheid's Dilemma', p. 57.

[77] Though some dissidents said they had initially hoped for guidance from their political or military leaders, they quickly realized they were on their own. E.g., interviews with Langford Ndiweni, 30 August 1995; Attempt Siziba, 25 September 1995.

[78] Interview with Saymore Nkomo, 26 September 1995.

[79] Interview with M.D., 18 December 1995.

Of course, the vast majority of former Zipra guerrillas did not react to 'the situation' by taking up arms again: a great many simply fled the country, along with many civilians, to Dukwe refugee camp in Botswana or to South Africa. Others sought to ride out the conflict in the army, at their rural homes, or in the relative anonymity of the cities. They (along with Zapu leaders) are often critical of their comrades who returned to 'the bush', seeing their choice as futile and destructive. Former NF2 commander Nicholas Nkomo dubbed the 1980s war 'the *mphehlo*'. *Umphehlo* refers to the second milking given a cow when a few more drops may be obtained – its use here is a comment on the scant rewards of the 1980s violence. However, the decision to take up arms once again was taken with great reluctance. Most of those who spoke to us simply felt their options had run out. Here we focus on a selection of personal accounts from former dissidents who operated in and around the Shangani to illustrate the routes by which they took up arms once again.

Langford Ndiweni was born in Nkayi in 1955.[80] He left for Botswana in 1975 with the intention of joining Zipra after several periods in detention. Once in Zambia, he was sent on to Tanzania where he encountered the bitter infighting between Zipra and Zanla during the period of their brief unification under Zipa. Finally, he entered the country in 1977 and made his way to the Shangani where he operated for the rest of the war, ending up in the rebel group Pamodzi. With the ceasefire, he entered Mike AP, and from there moved on to Entumbane where he was caught up in the clashes with Zanla. He hoped to join the ZNA but, like many others involved in the Entumbane fighting, was refused. When Langford demobilized in 1981, he had had ample experience of the bitter conflicts between Zipra and Zanla, and felt marginalized from the new order.

Langford returned home to Nkayi where he purchased 300 breeder fowls and four pigs, intending to take up a life of farming. Shortly thereafter, he began to hear rumours of armed people in his home area. He was picked up by soldiers, handcuffed, harrassed and insulted, and later detained at the Nkayi police camp where the CIO interrogated him about the presence of armed men in the area and his own political affiliation. Fearing for his life, Langford fled to Bulawayo where he heard rumours of developments in Nkayi, particularly about the depredations of the Fifth Brigade. He narrowly escaped capture in the army curfew and search operations in the city, due to the intervention of a former Zipra guerrilla then serving in the ZNA, and decided to flee again, back to the familiar safety of the dark forests of Nkayi, in late 1983. He stayed with friends outside his home area, moving from village to village so as not to be apprehended.

After living on the move for several weeks, he heard rumours that he was being looked for and felt it was only a matter of time before his capture. He decided to try to contact the dissidents:

> I made investigations and went out to them. They'd heard of me and we didn't trust each other. They ambushed me, 16 dissidents. They were all former Zipras. I was given the order that I was going to be shot. I stood still and the question was, 'Are you a soldier?' I said yes. I told them my training and all that. … They asked if I was sent to them. I said no. … They asked me a lot of things, why I'd left home. We went up to Makwateni where we met another group. … I didn't know any of them. I recognized some at Lupane. So after we met them, things were better. The fear was people were sent by the government and weren't genuine.

Langford stayed in the northern region, often in the same places he had operated in as a Zipra guerrilla, until the Amnesty for dissidents in 1988.

Gcobala Ncube was also born in Nkayi, and had operated in NF2 in the Chinamano

[80] Interview with Langford Ndiweni, 30 August 1995.

Detachment during the liberation war.[81] He entered Mike AP after the ceasefire and was later transferred to Entumbane where he was involved in the fighting with Zanla. He demobilized in the tense months of 1982 and returned home to southern Nkayi where he began to travel between Bulawayo and Nkayi, selling cloth. As Ncube recounted,

> Then came 1983, the reign of terror of the Fifth Brigade. I was at home, at about 4 pm, when these guys came. The first question they asked me was, 'Where are the dissidents?' My reply was, 'I don't know.' The response I received was a heavy beating, more like an assault. … I was beaten with a log, I was hit to the ground and lost consciousness. As a dream, I saw a wide open road. When I came round, it was as if I was wakening from a deep sleep. They told me not to go to hospital or anywhere as they would come back to finish me. I was home for two days. On the day they were supposed to come back, the third day, I woke up. What rang in my mind was to go to Bulawayo, but I had no money. The only way out was to double up, to walk to Bulawayo. I felt it was better to die on my way to Bulawayo than to be murdered by these ruthless people.

Ncube walked the 150 kilometres to Bulawayo, despite a fractured hip bone, keeping clear of the road. He received medical treatment from a private doctor: 'I couldn't go to [the government hospital] Mpilo because they would ask me how did I get this? And you can't say the soldiers beat you.' He hid in Bulawayo until 1984 when he received a visit from the CID, and decided to return to Nkayi before facing arrest. A local boy reported his return: 'He alerted the Nkayi security forces that the dissident was back again to exploit the villagers for money. I had a sleepless night. What rang in my mind was to recover my hidden weapon. This AK47 had been hidden at Mtshayibhuma valley.' Ncube travelled there, tested his weapon, and set off in search of the dissidents: 'I made my way in and out to join the other dissidents without any problem because I was armed.' He joined up with another man and they met a group of nine who accepted them after realizing that some of them had been in the Zipra training camps together. Ncube operated in the northern region, moving from Tsholotsho through to Kwekwe until the Amnesty of 1988.

Others also had decision-shaping experiences with the Fifth Brigade. Saymore Nkomo was one such, and his story of developments in Tsholotsho, to the west of Lupane, warrants exploration.[82] Saymore deserted from his ZNA Battalion following clashes between Zipra and Zanla guerrillas, and fled to Bulawayo. In Bulawayo, he met with others from his battalion and worriedly discussed rumours of the Fifth Brigade. Thereafter, he was very nearly caught in the door-to-door searches for deserters and others in the city. Deciding it was too dangerous to remain, he went home to what would turn out to be a far more volatile situation. His arrival coincided with that of the Fifth Brigade – Tsholotsho, like Nkayi and Lupane, suffered extreme repression at the brigade's hands. When Saymore arrived:

> My mother told me the Gukurahundi was here and [had] told her she should report my presence. And my mother said another neighbour's son had returned from Jo'burg and she had reported. The Gukurahundi had shot him. My uncle was the first person killed by the Gukurahundi in my area. Nine members of my uncle's family were killed on one day in Nemani, Tsholotsho. This uncle of mine was killed at a school where everyone was gathered. They shot him in the toilet. They saw someone who was mentally disturbed from my uncle's home and shot him, then they shot my elder uncle and his son. Some were running away.

---

[81] Interview by Japhet Masuku with Gcobala Ncube, December 1995.
[82] Interview with Saymore Nkomo, 26 September 1995.

Another uncle with his wife, having heard his brothers were killed, wanted to go to give condolences to the grandmother and they ran into the Gukurahundi on the way and were all shot dead. The Gukurahundi could never discuss, only shoot you. In some parts of Tsholotsho, they could put people in one room, and light the roof.

These events made his decision for him: 'I thought I should … run to Jo'burg [as some of his friends had], but if I was caught they'd send me back. That day I didn't sleep at home. I decided that day to look for those people in the bush.'

Mawobho Sibindi's turn to dissidency was different.[83] Mawobho came from Plumtree where his family was active in Zapu. He worked in Hwange and South Africa before returning home in 1977 and deciding to join the struggle. He operated in Tsholotsho until entering an AP in Plumtree, and was among one of the first groups taken for army integration. The integration process was fraught with tension, but not between Zipra and Zanla – it was the Rhodesians whom the guerrillas came to suspect of poisoning food. Mawobho and his Zipra and Zanla comrades went on 'strike' and were rounded up and imprisoned. After their release, they were sent to form 2:1 Battalion in Domboshawa. There were still few tensions between Zipra and Zanla guerrillas: the only overt friction was expressed through name-calling, the Zipra guerrillas being labelled 'mashuwashuwa', from a Zipra training chant. But then the Entumbane and related clashes took place. Mawobho was caught up in the second Entumbane conflict while on leave. When he made his way back to 2:1 Battalion, he was accused of having participated in the conflict and was severely punished. Tensions were raised in Mawobho's unit by Entumbane; they were also heightened by rumours of the Fifth Brigade's formation.

Subsequent to the kidnapping of the six foreign tourists just south of Lupane in July 1982, Mawobho's Battalion was posted to the region. His company was based at a school in Lupane where his commander, Mapfumo, told the soldiers:

We came to hunt dissidents. He said if we want to finish some dissidents, we must first finish those in the section. After that we go to the bush. I asked myself who a dissident was. … It became clear to me that Zanu says a dissident is a Ndebele. Zanu said that openly through the radios and newspapers. … I was thinking and analysing deeply about the words from Mapfumo. I knew clearly that a dissident within the section was a Zipra. … I was to think deeply how I could look after my life.

Some agonizing and fearful weeks later, Mawobho was on the point of suicide:

I became sad. I took my gun and went to a big tree. I opened the safety pin. I prayed. When I was praying, I heard a voice saying what are you doing? I opened my eyes and looked around. Nobody was there. I became afraid and shivered. I closed the safety pin and went back to my position. When I was in my position tears fell and I shivered more. I asked myself why I wanted to kill myself. I said I am not a coward but a brave soldier. This is the time I saw that it was better to leave the army and become a dissident.

Mawobho left with another Zipra guerrilla, and they were followed by three more. The group made its way to Botswana, but found themselves under pressure to join the South African-backed Super Zapu, and from the constant threat of deportation. Mawobho was put on a truck bound for Zimbabwe, but leapt off the back and escaped: 'It was clear to me that by the time I reached Zimbabwe and was in the hands of Zanu, I

[83] Autobiography of Mawobho Sibindi, 27 November 1995.

would be killed.'[84] Due to these pressures, and rumours of the massacres committed by the Fifth Brigade, Mawobho decided to return to Zimbabwe in early 1983. He operated in the Shangani region for the duration of the conflict.

For many, becoming a dissident was perceived primarily as a means of protecting one's life, a response to patterns of government repression and friction within the army. Often the decision to flee or demobilize was not initially a decision to take up arms again, and very rarely was the decision to take up arms politically motivated. Many of those who became dissidents were unaware of wider political developments. Though far from an orchestrated rising, the dissident phenomenon was certainly aided by the availability of guns and began to snowball as the chances of finding others 'in the bush' increased.

## Dissident Operational Strategy

The bulk of dissidents would come to organize themselves, however unsuccessfully, on the model of Zipra. In the early stages of the conflict, however, the ways in which dissidents operated differed from one region to the next, and communication among the small and scattered groups was scant. In southern and some parts of north-western Matabeleland, the process was greatly complicated by the existence of the South African-backed Super Zapu faction. The often bloody interactions with this group constituted a critical moment for many former Zipra guerrillas in which they affirmed themselves as 'pure Zipra' and sought to reconstitute Zipra's operational style.

Dissidents' accounts of Super Zapu largely match the piecemeal information available from other sources. It is generally accepted that Super Zapu was launched in late 1982 with South African backing in the shape of arms and other logistics, and that it operated largely in southern and western Matabeleland for a little over a year and with never more than 100 (and probably substantially fewer) members inside the country. Its leaders and some of its members were drawn from Zipra,[85] and its recruitment was in part dependent on the inhabitants of Dukwe refugee camp in Botswana (though dissidents add that others were recruited from among Zimbabwean migrant workers in South Africa, often with promises of further education), and that an upsurge in killings of white farmers was in part its work.[86]

Those who took to the bush or fled to Dukwe camp in 1982 regularly encountered Super Zapu. At first, most described confusion as to the credentials of this group: they did have senior Zipra members as commanders, they were offering sorely needed logistical support, and it was not immediately obvious that they were linked to South Africa. Operating with Super Zapu for any length of time, however, raised suspicions. Their Zipra commanders and members notwithstanding, the Super Zapu units were routinely brutal to former Zipra guerrillas who tried to join them in the field; they had

---

[84] Botswana came under great pressure to deport Zimbabweans from Dukwe camp and regularly did. See Engel, *The Foreign Policy of Zimbabwe*, pp. 209–10.

[85] Of those Super Zapu leaders drawn from Zipra mentioned in Martin and Johnson, 'Zimbabwe: Apartheid's Dilemma', pp. 57–60 and an article in *Parade* magazine of September 1990, the dissident accounts confirm the centrality of 'Tafara' but add those of Derek Nkomo, Zebedia, Brighton Majaha, Bazooka and Vela. It is difficult to pin names down as there were multiple aliases in use. Interviews with Innocent Gama, 27 September 1995; Langford Ndiweni, 10 September 1995.

[86] Whites living in Matabeleland's rural areas had largely escaped attack until late 1982 and 1983 when 33 white members of the farming community were killed. Martin and Johnson, 'Zimbabwe: Apartheid's Dilemma', p. 61, link Super Zapu to a number of these attacks through the use of police ballistics evidence: bullets recovered at the site of attacks were manufactured after 1980 and thus could not have come from Zipra caches, and were of a make used by the South African-supplied Renamo in Mozambique.

new AK-47s from which the original serial numbers had been removed and replaced; and, most importantly, they did not operate like Zipra. Some dissidents objected to Super Zapu's treatment of civilians, its methods of holding meetings, its brutality towards new recruits and, most vehemently, its alliance with South Africa. Zipra's historical link to the ANC's armed wing certainly disposed many against such an alliance, as did their knowledge of events in Angola where many had trained. Attempt Siziba simply stated: 'We said we don't want to be Unita.'[87] All the dissidents with whom we spoke (perhaps drawing on the benefits of hindsight) stressed that they were unwilling to form a new movement, that their loyalties remained with the Zipra High Command and Zapu leadership.

Super Zapu's hostility to former Zipras seems to have stemmed from its realization that they would object to an alliance with South Africa. Its commanders tried to stop Zipra guerrillas from questioning their authority through creating a reign of terror. Some Zipra guerrillas, like Mbacanga Viko, learned the hard way. Viko met a member of Super Zapu in Botswana after he fled Zimbabwe, and crossed back into the country with him where they joined a Super Zapu unit. Viko was interrogated, beaten and kept without a gun for a week, but he did not doubt the group's credentials because there were Zipras among their number. With time his doubts grew because, he explained:

> You could put across a very good idea, saying Zapu and Zipra never worked this way, then you would be ordered to lie down and be clobbered terribly. Later on we discovered as we tried to find out backgrounds, some had no Zapu or Zipra background, they were just working in South Africa, were given two weeks training, and sent in … They would say they'd trained in South Africa and had their own structure. One of the senior commanders was Tafara. This is what made people confused because Tafara was a senior Zipra intelligence man who had operated under the Northern Front. But now he was a different man. What further made us realise that they were different people was when people came from South Africa to join the unit they were wholeheartedly welcomed but ex-Zipras or people running from the ZNA were given a very hard time.[88]

Beatings and killings were common. Saymore Nkomo was another who had fallen in with a Super Zapu unit. At the first gathering of the unit, he and another guerrilla were badly beaten. One former Zipra guerrilla was killed:

> I had to ask, 'why are we being beaten?' but there was no answer. … As a military man, when all these beatings took place, I tried to find out why because there was no such thing in Zipra. I then thought the reason was to make us afraid of each other so we couldn't ask questions because then we might come with the truth about these people.

Saymore described how an *inyanga* was used to terrorize recruits. This man, 'would sniff around the guerrillas and he might say you are no good, and he would order you to be killed and you would be bayonetted to death. In this sniffing, the real Zipra guerrillas were the targets.'[89]

The demise of Super Zapu was certainly owed in part to protests made by the Zimbabwean government to South Africa and South Africa's own changing interests,[90] but it was also significantly owed to the actions of those dissidents who objected to an

[87] Interview with Attempt Siziba, 25 September 1995.
[88] Interview with Mbacanga Viko, 26 September 1995.
[89] Interview with Saymore Nkomo, 26 September 1995.
[90] Engel, *The Foreign Policy of Zimbabwe*, p. 211.

alliance with South Africa. Martin and Johnson, relying on the testimony of captured Super Zapu commanders, note that Super Zapu units had had several clashes with dissidents opposed to South African support in early 1983. In October 1983, a meeting was held in the Insuza forest on the southern Lupane border in which Tafara, the Super Zapu commander mentioned above, was beaten by Zipra dissidents unhappy with South African support.[91] This account is confirmed by former dissidents who said they had decided to 'crush this nonsense'.[92]

To do so, they instituted a territorial command structure which sought to mimic that of the 1970s Zipra. The southern dissidents linked this transition closely to the demise of Super Zapu: J.D. explained, 'On October 31, 1983, that's when these people ceased. That's when we organised ourselves into regions.'[93] Another said, 'We think they retreated because they heard the Nkayi, Tsholotsho and Gwanda comrades were talking about them as bad people. Some of them were shot. ...'[94] The hostility of these dissidents, in conjunction with clashes among the Super Zapu leadership, led many members of the movement to flee across the border to Dukwe.[95] In December 1983 there were clashes within Dukwe, and the Botswana government subsequently deported 199 Zimbabweans, among them many Super Zapu. While there were additional clashes with Super Zapu into mid-1984, the movement was in disarray.[96]

The dissidents modelled their 'regions' on those of the 1970s Zipra. There were three: a northern region encompassing Kwekwe, Nkayi, and Lupane, and stretching from the Bulawayo–Victoria Falls railway line to Silobela; a western region which ran south of the Falls railway line to the Plumtree rail line, and which included Tsholotsho and Plum- tree; and a southern region covering Kezi, Insiza, Gwanda and Beitbridge, running south and east from the Plumtree rail line to Mberengwa. Regions were not strictly sealed off from each other, and some groups did not establish communication with the regional structures until fairly late.[97] Each region had a commander and was broken down into platoons of 15 to 30 men and sections of around five. As in Zipra days, meetings or GPs (Gathering Points) were held within and among regions, reinforcements were sent to weaker areas, code words were established to identify different groups and prevent infiltration, and attempts were made to protect people's families by posting them to areas away from their homes. The first commander of the northern region even took the war name – 'Gilbert' – of his 1970s' Zipra predecessor, Nicholas Nkomo.

Despite their attempts to resurrect Zipra, the dissidents were a pale shadow of what Zipra had once been. Dissident numbers were far fewer: they probably numbered no more than 400 at their height.[98] Casualty rates and desertions were very high, probably

---

91  Martin and Johnson, 'Zimbabwe: Apartheid's Dilemma', pp. 57–60.
92  Interviews with K.M., 18 December 1995; Langford Ndiweni, 10 September 1995.
93  Interview with J.D., 18 December 1995.
94  Interview with M.D., 18 December 1995.
95  Dissidents note that Zebedia and Brighton Majaha, both former Zipra commanders and then Super Zapu commanders, were killed in in-fighting. Interviews with Saymore Nkomo, 26 September 1995; M.D., 18 December 1995.
96  *The Herald* of 7 May 1984 reported a clash between Super Zapu and 'local bandits' in Beitbridge. There may have been a subsequent round of Super Zapu. Martin and Johnson, 'Zimbabwe: Apartheid's Dilemma', p. 62, argue that there was further infiltration with South African support in November 1985, and link this to another upsurge in killings of white farmers. Most dissidents say that Super Zapu was largely wiped out by the end of 1983, but two accounts supported the idea that Super Zapu briefly re-emerged.
97  Interviews with Mbacanga Viko, 26 September 1995; Langford Ndiweni, 30 August 1995. Autobiography of Mawobho Sibindi, 27 November 1995.
98  Government figures provided by Engel, *The Foreign Policy of Zimbabwe*, p. 206, claim 342 dissi- dents were killed, and 275 were captured; 122 dissidents turned themselves in under the

between 50 and 75 per cent. M.D. recounted, 'When I joined the dissidents in 1983, we were around 200 [in the south]; by the amnesty we were around 54. Some were wounded, captured, died, or went to Botswana or South Africa. We had no hospitals so the wounded had to be taken out and maybe wouldn't come back.'[99] In the north, roughly half of all dissidents were captured, killed or deserted, leaving 41.[100] By the time of the Amnesty in 1988, only 122 dissidents would turn themselves in. The level of losses obviously affected command structures: all regions reported high turnovers and a lack of continuity. In the northern region in which the Shangani fell, the first commander, Gilbert Sitshela, was captured and later executed on charges of having murdered the six foreign tourists abducted in the region. He was followed by two further commanders, Mdawini and then Masikisela.

The dissidents also faced difficulties incorporating those civilians – refugees or others who fled repression – who joined them. They complained that these people were a risk because they were not trained fighters and did not know how to interact with civilians. Dissident units were also regularly infiltrated. As northern dissident Langford Ndiweni commented, 'We had a problem in our movement – some were not trained, and there was infiltration by the CIO. It made the whole thing very tough. When it came to orientation it was very difficult. We couldn't orient such people. Some were criminals among us' and would beat and rob civilians, causing a loss in support.[101]

With the rejection of South African support and crackdowns at Dukwe, the remaining dissidents lost any hope of an external supplier and the possibility of a secure cross-border refuge. Shortages of weapons, and especially ammunition, were common. Though many of the dissidents had left the army with their guns, or acquired them from caches left with civilians during the 1970s or established around APs, maintaining the war was a serious problem and generally relied on capturing arms from contacts with the army.[102] M.D. described how he, 'spent two years armed with a grenade only and a pistol with no spring, a toy. ... Imagine you're attacked by yourself, with no gun, and you'd see paratroopers. ... You think of going home, but you know that will end your life. You can go to Botswana and you will be sent back.'[103] The lack of ammunition forced a defensive strategy. Langford Ndiweni, who operated in the Shangani, commented:

> We had little ammunition, it was very rare for us to operate in the day, only in the night. We would get into a village and withdraw quickly. What is five bullets against an army? If we had a mission, we'd go during the night and move the whole night, so in the daybreak we were very far away. And we'd try to disguise our movements.[104]

All this contrasted powerfully with the liberation war, as northern dissident Mawobho Sibindi explained:

[98] (cont.) amnesty. That would mean a total of some 750 dissidents. This is surely an exaggeration: many of those claimed as killed or captured by the government were probably not dissidents but demobilized soldiers or civilians. Minister of State (Security) Emmerson Mnangagwa himself gave a far more likely estimate of around 300. See Lawyers' Committee for Human Rights, *Zimbabwe: Wages of War*, p. 16.

[99] Interview with M.D., 18 December 1995.

[100] According to Mawobho Sibindi, Interview, December 1994, six dissidents were captured in battles, 12 deserted, and 21 were killed. In the west, there were about 90 dissidents at their height. Interview with Mbacanga Viko, 26 September 1995.

[101] Interview with Langford Ndiweni, 30 August 1995.

[102] Interviews with Mbacanga Viko, 26 September 1995; Innocent Gama, 27 September 1995.

[103] Interview with M.D., 18 December 1995.

[104] Interview with Langford Ndiweni, 30 August 1995.

The first war was well known internationally. It was supported by super powers and small countries. ... Zapu and supreme commander Joshua Nkomo [were] organising clothes, food, weapons, ammunition and man power. ... Whatever we needed, it was easy to get. ... The second war of the 1980s was not supported by any political party or any country. ... Clothes, food, ammunition was difficult to get.[105]

The dissidents' small numbers, lack of supply lines and rear bases were not the only differences with the 1970s. Dissidents also maintained that the forces arrayed against them in the 1980s were significantly stronger than the Rhodesian Army of the 1970s. For all its notoriety, however, it was not the Fifth Brigade which concerned them militarily. Dissident accounts of the Gukurahundi were remarkably similar:

The Gukurahundi wasn't a good fighting unit. It was trained to reduce the Matabeleland population, it was just killing civilians. The Gukurahundi weren't soldiers – where do you see soldiers who sing when on patrol? They were looking for civilians not other soldiers so we would come across them singing and we would just take cover. Soon after you'd hear people crying in their homes. ... [W]e'd clash with them, but instead of following us, they'd call for the villagers. That's where they'd take revenge, that's where you'd hear bazookas and AKs firing into homes.[106]

Dissidents were far more concerned with the ZNA, with the elite paratroop units – a successor to the Rhodesian Light Infantry – and the paramilitary Support Unit, also based on, and containing many of the same members as, its pre-independence equivalent. The Support Unit was much feared for its expertise in tracking and accuracy in shooting:

With the Support Unit, those people didn't hurry, they weren't beating the civilians. They would monitor your movement as long as possible, seeing how and where you got relaxed. That's where they would pounce on you and kill you. They would discover your likes and dislikes and study them.

Using techniques developed by the Rhodesians, the paratroop units also posed a serious threat:

The advantage over us by the paras was they'd send out sticks of one or two to an OP [Observation Post, usually on a high place, a kopje or mountain] and would keep an eye on our movements from a concealed position. So if they saw us they'd radio for helicopters and drop men in a circle around us. You would have to fight hard to penetrate. It was a Rhodesian tactic.[107]

The intensity of government counter-insurgency was a key factor in preventing civilian support for dissidents. Most dissidents said they had very little support from local Zapu leaders because they came under such severe pressure and because the dissidents were unable to protect civilians against retribution – quite the opposite: their activities drew government crackdowns in which civilians suffered greatly. Here the Fifth Brigade did play an important role as it greatly contributed to a climate of fear and mistrust. One former dissident who had operated in the Shangani recalled: 'It was so

[105] Autobiography of Mawobho Sibindi, 27 November 1995.
[106] Interview with M.D., 18 December 1995.
[107] Interview with J.D., 18 December 1995.

hard to get support because people were so frightened and we had limited arms. It was very difficult for the party chairmen. ... [T]he Fifth Brigade would come and harass or kill them.'[108] Another Shangani-based former dissident remembered:

> Zapu wasn't supporting us. We took by force with a weapon. ... We didn't even have youth to support us, to get information. Zapu was saying they didn't know why we left the ZNA, they just heard of us in the forest. No one *could* support us. Each Zapu member was supposed to be killed then. Everything was so quiet ... even Nkomo ran away.[109]

Some have argued that dissidents may have built support by helping to express popular disaffection over land shortage. Dissidents did carry out attacks in the commercial, resettlement and forest areas of southern Lupane and neighbouring Nyamandlovu district, but this was not on the scale of similar activity in Matabeleland South, and dissidents consistently denied that attacks on resettlement schemes or white farmers had anything to do with a land redistribution agenda.[110] They said they had simply attacked individual white farmers where they had found them particularly hostile.[111] Regarding resettlement schemes, Attempt Siziba explained,

> We attacked them because we would clash with people in certain areas and those people would be moved to places in resettlement schemes. They could be spies at home and be given places in resettlement to hide. ... Also, militarily, economic sabotage was a goal – where government put money we destroyed that thing.[112]

The dissidents' 'economic sabotage' agenda was also not understood by them to be a bid for popular support. Nor did it build any: the primary victims of bus burnings, attacks on development projects and the like were civilians.

On the whole, dissidents did not succeed in building popular support. Dissidents admitted that there were problems of 'indiscipline' in their ranks but also often said that they were blamed for the work of government forces posing as dissidents. As we explore in Chapter 9, the dissidents elicited some sympathy initially, but their popularity, such as it was, rapidly waned. Civilians blamed dissidents for a wide range of abuses, describing them as cruel, uncontrollable and leaderless.

Though dissidents did not formulate a positive political programme, they were influenced by the pervasiveness of a tribalist discourse. Richard Werbner has argued that the 1980s' war polarized what he calls the 'super tribes' of the Shona and Ndebele, each of which was constructed from a mosaic of smaller ethnic and linguistic groups; he argues that this was the product of struggles for power within the new nation state.[113] The dissidents concurred with his views. For them, the 1980s' war had not only rendered the sacrifices of the liberation war meaningless, but dangerously sidelined ideological goals in favour of tribalism. Shangani-based former dissident Langford Ndiweni argued:

> During the [1970s] war we had soldiers, refugees, Zipras. When these came home, they were hunted by the Gukurahundi so people were confused and didn't know what to do, what they fought for, what they had trained for – even refugees, why had they become refugees? All were targets of the Gukurahundi. A party

---

[108] Interview with Langford Ndiweni, 30 August 1995.
[109] Interview with Gcobala Ncube, 5 December 1995.
[110] For details on dissident activity in Nyamandlovu, see CCJP/LRF, *Breaking the Silence*.
[111] Many of the attacks on whites were at any rate carried out by Super Zapu units, as noted above.
[112] Interview with Attempt Siziba, 25 September 1995.
[113] Werbner, *Tears of the Dead*, p. 159.

constitution, ideology, a court of discipline – those weren't there. It was a tribal war. People had lost discipline and ideology. ... Life was desperate. ... People were confused, they had no line, they were only trying to survive by carrying a gun to protect their lives. ... There was confusion.[114]

Langford's colleague Mawobho Sibindi explained that in the liberation war Zipra had fought against 'partyism, regionalism, racism and tribalism', but the 1980s war 'was on a tribal basis'. It could not even be construed as a war against Zanu(PF): 'we were not in the bush to fight Zanu, but we were fighting to defend ourselves against Zanu.'[115] Similar views came to be held by civilians, as we explore in the following chapter.

The politicization and polarization of ethnicity reshaped the dissidents' own views and tactics. In the 1970s, there had been a range of ethnic groups within Zipra, though it had been Ndebele dominated, and Zipra had operated successfully in Shona-speaking areas. But in the 1980s, there were no Shonas in the dissident ranks and Shona-speaking areas were described as extremely hostile. Gokwe District provides an interesting case. It is predominantly Shona speaking, but is inhabited by a wide range of ethnicities, including Tonga, Shangwe and Ndebele. The district was a Zipra operational area in the 1970s, but, as described in Chapter 6, the actions of the Rhodesian auxiliary forces had started to polarize the 'Shona' and 'Ndebele' in border areas. In the 1980s, Gokwe became a 'no-go' zone. Langford Ndiweni explained the transition from the dissident perspective: 'Since Gokwe is Shona, the leaders injected the spirit of tribalism and once one has that injection, the whole body becomes sick. As the leaders were Shona, [the Shonas in Gokwe] lost their discipline quicker and organized on tribal lines.' Gokwe did in fact have early desertions from Zapu to Zanu(PF). In early 1984 Gokwe's council chairman claimed the district was 100 per cent Zanu(PF), that 'vigilante groups' and a People's Militia had been established, thus preventing Gokwe from becoming dissident 'infested' like the 'Ndebele' district of Nkayi to the south.[116] Langford continued: 'If you went to Gokwe, ... people would shout and tell everyone, "There's a dissident!" and peasants were armed there by the government. Fortunately, Zapu is not a tribal party – otherwise we would have wiped out those Gokwe people.' Dissidents rarely ventured into Gokwe save to acquire guns from the People's Militia.[117]

Dissidents were not, however, immune to tribalist politics. Raids into border Shona areas were carried out specifically on the grounds that the government was only persecuting the Ndebele. One southern dissident explained:

During the curfew we went as far as Filabusi and further because there was no curfew there. We wanted to spread the curfew. ... We wanted to go to Belingwe [Mberengwa] because we knew that was where Zanu people were and we wanted them to be affected. Instead of beating people in Belingwe, the army would warn them we were coming and to give us food and everything and tell the army. This side, if people reported our presence, they would be shot.[118]

Shona-speaking civilians in Mberengwa and other border areas suffered particularly brutal attacks from dissidents.[119]

The combination of the dissidents' military weakness, lack of both leadership and support, and absence of a positive political ideology meant they were never able to

---

[114] Interview with Langford Ndiweni, 10 October 1995.
[115] Autobiography of Mawobho Sibindi, 27 November 1995.
[116] See report in *The Chronicle*, 25 April 1984.
[117] Interview with Langford Ndiweni, 10 October 1995.
[118] Interview with Saymore Nkomo, 26 September 1995.
[119] See CCJP/LRF, *Breaking the Silence*.

operate as Zipra had. The dissidents created a caricature of Zipra, parallel to (and partly in response to) the Fifth Brigade's gross distortion of Zanla. Nonetheless, dissidents' loyalty to Zipra remained firm, and they took pride in the vestiges of professionalism and discipline which survived to the end of the war. All the dissidents emphasized the ordered way in which they turned themselves in under the Presidential Amnesty of 1988. This included preparatory meetings among the three regions, and planned, group surrenders at police camps. In the Shangani, the northern dissidents sent a trusted civilian to bring police representatives to a meeting after which they held a 'regional Gathering Point' of the surviving 41 dissidents and decided to turn themselves in. They were finally disarmed on 29 April 1988.[120] The dissidents stressed that they came in because their leaders had asked them to. 'Our leaders said if you are really Zipra come home,' said Attempt Siziba.'We did because we were still taking orders from them' and that was 'proof that we were a disciplined force, banking our support on the political leadership and the High Command.'[121] The dissidents' continued allegiance to their leaders of the 1970s was key both to the restriction of South African influence in the early 1980s and to the rapid establishment of peace in 1988.

## Conclusion

The failures of Zimbabwe's transition to independence had deadly repercussions for former Zipra guerrillas. Those caught up in the internecine conflict of the 1980s – within the ZNA or outside it – were faced with an impossible situation. For some, the only option appeared to be a 'return' to the bush. But their memories of operations in the 1980s in no way paralleled their accounts of the 1970s. This was a war without political leadership, without civilian and party support, without hope of success, but only of survival. The parody of Zipra constructed by the dissidents highlighted for them the differences between a good war, fought for a legitimate goal, and a bad war, fought for nothing more than the hope of restoring the brief optimism of 1980. They could not, of course, achieve such a restoration, and for many former dissidents the costs were great. Nkayi's Gcobala Ncube counted the 'lasting effects on my life': 'A) I was crippled permanently in my hip; B) I was crippled permanently in society. The name dissident has had a psychological effect on me; C) Character wise, the society thinks I am a killer, the worst enemy of society; D) Educationally, I fell victim. ... ; E) When I look at the orphaned children whose fathers were abducted I feel sad.'[122] If former Zipra guerrillas lives were so marred by the violence of the 1980s, so too were the lives of civilians, to which we now turn.

[120] Autobiography of Mawobho Sibindi, 27 November 1995.
[121] Interview with Attempt Siziba, 25 September 1995.
[122] Interview by Japhet Masuku with Gcobala Ncube, December 1995.

# 9

# Civilian Perspectives on the 1980s Conflict

The post-independence history of rural Zapu has received as little attention as the dissident and rank-and-file Zipra perspectives we explored in the previous chapter. And it is no accident that the most detailed studies of areas loyal to Zapu have not been written by academics but by human rights organizations: state violence was a defining factor in Zapu's post-independence history.[1] In the Shangani, civilian memories of the violence of the 1980s overshadowed those of the liberation war. The war of the 1970s and its attendant suffering seemed purposeful and 'open' in comparison to the arbitrary and unacknowledged terror of the 1980s, unleashed not to achieve an intelligible and widely legitimate goal but for reasons which came to be interpreted as having party political and ethnic roots.

Although the violence of the 1980s was extreme, civilians did not tar the various forces of the state with one brush. Distinctions and moral judgements were made in the 1980s, just as they had been in the 1970s, and these would shape the political legacy of the period. The violence of the army's Fifth Brigade stands out as uniquely humiliating, tribalistic and political in civilian accounts. Operatives of the Central Intelligence Organisation (CIO) and police intelligence occupied a special category for their widespread abductions and torture, for their deceptions and secret night-time visits. The party Youth recruited by Zanu(PF) and deployed particularly during elections were seen as partisan and thuggish. All of these groups targeted primarily civilians. Others were not subject to the same approbation: most ZNA units and the police Support Unit

---

[1] By far the most detailed study of the 1980s' violence is the recently published Catholic Commission for Justice and Peace/Legal Resources Foundation document, *Breaking the Silence, Building True Peace. A Report on the Disturbances in Matabeleland and the Midlands 1980 to 1988* (Harare, CCJP/LRF, 1997). Also see Lawyers' Committee for Human Rights, *Zimbabwe: Wages of War. A Report on Human Rights* (New York, Lawyers' Committee for Human Rights, 1986), and R. Carver *A Break with the Past? Human Rights and Political Unity. An Africa Watch Report* (London, Africa Watch, 1989). The most penetrating published academic study to date is Richard Werbner's *Tears of the Dead: The Social Biography of an African Family* (Edinburgh, Edinburgh University Press, 1991). See also Katri Yap's unpublished papers, 'Voices from the Matabeleland Conflict: Perceptions on Violence, Ethnicity, and the Disruption of National Integration', Britain Zimbabwe Society Research Day, Oxford, 8 June 1996, and 'Arrested Resolution: Democracy, National Integration and the Politicization of Ethnic Identity with Regards to the Matabeleland Conflict (1981–1987)', International Conference on Historical Dimensions of Democracy and Human Rights in Zimbabwe, University of Zimbabwe, 9–14 September 1996.

were, on the whole, judged to be engaged in the military task of seeking out dissidents. And many members of the local state and police played a positive role, shielding civilians, or seeking to assist them to flee, and trying, often without success, to uphold the law as well as the ideal of an impartial civil service.

Before turning to the main period of violence and its aftermath, we consider the brief moment in which Zapu was able to operate relatively freely in the Shangani. We draw on interviews with civilian leaders conducted in all wards of the two districts, including councillors, former Zapu leaders, chiefs, headmen and their advisors, religious leaders, teachers and others.[2] Administrative records and human rights reports provide useful confirmation for many of the points raised in civilian testimony. On the basis of these sources, our account of Zapu's role in the 1980s is very different from that usually portrayed in 'official' narratives of post-independence politics, and in the contemporary media.[3]

## Reconciliation and Reconstruction, 1979–81

As we saw in the previous chapter, senior Zapu and Zipra leaders played a crucial role in containing conflicts associated with the process of guerrilla assembly after the ceasefire. Here we explore further aspects of the transition from war to peace, particularly the processes of reconciliation and reconstruction. While other accounts have focused on the activities of line ministries and NGOs,[4] we emphasize the role played by Zapu in attempting to uphold the official policy of reconciliation and in rebuilding civil authority and services. The task was, of course, a difficult one throughout the country. Insecurity and suspicion, coupled with high expectations for change, independent-minded local party structures, and the continued presence of guerrillas, everywhere hindered the quick re-establishment of order.[5] But in Matabeleland there was an additional complication – Zapu's electoral loss.

Zapu's loss at the polls came as a shock to many of its supporters, not least in the Shangani where there was virtually no support for, or campaigning by, Zanu(PF) and the UANC.[6] Many Zapu supporters – as well as Zipra guerrillas and the party's leadership – were convinced that Zanu(PF)'s victory could only have resulted from foul play.[7] In the Shangani, bitter disappointment sat alongside fears of favouritism, neglect

---

[2] More than 300 interviews were conducted in the two districts. We have withheld the names of interviewees where we have felt this is appropriate, or where the interviewee wished to remain anonymous, but all references indicate the place where the interview was conducted and where possible also indicate the position held by the informant.

[3] On the media's portrayal of the conflict, see J. Alexander and J. McGregor, 'Representing Violence in Matabeleland, Zimbabwe: Press and Internet Debates', in Tim Allen (ed.), *The Media of Conflict: War Reporting and Representations of Ethnic Violence* (London, Zed Books, 1999).

[4] E.g., see J. Jackson, 'Repatriation and Reconstruction in Zimbabwe during the 1980s', in T. Allen and H. Morsink (eds), *When Refugees Go Home* (UNRISD in association with James Currey, London, 1994).

[5] See T. Ranger, *Peasant Consciousness and Guerrilla War in Zimbabwe* (London, James Currey; Harare, Zimbabwe Publishing House, 1985), pp. 284-326; N. Kriger, *Zimbabwe's Guerrilla War. Peasant Voices* (Cambridge, Cambridge University Press, 1992), Chapter 6; J. Alexander, 'The State, Agrarian Policy and Rural Politics in Zimbabwe: Case Studies of Insiza and Chimanimani Districts, 1940-1990' (D.Phil, Oxford, 1993), Chapters 5 and 9.

[6] In Matabeleland North, Zapu won 9 out of 10 seats, receiving 313,435 votes while Zanu(PF) received 38,819. The Zanu(PF) votes came largely from Gokwe district. *The Chronicle*, 27 February 1980.

[7] See J. Nkomo, *The Story of My Life* (London, Methuen, 1984), p. 210.

or worse. Local Zapu leaders thought 'only freedom for Mashonaland' would follow.[8] A personalistic view of accountability was commonly voiced: 'Mugabe had never made us any promises, so how could we hold the government to account … ?' asked a provincial Zapu leader.[9]

Zapu's senior leaders were well aware of the potential dangers of such fears and suspicions. Joshua Nkomo did not put acceptance of the electoral results to a vote within the party because, 'there was a real danger that it might have gone the wrong way, unleashing forces that I could no longer control.'[10] Instead, Nkomo – who took up the post of Minister of Home Affairs in the new government, alongside a number of other Zapu ministers – threw his considerable weight behind enforcing acceptance of the new dispensation. He was not entirely successful: suspicion of the new government and its local political representatives and civil servants persisted, and would play into the conflicts which followed in later years.

In addition to the potentially explosive question of the electoral result, there were deep divisions to be overcome within communities. In the Shangani, reconciliation was not primarily about relations between blacks and whites, but about relations between local people who had served with the Rhodesians during the war and those who had supported Zapu. Communities all over the two districts were reluctant to accept demobilized Rhodesian soldiers and the much hated locally recruited District Security Assistants (DSAs) and auxiliaries into their communities. Though people often shrugged off the difficulty of post-war reconciliation in retrospect, casting former Rhodesian agents as 'victims of the situation' or simply asserting that 'war is war', those who had fought with the Rhodesians were in fact commonly rejected by their neighbours and publicly attacked as sellouts. Many former DSAs left for South Africa or Bulawayo, or built homes in new areas within Nkayi and Lupane, some choosing to stay close to the district offices in areas of Rhodesian wartime control.[11] As one former DSA recalled:

It was difficult for them [relatives who had also been DSAs] to go back to the rural areas. They were intimidated. People didn't trust them because they had taken their cattle. That created a big hatred. That is why … those relatives left to stay in places where they were not known. … As for me, well, I was OK because I never went back home. I stayed on and built my home just close to the township here [in Lupane].[12]

In other cases, former members of the Rhodesian military and paramilitary forces recall that their rejection came to an end when senior Zapu leaders intervened to demand reconciliation. A former Rhodesian soldier explained:

It was very difficult at independence because Lupane was full of Zapus who'd call us sellouts. … Then Nkomo came to Jotsholo to a rally and said, 'No, you have to live with them, the war is over. We'll jail all those who continue to say things like that.' So after that I had no problem.[13]

[8] Interview with former Zapu Provincial Committee member, Sobendle, 27 February 1996.
[9] Interview with former Zapu Provincial Committee member, Singwangombe, 3 February 1996.
[10] Nkomo, *The Story of My Life*, p. 211.
[11] E.g., interviews with former Zapu chairman, Mjena, 8 December 1995; Councillor, Malindi, 7 September 1995; household heads close to Lupane business centre, 5 February 1996, 1 March 1996.
[12] Interview with former DSA, Lupane, 27 August 1996.
[13] Interview with former Rhodesian soldier, Sobendle, 26 January 1996.

Similar interventions were made on behalf of other compromised figures such as chiefs. As we noted earlier, chiefs and headmen in the Shangani had almost without exception become targets for guerrillas, and had left their homes to live under government protection in the district centres or to settle in the relative safety of cities. After independence, some sought to return home. As elsewhere, their relationship with local communities depended partly on their political history.[14] A minority were straight-forwardly rejected, such as Headman Goduka, who had headed an auxiliary force during the war. But most chiefs were accommodated, partly because people recognized that they had occupied an impossible position during the war, partly because the district administrations and Zapu intervened to demand that communities accept them. The fact that chiefs' powers were greatly reduced in the new local government structures may also have eased their return – 'traditional authorities' continued to receive a stipend and some were granted ex-officio seats on the new councils, but they were stripped of their judicial, land and administrative powers.[15] Initially, however, many offices simply remained vacant. Some chiefs preferred to stay on in town, where they often had jobs. Others felt it was too dangerous to take up titles because of their association with collaboration.

Wartime legacies also posed much broader administrative problems in the first year of independence. Many Rhodesian-era administrative officials (both black and white) remained in office. They were highly visible to rural people who had come to see them as the enemy during the war, and who expected them to lose their jobs, if not face punishment. Suspicion over their continued tenure was heightened by the violence which accompanied the process of guerrilla assembly, Zapu's electoral loss, and the appointment of Shona-speaking former Zanla guerrillas to the position of Local Government Promotion Officer (LGPO).[16] In Nkayi, DC Ehrke summed up the situation in January 1981:

> I would class the whole of Nkai TTL [Tribal Trust Land] as a difficult TTL. It has a long history of lack of cooperation and dissatisfaction with the Government. Despite the fact that there is now a majority rule Government I do not think that the attitude of the tribesmen is likely to change as, being [Zapu] supporters, they do not feel that their government is in power yet. While this problem exists it is not insurmountable and can be overcome by extensive extension work to 'sell the idea of Local Government', etc, etc. However, the posting of Shona speaking Local Government Promotion Officers to Nkai does not help overcome the diffi-culties.[17]

Suspicion of administrative personnel led civilians to fear accusations of selling out should they cooperate with officials in reconstruction. After all, the closing of dips, schools and councils had been one of the main goals of guerrilla activity, and of nationalist politics before that. As Matabeleland North's Provincial Commissioner noted in April 1980, there was a reluctance to 'resume any services which the guerrillas closed'; people seemed to be waiting for 'permission'.[18] In addition, the belief that schools and clinics would be rebuilt on the people's behalf was widespread. Lupane's Acting DC Naryshkine reported 'general difficulties ... throughout the region in getting things done'. He noted the 'suspicion of the motives of the government in the belief that

[14] See Alexander, 'The State, Agrarian Policy and Rural Politics in Zimbabwe', Chapters 8 and 9.
[15] On government policy towards chiefs after independence, see Kriger, *Zimbabwe's Guerrilla War*, pp. 230–5; Alexander, 'The State, Agrarian Policy and Rural Politics in Zimbabwe', pp. 168–72.
[16] See Kusile District Council, 15 April 1981.
[17] DC A. Ehrke to PC, 21 January 1981, File LAN 23, Rural Planning, Dev 82/84, Nkayi.
[18] Quoted in *The Chronicle*, 12 April 1980.

everything is politically motivated', and the 'general belief that the government will provide'.[19] In this context, Zapu leaders were vital to overcoming suspicions and bolstering the authority of civil servants.

With regard to the councils, Zapu leaders and the new Zapu MPs worked to convince people that the proposed councils were not the same as their colonial predecessors. Zapu stalwarts contested the council elections of November 1980 and the new councils were dominated by veteran Zapu leaders, often with decades-long histories of political activism. In Nkayi, veteran nationalists swept the council elections; in Lupane it was only in one of 23 wards that suspicious local party officials sought to subvert the new council by electing a man discredited as a sellout.[20] Senior Zapu leaders and the new Zapu councillors held meetings and toured the rural areas to explain the merits of the councils, and to encourage participation in meetings. This was by no means an easy task. As Gonye ward's first councillor recalled, 'people didn't accept [the council] right off. Most said the introduction of this council is like a snake ... in the short or the long run it will live and bite us.'[21] The charisma and authority of Zapu leaders were crucial in overcoming these suspicions.

The establishment of new judicial authorities (called presiding officers) relied on a similar process of legitimization through Zapu's endorsement and participation. In August 1980, Joshua Nkomo told a rally in Lupane: 'I don't want to hear that any member of our party ... has held any trial in this part of the country.'[22] The new presiding officers in the Shangani were to a man (and they were all men) drawn from the local Zapu committees. The shift from the Rhodesian chiefs' and headmens' courts was not, however, a complete one: where 'traditional authorities' had a nationalist history they were often elected as presiding officers.[23] Zapu's efforts to supplant wartime court seems to have met with rapid success: the 'kangaroo courts' so regularly reported in the press and parliament in the first year of independence were largely a feature of Zanu(PF) areas.

The re-establishment of services presented additional problems. Perhaps the strongest popular resistance was reserved for veterinary services. The spread of anthrax in the last years of the war had heightened suspicions of state interventions with regard to cattle. In the Shangani, the veterinary department's efforts to vaccinate cattle against anthrax in 1980 were met with near total refusal: people preferred to travel to Bulawayo to buy the vaccine and administer it themselves.[24] Dips had long been a focus for nationalist attack, and were one of the few services whose destruction had met with widespread approval. Efforts to reopen dips failed almost completely in 1980. In January 1981, DC Ehrke reported that, of Nkayi's 50 dip tanks, 45 had been destroyed in the war. Eleven had since been restored, but only three were in use. It was only by working through the district's new Zapu councillors that the DC was able to 'overcome local suspicion'.[25]

---

[19] Acting DC Naryshkine to PC Matabeleland North, 29 December 1980, File Misc X GEN, DA's Office, Lupane.

[20] Interview with former Zapu Chairman, Jotsholo, 3 March 1996. This councillor was, however, rapidly ousted.

[21] Interview with former Zapu Chairman and Councillor, Gonye, 17 October 1995. Such accounts were the norm, e.g., interviews with former Zapu Chairman and former Councillor, Daluka, 25 January 1996; Councillor, Lupaka, 8 February 1996.

[22] See *The Chronicle*, 22 August 1980.

[23] This was less the case at the top of the 'traditional' hierarchy than it was at lower levels, particularly among headmen who had been ousted or arrested for their nationalist sympathies (such as Majaha), or who had helped in organising Zapu supply networks (e.g., Malindi). The great majority of kraalheads had sided with the nationalists, and were frequently chosen as presiding officers. This pattern was common elsewhere in the country.

[24] See reports in *The Chronicle*, 10 January 1980, 12 February 1980, 4 November 1980.

[25] See report in *The Chronicle*, 17 January 1981.

Schools also presented a great challenge, not only because they had been wartime targets but also because guerrillas had raised expectations by promising that the new government would not only foot the bill for rebuilding schools, but rebuild to a much higher level and provide new staff. The issue of schools was further complicated because Zapu had created its own schools for returning refugees in 1980. These were only integrated into the Ministry of Education in 1982. Before then, Zapu leaders had toured the district raising their own funds from local business people and party members.[26] Many civilians believed that the reason the government did not invest in schools in the manner they had anticipated was because Zanu(PF) had won the elections. In some cases, such as at Mateme, Lutsha and Saziyabana in Nkayi, parents initially refused to cooperate in rebuilding schools. At times, local Zapu leaders also blocked reconstruction. As one headmaster recalled:

> In 1980 when we reopened Lutsha school I said books have not yet been provided, so buy exercise books. But people said the government said it would do everything. They said, 'The government is failing, let it fall!' They didn't like the Mugabe government. I think I was the first to open a school. We were called to a meeting at Zenka Mission and there were strong Zapu people saying, 'You should not open the school, you are a sellout.' I said, 'No, the Ministry of Education said to open.' Slowly they did open, but people were against opening the schools, they were expecting teachers to come from Zambia.[27]

Zapu youth even burned two schools which had survived the guerrilla war, and they, as well as refugees from Botswana, often proved a disruptive force where they began to attend classes.[28] Zipra guerrillas who had refused to enter assembly points also shut down schools in northern Nkayi and elsewhere in mid-1980, presenting a real problem for local Zapu leaders, until they were rounded up by Zipra's regular forces.[29]

Clinics also faced problems from roaming Zipra guerrillas in 1980. The network of mission hospitals was slow to resume services, and a mobile clinic funded by Save the Children was the first health service to start operating. This service did not meet with popular resistance: nurses were in fact overwhelmed by people seeking treatment for a variety of diseases, ranging from malaria to anthrax. In Nkayi, the mobile clinic was able to operate in part because it was escorted by two Zipra guerrillas. These men assuaged suspicions, and protected the clinic from 'dissidents'. The danger was nonetheless judged too great after a series of dissident threats in July 1980, and the mobile clinic was withdrawn.[30] The reconstruction of government clinics and mission

---

[26] There were four such schools in Matabeleland (a boys' primary and secondary, and girls' equivalents), one of which was transferred from Wanezi in Filabusi to Fatima Mission in Lupane in May 1981. The schools occupied unused mission buildings with church leaders' authority, but faced opposition from government. In January 1982, the Ministry ordered that Fatima school be disbanded. However, many pupils remained and teaching continued for some months amidst suspicion that political motives lay behind the order. Finally an agreement was reached between Zapu, Fay Chung (then Director of the Zimbabwe Federation of Education with Production) and the Ministry of Education for the school to be developed under the Ministry's auspices. Interviews with Valo Mabi, former headmaster Fatima, 26 August 1996; Councillor Mahlamvana, former Zapu leader and fundraiser for Fatima, 27 August 1996; *Sunday News*, 1 February 1981.

[27] Interview with Headmaster, Lutsha, 3 October 1995.

[28] Interviews with former Teacher, Saziyabana, 3 October 1995; Councillor, Mateme, 1 December 1995. The Headmaster of Nkuba school recalled that refugees from Botswana and Zapu youth presented 'big disciplinary problems - they were smoking dagga, we had to use the cane to discipline them.' Interview, Nkuba, 25 November 1994.

[29] See Chapter 8.

[30] *The Chronicle*, 12 April 1980, 15 July 1980.

hospitals also ground to a halt at this time. Provincial Medical Officer Alan Pugh noted that Nkayi, Lupane and northern Plumtree districts were the only areas where such problems still existed.[31] By the end of 1980, however, the situation was judged to have improved greatly as a result of the sweeps carried out by Zipra regular forces, and the campaigning done by Zapu councillors and senior Zapu leaders.

Over time, Zapu leaders thus proved key in lowering expectations, promoting acceptance of reconstruction and reconciliation, and normalizing relations with Ministry officials amongst a fearful and suspicious population. Zapu drew heavily on the strength and legitimacy afforded by its lengthy history and strong local organization. Senior party leaders played a crucial role, stepping in where local committees and communities objected to the new dispensation. The successes which Zapu achieved were remarkable but also fragile, and were marred by distrust of the new Zanu(PF) government. The following section turns to the breakdown of this nascent new order, and the increasing constraints placed on Zapu's ability to mediate at both local and national levels.

### Constrained Mediation: Zapu, 1981–2

The arrival of a new wave of Zipra guerrillas as dissidents in 1981 and 1982 posed a far more serious problem for local Zapu leaders than had those Zipra guerrillas who had not entered, or had left, APs in 1980. Their arrival was significant not only for the increased numbers involved, but also because it paralleled the breakdown of national-level cooperation between Zanu(PF) and Zapu, the exclusion of senior Zapu and Zipra leaders from authority, and a growing government suspicion of all Zapu members. Over this period, not only would local Zapu committees lose their legitimacy in the eyes of the Zanu(PF) government, and hence much of their ability to mediate, but they would also lose the guiding hand of their national leaders.

Local Zapu leaders' reactions to this second round of Zipra dissidents changed over time. Initially, some greeted them with sympathy, feeling they had good cause, as opposed to those guerrillas who had failed to enter APs at all. As one councillor explained, 'After the deserters had arrived and we had been politicized, so then there was a little support. We heard how they had been persecuted and suffered in the army and we were sympathetic.'[32] Guerrillas fleeing the integrated ZNA told civilians, 'the situation was bad. Everything was now according to tribes. ... All Zanlas had done a good thing, and all Zipras had not.'[33] Some thought the dissidents' arrival heralded a return to war, and they resumed their support activities: 'We used to give them food and shelter', one councillor explained. 'It wasn't a question of force as such – we thought the war was going to start again.'[34] However, sympathy deteriorated rapidly for a number of reasons: senior Zapu leaders condemned dissidents, dissidents themselves began to treat people with disrespect and violence, and some blamed the dissidents for the heavy costs of the government repression that followed.

Many people had at any rate judged the dissidents' struggle a futile and illegitimate one from the outset. As one chief recalled: 'We didn't trust them, we thought they were government agents come to distort faith in independence.'[35] Many Zapu leaders criticized their indiscipline and refused to accept that this new war was analogous to

---

[31] *The Chronicle*, 29 July 1980.
[32] Interview with Councillor, Malunku, 6 March 1996. Also, e.g., interview with Councillor, Mateme, 12 December 1995.
[33] Interview with Councillor, Lupaka, 8 February 1996.
[34] Interview with Councillor, Tshongokwe, 6 December 1994.
[35] Group interview, Dongamuzi, 15 December 1994.

that of the 1970s. They stressed that independence had already been won, and that dissidents did not behave as Zipra guerrillas had in the war for independence.[36] Zapu leaders commonly explained, 'When they were still with Zipra they had to follow the rules, later they had the law in their own hands.'[37] The dissidents, 'had no strategy and no commander'.[38] A councillor elaborated:

> There was a problem with the dissidents. They forced you to cook a good meal, they wanted meat and tea and bread. If you didn't have these things, they would beat you. They were just taking young ladies. … Zipra and the dissidents were the same people but they were different. … Dissidents … couldn't be controlled, they were like wild animals, they had just deserted from others, they were cruel, they were criminals. … The difference between before and after independence is that they had now deserted from their leaders, from Zapu and Zipra. They were now alone. … There was no control over them, not from a commander or a chairman.[39]

The dissidents' physical appearance further undercut their claim to Zipra's mantle, and marked them as a far from credible fighting force. They were poorly clad and armed, they 'had no special uniform. One would be carrying an axe, one a shotgun, one an AK,' a councillor remembered.[40]

Dissidents' abuse of women throughout the conflict was a particular feature of civilian accounts, and one which was contrasted strongly to a (partly romanticized) memory of Zipra in the 1970s. A kraalhead recalled:

> If they found you had a young wife, they'd send the husband to fetch something and remain doing bad things with the wife. Or a daughter for that matter. If someone resisted, that was dangerous, you'd be killed as a sellout. … Such things were not allowed during the war.[41]

Administrative records also provide evidence of reported rapes attributed to dissidents in this period, such as that of two teachers.[42]

But perhaps above all, people associated dissidents with their unreasonable demands for good food: they were popularly known in the Shangani as 'silambe over', meaning 'we are very hungry' or as 'ozitshwala', a name derived from *isitshwala*, the staple maize porridge. Their demands were often contrasted to the moral economy of supply observed by the Zipra of the 1970s. As one man remembered, 'What really troubled us was these guerrillas no longer behaved like guerrillas – they'd go down the line having everyone cook for them, and spend a lot of time in one place,' hence straining local food supplies and placing families in unnecessary danger.[43] The

---

[36] Interview with elder Zapu activists, Zenka, 30 November 1994.

[37] Interview with Councillor, Lake Alice, 8 December 1994.

[38] Interview with church leader and Zapu activist, Somakantana, 29 August 1995.

[39] Interview with Councillor, Somakantana, 16 December 1994.

[40] Interview with Councillor, Lupaka, 8 February 1996. Also, e.g., interview, kraalhead and former Zipra guerrilla, Zinaphi, 21 September 1995.

[41] Group interview, Lupaka, 9 February 1996. Such stories were common: 'we were so hurt as parents' was a much repeated refrain. E.g., Interviews with Zapu chairman, Sebhumane, 30 November 1995; group interview, Chief Menyezwa's homestead, Dongamuzi, 15 December 1994; former Zapu chairman and kraalhead, Bububu, 23 March 1996. Certain dissidents, such as 'Kanka', were particularly notorious in this respect.

[42] Acting DA M. Simela to Under Secretary, 28 May 1982, Lupane Civil Defence Committee Minutes, DEF 7/2, DA's Office, Lupane.

[43] Interview with Zapu chairman, Sebhumane, 30 November 1995.

dissidents' arrival in numbers after 1981 also brought a wave of robberies of schools and shops, and attacks on buses, all of which civilians regarded as counter-productive.[44]

Former Zipra guerrillas comprised the core of the dissidents, but they were also joined by local youth, particularly as the conflict escalated and youth became a target for government forces. Civilians distinguished between these different types of dissident, casting the former Zipra guerrillas as better behaved and the local youth as thuggish, opportunist and criminal. A councillor explained:

> [The dissidents] were not so disciplined as the Zipra forces. Some had never been to war, many were local troublemakers who after committing an offence such as rape would go to join the dissidents. There was no discipline. But those who deserted from the army were good soldiers, it was the youngsters who were mischievous and opportunists.[45]

In areas where there were many refugees and Zapu youth who were targeted by government forces the situation was particularly bad. In Nkayi, the western Shangani valley became notorious both for the concentrations of Zipra dissidents in the area, and the large numbers of local refugees and former youth who joined them, or who simply engaged in criminal activities under cover of dissidency.[46]

Though dissidents were certainly violent, greedy and rapacious, civilian accounts do not portray them as anything like the efficient murderers of government propaganda. Analyses of dissident violence by Zanu(PF) officials and in the government-controlled press greatly exaggerated the violence attributable to dissidents, as well as dissident numbers.[47] Civilians consistently charged government agents with posing as dissidents, a tactic familiar from the Rhodesian Selous Scouts. In a story repeated in various ways throughout the Shangani, civilians reported being visited sequentially by 'dissidents' and then by government forces, yet they recognized the same individuals in both groups. One party leader described how he had followed a group of 'dissidents' and watched as they changed into government uniforms while hidden in the bush.[48] Others concluded that dissidents were government agents because of the response to reports of their presence: 'We thought they were government agents because when we went to report to the police, then no action was taken. ... They were testing us to see if we'd report dissidents.'[49] Some of the supposed 'dissidents' could not even speak Ndebele.[50]

Certain notorious incidents attributed to dissidents in the press were widely held to have been the acts of government agents. The murder of six clinic staff in Nkayi in 1987, for example, was judged by the Catholic Commission for Justice and Peace as more likely to be a CIO ambush than the work of dissidents.[51] The murder of Lupane's influential Chief Mabhikwa in October 1983 was also attributed to dissidents, and much

---

[44] Robberies are regularly documented in administrative records from late 1981. See, e.g., Kusile District Council, 21 August 1981; Civil Defence Committee, May 1982, DEF 7/2, DA's Office, Lupane.

[45] Interview with Councillor, Tshongokwe, 6 December 1994.

[46] Interviews with church leader and Zapu activist, Somakantana, 12 December 1994, 29 August 1995; Councillor, Somakantana, 16 December 1994.

[47] See CCJP/LRF, *Breaking the Silence*, *passim* and pp. 140-168 in which responsibility for violent abuses are analysed.

[48] Interview with former Zapu chair, Lupanda, 22 December 1994. Such accounts were common, e.g., interviews with Councillor, Fanisoni, 25 November 1994; Headmaster, Nkuba, 25 November 1994.

[49] Interview with former Zapu chairman, Jotsholo, 3 March 1996.

[50] See CCJP/LRF, *Breaking the Silence*, p. 17.

[51] CCJP/LRF, *Breaking the Silence*, p. 72.

covered in the press. The Deputy Minister of Local Government, John Chinengudu, told mourners at Mabhikwa's funeral that those who killed Mabhikwa were 'South African agents sent to this country to murder Zimbabweans'.[52] At a Lupane rally shortly after the murder, Minister Nyagumbo 'attacked the dissidents who had no aim and killed people like Mabhikwa, the link between us and our ancestral spirits'.[53] Many local people were, however, suspicious of the official account. Mabhikwa died on his way to Bulawayo where he was to attend the funeral of Lupane's Chief Gumede Menyezwa. He was picked up from his home in a vehicle arranged by the district authorities, and followed by an army van. A survivor of the ensuing attack returned home to report that the vehicle was stopped by soldiers, set alight, and the passengers burned and stabbed.[54]

Civilians in the two districts in fact attributed only an estimated 45 murders to dissidents between 1981 and 1987 (including some killings attributed locally to government agents disguised as dissidents, and other deaths for which youth – often only loosely connected with the Zipra dissidents – were responsible). Most of those killed were people accused of selling out. Individuals who joined Zanu(PF) were targeted (particularly after 1983), as were some civil servants, and members of the village development committees established in 1984/85. In a dynamic not unlike that of the liberation war, dissidents also killed people for 'selling out' based on flimsy evidence, such as travelling frequently to district offices, or as a result of the specious accusations of jealous neighbours: 'they would kill as they pleased, according to hatred among people', as one man put it.[55] But there were also differences with the liberation war. Dissidents are said to have killed a former Zipra guerrilla and at least one other for refusing to join them, and some dissident murders introduced a new level of sadistic cruelty. In an infamous Lupane case, a headmaster's wife was forced to cut off her husband's head.[56] In another instance, a son was forced to kill his father after the latter was accused of informing on a dissident.[57] In a widely cited Nkayi case, a second wife was forced to cut off the hands of her husband.[58] Civilians also testified to two cases of mutilation by cutting off lips or ears.[59] Dissidents did not, however, kill witches, possibly because they did not claim, and nor were they accorded, the community authority necessary to pass judgement in such cases.[60]

When this second wave of dissidents first arrived, local Zapu leaders sought clarification from their superiors as to how they should be received. The district council in Lupane organized a delegation to visit Joshua Nkomo; other councillors and Zapu leaders sought out Nkomo individually. They were told that the dissidents were 'not under Zapu control', that they should be fed and told to go, that if they remained in the area they should be reported to the police.[61] Nkomo reiterated this message repeatedly

52  *The Chronicle*, 25 October 1983. See also, *The Chronicle*, 26 October 1983.
53  *The Chronicle*, 7 November 1983. On 4 January 1984, *The Chronicle* reported on the trial of an Insuza man who was accused of failing to report the dissidents said to have murdered Mabhikwa.
54  Interview, Jotsholo, 20 November 1994.
55  Interview with church leader and Zapu activist, Somakantana, 29 August 1995. Local youth associated with the dissidents at times also killed civilians: in one case, a nurse was killed by local youth after dissidents let her go, out of fear that she would report them. Interview with former councillor, Daluka, 25 January 1996.
56  Group interview, Malunku, 6 March 1996.
57  Interview, St Paul's, 12 September 1995.
58  Interview with elder Zapu activists, Zenka, 30 November 1994.
59  Interviews, Pupu, 2 April 1996; St Paul's, 12 September 1995.
60  This was the view propounded by Nathaniel Mpofu, interview, Somakantana, 29 August 1995.
61  Interviews with former MP, Lupane, 16 September 1995; former Zapu District Chairman, Lupanda, 22 December 1994.

at public meetings.[62] These instructions notwithstanding, councillors and party chairmen in Nkayi and Lupane often emphasized the awkwardness of their position, the lack of clear direction, the hushed silence. Faced with armed men demanding support, they often had little choice as to their response. Reporting the presence of dissidents was extremely dangerous, and Zapu leaders were often considered by definition suspect by government forces.[63]

Nkayi and Lupane's Zapu leaders tried to walk a fine line. They gave dissidents food but refused to mobilize communities on their behalf as they had for Zipra in the liberation war. At considerable risk to themselves, some debated with dissidents, arguing that they were not a credible armed force, that they lacked political leadership, that Nkomo did not support them, that their behaviour was unacceptable. As Lupane's then council chairman, Nkosembi Khumalo, recalled:

> I told them they were the youth and should listen to us and have senior people like Joshua Nkomo. As they didn't listen to me and had no support from Nkomo, so we wouldn't support them. [But] the government couldn't believe that Zapu was not supporting the dissidents.[64]

Veteran nationalist D.C. Moyo scolded a group of dissidents who had come to his home:

> I said, '… you are here with us responsible for your life. We gave you food, water, blankets, but you don't respect us – you hit your father, brother, sister, mother – what type of people are you? You are very different from freedom fighters.'

Though the dissidents accused Moyo of selling out, he claims their behaviour improved.[65]

In 1981 and the first half of 1982, Zapu chairmen and councillors continued to live and work within the rural areas, though under tense and difficult circumstances.[66] They were not in this period primary targets for the ZNA battalions that moved into the districts in early 1981.[67] Though councillors lodged complaints about soldiers harassing women and old people, the government forces were described as largely focused upon looking for armed dissidents, and only selectively beating civilians they suspected of hiding information.[68] However, the situation deteriorated rapidly in July 1982 following the notorious abduction and murder of six foreign tourists.[69]

The tourist abduction has not been fully explained. The government blamed it on dissidents: two former Zipra guerrillas were eventually captured, confessed to the abduction, and were executed. But more recent testimony from two former Rhodesian Selous Scouts suggests South African involvement, and there may have been a South African agent amongst those responsible for the abduction.[70] The question remains

---

[62] See, e.g., *The Chronicle*, 26 June 1982, 26 August 1982, 30 August 1982.

[63] E.g., interviews with former Zapu chairman, Sebhumane, 30 November 1995; former Zapu youth chairman, Mathendele, 13 September 1995; Councillor, Lupaka, 8 February 1996.

[64] Interview with former Council Chairman, Lupane, 16 September 1995.

[65] Interview, Gonye, 17 October 1995.

[66] Incidents of armed robberies, assaults and the like were reported by police to have declined significantly over 1981. See *The Chronicle*, 17 December 1981. The process of reconstruction continued slowly in this period. See, e.g., Nkayi District Team, 26 May 1982, DA's Office, Nkayi.

[67] It seems the first ZNA battalion was deployed to Nkayi in mid-March 1981. See *The Chronicle*, 17 March 1981, 17 December 1981.

[68] See comments from Nkayi's District Council Chairman, Welshman Mabhena, in Nkayi District Team Meeting, Nkayi, 12 October 1981, File: District Development Committee 1985, Nkayi.

[69] See discussion of this period in D. Auret, *Reaching for Justice. The Catholic Commission for Justice and Peace, 1972–1992* (Gweru, Mambo Press and CCJP, 1992), pp. 148–50.

[70] The ex-Rhodesian South African agents' confession is discussed in *Moto*, October 1996, p. 7, and

unresolved and it is one of the few still deemed too controversial to discuss by the many dissidents we interviewed. Whoever was responsible, the abduction of the tourists certainly marked a significant escalation of violence in eastern Lupane and neighbouring areas where government intelligence suggested the tourists were being held.[71] Mugabe and other Zanu(PF) officials justified the clampdown by arguing that local people were helping the dissidents, and that Zapu was masterminding their operations from the highest levels. Mugabe promised to use 'extra legal' means to destroy 'these harmful pests and their deceitful mentors'.[72] Joshua Nkomo desperately tried to control the situation: he travelled to Nkayi and Lupane where he denounced dissidents, appealed for information on the whereabouts of the (already dead) tourists, and even defended the harsh measures taken by the security forces.[73]

Security force measures were indeed increasingly harsh following the tourist abduction. A 'Task Force' was deployed in Matabeleland under the command of Lionel Dyke with instructions (in Dyke's words) to 'hunt and destroy the dissidents'. Dyke recalls that the Task Force was 'a very big operation', comprising four or five battalions.[74] The Force's deployment was accompanied by a curfew, which lasted until mid-October, in Lupane and Tsholotsho.[75] In September 1982, the army's 3:3 Battalion, commanded by Major Kruger, arrived in Nkayi, and the Lupane curfew was extended to the district. Major Kruger told civil servants and councillors in Nkayi that his battalion, 'was a task force relayed under the command of the Prime Minister to deal with all dissident activity in the region'. No vehicles were to enter the district without a permit. The public were to be instructed not to 'move in any manner that would raise any suspicion to those maintaining law and order'; no member of the public was to be 'out of a distance of 100m from his lodgings' from dusk to dawn; 'All mujibas or persons looking suspicious will be picked up and placed in police custody till such time as the government will have prepared a place for such persons, where they would undergo re-education'. Kruger added that, 'drought-relief aid was to cease in the region because it had been established that a lot of food supplied to the public ended up in the wrong mouths'. Nkayi's councillors and officials were shocked. Mr Masuku, the District Literacy Coordinator, 'wanted to know exactly how these mujibas would be distinguished from any innocent male'. Council Chairman Welshman Mabhena expressed concern that, 'it was ever hard for people to distinguish between a robber and an army personal [sic] as they all appeared in the same type of clothing, at the same time with the same type of arms'. Zapu representative Mr Gumpo, 'appealed to the Government to arrange a means whereby food could reach the hungry, because as this situation existed some people would die of hunger'.[76]

The Task Force quickly set to work in Nkayi and Lupane. Following a dissident

---

[70] (cont.) CCJP/LRF, *Breaking the Silence*, p. 43. Also see 'Tourist Killers Still at Large', *Parade*, September 1990. The testimony of one of the two ex-Zipra dissidents who confessed to the abduction is regarded as particularly unreliable. See CCJP/LRF, *Breaking the Silence*, p.43, and Lawyers' Committee for Human Rights, *Zimbabwe: Wages of War*, p. 21.

[71] The tourists' bodies were eventually found close to the Victoria Falls road, outside Lupane's western border, having apparently been killed within a few days of their capture. It is not clear if they ever entered Lupane, though one Zapu leader close to Lupane's eastern border claims to have been approached by agents of the dissident 'Sitshela' to cook for the tourists. Interview, Singwangombe, 21 February 1996.

[72] See Mugabe's comments in parliament, reported in *The Chronicle*, 30 July 1982, and other reports in *The Chronicle*, 4 August 1982, 18 August 1982, 15 September 1982.

[73] See *The Chronicle*, 26 August 1982, 30 August 1982.

[74] Quoted in Yap, 'Voices from the Matabeleland Conflict', p. 9.

[75] See *The Chronicle*, 26, 28, 29 July 1982.

[76] Nkayi District Team Meeting, 9 September 1982, DA's Office, Nkayi.

attack on a Support Unit camp near St Paul's Mission shortly after the tourist abduction, the Task Force undertook house to house sweeps in the vicinity, arrested local youth indiscriminately and established a large detention camp at St Paul's. The ZNA guarded the camp while a much expanded CIO contingent interrogated and tortured inmates.[77] Detainees from both Nkayi and Lupane were questioned about dissidents in general and the abduction of the tourists in particular. Other detention centres were established at Nkayi and Lupane district centres.[78] Lobengula barracks in Nkayi became for some months a mass detention centre for Zipra guerrillas caught in sweeps throughout the region. As one former Zipra guerrilla remembered, 'Some of those were taken at night and killed … There are mass graves at Sivomo.'[79] Sweeps in Bulawayo were coordinated with those in the rural areas to catch those who had fled to town.[80]

In this period, increasing numbers of Zapu leaders, councillors and civil servants were rounded up and sometimes tortured and killed. Teachers came under great pressure. Lupane's council chairman, Education Officer, Assistant Education Officer and Secretary were detained by the Lupane police in August 1982, 'on suspicion of not encouraging teachers to report the presence of dissidents'.[81] Nkayi's council chairman complained that soldiers had beaten teachers and students at Gwitshi and Guwe schools, causing their closure.[82] The Nkayi administrative files document a number of violent attacks on school teachers, including the shooting of teacher Douglas Sikhosana in November 1982:

> According to the headmaster's report … members of the security forces were seen approaching the teachers' cottages shooting. On arrival D. Sikhosana was asked the whereabouts of dissidents, he was then instantly shot before expressing himself for a long time. The headmaster, Mr J. Ndlovu, also had his left radius and ulna fractured.[83]

Councillors were also routinely interrogated: 'It was assumed that we knew and collaborated with the dissidents in the bush. The police began to interrogate us in a harsh way,' commented one.[84] Those suspected of having had anything to do with the tourists' abduction met with particularly harsh treatment.[85]

Interpretations of this heightened violence differed. Some argued that the increasing dissident activity 'invited gukura', a reference to the Fifth Brigade which was soon to initiate the worst period of repression in the Shangani.[86] But most held that the dissidents – and the tourist abduction – were part of a government plot designed to justify repression.[87]

Mid-1982 thus marked the beginning of what would become an almost total break-

---

[77] Interviews with former Zapu youth chairman, Mathendele, 13 September 1995; Councillor, Malunku, 6 March 1996.

[78] Interview with Councillor, Malunku, 6 March 1996. Also see Auret, *Reaching for Justice*, p. 150 on St Paul's and other detention centres.

[79] Interview with former Zipra guerrilla, Dakamela, 15 September 1995.

[80] CCJP/LRF, *Breaking the Silence*, p. 43; Auret, *Reaching for Justice*, pp. 149–50.

[81] Interview with Executive Officer Administration, Nkayi, 14 and 17 December 1995.

[82] Nkayi District Team Meeting, 9 September 1982, DA's Office, Nkayi.

[83] R. Siziba, for CEO to the Director of Education, 5 November 1982, File: Council General 182, Nkayi.

[84] Interview with Councillor, Gwampa, 1 March 1996.

[85] Interview with former provincial Zapu committee member, Singwangombe, 21 February 1996.

[86] Interview with former Zapu leaders, Bububu, 23 March 1996.

[87] E.g., interviews with former Zapu Chairman, Lupanda, 22 December 1994; Nkayi Council Chairman, Nkayi, 15 December 1994.

down in the mediating and leadership roles played by Zapu and the councils. In 1983, the local political leadership would no longer be able to play a public role, and reconstruction efforts were much hampered. Civil servants were increasingly unable to move outside district centres and themselves came under suspicion. Joshua Nkomo had been dismissed from government following the arms caches incident of early 1982, and fled the country in early 1983. People felt confused and abandoned:

> Before 1980 it was clear. Everyone was Zapu, and we knew what we were after. But during the dissident times there was a big mist. … People didn't understand what had happened, the two leaders weren't even trying to side with the people. People felt neglected, they had no place to go, no one to go to.[88]

## The Fifth Brigade, 1983

The deployment of the Fifth Brigade in early 1983 introduced terror and hardship on a scale civilians had known neither in the mounting insecurity of the 1980s nor at the height of the guerrilla war. The Fifth Brigade's exercise of violence was concentrated within a relatively short period – just under a year – and was perceived as unique. The Fifth Brigade overtly justified its violence in political and tribal terms. It not only systematically attacked Zapu and other community leaders but it also attacked civilians at large, civil servants, and even other ZNA units and the police. The death toll was high. Based on interviews in all wards of Nkayi and Lupane Districts, we conservatively estimate that 1,250 people died during the Fifth Brigade's tenure (a minimum of 750 in Lupane and 500 in Nkayi), not including the many people who 'disappeared'.[89] Many more were beaten and detained. The curfew and ban on travel left thousands short of food in the midst of an extremely severe drought.[90]

The Fifth Brigade's tenure intensified the already severe erosion of Zapu's ability to act as a mediating force between local communities and the state. Five councillors were killed in the 1980s, three in Nkayi, two in Lupane; the party was forced underground once again; councils could no longer meet; chiefs, teachers and nurses fled the rural areas; and local state representatives were themselves subject to attack. The Fifth Brigade's arrival was calculated to establish it as firmly outside normal authority structures. In Nkayi, Fifth Brigade soldiers immediately beat policemen, as well as soldiers from another ZNA unit.[91] In a symbolic move, they destroyed the signs which bore the name of Nkayi's barracks, 'Lobengula'. Nkayi's council chairman, Leonard Nkomo, recalled visiting the Member in Charge the next day: 'He was shivering from

---

[88] Interview with Headmaster, Nkuba, 25 November 1994.

[89] CCJP records list 450 *named* individuals killed in Lupane (comparable figures are not available for Nkayi). Overall, the CCJP/LRF report estimated that the number of dead was likely to be over 6,000, and that the Fifth Brigade was responsible for over 80% of all offences. CCJP/LRF, *Breaking the Silence*, pp. 143, 157.

[90] On the suspension of drought relief and its consequences during the curfews in 1982 and 1983 in Nkayi, see DA Maphosa to Under Secretary, Development, 9 June 1983, and other correspondence in File: AGR 19, Nkayi.

[91] Interview with former Zapu activists, Sibangelana, 7 December 1994. Serving in the ZNA was no protection against the Fifth Brigade: in a much publicised case, Fifth Brigade soldiers killed ZNA Lieutenant Ndlovu and three civilians who were travelling through Lupane to Bulawayo. As *The Chronicle* of 5 October 1983 reported, 'Lt Ndlovu and his passengers were accused of being dissidents and were bayonetted to death – despite the fact that they had produced their identification particulars.'

having been beaten the night before. He said, "Even we, the police, have been beaten. We don't know why the government sent these people."'[92]

In March 1983, Lupane's DA told a District Team Meeting that the 'link with the peasant had gone', that 'schools were deserted'.[93] Reports of assaults and killings at schools multiplied. The treatment meted out at Nkayi school is indicative. The Headmaster reported that four soldiers arrived on 23 January and assaulted him as well as teachers, some to the point of unconsciousness:

> On hearing that we were being beaten because it was believed that the dissidents had been at the school that day, we were much surprised for we had not seen or heard of any around the school. On trying to prove and explain to them we just found ourselves being beaten again because of not knowing Shona language which they were using.[94]

Teachers resigned, requested transfers or simply fled. In the first weeks of the Fifth Brigade's tenure in Nkayi, over 100 teachers were absent due to the 'security clampdown'.[95] The situation was even worse in Lupane. In 1983, at least five teachers were killed by the Fifth Brigade; 60 teachers left the district, including four head-masters, and no-one would come forward to teach the following year.[96] Health staff, particularly the nurses who were former Zipra guerrillas, were also attacked.[97] One such who served at Nkayi hospital recalled how the Fifth Brigade, 'came to look for the Zipras, and a number who worked at the hospital were killed. ... The Fifth Brigade used to come into the hospital ordering us not to treat the casualties who were locals. We treated them under difficult circumstances.'[98]

The Brigade's operations were crucial in amplifying both a political and an ethnic interpretation of violence: the almost entirely Shona-speaking Fifth Brigade regularly used an overtly tribal and political discourse, and its all-encompassing violence could not be explained as militarily motivated.[99] In local accounts, people make strong distinctions between the Fifth Brigade – easily identified not only by its behaviour but also by its distinctive red berets – and other arms of the state. Throughout the 1980s, other ZNA units and the Support Unit were seen as largely focused on combatting dissidents themselves. Some administrators and police were cast as helpless in the face of, but certainly not happy participants in, this most extreme period of violence. They in fact often sought to protect people from the Fifth Brigade and the CIO, helping those in danger to hide or flee, and lodging protests with their superiors or with the Brigade itself.[100] In

[92] Interview with Council Chairman Leonard Nkomo, Nkayi, 15 December 1994.

[93] Lupane District Team Meeting, 25 March 1983, DA's Office, Lupane.

[94] Headmaster, Nkayi School, 26 January 1983, File: Council General 182, Nkayi.

[95] See R.R. Siziba, EO Education, Nkayi District Council, 'Term End Report', June 1983, and other correspondence in File: Council General 182, Nkayi.

[96] See Kusile District Council, 31 December 1983; 31 January 1984. Interview sources reveal that the Fifth Brigade killed the headmasters of Dandanda and Ndwane schools, two teachers in Mzola and one in Nono. Interviews with Councillor, Jibajiba, 14 September 1996; headmaster's wife, Dandanda, 30 March 1996; former Council Chairman, Matshokotska, 5 April 1996.

[97] In Jotsholo clinic, for example, the (former Zipra) nurse was taken by the Fifth Brigade and never seen again.

[98] Interview with former Zipra guerrilla, Dakamela, 15 September 1995.

[99] Though the Fifth Brigade was dominated by Shona-speakers, civilians make repeated reference to non-Zimbabweans within their ranks. They are usually identified as Mozambicans, due to their use of Portuguese or Sena. Others refer to some soldiers having nose rings, a complexion which was darker than normal for Zimbabwe, or other strange features.

[100] Interview with Council Chairman, Nkayi, 15 December 1994.

Tshongokwe, for example, people 'flocked to the police' for protection on the day the Fifth Brigade arrived.[101] In Maphanabomu, the police sought out Zapu leaders to warn them to flee, saying 'something terrible is going to happen. Go to Bulawayo at once.'[102] One headmaster, whose son was charged with joining the dissidents, was picked up by the Fifth Brigade and taken for interrogation by the CIO in March 1983, but was protected by the police: 'I was detained for two days. On the second day, I was to be taken at night to be hanged or shot. But there was a policeman there and he protected me, he refused to kill me.'[103]

Where appeals to the police or administration failed, as they often did, people also sought help from the network of Catholic priests and doctors. These tried to shelter or protect those persecuted by the Fifth Brigade, often becoming targets themselves as a result. As one kraalhead recalled, when the Fifth Brigade came, 'Many ran for cover at Fatima [mission]. Few remained behind. ... The Brother went to Jotsholo to phone ... the DA to tell them to stop. But at Jotsholo, another Brother was beaten up.'[104] Large 'refugee' populations camped outside St Luke's mission as well, where Dr Davis was credited with saving many lives. One councillor recalled, 'I fled to St Luke's – they came looking for me at home and also in town. When the Doctor saw me, she hid me and then helped me to get to Bulawayo. Dr Davis should be thanked – many people camped out around the hospital, she organized food for them and no one was killed at the hospital.'[105] As curfews limited movement through the districts during the Fifth Brigade's operations, reports written by mission staff provided some of the main contemporary records of violence, and served as a basis for the Catholic Commission of Justice and Peace to lodge appeals to Mugabe.[106]

Below, we discuss the Fifth Brigade's methods before turning to local interpretations of the Brigade's violence.

### Understanding the Fifth Brigade: Operations and Interpretations

Fifth Brigade operations followed distinct patterns. Its units established permanent bases at Nkayi and Lupane district centres, as well as semi-permanent bases at outlying sub-offices, missions or police camps. Schools, boreholes and other sites were also occupied for shorter periods. Areas close to the Brigade's semi-permanent camps and bases were always severely affected by violence, but the Brigade made forays into all parts of the two districts, and there were no wards in which deaths did not occur. Some, however, suffered more than others: the villages of the Lupane valley had the highest death toll, possibly because of their proximity to the Zipra headquarters of the 1970s and to St Paul's AP, and because of suspicions that the area had been used to hide the abducted tourists. The densely forested areas along the Shangani river in both districts were also targeted – they were key areas of refuge for dissidents and home to large numbers of Zapu youth.

The Brigade's arrival in any area was almost always characterized by a spate of killings. Those killed were sometimes Zapu leaders identified at public meetings, through interrogations or from lists which the Fifth Brigade carried with it. At first, people were often ignorant of the Fifth Brigade's intentions, and readily identified Zapu leaders. As news spread that identifying these leaders was as good as signing their death warrant, evasion became the norm: people lied about the whereabouts of Zapu

[101] Interview with former Zapu district office holder, Sobendle, 27 February 1996.
[102] Interview with former Zapu district office holder, Pupu, 19 February 1996.
[103] Interview with Headmaster, Nkuba, 25 November 1994.
[104] Interview with kraalhead, Jabachava, 23 January 1996.
[105] Interview with former councillor, Daluka, 25 January 1996.
[106] This record is discussed in CCJP/LRF, *Breaking the Silence*, pp. 9–11 and *passim*, and Auret, *Reaching for Justice*.

leaders or claimed they had all died in the war for independence.[107] Many Zapu leaders narrowly escaped death by walking huge distances, adopting disguises, speaking convincingly in Shona, or by other means. Others were not so lucky. Lupanda's veteran Zapu activist, who was by then a central committee member as well as the chairman of the Zimbabwe National Farmer's Union and the organizer of a Save the Children Fund project, had been warned not to return home because the Fifth Brigade was looking for him. He returned nonetheless to try to protect his family, saying, '"How can I stay away when others are dying? Better for me to die than my children."' He died with six others: they were made to squat with their hands clasped behind their knees, then shot and buried in a shallow grave close to Lupanda's Sipopoma school.[108]

Other groups such as former guerrillas, former Rhodesian soldiers, migrant labourers and refugees were also sought out and often killed by the Fifth Brigade. Many killings, however, seemed indiscriminate – victims included people met on patrol who could not speak Shona, mothers who could not account for the whereabouts of a son, individuals who did not answer questions quickly enough.[109]

Sometimes killings were on a grand scale. The largest single massacre – of 55 people – occurred in Ciwale in northern Lupane.[110] In the Lupane valley, Fifth Brigade soldiers killed people systematically in each home they visited: in the village of Isilwane in Jibajiba ward, for example, 52 people were killed as the soldiers moved from home to home on February 6, 1983; 22 people were registered in St Luke's hospital with gunshot wounds and many others were admitted with injuries from severe beating, including fractured and broken limbs. A kraalhead recalled the pattern of killings:

> There were two local boys killed here [in this home] and in the next home they killed two visitors, the host, his two wives and daughter-in-law. In another home they killed twelve people. ... They were all shot. Next door to the twelve, they killed two. ... Over the river there was one young boy [killed], and then seven in one home and five in another. At the business centre people had been taken from their homes and grouped there and killed. They were seven. Then close to the business centre there were three killed in one home (a man, his wife and son), there was another boy and then another three in another home. Next door to that home, there was another one. Plus two other boys. All this killing was between 6:30 and 10 am.[111]

In the devastated Tshongokwe ward in Lupane, staff of the Catholic mission recorded

---

[107] Interview with Church leader and Zapu activist, Somakantana, 12 December 1994.

[108] Interview with widow, Lupanda, 14 March 1996. These were not the only Fifth Brigade killings in Lupanda. In the Sipopoma area of Lupanda alone, at least twelve people were killed.

[109] Such accounts were common. E.g., interviews with Councillor and Zapu Chairmen, Malindi, 12 September 1995; Kraalhead, Dwala, 9 December 1995; Zapu Chairman, Jibajiba, 21 February 1996; senior kraalhead and Provincial Zapu committee member, St Paul's, 12 September 1995; Council Chairman, Nkayi, 15 December 1994; Group interview, Mbembesi, 14 February 1996.

[110] See account in CCJP/LRF, *Breaking the Silence*, p. 48, which includes the testimony of one of the seven survivors of this massacre.

[111] Interview, 14 September 1995. For confirmation of the numbers killed and a contemporary account of the Isilwane killings and St Luke's medical records, see CCJP/LRF, *Breaking the Silence*, pp. 226, 238–9. Neighbouring villages in the same ward also suffered severe casualties. In Ndwane village, for example, fifteen people were killed on the first day of the Brigade's deployment, including the headmaster of the primary school, three women, a girl and six boys: 'they said they wanted dissidents, but they said everyone was a dissident. ... All these people died on the one day, February sixth.' Interview with Councillor, Jibajiba, 14 September 1995. When the Fifth Brigade moved on to Keswa village, at least five more were killed on the first day.

33 deaths.[112] Though these cases were extreme, all around the Shangani large numbers were killed in the first days of the Fifth Brigade's operations.

The Fifth Brigade also established large detention centres to which people were brought from all over the district. At St Paul's detention centre, local leaders reported at least fifty killed.[113] And there were other killing zones to which people were brought from around the districts and elsewhere. In Lupane business centre, locals recalled people being pulled from buses and killed in the river valley beside the road. There are similar accounts for a bridge in the Mbembesi Forest Area adjacent to the main Victoria Falls Road. Civilians report government trucks returning to remove the bones from such areas 'so no one would find any bodies'.[114] In Nkayi, the forested areas around Fanisoni, and an abandoned mine shaft in the same area were used for dumping bodies on a regular basis: in 1983, 'every evening the army would drive there into the bush, taking people, and not bringing them back,' recalled the local councillor.[115] Mass graves are now a well-known, and deeply disturbing, feature of the Shangani's landscape.

Subsequent to initial spates of killing, the Fifth Brigade units tended to settle into a lower (though often still deadly) level of violence. 'Supposing you were home, they'd thrash you there. You go to the stream, you'd be thrashed. You go to the field, you'd be hit for no reason,' recalled a group of party activists.[116] This violence was often humiliating and dehumanizing. Women were raped, sometimes systematically: 'The Fifth Brigade was taking women by force from schools. The Fifth Brigade commander ... had a policy of ordering the soldiers to take women,' Nkayi's Council Chairman asserted.[117] The Headmaster of Nkuba School vividly remembered a visit by Fifth Brigade soldiers. They had beaten teachers with logs, forced teachers to engage in boxing matches with each other, forced them to climb trees and then fall out. 'They would laugh and laugh,' he recalled. One teacher was found to have an airgun. He was taken to a nearby tree and made to dig his 'grave' with his fingers. He was then forced to fight with his brother until 'his teeth were broken'.[118] Mr Masuku, a distinguished longtime nationalist, recounted how Fifth Brigade soldiers had found a photo of Joshua Nkomo in his younger brother's home. They beat Masuku's nephew, breaking his arm, and then found Masuku himself preparing to cook liver. Masuku was forced to eat the meat raw, on his hands and knees, 'like a dog'. He was then beaten while his wife was made to serve the soldiers melons.[119] Such cases were daily fare for Fifth Brigade soldiers. We cannot possibly do justice to the numerous such incidents which were so painfully recounted to us. The injury which they left in their wake cannot be over-emphasized, both on psychological and physical levels. It is commonly said that people are 'still dying' from the wounds inflicted by the Fifth Brigade.

The Fifth Brigade also directed its energies to political 'mobilization', what Ranger and Bhebe aptly describe as 'politicization without politics'.[120] The Fifth Brigade forced

---

[112] Interview with Father Francis, Gomoza, 4 March 1996.

[113] Group interview, Malunku, 13 September 1995.

[114] At Lupane business centre, 'Down Store [adjacent to the Victoria Falls Road] was a venue for killing. Many were drawn off the buses. When they were collecting bones, they filled up a whole lorry. The government called us all ... to collect the bones to clear up the area.' Interview with kraalhead, Matshiya, 19 September 1995.

[115] Interview with Councillor, Fanisoni, 25 November 1994. Also see interview with Headmaster, Nkuba, 25 November 1994.

[116] Group interview, Mateme, 14 September 1995.

[117] Interview, Leonard Nkomo, Nkayi, 15 December 1994.

[118] Interview with Headmaster, Nkuba, 25 November 1994.

[119] Interview, Sebhumane, 30 November 1995.

[120] N. Bhebe and T. Ranger, 'Volume Introduction: Soldiers in Zimbabwe's Liberation War', in N. Bhebe and T. Ranger (eds), *Soldiers in Zimbabwe's Liberation War* (London, James Currey, 1995), p. 19.

people to attend Zanu(PF) meetings, and held Zanla-style pungwes at which people were made to sing Zanu(PF) songs and chant Zanu(PF) slogans in Shona, to denounce Zapu, and to engage in a kind of forced revelry of dance and music. One Zapu veteran remembered,

> They used to round up people, take them to Sagonda and have a pungwe. We'd be there the whole day, ... singing and dancing. After that they'd say, 'Those who have seen dissidents on this side, the others on that side'. Those who didn't see dissidents were made to take off their shirts and lie down. ... Then they'd ask ... where the dissidents were, holding a big long stick for thrashing. And you'd be thrashed. The second day three people were already dead and they were roasted on a fire.[121]

Such accounts are, again, too numerous to recount here: all follow a similar pattern of forced singing, dancing and sloganeering, often accompanied by grotesque forms of violence, as well as lesser humiliations – old men and women whose dancing did not appeal to the soldiers, or who could not sing Shona songs, were forced to dance for hours as they were beaten, or were held up for ridicule and special punishment.

How can this *modus operandi* be explained? Certainly the Fifth Brigade differed from other ZNA units in that it was trained by the North Koreans; certainly its domination by former Zanla guerrillas shaped its propensity for using Zanla mobilization methods such as the pungwe. But the excessive and exceptional violence of the Brigade cannot be explained, as some have sought to, as a consequence of 'indiscipline, drunkenness and boredom'.[122] Perhaps the only reasonable explanation is that the Fifth Brigade was simply acting under orders, an hypothesis made the more credible by the consistency in its behaviour and self-presentation in the two districts.

Local testimonies include many instances of Fifth Brigade commanders and soldiers explaining their orders. They told people that they had been ordered to 'wipe out the people in the area', to 'kill anything that was human'.[123] They said they had been told that all Ndebeles were dissidents, making women and children as well as men targets: 'The child of a snake is also a snake', as one put it.[124] Others said they were taking revenge for nineteenth-century Ndebele raids against their Shona ancestors: 'They said, "Your forefathers ate our cattle – where are they?" We were attacked for being Ndebele. They were actually saying it,' recalled a group of party activists.[125] A Zapu chairman in Lupanda remembered, 'they didn't hide their real motive: "You have been killing our forefathers, you Mandebele." '[126] Fifth Brigade commanders drew on biblical metaphors to describe their unlimited powers. A Zapu chairman in Nkayi gave the following account of the first speech given by Fifth Brigade commander O. M. Pongweni, better known as Jesus, in 1983:

> Jesus said, 'We know the dissidents don't live on their own, they live with you. If

---

[121] Interview with former Zapu chairman, Mjena, 8 December 1995.

[122] See discussion in CCJP/LRF, *Breaking the Silence*, p. 50. The Lawyers' Committee for Human Rights, *Zimbabwe: Wages of War*, p. 32, and A. Alao, 'The Metamorphosis of the "Unorthodox": The Integration and Early Development of the Zimbabwe National Army', in N. Bhebe and T. Ranger (eds), *Soldiers in Zimbabwe's Liberation War* (London, James Currey, 1995), p. 114, make this argument.

[123] Interviews with former Zapu Provincial committee member, St Paul's, 12 September 1995; Councillor, Lupaka, 8 February 1996.

[124] Interview with Kraalhead, Mzola, 1 February 1996.

[125] Group interview, Mateme, 14 September 1995.

[126] Interview with former Zapu district chairman, Lupanda, 22 December 1994. There were many such cases: e.g., interview with Executive Office Administration, Nkayi, 17 December 1995.

you don't report [the presence of dissidents] tomorrow morning, I'm giving you one week, and then I'll send my angels. If I tell my angels I want more than 200 heads chopped off, they will bring them here, they will do that if I order it as Jesus.'[127]

Exceptionally, people also told of soldiers who repented of their actions, who believed they had been misled into thinking that all Ndebele were dissidents. One commander stated at a public meeting that he did not agree with his orders and would not carry them out.[128]

The belief that the Fifth Brigade's particular brand of violence was not an aberration but part of a plan orchestrated by Zanu(PF)'s leaders shaped people's perceptions of the goals of the 1980s war. They came to see the conflict not as one fought against the dissidents but against the Ndebele and Zapu. In local accounts, there is a constant slippage between an emphasis on tribalism and on inter-party conflict as the motive force behind the Fifth Brigade's violence. The ethnic interpretation drew heavily on the indiscriminate nature of Fifth Brigade violence, the Brigade's use of Shona, and its frequent recourse to tribalist justifications. The political interpretation drew on the targeting of Zapu leaders.

Acts of violence perpetrated by the Fifth Brigade were given specific meanings as a result of its tribalist rhetoric. For example, while rapes committed by dissidents or ZNA soldiers might be described simply as an abuse of power, rapes committed by the Fifth Brigade were perceived as a systematic attempt to create a generation of Shona children. Such interpretations extended to the Fifth Brigade's bizarre involvement in building schools: these initiatives were not seen as developmental in intent but as heralding the introduction of Shona students to Matabeleland.[129] Tribalist interpretations were also used to explain the pattern of violence in areas which bordered on Shona-speaking regions, or where some people were themselves able to speak Shona. In such contexts people claimed that the Fifth Brigade did not attack their cross-border neighbours, despite dissidents operating in those areas, or that they were themselves spared attack because they could speak Shona.[130]

Others, particularly the districts' senior Zapu leaders, stressed the Fifth Brigade's role in destroying Zapu. They noted that, while the Fifth Brigade's violence was at times indiscriminate, many of its actions, as well as those of the CIO, were directed specifically against Zapu. They saw the war as a whole, sometimes even including the actions of dissidents, as orchestrated to this end.[131] Most commonly, however, people elided the categories of Ndebele and Zapu: an attack on the Ndebele was an attack on Zapu, an attack on Zapu was an attack on the Ndebele; and attacks on Zapu *as* Ndebele made even those Zapu members who were not Ndebele come to see themselves as such. Such attacks struck at the root of people's most cherished social and political identity.

---

[127] Interview with former Zapu chairman, Malindi, 12 September 1995. A Fifth Brigade commander stationed in Lupane district also referred to himself as 'Jesus', as did the Fifth Brigade's overall commander, Perence Shiri. Interview with Councillor, Lupaka, 8 February 1996.

[128] Interviews with Councillor, Kwesengulube, 1 December 1995; Councillor, Malindi, 12 September 1995.

[129] Interview with Councillor and former Zapu chairmen, Gwelutshena area, 6 December 1994.

[130] Interviews with Councillor and Vidco chairman, Kana, 5 December 1995, 28 November 1995; Councillor and former Zapu chairmen, Mateme, 7 December 1995; kraalhead, Dwala, 9 December 1995; Group interview, Mateme, 15 September 1995; kraalhead, Mapendere, 3 December 1994; farm owner, Lupanda, 28 March 1996.

[131] E.g., interviews with Nkayi Council Chairman, Nkayi, 15 December 1994; former Zapu Chairman and Councillor, Daluka, 25 January 1996; Councillor and former Zapu chairmen, Mateme, 7 December 1995.

Lupane's council chairman, Gabheni Sibanda, aptly summed-up such perceptions when he described the pungwe songs in which he was forced to denounce Zapu in Shona as 'songs of self denial'.[132]

The Fifth Brigade's greatest 'success' may have been in hardening ethnic prejudice, and in bolstering a strong identification between ethnicity and political affiliation. It also greatly undercut the capacity of local institutions – the party, the council – to represent their constituencies, and to mediate with the state. In the following section, we discuss the greatly circumscribed role of local institutions during the Fifth Brigade's tenure and after.

### Absent Mediation

For councillors, Zapu leaders and others in Nkayi and Lupane, the period from 1983 on was a time of detention and torture, disappearance and flight. Their political and developmental activities were totally paralysed. Officials repeatedly raised the problems posed for communication and development by councillors' absence.[133] Chiefs fled the rural areas, some after suffering beatings and threats.[134] During and after the Fifth Brigade's depredations, the CIO and Zanu(PF) Youth carried out a more targeted programme of political violence. The local and national elections of 1985 heralded a concerted campaign on the part of Zanu(PF) directed at the conversion, elimination and intimidation of Zapu cadres. Repression largely failed as a means of changing political allegiance, but it did cripple the Zapu leadership. In the absence of Zapu mediation, people greeted developmental initiatives with great suspicion and non-cooperation, while DAs and other civil servants found themselves in the invidious position of being both threatened by the security forces and dependent on them for protection from dissidents. Many struggled to maintain neutrality, others were forced out of the districts or fled.

The CIO was central in orchestrating the detentions and disappearances of Zapu leaders, councillors and others such as Zipra guerrillas. CIO agents sometimes accompanied army units, or arrived in their aftermath. They were often described as having been friendly and helpful in daytime, only to return at night as 'thieves, stealing people' from their homes.[135] In both Nkayi and Lupane, people believe that the CIO and soldiers orchestrated simultaneous night time sweeps throughout Matabeleland in an effort to surprise and capture key Zapu activists.[136] An old Zapu activist likened the CIO to 'an animal called *imvukuzane* which moves at night and can't be seen in the day' and which witches used 'to destroy you quietly'.[137]

---

[132] Interview with Lupane Council Chairman, 19 February 1996. Similar comments were made in interview with a Kraalhead and others, Menyezwa, 24 September 1995.

[133] See interventions by Comrade Mamiyo (responsible for youth) who 'queried whether it was a normal situation that councillors should be left out from the meeting'; Ncube of Agritex, who 'queried why councillors had been left out of [ward and vidco] delineation teams', Nkayi District Development Committee, 4 March 1984. See also Nkayi District Development Committee, 7 March 1985, on the 'vacuum' created by the absence of the councillors who are a 'pivot in the development process'; DA's monthly report April 1985; May 1985, Nkayi.

[134] DA's monthly reports, Nkayi, April 1985, November 1985 note that all chiefs were 'in exile', mostly in Bulawayo. Chief Madliwa had been badly beaten by the Fifth Brigade. Interview with Chief Madliwa, Nesigwe, 2 December 1994.

[135] Interviews with former Zapu chairmen, Gampinya, 19 October 1995; former Zapu chairmen, Zenka, 30 November 1994.

[136] The dates for rural sweeps given in interviews were not consistent. See CCJP/LRF, *Breaking the Silence*, pp. 55–6, 63–8, on the CIO and disappearances.

[137] Interview with former Zapu chairman and Councillor, Gonye, 17 October 1995.

Parallel to the activities of the CIO, Zanu(PF) recruitment and campaigning was stepped up. The Zanu(PF) Youth became prominent agents of violence in this process, as did certain key defectors from Zapu structures. Defections to Zanu(PF), while devastating in their impact in some instances, were small in scale, and defectors failed to achieve popular legitimacy. In Lupane, Zanu(PF) recruited from those labelled as sell outs in the days of the liberation war, people who for the most part lived around the district offices. They included former Rhodesian paramilitaries, a 'Shona' from Gokwe District, and people living in the immediate vicinity of the business centre such as a storekeeper widely held to have stocked poisoned clothing during the liberation war.[138] In Jotsholo, a teacher who defected from Zapu tried (largely unsuccessfully) to mobilize other teachers. In Nkayi, the locally recruited Zanu(PF) leadership numbered only a handful of former Zapu activists who lived in the vicinity of Nkayi centre. These defectors were described as people of weak character, people who were greedy and power-hungry, and who had in some instances been accused of corruption within Zapu.[139] Elsewhere, Zapu committees were forced to rename themselves Zanu(PF), but this did not entail a change in allegiance: 'it was just on paper – we were all Zapu members,' recalled one 'convert'.[140]

Though weak, the Zanu(PF) structures – and particularly the genuine Zapu defectors – were extremely dangerous to Zapu cadres for their ability to identify, locate and inform on key activists. They also played an important role in leading the Zanu(PF) Youth. The Youth were partly locally recruited, and partly brought in by bus from other districts. Though many local youth fled the rural areas to avoid recruitment, others were described as relishing the power which they wielded over their elders as Zanu(PF) Youth.[141] They operated mainly around the districts' centres and gained notoriety for the beatings they administered. For their excesses, they faced criticism from the administration, council and police, though none of these forces was able to control them. As one of Lupane's executive officers recalled, 'The police were completely impotent. They couldn't arrest the youth or the paramilitaries for beating people. People went to them but they were powerless.'[142] In Nkayi, the Zanu(PF) Youth under the leadership of a key Zapu defector burned down the house of the council chairman with impunity, and regularly beat people arriving in the district on buses who did not hold Zanu(PF) cards. The cards came to be called 'bus passes' as a result.

The massive force at its disposal notwithstanding, Zanu(PF) efforts at mobilization manifestly failed to create a viable party structure or significantly change allegiances. Fear of reprisals by dissidents was a factor. Dissidents targeted those who joined Zanu(PF) as well as government officials and those thought to be cooperating with officials more generally. For example, they massacred the family of a prominent Zanu(PF) convert in Nkayi and killed the Zanu(PF) chairman and another Zanu(PF) committee member in Daluka. Teachers, as civil servants, were also prominent among dissidents' targets, particularly after Zanu(PF) tried to forcibly recruit them.[143] But more important in limiting Zanu(PF)'s success was an unswerving and profound loyalty to

---

[138] Interview with former Zanu(PF) district chairman, Lupane, 27 August 1996.

[139] Interview with former Zapu chairmen and Councillor, Malindi, 12 September 1995.

[140] Group interview, Mateme, 14 September 1995.

[141] Interviews with former Zapu chairmen and Councillor, Malindi, 12 September 1995; Councillor, Nkalakatha, 31 November 1994; Kraalhead, Matshiya, 19 September 1995.

[142] Interview with Senior Executive Officer, Lupane, 3 April 1996. The SEO's attempts to ban Zanu(PF) Youth meetings are detailed in Lupane District Team Minutes, 17 July 1984 and 5 September 1984, file ADM 33/2, DA's Office, Lupane.

[143] In Lupane, three teachers were killed by dissidents. Interviews, Dongamuzi, 15 December 1994; Tshongokwe, 6 December 1994. In another incident, dissidents shot the police constable guarding a teacher who was a Zanu(PF) activist. Interview, Jotsholo, 11 March 1996.

Zapu, which many people ascribed to the 'Ndebele character', and which had firm roots in Zapu's long history of resistance. Rather than changing allegiances, many maintained that repression 'hardened' people's convictions.[144]

Zanu(PF)'s failure at 'mobilization' was mirrored in its efforts to win seats on the district councils. The local elections of January 1985 were preceded by a wave of detentions and attacks which affected many Zapu candidates. In Nkayi, the Zapu offices were attacked by soldiers in late June 1984: the Zapu administrator managed to take refuge in the DA's office where he hid for three days before the DA smuggled him to Bulawayo.[145] The position of DAs became increasingly difficult as they began to come under sustained pressure from their superiors and Zanu(PF) officials. Just prior to the council elections, the Provincial Administrator castigated DAs 'for their lack of cooperation and disloyalty to the ruling party and government'. The Minister of Mines and Provincial Chairman of Zanu(PF), Callistus Ndlovu, told DAs that, 'as civil servants' they 'should remain either neutral or support the ruling party and government in carrying out their activities'. He said that some DAs had been a stumbling block to the activities of the ruling party in the districts. The DAs were warned that the ruling party would recommend dismissal of such undesirable elements. The DAs responded that they were victims of 'malicious rumours spread by ruling party cadres' who were finding it difficult to 'organize the people' and who made unacceptable demands such as that the administration provide vehicles for their 'political duties'.[146]

During the elections, many councillors not already in hiding in Bulawayo fled, and people pleaded for police protection at polling sites.[147] Zanu(PF) was nonetheless driven to sometimes ludicrous measures even to field candidates. Some candidates were nominated against their will or without their knowledge; teachers and other civil servants were intimidated into standing for Zanu(PF); some Zapu candidates were proposed, much to their outrage, on the Zanu(PF) ticket.[148] In the event, people voted in Zapu candidates even where they were in detention. As Lupane's council chairman, Nkosembi Khumalo, recalled, 'when the time for the elections came, I was in prison, so there was no Zapu candidate. So then someone picked up a stone and said, "This is Nkosembi". Then everyone voted for the stone. The Zanu candidate was only supported by his two wives.'[149] Only one Zanu(PF) candidate gained office in Lupane, and he hailed from a ward where Fifth Brigade massacres had been extreme. In Nkayi, not one Zanu(PF) candidate won.

Zapu's victory did not, however, give it a renewed ability to act. Instead, it brought retaliation. In Nkayi, Zanu(PF) Youth and soldiers assaulted the DA, councillors, and

---

[144] E.g., interviews with former Councillor, Daluka, 25 January 1996; Executive Officer Administration, Nkayi, 17 December 1995; former Zapu chairmen, Mateme, 7 December 1995.

[145] Interview with Councillor, Nkayi, 31 November 1994. This man stayed in Bulawayo as a 'refugee' until 1989. He became a councillor on his return to the district.

[146] Minutes of a Meeting [with DAs, PA and others], 5 January 1985, File: DM 3/85 'District Administrators' Conferences and District Administrators' Minutes from the Permanent Secretary', Nkayi.

[147] Interviews with Councillor, Sobendle, 18 December 1996; former Council Chairman, Lupane, 16 September 1995; Councillor, Nkalakatha, 31 November 1994; Chief and adviser, Dongamuzi, 15 December 1996.

[148] In Lake Alice, the Zapu candidate was also listed as a Zanu(PF) candidate, though he did not know it. When he was elected, and discovered he was on the Zanu(PF) list, he lodged a formal complaint and resigned. See letter in Lupane DA's Office, 12 June 1985. Similarly, a Zapu candidate from Mpande Ward in Nkayi was listed on the Zanu(PF) ticket. He called a meeting with the DA and Zanu(PF) representatives before the elections, demanding he be taken off the Zanu(PF) list. Interview with DA, Nkayi, 19 December 1994; Minutes on District Council Elections Meeting, DA's Office, Nkayi, 8 January 1985, File: EL/5 Elections, Nkayi.

[149] Interview with former Council Chair and MP, Lupane, 16 September 1995.

council and hospital staff under the watchful eye of Provincial Governor Mudenda. Many civil servants and councillors fled as a result and the district offices were closed. Nkayi's DA was lucky to survive. The DA, Inyathi, subsequently made strong protestations to his Ministry, threatening to resign if civil servants and police were not allowed to carry out their duties without political interference and violence.[150] Nonetheless, this round of repression again failed to change voting patterns: in the July 1985 national elections Zapu was returned with an overwhelming majority in both Nkayi and Lupane.[151] But the councils could not function – most councillors did not even reside within their districts. Many of Nkayi's councillors were detained for a week in 1986, and both the Lupane and Nkayi councils were suspended in 1987, and placed under the 'management' of civil servants.[152] DAs continued to come under pressure and criticism for being 'resistant to government policies'.[153]

In Lupane, Zanu(PF) 'councillors' were appointed in 1987, each responsible for several constituencies. These councillors rarely set foot in their wards: 'Their constituency was the office,' remarked Lupane's (Zapu) Council Chairman.[154] Lupane Council Minutes record Zanu(PF) Minister Maurice Nyagumbo's Orwellian justification for the imposition of councillors:

> Since 1981, those who did not support PF Zapu in Matabeleland have been killed, denied drought relief food, denied water supplies and forced to abandon their kraals or seek refuge near police stations and cities. On the contrary, in Mashonaland, PF Zapu supporters are not being killed or harassed. The Minister told the PF Zapu councillors that they were no longer going to go on as councillors. The council is going to be run by Zanu(PF) Councillors and this position is going to continue as long as Zanu(PF) is in power.[155]

A Zapu councillor recalled his interpretation of the same meeting:

> The Zanu Secretary General [Nyagumbo] must not have been happy with Zapu candidates winning. ... It was a very tense atmosphere. At the meeting the Zapus were marginalised. The Zanu's were joyful, [they] filled the room. We smelled a rat. Nyagumbo ... [said,] 'Ever since elections started, Zanu has won straight out. You can't have two bulls in a kraal.' So that is why we were dismissed. 'You go and be councillors of your dissidents,' he told us. So we left. ... Within two weeks,

---

[150] Interview with DA, Nkayi (former DA, Inyathi), Nkayi, 19 December 1994. Also see, Minutes of a Meeting held at the District Council Boardroom to Discuss the Problems Causing the Closure of the District Council Offices, Nkayi, 21 February 1985, File Council General 182, Nkayi, which record descriptions from council staff of their beatings and flight to Bulawayo. The Acting DA, L. Chitawi, who replaced the DA who had been beaten, threatened to withhold their salaries if they did not return to their offices.

[151] In Nkayi, Zapu won 25,874 votes to Zanu(PF)'s 760 and the UANC's 366. There were 1,170 spoilt votes. See Report, 12 July 1985, File: EL/5 Elections (General), Nkayi.

[152] Kusile District Council, 7 September 1987; Nkayi District Council, 17 August 1987; District Development Committee, Nkayi, October 1987. In 1983, the Emergency Powers had been amended to allow the Prime Minister to suspend individual councillors or entire councils. In Matabeleland South, Insiza's council was suspended in 1983 and again in 1987. See Alexander, 'The State, Agrarian Policy and Rural Politics in Zimbabwe', pp. 283–94.

[153] Minutes of a Meeting between DAs and PA, Lupane, 10 December 1985, File: DM 3/85 'District Administrators' Conferences and District Administrators' Minutes from the Permanent Secretary', Nkayi.

[154] Interview with Council Chairman, Lupane, 9 November 1994.

[155] Kusile District Council, 7 September 1987.

[Provincial Governor] Mudenda and the CIO came dressed in combat gear to order my arrest. ... When I got to the cells, I found all the other councillors.[156]

Political conflict and the absence of councillors also severely disrupted the establishment of village development committees (vidcos) in 1984 and 1985. Vidcos, intended to be a lower-level rung of the council, spread at a snail's pace for a number of reasons. Civil servants found it difficult to travel outside the administrative centres due to the threat of attack by dissidents, and constantly complained of shortages of military escorts. Some civil servants were distrusted and had difficulty communicating because they were Shona speakers. This applied particularly to Local Government Promotion Officers (LGPOs), many of whom were former Zanla guerrillas, and who played the sensitive role of introducing the vidcos. People were afraid to be counted for the vidco delineation exercise as they associated being counted for the census in 1982 with the curfew and repression which followed immediately thereafter. People also regularly refused to cooperate with government officials in the absence of their councillors. This latter was a common complaint from LGPOs, and was at once a strategy of non-cooperation, a real indication of people's allegiance to their Zapu leaders, and a sign of fear of reprisals.[157]

In some areas, people interpreted vidcos as a mechanism for Zanu(PF) control. As one councillor commented, 'When the vidcos were formed, we were very suspicious. They were to be part of the Zanu government.'[158] And those who joined the vidco structures were often branded as sellouts. At least one was killed by dissidents.[159] Participating in development projects even where these were popular had become a dangerous exercise.[160] On the other hand, if people did not cooperate, they were accused of siding with dissidents by the government.[161] As a result, people often feared to come forward for any government office: in Kana, where the Fifth Brigade had killed the presiding officer, people recalled, 'it was the ones in positions of authority they wanted. You couldn't be elected after that. You'd shiver and say to yourself, no, I don't want to be elected for anything.'[162] The suspicion of all government initiatives combined with other problems – a lack of staff and finance, constraints on travel – to undermine development during the 1980s.[163] The (not insignificant) development which did take place stood as a testament to the impartial functioning of the line ministries in the context of political turmoil. Nonetheless, the expansion of schools and clinics in the 1980s looked more impressive on paper than on the ground: though their numbers multiplied, they were not always able to function. Perhaps more importantly, they were not perceived as responses to the demands and desires of the Shangani's own people and representatives.

Despite the unity of support for Zapu during elections, developmental initiatives in

---

[156] Interview with Councillor, Menyezwa, 22 January 1996.
[157] See DA G.S. Maphosa to PA, 30 August 1984; DA's monthly reports for 1985, File: Report Gen/85, Nkayi; Nkayi District Development Committee, 4 March 1984, 13 March 1985, File: DDC 1985, Nkayi; G. Nyamawaro, LGPO's Report, March 1985, File: ADF 6/2, Nkayi.
[158] Interview with Councillor, Kwesengulube, 1 December 1995.
[159] Group interview, Lusulu, 26 February 1996.
[160] See, for example, D.B. Ntini, 'Report. Sihlengeni-Gwelutshena Pipe Line', 1 August 1985, File: ADF6/2, Nkayi, which notes the prevasiveness of sell-out accusations against those who co-operated with the pipeline's construction and blames councillors for this.
[161] E.g, interviews with elders, Menyezwa, 24 September 1995; Councillor, Kwesengulube, 1 December 1995.
[162] Interview, Kana, 1 February 1996.
[163] See File: LAN 23, Rural Planning, Dev 82/84, Nkayi; File: Report Gen/85, Nkayi; File: Council General 182, Nkayi; File: DDC 1985, Nkayi, for ample evidence of these problems.

the context of political repression created bitter divisions within communities (as well as among civil servants), a reluctance to stand for any position of authority, and a pervasive discourse of selloutism. These have remained important features of local politics, and constitute a key legacy of the 1980s violence.

## Conclusion: 'Unity First, Solutions Later'

The Unity agreement of December 1987 led to the merger of Zanu(PF) and Zapu under the name Zanu(PF), and finally brought peace to Matabeleland. Negotiations had begun shortly after the 1985 national elections and plodded on for over two years. The obstacles encountered were indicative of what was at stake in the stand-off between the two parties. It was not the composition of a unified leadership which caused discord; it was not ideology or policy which occasioned debate; and nor was it even the violence of the 1980s itself that produced division. From the beginning of the negotiations, it was the unified party's name which stood at the centre of dispute. Zanu(PF) negotiators held from the outset that the unified party should be called Zanu(PF), as Zanu(PF) would continue to constitute the majority. Joshua Nkomo argued it would be difficult to convince his supporters to accept an unmodified name, that it would leave Zapu with no recognition of its lengthy history. Nkomo was reduced to pleading that the brackets which surrounded the PF which followed the name Zanu be changed to a dash. Zanu(PF) refused to budge and Zapu was forced to concede.[164]

The Unity agreement was nonetheless an historic achievement, and one which brought rapid, if not always expected, change. Zanu(PF)'s leaders had expected Unity to open the way for a one-party state. Instead, it brought a flowering of political dissent. The Zimbabwe Unity Movement and other opposition parties emerged on the national political scene; throughout the country, students, trade unions, the media and politicians voiced criticisms of the government.[165] In Matabeleland, however, Unity heralded rather different changes in the political climate.

Despite a great desire for peace, Unity was greeted with deep suspicion in the Shangani. As one of Lupane's veteran nationalists recalled, 'At first we refused. Nkomo told us: "Unity first, solutions later". It was hard for us leaders to tell the people that – after all the killing, they were afraid. [They asked,] "How can we join our enemies?".'[166] Though Unity was accepted, it was an ambiguous acceptance. In practice, Zapu was incorporated as an entity within Zanu(PF). Unity is often described as less than 'real', as subsuming a 'broken and bent' Zapu inside Zanu(PF).[167] Loyalty to Zapu leaders was maintained as was a Zapu identity – people talk of being 'Zapu underneath' or 'Zapu in heart' – and loyalty is cast as an essential feature of Zapu's political culture and of being Ndebele. Nonetheless, former Zapu areas remain some of the safest seats for Zanu(PF). In our many interviews, the possibility of joining an opposition party was never

---

[164] For a fascinating blow by blow account of the negotiations, see W. Chiwewe, 'Unity Negotiations', in C. Banana (ed.), *Turmoil and Tenacity: Zimbabwe 1890-1990* (Harare, College Press, 1989), pp. 242–87.

[165] For a discussion of the politics of Unity and subsequent developments, see J. Moyo, *Voting for Democracy. Electoral Politics in Zimbabwe* (Harare, University of Zimbabwe Publications, 1992); B. Raftopoulos, 'Beyond the House of Hunger: The Struggle for Democratic Development in Zimbabwe', in L. Lauridsen (ed.), *Bringing Institutions Back In: The Role of Institutions in Civil Society, State and Economy* (IDS Occasional Paper No. 8, Roskilde University, 1993); W. Ncube, 'The Post-Unity Period: Developments, Benefits and Problems', in C. Banana (ed.), *Turmoil and Tenacity: Zimbabwe 1890–1990* (Harare, College Press, 1989).

[166] Interview with former Zapu Chairman, Lupanda, 22 December 1994.

[167] Interview with Councillor, Kwesengulube, 1 December 1995.

mooted, and was in fact perceived as traitorous, in large part because of Joshua Nkomo's commitment to the new Zanu(PF). As Nicholas Nkomo commented, 'Ndebeles take time to grapple with a situation, and when they do they won't stop. ... Once they joined [Zanu], they're more Zanu than Zanu, and you find these Zanu splitting all over!'[168]

These contradictions are encapsulated in a popular metaphor used to describe Unity, that of marriage. One former Zapu activist used this metaphor to explain that accepting Unity was more a matter of loyalty than good sense:

> For us, it is in the blood. We have chosen leaders, we are loyal to that person until the end whatever the circumstances and whatever he does, good or bad ... Surely, we are now living under Mugabe's Zanu government, but we are there through marriage, not that we've now switched to Mugabe, but that we followed our leaders loyally into that marriage. But we're still Zapu in that marriage: a woman doesn't lose her maiden name even if she uses her husband's name.[169]

If a Zapu allegiance and identity have survived Unity, so have many of the long-standing Zapu leaders of Nkayi and Lupane. There have of course been losses along the way. Some prominent leaders died or were killed; others have refused to accept the post-Unity order and withdrawn from politics; some have stayed in town in fear of renewed violence; while several of the post-Unity councillors were elected on a development ticket and not by right of their nationalist past. Nonetheless, it was Zapu's nationalist stalwarts who once again dominated the councils of Nkayi and Lupane.

The surviving Zapu veterans, and people more widely, could not, however, return to the status quo ante of 1980. The failure publicly to debate the painful history of the 1980s allowed resentment and fear to prosper. A discussion between a councillor and headman in Lupane aptly illustrates this process. The councillor argued:

> When there is war, there are so many effects. What should have followed was education. The government should have come to say, 'Now the war is finished so let's build the country'. But people didn't understand anything but death. If you tried to gather people for anything, they'd suspect death. They were very seriously damaged psychologically during this violence.

The headman agreed:

> Such issues are never brought up. We're still not free. ... We still can be eliminated at any time. ... This wound is huge and deep. I have young children, but they've never set foot here and don't intend to. ... I'm staying alone like a mad person. There are still barriers. ... The liberation war was painful, but it had a purpose, it was planned, face to face. The war that followed was much worse. It was fearful, unforgettable and unacknowledged.[170]

As we explore in the following chapter, the legacies of the 1980s violence have had a pervasive impact on attitudes to the state, development and ethnicity in the post-Unity period. In the absence of state acknowledgement of the violence, a feeling of alienation from the national body politic pervades Matabeleland. In such a context, it is unsurprising that the tribalist antagonisms fostered during the 1980s continued to prosper, and were regularly invoked as a means of explaining what was firmly believed

---

[168] Interview with Nicholas Nkomo, Nkayi, 10 September 1995.
[169] Discussion, former Lupane MP and Headmaster, 16 September 1995.
[170] Interview with Councillor and headman, Malunku, 6 March 1996.

to be Matabeleland's neglect. Continued fears of persecution and strategies of non-cooperation sat side by side with a broader sense of hurt for wrongs committed and unacknowledged. On a less negative note, local understandings of the source and agents of violence drew on a subtly differentiated understanding of the state, and of the relationship between party and state. The local state as well as service ministries emerged relatively unscathed in popular understandings, allowing for at least the possibility of re-building state legitimacy.

# 10

# *The Politics of Development after Unity*

The Unity agreement of December 1987 raised high hopes for development within Matabeleland. Many in the region expected to be rewarded for accepting Unity, and anticipated a programme of reconstruction to compensate for the years of violence. However, Zanu(PF)'s old guard did not see Unity as cause for reward, save in terms of the incorporation of senior Zapu leaders into government. Nor was the post-Unity context a propitious one in which to meet expectations for state investment. By the late 1980s, the expansion in rural services which had followed independence had long since ended. In the 1990s, state expenditure was restricted under the provisions of Zimbabwe's structural adjustment programmes, and severe drought further stretched state resources. Throughout the country, the state's role in development came under critical scrutiny as the optimism and enthusiasm of independence gave way to resentment of leaders perceived as increasingly corrupt, self-interested and authoritarian.

In this chapter, we discuss development in the post-Unity period and, through three case studies, we explore attitudes toward the central state, local institutions and political leaders. We consider efforts to implement land use planning, conflicts over the attempt to establish a community-based wildlife programme known as Campfire, and attitudes towards state bio-medical services in the context of the exceptionally severe malaria epidemic of 1996. Though the cases are specific ones, they touch on wider issues pertinent to an understanding of the political, economic and ideological forces at work in struggles over rural development. They illustrate the different ways in which the history of the liberation and post-liberation wars, as well as memories of colonial policies and aspirations dating from the evictees' efforts to 'civilize' their new and wild home, affected local attitudes towards the state and development. In none of the three cases were the failures of development unique to Matabeleland. Interpretations did, however, differ. For many people in the Shangani, the legacies of the war years reinforced a conviction that political and ethnic discrimination lay behind developmental neglect. The views of many officials continued to be shaped by the notorious reputation which Matabeleland had gained for belligerence and obstruction of state development in the colonial and post-colonial periods.

Before turning to our case studies, we briefly set out the context of district development in the 1990s.

## The Political and Economic Context of Post-Unity Development

The 1990s ushered in the era of structural adjustment in Zimbabwe, with severe repercussions for state expenditure on developmental initiatives. Central government grants to district councils were drastically cut back and councils struggled to fill a growing funding gap amidst a series of severe droughts.[1] In Nkayi and Lupane, the high expectations for an immediate boom in development after Unity were dis-appointed:[2] the councils' lack of resources created deep frustration and hardened a widespread perception of discrimination and neglect.

The Shangani's councils subsisted on a scant material base. They relied heavily on sales of beer and, particularly, indigenous hardwoods for revenue.[3] The high levels of commercial timber extraction were not, however, sustainable: councils continued to grant concessions into the mid-1990s largely due to the lack of alternative sources of funding.[4] Revenue from beer sales was hard hit in times of drought when rural purchasing power declined. In the series of droughts in the 1980s and early 1990s, large parts of Nkayi and Lupane relied on state-supplied drought relief or grain loans. Frequent entries in council minutes lamented the lack of funds for 'viable projects', the elusiveness of 'development'.[5]

Other sources of revenue, like the collection of household rates, faced political obstacles. Opposition to direct taxation had long been on the nationalist agenda – councillors knew that reintroducing taxes would undermine their popularity and make a mockery of their nationalist promises.[6] In the 1980s, the combination of drought and violence meant rates had only been haphazardly collected.[7] After Unity, anger over the enforcement of rates and other fees provoked deep bitterness in the Shangani, not least among the veteran nationalists. As two such commented with great exasperation: 'We worked so hard for nothing. We have taxes again – dog, bicycle, scotchcart. A scotchcart is 10 dollars, a person is 10 dollars, a dog is five dollars! We have to pay taxes for dogs!' His colleague elaborated: 'I remember when Hunt was still the [District Commissioner, in the colonial period], we asked why we pay tax for a dog – we feed it, we keep it. He

---

[1] The decline in central funding for councils was well underway before the introduction of structural adjustment: central government grants on average comprised over 85% of council budgets in 1980, but had dropped to under 45% by 1986. See J. Petersen, *Campfire: A Zimbabwean Approach to Sustainable Development and Community Empowerment Through Wildlife Utilization* (Harare, CASS, UZ, 1991); A.H.J. Helmsing, 'Rural Local Government Finance. Past Trends and Future Options', in A.H.J. Helmsing *et al.*, *Limits to Decentralization in Zimbabwe: Essays on the Decentralization of Government and Planning in the 1980s* (The Hague, Institute of Social Studies, 1991). For criticisms of council finance in the 1990s, see L. Mhlanga, 'Rural District Councils Financing "New Born Child"', Association of Rural District Councils, 31 May 1994, Lupane DA's Office.

[2] On expectations for development, see, e.g., Nkayi District Council, August 1988.

[3] In Lupane, timber revenues were approximately Z$800,000 to 900,000 per annum, according to estimates provided by the Chief Executive Officer of Kusile District Council. Interview, Lupane, 26 August 1996.

[4] The Nkayi District Council resolved to end all timber concessions in 1987 because 'there is no more timber'; the Forestry Commission recommended cutting back on concessions, warning of depletion, in 1988. The council halted operations in 1989, only to start them up again: though 'timber resources were being mercilessly depleted', ending concessions would lose the district 100 jobs, as well as monthly royalties of around Z$15,000. See Nkayi District Council, 14 June 1987, 19 December 1988, 30 January 1989.

[5] E.g., Kusile District Council, 4 July 1994; Nkayi District Council, 26 November 1990, 24 June 1991, 18 November 1994.

[6] See, e.g., Nkayi District Council, 30 July 1985.

[7] E.g., In the drought year of 1986, no taxes were collected in Nkayi, and in Lupane only Z$1,600 was collected out of an expected (but still paltry) Z$50,000. Kusile District Council, District Development Committee, 4 June 1988.

said, "You are a bank for us. We whites eat from you." ... I remember Hunt's words, and I look at what is happening here.'[8] Many councillors were themselves less than meticulous in paying their taxes, and in collecting those of others: lists of defaulting councillors appeared in council minutes; regular calls were made for councillors to 'motivate' and 'mobilize' people to pay.[9] Councillors proved ineffective tax collectors for other reasons as well – it was near impossible for them to travel the length and breadth of their wards in search of defaulters.

The political and logistical obstacles facing councillors led them to turn to the tax collectors of the colonial period. The Nkayi council called for headmen and kraalheads to register all ratepayers and to take action against defaulters from 1990 while the Lupane council offered kraalheads financial incentives to perform this unpopular duty at the rate of 10 per cent of every Z$500 collected.[10]

Councillors throughout the country had hoped that the tax base of their districts would be expanded with the implementation of the Rural District Councils Act of 1988. The Act provided for the amalgamation of the Rural Councils (which served the former 'European', now 'large-scale commercial', farming areas) with the District Councils (serving African communal and small-scale commercial farming areas) under new unitary Rural District Councils. However, hopes of an expanded tax base were not realized when the Act was finally implemented in the mid-1990s. The Nkayi Rural District Council gained control over a resettlement area (against the wishes of the settlers), but not over any commercial farming areas. In Lupane, the commercial farmers of the Gwaai Valley Rural Council voted unanimously to leave Lupane District, preferring to join the much larger community of commercial farmers in neighbouring Hwange. Councillors in Lupane, well aware of the financial repercussions, unsuccessfully tried to mount a legal challenge to the commercial farmers' departure.

The councils' inadequate financial base deeply undermined their autonomy and reputation. In Lupane, all council vehicles were sold in 1992, leaving council officers with no independent means of transport; delayed payments from timber concessionaires led to delayed payment of council employees' salaries. In this context of dearth and demoralization, development depended ever more on the resources, interests and vision of government ministries and foreign donors. The central ministries had always held a powerful position with regard to councils: efforts to decentralize power to provincial and district levels, instituted from the mid-1980s, had proved ineffective, largely due to the maintenance of financial control and technical expertise at head offices. Reports from lower levels were bitterly sarcastic about the rhetoric of decentralization. Matabeleland North's Provincial Administrator wrote that the problem with provincial planning was that it was wholly ignored – instead, projects funded through line ministries and donors 'mushroom haphazardly'. The Provincial

---

[8] Interview with Paul Mapetshwana Moyo and Paul Sibanda, Gampinya, 19 October 1995.

[9] E.g., see Nkayi District Council, 21 August 1989, 25 June 1990, 26 January 1990. In Lupane, the overwhelming majority of councillors were issued with notices of dismissal in 1996 because they had not paid their taxes, let alone collected them from others, despite repeated threats from the Ministry of Local Government. Ministry of Local Government, Rural and Urban Development, Minute of 19 February 1996, announced the future disqualification of councillors in arrears of council rates.

[10] Kusile District Council, 6 February 1996; Nkayi District Council, 14 May 1990, 24 June 1991. Also see continued discussions, casting kraalheads and headmen in an increasingly punitive role in Nkayi District Council, 17 June 1994. At the time of our research, kraalheads were once again armed with the 'books' of taxpayers which had been the source of their title 'sabhuku' in the colonial period. Elsewhere in Zimbabwe, kraalheads had been coopted by councils to collect taxes even earlier. See Alexander, 'The State, Agrarian Policy and Rural Politics in Zimbabwe', pp. 336–43.

Governor argued that 'provincial plans are nothing but a waste of man hours' due to the government's 'top down approach'.[11] Provincial planners queried whether there was a way legally to avoid planning altogether; they condemned planning as the 'most difficult and frustrating activity', and the plans themselves as '"Tiger Documents" that continuously decorate our shelves without the slightest chance of implementation.'[12]

Resentment over the failures of decentralization was expressed countrywide.[13] In Matabeleland it was compounded by the expectations that followed Unity and the powerful perception of past and present neglect and discrimination. The popular perception of discrimination – voiced in beerhalls, homes and meetings throughout the Shangani – was mirrored by officials. Post-Unity provincial plans noted that Matabeleland 'lagged well behind other Provinces' due to the 'security situation' of the 1980s, and that this 'imbalance' had not been redressed.[14] Complaints were regularly voiced in provincial council meetings. In an angry debate over the lack of government action with regard to water shortage in Matabeleland, then deeply aggravated by severe drought, Nkayi's council chairman maintained: 'In terms of government policy, there is no precise reason why other regions are more developed than Matabeleland ... The big question which the Ministers across the government spectrum need to answer is WHY SO?' A civil servant added, 'It appears there is no obligation on the part of government to effect equal regional development.'[15]

The careful wording of the provincial council minutes hid the more popular interpretation of neglect as a product of ethnic discrimination. Ethnic interpretations in rural Matabeleland drew on memories of the Fifth Brigade's explicitly tribal and political attacks. People had often expected Shona-speaking officials and Zanu(PF) 'sellouts' to be removed after Unity. Many were not, and Shona-speaking civil servants working at district level were seen as the most proximate embodiment of a discriminatory central government strategy. They were often treated with suspicion and contempt and were commonly criticized for benefiting from a nepotistic government which denied equal opportunity to 'the Ndebele'.[16] Local people bantered – at times acrimoniously – with Shona-speaking officials, using mutually derogatory ethnic labels ('amasvina' or 'dirt' for Shona and 'amadzviti' or 'raiders' for Ndebele). Shona-speaking officials stationed in Matabeleland shortly after Unity feared leaving their homes or talking to people, thinking everyone a dangerous dissident.[17] Encounters with

---

[11] Minutes of the One Day District Planning Workshop held at Tsholotsho DDF Training Centre, n.d. [c. 1990], File: District Development Plans, Lan/22/84, PA's Office, Bulawayo.

[12] Provincial Planning Officer to PA, Bulawayo, 2 November 1990; 'Review of Development Programmes and Development Planning: In Matabeleland North Province', n.d. [c. 1990], File: Matabeleland North Provincial Development Plan, Lan/22/86, PA's Office, Bulawayo.

[13] See Alexander, 'The State, Agrarian Policy and Rural Politics', pp. 165–78.

[14] *Matabeleland North Provincial Five Year Development Plan, 1990-1995* (Bulawayo, Provincial Development Committee, 1991), p. 2.

[15] Minutes of the First Provincial Council 1993 Meetings, Elangeni Public Service National Training Centre, 29 November 1993, Provincial Council Committee, Minutes of Meetings, DMN/ZPC, PA's Office, Bulawayo. This debate took place at a time when water shortage in Matabeleland was hotly debated, notably by the high profile Matabeleland Zimbabwe Water Project Trust, then fronted by Minister Dumiso Dabengwa and Provincial Governor J.B. Maseko, and tasked with studying the possibility of establishing a pipeline from the Zambezi to Bulawayo.

[16] The Nkayi council was accused of trying to dismiss all Shona speakers from its District Development Fund workshop in 1994, though the council chairman argued it was merely seeking 'clarification of the D.D.F. policy of creating employment for locals'. Nkayi District Council, 18 November 1994. Whichever was the case, popular views with regard to hiring Shona speakers were decidedly negative.

[17] Forestry officer, personal communication, 1997.

locals who angrily held them – as Shona – collectively responsible for the violence of the past, reinforced such notions.[18] Some officials were accused of arrogantly refusing even to try to speak Ndebele – they travelled the districts with interpreters, addressing community meetings in English through a translator. Rather than breaking down exclusive notions of other built through the years of conflict, these exchanges reinforced ideas of difference. They enhanced perceptions of a discriminatory 'Shona' government on the one hand and of irrational, destructive and stubborn opposition as part of a 'Ndebele' character on the other. Needless to say, such a context was far from propitious for development.

Criticism was not, however, reserved solely for those conceived of as outsiders. The councillors – people with years of service in Zapu – also came in for harsh criticism. The failure to deliver development came to be blamed at least in part on their corruption and self-interest. Unlike central government officials, councillors lived among and interacted with their constituents on a daily basis. It was incumbent on them to try to justify and promote development initiatives, as well as to defend the many inevitable delays and failures. Councillors' electoral campaigning depended not only on an invocation of nationalist history, but also on (often exaggerated) promises of development. When development did not materialize, people accused councillors of 'eating' funds, whether or not such funds actually existed. As one man put it, 'You know this small blue bird that makes its nest from other birds' feathers? That is a councillor!'[19]

The context for development after Unity was thus marked by severe financial constraints on local institutions and priorities dictated by ministries and donors, by tense and suspicious relationships between local communities and officials, and by a pervasive perception of neglect and discrimination. On the part of the former Zapu councillors, provincial and district authorities, it was also marked by an adherence to authoritarian modernization, on the same model as that promoted by Zanu(PF) throughout the country. Below, we turn to several specific policies promoted in this context.

## Land Use Planning Revisited

By the time peace returned to Matabeleland, state development programmes had undergone a major shift from the populist ethic of redistribution of the early years of independence. With regard to agrarian policy, land redistribution had been greatly scaled down, and much emphasis was instead placed on a programme of 'internal' resettlement within the communal areas.[20] The Communal Area Reorganization Programme in essence replicated the Land Husbandry reforms of the 1950s. It involved a spatial reorganization of the communal areas, separating arable from grazing land and concentrating settlement through a programme of villagization. The programme was top-down in its formulation, and technocratic in its implementation requirements.

The resurrection of unpopular policies was justified in official circles by arguing that colonial land use planning failed not because of its technical flaws, but because of its political context.[21] To the extent that councillors endorsed land use planning, they used

---

[18] While trying to investigate poaching in forest areas, one Shona speaking researcher visiting from Harare was threatened with an axe by a woman who angrily accused him of killing her sons. He decided to choose another study area outside Matabeleland. Personal communication, 1997.

[19] Interview with Paul Mapetshwana Moyo, Gampinya, 19 October 1995.

[20] See J. Alexander, 'State, Peasantry and Resettlement in Zimbabwe', *Review of African Political Economy*, 61, 1994, pp. 325–45; M. Drinkwater, 'Technical Development and Peasant Impoverishment: Land Use Policy in Zimbabwe's Midlands Province', *Journal of Southern African Studies*, 15, 2, 1989, pp. 287–305.

[21] Alexander, 'State, Peasantry and Resettlement', p. 332.

a not dissimilar logic: they reinterpreted their own colonial era stance as political, while emphasizing the importance and benefits of 'modern' development, defined in colonial terms. Nkayi's former council chairman, now the Provincial Governor, even argued for working through the young who would not remember the resistance of the colonial period.[22] Some councillors found new reasons to back land use planning, seeking to use it as a basis for evicting 'squatters' from areas designated as grazing land, and for controlling untaxed timber felling.[23] Certainly, the constant reiterations of the importance of land use planning by officials and senior political figures swayed some councillors into at least tacit – and sometimes enthusiastic – agreement. In the first post-Unity council meetings, the Provincial Governor put Communal Area Reorganization and villagization top of the list of the councils' 'areas of development challenge', reflecting the priorities of senior ministerial officials.[24]

Not all councillors were, however, convinced of the merits of land use planning. Some objected vehemently to the lack of a link to land redistribution, and the displacement within communal areas that would result.[25] These and other objections were often raised at local levels, but they met with little sympathy from officials who (again like their pre-independence predecessors) regularly cast objectors as self-interested, simply anti-government, or steeped in irrational beliefs. Such characterizations were, however, far off the mark, much as they had been in the colonial period: resistance to land use planning was more than simply stubborn obstruction or a backward-looking rejection of 'modern' development. Rather, land use planning had immediate costs which were perceived to outweigh potential future benefits – benefits which were often at any rate perceived as the province of particular individuals or groups, or the council, rather than the wider community.

Despite the primacy of Communal Area Reorganization in ministerial and council development priorities from the mid-1980s, little or no progress was made in the subsequent decade. In Lupane, the government agricultural extension services (Agritex) had only begun to plan five of the district's 23 wards by 1996. Even this achievement had been dependent on considerable outside support from the FAO and a Dutch Planning Institute.[26] In Nkayi, work had begun on three wards, but progress on the

---

[22] Interview with Provincial Governor Welshman Mabhena, Bulawayo, 27 October 1994.

[23] The Nkayi Council repeatedly called on Agritex, the Department of Physical Planning, the Natural Resources Board and the police in an effort to enforce what it considered to be land use plans, though these were not officially regarded as such. Its failures in this regard led to a long drawn out process of trying to implement land use by-laws so as to give the council added coercive power. See Nkayi District Council, 16 February 1987, 30 September 1991, 25 November 1991, 27 January 1992, 29 June 1992, 3 August 1992, 28 September 1992, 18 June 1993, 19 November 1993, 3 February 1995, 25 August 1995.

[24] Kusile/Tsholotsho District Councils, Minutes of Joint Meeting on Governor's Programme, 23 August 1988; Minutes of the Governor's Meeting held at Nkayi District Council, 22 August 1988. See also address by Minister of Local Government E.C. Chikowore, Association of District Councils, Fifth Annual Congress, Record of Proceedings, 8-10 February 1989.

[25] See objections raised by council representatives in Association of District Councils, 'Minutes of the Third Annual Congress', Kariba, 15-17 October 1986.

[26] The FAO project, intended to strengthen Agritex's capacity, had been instrumental in the planning of one ward, but had also brought problems due to differences in survey methods, data collection, and techniques for describing farming systems and zones. See 'Land Use Plans (village)', FAO, File F/28/1, Agritex, Lupane; 'FAO Programme of Assistance to Agritex Zim/91/005'; E.P. Goto and L.S. Dube, 'Implementation of the Development Sequence. The Field Experience of Gokwe and Lupane Districts', Internal Review Workshop, 11–12 November, 1993. Two further wards had been planned with Dutch assistance but similar problems had occurred and the first plan had to be re-done.

ground was slow due to a lack of resources and local opposition. Agritex officials stated that part of the problem was the village boundaries they were working with. These had been drawn by LGPOs in the mid-1980s, at the height of the violence, largely in the district offices. They often left villages with no arable land, or no grazing land, whatsoever.[27]

Such inertia was characteristic of the country as a whole. The national Land Tenure Commission report of 1994 explained the lack of progress in terms of the 'over-centralisation of government with the relevant technical ministries using top-down methods of planning and implementation', coupled with high short-term costs and risks, and poor coordination between ministries. Like its Rhodesian predecessor, land use planning was extremely costly in terms of resources (which often proved un-available) as well as technical officers' time (which was often in demand elsewhere). There were few incentives for communal area farmers to participate, and good reason for opposition: 'In some areas, the commission could not understand or see how people could be reorganized without many losing current land rights. … The villagers are therefore strongly suspicious of this programme and it will be difficult to implement the programme under the present framework.' The Commission recommended that Communal Area Reorganization be re-linked to land redistribution and that planning be further decentralized.[28]

The Commission's recommendations did not, however, filter down to district levels. Councils, officials and donors maintained their commitment to – and faith in – land use planning: 'We need proposals for land-use planning, we feel it's critical for everything, we need plans for everything,' enthused Lupane's Projects Officer.[29] Nkayi and Lupane's councils tried to overcome popular resistance by linking land-use planning to other donor-funded projects, such as the water and sanitation project, a sizeable pro-gramme to be financed by the British government. They also proved increasingly ready to adopt an authoritarian stance.

It is to one such attempt to link land use planning with other investments that we now turn. The Jotsholo Pilot Conservation Project, funded by NORAD, provided the only example within the two districts of a ward land use plan which had begun to be implemented.[30] The project received considerable publicity and was portrayed as a 'success' on Zimbabwean Television. The council hoped it would provide an encourag-ing demonstration to other wards of the benefits of land use planning and conservation. At least one other councillor, having seen the extensive funds poured into the project – Z$1,700,000 for 98 kilometres of fencing, boreholes, small dams, workshops and meetings – claimed that the people of his ward were 'demanding that land use planning be implemented with utmost urgency'.[31] However, the lessons of the Jotsholo pilot were ambiguous. The debates and conflicts which it provoked illustrated the broader problems of land use planning discussed above, as well as issues particular to Matabeleland, notably the effects of the fearful legacy of the 1980s, and historical memories of nationalist resistance to imposed development.

The Jotsholo pilot scheme was initiated in 1986, before the Unity agreement had been signed and while many councillors were still in detention. It may be significant that Jotsholo ward was alone in being represented by a councillor who had joined and

[27] Interview with N. Dube, Cartographical Section, Agritex, Nkayi, 26 August 1996.
[28] *Report of the Commission of Inquiry into Appropriate Agricultural Land Tenure Systems. Volume One: Main Report,* Chaired by Professor M. Rukuni, pp. 35–6, 53.
[29] Interview, Projects Officer, Kusile District Council, Lupane, 27 August 1996.
[30] This section is based on the minutes of the Jotsholo Pilot Conservation Scheme, and the minutes of the Kusile District Council's conservation committee, full council, and development com-mittee meetings.
[31] Kusile District Council, 25 March 1991.

actively supported Zanu(PF) before the Unity agreement. The tense circumstances of the pre-Unity period undoubtedly contributed to the lack of objections documented at early meetings. The project started with a pilot workshop at ward level, followed by 'conservation awareness' workshops in each of the ward's six vidcos. Plans were made and 'approved' for each village. They included proposals for water development, gulley reclamation, woodlots, fenced grazing schemes, the relocation of fields, and villagization. Implementation of the land use plan was to be the first step. It required the relocation within the ward of a full 245 families. Records noted that the 'project started with full consent of locals', but there was in fact bitter opposition to such movement.[32] Officials were eventually forced to drop the demand for resettlement almost entirely.

This was not the end of the project's problems. Boundary disputes soon proliferated as a result of efforts to define the limits of, and to fence, the grazing areas of each village, and the borders with the communities of adjacent wards. Once again, proposals 'approved' at meetings where people did not speak out were no indication of full agreement. The Council Projects Officer noted: 'Plans are only the first stage. … As we saw from the Jotsholo project, a lot of problems can emerge even after the document is approved – boundary problems and the like. … There are problems of impounding cattle, there have been some scuffles.'[33] Defining the boundaries of grazing lands and mobilizing labour for fencing proved time consuming and divisive. Those without cattle were reluctant to work on fencing as they would not benefit directly from so doing. Disputes erupted between absentee owners of sizeable herds and locals.[34]

Opposition was also shaped by memories of colonial paddocking schemes, schemes which had been imposed despite a rhetoric of community participation. As one disgruntled farmer explained, the Jotsholo project was 'an old scheme, initiated by whites. I remember … that system of paddocks. It's not a new thing'. He argued that, just as the chief's word had allowed objections to be overridden in the colonial period, so too with the current project:

> When the chief had approved that thing, no one had any choice. Things were done for us and we were then told. We had little option to say anything. Now also we are moving with our eyes shut. Someone else is seeing for us … Village lines are an old plan, we discuss that every meeting, but we don't want it. What is prepared in a plan, we'll agree, good or bad. If you refuse you'll be expelled. It's just the same as the colonial plans.[35]

Faced with opposition to the 'approved' plans, the local councillor advocated force. As the project minutes record, he 'advised that technocrats should not listen to individuals but go as per their maps. If that means going over somebody's house just do it …' The party district chairman, DA and other officials supported his view, and voiced surprise at the degree of opposition. They were 'depressed by statements of boundary disputes' which had supposedly been resolved seven years previously: 'where is the mess now coming from?' bemused project officials asked.[36]

By far the most serious dispute the project provoked was between Jotsholo ward where the project was based and adjacent Menyezwa ward which had lost substantial grazing land as well as fields to the project. The council Projects Officer argued that, 'Resettlement is the solution. We can't say to the donors, no we made a mistake and

---

[32] Natural Resources Officer, quoted in Kusile District Council, 10 March 1988.

[33] Interview with Projects Officer, Kusile District Council, 27 August 1996.

[34] Interview with C. Mkwananzi, Jotsholo, 2 February 1996; Minutes, Jotsholo Pilot Conservation Project, 15 September 1994.

[35] Group interview, Gondo, Jotsholo, 2 February 1996.

[36] Minutes, Jotsholo Pilot Conservation Project, 15 September 1994.

took Menyezwa's grazing land.'[37] Others argued that resettlement was justified on conservationist grounds as the ward was 'so eroded'.[38] Faced with the loss of their grazing land and fields, people in Menyezwa turned to resistance. They contacted the press, and continued to use what they regarded as their land. They drove cattle onto 'project' land and objected when they were impounded; they cut fencing; and rumours circulated that they had started a series of forest fires in the contested area. They spoke of the betrayal of the promises of independence, the need to resort once again to violence. The councillor of the aggrieved ward explained:

> Now we are fighting for our freedom again. ... We are planting and grazing our stock by force – if they lock the gates in the fence, we'll cut the wire. We have no other land. We are all Zimbabweans. ... [W]e don't want to be resettled, we want our grazing area. Now we are stateless. ... NORAD said the project is to be for everyone. But now that NORAD has poured the money in, the Jotsholo people say, 'No, it's our project'. ... There is a lot of hatred. ... I castigate NORAD for dividing people who once lived joyfully together.[39]

Councillors, district and provincial officials as well as party office holders also came in for harsh criticism.

Given the alignment of powerful interests within the district, it was unclear whether Menyezwa's loss of grazing land would be reversed. The council, the district party structures, as well as government officials all had an interest in the success of the project: it had brought publicity to development work within the district, and had received significant donor investment. Though the project had brought benefits and prestige to some, for others it was perceived as tantamount to the top-down, technical planning schemes of the Rhodesian era. It had created insecurity and fear, and raised the prospect of eviction once again for communities who had been forcibly displaced time and again. Some of the problems the project encountered were typical of comparable efforts elsewhere. They were rooted in conflicting interests between villages, between cattle-owners and the cattle-less, between those absent in town and those resident locally, between those inside and those outside the project. But in the context of Matabeleland, the elevated fear of speaking out in public meetings in the wake of the violence of the 1980s enhanced the problem of trying to secure 'participation'. For those outside the project boundaries, the threat of eviction provoked a confrontational stance which drew on the rhetoric of the liberation war and appealed to the inclusive goals of nationalism.

Such dynamics marred other development initiatives as well, as we explore below.

## Campfire[40]

Campfire, the Communal Areas Management Programme for Indigenous Resources, was developed as a means of overcoming the legacies of the colonial era development

---

[37] Projects Officer, quoted in Kusile District Council, 27 August 1996. Historical arguments were also drawn upon to justify the proposed relocation: in the 1960s, Chief Menyezwa, then resident in the currently dispossessed ward, had moved to the settlement frontier in the north of the district and his followers were given the choice of moving or staying, with those remaining to fall under Chief Mabhikwa in Jotsholo ward. In discussions over the project, it was argued that the people of Menyezwa ward should follow their chief.

[38] Interview with Mr Jubane, MP for Lupane, 3 February 1996.

[39] Interview with Petrus Ndlovu, Menyezwa, 22 January 1996.

[40] For a more detailed consideration of the Campfire initiative in Nkayi and Lupane, see J. Alexander and J. McGregor, 'Wildlife and Politics: Campfire in Zimbabwe', *Development and Change*, 31, 3, 2000.

initiatives which Communal Area Reorganization essentially replicated. It was intended to reverse the impact of programmes which focused on technical prescription and coercive implementation and which undermined people's control over their environment, in this case particularly wildlife.[41] Campfire has been hailed internationally for its participatory approach and its innovative strategies for confronting the developmental and conservation problems of some of the most marginal rural areas. In the Shangani, however, Campfire quickly gained a totally different reputation. By the mid-1990s, mention of Campfire was enough to provoke threats of violence from the residents of the Gwampa valley in which the project was based. Councillors associated with the project were afraid to travel to the valley, police monitored meetings and detained protesters, and angry exchanges were recorded in the press. Before exploring the causes of this bitter impasse, let us first take a brief look at debates over Campfire more widely.

Two years after independence, the legal basis for Campfire was laid through an amendment to the Parks and Wildlife Act which allowed councils to apply for 'appropriate authority' status and gave them the right to exploit wildlife and other natural resources within their jurisdiction. Between 1988 and the end of 1989, a full 11 district councils signed up for Campfire. These projects encountered a range of problems and by the early 1990s had given rise to much debate. Debate focused on the appropriate way to define and organize the beneficiary 'community',[42] the long-term economic viability of the projects in the absence of donor funding,[43] and the efficacy of the 'empowerment' aspects of Campfire.[44] Most commentators stressed economic solutions to these problems. They argued that if local communities became 'stakeholders' in wildlife, conservationist attitudes towards game, and a basis for institution-building, would follow.[45] Some argued that financial returns alone would deliver the desired changes in attitude and practice.[46]

[41] Colonial laws had effectively classified Africans' use of game as poaching. See J. Mackenzie, 'Chivalry, Social Darwinism and Ritualized Killing: The Hunting Ethos in Central Africa up to 1914', in R. Grove and D. Anderson (eds), *Conservation in Africa: People, Policies and Practice* (Cambridge, Cambridge University Press, 1987), pp. 56–7. Discussions of the history and objectives of Campfire can be found in, *inter alia*, Environmental Consultants, *People, Wildlife and Natural Resources – The Campfire Approach to Rural Development in Zimbabwe* (Zimbabwe Trust, DNPWM and Campfire Association, Harare, 1990), pp. 5–6; R.B. Martin, 'Communal Areas Management Programme for Indigenous Resources (CAMPFIRE)', Working Document 1/86 (DNPWM, Harare, 1986).

[42] See S.J. Thomas, 'The Legacy of Dualism and Decision-Making: The Prospects for Local Institutional Development in "Campfire"', Harare, CASS, 1991; J. Murombedzi, 'Decentralizing Common Property Resource Management: A Case Study of Nyaminyami District Council of Zimbabwe's Wildlife Management Programme', *Dry Land Networks Programme*, International Institute for Environment and Development, London, Paper No. 30, 1991; B. Child and J.H. Peterson, *Campfire in Rural Development: The Beitbridge Experience* (Harare, CASS and DNPWM, 1991).

[43] See Murombedzi, 'Decentralizing Common Property Resource Management', pp. 14–15.

[44] Some have argued that Campfire had the potential to re-centralize state authority, and to extend state power to remote areas. J. Murombedzi, *Decentralization or Recentralization? Implementing Campfire in the Omay Communal Lands of Nyaminyami District* (Harare, CASS, 1992); K. Hill, 'Zimbabwe's Wildlife Utilization Programs: Grassroots Democracy or an Extension of State Power?', *African Studies Review*, 39, 1, 1996, pp. 103–19.

[45] Thomas, 'The Legacy of Dualism and Decision-Making'; Environmental Consultants, *People, Wildlife and Natural Resources*; Murombedzi, 'Decentralizing Common Property Resource Management'.

[46] Child and Peterson, *Campfire in Rural Development*, p. 67. Murombedzi, *Decentralization or Recentralization?*, p. 41, provides an excellent critique of the idea that 'cash is the best extension agent'.

However, the assumption that people's hostility to wildlife – historically and at present – lay principally in their exclusion from its economic benefits was deeply problematic in the Shangani. The colonial period had not only been about the exclusion of Africans from the benefits of game; attitudes towards game were (and are) based on much more than economic calculation. As explored in earlier chapters, the Rhodesian government's tsetse clearance programme had involved the large-scale slaughter of game and employed large numbers of the early settlers of the Shangani. While certain aspects of the programme were resented, there were significant benefits: 'big men' established themselves by converting their wealth in game meat into wives and, as the tsetse belt was driven north, into cattle.

Exclusion from game and discriminatory legislation were not the sole or even the most important features of early settlers' memories of wildlife – nor were they the most prominent feature of the accounts of the evictees of the 1940s and 1950s. The modernizing, cattle-holding evictees saw the Shangani's natural environment as dangerous and uncivilized. For them, the clearing of game was both a necessity for stock rearing, and an important part of 'taming' a wild place. The people of the Shangani as a whole committed themselves to cattle husbandry and agricultural production, and they preferred it to wildlife management.[47] People's productive aspirations had long been shaped by their ideas about modernity, by a desire to leave behind a life of 'suffering in the bush with wild animals'. Game was associated with the primitive and backward, with neglect and hardship. In addition, attitudes to land were powerfully influenced by colonial evictions, and the belief that the liberation war had been fought to right these past wrongs. The notion that the land had been stolen from its rightful owners was much more strongly developed than any comparable notion of lost proprietorship over game.[48]

These attitudes to game, land and development were important in shaping the fate of the Gwampa Valley Campfire project; so too were institutional factors. In this case, as in other Campfire projects, the district councils played a crucial role: as the 'appropriate authority' they were responsible for negotiating an agreement with 'producer communities' regarding the management of, and division of benefits from, wildlife and other natural resources. The councils had also to negotiate agreements with third parties – in this case, the Forestry Commission, foreign donors, and the central government. The attitudes of councillors in the Shangani were shaped by their desire to deliver development following Unity, and by the extreme economic constraints of the period. With intense pressure on councils to find alternative sources of income, and with the demands of councillors' constituents for development, Campfire and its attendant donor funding appeared a Godsend. These pressures helped to explain why councillors with a long nationalist history of opposing eviction and coercive state development embraced a programme which involved eviction, and have advocated coercion as a means of overriding opposition.

Of course, the councillors did not operate in a vacuum. They were strongly influenced by the attitudes and advice of the technical officers who dominated the district development committees, as well as by the interests of the Forestry Commission and donors. The Commission held jurisdiction over the Gwampa and Lake Alice forests, which were to form the southern half of the Campfire area. Its interests lay not in the development of the communal areas, but in establishing a buffer zone around its

---

[47] This is also the case elsewhere. On Gokwe, see J. Peterson, *CAMPFIRE: A Zimbabwean Approach to Sustainable Development and Community Empowerment through Wildlife Utilization* (Harare, CASS, 1991), p. 52. On Binga, see E. Madzudzo and V. Dzingirai, 'A Comparative Study of the Implications of Ethnicity on Campfire in Bulilimamangwe and Binga' (Harare, CASS, 1995).

[48] Child and Peterson, *Campfire in Rural Development*, pp. 73–4, also note the weakly developed sense of ownership of game, but they see it as a product of colonial era game regulations.

forests and curbing the poaching of game and other resources. Donors wielded tremendous influence by right of their control over resources. As in the case of the NORAD-funded conservation project, their endorsement of, and decision to fund and supply staff for the Gwampa project, granted it a momentum it would otherwise have lacked.

These various actors sought to intervene in an area in which people not only did not value game *per se*, but which also had a long history of insecure tenure and conflict with the Forestry Commission. Many Gwampa residents had been evicted not once, but several times, including being forced out of Forestry Commission land in the 1930s and again in the 1970s.[49] Those moved felt tricked by the Forestry Commission and nursed a bitter sense of betrayal.[50] Even people living within the communal area side of the Gwampa had not escaped forced movement from the valley in the 1950s and 1960s. The Gwampa game and bird sanctuary initiatives of the 1970s, discussed in previous chapters, convinced many that introducing game and depriving people of land went hand in hand.

During the liberation war and in its aftermath, large numbers of people had moved into the state forests once again, encouraged by Zipra and Zapu. People expected their occupation to be sanctioned by the new government. However, it was only the conflicts of the 1980s which (largely) prevented the Forestry Commission from taking action against them. After Unity, the Commission launched 'a new kind of war, a war waged ... against forest occupants ...', and forest neighbours, who come into the forest to collect minor forest products such as thatching grass or to hunt small game animals to meet their subsistence needs.'[51] In Lupane's forest areas, people speak of the 'forest war' which followed the 'dissident war'. The Forestry Commission adopted the view that all occupants should be removed from its land.[52] In the course of evictions, homes and grain stores were burnt and people were beaten. Lengthy and acrimonious negotiations between the Forestry Commission and Lupane's councillors and MPs who tried to prevent evictions had reached an uncomfortable impasse by 1995: evictions were delayed, but remained a constant threat. In the meantime, people in the forest areas were denied the right to exploit any natural resources, were prohibited from repairing or improving homes and schools, and had their grazing land drastically reduced.[53]

It was in this context that the Gwampa Valley Campfire programme, a joint endeavour of the Forestry Commission and the councils of Nkayi and Lupane, was introduced. It followed in the footsteps not only of the failed bird and animal sanctuary initiatives of the 1970s, but also the more recent rejection of yet another wildlife project. In 1989, Gwampa residents had 'vehemently turned down' this latest proposal, arguing that they 'can't reside with animals in their midst'.[54] But the Campfire project developed a greater momentum than its predecessors. This was in part due to the funding pledged (though not secured) by the Canadian International Development Agency (CIDA) and the central government. The Danish NGO, MS-Zimbabwe, had also, since 1993,

---

[49] G. Judge (ed.), 'The Kalahari Sands Forests of Rhodesia: Management Report', Forestry Commission, Harare, 1975, Chapter 2, p. 3 and Chapter 6, p. 4; F. Matose and J. Clarke, 'Who is the Guardian of the Indigenous Forests?', Forestry Commission, Harare, 1993.

[50] Interview with Musa Dube, Aaron Dube and Ken Moyo, Mtupane, Lake Alice Ward, Lupane, 19 February 1996.

[51] Matose and Clarke, 'Who is the Guardian of the Indigenous Forests?', p. 15.

[52] See discussion in Matose and Clarke, 'Who is the Guardian of the Indigenous Forests', pp. 15–16. The Forestry Commission came up with alternative solutions, such as the resettlement of occupants of state forests, the redesignation of certain state lands as communal land, and resource sharing schemes. These were not, however, implemented.

[53] Interviews, Ilihlo, 29 March 1996; Masungamala, 7 February 1996.

[54] Kusile District Council, Conservation Committee, 2 October 1989.

provided support in terms of personnel and vehicles, largely for educational and training purposes. The councils were impressed by the large sums of money involved, and the project appealed to donors and councillors alike for its promise of development and conservation: it envisaged stocking the Gwampa Valley with wildlife (little in the way of big game inhabited the area) that would attract photo safaris. The Campfire project appealed to the Forestry Commission in part because it involved moving substantial numbers of valley residents out of a strip of land running the valley's length, measuring 1.5 to 2 kilometres from the river itself.[55] This boundary would then be fenced so that game could move freely between the Forestry Commission's lands and the water sources of the valley. The fence would also go some way to solving the Commission's problems with incursions from the communal areas.

In the rush to agree to the Gwampa Campfire proposal, only cursory discussions took place at the local level – and reports of total support were recorded.[56] Later, however, local communities adamantly rejected the project at meeting after meeting. By the time of our fieldwork in 1994 and 1995, Campfire had become an explosive issue.

The view propounded by many (though not all) councillors, and the civil servants who supported them, was that the project was an unmitigated good that would bring vast wealth to the districts and provide a means for achieving real development. The Provincial Governor, the two DAs and the chief executive officers of the councils were ardently committed to the project and dismissive of objections. Nkayi's DA classed resistance as the work of a handful of troublemakers, people who were politically ambitious, or absentee cattle owners who were threatened by the loss of water sources and grazing in the valley. He was quoted in the local press as attributing opposition to 'only seven troublesome villagers' who were resident in Bulawayo and were 'busy discouraging villagers because they wanted cheap labour from the local communities'.[57] Executive officers and DAs argued that development was necessarily coercive, and that obstructive minorities should not hold back entire districts. The Provincial Governor asserted that people in the valley were backward and had nothing to lose because they lived in 'grass huts'.[58]

The views of those who lived in the valley could not have been more different. They drew on historical arguments which likened the current initiative to the most hated of colonial interventions. Campfire was regularly cast as a betrayal of the promises of independence, and resistance to it as an attempt to preserve a hard-won 'civilized' existence. The prospect of eviction under the project caused grave concern, and raised memories of past evictions and the unmet promises of land made in the liberation war. In Mtupane, people argued: 'Land is what we fought the war for. Squatters are clamouring for land. The government says no land is available, but there is this land for animals.'[59] The prospect of movement created extreme anger and distrust. Campfire was described as 'another gukura', a reference to the violent conflict of the 1980s.[60]

The costs of movement were high. Schools, clinics, roads and boreholes were within the area to be vacated, in addition to many homes, and would have to be rebuilt. Based on prior experiences of eviction, people did not trust the government to compensate them for their individual and community investments. The threat of eviction discouraged

---

[55] Whereas the Nkayi valley population would be moved out of the valley bottom up onto the watershed, Lupane's affected settlements would be moved to an (as yet) unidentified place due to land shortage.

[56] E.g., see Nkayi District Council, 17 June 1994, 18 November 1994.

[57] *Indonsakusa Ilanga*, 8 September 1995.

[58] Cited in *The Chronicle* in mid-January 1995.

[59] Interview with kraalheads and others, Mtupane, 19 February 1996.

[60] Interview with Councillor Joshua Ncube, Mtupane, 19 February 1996.

on-going development projects and home improvement. An elderly kraalhead from Dwala complained:

> the pegs are about 1.5 kilometres north of here in the highland. So I'm expected to leave this home and live up there. This has disturbed the community, so we see no point in developing the school and clinic. I would like to thatch here – see the piles of grass? – but I can't because we will be moved. ... You see us so thin, we are over worried. Look at the energy I put into this home, look at my age – how will I build again? We even think the white government was much better than the government we're under now.

Moving up the watershed into infertile, sandy *gusu* soils would undermine agricultural production. As the old man continued: 'If we move up there, we'll have very little pasture, we'll have to destock to five animals and we'll have to open new fields in poorer soils.' He went on to contend that he and others had been given no choice in supporting Campfire:

> People were not consulted, it was a forced matter. They say we are in the communal area, so we can be moved anywhere, anytime, for any development project ... No one in this valley supports [Campfire]. The people who support it are the committee members who we believe will gain in some way from the project. They are people who live outside the valley. ... We have had plenty of meetings and we always say we are against moving.[61]

The desperation of people in the valley led them to adopt a variety of tactics. They contacted the local press and the Bulawayo *Chronicle* which then ran a series of articles on the conflict. They contacted lawyers in Bulawayo.[62] They proposed alternative development projects and, in the last instance, they showed themselves ready to resist.[63] In Lupane's Lake Alice ward, the councillor was elected on an anti-Campfire platform. He held that, 'Campfire has come to destroy the country because it is to deprive the people of land and give it to animals.'[64] The community staged a large protest to greet a Campfire delegation from the council.[65] They mounted placards which read, 'Down with Campfire, Down with the council chair.' Women danced and sang, 'We don't want Campfire. Our sons didn't die for animals.' An ex-combatant raised his arms, which had been amputated at the wrists, to the delegation and asked, 'How am I going to build a new home? Who will help me?' Mtupane youth threatened to smash the vehicle in which the delegation arrived.

All along the valley, foreboding surrounded the Campfire project. In Nkayi, fear had been compounded by arrests.[66] Councillors from the Nkayi end of the valley who backed Campfire were branded as sellouts by their constituencies. They refused to visit the valley on the grounds that they would be killed or beaten. One commented: 'I went to a meeting in Gwampa and I had to run away – the people wanted to kill me. I won't go down there again unless the police come with me.'[67] At Lehumbe on the Nkayi/

---

[61] Interview with Kraalhead, Dwala, 9 December 1995.

[62] See 'Gwampa Harrassment', *The Chronicle*, 13 October 1995.

[63] E.g., Interviews with Kraalhead, Dwala, 9 December 1995; Mhlotshwa Majaha Moyo, Majaha, 5 October 1995; Sipho Moyo, 1 October 1995, Nkayi.

[64] Interview with Councillor J. Ncube, Lake Alice Ward, 19 February 1996.

[65] The demonstration was described in a group interview, Mtupane, 19 February 1996, and in discussion with the Lupane Council Chairman.

[66] See 'Gwampa Harrassment', *The Chronicle*, 13 October 1995.

[67] Interview with Councillor Albert Hadebe, Lutsha, 4 October 1995.

Lupane border, a school play was staged about Campfire in which the councillor was portrayed as a trickster who abused his power as a translator at meetings between local people and foreign donors, and who was distanced from the community by virtue of his education and interest in his own status and wealth. The play ended with the community resolving to use violence if all else failed.[68]

Opposition was significant in altering the commitment of some to Campfire, notably the Lupane Council Chairman, and party leaders more widely in both districts. They argued that projects that provoked so much resistance did more harm than good to the authority of the council and party. But the commitment to Campfire remained. The councils sought to downplay resistance, to misrepresent the attitudes of those in the valley to other interested parties. They falsified minutes of meetings to make it appear that communities had accepted the project. They called on the Governor and DAs to address meetings. They backed (donor funded) visits of groups from the Gwampa valley to a Campfire project in Tsholotsho. The Lupane council dissolved committees which resisted Campfire and handpicked new ones.[69] Councillors called on the police for escorts, raising all too recent memories of state violence: 'Once you are identified as outspoken – like at these Campfire meetings – the CIO is there, so the threat of abduction is still prevalent.'[70] Finally, the councils argued that communal area land belonged to the state, and that the council had the legal right to decide what to do with it. Therefore, they could force people to move should they so desire.[71]

Obviously, these events brought Campfire a long way from its stated goals of giving local communities a stake in managing and benefiting from their own resources. A report compiled in December 1995 by the Zimbabwean Campfire adviser and Danish Campfire manager employed by MS-Zimbabwe in Nkayi revealed the levels of frustration and concern that had emerged.[72] The report noted that the councils had not been adequately involved in planning meetings held by the Forestry Commission-chaired Steering Committee, and that the Campfire adviser and manager themselves had not been kept abreast of changes. Moreover, they and the councils had 'always been told by the Forestry Commission that CIDA [the main donor] was not releasing the funds, but it is now clear that the reason for that is that the Government is not prepared to fulfill its [financial] obligation'. Without the release of the CIDA funds, the project could not go ahead and it now appeared that the Forestry Commission wanted to use the funds elsewhere. The viability of the project even with the donor funds was at any rate called into question by a study carried out by the WWF in late 1994. The study 'did not rate the proposed project as very viable'. But this apparently damning report had never been distributed, despite requests to see it.

And there were other problems. The report outlined serious misgivings regarding the councils' commitment to the Campfire philosophy. The report developed this criticism with regard to the Nkayi council's management of natural resources it already exploited, principally timber:

---

[68] School play by Shylock Mathiya, Lehumbe school, November, 1994.
[69] In Mtupane, committee members refused to acknowledge they were a committee, or that they could talk on behalf of the community. They were fearful that the mere existence of a committee could be used as evidence that the community supported Campfire. When the council went to Mtupane, they had to spend hours driving around in order to fetch the reluctant committee members from their homes.
[70] Group interview, Mathendele, 13 September 1995.
[71] 'Gwampa Harrassment', *The Chronicle*, 13 October 1995.
[72] See Alois N. Sikuka, Campfire Manager, and Ole Thompson, Campfire Adviser, *Campfire Department, Nkayi Rural District Council. Annual Report to MS, Second year, for the Period November 1, 1994 to December 1, 1995* (MS-DW, Nkayi, 1 December 1995).

Unfortunately the leadership of Nkayi District is of the opinion that ... it only has to follow the Campfire principles in some wards. This has been evidenced through a lot of discussions – latest in a very heated debate with the Council Chairman in a Natural Resources Committee Meeting – where the [Campfire] Department has advocated that at least some of the revenue from the District's timber utilisation should be ploughed back. ... Timber poaching is an increasing problem in Nkayi District, but the official opinion seems to be that this problem is solved now where the District's by-laws have been gazetted and the Council therefore can prosecute poachers. Time will show whether this is the case or the Campfire Department's argument that letting the producer community benefit directly is the solution.

In order to protect its most important source of revenue, the council had thus abrogated the most basic of Campfire tenets and sought to use legal penalties rather than economic incentives to control local people's use of timber resources.[73] The principal motive was, of course, to fill the councils' empty coffers. Under these circumstances, the Campfire scheme began to look increasingly uncertain. The MS report noted that efforts to peg the Campfire boundary along the valley had 'met massive resistance' and concluded that 'at the moment it looks like the project is in a deadlock situation'.

Even if the project is abandoned, the damage done is likely to last. Distrust and fear were, in the end, among the most important products of the Gwampa Campfire initiative. Local people no longer believed that the councillors supporting the project were acting in their interests. The programme's emphasis on game, and the necessity of eviction from the valley, threatened both local livelihoods and people's sense of having struggled for the land, of having brought their own version of development to a backward place. Not only did they believe their voices had been ignored, but they feared persecution for speaking out. Such views led to a breakdown of communication between the councils and their Gwampa constituents. The finance-strapped councils, desperately seeking sources of revenue, had succeeded not only in creating serious problems for their income-generating activites, but had also greatly undermined their own legitimacy. The ironies of the situation were manifest. A development initiative with democratic potential had become a focus of fear and resistance. People who saw themselves as progressive and modernizing, who desired development, had been cast as obstacles to development once again. This time, however, it was the grassroots political leaders, the men who had survived and mobilized through decades of resistance to oppression, who had taken on the mantle of the oppressor. In local eyes, the councils appeared to be playing the role of the colonial 'developers' they (along with many of the councillors) had fought so hard to dislodge.

## Malaria and State Bio-medical Services

Unlike the inertia and conflict that characterized land use planning and the explosive situation produced by Campfire, the dramatic expansion in state-provided medical services after independence was, along with the expansion of education, one of the

---

[73] The Nkayi council's attitude towards timber had provoked local attempts to use the Campfire rhetoric against the council: in Mdlawuzeni, local leaders were writing their 'own constitution' for their 'own Campfire': 'We've seen all the money from the timber felling going to the council without benefitting us, so this is our own, for the ward'. Interview with Kraalhead and Vidco Chairman, Mdlawuzeni, 11 September 1995. The Nkayi council was not alone in its attitude to timber revenues: see C. Bird *et al.*, 'Was Mrs Mutendi only Joking? A Critique of Timber Concessions in the Communal Areas of Zimbabwe', Harare, 1993.

most notable and popular achievements of the independent state.[74] Criticisms focused
largely on charges that the state invested too little. In Matabeleland, such criticisms
were underlain by the widespread perception that the region had been neglected for
political and ethnic reasons, a sentiment which was deepened in the course of the
exceptionally severe malaria epidemic of 1996. Before turning to the debates provoked
by the epidemic, we first explore the state's efforts to rectify colonial legacies of neglect
in the 1980s.

As we explored in earlier chapters, the Shangani region's notoriety as a disease-
ridden wilderness had sparked demands from chiefs and, more vociferously, the
evictees of the 1940s and 1950s, for investment in health services. On their arrival, the
evictees had suffered devastating mortality levels from malaria, far higher than the
longer-term settlers of the region, in part due to their lack of resistance to the disease.[75]
Though some improvements were made before independence, Matabeleland North as a
whole lagged well behind other provinces in 1980. Clinics multiplied in the 1980s, but
failed to overcome the colonial legacy of neglect.[76] Moreover, due to the 'security
situation', the new rural health centres were regularly closed or inaccessible; health staff
(notably the large number of former Zipra guerrillas employed as nurses) were subject
to attack from Fifth Brigade soldiers; and the new village health workers were vulnerable to dissidents who accused them of selling out.[77] Malaria cases increased generally
in the post-independence period, partly due to the interruption of environmental
spraying during the liberation war and the disruptions of the 1980s conflict.[78]

After Unity, public investments in health services were dramatically undercut by
Zimbabwe's structural adjustment programme. Real per capita expenditure on health
fell through the 1990s and the commitment to free health care for all was abandoned.
Though the collection of fees at rural clinics was suspended during the severe 1991–2
drought, charges were reintroduced in 1993, and dramatically increased in subsequent
years. Efforts to minimize the costs for the poor through the Social Development Fund
and other measures had only a small impact, especially in rural areas, due to 'grossly
inadequate initial funding' and cumbersome application procedures.[79]

[74] See C. Stoneman and L. Cliffe, *Zimbabwe: Politics, Economics and Society* (London and New York,
Pinter Publishers, 1989), pp. 168–76; R. Lowenson and D. Saunders, 'The Political Economy of
Health and Nutrition', in C. Stoneman (ed.), *Zimbabwe's Prospects. Issues of Race, State, Class and
Capital in Southern Africa* (London, Macmillan, 1988), pp. 133–52.
[75] For further detail on debates over malaria, see J. McGregor and T. Ranger, 'Displacement and
Disease: Epidemics and Ideas About Malaria in Matabeleland, Zimbabwe, 1945–1996', *Past and
Present*, forthcoming.
[76] Matabeleland North had only 5.98 rural health centres per 100,000 people in 1980, in contrast to
a national average of 9.49. Though the number of health centres doubled in the first five years of
independence, Matabeleland North remained the least well-served province in the country. See
J. Herbst, *State Politics in Zimbabwe* (Harare, University of Zimbabwe Publications, 1990),
pp. 174–5, citing Ministry of Health, 'The Health Institutions of Zimbabwe' (Harare, Ministry of
Health, 1985); Central Statistical Office, *Main Demographic Features of the Population of Zimbabwe*
(Harare, CSO, 1985).
[77] See Chapter 9. On village health workers specifically, see Nkayi District Council, 14 December
1983.
[78] P. Taylor and L. Mutamba, 'A Review of the Malaria Situation in Zimbabwe with Special
Reference to the Period 1972–81', *Transactions of the Royal Society of Tropical Medicine and Hygiene*,
80, 1986, pp. 12–19.
[79] L. Bijlmakers, M. Basset and D. Saunders, 'Health and Structural Adjustment in Rural and Urban
Zimbabwe', *Research Report No. 101* (Nordiska Afrikainstitutet, Uppsala, 1996), pp. 13–16, 67.
Also see M. Chisvo and L. Munro, *A Review of Social Dimensions of Adjustment in Zimbabwe
1990–94* (Harare, UNICEF, 1994).

It was in this context that the exceptionally severe malaria epidemic of 1996 struck. Matabeleland North was hit harder than other parts of the country: an estimated 398 people died from malaria in Lupane hospital between January and June of 1996; an unknown number died at home or on their way to clinics and hospitals; and 52,932 people were treated for malaria by the overstretched district health services.[80] The Bulawayo *Chronicle* reported that thousands were 'under siege' in the province, that health facilities were 'virtually unable to cope', and called for emergency measures.[81] The 1996 epidemic was so devastating for a combination of reasons. First, areas of endemic malaria had expanded after 1980, and resistance to chloroquine had grown.[82] Second, the heavy rains of 1996 followed a series of droughts during which resistance to malaria had declined. AIDS may also have elevated mortality. Third, state health services had, according to the Provincial Medical Officer, 'stopped prioritizing malaria. ... So then when the malaria struck, we were not prepared for it.'[83] The result was an epidemic on a scale unequalled in popular memory since the 1950s.

The 1996 epidemic profoundly altered local debates over the causes of disease, as well as attitudes towards bio-medical services, the state and development. It stimulated a re-evaluation of past epidemics and of colonial history. Much criticism focused on the effects of declining state investment in bio-medical services. Matabeleland's MPs accused the Minister of Health of inadequate and delayed spraying, and of over-diluting chemicals.[84] People in the Shangani maintained, 'We and our cattle live like kudu in the forest. The government doesn't care.'[85] They emphasized the prohibitive costs of repellents and nets, as well as of the fees charged at hospitals and clinics. Fees had also been introduced for rural ambulances: in the wake of successive droughts, these charges proved to be too much. The post-independent state was regularly compared unfavourably with its colonial predecessor. Despite the terrible effects of the 1950s epidemic, some thought they had been greatly helped by the distribution of pills and spraying. The high mortality of the 1990s was thus cast as a failure of the independent government to take similar measures. Some even went so far as to argue that malaria had been unknown in the colonial period.

People's understanding of malaria more generally also shaped their reactions to the 1996 epidemic. People had incorporated health-education messages into their under-standing of the causes of malaria, its prevention and cure in diverse ways.[86] They often did not connect mosquitoes and malaria,[87] and tended to interpret the diseases of the rainy season as a whole as non-fatal. Such ideas discouraged them from taking

---

[80] Malaria De-Brief Meeting Report, Matabeleland North Province, 23–27 September 1996.

[81] *The Chronicle*, 4 April 1996.

[82] S. Mharakurwa and T. Mugochi, 'Chloroquine Resistant Falciparum Malaria in an Area of Rising Endemicity in Zimbabwe', *Journal of Tropical Medicine and Hygiene*, 1994, 97, 1, pp. 39–45.

[83] Interview with Provincial Medical Director, Matabeleland North, 17 September 1996.

[84] *The Chronicle*, 4 April 1996. There were, however, problems with environmental spraying: it is expensive and difficult to carry out on a large scale, and the efficacy of spraying homes is unclear when people spend much of their time outside them. Interview, Provincial Medical Director, Matabeleland North, 17 September 1996. Also see Malaria De-Brief Report, Matabeleland North Province, 17–23 September 1996.

[85] Group interview, Ndimimbili, 11 March 1996.

[86] On attitudes to spraying operations, see C. Vundule and S. Mharakurwa, 'Knowledge, Practices, and Perceptions about Malaria in Rural Communities of Zimbabwe: Relevance to Malaria Control', *Bulletin of the World Health Organisation*, 74, 1, 1996, pp. 55–60. On attitudes to malaria more generally, see McGregor and Ranger, 'Displacement and Disease'.

[87] Surveys in other parts of the country have estimated that 44% of the rural population did not link malaria to mosquitoes. See A.A. Van Geldermansen and R. Munochivoyi, *Central African Journal of Medicine*, 41, 1, 1995, pp. 104–12.

preventive measures against being bitten by mosquitoes and from visiting the clinic. In the context of the 1996 epidemic, the association between 'malaria' and the Ndebele category of disease known as *'inyongo'* was key to how people in the Shangani interpreted illness and in the treatment they sought. *Inyongo* was usually defined as a non-fatal disease of the rainy season, associated not with mosquitoes but with gorging on the first fruits. Some saw both *inyongo* and 'malaria' as ultimately environmental, held in the breath of animals, in the soil, vegetation and air.[88] But in 1996, distinctions were drawn between the non-fatal seasonal disease of the past (*inyongo*) and the new fatal disease, which was referred to variously as 'a new type of *inyongo*' or 'malaria'. This new disease was distinctive for failing to respond to traditional cures, for its association with other killer diseases such as AIDS, for striking out of season and for afflicting everyone (rather than primarily the evictees, as in the 1950s).

If the malaria epidemics of the 1950s had acted to reinforce suspicion between evictees and locals, the 'new' disease of the 1990s brought different reactions. People were preoccupied not only with the inadequacy of health facilities and how the disease could be contracted, but also raised political questions about the timing and impact of the epidemic and sought explanations beyond the field of conventional medicine. Many blamed the Mugabe government both for exacerbating the epidemic by 'under-developing' Matabeleland and for directly causing the disease by failing to deal with the legacies of war.

The connection between violence and disease was made in different ways, sometimes explicitly and sometimes by association: bloodshed, the pollution of gunfire and smoke, and the lack of cleansing were all invoked. As a group of elders commented:

> Several new diseases arose during the war and have continued: we have had new ticks, anthrax and black leg. The latter two are caused by the poison of the gunfire. There should have been cleansing after the war. Even with people, we now have several diseases which were not there before the war: there is AIDS and there is this headache which leads to death [malaria].[89]

Some contrasted the polluting guns of war with the non-polluting effect of the guns used to shoot animals in the colonial era tsetse eradication campaign, a campaign remembered as having helped to rid the environment of the polluting breath of wild animals:

> The guns introduced by the [Rhodesian] government to kill animals didn't bring disease, only the ones brought to kill people, these bazookas and land mines, all that smoke. These are the things which brought these incurable diseases here.[90]

The association between war and disease was further strengthened by memories of the 1918 influenza epidemic, locally known as *ifureza*.[91] *Ifureza* followed World War One just as the 1996 epidemic followed *'gukura'*, the violence of the 1980s:

> *Ifureza* was caused by the war with the Germans. ... People died running from the mines. They died in the bushes before they reached home. ... You see, when blood

---

[88] See McGregor and Ranger, 'Displacement and Disease'.

[89] Group interview, Lupaka, 9 February 1996.

[90] Interview with Mudenda Dube, Lubimbi, 26 March 1996.

[91] Accounts of *ifureza* in the Shangani are remarkably similar to those noted by Z. Ndava, 'A Study of the 1918–1919 Influenza Pandemic', cited in T. Ranger, 'Plagues of Beast and Men', in T. O. Ranger and P. Slack (eds), *Epidemics and Ideas* (Cambridge, Cambridge University Press, 1993). See also T. Ranger, 'The Influenza Pandemic in Southern Rhodesia: A Crisis of Comprehension', in D. Arnold (ed.), *Imperial Medicine and Indigenous Societies* (Manchester, Manchester University Press, 1988).

is spilt all over the land and is blown in all directions by the wind it causes diseases. After gukura people again started to die. In gukura, so many were killed and God didn't like that. ... *Inyongo* in the past ... had its own time, after the *insewula* [first heavy rains], when the grass was at knee height and you'd be eating the first fruits. It wasn't serious, it never killed anyone and you could vomit it away. The war then gave birth to this new disease, just like *ifureza*.[92]

If explanations for the severity of the 1996 epidemic were diverse, so too were ideas about how to respond. Some people lobbied councillors and MPs for free transport between clinics and hospitals, for training of additional community workers, and for the distribution of drugs, mosquito repellent and nets. Many, however, believed the state would not respond, or that bio-medicine in general and anti-malarial drugs in particular were no longer effective: 'Pills don't cure you for good. If you go one year for the pills, you go back next year', was a typical attitude. Some held that the reliance on pills and injections had in fact weakened people, leaving children in particular less strong than in the past.[93] Given the spread of chloroquine resistant malaria, such a lack of confidence in bio-medical interventions was not unfounded. Many people sought to supplement treatment provided by state health facilities with purging and cleansing herbs, and visits to traditional healers such as *izinyanga* and *izangoma* spirit mediums. But these latter were often judged impotent in the face of the 1996 epidemic: they could treat '*inyongo*', but not '*malaria*'.

The arguments which linked the epidemic to war, to the failure to carry out cleansing (as well as, more broadly, the Mugabe government's lack of respect for 'tradition'), contributed to the major resurgence of activity around the rainshrines of Matabeleland, as we discuss in the next chapter. However, the malaria epidemic did not bring a revival of those aspects of traditional religious practice most closely associated with disease control, notably the first fruits ceremonies. These were rarely organized at the house-hold, let alone the community, level. Instead, people tended to turn to *izinyanga* and the independent churches which offered healing, such as the Zionists and Apostolics. These latter had flourished during the wars of the 1970s and 1980s, and they continued to do so during the malaria epidemic. The daily purging which they advocated resonated with older ideas of how to cleanse the body. In many respects, however, malaria – and in effect the environment itself – was often seen as beyond local control.

People's assessment of bio-medical services and their responses to malaria in the 1990s have to be set against the current financial crisis in the provision of bio-medical care, the spread of resistant strains of malaria, and the interactive effects of malaria and AIDS in elevating mortality. The health services have failed to cope with recent malaria epidemics; tablets are increasingly seen as ineffective. Despite the significant state investments in health care in the 1980s, the debates over the malaria epidemic of 1996 reinforced a sense of marginalization and discrimination. Broadly, people compared the government's response to malaria unfavourably with memories of government inter-vention in past epidemics. Specifically, they linked their current suffering to the history of state violence, and the government's failure to undertake post-war cleansing.

## Conclusion

The debates surrounding the three aspects of development which we have considered in this chapter reveal common themes despite their very different nature. All three cases illustrate the crippling effect on local government and state services of growing

---

[92] Interview with M. Mathe, Endamuleni, 7 March 1996.
[93] Group interview, Lupaka, 9 February 1996.

financial constraints. All show how such constraints undermined attempts to make local and central government accountable. These problems were, of course, national: local and central government faced a deepening crisis of finance and legitimacy throughout the country. Everywhere, the state was increasingly directed by donor priorities. Even in more specific terms, the problems which development faced nation-wide were similar to the problems we have described in Matabeleland: land use planning produced parallel conflicts over boundaries and the movement of homes in all parts of the country and was only rarely fully implemented; Campfire projects have been less explosive in other parts of Zimbabwe, but have often also provoked conflicts and a breach of confidence between councils and local communities; bio-medical services have proved ineffective in the face of the growing threat of malaria nationwide.

But our discussion has also illustrated the ways in which historical memories specific to Matabeleland were drawn upon in debating the problems of development. Perhaps above all, each of these very different cases reinforced a powerful conviction that Matabeleland remained the victim of neglect and discrimination, that the good state people had imagined and fought for remained unattained (the post-Unity absorption of so many former Zapu leaders into the state and councils notwith-standing). In each case, people drew on their memories of forced movement, of battles to build and defend their lives and dignity against disease, dearth, animals and the dark forests themselves, of colonial and post-colonial coercion and repression. Post-Unity development left the goals of nationalism unmet, the legacies of violence unaddressed and unresolved. In the next – and final – chapter we turn to some of the initiatives that people themselves have taken to try to address these legacies.

# 11

## Resolving the Legacies of War?

### Accountability, Commemoration & Cleansing

This book has described a long sequence of violence in the history of the Shangani, stretching over more than a hundred years and rising to an obscene climax in the 1980s. We have seen how the imagery of the *gusu* forests as 'dark' and 'threatening', as peopled with wild animals, outcasts and rebels, is invoked time and again in the telling of this history. Today the Shangani is at peace but the memories of violence live on, and continue to influence many aspects of life in the *gusu*. In the previous chapter, we discussed development; here we explore the attempts that have been made since 1988 to cope with past violence – to commemorate its victims and heroes, to cleanse the land and the people from its effects, to heal individuals, families and fighters.

Although the violence of the 1980s has left the most recent and painful memories, efforts to interpret it or to heal its legacies have looked to past eras of violence. The past has provided sources of comparison and contrast, has offered 'traditions' of commemoration, cleansing and healing, and has itself been given new meaning and significance in the process. As we will show, the attempts which have been made in the 1990s to deal with past violence have summoned up many aspects of Shangani history. Commemoration of the 'heroes' of the liberation war, attempted at the symbolic site of Pupu, invoked the need for repentance and cleansing of more than a century of conquest and terror – the overthrow of the Rozwi Mambo and the displacement of his people; the killing of blacks and whites in 1893; as well as the deaths of Zipra guerrillas in the 1970s and the violence of the 1980s. The search by guerrillas and dissidents for healing has involved a revival of old traditions of spiritual absolution and a new focus on the Mwali shrines. The quest to understand the most recent droughts and epidemics has led to a re-evaluation of those of the past, a questioning of leaders at all levels, and debates over spiritual responsibility for the land. All this makes this chapter a commentary on the themes of the whole book.

The context in which we explore emergent debates over the legacies of violence was shaped by the more open political climate created by the Unity agreement. It was a time of devastating drought and growing economic hardship in which popular disaffection spread, and the ruling elite faced challenges from all over the country on a wide range of issues. Criticisms were made not just of the Zanu(PF) government's developmentalist claims, but also of the second great plank of its legitimacy: the struggle for national liberation. In the 1990s, the government's use of nationalist history – and its exploitation of national wealth – came under sustained challenge. There were appeals to unfulfilled nationalist promises, charges of misappropriation of the benefits of independence, and challenges to the government's exclusive version of heroic nationalism. Zapu and Zipra were central players in attempts to re-write official history. They sought to assert their long sidelined contribution to the nationalist struggle; they sought official recognition in the pantheon of heroes for their members who had died in the liberation war or thereafter. Claims for recognition of the wholly unacknowledged post-independence violence posed a different challenge to nationalist narrative: they threatened the new myth of Unity to which both the former Zapu leaders and Zanu(PF) now subscribed.

In the Shangani, public debates in the 1990s over the unresolved legacies of war were revealing of the ways in which people understood their relationships with the state and individual members of the government, their ideas about how national leaders could be held to account, and the extent to which local leaders could confront the legacies of war. Nationalism was perceived to be the most powerful idiom through which claims could be made on leaders. Arguments about accountability drew on both the nationalist appeal to the rights of citizens, and on a 'traditionalist' idiom which invoked the support and legitimacy which nationalist leaders had sought from ancestral spirits and the High God Mwali. As Werbner has argued, this traditionalist idiom was rooted in the idea of a 'moral partnership' between the living and the dead, the breach of which required ritual resolution.[1] Demands on leaders thus combined calls for public acknowledgment of human rights abuses, calls for commemoration of those who died, and calls for the appeasement of ancestral spirits and Mwali.

Before turning to commemorative and cleansing initiatives in the Shangani, we first discuss the vociferous challenges at the national level to the governing elite's manipulation of the narratives, symbols and benefits of nationalism in the post-Unity period.

## National Post-Unity Debates Over the Legacies of War

Post-Unity debates over the legacies of war focused on both the 1970s and the 1980s, but in very different ways. The plight of the veterans of both liberation armies, their material conditions and the commemoration of their role in national liberation came to the fore in a variety of public fora, and led to strident demands for material compensation. Public revelations about the violence in Matabeleland, by contrast, led to demands from within the region for what Richard Werbner has termed 'recountability' – i.e., the right 'to make a citizen's memory known, and acknowledged in the public sphere'.[2] At this stage, these demands were not primarily material in focus.[3]

The debates of the 1990s did not start from a blank slate. As Norma Kriger has written, Zanu(PF) had since independence sought to ground the nation's identity as well as its own political legitimacy in the liberation war. The government had established a hierarchy of 'Heroes' Acres' – burial grounds for guerrillas and nationalists – at national, provincial and district levels, thus symbolically enshrining the nationalist

---

[1]  R. Werbner, 'Human Rights and Moral Knowledge. Arguments of accountability in Zimbabwe', in M. Strathern (ed.), *Shifting Contexts. Transformations in Anthropological Knowledge* (Routledge, London, 1995).

[2]  Richard Werbner, 'Beyond Oblivion: Confronting Memory Crisis', in Richard Werbner (ed.), *Memory and the Postcolony: African Anthropology and the Critique of Power* (Zed Books, London, 1998), p. 1.

[3]  The CCJP/LRF report, *Breaking the Silence, Building True Peace. A Report on the Disturbances in Matabeleland and the Midlands 1980 to 1988* (CCJP/LRF, Harare, 1997), does make claims for compensation, but such claims were not strongly voiced by people in the Shangani with whom we spoke. For them, acknowledgement and commemoration seemed more important. Interestingly, it was material losses suffered in the liberation war which were more often the focus of hopes for compensation.

past. But this hierarchy had proved divisive – it had come to symbolize not a unifying nationalism, but one fissured with divisions between the elite and the 'povo', between Zanu(PF) and Zapu. Those with connections to Zanu(PF)'s elite enjoyed opulent state burials at the national Heroes' Acre in Harare. Others were relegated to provincial and district levels where their friends and family were left to foot the bill. Zapu heroes gained scant recognition.[4]

Zapu leaders (and others as well) lodged strong objections to the government's commemoration of heroes in the 1980s. They attacked the designation of heroes as partisan, criticized the idea of a hierarchy of heroes, and argued that it went against Ndebele tradition to move and rebury the remains of the dead. The failure to recognize Lookout Masuku as a hero following his death in April 1986 provoked the most heated response. Masuku had been Zipra's last commander-in-chief, and had spent his final years in detention on charges of treason (though a court had acquitted him) – treatment which many, including Joshua Nkomo, believed had hastened his death. Nkomo's speech at Masuku's funeral, in front of a crowd of some 20,000 in Bulawayo, was filled with rage:

> If Lookout Masuku is not a hero, who then is a hero of this country? … We accused former colonisers who used detention without trial as well as torture and yet do exactly what they did, if not worse. We accused Whites of discrimination on grounds of colour yet we have discriminated on political and ethnic grounds.[5]

After Unity, Zapu began to take its own steps to identify and commemorate its war dead, significantly at the behest of Dumiso Dabengwa, Zipra's former head of intelligence who had himself only been released from jail in December 1986. In March 1989, the Zipra War Shrines Committee was established by the (still extant) Zapu Central Committee. Dabengwa, who had by then taken up the post of Deputy Minister of Home Affairs, headed the Committee. It was charged with locating the graves of Zipra guerrillas, and with identifying the names of all Zipra and Zapu members who had died in the liberation war. In line with Zapu's earlier objections to reburial of the dead, the Committee intended to mark the grave sites, but not to disturb the remains. The Committee's work was continued by the Mafela Trust from September 1990. Mafela, or 'the fallen one', had been Lookout Masuku's war name. The Mafela Trust published the names of the dead in *Parade* magazine in August and December 1990. By the end of 1991, the Trust's researchers had identified 1,087 graves and 1,414 dead.[6]

Alongside these specifically Zapu/Zipra initiatives, a much more wide-ranging critique of the official heroes hierarchy began to be voiced. The National Liberation War Veterans' Association, formed in 1989 and representing both guerrilla armies, expressed ex-combatants' desire for a say in the process of choosing heroes and organizing their commemoration. The association was critical of the graded heroes' acres, and the anomolies in those chosen as heroes. Their case was taken up by MPs, some of them ex-combatants, in parliamentary debates. Questions were also raised in parliament and the press about the government's treatment of living ex-combatants and disabled civilians. The nation's leaders were charged with abandoning their former comrades, with forsaking those responsible for the country's independence. They were condemned

---

[4] See N. Kriger, 'The Politics of Creating National Heroes: The Search for Political Legitimacy and National Identity', in N. Bhebe and T. Ranger (eds), *Soldiers in Zimbabwe's Liberation War* (London, James Currey, 1995), pp. 139–62.

[5] Quoted in Kriger, 'The Politics of Creating National Heroes', p. 153. Also see Jeremy Brickhill, 'Making Peace with the Past: War Victims and the Work of the Mafela Trust', in N. Bhebe and T. Ranger (eds), *Soldiers in Zimbabwe's Liberation War* (London, James Currey, 1995), pp. 163–73.

[6] Brickhill, 'Making Peace with the Past', pp. 166–8. Brickhill explores the difficulties which the researchers encountered in the field, and the wave of popular responses to the Trust's project.

for living in great luxury while the 'forgotten fighters' languished in poverty.[7]

The attack on the ruling elites' attempts to use the liberation war as a means of legitimizing its rule while at the same time excluding the 'living heroes' from sharing in the nation's wealth gained force in the 1990s. A full 15 years after independence, the War Veterans' Association received promises of compensation – but the compensation process, in which vast sums of money were at stake, quickly foundered under accusations of corruption.[8] The same elite who had monopolized the liberation war's symbolic capital for its own ends now stood accused of seeking to monopolize the funds tardily made available for ex-combatants as a whole. War veterans took to the streets, rioted and heckled Mugabe's Heroes' Day speech in 1997. In the face of such unprecedented protest, Mugabe responded with both a Commission of Inquiry into the misuse of funds, and a promise of a lump sum pay-out to all ex-combatants of Z$50,000 in addition to pensions of Z$2,000 a month.[9]

Far from bringing the debate over the nationalist leaders' debts to an end, the promise of compensation to ex-combatants sparked further claims. Early on, ex-detainees had formed their own organization to press for recognition and compensation. The youth who had aided guerrillas during the war formed the oddly named Zimbabwe National Liberation War Collaborators' Association, and heatedly harrassed Zanu(PF) meetings in search of their own compensation.[10] The promise of huge payments to war veterans helped trigger the collapse of the Zimbabwe dollar. Mugabe's attempts to impose tax increases to fund the war veterans' payments deepened the crisis: they were met with massive street demonstrations organized by the Zimbabwe Congress of Trade Unions. Union members and influential voices in the press asked 'Who is not a war veteran?' Civilians, youth and detainees, as well as guerrillas, had paid a high price during the liberation war: the wounds of war were inflicted on the nation as a whole.[11]

These protests, and the earlier objections to the government's hierarchical and exclusive handling of liberation war heroes, showed a renewed willingness to question the very basis of the government's claims to legitimacy. The memory of the liberation war proved difficult to monopolize as alternative views of the debts it had left, of the ideals which had been fought for, were forcefully put forward. The memories of the violence of the 1980s would prove equally difficult to manage in the newly open post-Unity period.

[7] See Kriger's detailed discussion, 'The Politics of Creating National Heroes', pp. 155–60. Later debates also charged the leadership with selfishly confining hero status to their own generation, and not acknowledging fully the role of the heroes of the first Chimurenga. See parliamentary debates in the *Hansard*, 15 August 1996.

[8] For discussion of misuse of the compensation funds see, e.g., 'The great war victims rip off', *Horizon*, June 1997; 'Meetings with war veterans turn nasty', *The Herald*, 21 July 1997; *Financial Times*, 21 November 1997; 'Ex-Zipra Fighters Cry Foul over Compensation Fund', *Moto*, October 1997; 'War Victims' Trauma Assessment a Scandal', *Horizon*, November 1997. A massive Z$1.7 billion was paid out of the compensation fund between 1992 and 1997, much of it to dubious recipients. See *Mail and Guardian* (electronic), 1 September 1997.

[9] Other concessions were also made, such as promises of benefits to the dependents of provincial and district heroes. (Previously only national heroes' dependents had been eligible.) See R. Werbner, 'Smoke from the Barrel of a Gun: Postwars of the Dead, Memory and Reinscription in Zimbabwe', in Werbner (ed.), *Memory and the Postcolony*, p. 78.

[10] See R. Chinodafuka, 'Liberation war collaborators spill the beans', *Moto*, May 1998, p. 8. The 'collaborators' threatened to reveal the 'skeletons in the war heroes' cupboards' if they were ignored. They referred particularly to the rape of young women and the killings of falsely accused sellouts by guerrillas.

[11] Tendai Mandinah, *Horizon*, November 1997, p. 6. Also see J. Todd in the *Zimbabwe Independent*, 31 August 1997.

Amidst the wider debates over the treatment to be given the dead and the living combatants of Zimbabwe's liberation war, the independent press began to revisit the Matabeleland conflict of the 1980s. From 1988, coverage was given to the government's failure to release certain Zapu and Zipra prisoners under its general Amnesty; wide-ranging discussions of the implications of the violence were published; the particular problems of individuals in obtaining death certificates for those killed in the 1980s, and attempts by victims of violence to obtain compensation, were explored.[12] In the next years, cases of massacres and 'disappearances' were increasingly reported, often drawing on information collected by the ever-active Catholic Commission for Justice and Peace (CCJP). These included a mass grave uncovered at Mpindo by heavy rains, the case of the 'Silobela 9' and other lower level Zapu officials who had 'disappeared' at the time of the 1985 elections, and the discovery of mine shafts filled with bodies at Antelope and Silobela.[13]

In each case, the government was called upon to respond. Zanu(PF) leaders consistently either denied responsibility or maintained that violence had been justified by the threat posed by dissidents. More surprisingly, senior members of the former Zapu (who were now in government) made a quick conversion to the merits of silence, maintaining that 'old wounds should not be reopened'. For many – though not all – of them, the violence of the 1980s had become embarrassing, troublesome, an obstacle to their consolidation of a new myth of Unity.[14] Local police and the CIO were reported to have threatened those who had come forward with information, or who sought to visit places where mass graves had been found: at Antelope Mine, police immediately mounted a guard post at the site, and the CIO kept locals away; at the Silobela mineshaft, police threatened the mine-owner (a local man), intimidated others, and tampered with evidence. Such threats, coming so soon after the violence of the 1980s, were terrifying for local people.[15] Despite the hostile government response, these reports played an important role within Matabeleland for their public confirmation for the first time of the existence of government atrocities, and their sparking of a public debate about the need for acknowledgement and healing.[16]

[12] E.g., see 'The forgotten prisoners', *Moto*, December 1988/January 1989; B. Sodindwa, 'The people and their wounds' and A.Z. Nhamo, 'Shock and disbelief in Matabeleland' both in *Moto*, January 1993; Collet Nkala, 'Matabeleland's missing persons mystery', *Horizon*, November 1991; 'Looking back over the decade', *Parade*, April 1990; Collet Nkala, 'Tsholotsho folk challenge death certificate ruling', *Horizon*, October 1990. *Horizon* magazine also ran a series of articles on South African involvement in the 1980s violence, and on Zipra. The latter was an important effort to right some of the historical distortion of that army's contribution to the liberation struggle.

[13] See, e.g., Thabo Kunene, 'Gukurahundi murders exposed', *Horizon*, March 1992; Thabo Kunene, 'Matabeleland massacres spark outcry', *Financial Gazette*, 23 July 1992; 'Silobela abductees declared dead' and 'The mystery continues', *Horizon*, June 1992; 'Tragedy at Tsholotsho', *Horizon*, July 1992; 'Missing men mystery: no records from state' and 'CCJP wants army atrocities published', *Parade*, November 1991; 'Human remains continue to surface in Matabeleland', *Parade*, October 1992; 'Miner who found Silobela bones now fears for his life', *Parade*, April 1993; 'Villagers blame Fifth Brigade atrocities for drought as famine hits Matabeleland', *Parade*, January 1996.

[14] In 1992, confronted with the discovery of human remains at Antelope Mine in Kezi District (his home area and political stronghold), former Zapu leader and then Vice President Joshua Nkomo told assembled crowds that he 'could not answer any questions in the absence of his colleague [and co-Vice President], Simon Muzenda'. See 'Human remains continue to surface in Matabeleland', *Parade*, October 1992. Other, less senior, Zapu leaders were less willing to keep quiet.

[15] See 'Human remains continue to surface in Matabeleland', *Parade*, October 1992, and 'Miner who found Silobela bones now fears for his life', *Parade*, April 1993.

[16] E.g, see Letters to Editor page of *Horizon*, September 1992. We were often told that the coverage of the Antelope Mine discoveries was important in local eyes for confirming people's long denied grievances.

The most far-reaching debate on the conflict followed the publication in 1997 of a human rights report by the CCJP and Legal Resources Foundation, entitled *Breaking the Silence, Building True Peace: A Report on the Disturbances in Matabeleland and the Midlands 1980-1988.*[17] The report explored in painstaking detail the course of violence in the 1980s. It weighed the organized violence of the state and party – the Fifth Brigade, ZNA, Zanu(PF) Youth League, CIO and police – against the relatively small impact of the dissidents they were ostensibly countering. The report explored the conflict's background, examining the relationship between Zapu and Zanu(PF), the problems encountered in creating a unified army after independence, and the role of South African agents. It concluded that two wars had been fought, one against the dissidents themselves, one against the people of Matabeleland, the latter having ethnic and political overtones and motives. The report called on the government to acknowledge human rights abuses in the interests of a lasting peace and proposed a 'reconciliation trust' to provide compensation to affected areas in the form of funds for community projects and memorials.

President Mugabe was handed a copy of the report in March 1997. The report was not to be publicly circulated until after Mugabe had had a chance to respond. A copy was nonetheless leaked to the South African *Weekly Mail and Guardian* in the first week in May. The *Mail and Guardian* (which is readily available in Zimbabwe's main cities) published long excerpts, and made the report available on its website. *Breaking the Silence* subsequently received extensive and positive coverage in the independent press.[18] It was, however, largely ignored by the government-controlled press, and where it was not ignored it was attacked as a divisive tool designed to divert attention from the Zanu(PF) government's positive programmes.[19]

Mugabe was forced to respond, but did so ambiguously. While addressing mourning crowds at the funeral of Zapu leader Stephen Vuma at Heroes' Acre, he criticized the Bishops for opening old wounds and threatening the nation's unity, implicitly suggesting that it was the publication of their report, rather than the violence about which it was written, which would dangerously divide the nation: 'If we dig up history, then we wreck the nation ... and we tear our people apart into factions, into tribes.' He nonetheless seemed to take a small step towards acknowledging government human rights abuses: 'The [historical] register or record will remind us what never to do. If that was wrong, if that went against the sacred tenets of humanity, we must never repeat it.'[20] Though decidedly tentative, Mugabe's response marked an important shift from previous blanket denials of security force abuses. It also pointed to the paradoxes of remembering state violence used against the state's own citizens: violence had to be remembered to be avoided in future, it had to be forgotten to ensure the unity of the nation.[21]

This ambiguity was expressed not only by Mugabe but also in the popular media.

---

[17] The report is based on interviews with victims in two case study districts of Matabeleland (Tsholotsho in Nyamandhlovu and Matobo in Kezi), cross referenced with and supplemented by a compilation of all other available material, from hospital records, CCJP correspondence and reports, legal cases, press and human rights reports. It is an exemplary case of careful and nuanced reporting, and was praised as such by Amnesty International.

[18] See, e.g., *The Zimbabwe Independent*, 9 May to 15 May 1997; *Financial Gazette*, 8 May 1997; 'Zimbabwe's killing fields', *Horizon*, July 1997; 'Are Catholic Bishops developing cold feet over explosive report?', *Parade*, June 1997; 'Mugabe taken to task over human rights', *Parade*, August 1997.

[19] See analysis in Iden Wetherell, 'The Matabeleland Report: A lot to hide', *Southern African Report*, June 1997, pp. 21–2.

[20] *The Sunday Mail*, 11 May 1997.

[21] See Werbner, 'Smoke from the Barrel of a Gun', pp. 96–7, on the paradoxes of remembering and forgetting in the construction of nationhood.

Following the publication of an article on 1980s' army atrocities in Gwanda in *Moto* magazine, the letters to the editor recorded the following exchange. One writer asked, 'What did your magazine expect to gain by publishing the Matabeleland story? Firstly, it is opening old wounds. Secondly, don't you realise that publishing such a story at a time when some Ndebeles are calling for an anti-Shona crusade ... kindles hatred?' Another correspondent took the opposite view. He praised the article as 'an important historical document that will play an important role in emboldening people to come forward so that the story can be told'; he argued that, 'It will also help cleanse the blood on our hands for not having dared to speak out when we knew terrible things were happening in our midst. ... We need to know our sins, both to accelerate the healing of the pain for the victim's families, and to prevent such terrorism in future.'[22]

The metaphor of 'opening old wounds' was a powerful one, invoked by former Zapu and Zanu(PF) politicians as well as by ordinary citizens and human rights groups. The 'wounds' stood as markers of a history of violence, inscribed on both individuals and the body politic; 'opening' them meant public probing. Whether they had ever healed, and hence stood to be 'opened', whether 'opening' them constituted a destructive or a healing act, were subjects of contention which begged a range of questions regarding the proper commemoration of the dead and the appropriate ways in which history might be invoked in the present without 'tearing the nation apart'.

## Commemoration in the Shangani: Pupu and Daluka

The national debates over the government's manipulation of the benefits, symbols and narratives of the nation, and its silence over the violence of the 1980s, set the scene for regional and local initiatives to memorialize those who had been excluded from the official nationalist narrative. Below, we discuss two such attempts within the Shangani: the high profile effort to annoint Pupu in Lupane as a shrine and provincial Heroes' Acre, and the very local attempt to commemorate victims of the Fifth Brigade's violence at Daluka. Both initiatives revealed the demand for commemoration, the need for public acknowledgement and ritual resolution of the history of violence, as well as the great controversy which continued to surround even the smallest of efforts to mark that history on the landscape, and in public memory.

The Pupu site is redolent with the history of violence, as we've discussed in previous chapters. It was here that Lobengula's Insukamini regiment wiped out to a man the forces of Alan Wilson's pioneer column on December 4, 1893; it was here, after that fateful battle, that Lobengula disappeared, never to be seen again. The battlefield remained scattered with bones until colonial officials collected them in a single grave in preparation for the settlement of the area by evictees from Matabeleland South; local people and the evictees organized their own cleansing ceremony. An obelisk established by the Rhodesians commemorated the white dead. Both the obelisk and a *mtswiri* tree, which had acted as Lobengula's 'command post' and last resting place, were annually visited by the colonial District Commissioner and 'cleaned' by local traditional leaders.[23] In the early 1960s, Pupu was again racked by violence: it was here that some of the most violent confrontations between Zapu nationalists and the Rhodesian police and army took place. In the 1970s, Pupu became a Zipra stronghold. The grave and *mtswiri* tree were regularly visited by guerrillas who encouraged the performance of ceremonies to gain ancestral spirit support. Pupu was thus highly significant in Ndebele, Zapu and Zipra – as well as Rhodesian – identity and history.

---

[22] *Moto*, April 1995, p. 2.
[23] Interviews with Kraalhead Magwaza Ndlovu, Pupu, 20 February 1996; Pilot Ncube and Daveti Sibanda, Pupu, 2 April 1996.

When the central government called on provincial and district levels to designate sites for heroes' acres, it was not surprising that Pupu should play a central role. There were, however, obstacles in the pre-Unity period for the obvious reason that Matabeleland's living local heroes were on the run, in detention, or otherwise facing persecution. The Nkayi District Council first debated the subject of a District Heroes' Acre in 1984, but no action was taken.[24] The question arose again in 1986. Nkayi councillors decided to approach their opposite numbers in Lupane with a proposal for a joint Heroes' Acre at Pupu; Lupane agreed to the idea.[25] The Lupane council established a committee 'to identify fallen heroes', but found it 'impossible to move to villages to assess cases without funds'.[26] In Nkayi, the composition of the council's Heroes' Acre committee was hardly calculated to inspire trust: the CIO, army and police were all represented.[27] No action was taken until after Unity when the Provincial Governor once again called on councils to urgently designate district sites for the burial of heroes.[28] Nkayi's council reiterated its preference for Pupu, but was told each district had to have a separate shrine.[29] In early 1989, the Nkayi council chairman, who had been in touch with leading Zapu figures, informed the council that the Zapu Central Committee had decided that all places where guerrillas were buried would be declared 'shrines', but not 'heroes' acres'.[30] Representatives of the Zapu War Shrines Committee visited the district shortly thereafter in search of guerrilla graves.[31] But again, no action was taken to mark graves, or to designate a heroes' acre.

It was only in 1992 that Pupu became a site for commemoration. It was not, however, to be a conventional heroes' acre, and nor did the impetus for action come primarily through official channels. A National Monuments memorandum of February 1992 noted that local people wanted a memorial to Lobengula's warriors, that they wanted the *mtswiri* tree to be preserved as the last resting place of Lobengula, that they saw the liberation war as a 'logical conclusion to the 1893 war', and that the 'proposed developments' should be completed for the centenary of Lobengula's last battle.[32] But it was the Mafela Trust (successor of the Zapu War Shrines Committee) which took the initiative in 1992, organizing a Heroes' Day celebration at Pupu with the intention of establishing a shrine to Zipra at the site. Lupane's council also envisioned a museum and caretaker's home, but worried that 'there had been no go ahead from the top', that the council's committee had 'not succeeded in seeing Mr [Joshua] Nkomo about this'.[33] The Mafela Trust activists – principally Jeremy Brickhill, Dumiso Dabengwa, Richard Dube and Nicholas Nkomo – went ahead nonetheless. They were well-known figures: Dube and Nkomo had worked in Lupane and other Matabeleland districts while identifying Zipra graves; Nkomo had been wartime commander of this entire region; Dabengwa was, of course, a high profile figure. All were former Zipra and Zapu, and they drew on the legitimacy which that history gave them. They consulted widely with local leaders, including Chiefs Mabhikwa and Menyezwa; MP Nkosembi Khumalo, the grandson of Lobengula; district councillors, particularly Zipra ex-combatant K.K. Nyathi in whose ward Pupu fell; and spiritual leaders and elders of the area. Joshua Nkomo was, in the end, drawn into the arrangements.

24  Nkayi District Council, 12 March 1984.
25  Nkayi District Council, 29 September 1986; Kusile District Council, 26 January 1987.
26  Kusile District Council, 23 January 1987.
27  Nkayi District Council, 17 August 1987.
28  Minutes of the Governor's Meeting held at Nkayi District Council, 22 August 1988.
29  Nkayi District Council, 26 September 1988.
30  Nkayi District Council, 20 March 1989.
31  Nkayi District Council, 19 June 1989, 21 August 1989.
32  Quoted in T. Ranger, 'Indigenous Ideas: Accounting for Drought, Making Rain and Healing History in Matabeleland, 1992', ms., Oxford, 1992, pp. 10–11.
33  Kusile District Council, 8 June 1992.

In the event, some 5,000 people arrived at Pupu for the August 11 ceremony. The night before, groups gathered around fires. They included chiefs and headmen, war veterans and elders, old and young, men and women, locals and visitors, whites and blacks. Rites of propitiation were carried out for the spirits of the white and black dead; praise poems were chanted to Mzilikazi and Lobengula; a medium of Mambo danced and sang, invoking an earlier history of violence and displacement. The following day, Ndebele war songs and praise poems were performed, there were Kalanga spirit dances, and the Mambo medium had his say.[34] This was certainly an extraordinary event, far more popular, multi-voiced and historically sweeping than the official enactments at Heroes' Acres. As *Horizon* reporter Thabo Kunene wrote, 'As a people's celebration, it was in remarkable contrast to the near-empty stands seen at other official provincial Heroes' Day festivals. At Pupu the feasting and dancing went on all night.' This 'people's celebration of their history', however, was more problematic than it seemed.[35]

South-African journalist Allister Sparks wrote a revealing account of the ceremony on the basis of information supplied by Mafela Trust organizer Jeremy Brickhill before the fact. He recorded, wrongly as it turned out, that Zanla ex-combatants, including 'the Minister of State Security [Emmerson Mnangagwa] who sent the ruthless Fifth Brigade into Matabeleland in the 1980s', had gathered alongside their Zipra counterparts, 'To stand together and admit what was done and read out the names of those that died at one another's hands.'[36] Zanla representatives were not in fact present and no names were read out. Mnangagwa had visited Pupu earlier, but he did not attend the ceremony. Not only was the chance for a public exchange between the former leaders of Zipra and Zanla lost, but so was the opportunity for recognition of an older, pre-nationalist unity: Mnangagwa's grandfather had, in fact, fought at Pupu with Lobengula's Insukamini regiment. Zipra proved a problematic subject even within its own ranks. Zipra representatives were not given a voice during the public speeches, which were instead dominated by Joshua Nkomo. He took the opportunity to promote the cause of Unity. The most senior Zipra representative involved in the ceremony's organization, Dumiso Dabengwa, was unable to attend: he was required to appear at the national Heroes' Day ceremonies in Harare instead.

Perhaps most importantly, the Mafela Trust was not, in the end, able to establish a shrine to the Zipra dead. Local elders and spiritual leaders insisted that the shrine had to wait until the proper ceremonies had been carried out for the dead of 1893, until the spirit of Lobengula had been asked to return in an *umbuyiso* ceremony.[37] This has, to date, not occurred, despite the fact that a high-profile meeting with Joshua Nkomo, MPs, chiefs, headmen, councillors, party representatives and others endorsed the calls for a shrine for both guerrillas and Lobengula's warriors at Pupu shortly after the 1992 ceremony,[38] and the fact that another celebration was planned for the following year at

[34] See accounts in the October 1992 issue of *Horizon*: J. Brickhill, 'Matabeleland Makes Peace with its Past', pp. 16–17, 19; T. Ranger, 'Healing the Land', pp. 16, 23; T. Kunene, 'The Pupu Pungwe – a new way to mark Heroes' Day', p. 17, and 'Lobhengula's Last Day', p. 18.

[35] Kunene, 'The Pupu Pungwe', p. 17.

[36] Quoted in Ranger, 'Indigenous Ideas', p. 12.

[37] Kunene, 'Lobhengula's Last Day', p. 18; Brickhill, 'Matabeleland Makes Peace with its Past', p. 19.

[38] Minutes of the Vice-President's Meeting, the Honourable Dr. J.M. Nkomo, with Chiefs and Headmen, Elders, Members of Parliament, ZANU (P.F.) Party Officials, Government Officials and Councillors, Mguza Training Centre, 5 September 1992, File: CHK 14, DA's Office, Nkayi. The Matabeleland North Provincial Council also backed calls for a shrine, and officially upgraded Pupu to the status of Provincial Heroes' Acre in October 1992. Minutes of the Provincial Council Meeting, Bulawayo, 30 October 1992, File: Provincial Council Committee, Minutes of Meetings, DMN/ZPC, PA's Office, Bulawayo.

which the centenary of Lobengula's death would be marked. In September 1993, the Lupane Council Heroes' Committee noted that 'the people of Pupu were prepared to offer anything for a celebration but the Provincial Administrator's office advised against conducting a celebration at Pupu'.[39] The much-anticipated follow-up to the 1992 ceremony was thus never realized. Instead, a full five years later, an official monument to the unknown soldier was unveiled by the provincial governor near Lupane administrative centre. The ceremony, held on Heroes' Day in 1998 as part of nationwide festivities, and the monument itself were met with scepticism and apathy. Few attended, and those who did found the symbolism of the much delayed monument singularly inappropriate: former guerrillas who were present wondered how a soldier could be unknown – they wanted to know who he was, where he was from, and they wondered what purpose a single soldier served. This was a far cry from the all-encompassing aspirations of the Pupu ceremony and its hoped for follow-up.[40]

The absences and silences at the 1992 ceremony, the failure to build the planned shrines, and the eventual official substitution of the unknown soldier for the many hoped for historical figures, indicated still controversial aspects of the nation's memory and politics – the recognition to be given the nineteenth-century Ndebele state, Zipra's contribution to the war, and the shadowy presence of the victims of the violence of the 1980s. The latter were perhaps the most threatening, as subsequent events would reveal.

In February 1997, a different commemoration of the dead was planned in Lupane, this time with the explicit goal of memorializing those killed in the violence of the 1980s. Unlike the Pupu event, this was a local initiative which sought to 'break the silence' of the Gukurahundi period. The initiative preceded the publication and public discussion of the CCJP/LRF report on human rights abuses in Matabeleland. It was truly a ground-breaking effort. The community of Gandangula in Daluka planned a large public ceremony at the site of one of the district's mass graves. They intended to erect a gravestone inscribed with the names of five Fifth Brigade victims. The organizers, who included the school's headmaster, kraalheads and other local leaders, raised more then Z\$4,000 from the Gandangula community, in addition to which local families each donated one bag of cement. Well over one thousand people were invited. It was hoped that the local MP and Provincial Governor would address the meeting.[41]

Organizers publicized their plans for the event in the *Zimbabwe Independent* newspaper in January 1997. The article showed how deeply disturbing was the silence over the 1980s conflict, how unsettling was the presence of unacknowledged mass graves, and how important it was that the killings should be publicly spoken about and the dead commemorated:

> The Gandangula community said the commemoration was to help affected families speak out on the issue, which has been kept quiet in Matabeleland since the signing of the unity accord in 1987. 'On February 12, 1983, the Gandangula area had the blackest day in history. It has taken 14 years without anyone raising the issue or talking about it,' said a statement from the organisers of the commemoration day. The organisers of the event said the planned commemoration, which had been cleared by the police in Lupane, was the first step towards breaking the silence. Five people from Gandangula Village, 20 km east of Lupane shopping centre, were killed in 1983 and buried in a shallow grave within the grounds of a local primary school. The five people, one of whom was a visitor to

---

[39] Kusile District Council, 9 September 1993.

[40] Personal communication from Japhet Masusu, Nkayi, August 1998, and contemporary ZBC coverage of the event. Other unveilings of monuments in Matabeleland and elsewhere were met with similar scepticism.

[41] *Zimbabwe Independent*, 7–13 March 1997.

the area, were shot in cold blood. 'Since it happened no person has talked about it publicly and no traditional proceedings have been carried out. Community members think misfortunes occurring within the village may be caused by the non-recognition of the deceased, who share one grave' ... The highlight of the ceremony will be the erection of a memorial stone and the fencing of the area where the victims are buried. While the coordinators said they could not establish the actual motive behind the killing of the five Lupane villagers, all of whom were male, it is known that the killings were carried out by the Fifth Brigade.[42]

Local accounts of the events of 12 February 1983 mirrored so many other memories of Fifth Brigade killings in Matabeleland North. One Gandangula leader described how the Fifth Brigade soldiers had asked, '"Have you ever seen how people are killed? Well, we'll show you today!" They had rounded people up at the school and shot the five in front of a meeting. The people were asked to dig a shallow grave for them.'[43] The Fifth Brigade had targeted Zapu office holders and ex-Zipra combatants. As another local man recalled, the Fifth Brigade's 'system was first to discover all the people who were [Zapu] office bearers and ex-Zipra and wipe them all out – anyone who had left the country as a refugee, they too were targets. ... At the school, four Zapus were killed and one ex-Zipra.'[44] The soldiers went on to burn down the homes of those they killed. And these were not the only killings in Gandangula: others were killed at the township or 'disappeared'. These included one particularly poignant killing of a demobilized Zipra guerrilla: 'He had returned home and was conducting a ceremony of remembrance for his father, who had died in the liberation struggle as a sellout and informer. On the day he conducted the remembrance of his father, [the Fifth Brigade soldiers] took him from his home and he never returned.'[45] As a result of the killings, 'People fled. ... At the township, they wanted people who had boarded buses. ... They terrorised, there was mass killing and mass beating. ... One person was left dead on the main road. ... The head was too damaged to know who it was.'[46] Many people gathered at nearby St. Luke's hospital, where the wounded were treated and others camped outside in the hope that the mission could provide a degree of protection. Commemorating the five men who lay in the school's shallow grave would clearly be only a small step towards a public acknowledgement of the 1980s violence.

Local organizers of the Daluka ceremony were well aware of the sensitivity of publicly remembering such events in the context of national denial. They had taken care to inform political and other authorities of the event; the Lupane police had cleared the commemoration, saying 'the event was not governed by any laws except if it violated public peace'.[47] Minister of Home Affairs Dumiso Dabengwa had been informed in a briefing from his commanding officer for Matabeleland North: '"People do not need permission to hold such ceremonies. ... I knew about it," said Dabengwa who said his offices had a hand in the holding of the event.' Despite the precautions taken to inform and involve the authorities, the public ceremony was called off at the last minute in the face of CIO intimidation. As the *Zimbabwe Independent* reported: 'Intimidation of Gandangula villagers by the Central Intelligence Organisation reduced ... [the] ceremony held to commemorate Fifth Brigade victims in Lupane to a "private event" attended by a handful of terrified people.' Provincial Governor Welshman Mabhena denied all knowledge of the event, despite claims by the organizers to have sent him

---

[42] *Zimbabwe Independent*, 24 January 1997.
[43] Interview, Daluka, 5 December 1994.
[44] Interview, Daluka, 20 December 1994.
[45] Interview, Daluka, 5 December 1994.
[46] Interview, Daluka, 20 December 1994.
[47] *Zimbabwe Independent*, 24 January 1997.

three letters. He maintained, '"I was not invited. I got the news of the ceremony through other people. I was not consulted at all. Besides it does not help development. I did not know, had I known, I would have told the police to tell the people not to do it."' In place of the planned public ceremony, the 'families of the victims built a make-shift grave, located near one of the classroom blocks within the school grounds. A headstone with the inscription of the names of the deceased villagers was not erected, contrary to original plans. ... The only inscription on the mass grave indicated was Saturday's date.' The school headmaster, who had been central to organizing the event, stayed away from the ceremony. So did the invited officials.[48]

Ten years after Unity, the Zimbabwean polity still struggled with the memory of the 1980s violence. The CIO had made its presence known – and effectively over-ruled the more generous police. Former Zapu politicians like Provincial Governor Mabhena, who had themselves suffered so much in the 1980s, did not defend these local attempts to 'break the silence', to offer respect to the dead. Their narrative of the nation was now one of unity and development, a narrative which could not brook the inscription on the landscape of the names of those who had died in a moment of national division. The ambiguously marked gravestone, the 'private' ceremony at the school, stood as evidence not of a community reconciled with its dead but of a nation unwilling to remember.[49]

That the efforts to establish shrines at Pupu and Daluka should inspire such heavy-handed obstruction is only surprising if they are removed from the context of independent Zimbabwe's politics of commemoration. The rigid, top-down control of the nation's 'heroes' could not be easily relinquished: they symbolized the ruling elite's legitimacy, they created a national identity. Bottom-up efforts to add new names to the list of heroes, to include the 1980s violence in the nation's narrative, struck a blow at that control. The linking of the 1970s war with that of the 1890s threatened to provide a basis for regionalist – if not tribalist – politics which might build on the uneasy legacy of ethnic antagonism left in the wake of the post-independence violence. The first efforts to mark the graves of the victims of the Gukurahundi, if left to spread, might well spark a much wider call to account – and to recount. The control exercised by the ruling elite – both Zanu-PF and former Zapu – over the nation's memory began to fray as never before in the post-Unity period. But though it frayed largely as a result of popular pressures for acknowledgement, these pressures were still susceptible to limitation and repression: initiatives depended upon an intimate interaction between leaders and led. Such conditions also applied to the broader debates over accountability which were sparked by drought and the perceived need for cleansing. It is to these that we now turn.

## Drought, Cleansing and Accountability in the 1990s

The controversies over commemoration were not the only ones to reflect the difficulties of resolving the legacies of war. The devastating nation-wide droughts of 1991–2 and 1994–5 provided the impetus for a profound and new critique of Zimbabwe's leaders, and triggered a far-reaching moral and religious reappraisal of the state and nation.[50] In

[48] See account in the *Zimbabwe Independent*, 7–13 March 1997.
[49] See Werbner's discussion, 'Smoke from the Barrel of a Gun', p. 98.
[50] See the excellent contributions to the special issue of the *Journal of Religion in Africa*, 1995, 25, 3: H. Mafu, 'The 1991–92 Zimbabwean Drought and Some Religious Reactions', pp. 288–309; A. Mawere and K. Wilson, 'Socio-Religious Movements, The State and Community Change: Some Reflections on the Ambuya Juliana Cult of Southern Zimbabwe', pp. 252–88; T. Ranger, 'Religious Pluralism in Zimbabwe', pp. 226–52.

Matabeleland, the search to understand the causes of, and remedies for, drought operated at a number of levels, and was closely linked to the desire for a cleansing of the metaphysical and physical traces of violence. At one level, debates focused on the legitimacy of the national leaders, and returned persistently to the unresolved legacies of the liberation and post-independence wars. These debates drew on a notion of accountability which looked not to the idiom of 'belly politics' but to concepts of leaders' responsibilities to God, the ancestors, and through them their followers, in times of drought and war. These concepts drew heavily on nineteenth-century precedents and nationalist history. At another level, criticisms focused on more accessible local spiritual and secular leaders, and were very much about both the consumptive excesses of these leaders and ongoing social struggles within communities. These two levels of debate at times intersected in the initiatives taken by both local and regional actors to confront drought and the legacies of war, illustrating the complex interplay of local struggles and national politics.

### Omissions and Commissions of the Leaders

The widespread belief that Zimbabwe's liberation war had been supported by the ancestors and the powers of both the Matopos rainshrines in Matabeleland South and the Nevana medium to the north, formed the basis for a critique of national leaders and a common thread in debates over post-war cleansing and drought.[51] People in Matabeleland charged national leaders with neglecting the rainshrines after they had come to power. They had failed to 'report' properly to the shrines, to thank the spirits and Mwali for their support, to offer an apology for the violence, and to lead the way in cleansing the nation of the effects of war.

In the Shangani, people remembered how nationalist leaders and guerrillas had consulted the Nevana medium in Gokwe district and the Matopos shrines in Matabeleland South, how the spirits had actively supported nationalism and later guerrilla war. Zapu's nationalism had invoked the goals of freedom, equality and 'one man one vote', but had also cast Zapu leader Joshua Nkomo as the 'father of the nation', endorsed by the Matopos shrines and the ancestors. His trip to the Dula shrine in the Matopos in the 1950s, where he asked for guidance and strength in the struggle for independence, was much recounted. Former Zapu leaders in the Shangani often described Nkomo as the 'holder of the *inkezo*', or calabash, a position which had two related meanings: first, as the head of an extended family, the holder of the *inkezo* was responsible for solving problems within the family and maintaining relations with the ancestors; second, the holder of the *inkezo* was someone with particular duties and powers with regard to rainmaking.[52] Local party leaders held that Nkomo's powers were such that his rallies themselves brought rain: 'when we were still fighting for our freedom, Nkomo could call meetings in Wankie, in Harare, anywhere, and it would be raining throughout. Trucks would get stuck in the heavy rains.'[53]

For many former Zapu leaders in the Shangani, this understanding of Nkomo's leadership meant that only he could legitimately rule the new nation. One party chairwoman asserted that Nkomo had been 'given the mandate to rule in 1957 on his

---

[51] See T. Ranger, *Voices from the Rocks. Nature, Culture and History in the Matopos Hills of Zimbabwe* (Oxford, James Currey, 1999), Chapters 7 and 8, for a broad discussion of these themes in Matabeleland generally and with regard to the Njelele shrine particularly.

[52] See discussion of the position of holder of the *inkezo* generally in Leslie Nthoi, 'The Social Perspective of Religion: A Study of the Mwali Cult of Southern Africa', Ph.D., University of Manchester, 1995, p. 179.

[53] Interview with Paul Mapetshwana Moyo, Gampinya, 19 October 1995. Also see interview with Mpulazi Msipa, Lupanda, 28 March 1996.

first visit [to the Dula shrine], so it can only be him'.[54] The fact that Nkomo did not win the 1980 elections was deeply problematic. 'The way I look at it,' a former Zapu political commissar explained, 'Joshua Nkomo was chosen by the ancestors to lead the country. But when it came to independence, that power was usurped from him and given to another man and from there the ancestors and God turned against us.'[55] It was Nkomo and not Mugabe who held the *inkezo*, and hence could bring fertility and rain: 'How can rain come to someone who has no *inkezo*? Josh is the holder of the *inkezo* and it is empty,' lamented another local leader.[56]

Notwithstanding his weighty status as holder of the *inkezo* and father of the nation, Joshua Nkomo's involvement with Njelele after independence was deeply controversial in Matabeleland. Nkomo was responsible for two ceremonies. The first, a celebration of independence, was held in 1980. Nkomo subsequently established a Committee for National Shrines to advise on shrine affairs (the *Inkundla ye Litshe Lemvelo*). This Committee organized a second meeting in 1982. It was presided over by the controversial shrine keeper Sitwanyana, who Nkomo had long backed and who he had reinstalled at the shrine after his eviction by guerrillas in the 1970s. The ceremony appealed to the 'traditional chiefs' to uphold 'the traditions, culture and customs of our people'. However, the Matopos chiefs, as well as many local people, were strong critics of Sitwanyana, considering him corrupt and illegitimate. They remained unconvinced by Nkomo's endorsement. In 1985, dissidents, acting on local resentments much as guerrillas had done before them, drove Sitwanyana from the shrine once again, forcing him to take refuge on one of Nkomo's farms.[57]

Though people in the Shangani were not nearly so aware of the complex machinations at the shrines as the people and chiefs of the Matopos, they also interpreted Nkomo's interventions there as problematic and incomplete. Some said he had not invited the proper people to the ceremonies, that he had not used these occasions to thank those who had suffered and died in the war. He had been overly concerned with trumpeting his own glory and had neglected the guerrillas and ordinary people who made up his political and military following. 'There had been too much blood spilt on the ground,' argued Ndaleka Mapala. 'When Nkomo went to Njelele he didn't report all the dead.'[58] And the opportunity had not been taken to cleanse the effects of 'the guns, gases and bombs – all the things of war'.[59]

The Nevana medium in the north was the object of a similar, if less elaborate, popular discourse of leaders' neglect. Nevana had supported Zipra guerrillas during the war; he had been visited by senior Zapu politicians. In retaliation, the Rhodesians had bombed his home, and he was said to have miraculously escaped due to his great powers. But people stressed that no apology had ever been made by Nkomo or anyone else for Nevana's consequent displacement from his father's home – nor had the leaders acknowledged his role in the struggle.[60] The Nevana medium himself explained, 'The

---

[54] Interview with Ivy Ndlovu, Mateme, 23 November 1995.
[55] Interview with Moffat Mbombo, Mateme, 23 November 1995.
[56] Interview with Matshaya Mpofu, Mateme, 23 November 1995.
[57] See Ranger, *Voices from the Rocks*, chapter 8; J. Alexander, 'Dissident Perspectives on Zimbabwe's Post-independence War', *Africa*, 68, 2, 1998. Zapu politicians made other appeals to the Matopos shrines, reportedly asking them for advice during the violence of the 1980s, and during the Unity Accord negotiations. See Ranger, *Voices from the Rocks*, chapter 8; Nthoi, 'The Social Perspective of Religion', pp. 222–3.
[58] Interview with Ndaleka Mapala, Dakamela, 11 September 1995. Also see interview with Madoda Ndhlovu, Gampinya, 8 December 1994.
[59] Interview with Luka Mpofu, Mtshabi, 12 October 1995.
[60] Interviews with Luka Mpofu, Mtshabi, 12 October 1995; Mlingo Ncube, Dakamela, 25 August 1995; Christopher Ngwenya, Mzola 28 January 1996.

leaders have not come to thank me for my help. Immediately after the war, no leader came to say we have conquered, the country is in our hands. The spirits don't know the country is independent up to now.'[61]

If Nkomo's initiatives were considered to be inconclusive at best, Mugabe's interventions were considered wholly illegitimate. His offences were limited to the Njelele shrine. Zanu(PF) ministers had made heavy-handed attempts to install Shona-speaking shrine keepers and, in 1982, government forces had attacked Njelele.[62] One shrine adept explained, 'At independence the government made a blunder by fighting someone who wasn't fighting them – they broke the clay pots at Elitsheni [the Njelele shrine].'[63] A group of elderly kraalheads made a similar case:

> During the war [in the 1980s] people were not together. Ceremonies were not properly done at Elitsheni. People were divided. These wosanas had no time to celebrate there. It seemed everything was at a standstill. And, at the Njelele shrine, there are earthen pots which are kept full of water – during the war Mugabe's soldiers were sent there to go inside the cave and take the pots. Where they've gone, no one knows. The normal practice was, if there's going to be plenty of rain you'd find these pots full of water, but now they're not there. ... It was disrespect. There was also shooting inside [the cave].[64]

Mugabe had made the gravest of mistakes – he had 'erred against our ancestors' by 'using ammunition at Njelele'.[65]

More generally, the post-independence violence in Matabeleland was cast as the action of an illegitimate ruler. Mugabe was said to have 'angered God' and hence brought drought. Drought was 'an act of government because the government is not governing in an acceptable way'.[66] An old activist reflected, 'Mugabe should go and apologize sincerely to the spirits – without a personal apology, I don't foresee change.'[67] Others elaborated on this point through biblical comparisons:

> Mwali doesn't like Mugabe, he doesn't care for people, so Mwali stopped the rain. There are bones in the forests and gulleys – you wouldn't have someone killed just anywhere if the President was good to people. It's like King Nebuchadnezzar in the bible – God hated him and sent drought. If the nation's not quite good, then God will destroy everything.[68]

The crucial role attributed to nationalist leaders in these accounts highlighted the continued potency of the political and spiritual relationships defined through decades of building rural nationalism. These were powerful ties, and it is certainly true that African religion 'offered a critique of the state which gave rural people a voice'.[69] It was

---

[61] Interview with Sampson Tewasira, Gokwe, 19 September 1995.

[62] On these events, see Ranger, *Voices from the Rocks*, chapter 8.

[63] Interview with *wosana* England Ngwenya, Tshakalisa, 6 December 1995.

[64] Interview, Mabayi, 21 September 1995. This was a very widely held view. E.g., interviews with Lazarus Sibanda, Johnson Mpofu and Alson Tshabalala, Malindi, 12 September 1995; Enos Kanye, Tshugulu, 27 November 1995; Phineas Ncube, Somakantana, 16 December 1994.

[65] Interview with V.J. Ndhlovu, Mateme, 23 November 1995.

[66] Interview with Fakasi Mthwasa, Menyezwa, 30 January 1996. Similar points were made in many interviews: e.g., Paul Mapetshwana Moyo, Gampinya, 19 October 1995; Anderson Ncube and Round Sibanda, Mzola, 1 February 1996.

[67] Interview with Mhanqwa Ndlovu, Ngondo, 2 February 1996.

[68] Interview with Phineas Ncube, Somakantana, 16 December 1994.

[69] Ranger, 'Religious Pluralism in Zimbabwe', p. 241.

not, however, a voice which could command – such was not the nature of the relation-ship between nationalist leaders and their followers. As a Zapu veteran in Nkayi explained, 'the droughts come from the leaders failing to go to the shrines – they are our fathers, they should go', but he could not ask them to do that: 'We can't ask them – you can't ask the President!'[70]

There were others who were, however, more readily confronted and criticized in debates about the causes of drought. The Njelele shrine keepers themselves, the many shrine messengers and *wosana*, the Nevana medium and local chiefs were all accorded a share of the blame. These criticisms were born of different kinds of relationships from those with nationalist leaders and they were expressed in a different idiom. They were very much about the 'belly politics' which was not central to discussions of the failings of nationalist leaders, and they were powerfully shaped by the longstanding divisions within communities between Christians and 'traditionalists', evictees and earlier settlers of the Shangani.

Both the keepers at Njelele and the Nevana medium came in for trenchant criticism. Much of the detail of the complex machinations at the Njelele shrine were unknown in the Shangani, but intimations of corruption, of keepers using the shrine for personal profit were nonetheless common. Some alleged that shrine delegates waited for pilgrims at the bus stop and charged them fees. Others complained of the use of the shrine by *izinyanga* for their own business, or of the damaging effects of the rivalries among keepers.[71] In the case of the Nevana medium, criticisms focused on his overly 'modern' predelictions for cars and fine clothes, women and brandy. People in the Shangani had had occasion to observe him directly as he travelled periodically to the homes of Chiefs Sikhobokhobo, Dakamela and Mabhikwa to carry out ceremonies. Luka Sibanda complained:

> The former Nevana used to walk [when he came to Nkayi] and when he crossed the Kana we would carry him on our backs, and the same for the Shangani. But the current Nevana is a gentleman: he crosses with a car or on foot and he can walk into a bottlestore and buy beer and even drink hot stuff. That's what he does but the spirit does not wish him to do this. Nevana shouldn't be wearing fancy clothes – he should just wear a black cloth to cover his private parts. To show the spirits were against this, Nevana put on a suit to visit a girlfriend and the suit burnt to ashes while he was wearing it. A second time he was going to a girlfriend and he got into a car and a big wind developed and he couldn't drive to the place.[72]

A Nevana messenger blamed excessive thunder and wind on Nevana's use of a car, and criticized the chiefs for not addressing the problem.[73] Others condemned the medium for travelling to areas south of the Shangani in an effort to extend his influence.[74]

Criticism was also directed against individuals and groups within the Shangani,

---

[70] Interview with Goodenough Mpunzi, Sibangelana, 6 December 1994.

[71] E.g., interviews with Luka Mpofu, Mtshabi, 12 October 1995; Enos Kanye, Tshugulu, 27 November 1995; Mlingo Ncube, Dakamela, 25 August 1995; L. Malaba, Maphanabomu, 12 September 1995.

[72] Interview with Luka Sibanda, Kana, 5 December 1995.

[73] Interview with Mlingo Ncube, Dakamela, 25 August 1995. Ncube wanted Nkayi's chiefs to 'gather and tell Nevana not to use a motor car. The chiefs are now making money and they are young boys and so they don't mind Nevana's car and women. These chiefs are being told by local people what to do, told by just anybody. Sikhobokhobo is too old and Sivalo goes to church. Dakamela and Nkalakatha are too young.'

[74] Interview with *wosana* England Ngwenya, Tshakalisa, 6 December 1995.

illustrating the lack of consensus on the causes of drought, and the perennial nature of local divisions. Rainshrine messengers, *wosana* and chiefs came under attack for their ignorance, lack of commitment, their youth, or for diverting funds meant for ritual purposes to their own use in the context of the 1990s' droughts. Disputes over successors to famous local rainmakers and shrine messengers reflected a variety of longstanding social cleavages – between different generations of migrants, between those favouring Nevana and those favouring Njelele, between chiefs and their subjects. Those involved in 'traditional' religion at times levelled their criticisms against social groups, primarily youth and Christians. They were charged with failing to maintain, or even directly desecrating, local sacred places, as well as with a refusal to observe the rest days mandated by the spiritual centres.[75] Some Christian churches – most notably the Catholics – responded to such charges by organizing joint ceremonies to pray for rain; others simply ridiculed traditional beliefs about rainmaking, and the shrine adepts themselves.[76] They offered biblical, and sometimes apocalyptic, counter-explanations for drought. As one Seventh Day Adventist churchgoer and party chairwoman explained: 'The drought is biblical. It is a fulfillment of the prediction of famine and thirst, incurable diseases like AIDS, war and false prophets [a reference to witch-cleansers]. We erred and killed each other. The bible has been fulfilled. Then comes the end of the world.'[77]

The charges levelled at national leaders, and the much divided and contested local context, set the scene for a variety of initiatives intended to bring an end to drought and to cleanse the effects of war.

## Taking Action: Local and Regional Initiatives

The many local initiatives taken in the face of what was seen as a disrupted natural and political order were cast as partial measures, and certainly not as a substitute for nationalist leaders' actions. Nonetheless, they brought a sense of achievement, and altered the relative influence of various religious centres and figures. Some were strictly local initiatives, others sought to make wider links and operated in interaction with the regional and national politics of chieftaincy, war veterans and the Njelele shrine.

The two most common responses to drought in villages all over the Shangani were gatherings to 'clean' the forests, known as *ukwebula inxoza* or *mqawule*, and ceremonies at local rainshrines or *mtolos*. The former were generally uncontroversial. They were organized by secular leaders (kraalheads, headmen and chiefs) and did not involve ancestral or territorial spirit mediums. The latter involved *wosanas*, messengers to the major rainshrines (*abahambi bendlela*) as well as secular leaders, and were the focus of much contestation. Sometimes the two ceremonies were linked – forests were cleaned prior to a visit to one of the regional raincentres or a *mtolo* ceremony – and both were important in reinforcing the popular association between drought and war.

In cleaning ceremonies, the chief, headman or kraalhead called upon men to search the forests, removing bones, birds' nests, the branches of trees hit by lightning, and killing animals encountered on the way.[78] These items were piled up and burnt, the meat was roasted and eaten unsalted, and finally participants washed in nearby rivers

---

[75] E.g., interviews with Kraalhead Wilson Ncube, Mateme, 23 November 1995; Julia Sibanda and Kedemon Ziyapapa Tshuma, Matshokotsha, 4 April 1996.

[76] On Catholic endeavours to incorporate 'traditions', see interview with Jeremiah Moyo, Gomoza, 13 March 1996. On ridiculing rainmakers, see interview with Councillor Timothy Mthethwa, Kwesengulube, 1 December 1995.

[77] Interview with Ivy Ndlovu, Mateme, 23 November 1995. See also interview with members of the Apostolic Faith Mission Church in Zion, Maponawemvu, 28 August 1996; Councillor Dume-sweni, Matshiya, 18 September 1995.

[78] These ceremonies are described in Rev. W. Bozongwana, *Ndebele Religion and Customs* (Gweru, Mambo Press, 1983). We also have many interview accounts of this practice.

or pools. This was a longstanding practice, and the bones gathered were usually those of animals, but the existence of human bones in the forest, scattered or in mass graves, heightened the association between drought and the legacies of war and was a cause of great concern. One group of elders spoke of the 'human skeletons in the forest – that is taboo'.[79] Others spoke of 'people killed in the war, eaten by birds and never buried. It is not right that a person's skeleton should be left lying around like that.'[80] The years of violence had also disrupted cleaning ceremonies. Some people said they had been too afraid to clean the forests, which were the sites of so much killing, during the wars.[81] Others pointed to the problem of organizing any community activity in the wake of violence: 'We thought of cleaning the forest after the [1980s] war, but no one wanted to make a meeting, as it would be thought you were trying to make a revival of what we had just been through.'[82] However, by the time of our research – a full seven years after Unity – most communities had succeeded in organizing such events.

Ceremonies held at *mtolo* trees, of which there are dozens in the Shangani, were altogether more controversial affairs. As discussed in earlier chapters, the divisions between evictees and locals, between practitioners of traditional and Christian religions, expressed themselves in contestations over the authenticity and efficacy of particular *mtolos* and rainshrine adepts, and over the *mtolo* ceremonies as a whole. The advent of nationalism, and particularly the guerrilla war, had strengthened the hand of 'traditional-ists' against Christians, a shift which favoured the early settlers of the Shangani. The severe droughts and epidemics of the 1990s, and the perceived need for a response to the legacies of war, tended to reinforce this shift, as well as to spark wider debates about customary practices.

The drought, disease and war-related revitalization of traditional religion received a further boost from the attention paid to chiefs by both politicians and the Ministry of Local Government in the 1990s.[83] The role of chiefs as 'cultural custodians' was much emphasized, providing a stimulus to their interventions in religious practice, if in no way making these interventions less controversial. In Matabeleland, in the midst of the severe drought of 1992, Joshua Nkomo told chiefs that there were 'a lot of confusing stories' about Njelele, and this 'was one of the areas of concern where chiefs' advice was being sought'. The meeting agreed that 'chiefs should consider themselves as our traditional leaders, custodians of our culture who should play a vital role in the cultural procedures with particular emphasis on rain-making ceremonies.'[84] Chiefs and their

---

[79] Group interview, Ndlovu school, Matshiya, 18 September 1995.

[80] Interview with Mhanqwa Ndlovu, Ngondo, 2 February 1996. Such sentiments were very commonly expressed, e.g., interviews with M. Kheswa, Jotsholo, 3 February 1996; Faneni Khumalo, Mateme, 23 November 1995.

[81] E.g., interview with Headman Fanisoni, Fanisoni, 24 November 1994.

[82] Interviews with Mavelalitshone Mpofu, Matshiya, 19 January 1996; Anderson Ncube and Round Sibanda, Mzola, 1 February 1996.

[83] Government policy with regard to chiefs had long been ambivalent. Though chiefs had lost many of their colonial powers at independence, they were still credited with a 'cultural' role. In 1985, they were promised the return of their courts, a measure which began to be implemented in the 1990s. In 1988, President Mugabe had called on DAs to urgently consult with chiefs on a range of issues from bride price to the status of women, to land allocation. See PA, Matabeleland North, to all DAs, 8 March 1989; Meeting of Matabeleland North Chiefs' Provincial Assembly, Ntabazinduna Chiefs' Hall, 14 March 1989, File: CHK 14, DA's Office, Nkayi.

[84] Minutes of the Vice President's Meeting, the Honourable Dr. J.M. Nkomo, with Chiefs and Headmen, Elders, Members of Parliament, ZANU (P.F.) Party Officials, Government Officials and Councillors, Mguza Training Centre, 5 September 1992, File: CHK 14, DA's Office, Nkayi. Also see Minutes of the Chief's Meeting, Ntabazinduna Chiefs' Hall, 1 September 1992, in the same file.

subordinates in the Shangani began to try to enforce the rest days demanded by Njelele (Wednesday) and Nevana (Thursday). In Lupane, Chief Mabhikwa sent a letter to all kraalheads and headmen in July 1993 authorizing them to punish those found working on a rest day with a 200 dollar fine.[85] Several headmen in Nkayi authorized followers to fine or confiscate the ploughs or oxen of those found in their fields on rest days, practices sometimes endorsed by the Nevana medium.[86] Such actions were applauded by many but deeply offended Christians – they pointed out that observance of the Sabbath was not upheld by fines.

Chiefs also tried to establish the Shangani River as a formal boundary between the spheres of influence of the Matopos shrines to the south and Nevana to the north. Where the new boundary altered previous practices it was a source of much discontent. Chief Mabhikwa's efforts to convert an area under his authority from Njelele to Nevana provoked charges that the switch had caused the disappearance of ancestral bees and snakes: 'Nevana is the cause of that disappearance, because those things are related to Njelele. ... Nevana's proper area of work is over the other side [of the river]. This side he comes as an intruder and a causer of discord and drought.'[87] Others rejected the chiefs' initiative on different grounds. A councillor argued: 'It is the spirit and not another person who has the right to tell you where to go. The government says in the Constitution of Zimbabwe we all have freedom of worship, so that means you can go to where your spirits are satisfied.'[88]

Amidst these divisive assertions of chiefly power, there were others which involved a much wider set of actors and which sought to bring local initiatives into a regional context, and into interaction with national leaders. By far the most ambitious set of initiatives to combat drought, to intervene at Njelele and to cleanse guerrillas, was largely the result of the efforts of one Jonathon Nkanyezi Sibanda. Nkanyezi, who came from Nkayi and now worked for the Bulawayo City Council, wore many hats: he was an ex-Zipra combatant and executive officer of the provincial War Veterans' Association (WVA); he was an influential *inyanga* who had held the post of president of the provincial Zimbabwe National Traditional Healers' Association (Zinatha); he had long been interested in the workings of Njelele – his spirits had told him that an offering needed to be made at the shrine, that the proper keeper needed to be installed. His desire to intervene at the Njelele shrine found a receptive audience in Nkayi. At a meeting of chiefs, headmen, councillors, Zinatha and Arts Council representatives in Nkayi, Nkanyezi 'emphasised the need for the restoration of the situation at Njelele'. Others present stressed the need for shrines to be given 'due respect', noting that politicians had called on the shrines in time of war, 'but forgot to do the same when they came back victorious'. They resolved to contact the key Matopos chiefs with regard to Njelele; they stressed the crucial role chiefs had to play in 'restoring culture'.[89]

The model established for righting what had gone wrong at the shrine invoked the practices of Mzilikazi, King of the nineteenth-century Ndebele state. As Luka Mpofu, an active member of Nkayi's National Arts Council, explained:

> We asked why is this country in this state? What can we do? We agreed to follow the example of Mzilikazi. When Mzilikazi came into this country, he sent black cows to Njelele. Those were meant for good living between Mzilikazi and [the

[85] Interview with Mavelalitshone Mpofu, Matshiya, 19 January 1996.
[86] Interviews with *wosana* England Ngwenya, Tshakalisa, 6 December 1995; Kraalhead M.S. Ndlovu, Dwala, 9 December 1995; Councillor Elias Sibanda and Daniel Ncube, Kana, 28 November 1995.
[87] Interview with L. Malaba, Maphanabomu, 12 September 1995.
[88] Interview with Councillor Ruben Dube, Malunku, 6 March 1996.
[89] Meeting of Chiefs and Headmen in the DA's Office, Nkayi, 30 June, 1992, File: CHK14, DA's Office, Nkayi.

autochthonous ruler] Mambo, so there was peace and tranquility and no war
between the two.[90]

The Nkayi chiefs proceeded carefully: they consulted with chiefs in the Matopos, as
well as the Provincial Administrator, before acting. With official approval, they began to
collect money to purchase several beasts, a process which involved organizing and
raising substantial funds from local people.[91] After four cows had been purchased,
ceremonies were organized by the chiefs, and prominent *wosanas* were drafted in to
bless the cattle. The cows were then sent to Njelele, accompanied by four rainshrine
messengers, each representing one of the chieftaincies that had donated a beast.

The initiative was remarkable as an organizational feat, but its fate illustrated the
tremendous sensitivity required in overcoming local differences, and the complex
politics of the shrines themselves. Nkanyezi and the Matopos chiefs favoured the shrine-
keeper Ngcathu Ncube (MaNcube), on whose behalf Nkanyezi had been running a
campaign for some time, and who had only recently been reinstalled at the shrine. They
were strongly opposed to Joshua Nkomo's candidate, Sitwanyana, who was MaNcube's
estranged husband and the man she held responsible for unjustly ousting her, with
Nkomo's backing, from Njelele.[92] This was a bitter and volatile battlefield: despite their
careful preparations, the Nkayi contingent quickly fell foul of the Matopos players. One
of Nkayi's most prominent *wosanas*, a woman named Sibongo, was delegated to travel
on ahead of the cattle to make preparations for their arrival. She went to Sitwanyana,
considering him the proper keeper of the shrine, and not MaNcube. The Matopos chiefs
reacted with outrage and nearly put an end to the entire effort. When the movement of
the cattle got underway once again, the messengers who accompanied them fell out,
launching vitriolic attacks on each other's authority in spiritual and ethnic terms.[93]
When the cows finally arrived at Njelele they were taken to MaNcube, but no preparations had been made for their arrival, and they were sacrificed before the Nkayi *wosanas*
and other dignitaries had arrived. Some blamed Nkanyezi, others blamed MaNcube,
and still others blamed the quarrelling messengers for this mistake. Whoever was
responsible, the result was disastrous: the proper ceremonies had not been carried out,
the cows had not been blessed, beer had not been brewed. Nkayi's *wosanas* fell ill;
Sibongo refused to have anything further to do with Njelele until the matter was
resolved;[94] and MaNcube nursed suspicions that two cows had been stolen.

[90] Interview with Luka Mpofu, Mtshabi, 12 October 1995. Similar views were expressed by Enos
Khanye, Tshugulu, 27 November 1995, and by Nkanyezi Sibanda himself, Bulawayo, 4 September 1996.
[91] Of the six Nkayi chiefs, two did not contribute. Chief Nkalakatha considered himself too young
and ignorant and in the end contributed only cash, while Chief Sivalo maintained his distance as
a staunch Christian. The four participating chiefs were Sikhobokhobo, Madliwa, Tshugulu and
Dakamela.
[92] The Matopos chiefs and their allies had been publicly denouncing and calling for the expulsion
of Sitwanyana since at least the mid-1980s. By 1992, they felt the shrine to be in such disarray
that they sought to close it down. See Nthoi, 'The Social Perspective of Religion', pp. 246–9 and
*passim*; Ranger, 'Indigenous Ideas', pp. 4–5.
[93] Charges were made of improper methods of driving the cattle, of improper approaches to the
chiefs of the Matopos, and to the shrine itself. The disputes took on an ethnic dimension, related
to the history of the Njelele shrine: one messenger maintained that another was Nguni and
hence had no business approaching the shrine which belonged to the Mambos who had lived in
the region before the arrival of the Ndebele; another maintained that the trouble was caused by
one messenger's ignorance of how to approach Nguni chiefs.
[94] Interviews with Matshisa Mathema and Simon Ndhlovu (representatives of Sibongo), Manomano, 17 October 1995; *wosana* Chithekile Mhlanga, Mdlawuzweni, 11 September 1995. Sibongo's

The outcome of the initiative for the Nkayi delegation was thus a mixed one: while they had succeeded in the momentous task of purchasing, blessing and delivering four cows to Njelele in accordance with what they believed to be the correct nineteenth-century precedents, they had fallen foul of the shrine's own politics in such a way as to severely strain relations between the *wosanas* and chiefs of Nkayi and the shrine. Nkanyezi was, however, able to use the trip as part of his larger project: for him, sending the cows was to play a 'multi-purpose role – drought, cleansing, the installation of the old lady [MaNcube], setting the house in order'. He said that he subsequently brought Joshua Nkomo to the shrine and effected what he saw as a reconciliation between the 'father of the nation' and MaNcube, thereby displacing Sitwanyana as Nkomo's favoured keeper (Sitwanyana nonetheless remained at his Njelele home, in close proximity to, and in direct competition with, MaNcube for some time). For Nkanyezi, this was merely the start to further efforts to 'restore' the shrine.[95]

Nkanyezi's next step required him to don his ex-combatant's cap. He now set about initiating a cleansing, or at least a pre-cleansing, ceremony for guerrillas, to be held at Njelele under the authority of MaNcube. 'We ex-combatants,' he explained:

> realizing that the top leaders were doing nothing, knowing that cleansing must be done whenever people come from war, it was then that we realized 15 years had elapsed and we would do it on our own. We told the leaders we are doing our own thing, because you – Nkomo, former Zapu – have done nothing … and they said go ahead. Because I had the knowledge and light of how things should be done, I initiated the move.[96]

Here he hit a chord with many ex-combatants who were less well connected than himself. In our interviews, former guerrillas often voiced concern over the fact that they had not been properly cleansed, that their return from war had not been reported to Mwali, Nevana and the spirits and thus they were not truly at peace.[97] One such explained: 'I still feel we haven't laid down our weapons because we haven't said we're back. When I dream, I'm carrying a gun, doing operations, I'm still at war, I'm not liberated yet.'[98] In some cases former guerrillas had undergone family cleansing ceremonies. The ex-dissidents had themselves organized several trips to the shrines in an effort to seek cleansing and to alert the spirits and Mwali of the end of war, but felt that they had not yet succeeded, largely because of the lack of support of the nationalist leaders.[99] Cleansing and reporting back after war were held to be intimately linked and were often spoken of together, as part of the same process. That they were linked made the involvement of the political, military and spiritual leaders who had initiated and endorsed war necessary. This sort of cleansing was not about individual wrongs and acts of violence but about the violence of war as a whole, of an army.[100]

---

[94] (cont.) representatives were particularly bitter. They held that the event 'didn't serve a purpose. It hurt the nation, it hurt the people, it was destructive to the ancestors and the whole country.'

[95] Interview with Nkanyezi Sibanda, Bulawayo, 4 September 1996.

[96] Interview with Nkanyezi Sibanda, Bulawayo, 4 September 1996.

[97] Apparently there had been efforts to organize a joint cleansing ceremonies for guerrillas in the Assembly Points after independence, but they had not come to fruition. Interview with Nicholas Nkomo, Nkayi, 15 December 1995. Also see comments from Luka Mpofu, the Nkayi rain messenger, in 'Ex-combatants troubled by evil spirits – claim', *The Sunday News*, 17 September 1995.

[98] Interview with Micah Bhebe, Saziyabana, 14 October 1995.

[99] See Alexander, 'Dissident Perspectives', for further on specifically dissident initiatives in this regard.

[100] Of course, civilians also often perceived a need for post-war cleansing. Here, we confine our comments to ex-combatants.

Nkanyezi, with his connections to the Njelele shrine, his credentials as an ex-combatant and *inyanga*, and his links with senior Zapu politicians, was able to act far more effectively than individual guerrillas, or the suspiciously regarded dissidents. Nkanyezi wrote letters to all DAs and district WVA committees; he approached Dumiso Dabengwa (now Minister of Home Affairs) who agreed to support the effort with the provision of a police lorry to carry ex-combatants to the shrine. Contacts were then made with MaNcube. She explained:

> The freedom fighters came to me – Nkanyezi, Dlomo [another *inyanga*], Dabengwa also, saying, we are not happy about how the country is independent. We are affected by many diseases, instability in the country. We were promised farms but they don't come. We are promised compensation, but we don't see it. The main request was we want our leaders to report to our ancestors that we are back. And there are very many ex-combatants who are mad, who are sick. Our ex-nationalists haven't done enough, they haven't reported back. They wanted to tell the ancestors.[101]

The cleansing ceremony, like Nkanyezi's previous initiatives, drew its form and legitimacy from memories of the wartime practices of the nineteenth century Ndebele king, Mzilikazi. Nkanyezi had consulted elders of the Khumalo clan for guidance concerning pre-colonial precedent. This made sense to those involved in the ceremony as they saw the liberation war as a continuation of the Ndebele state's struggle against colonial conquest. According to Nkanyezi, 'The truth is that the [liberation] war we fought is like that of our forefathers. … It is a continuation of that war. Our forefather's spirit is still with us.'[102] However, by incorporating nineteenth-century precedents into the post-Unity context of ethnic antagonism, he gave old practices new and exclusive overtones. Whereas the shrine's constituency in Mzilikazi's time had included the multi-ethnic warriors of the polity as a whole and also served a much larger, non-Ndebele constituency, Nkanyezi maintained that the cleansing ceremony he was organizing was only for Zipra guerrillas – others should go to their own shrines.

The ceremony was attended by about 30 former Zipra guerrillas, *wosanas* from all over Matabeleland, and the shrine keeper MaNcube.[103] The participants gathered in a clearing at the base of the cave from which the voice of Mwali speaks at Njelele. They spent the night seated around fires while the *wosanas* sang, beat drums and danced. In the early morning, the former guerrillas went to the cave where they made a wide variety of requests relating to their misfortunes and ambitions – many complained of their current economic situation. A bull and sheep were sacrificed in front of the shrine (the bull being the offspring of one of the cows brought from Nkayi). The blood of the bull was drained into a bucket and Nkanyezi mixed it with herbs and soil from inside the cave. The guerrillas were called to the cave where they were sprinkled with the blood mixture. MaNcube used the occasion to make an overtly political speech denouncing those she saw as her enemies, notably Joshua Nkomo and the rival shrine keeper Sitwanyana. A feast of roasted meat followed and the participants left with gifts of black cloth and tobacco from MaNcube.

There were different interpretations of the ceremony. For the Nkayi guerrillas whom

---

[101] Interview with MaNcube, Njelele, 2 September 1996.
[102] Interview with Nkanyezi Sibanda, Bulawayo, 4 September 1996.
[103] Some former guerrillas came from as far away as Manicaland, but most came from nearby areas, from Bulawayo or from Nkanyezi's home area of Nkayi. Many more would likely have attended had it not been for the coincident national strike, which severely hindered communication and transport. The following account is based on J. Alexander and J. McGregor's attendance at the ceremony.

we accompanied, the event had been about cleansing and reporting their return. They left in high spirits, and with a new found loyalty to MaNcube. MaNcube interpreted the ceremony similarly:

> What I was doing there was cleansing. I went in with the ex-fighters, reporting to the ancestors, here are the children. ... You remember the sprinkling of blood – that was to open the way for all ex-combatants to have success in whatever they were doing, to cleanse from sickness. Remember in Mzilikazi's time when soldiers came from war they went into the bush and got some herbs and mixed them up into a concoction to treat those who came from war. At war they met death, killing. Take those guerrillas, those who used to kill innocent people. Some used to kill people because they were rich, to take their clothes. So many lost their senses. So I was asking for Njelele to open their way, to forgive them because it was war.

Though Njelele was not specifically a venue for cleansing and though MaNcube was not in fact capable of cleansing herself – that task was held to be the responsibility of the *izinyanga* – she felt Njelele was an appropriate site for the ceremony. In contrast to Nkanyezi's more partisan depiction of the Njelele ceremony, she argued, '... this place is a national place so it was wise for the cleansing to be held here. ... Njelele is a national thing ... it caters for everybody, it is for the whole world, it enshrines everything.'[104]

In contrast, Nkanyezi saw the ceremony not as a full cleansing, but an apology, and the first step in a long process which would eventually result in cleansing:

> What you saw at Njelele was just the beginning, the first step. We went back to report to the spirits that we fought, that some came back, that some died, that some were mentally disturbed. Now we will carry out the real cleansing at Dula [another Matopos shrine]. ... People will be rinsed, washed, cleansed with lots of herbs. At Dula it will be a proper cleansing, not just rinsing. ... That blood at Njelele was spread to cool down tensions. That wasn't cleansing, [it was] just to cool tensions because people are just dying. It's a cooling down of tempers ceremony, an apology ... because the leaders didn't report for so long.[105]

Nkanyezi was busily engaged in further discussions with Khumalo elders and politicians, intent on planning a second gathering of guerrillas. Two years later, his plans were realized, though not at Dula (a shrine also vexed by competing keepers) as had been hoped, and not without provoking considerable controversy.

Nkanyezi again used his many connections to mobilize support, and this time some 3–5,000 guerrillas from all over the country, though primarily from Matabeleland, attended a second cleansing ceremony at Njelele. On their arrival, they found that the shrine had been damaged by fire – logs used to cover the cave entrance, ancient sacred pots, trees in the area, were all damaged or destroyed.[106] At the ceremony itself, MaNcube informed the gathered guerrillas that her rival Sitwanyana had been responsible, and that he had only narrowly been prevented from stealing the sacred pair of ivory tusks held at the shrine. The guerrillas decided to remove him on the spot,

---

[104] Interview with MaNcube, Njelele, 2 September 1996. MaNcube was not, however, without complaints: she was angry that key notables such as the Matopos chiefs and Dabengwa himself had not attended the ceremony.

[105] Interview with Nkanyezi Sibanda, Bulawayo, 4 September 1996.

[106] See *The Chronicle*, 18 September 1998. The shrine was reportedly attacked on 1 September by unidentified assailants. *The Chronicle* called for their punishment for 'a crime against the Zimbabwean nation'.

sending a contingent of 12 men to his home. A sheep was killed in order to 'restore' the shrine before the cleansing continued. This time the rituals took place on a neigh-bouring hilltop, on which guerrillas knelt and were sprinkled with a special concoction, a process which went on all day. Two black beasts were subsequently sacrificed at the shrine and, on their departure, guerrillas were anointed on the forehead, and given black cloth and tobacco to take home with them. Despite a shortage of beer and food, the guerrillas left in celebratory mood.[107]

While certainly a grander affair than the first ceremony, this one also had its missing cast of characters – notably the nationalist leaders themselves. They were once again chastised for their negligence; for calling on the guerrillas to fight, for appealing to the shrine in wartime but failing to cleanse the blood spilt during the war in its aftermath.[108] The ousting of Sitwanyana caused further controversy: some of those guerrillas involved in his eviction, and the subsequent burning of his home, appeared in court in October 1998 to answer charges. And it seems that senior nationalists, including Joshua Nkomo, still harboured hopes of re-installing the now thrice-evicted keeper.[109] The complex interaction of the shrines, the demands of guerrillas, and the ommissions and commissions of the nationalists looked set to continue.

Like the efforts at memorialization and commemoration, cleansing and drought-related initiatives invoked a lengthy history. They delved into the nineteenth-century past, and drew on the political and spiritual links between leaders and led, constructed through nationalism and guerrilla war. They did not, however, provoke the heavy-handed responses which greeted efforts to mark the landscape with the memory and names of the war dead. Casting drought or the need for cleansing as legacies of war was in some ways less threatening for the nationalist leaders, less challenging to their vision of the nation's history. This was in part due to the deep local divisions over such questions and the wide distribution of blame over time, space and a huge cast of actors. It was also due to the ways in which relationships with nationalist leaders were constructed: while they were held personally responsible for acting to ensure the land's fertility and for cleansing the fighters they had sent to war, they were also cast as 'fathers' from whom action could not be demanded. Their inaction – or inappropriate action – left a vacuum into which others stepped. Alternative visions with potentially divisive consequences were put forward, notably with regard to the attempts to add an element of Ndebele exclusivism to the guerrilla-cleansing ceremonies at the 'national' shrine of Njelele.

## Conclusion

In the post-Unity period, demands for the ritual resolution of the legacies of war, for public commemoration and acknowledgement, drew not on the duties of an abstract state but on a personalized notion of national leaders' responsibilities developed over the course of the nationalist struggle.[110] In Matabeleland, people's demands were directed not at the government generally, but at their (former) Zapu leaders, at those

[107] Personal communication from Japhet Masuku, Nkayi, 23 September 1998. An ex-combatant, Japhet had long worked with us during our research, and had attended the first cleansing ceremony as well as the second.
[108] See report in *The Sunday News*, 13 September 1998, including an interview with Nkanyezi, and personal communication from Japhet Masuku, Nkayi, 23 September 1998.
[109] Personal communication from Pathisa Nyathi, Bulawayo, 15 October 1998. Nyathi reports that a meeting, at which Joshua Nkomo, John Nkomo and Dumiso Dabengwa were present, was held in the hope of installing Sitwanyana once again. It was not, however, successful.
[110] See also Werbner, 'Crisis and Cosmos'.

who had led them in the struggle for liberation. The main route by which people perceived they were able to reach Mugabe, and Zanu(PF) leaders generally, was indirectly, through Zapu. But Zapu's reaction was ambiguous: while some Zapu leaders responded to local demands for commemoration and cleansing with a degree of support, others, and most significantly Joshua Nkomo, upheld the new narrative of Unity, a narrative which could not easily incorporate Matabeleland's turbulent history, particularly the violence of the 1980s, but also that of the 1890s and 1970s.

The tight control exercised by nationalist leaders over public memory in Matabeleland was not, however, wholly successful. And although local attempts to address the legacies of war were sometimes stifled or divisive, they were far from totally counter-productive. The outcome of efforts to hold nationalist leaders accountable and to make memory publicly recountable were ambivalent. They produced effects which were difficult to predict, much less to control. The Pupu ceremony may have failed in bringing together former Zanla and Zipra, and in memorializing Zipra and Lobengula, but it did offer a forum for the expression of a multi-voiced and historical understanding of ethnicity and violence in the region. Some aspects of history were debated and commemorated, even if all memories could not be voiced and were not accorded official recognition. The repression of the Daluka initiative served as a reminder of the intimidatory capacity of the CIO in local people's eyes, and of the silences still enforced in the nation's narrative in the name of development and Unity, even by senior office-holders of the former Zapu. But the local state and the police were not tarred with the same brush as the CIO, and the nameless marker in the Gandangula school grounds will stand as a constant reminder of what was *not* commemorated. The human rights report of the CCJP and LRF may have 'opened old wounds' in the eyes of some, but it was also a triumph of rights-based investigation and an important affirmation of the existence of past wrongs for those who had suffered at the hands of the security forces. Its circulation in the public sphere has already provoked wide-ranging debate and will surely continue to do so.

Drought and cleansing produced similarly complex results. The extraordinary effort to recreate Mzilikazi's homage to Njelele by sending cattle to the Matopos shrine to bring an end to drought, met an unhappy end, victim to the rocky politics of the shrine itself and the spiritual and other divisions within the Shangani. Nonetheless, the effort marked a new level of initiative and cooperation, and set in train the sequence of events which opened the way for the first efforts to cleanse guerrillas collectively. The cleansing ceremonies at Njelele, like the initiatives related to drought, drew legitimacy from a nineteenth-century model, but were given a newly exclusive tone. Zipra and Zanla nonetheless joined together as never before under the umbrella of the War Veterans' Association to effectively express demands for material compensation. These demands had their own effects: by challenging the distribution of the nation's rewards, the door was opened to challenges from the many other groups who had suffered in the name of the nationalist cause.

The politics of memory and violence in the Shangani's dark forests are far from resolved: in coming years, they will continue to shape the relationships between people and their leaders, they will continue to impinge upon the religious and moral in local and national realms, they will continue to shape people's identities and aspirations. For the people of the Shangani the great markers of violence – conquest, eviction, nationalist struggle, guerrilla war and post-independence repression – will remain central to their understanding of their role as citizens of Zimbabwe.

# Sources & References

## ARCHIVAL SOURCES

National Archives of Zimbabwe, Harare

A 3/18/39/21 Methodist petition.

| | |
|---|---|
| C-8130 | Evidence of Umjane, 16 October 1894, *Matabeleland. Report of the Land Commission of 1894 and Correspondence Relating Thereto*, June 1896. |
| Cmnd. 4964 | *Report of the Commission on Rhodesian Opinion under the Chairmanship of the Right Honourable the Lord Pearce*, London, 1972. |
| D 3/8/1 | Criminal cases, Sebungwe District. |
| D 3/23/1 | Rex v Mzungu and Simelwane, 19 October 1909. |
| D 3/23/2-3 | Rex v J.H. Hoare, 26 May 1913. |
| | Rex v W.T. Dymott, 21 August 1914. |
| | Rex v N.G. Von Petty, 9 February 1915. |
| | Rex v J.W. Morrison, 22 April 1915. |
| D 3/23/4 | Rex v Magodi, 19 October 1917. |
| G 1/3/2/16 | Native Commissioner, Bubi to Superintendent of Natives, Bulawayo, 18 May 1922. |
| L 2/2/117/43 | CNC to Chief Secretary, 26 April 1906. |
| | CNC to Chief Secretary, 18 June 1906. |
| LS 100/3B/50 | CNC to NC Lupane, 7 November 1950. |
| N 3/19/3 | Memorandum by CNC, 17 August 1914. |
| | N.C. Carbutt to Superintendent of Natives, Bulawayo, 29 July 1919. |
| N 3/19/4 | Interview with Nyamanda, 19 April 1920. |
| N 6/1/3 | Annual Report, Sebungwe/Mafungabusi, 31 March 1903. |
| N 6/4/7 | Monthly Report, Sebungwe, January 1906. |
| N 6/4/10 | Annual Report, Bubi, October 1909. |
| N 9/1/22 | Annual Report, Bubi, 1919-20. |
| N 9/1/24 | Annual Report, Bubi, 1921. |
| NB 6/1/1 | Annual Report, CNC, 31 March 1898. |
| | Annual Report, Inyati, March 1898. |
| NB 6/5/2/2 | Val Gielgud's patrol to the Zambezi, 8 January 1898. |
| NB 6/5/2/5 | Report by Green to Robert Lanning, Native Commissioner, Shiloh, 14 December 1897. |
| NBG2/4/1 | Nielsen to Chief Staff Officer, 21 March 1919. |

| | |
|---|---|
| S 1051 | Annual Report, Shangani Reserve, 1943, 1947. |
| | Annual Reports, Nyamandhlovu and Shangani Reserve, 1945. |
| S 138 92 | Superintendent of Natives, Bulawayo, to CNC, 15 November 1926. |
| | J.W. Posselt to CNC, November 1926. |
| S 138 92 | Files, 1923-33. |
| S 1516/47 | Minister of Agriculture, memo, 1 September 1947. |
| S 2086/1995 | C. Bisset to Mr Powys Jones, 2 October 1950. |
| | NC Lupane to PNC, 2 October 1950. |
| S 2208/1/25 | J. Richardson, LDO, Shangani Reserve, 'Report on Area C', January 1958. |
| | Report on Zone B, January 1958. |
| S 2263 | Rex v Sibuzana, 27 July 1951. |
| S 235 503 | Annual Report, Bubi, 1925. |
| S 235/506 | Annual Report, Gwelo, 1928. |
| S 235/510 | Annual Report, Shangani Reserve, 1932. |
| S 235/511 | Annual Report, Shangani Reserve, 1933. |
| S 235/517 | Annual Report, Shangani Reserve, 1939. |
| S 235/518 | Annual Report, Shangani Reserve, 1946. |
| S 2403/2681 | Annual Report, Hartley, 1952. |
| | Annual Report, Bubi, 1952. |
| | Annual Report, Shangani Reserve 1952. |
| S 2413/400/78/8 | Draft answers to WHO questionnaire, May 1950. |
| | D.M. Blair, 'Malarial Control. Southern Rhodesia', August 1950. |
| S 2588/1978 | D.E. Williams to Minister of Agriculture, 22 July 1942. |
| | J. Tulloch, Ingwenya, to Chief Native Commissioner, 8 December 1945. |
| | CNC to Acting PNC, 21 January 1946. |
| | NC Bubi to PNC, 6 February 1946. |
| S 2796/2/1 | Minutes of the Midlands Provincial Assembly, 1951–2. |
| S 2808/1/25 | Report on Area 2, A.G. Pilditch, 10 June 1959. |
| | NC Nkayi to PNC, 29 June 1954, 4 April 1955, 4 December 1958. |
| | Memo to Minister of Native Affairs, 8 August 1955. |
| | Report on Zone A1, W.L. Moncrieff, Field Assistant, NHLA, 24 May 1956. |
| | Pasture Research Officer, Memo, 22 May 1956. |
| | Reports on Zone A2 and C. |
| | Report on Zone B, January 1958. |
| | Assessment Committee Report, 17 July 1959. |
| | Director of Native Agriculture to Under Secretary, 1 May 1959. |
| | Under Secretary to PNC, Matabeleland, 2 May 1959. |
| | E.D.K. McLean 'Native Land Husbandry Act – Start of Implementation in Residual Area of District', 19 May 1961. |
| S 2827/2/2/2 | Annual Report, Nkayi, 1955. |
| S 2827/2/2/3 | Annual Report, Lupane, 1955. |
| S 2827/2/2/4 | Annual Reports, Nkayi and Lupane, 1956. |
| S 2827/2/2/5 | Annual Reports, Lupane and Nkayi, 1957. |
| S 2827/2/2/6 | Annual Report, Lupane, 1958. |
| S 2827/2/2/7 | Annual Report, Nkayi, 1958-59. |
| S 2827/2/2/8 | Annual Report, Nkayi, 1961. |
| S 2929 | Delineation Report, Nkayi, Chief Madhliwa, June 1965. |
| | Delineation Report, Nkayi, Headman Mankambini. |
| | Delineation of Communities: Interim Report, A.D. Elliott, June 1965. |
| S 2929/7/3 | Delineation Reports, Gokwe: Chiefs, Mfungo and Mkoka. |
| S 2929/5/1/1 | Delineation Report, Binga. |
| | Delineation report on Chief Sinampande, C.J.K.Latham, March 1967. |
| S 3024/1/1 | NC Inyathi to S/N/Bulawayo, 9 January 1932. |

|  | CNC to S/N/Bulawayo, 20 March 1933. |
| --- | --- |
|  | ANC, Shangani Reserve, to NC Inyathi, 20 March 1941. |
| S 607 | Meeting between NC Bubi and Inyathi chiefs, 1925. |
|  | Meeting between the Governor and chiefs, Shangani Reserve, 6 August 1925. |
| S 84/1/301 | Citations of ICU speeches. |
| ORAL/22 | Interview with Richard John Powell, 3 July, 21 August and 5 September 1978. |
| ORAL/240 | Interview with Noel Hunt, 27 November 1983. |
| ORAL/241 | Interview with Rupert Meredith Davies, 17 November 1983. |

**Provincial Administrator's Office, Bulawayo**

| CHK 6/LU | M.E. Hayes, reports on Headman Ndabambi, Headman Goduka, Chief Mabhikwa and Headman Matenjwa, November 1975. |
| --- | --- |
|  | DC to PC, 15 September 1969. |
|  | DC to PC, 27 February 1973. |
| CHK 6/Nkayi | M.E. Hayes, reports on Chiefs Madhliwa and Sikobokobo, October 1975 |
| DMN/ZPC | Provincial Council Committee Minutes. Minutes of the First Provincial Council 1993 Meetings, 29 November 1993; 30 October 1992. |
| H/M | Headmen's files: Manguni, Mlume (Majaha). |
| LAN 22/84. | District Development Plans. Minutes of the One Day District Planning Workshop Held at Tsholotsho DDF Training Centre, n.d. (c.1990). |
| LAN 22/86. | Matabeleland North Provincial Development Plan. |
|  | Provincial Planning Officer to PA, Bulawayo, 2 November 1990. |
|  | 'Review of Development Programmes and Development Planning in Matabeleland North Province', n.d. (c. 1990). |

*Matabeleland North Provincial Five Year Development Plan, 1990–1995* (Bulawayo, Provincial Development-ment Committee, 1991).

**District Administrator's Office, Nkayi**

| ADF 6/2 | G. Nyamawaro, LGPO's Report, March 1985; D.B. Ntini, 'Report. Sihlengeni-Gwelutshena Pipe Line', 1 August 1985. |
| --- | --- |
| AGR 19 | DA Maphosa to Under Secretary, Development, 9 June 1983. |
| CHK 6 Nkayi. | Chiefs Myinga Dakamela, Madliwa, Tshugulu and Sikobokobo, Correspondence 1956–75. Reports by M.E. Hayes on Headmen Mpande, Malundu and Fanisoni, October 1975. |
| CHK 14 | Minutes of the Vice President's Meeting, 5 September 1992, PA Matabeleland North to all DAs, 8 March 1989. |
|  | Meeting of Matableland North Chiefs' Provincial Assembly, 14 March 1989, 1 September 1992. |
|  | Meeting of Chiefs and Headmen, 30 June 1992. |
|  | DC Nkayi to PC, 16 June 1964, 27 February 1973, 10 November 1976. |

Council General 182. Headmaster, Nkayi School, 26 January 1983.

| | R.R. Siziba, EO Education, 'Term End Report', June 1983. |
| --- | --- |
| | Minutes of Meeting to Discuss the Problems Causing the Closure of the District Council Offices, Nkayi, 21 February, 1985. |

DAs Monthly Report, April 1985, May 1985, November 1985.

District Council Minutes, Nkayi, 1984-95.

District Development Committee Meeting, Minutes, 1984-85.

District Team Meeting Minutes.

DM 3/85 District Administrators' Conferences and Districts Administrators' Minutes from the Permanent Secretary.

| EL/5 | Elections. Minutes on District Council Elections Meeting, December 1994; 8 January 1985. |
| --- | --- |
|  | Report, 12 July 1985. |

File X 461/44 Nkayi. DC Nkayi to SIA, 8 December 1978.
LAN GEN/1/1962–70, Nkayi. Internal Affairs correspondence and reports, 1963–70.
LAN GEN/1/1967–70, Nkayi. Internal Affairs correspondence and reports, 1967–70.
LAN 22/1972–78 Memorandum DC Nkayi to PC, 22 September 1972.
LAN 23, Rural Planning, Dev 82/84. Internal Affairs, Conservation and Forestry, correspondence and reports, 1970–81.
Report Gen/85 DA to PA 30 August 1984; DAs monthly reports.
SMO Miscellaneous 1974 and 1975, Nkayi. Correspondence, N. Hunt to PC, 9 May 1975; DC Nkayi to PC, 27 May 1975.


District Administrator's Office, Lupane

ADC                    Association of District Councils. L. Mhlanga, 'Rural District Councils Financing "New Born Child"', 31 May 1994.
                       Address by Minister of Local Government E.C. Chikowore, Association of District Councils, Fifth Annual Congress, Record of Proceedings, 8–10 February 1989.
                       Minutes of Third Annual Congress, Kariba, 15–17 October 1986.
ADM 33/2               Lupane District Team Minutes, 17 July 1984, 5 September 1984.
AGR 16                 Tilcor Irrigation Projects, General.
DEF 7/2                Civil Defence Committee Minutes, May 1982.
                       DA Martin Simela to Under Secretary, 28 May 1982.
District Development Committee Minutes, 4 June 1988.
District Team Meeting, Minutes, 25 March 1983.
F/28/1, Agritex FAO, 'Land Use Plans (village)'.
                       'FAO Programme of Assistance to Agritex Zim/91/005'.
                       E.P. Goto and L.S. Dube, 'Implementation of the Development Sequence. The Field Experience of Gokwe and Lupane Districts', Internal Review Workshop, 11–12 November 1993.
File His 3, District and Tribal History and Custom, Lupane. 'Notes on the Role of the Ministry of Internal Affairs During the War: Lupane'.
File Misc X Gen. ADC Naryshkine to PC Matabeleland North, 29 December 1980.
Jotsholo Pilot Project Committee Minutes. 1987–96.
Kusile District Council Meeting, Minutes 1981–96.
Kusile/Tsholotsho District Councils, Minutes of Joint Meeting on Governor's Programme, 23 August 1988.
Kusile District Council Conservation Committee Minutes. 2 October 1989.
LAN 9                  Tribal Trust Lands, General.
Ministry of Local Government, Rural and Urban Development, Minute of 19 February 1996.


OTHER ARCHIVES

Samkange Archives, The Castle, Harare.

School of Oriental and African Studies, University of London.
Box 76, Folder 4, Bowen Rees to Mr Hawkins, 23 July 1914, CWM, South Africa Incoming.
Box 76, Folder 4, Bowen Rees, 'Lions on the Path', 23 July 1914, CWM, South Africa Incoming.
CWM Incoming, Inyati Report, 1914.
LMS South Africa 1936, W.W. Anderson to T. Coker Brown, 3 March 1936.

## NEWSPAPER SOURCES

Newspaper Sources held in the Zimbabwe National Archives
*Daily News*
*Rhodesia Herald*
*Bantu Mirror*
*Times of Zambia*

Newspaper Sources held in the Bulawayo Record Office
*Chronicle*

Contemporary press sources
*Financial Gazette*
*Herald*
*Horizon*
*Indonakusa Ilanga*
*Mail and Guardian*
*Moto*
*Parade*
*Sunday Mail*
*Zimbabwe Independent*

## PUBLISHED SOURCES

Alao, A., 'The Metamorphosis of the "Unorthodox": The Integration and Early Development of the Zimbabwe National Army', in N. Bhebe and T. Ranger (eds), *Soldiers in Zimbabwe's Liberation War* (London, James Currey, 1995).

Alexander, J., 'State, Peasantry and Resettlement in Zimbabwe', *Review of African Political Economy*, 61, 1994, pp. 325–45.

—— 'Dissident Perspectives on Zimbabwe's Post-Independence War', *Africa*, 68, 2, 1998, pp. 151–2.

Alexander, J. and J. McGregor, 'Modernity and Ethnicity in a Frontier Society: Understanding Difference in Northwestern Zimbabwe', *Journal of Southern African Studies*, 23, 2, 1997, pp. 187–201.

—— 'Representing Violence in Matabeleland, Zimbabwe: Press and Internet Debates', in T. Allen (ed.), *The Media of Conflict: War Reporting and the Representation of Ethnic Violence* (London, Zed Books, 1999).

—— 'Wildlife and Politics: Campfire in Zimbabwe', *Development and Change*, 31, 3, 2000.

Alexander, J. and T. Ranger, 'Competition and Integration in The Religious History of North-Western Zimbabwe', *Journal of Religion in Africa*, 28, 1, 1998, pp. 3– 31.

Alexander, J., J. McGregor and T. Ranger, 'Ethnicity and the Politics of Conflict: The Case of Matabeleland, Zimbabwe', in E.W. Nafziger, F. Stewart and R. Väyrynen (eds), *The Origins of Humanitarian Emergencies: War and Displacement in Developing Countries* (Oxford, Oxford University Press, forthcoming).

Auret, D., *Reaching for Justice: The Catholic Commission for Justice and Peace 1972– 1992* (Gweru, Mambo Press, 1992).

Banana, C., (ed.), *Turmoil and Tenacity: Zimbabwe 1890–1990* (Harare, College Press, 1989).

Barnes, T., 'The Heroes' Struggle: Life After the Liberation War for Four Ex-Combatants', in N. Bhebe and T. Ranger (eds), *Soldiers in Zimbabwe's Liberation War* (London, James Currey, 1995).

Bayart, J.F., *The State in Africa. The Politics of the Belly* (London, Longman, 1993).

Bayart, J.F., S. Ellis and B. Hibou, *The Criminalization of the State in Africa* (Oxford, James Currey, 1999).

Beach, D., *The Shona and Zimbabwe, 900–1850* (Gweru, Mambo Press, 1980).

—— *A Zimbabwean Past: Shona Dynastic Histories and Oral Traditions* (Gweru, Mambo Press, 1995).

Berman, B. and J. Lonsdale, *Unhappy Valley 2. Violence and Ethnicity* (London, James Currey, 1992).

Bhebe, N., *Benjamin Burombo: African Politics in Zimbabwe* (Harare, College Press, 1989).

—— *Zapu and Zanu. Guerrilla Warfare and the Evangelical Church in Zimbabwe* (Gweru, Mambo Press, 1999).

Bhebe, N. and T. Ranger (eds), *Soldiers in Zimbabwe's Liberation War* (London, James Currey, 1995).

—— *Society in Zimbabwe's Liberation War* (London, James Currey, 1995).

Bijlmakers, L., M. Basset and D. Saunders, 'Health and Structural Adjustment in Rural and Urban Zimbabwe', *Research Report No. 101* (Uppsala, Nordiska Afrika Institutet, 1996).

Bozongwana, W., *Ndebele Religion and Customs* (Gweru, Mambo Press, 1983).

Brickhill, J., 'Zimbabwe's Poisoned Legacy: Secret War in Southern Africa', *Covert Action*, 43, 1992–93, pp. 4–59.

—— 'Daring to Storm the Heavens: The Military Strategy of Zapu, 1976–1979', in N. Bhebe and T. Ranger (eds), *Soldiers in Zimbabwe's Liberation War* (London, James Currey, 1995).

—— 'Making Peace with the Past: War Victims and the Work of the Mafela Trust', in N. Bhebe and T. Ranger (eds), *Soldiers in Zimbabwe's Liberation War* (London, James Currey, 1995).

Carbutt, C.L., 'Reminiscences of a Native Commissioner', *Native Affairs Department Annual*, 1924.

Carver, R., *A Break with the Past? Human Rights and Political Unity. An Africa Watch Report* (London, Africa Watch, 1989).

Catholic Commission for Justice and Peace/Legal Resources Foundation, *Breaking the Silence, Building True Peace: A Report on the Disturbances in Matabeleland and the Midlands, 1980 to 1988* (Harare, CCJP/LRF, 1997).

Chabal, P., *Power in Africa. An Essay in Political Interpretation* (London, Macmillan, 1994).

—— 'The African Crisis: Context and Interpretation', in R. Werbner and T.O. Ranger (eds), Chabal, *Postcolonial Identities in Africa* (London, Zed Books, 1996), pp. 29–55.

Chabal, P. and J.P. Daloz, *Africa Works. Disorder as Political Instrument* (Oxford, James Currey, 1999).

Child, B. and J.H. Peterson, *Campfire in Rural Development: The Beitbridge Experience* (Harare, Centre for Applied Social Studies and Department of National Parks and Wildlife Management, Harare, 1991).

Chipungu, S.N. (ed.), *Guardians in Their Time. Experiences of Zambians Under Colonial Rule 1890–1964* (London, Macmillan, 1992).

Chisvo, M. and L. Munro, *A Review of Social Dimensions of Adjustment in Zimbabwe 1990–1994* (Harare, UNICEF, 1994).

Chiwewe, W., 'Unity Negotiations', in C. Banana (ed.), *Turmoil and Tenacity: Zimbabwe 1890–1990* (Harare, College Press, 1989).

Clapham, C. (ed.), *African Guerrillas* (Oxford, James Currey, 1998).

Cleaver, F., 'Water as a Weapon: The History of Water Supply Development in Nkayi District, Zimbabwe', *Environment and History*, 1, 3, 1995, pp. 313–35.

Cliffe, L., J. Mpofu and B. Munslow, 'Nationalist Politics in Zimbabwe: The 1980 Elections and Beyond', *Review of African Political Economy*, 18, 1980, pp. 44–67.

Clinton, I., *These Vessels. The Story of Inyati, 1859–1959* (Bulawayo, Stuart Manning, 1959).

Comaroff, J. and J. Comaroff, 'Through the Looking Glass: Colonial Encounters of the First Kind', *Journal of Historical Sociology*, 1, 1, 1998.

Crummey, D., (ed.), *Banditry, Rebellion and Social Protest in Africa* (London, James Currey, 1986).

Dabengwa, D., 'Zipra in the Zimbabwe War of National Liberation', in N. Bhebe and T. Ranger (eds), *Soldiers in Zimbabwe's Liberation War* (London, James Currey, 1995).

Davidson, B., *The Black Man's Burden: Africa and the Curse of the Nation State* (London, James Currey, 1992).

Davies, J.C.A., 'A Major Epidemic of Anthrax in Zimbabwe', *Central African Journal of Medicine*, 29, 1983, pp. 8–12.

De Boek, F., 'Beyond the Grave: History, Memory and Death in Postcolonial Congo/Zaire', in R. Werbner, (ed.), *Memory and the Post Colony. African Anthropology and the Critique of Power* (London, Zed Books, 1998), pp. 21–57.

Delius, P., *A Lion amongst the Cattle: Reconstruction and Resistance in the Northern Transvaal* (London, James Currey, 1996).

Drinkwater, M., 'Technical Development and Peasant Impoverishment: Land Use Policy in Zimbabwe's Midlands Province', *Journal of Southern African Studies*, 15, 2, 1989, pp. 287–305.
—— *The State and Agrarian Change in Zimbabwe's Rural Areas* (London, Macmillan, 1991).
Ellert, H., *Rhodesian Front War: Counter-insurgency and Guerrilla Warfare 1962–1980* (Gweru, Mambo Press, Second Edition, 1993).
Ellis, S. (ed.), *Africa Now. People, Politics and Institutions* (London, James Currey, 1996).
Elphick, R. and R. Davenport (eds), *Christianity in South Africa. A Political, Social and Cultural History* (Oxford, James Currey, 1997).
Engel, U., *The Foreign Policy of Zimbabwe* (Hamburg, Institut für Afrika-Kunde, 1994).
Environmental Consultants, *People, Wildlife and Natural Resources – The Campfire Approach to Rural Development in Zimbabwe* (Harare, Zimbabwe Trust, DNPWM and Campfire Association, 1990).
Feierman, S., *Peasant Intellectuals: Anthropology and History in Tanzania* (Madison, University of Wisconsin Press, 1990).
Flower, K., *Serving Secretly. An Intelligence Chief on Record, Rhodesia into Zimbabwe 1964–1981* (London, John Murray, 1987).
Ford, J., *The Role of Trypanosomiases in African Ecology* (Oxford, Clarendon Press, 1971).
Frederikse, J., *None But Ourselves: Masses Versus the Media in the Making of Zimbabwe* (London, James Currey, 1982).
Fukui, K. and J. Markakis (eds), *Ethnicity and Conflict in the Horn of Africa* (Oxford, James Currey, 1994).
Geffray, C., *A Causa das Armas. Antropologia da Guerra Contemporanea em Moçambique* (Porto, Ediçoes Afrontamento, 1991).
Geiger, S., *Tanu Women. Gender and Culture in the Making of Tanganyikan Nationalism, 1955–1965* (Oxford, James Currey, 1997).
Glaser, C., '"We Must Infiltrate the *Tsotsis*". School Politics and Youth Gangs in Soweto', *Journal of Southern African Studies*, 24, 2, 1998, pp. 301–25.
Government of Zimbabwe, *Report of the Commission of Inquiry into Appropriate Agricultural Land Tenure Systems. Volume One: Main Report.* Chaired by Professor M. Rukuni (Harare, Government Printer, 1994).
Hanlon, J., *Apartheid's Second Front: South Africa's War Against its Neighbours* (Harmondsworth, Penguin, 1986).
—— *Beggar Your Neighbours: Apartheid Power in Southern Africa* (London, CIIR, 1986).
Helmsing, A.H.J., 'Rural Local Government Finance. Past Trends and Future Options', in A.H.J. Helmsing *et al.* (eds), *Limits to Decentralization in Zimbabwe: Essays on the Decentralization of Government and Planning in the 1980s* (The Hague, Institute of Social Studies, 1991).
Henderson, H.J.R., 'Legislation and Land-use Planning in Rhodesia: An Example of Recent Land-scape Evolution in the Nkai Tribal Trust Land', *Swansea Geographer*, 15, 1977, pp. 56–9.
Herbst, J., *State Politics in Zimbabwe* (Harare, University of Zimbabwe Publications, 1990).
Hill, K., 'Zimbabwe's Wildlife Utilization Programs: Grassroots Democracy or an Extension of State Power', *African Studies Review*, 39, 1, 1996, pp. 103–19.
Hobsbawm, E., *The Age of Extremes. The Short Twentieth Century, 1914–1991* (London, Abacus, 1995).
Hodder-Williams, R., 'Conflict in Zimbabwe: The Matabeleland Problem', *Conflict Studies*, 151, 1983, The Institute for the Study of Conflict, London.
Iliffe, J., *A Modern History of Tanganyika* (Cambridge, Cambridge University Press, 1979).
Jackson, J., 'Repatriation and Reconstruction in Zimbabwe during the 1980s', in T. Allen and H. Morsink (eds), *When Refugees Go Home* (London, UNRISD in association with James Currey, 1994).
James, W., 'War and "Ethnic Visibility": the Uduk on the Sudan–Ethiopia Border', in K. Fukui and J. Markakis (eds), *Ethnicity and Conflict in the Horn* (Oxford, James Currey, 1994).
Kershaw, G., *Mau Mau from Below* (Oxford, James Currey, 1997).
Kesby, M., 'Arenas for Control, Terrains of Gender Contestation: Guerrilla Struggle and Counter-Insurgency Warfare in Zimbabwe 1972–1980', *Journal of Southern African Studies*, 22, 4, 1996, pp. 561–85.
King, P.S., 'Post-War Expansion', in Iris Clinton, *These Vessels. The Story of Inyati, 1859–1959* (Bulawayo, Stuart Manning, 1959).

Kriger, N., *Zimbabwe's Guerrilla War. Peasant Voices* (Cambridge, Cambridge University Press, 1992).
—— 'The Politics of Creating National Heroes: The Search for Political Legitimacy and National Identity', in N. Bhebe and T. Ranger (eds), *Soldiers in Zimbabwe's Liberation War* (London, James Currey, 1995).
Lan, D., *Guns and Rain. Guerrillas and Spirit Mediums in Zimbabwe* (London, James Currey, 1985).
Lancaster, C., *The Goba of the Zambezi: Sex Roles, Economics and Change* (Norman, University of Oklahoma Press, 1981).
Lawyers Committee for Human Rights, *Zimbabwe: Wages of War* (New York, LCHR, 1986).
Lemarchand, R., *Burundi: Ethnic Conflict and Genocide* (Cambridge, Cambridge University Press, 1995).
Low, D.A and J.M. Lonsdale, 'Introduction: Towards the New Order 1945–1963', in D.A. Low and Alison Smith (eds), *History of East Africa: Volume Three* (Oxford, Oxford University Press, 1976).
Lowenson, R. and D. Saunders, 'The Political Economy of Health and Nutrition', in C. Stoneman (ed.), *Zimbabwe's Prospects. Issues of Race, State, Class and Capital in Southern Africa* (London, Macmillan, 1988).
Mackenzie, J., 'Chivalry, Social Darwinism and Ritualized Killing: the Hunting Ethos in Central Africa up to 1914', in R. Grove and D. Anderson (eds), *Conservation in Africa: People, Policies and Practice* (Cambridge, Cambridge University Press, 1987).
Madzana, I., 'Decolonizing Minds', *Moto*, 195 (April 1999), p. 2.
Madzudzo, E. and Dzingirai, V., *A Comparative Study of the Implications of Ethnicity on Campfire in Bulilimamangwe and Binga* (Harare, Centre for Applied Social Studies, 1995).
Mafu, H., 'The 1991–92 Zimbabwean Drought and Some Religious Reactions', *Journal of Religion in Africa*, 1995, 25, 3, pp. 288–309.
Makambe, E.P., *Marginalising the Human Rights Campaign: The Dissident Factor and the Politics of Violence in Zimbabwe 1980–1987* (Lesotho, Institute of Southern African Studies, 1992).
Mamdani, M., *Citizen and Subject. Contemporary Africa and the Legacy of Late Colonialism* (Oxford, James Currey, 1996).
Martin, D. and P. Johnson, *The Struggle for Zimbabwe* (London, Faber and Faber, 1981).
—— 'Zimbabwe: Apartheid's Dilemma', in D. Martin and P. Johnson (eds), *Destructive Engagement: Southern Africa at War* (Harare, Zimbabwe Publishing House, 1986).
Mawere, A. and K. Wilson, 'Socio-Religious Movements, The State and Community Change: Some Reflections on the Ambuya Juliana Cult of Southern Zimbabwe', *Journal of Religion in Africa*, 25, 3, pp. 252–88.
Maxwell, D., *Christians and Chiefs in Zimbabwe. A Social History of the Hwesa People, c. 1870s–1990s* (Edinburgh, IAI, 1999).
Mbembe, A., 'Provisional Notes on the Postcolony', *Africa*, 62, 1 (1992), pp. 3–37.
—— 'The Banality of Power and the Aesthetics of Vulgarity in the Post-Colony', *Public Culture*, 4, 2 (1992), pp. 1–30.
Mbizo, 'Mtikana ka Mafu', *NADA*, 1926, pp. 56–7.
McGregor, J., 'Containing Violence: Poisoning and Guerrilla/Civilian Relations in Memories of Zimbabwe's Liberation War', in K. Lacy Rogers, S. Leydesdorff and G. Dawson (eds), *Trauma and Life Stories: International Perspectives* (London, Routledge, 1999), pp. 131–59.
McGregor, J. and T. Ranger, 'Displacement and Disease. Epidemics and Ideas about Malaria in Matabeleland, 1945–1996', *Past and Present*, 2000, No. 167.
Meredith, M., *The Past is Another Country* (London, Pan, 1980).
Mharakurwa, S., 'Knowledge, Practices and Perceptions About Malaria in Rural Communities in Zimbabwe: Relevance to Malaria Control', *Bulletin of the World Health Organisation*, 74, 1, 1996.
Mharakurwa, S. and T. Mugochi, 'Chloroquine Resistant Falciparum Malaria in an Area of Rising Endemicity in Zimbabwe', *Journal of Tropical Medicine and Hygiene*, 97, 1, 1994, pp. 39–45.
Middleton, K., '"Who Killed Malagasy Cactus?" Science, Environment and Colonialism in Southern Madagascar (1924–1930)', *Journal of Southern African Studies*, 25, 2, 1999.
Ministry of Information, Posts and Telecommunications, *A Chronicle of Dissidency in Zimbabwe* (Harare, Government Printer, 1984).
Mohr, E., *To the Western Falls of the Zambesi* (London, Sampson Law, 1876).

Minter, W., *Apartheid's Contras. An Inquiry into the Roots of War in Angola and Mozambique* (London, Zed Books, 1994).

Moorcroft, P. and P. McLaughlin, *Chimurenga! The War in Rhodesia 1965–80* (Marshalltown, Sygma/Collins, 1982).

Moore, D., 'The Zimbabwe People's Army: Strategic Innovation or More of the Same?', in N. Bhebe and T. Ranger (eds), *Soldiers in Zimbabwe's Liberation War* (London, James Currey, 1995).

——— 'Clear Waters and Muddied Histories: Competing Claims to the Kaerezi River', *Journal of Southern African Studies*, 24, 2, 1998, pp. 377–405.

Moore, H. and M. Vaughan, *Cutting Down Trees. Gender, Nutrition and Agricultural Change in the Northern Province of Zambia, 1890–1990* (London, James Currey, 1994).

Moyo, J., *Voting for Democracy. Electoral Politics in Zimbabwe* (Harare, University of Zimbabwe Publications, 1992).

Murombedzi, J., 'Decentralizing Common Property Resource Management: A Case Study of Nyaminyami District Council of Zimbabwe's Wildlife Management Programme', *Dryland Networks Programme*, International Institute for Environment and Development, London, Paper No. 30, 1991.

——— *Decentralization or Recentralization? Implementing Campfire in the Omay Communal Lands of Nyaminyami District* (Harare, Centre for Applied Social Studies, 1992).

Nass, M., 'Zimbabwe's Anthrax Epizootic', *Covert Action*, 32, Winter 1992/93.

Ncube, W., 'The Post-Unity Period: Developments, Benefits and Problems', in C. Banana, (ed.), *Turmoil and Tenacity: Zimbabwe 1890–1990* (Harare, College Press, 1989).

Nkomo, J., *The Story of My Life* (London, Methuen, 1984).

Nugent, P. and A.I. Asiwaju (eds), *African Boundaries: Barriers, Conduits and Opportunities* (London, Pinter, 1986).

Nyagoni, W., *African Nationalism in Zimbabwe* (Washington, University Press of America, 1978).

Oates, C.G. (ed.), *Frank Oates, Matabeleland and the Victoria Falls* (London, Kegan Paul, Trench and Co., 1889).

Parkinson, D.K., 'Lupane Notes', *NADA*, 1980.

Penvenne, J., 'Mozambique: A Tapestry of Conflict', in D. Birmingham and P. Martin (eds), *History of Central Africa. The Contemporary Years since 1960* (London, Longman, 1998).

Petersen, J., *Campfire: A Zimbabwean Approach to Sustainable Development and Community Empowerment through Wildlife Utilization* (Harare, Centre for Applied Social Studies, 1992).

Prescott, J.R.V., 'Overpopulation and Overstocking in the Native Areas of Matabeleland', *Geographical Journal*, 52, 1961.

Prunier, G., *The Rwanda Crisis: 1959–1964. History of a Genocide* (London, Hurst, 1995).

Raftopoulos, B., 'Beyond the House of Hunger: The Struggle for Democratic Development in Zimbabwe', in L. Lauridsen (ed.), *Bringing Institutions Back In: The Role of Institutions in Civil Society, State and Economy* (Roskilde University, Institute of Development Studies, Occasional Paper No. 8, 1993).

Raftopoulos, B. and I. Phimister, *Keep on Knocking: A History of the Labour Movement in Zimbabwe, 1900–1997* (Harare, Baobab, 1998).

Ranger, T., *Peasant Consciousness and Guerrilla War in Zimbabwe* (London, James Currey, 1985).

——— 'Bandits and Guerrillas: The Case of Zimbabwe', in D. Crummey (ed.), *Banditry, Rebellion and Social Protest in Africa* (James Currey, London, 1986).

——— 'The Influenza Pandemic in Southern Rhodesia: A Crisis of Comprehension', in D. Arnold (ed.), *Imperial Medicine and Indigenous Societies* (Manchester, Manchester University Press, 1988).

——— 'Religious Pluralism in Zimbabwe', *Journal of Religion in Africa*, 25, 3, 1995, pp. 226–52.

——— 'African Identities: Ethnicity, Nationality and History. The Case of Matabeleland, 1893–1993', in Joachim Heidrich (ed.), *Changing Identities. The Transformation of Asian and African Identities Under Colonialism* (Berlin, Centre for Modern Oriental Studies, 1994).

——— *Are We not Also Men? The Samkange Family and African Politics in Zimbabwe 1920–64* (London, James Currey, 1995).

——— 'The Moral Economy of Identity in Northern Matabeleland', in Louise de la Gorgendière, *et al.* (eds), *Ethnicity in Africa* (Edinburgh, African Studies Centre, 1996).

——— 'Zimbabwe and the Long Search for Independence', in D. Birmingham and P.M. Martin (eds),

*History of Central Africa. The Contemporary Years Since 1960* (London, Longman, 1998).
—— *Voices from the Rocks. Nature, Culture and History in the Matopos Hills of Zimbabwe* (Oxford, James Currey, 1999).
Ranger, T. and M. Ncube, 'Religion in the Guerrilla War: The Case of Southern Matabeleland', in N. Bhebe and T. Ranger (eds), *Society in Zimbabwe's Liberation War* (London, James Currey, 1995).
Ranger, T. and P. Slack (eds), *Epidemics and Ideas* (Cambridge, Cambridge University Press, 1993).
Reid Daly, R. and P. Stiff, *Selous Scouts. Top Secret War* (Alberton, Galago, 1982).
Richards, P., *Fighting for the Rainforest. War, Youth and Resources in Sierra Leone* (Oxford, James Currey, 1996).
Schmidt, H., 'Love and Healing in Forced Communities: Borderlands in Zimbabwe's War of Liberation', in P. Nugent and A.I. Asiwaju (eds), *African Boundaries: Barriers, Conduits and Opportunities* (London, Pinter, 1986).
Seeger, A., 'Revolutionary Armies of Africa: Mozambique and Zimbabwe', in S. Baynham (ed.), *Military Power and Politics in Black Africa* (London and Sydney, Croom Helm, 1986).
Selous, F.C., *A Hunter's Wanderings in Africa* (London, Richard Bentley, 1895).
SGP, 'Native Nomenclature', *NADA*, 1934.
Shamuyarira, N., *Crisis in Rhodesia* (London, Deutsch, 1965).
Sithole, M., *Zimbabwe: Struggles Within the Struggle* (Salisbury, Rujeko, 1979).
Spring, A., *The Long Fields: Zimbabwe Since Independence* (Basingstoke, Pickering and Inglis, 1986).
Stiff, R., *See You in November. Rhodesia's No-holds Barred Intelligence War* (Alberton, Galago, 1985).
Stoneman, C. and L. Cliffe, *Zimbabwe: Politics, Economics and Society* (London and New York, Pinter Publishers, 1989).
Taylor, P. and L. Mutamba, 'A Review of the Malaria Situation in Zimbabwe with Special Reference to the Period 1972–1981', *Transactions of the Royal Society of Tropical Medicine and Hygiene*, 80, 1986, pp. 12–19.
Thomas, S.J., 'The Legacy of Dualism and Decision-Making: The Prospects for Local Institutional Development in "Campfire"' (Harare, Centre for Applied Social Studies, 1991).
Thomas, T.M., *Eleven Years in Central Africa* (London, Snow, 1872).
Tshabangu, O., *The March 11 Movement in Zapu – Revolution Within the Revolution for Zimbabwe* (Heslington, Tiger Papers, 1979).
Turton, D., 'Mursi Political Identity and Warfare: The Survival of an Idea', in K. Fukui and J. Markakis (eds), *Ethnicity and Conflict in the Horn* (London, James Currey, 1994).
Turton, D., *War and Ethnicity: Global Connections and Local Violence* (New York, University of Rochester Press, 1997).
Van Geldermansen and R. Munochivoyi, *Central African Journal of Medicine*, 41, 1, 1995, pp. 104–12.
Wason, E., *Banned: The Story of the African Daily News* (London, Hamish Hamilton, 1976).
Werbner, R., *Tears of the Dead: The Social Biography of an African Family* (Edinburgh, Edinburgh University Press, 1991).
—— 'Human Rights and Moral Knowledge. Arguments of Accountability in Zimbabwe', in M. Strathern (ed.), *Shifting Contexts. Transformations in Anthropological Knowledge* (London, Routledge, 1995).
—— 'Beyond Oblivion: Confronting Memory Crisis', in R. Werbner (ed.), *Memory and the Postcolony: African Anthropology and the Critique of Power* (London, Zed Books, 1998).
—— 'Smoke from the Barrel of a Gun: Postwars of the Dead, Memory and Reinscription in Zimbabwe', in R. Werbner (ed.), *Memory and the Postcolony: African Anthropology and the Critique of Power* (London, Zed Books, 1998).
Wetherell, I., 'The Matabeleland Report: A Lot to Hide', *Southern African Report*, June 1997, pp. 21–2.
Wilson, K., 'Cults of Violence and Counter Violence in Mozambique', *Journal of Southern African Studies*, 18, 3 (1992), pp. 527–82.
Windrich, E., *The Mass Media in the Struggle for Zimbabwe* (Gwelo, Mambo Press, 1981).
Worby, E., 'Maps, Names, and Ethnic Games: The Epistemology and Iconography of Colonial Power in Northwestern Zimbabwe', *Journal of Southern African Studies*, 20, 3 (1994), pp. 371–92.
—— 'Tyranny, Parody and Ethnic Polarity: Ritual Engagements with the State in Northwestern Zimbabwe', *Journal of Southern African Studies*, 24, 3 (1998), pp. 561–78.

## UNPUBLISHED SOURCES

Alexander, J., 'The State, Agrarian Policy and Rural Politics in Zimbabwe: Case Studies of Insiza and Chimanimani Districts', PhD, Oxford, 1993.

Alexander, J. and J. McGregor, 'Zipra Guerrilla Narratives', ms, 1998.

Anon., 'Mission Work of the Mariannhill Missionaries in Zimbabwe, 1896–1980', ms, Bulawayo, 1982.

Bird, C. et al., 'Was Mrs Mutendi only Joking? A Critique of Timber Concessions in the Communal Areas of Zimabwe', ms., Forestry Commission, Harare, 1993.

Bowen Rees, 'Social Conditions of Native Populations', ms, circa 1910.

Cobbing, J., 'The Ndebele Under the Khumalos, 1820–1896', PhD, University of London, 1976.

Floyd, B.N., 'Changing Patterns of Land Use in Southern Rhodesia', PhD, Syracuse, 1959.

Grignon, F., 'Understanding African States' Governmentalities: The Case of Kenya', paper presented at the Institute of Commonwealth Studies, London, December 1996.

Holst, R., 'Continuity and Change. The Productive Dynamics of Social and Productive Relations in Hwange, Zimbabwe, 1870–1960', M.Phil, University of Liverpool, 1993.

Judge, G. (ed.), 'The Kalahari Sands Forests of Rhodesia: Management Report', Forestry Commission, Harare, 1975.

Kriger, N., Zimbabwe's Guerrilla Integration: Entitlement Politics (ms, 1996).

Martin, R.B., 'Communal Areas Management Programme for Indigenous Resources (Campfire)', Working Document 1/86, Harare, Department of National Parks and Wildlife Management, 1986.

Matabeleland North Province, 'Malaria De-Brief Report', 17–23 September 1996.

Matose, R. and J. Clarke, 'Who is the Guardian of the Indigenous Forests?', ms, Forestry Commission, Harare, 1993.

Mhlabi, S.J., 'The effects of and African responses to the Land Husbandry Act of 1951 with special reference to Ntabazinduna Communal Land', BA History Honours thesis, University of Zimbabwe, 1984.

Ncube, C., 'Tonga Ritual: A Way of Constructing Reality', BA Honours thesis, Religious Studies, University of Zimbabwe, 1987.

Ncube, G.T., 'A History of North West Zimbabwe, 1850–1950s: Comparative Change in Three Worlds', M.Phil., University of Zimbabwe, 1994.

Nhongo-Simbanegavi, J., 'Zimbabwean Women in the Liberation Struggle: Zanla and its Legacy, 1972–1985', PhD, University of Oxford, 1997.

Nkomo, N., 'Between the Hammer and the Anvil: The Autobiography of Nicholas Nkomo', ms, 1996.

Nthoi, L., 'The Social Perspective of Religion: A Study of the Mwali Cult of Southern Africa', PhD, University of Manchester, 1995.

Ranger, T., 'Indigenous Ideas: Accounting for Drought, Making Rain and Healing History in Matabeleland, 1992', ms, Oxford, 1992.

—— 'Patterns of Witchcraft Belief and Control in Northern Matabeleland', November 1996.

Schmidt, H., 'The Social and Economic Impact of Political Violence in Zimbabwe, 1890–1990: A Case Study of the Honde Valley', PhD, University of Oxford, 1996.

Sikuka, A.N. and O. Thompson, Campfire Department, Nkayi Rural District Council. Annual Report to MS, Second Year, for the Period November 1 1994 to December 1 1995 (MS-DW, Nkayi, December 1995).

Thomas, Charles Celt, 'Thomas Morgan Thomas. Pioneer Missionary, 1828–1884', ms.

Thompson, G., 'Cultivating Conflict: the Native Land Husbandry Act in Colonial Zimbabwe', PhD, University of Minnesota, 1998.

Worby, E., 'Remaking Labour, Reshaping Identity: Cotton, Commodification, and the Culture of Modernity in Northwestern Zimbabwe', PhD, McGill University, 1992.

Yap, K., 'Voices from the Matabeleland Conflict: Perceptions on Violence, Ethnicity and the Disruption of National Integration', Britain Zimbabwe Society Research Day, Oxford, 8 June 1996.

—— 'Arrested Resolution: Democracy, National Integration and the Politicization of Ethnic Identity with Regards to the Matabeleland Conflict (1981–1987)', paper presented at the International Conference on Historical Dimensions of Democracy and Human Rights in Zimbabwe, University of Zimbabwe, 9–14 September 1996.

# Index